PACIFIC SEMINAR 3

What is an Ethical Life?

XanEdu

Acknowledgments:

pp. 2–17: As appeared in the *Journal of Moral Education*, Vol. 31, 2002. Copyright © 2002 by Taylor and Francis Informa UK. Reprinted by permission of the publisher via the Copyright Clearance Center.

pp. 18–24: As appeared in *The Forum for Family and Consumer Issues*, Vol. 3, No. 3, Fall/Winter, 1998. Copyright © 1998 by Robert Flashman, Melissa Flashman, Libby Noble, and Sam Quick. Reprinted courtesy of The Forum for Family and Consumer Issues, North Carolina Cooperative Extension, and North Carolina State University.

pp. 25–33: From *Willing to Learn: Passages of Personal Discovery* by Mary Catherine Bateson. Copyright 2004 by Steerforth Press. Reprinted by permission.

pp. 34–53: From the "Business Roundtable Institute for Corporate Ethics Bridge Paper" by Patricia Werhane and Brian Moriarty. Copyright © 2009 by Patricia Werhane and Brian Moriarty. Reprinted by permission of the authors and the Business Roundtable Institute for Corporate Ethics. http://www.corporate-ethics.org/

pp. 56–74: From *Essays on Moral Development: The Philosophy of Moral Development*, Volume 1, by Lawrence Kohlberg. Copyright © 1981 by Lawrence Kohlberg. Reprinted by permission of HarperCollins Publishers.

pp. 75–90: As appeared in *American Journal of Orthopsychiatry: Interdisciplinary Approaches to Mental Health*, 1982. Copyright © 1982 by the American Psychological Association. Reprinted by permission of the publisher via the Copyright Clearance Center.

pp. 91–103: As appeared in *The Nation*, December 28, 1992. Copyright © 1992 by Katha Pollitt. Reprinted by permission of the author.

104–116: From *An Ethic of Care: Feminist and Interdisciplinary Perspectives* by Gertrud Nunner-Winkler. Copyright © 1993 by Taylor & Francis Group, LLC. Reprinted by permission of the publisher via the Copyright Clearance Center.

Change the course.

530 Great Road
Acton, MA 01720
800-562-2147

Table of Contents

Acknowledgements

"Pacific Seminar 003: What is An Ethical Life? (PACS 003)" is the current incarnation of a core general education course developed for University of the Pacific seniors. While the name of the course has changed over time from "Mentor Seminar 003: Ethical Applications of Knowledge" to "Pacific Seminar 003: The Ethics of Family, Work, and Citizenship" to the current title, the course itself has consistently emphasized the interplay of narrative and theory informing the development of moral imagination, reasoning, and behavior. The course we offer in 2014 is very much the same course that Pacific introduced in 1996. In that sense, this edition of the PACS 003 reader builds on the foundations laid two decades ago by Dean Robert Benedetti, and legendary faculty members like Bob Blaney, Gwenn Browne, Bob Orpinela, Margaret Payne, and Jon Schamber.

The work of preparing the series of readers for the course has been taken up by several planning committees. During the last years of the Mentor Seminar 003 era, Eleanor Wittrup and Linda Thomas prepared the first edited readers for the course. In 2005–2006, a faculty committee comprising Brian Klunk, Carolynn Kohn, Randall Koper, Peter Meyer, Stefanie Naumann, Dari Sylvester, Thomas, and Wittrup produced the first reader for Pacific Seminar 003. The second edition of the PACS 003 anthology appeared during 2008–2010; it was edited by Klunk, Koper, Lou Matz, and Larry Thiel. Their revision profited from a meeting with Dr. Elliot Turiel from the Graduate School of Education at UC Berkeley, who made valuable suggestions about the content of the moral development chapter and the general organization of the reader. The next edition, prepared for 2010–2012, was edited by Caroline Cox, Klunk, Koper, AmyJo Mattheis, Matz, and Thiel. A committee that included Jeffrey Becker, Cox, Rex Hamilton, Matz, and Ty Raterman oversaw the 2012–2014 reader.

The current editorial team (Becker, Marilyn Draheim, Hamilton, Klunk, Thiel, and Wittrup) wishes to thank Pacific's Director of General Education Gesine Gerhard for her support in the development of this anthology. The team also wishes to recognize our new partners at XanEdu for their assistance as Pacific moves the PACS 003 reader online for the first time. Finally, gratitude is due to Brett DeBoer of Pacific's Visual Arts Department, whose Graphic Design students produced many wonderful candidates for the reader's cover art. Sadly, we could only use one.

Chapter 1

Ethics and Narrative

"So, How Did You Arrive at that Decision?" Connecting Moral Imagination and Moral Judgement

Michael J. Pardales

Michael J. Pardales *(1969–) is Vice President and Chief Learning Officer at St. Joseph's College of Maine. His academic background is in educational psychology. His publications range over a number of interests in educational psychology including the use of students' autobiographies.*

ABSTRACT—Using theoretical understandings from many fields, this article makes a detailed argument for how it is that reading literature is one of the best ways to cultivate the moral imagination. Drawing on sources from cognitive science, philosophy, literature and education, I analyse the inter-relationship between literature, moral imagination and moral judgement by connecting the cognitive underpinnings of the moral imagination (prototypes, metaphor, and narrative) to the process of moral judgement. Furthermore, this article argues that a cultivated moral imagination will have greater ability to make sound moral judgements. In this way, an explanation of how we actually make decisions in matters of moral significance is put forth and applied to educational pursuits.

Judgement

Judgement plays an important role in our attempt to lead meaningful lives. How we deliberate and decide what to do in complex situations is very important, because the consequences of our actions impact on our daily life, and our relationships with others. Sometimes the information we have in deliberating over moral matters is incomplete and uncertain, yet we must often take action, even though the information we have is partial. As we attempt to lead our lives we are confronted by situations that admit of great variety and complexity; this variety and complexity defy the possibility that there is one valid moral theory that can, more or less mechanically, tells us how to act in every possible moral situation that might arise.

We need to look at monistic systems, such as Utilitarianism or Kantian ethical theory, differently. We need to ask of these theories what they tell us about how we make judgements in complex moral situations. Utilitarianism tells us that one concern we might have in a moral dilemma is: will there be a measurably good outcome from our decision (Smart & Williams, 1973)? I think this is a reasonable concern, as long as it is not the only concern. I think most would agree that treating people as autonomous individuals who should be respected as ends in themselves is an important concern (Kant, 1988). Again, it is not the only concern; it is just one of the concerns that is good to have.

Making a judgement is not simply the application of a rule, and it is not the expression of mere taste or preference. While either of these might be involved in the process of judgement, neither makes it up entirely. It is like the difference between judging the 50-metre freestyle race and diving in a swimming competition. In the 50-metre freestyle race, the winner can be determined by appealing to an objective standard: the stopwatch. In high-diving, a team of judges must be assembled; these judges must take into account various aspects of the diver's performance. There is the difficulty of the dive, the entry into the water, the execution of the moves and so on. These judges are usually considered experts in the sport of diving and each may weigh his or her considerations differently; one judge may put more emphasis on the difficulty of the dive, while another may put more emphasis on the diver's entry into the water. We call these people judges because they must take into consideration several factors, compare them to their body of knowledge and expertise in the field and make a decision about what a particular dive is worth. We can see, from this example, that judgement is not simply applying rules and is more sophisticated than arbitrary choice. Judgement involves perception, knowledge and action (among other things).

Judgement even pervades the sciences: a place regarded for precision, exactness and objectivity. Thomas Kuhn (1977) has written about the role of judgement in choosing between opposing comprehensive scientific theories. Kuhn explains that there are five criteria that scientists use to decide between competing theories: consistency, accuracy, scope, simplicity and fruitfulness. He thinks that while scientists do agree on these criteria, they do not agree on exactly how they are applied; they may make different judgements regarding how any one of these criteria may be applied in evaluating a theory. He states, "Individually the criteria are imprecise: individuals may legitimately differ about their application to concrete cases. In addition, when deployed together, they repeatedly prove to conflict with one another; accuracy may, for example, dictate the choice of one theory, scope the choice of its competitor" (p. 322). It is not always obvious why these different criteria are given more consideration. Sometimes it is a matter of temperament: one scientist may believe, due to her enculturation, that accuracy must always take precedence over scope; another scientist might be willing to sacrifice some accuracy if a theory is fruitful. We begin to see that making judgements is connected intimately with valuation. Where there are differing value schemes, judgement takes on a more important, and more difficult, role.

Nagel (1979) identifies some of the conflicting and incommensurable values that make judgement-making so difficult in particular situations:

> obligations, rights, utility, perfectionist ends, and private commitments—these values enter into our decisions constantly, and conflicts among them, and within them, arise in medical research, in politics, in personal life, or wherever the grounds of action are not artificially restricted. What should it mean to give a system of priorities among them? A simpler moral conception might permit a solution in terms of a short list of clear prohibitions and injunctions, with the balance of decision left to personal preference or discretion, but that will not work with so mixed a collection (p. 131).

A permanent ordering of the values Nagel described will be just as problematic as trying to operate with only the principle of utility. In questions of justice, rights may win out over perfectionist ends. In questions of personal relationships, obligations might take precedence over fairness. Particular situations may demand that we order our values differently. Total agreement, especially in moral matters, is rarely ever found. Isaiah Berlin (1991) thought this was the case, but he did not see disagreement as a problem so much as evidence that a plurality of conflicting and incommensurable values and conceptions of the good is a permanent feature of human life:

> What is clear is that values can clash—that is why civilizations are incompatible. They can be incompatible between cultures, or groups in the same culture, or between you and me. You believe in always telling the truth, no matter what; I do not, because I believe that it can sometimes be too painful and too destructive. We can discuss each other's point of view, we can try to reach common ground, but in the end what you pursue may not be reconciled with the ends to which I find I have dedicated my life. Values may easily clash within the breast of a single individual; and it does not follow that, if they do, some must be true and others false (p. 10).

Berlin is saying that we must recognise that a plurality of values and conceptions of the good life exists, and they are often not compatible with one another. This incommensurability is not due to the fact that one conception of the good is wrong and another right. It is due to the fact that there are many different, reasonable values and conceptions of the good life that can be held and pursued within the same society. Where there are serious moral dilemmas, with particularities that defy the application of an abstract rule only, some ability to exercise judgement becomes necessary.

In particular, I think we need a better understanding of how we actually make decisions about complex moral matters; this understanding would help us evaluate the thought process we go through, the factors we weigh, and would shed some light on how we handle these difficult situations. Nagel (1979) describes the faculty of judgement, which helps us in morally complex situations that we encounter in our particular life circumstances:

> What makes this [deciding what to do in morally complex situations] possible is judgment—essentially the faculty Aristotle described as practical wisdom, which reveals itself over time in individual decisions rather than in the enunciation of general principles. It will not always yield a solution: there are true practical dilemmas that have no solution, and there are also conflicts so complex that judgment cannot operate confidently. But in many cases it can be relied on to take up the slack that remains beyond the limits of explicit rational arguments (p. 135).

My point is, because of the many complex moral situations we face (and may face in the future), we need to be armed with more than just rules and principles.[1] What, I think, we are in need of is an understanding of how we decide and how our decisions are informed as we negotiate morally complex situations.

Moral Judgement

Moral judgement is connected intimately to moral imagination. Within the scope of the moral imagination there are certain elements that inform, vitally, our process of deliberation and action. Mark Johnson (1993) describes eloquently what having some understanding of this process can mean:

> Profound moral self-examination of this sort can free us by giving us a psychologically and philosophically realistic understanding of morality. Recent empirical research in the cognitive sciences has revealed that both our concepts and our reasoning about them are grounded in the nature of our bodily experiences and are structured by various kinds of imaginative processes. Consequently, since moral reasoning makes use of these same general cognitive capacities, it, too, is grounded in embodied structures of meaning and is imaginative through and through (p. 1).

The rest of the article will consist of a side-by-side account of moral imagination and the corollary aspect of moral judgement it is connected with. I will argue for how moral imagination (and hence moral judgement) can be cultivated, and claim that a cultivated moral imagination is more likely to lead to sound moral judgement, while an uncultivated moral imagination will be lacking.

Moral Imagination and Moral Judgement

Simply understood, moral imagination is a psychological faculty that allows individuals to explore various possibilities for their lives. In *The Morality of Pluralism*, John Kekes (1993) examines four activities that the human imagination makes possible, of which the fourth is critical to moral imagination:

> The first is the formation of images, like the face of an absent friend; the second is resourceful problem solving, exemplified, for instance, by nonlinear thinking; the third is the falsification of some aspects of reality, as when we fantasize that the facts are other than they are; and the fourth is the mental exploration of what it would be like to realize possibilities, such as being very rich. Moral imagination belongs to the fourth kind of imaginative activity. It is moral because one central concern of the agents engaged in it is with evaluating the possibilities they envisage as good or evil (p. 101).

Evaluating these possibilities is critical to how we live our lives. If we could not imagine and evaluate the possibilities of life, it would be very difficult to understand the behaviour of other people and ourselves. We would have great difficulty considering what actions were beneficial or harmful to us, so one function of the moral imagination is that it allows us to envisage possibilities for our lives. These could be what career to choose, with whom to have intimate relations, what food to eat, and so forth.

The components of the moral imagination I will discuss are: prototypes, metaphor, narrative and moral perception; prototypes, metaphor and narrative are *sources of knowledge* for us to draw upon, while moral perception is a capacity to recognise morally salient events in our life. When I use the phrase "source of knowledge", I mean that prototypes, metaphor and narrative are sources that inform our process of deliberation over moral matters. In this way prototypes, metaphor and narrative are sources of knowledge that we can reflect upon to inform our process of moral judgement (although we may not always engage in this reflection). After I have explained one element of the moral imagination, I will show how that element can affect our process of moral judgement.

Prototypes

The notion of a prototype comes from work done in the field of cognitive science (Churchland, 1989). In the introduction to their edited book, *Minds and Morals*, Friedman and Clark (1996) give a very clear explanation of what a prototype is, while distinguishing it from other important concepts:

We should carefully distinguish exemplars, stereotypes, and prototypes. Exemplars are the concrete instances we encounter during training or learning. Stereotypes are the socially constructed images of "typical" exemplars of a concept or category (e.g., the stereotypic nurse).

Prototypes (as used in most cognitive scientific literature) are the internally represented results of a process that extracts statistical central tendency information from the specific set of exemplars to which an individual system has been exposed. Statistical central tendency information is information concerning which features are most common to the exemplars of some class. One of the central tendencies of the "pet" class may be the feature "furry". The idea of a prototype is thus the idea of a body of features united as the most statistically common characteristics of the exemplars to which a system has been exposed (pp. 5–6).

What is important about the use of a prototype model in moral theory is the fact that we derive central tendency information from a set of exemplars. Applied to the moral realm, we form prototypes of love, justice and harm based on exemplars that we have experienced throughout our lives.[2] For example, as children we begin forming a prototype of fairness. By playing games and watching people play by or break rules, we begin to derive statistical tendencies from these exemplars; our prototype for fairness is the statistical average of all these exemplars. When we hear people say that a particular action is fair or unfair, or we read stories about people who cheat and are then scolded because cheating is not fair, we factor these exemplars into our prototype; when we transgress a rule that cheats someone else, and are scolded for not being fair, we factor that exemplar into our prototype as well. All the exemplars of fairness that we experience in our lives become part of our prototype of fairness. Johnson (1993) explains that prototypes have affective dimensions as well:

These basic prototypes carry with them the affective dimensions of the concrete situations in which they arise. They thus evoke emotions, moods, erotic desire, empathy, and a host of typical affective states that motivate our actions. In this way, our basic moral concepts are never pure abstractions, but are always permeated with passion and emotion that move us to action (p. 191).

At any given moment, our prototype of any moral concept is the average of all of our experiences of situations where that concept played a role. Because we are always having new experiences, our prototypes are always being refined. We have prototypes for other moral concepts like love, justice, human rights and harm as well. Now let us examine how this correlates with moral judgement.

I have said that moral judgement is a process of taking many factors into consideration, and acting in a particular moral situation. Our prototypes of various moral concepts are one of the factors that factor into this process. When a moral dilemma arises that requires me to judge what is a fair thing for me to do my prototype for fairness informs how this new situation compares with what, in my own mind, is fair or unfair. Explaining exactly what enacting a prototype is is a difficult matter, because enacting a prototype could happen in several ways. We could invoke images, linguistic rules, even sounds and smells. Andy Clark (1996) explains how this happens:

> Moral rules and principles, on this account, are nothing more than one possible kind of context-fixing input among many. Others could include well-chosen images or non-rule-invoking discourse. Thus understood, language simply provides one fast and flexible means of manipulating activity within already developed prototype spaces (p. 118).

By recognising that our moral concepts have prototypical structure, we can consider what events have gone into the construction of our prototype; we can consider how we have acted in past instances where we had to exercise our moral prototypes, and see what result our decisions led to. In this way, our prototypes become one source of knowledge for us to draw upon, as we engage in the process of moral judgement.

Metaphor

Mark Johnson (1996) has offered very convincing arguments for the view that our human conceptual system is fundamentally metaphorical.[3] A conceptual metaphor is a mapping of conceptual structure from a source domain, which is typically some aspect of our concrete bodily experience, onto a more abstract or less highly articulated target domain. It is crucial to keep in mind that conceptual metaphors are structures in our conceptual system, not merely propositions or linguistic entities. They invoke conceptual structure, the basis for the inferences we draw from the metaphor. The content and logic of the source domain thus determines our understanding of the target domain. In other words, the reasoning we do about the target domain is based on the embodied corporeal logic of the source domain (p. 51).

Let us look at some examples of the way our conceptual system is metaphoric. Johnson explains that one of our metaphors for moral understanding is an accounting metaphor (ibid, p. 53). If A does a favour for B, then B is said to be indebted to A; "I owe you one". If A knows that B has always paid back his debts, A may even say, "your credit is always good with me". This metaphor becomes extended into a *wealth as well-being* metaphor; consider these examples: "I've had a *wealth* of happiness in my life. The cynics of the world lead *impoverished* lives. Nothing can compare to the *riches* of family and friends. Doing disaster relief work has *enriched* Sarah's life immeasurably" (ibid., p. 54). Notice that, when we utter sentences like this, we are not only using the metaphor in the linguistic sense, we are conceptually understanding the metaphor of *wealth as well-being*. We may actually "think" that, if we have family, friends and loved ones, we are "wealthy" (and this is prob-ably the case). We begin to see the influence that metaphor has on our most basic conceptual understanding and, hence, our way of conversing. For this reason, we articulate many of our moral concepts metaphorically. What I have provided, of course, is only a brief account of a very complex argument.

The metaphorical nature of our conceptual understanding has important implications for moral judgement. When we find ourselves uncertain about how to act in morally ambiguous situations, metaphorical understanding provides us with another source of knowledge from which to inform our process of moral judgement. By reflecting on the metaphors that we use personally, we can learn something about the way we approach moral situations.[4] We may even learn that, in some cases, our use of metaphor hinders our process of deliberating over moral matters, and that we need to reconceptualise our basic understanding of moral concepts. By examining the metaphors we use we can evaluate whether they are really appropriate. For example, the moral accounting metaphor might not be appropriate in matters of love and marriage. We may not even want to use it in relationships with close friends. If I conduct my friendships, or loving relation-ships, in such a way that I keep minute track of what people have done for me, and what I have done for them, this might seriously restrict my relationships. If I will not give my friend a ride to school because he currently owes me two favours that he has not re-paid, I am not likely to keep this friend or any other. I may learn by reflecting on how I conduct my friendships, and how my past friendships have been, that I need to revise my understanding of friendship; a moral accounting metaphor may not be the best metaphor for thinking about personal relationships.

Reflective knowledge of the metaphorical nature of our conceptual under-standing broadens our ability to evaluate the morally complex situations in which we find ourselves. This evaluation of ourselves and our relations is likely to assist us in the process of moral judgement. I agree with Johnson (1993) that, under-standing that we use particular metaphors, should suggest that ours is only one of the possible ways of understanding moral concepts: "Such knowledge of the metaphors we live by should engender a modesty about our own moral claims and a recognition of the variety of morally possible ways of living" (p. 195). The metaphorical aspect of our moral imagination is but another source of *knowledge* to inform our process of moral judgement.

Narrative

The third element of the moral imagination is the narrative element. Johnson, among others, has argued that our lives ultimately have a narrative structure.[5] "It is in sustained narratives, therefore, that we come closest to observing and participating in the reality of life as it is actually experienced and lived" (ibid., p. 196). By viewing our lives and the lives of others as extended narratives we come to an understanding of our moral thinking across time. We can examine particular situations that have impacted the course our life has taken and reflect on why our personality has formed the way it has. This element, of the moral imagination, presents us with a way to examine our life story. "An adequate moral theory", Johnson claims, "must acknowledge the way we try to construct narrative unities that give us the means to criticize our present situation, explore avenues of possible action, and transform our identity in the process" (ibid., p. 154).

Understanding that our lives have a narrative element means, to some degree, thinking about ourselves as a character in a story. Our lives have a beginning, middle and an end. There are main and supporting characters. We live in a particular context of time, place and culture. By reflecting on our lives as narrative we notice patterns and can question what caused or causes us to act a certain way in particular situations. This aspect of the moral imagination gives us critical insight into the novel that is our life. The knowledge gained from this is vital to our process of moral judgement. By reflecting on the narrative structure of our lives we reflect back on our story and see if it makes sense. We try to understand key decisions we made in our lives and how those decisions have impacted us. We examine the factors that surround us (upbringing, family, time, place, etc.) and determine what role these factors may have on the decisions we make. We may notice patterns of judgement that we should change or hopefully we recognise patterns of judgement that have brought us success. This can lead us to reflect on and revise our prototypes and metaphors as well. In this way, the narrative element of the moral imagination provides another *source of knowledge* to inform our process of moral judgement, at the same time that it provides us with a valuable perspective on our life story.

Moral Perception

The final component of the moral imagination that I would like to discuss is moral perception. This perceptive faculty of our moral imagination is what allows us to recognise the morally salient in our lives. John Martin Fischer (1995) describes how this faculty operates:

> We often face highly nuanced, complicated, and ambiguous situations in which we must first identify the ethically relevant features. Before we can properly decide how to respond or what to do, we must—either explicitly or implicitly— see what is morally relevant and important. As we confront the situation, we "frame the moral issues": we give a structure to a moral situation, identifying and making salient (admittedly sometimes in inchoate fashion) the features that are relevant to a moral assessment and to an appropriate response (p. 7).

If we cannot recognise an act of racism, harm or injustice we cannot react to the situation. Our moral imagination heightens our ability to perceive relevant situations that demand our attention. For example, if I am a passenger on a crowded train and notice several other people who do not have seats, moral perception may help me notice if one of those unseated people needs my seat because of a disability, or because they are elderly; dull moral perception may cause me to disregard the fact that there are others on the train that need a seat much more than I do. Heightened moral perception makes us sensitive to situations that we might be callous to otherwise.

In addition to perceiving the morally relevant, the moral imagination gives us the power to frame these perceptions within a context. It is one thing to witness a person assault someone on a street corner; it is another thing to witness a person assault someone on a theatre stage.

It is obvious that this perception is necessary for us to make moral judgements. If we are not aware of morally relevant situations when they present themselves to us, our process of moral judgement will certainly be lacking. This element of the moral imagination works a little differently to the others we have examined. This awareness is not a source of knowledge *per se*, but it is a capacity to perceive, an ability to recognise the morally salient in our lives.

This brings us to the end of my examination of the connections between the moral imagination and the process of moral judgement. Prototypes, metaphor and narrative all inform, in important ways, the process of moral judgement, and our capacity for moral perception is what sets the process in motion. I hope I have made a clear enough presentation of the elements of the moral imagination and their connection to moral judgement to show that the two are intimately connected. If I have made these connections clearly and plausibly, the need for a cultivated moral imagination should become apparent: "This means that the quality of our moral understanding and deliberation depends crucially on the cultivation of our moral imagination" (Johnson, 1993, p. 1).

Cultivating the Moral Imagination

In this section of my article I will show how literature is one of the best cultivators of the moral imagination, and in cultivating the moral imagination, reading literature greatly enhances the process of moral judgement. The main thesis in this section is: a cultivated moral imagination will have a greater store of and more complex prototypes and metaphors, a richer sense of narrative and a heightened sense of moral perception. The corollary to this is an uncultivated moral imagination will probably have impoverished prototypes and metaphors, a weaker sense of narrative and dull moral perception. It follows then, that an uncultivated moral imagination will impede the process of moral judgement, while a cultivated moral imagination will greatly enhance the process of moral judgement.

The moral imagination is cultivated by reading novels. One of the most extended arguments on this matter has been made by Martha Nussbaum (1990):

Why novels and not histories or biographies? My central subject is the ability to imagine what it is like to live the life of another person who might, given changes in circumstances, be oneself or one of one's loved ones . . . In other words, history simply records what in fact occurred, whether or not it represents a general possibility for human lives. Literature focuses on the possible, inviting its readers to wonder about themselves (p. 5).

Cultivating the moral imagination with the novel can have the effect (and affect) of fostering the various elements of the moral imagination.[6] We engage literature in a way that actually adds significant dimensionality to our experience. Nussbaum comments on this:

We can clarify and extend this point by emphasizing that novels do not function, . . . As pieces of "raw" life: they are a close and careful interpretive description. All living is interpreting; all action requires seeing the world *as* something. So in this sense, no life is "raw", and . . . Throughout our living we are, in a sense, makers of fictions. The point is that in the activity of literary imagining we are led to imagine and describe with greater precision, focusing our attention on each word, feeling each event more keenly-whereas much of actual life goes by without that heightened awareness, and is thus, in a certain sense, not fully or thoroughly lived (ibid., p. 47).

In this way, literature actually *adds* to our experience in a way that daily living, alone, often cannot. Through literature we can have experiences that we may not be able to have otherwise. We get a glimpse into the lives of characters that may be very different from our own, or to which we would not otherwise have access.

We can begin to see how this is important for our prototypes, metaphors, narrative and moral perception. Through literature we experience new exemplars that increase significantly the statistical sampling base of our prototypes of moral concepts (love, fairness, harm, justice, etc.). By informing our prototypes in this way, we enrich them and increase our statistical sampling base; and not only will we have more complex prototypes, we may even have a greater number of prototypes. For example, we may have more specialised prototypes for fairness: fairness in love, fairness in economic matters and fairness in friendship. One example of this from literature occurs in Charles Dickens's (1990) novel *Hard Times*. In this novel there are questions about economic fairness, fairness in matters of social justice and fairness in matters of love and family relationships. One specific example is when a young character named Sissy Jupe is being tutored relentlessly in the popular Utilitarian Calculus of the day. Sissy is a young girl who is particularly sensitive to the plight of everyday people, and is having trouble understanding the economic theory that her teacher, M'Choakumchild, is tutoring her in. He is trying to point out to her that, within the current economic system, it is totally acceptable for some people to be starved to death in the streets, given that the majority of the population does not share their plight.

Then Mr. M'Choakumchild said, "This schoolroom is an immense town, and in it there are a million inhabitants, and only five-and-twenty are starved to death in the streets, in the course of a year. What is your remark on that proportion?" And my remark was—for I couldn't think of a better one—that I thought it must be just as hard upon those who were starved, whether the others were a million, or a million million. And that was wrong, too (p. 48).

Sissy was not able to think as her teacher wanted her to; to her, it must have been just as hard to those starving in the streets regardless of what proportion of the total population they comprised. This is a wonderful illustration of one little girl's take on fairness in economic matters. Sissy identifies with a different group of people than her teacher. To her, it seems unfair to have any people starving in the streets regardless of how many people are not starving. It is examples such as this, which rich literature offers in abundance, that can help cultivate our prototypes. Having more complex and specific prototypes increases our ability to approach different moral situations with more specificity and refinement. This has the effect of improving our process of moral judgement. With more sophisticated prototypes, and more prototypes in general, we have a larger knowledge base from which to draw upon. Having a larger knowledge base can only help us make better moral judgements, as we will be acting on more information. This same notion applies to metaphor.

If, as discussed earlier, our conceptual understanding is fundamentally metaphorical, exposure to literature is likely to broaden our conceptual abilities as well. Literature exposes us to metaphor in many ways and gives us the opportunity to learn new metaphors. In this way, as with prototypes, cultivating the literary imagination can have the effect of providing our moral imagination with more complex and varied metaphors with which to inform our process of moral judgement. For example, here is one passage from *Hard Times,* where Dickens describes the mechanical looking Thomas Gradgrind, who is about to address the same classroom that I referred to in the above example. "He seemed a galvanizing apparatus, too, charged with a grim mechanical substitute for the tender young imaginations that were to be stormed away" (ibid., p. 8). In this passage, Dickens uses the metaphor of a cold, hard, galvanising machine to describe Thomas Gradgrind. He does this because Thomas Gradgrind believes in an education that mandates only the learning of calculation and fact, never imagination and creativity. In this example, Dickens's use of metaphor gives us a new way to think about a particular style of education and the somewhat deformed personality it takes to generate it. This is just one sentence in a whole novel. It becomes apparent that, in literature, we are likely to run into new and unusual uses of metaphor that will generously cultivate our own sense and use of metaphor. This will, of course, richly inform the process of moral judgement.

The implications of this on the narrative element of the moral imagination are significant. Consider the narrative way that our moral imagination allows us to view our lives; this, then, becomes richly informed by the reading of novels. Reading novels involves us with the narratives of others. We are able to assess their actions, decisions, emotional states and the rich particularity of their lives. Johnson (1993) comments on the richness of narrative:

> Tracing out over an extended time period the consequences of various moral deliberations is therefore crucial to our moral knowledge, and it is essential for moral education. It is through sustained life narrative—through the narratives we live out and construct, and through the fictional narratives we imaginatively inhabit—that we can perform these essential reflections and moral inquiries (p. 197).

Reading multiple and diverse narrative accounts of others gives us new experiences (experiences we may never have) and hence, increases our knowledge base. The increased knowledge base will better inform our process of moral judgement. Of course, our moral perception will be greatly enhanced as well.

By reading novels we bear witness to various particular circumstances that can enhance our moral perception and expose us to more, morally salient situations than we are likely to face in our real world experience alone. Nussbaum (1995) explains how reading Richard Wright's (1993) novel, *Native Son,* can expose us to the life of a black man tormented by inequity and hatred in a way that broadens our experience and may heighten our ability to be sensitive to issues of race and social justice:

> One such novel is Richard Wright's *Native Son.* As I taught this novel to an almost entirely white group of law students in the very place where the novel is set, we recognized that most of us were . . . well-meaning but grossly ignorant and underdeveloped in sympathy, desirous of knowing what it is like to live the other side of "the line", . . . The experience of reading and discussing the novel at least begins to give white readers a knowledge of their ignorance, and to introduce habits of "fancying" that it is crucial to develop if we are to deliberate well about race (p. 93).

Novels draw us into the lives of characters; when a character faces a moral situation, so do we. This heightened moral perception, as we have seen, is a crucial step in the process of moral judgement. After all, we need to recognise that a situation demands action before we can engage in the process of moral judgement.

Although my explanation of how literature can cultivate the moral imagination was brief, I hope it has become apparent that cultivating the moral imagination, through literature, directly impacts our process of moral judgement. A cultivated moral imagination increases the background knowledge that informs our process of moral judgement; it also heightens our capacity to recognise morally relevant situations. An uncultivated moral imagination will have fewer resources and yield a process of moral judgement that is based on less information. The resulting judgements are likely to be significantly less informed.

Educational Import

When originally conceiving this article there was one particular motivation that inspired me to continue. If there is some plausibility to my belief that there are important connections between the moral imagination and moral judgement, and if engaging with rich literature can contribute to the cultivation of the moral imagination (and hence moral judgement), then this will have vital implications for education.

Because our moral imagination allows us to envision the possibilities for our life, it is inherently bound up with *leading a life.* Our moral imagination is critical to answering the question, "how should I lead my life?" That is, if we do not reduce what is moral to only our actions in morally ambiguous situations, we open up discussion of morality to the age-old question with which both Plato and Aristotle were concerned: "How should one live?" The complexity of particular lives requires that we make judgements in the midst of great uncertainty. More of our educational endeavours and goals should be inspired by this question rather than the disintegrated curricula inspired by standardised testing and accountability.

In USA education the K–12 level there already exists literary education (language arts), but we may want to re-examine how literature is taught. Quizzing students on the plot and characters will not be sufficient. By discussing works of literature in a literary "community of inquiry" (Lipman, 1991), students will be in an atmosphere where they can engage with the literature, the thoughts of their classmates and, most importantly, their own thoughts. This notion of a literary community of inquiry is not unlike what is supposed to happen in a seminar, where the emphasis is more on rigorous discussion, the sharing of ideas, mutual respect and concern for all involved and the pursuit of a line of inquiry of interest to the participants. Participation in a literary community of inquiry provides us with the opportunity to try out our process of moral judgement and examine the elements of moral imagination in an environment where the consequences of our actions are not so severe (as opposed to trying them out "live" in our relationships with others).

As I have argued above, literature has the power to cultivate the elements of a student's moral imagination. Reading and discussing the morally relevant aspects of works of literature in a community of inquiry will help cultivate students' prototypes, use of metaphor and narrative and heighten their moral perception. We may also find that we want to expose students to literature that is morally engaging and reflective of diverse perspectives; morally engaging literature will have interesting characters that become embroiled in rich stories and situations where there is moral uncertainty and sophistication (much like and unlike our students' lives).

At the high school and college level these ideas will translate into ethics courses that use works of literature (e.g., *Hard Times)*, as well as philosophical works (e.g., Mill's *Utilitarianism).* That is because, as I have argued earlier in the article, general rules and principles can offer only partial insight into moral situations; they often cannot tell us what to do. They can never account fully for the richness of particular lives. When they are applied to the more streamlined examples that are used most often in the exposition of theory they work quite well; but that is because there are no particularities to confound their application.

This points to the usefulness of using both literature and theoretical texts in ethics classes. By using both, students become used to thinking about both the general and the particular. Not only will they engage Utilitarian theory in Mill's *Utilitarianism,* they will see how utilitarianism might appear to the lives of particular people in Dickens's *Hard Times.* This is not to suggest that literature should be used only to illustrate theory; it is there to cultivate the moral imagination. It is there to add an element of the particular to the generality and abstractness of theory; it gives a human face to theories that sometimes do not seem connected to human affairs and deliberation. One without the other will produce an imbalanced approach to the teaching of ethics.

Notes

1. One field where this is certainly the case is medical ethics. As new technology develops, such as the ability to keep people alive when most of their brain has been destroyed, or new cloning technology that is now being studied, new moral questions emerge that could not have been predicted. It is not reasonable to expect one rule or principle to accommodate all the moral and ethical dilemmas that could ever arise.

2. I am using the term "experience" here in the broadest sense. An exemplar can be experienced by living through a situation, reading a story, hearing a story, witnessing an event, seeing a movie, etc.

3. He has done this in the 1993 book that I have already cited, and in *The Body in the Mind: The Bodily Basis of Meaning, Imagination, and Reason* (Chicago, University of Chicago Press, 1987). See also George Lakoff (1987) in *Women, Fire and Dangerous Things: What Categories Reveal About the Mind* (Chicago, University of Chicago Press). Lakoff and Johnson have conducted some of their work in this field in collaboration with one another.

4. The methods of discourse analysis can be extremely valuable in helping us determine our metaphorical understandings. By paying very close attention to what we say we can uncover the linguistic and conceptual metaphors by which we live.

5. This argument has been made by Johnson in his book already cited called *Moral Imagination*. It has also been made by Martha Nussbaum (1990) in *Love's Knowledge: Essays on Philosophy and Literature* (Oxford, Oxford University Press). Richard Rorty (1990) has argued for this in *Contingency, Irony, and Solidarity* (Cambridge, Cambridge University Press). Alasdair MacIntyre (1981) has argued for this in chapter 15 of his book, *After Virtue* (Notre Dame, University of Notre Dame Press). Jerome Bruner (1996) has argued for this in *The Culture of Education* (Cambridge, Harvard University Press).

6. While I think the novel is one of the most efficient and reliable tools for cultivating the moral imagination, a good argument can be made for the role that some film, ethnography and storytelling might play as cultivators of the moral imagination.

References

Berlin, I. (1991) *The Crooked Timber of Humanity: Chapters in the History of Ideas* (New York, Knopf).

Churchland, P. (1989) *A Neurocomputational Perspective: The Nature of Mind and the Structure of Science* (Cambridge, MIT Press).

Clark, A. (1996) Connectionism, moral cognition, and collaborative problem solving, in: L. May, M. Friedman, and A. Clark (Eds) *Minds and Morals,* pp. 109–128 (Cambridge, MIT Press).

Dickens, C. (1990) *Hard Times* (New York, W. W. Norton and Co.).

Fischer, J. M. (1995) Stories, *Midwest Studies in Philosophy,* XX, pp. 64–78.

Friedman, M., and Clark, A. (1996) Introduction, in: L. May, M. Friedman and A. Clark (Eds) *Minds and Morals,* pp. 1–15 (Cambridge, MIT Press).

Johnson, M. (1993) *Moral Imagination: Implications of Cognitive Science for Ethics* (Chicago, University of Chicago Press).

Johnson, M. (1996) How moral psychology changes moral theory, in: L. May, M. Friedman, and A. Clark (Eds) *Minds and Morals,* pp. 45–68 (Cambridge, MIT Press).

Kant, I. (1988) On the Metaphysics of Morals, in: L. W. Beck (Trans) *Kant: Selections* (New York, Macmillan Publishing Co.).

Kekes, J. (1993) *The Morality of Pluralism* (Princeton, Princeton University Press).

Kuhn, T. S. (1977) *The Essential Tension: Selected Studies in Scientific Tradition and Change* (Chicago, University of Chicago Press).

Lipman, M. (1991) *Thinking in Education* (Cambridge, Cambridge University Press).

Nagel, T. (1979) *Mortal Questions* (Cambridge, Cambridge University Press).

Nussbaum, M. (1990) *Love's Knowledge* (Oxford, Oxford University Press).

Nussbaum, M. (1995) *Poetic Justice: The Literary Imagination and Public Life* (Boston, Beacon Press).

Smart, J. J. C., and Williams, B. (1973) *Utilitarianism: For and Against* (Cambridge, Cambridge University Press).

Wright, R. (1993) *Native Son* (New York, Harper).

Ethical Wills
Passing on Treasures of the Heart

Robert H. Flashman, Melissa Flashman,
Libby Noble, and Sam Quick

Robert H. Flashman *earned a PhD from The Ohio State University and is currently a professor and state specialist in Family Resource Management in the Department of Family Studies at the University of Kentucky.* **Melissa Flashman** *is a graduate of Wesleyan University;* **Libby Noble** *is a freelance editor; and* **Sam Quick** *earned a PhD from Florida State University and is currently a Human Development and Family Relations Specialist with the University of Kentucky Cooperative Extension Service.*

Ethical Wills have received considerable media attention in recent years. They are documents in which people describe their non-material legacy, the values and life lessons they wish to pass on to those who will survive them.

Quietly flakes of snow bounced off the large bedroom window. It was February 1921 and Tyrone knew he would soon die. Gently he ran his hand over the cover of the journal that had become his friend over the past two years. Soon after he learned his illness was probably terminal, he decided he wanted his family to have a part of him to hold onto long after he was gone. Tyrone penned an "ethical will—a document filled with thoughts, values, life events, and wisdom—things that were important to him. It was his gift, a lasting heritage to his wife, their children, and their children's children. Now, some 70 years later, Tyrone's journal has aged, its pages brown and worn from the loving touch of many hands.

Unlike traditional wills that transfer worldly possessions, an ethical will bequeaths values, ideas, and personal reflections to family members and other loved ones.

Longer ethical wills, such as Tyrone's, can include descriptions of significant events from one's lifetime.

But an ethical will need not be lengthy or time consuming to produce. A few well-stated paragraphs can be just as meaningful as numerous pages of writing. And you don't have to be an experienced writer to compose an ethical will. If the message you leave is from the heart, spelling and grammatical mistakes will be inconsequential to the loved ones reading your words.

A Sense of Control, Preparation, and Closure

An ethical will helps the writer confront and accept death in a healthy way. It also helps to provide a sense of control and a feeling of closure. This is important, because death is one of the things in life we have very little control over. We do not know when we will die, and we generally do not want to know. In fact, most of us avoid thinking about death as much as possible. Some individuals even believe that talking about death will hasten their own demise. Fear and dread of the unknown cause us to evade the topic of death.

Research supports the premise that attitudes toward death and dying affect one's longevity and general well-being. The role of attitudes adds a measure of control to your life, in that you can sometimes delay or hasten death by the way you feel about your own health or about death overall. For example, in one study (Sobel and Ornstein 1996), a positive outlook about their health was shown to prolong the lives of the subjects, even though they had been given less optimistic prognoses by their physicians.

Further substantiating these findings, Viktor Frankl (1962), well-known existential psychiatrist and concentration camp survivor, wrote that the risk of death in concentration camps was greatly increased if the prisoner could perceive no sense of purpose or meaning in life, both of which undergird personal control and militate against giving up.

In spite of the advantages (emotional, psychological, and financial) of preparation, most individuals choose not to plan for or talk about death. A good example of this relates to funeral arrangements. A recent research study (Bern-Klug 1996) shows that consumers usually overpaid for funeral arrangement expenses because of not preplanning for their funeral. In this study, more than 90 percent of the families met with the funeral home director for two hours or less in planning the funeral and did not shop around. This is in stark contrast to the many months the typical family spends making wedding plans by looking at numerous options and comparing prices. Those who do comparison shop and make funeral arrangements according to their own preferences can save thousands of dollars.

Adequate financial and legal preparation for death imparts a sense of control. The notion of "taking care of business" can be fulfilled through pre-planning a funeral, writing a will, purchasing adequate life insurance, and forming a trust or making other financial arrangements to ensure proper financial provision for survivors. Similarly, another practical and meaningful way to take charge and prepare wisely for death is through the penning of an ethical will.

An Ancient Tradition

Primarily a Jewish tradition, the roots of which stem from early Biblical times, ethical wills have gained broad popularity in recent years. The earliest ethical wills were most likely passed on orally, while those of later generations were recorded on paper. Actual wills dating from the Medieval and Renaissance periods have even been preserved to modern times.

Jack Riemer (1991), co-author of *Ethical Wills: A Modern Jewish Treasury* (1983), has found that ethical wills may be more commonplace today than most of us realize: "I was on the Today Show, talking about this custom. And for two weeks after the broadcast, I was inundated with letters from all over the country, from people who wanted to tell me that they had ethical wills in their possession. . . . They all said that they treasured these wills and took them out and reread them often."

An Expression of Your Unique Personality

There is no magical formula that dictates the format or content of an ethical will. What is important is that it expresses the essence of your heart and your personality. If you enjoy writing poetry or songs, consider including an original composition in your will. If you are not good with written words or you are no longer able to manage a writing instrument, try dictating your ethical will onto a cassette tape or use a video recorder. Perhaps your penmanship is poor; think about using a typewriter or word processor. Your creativity is your only limitation.

You can address your ethical will to your spouse or children, to a special friend, or "To My Family." Of course, you may wish to compose more than one ethical will. Listen to your inner guidance; you will know how to proceed.

To be certain that your ethical will remains intact for many years to come, use acid-free paper that will not disintegrate, mold, or fade. Think about the size and type of paper as well. You may prefer a bound book over loose-leaf sheets, and you should use only high-quality, fade-resistant ink.

What You Have to Say is Important

If you're thinking to yourself, "Well, I don't really have anything all that important to write about," think again. You are unique! You have lived and learned in your own special way, and you have important thoughts, experiences and feelings to pass on to those around you. To write an ethical will you don't need to be a sage or a saint; you just need to be yourself. Open your heart and write what comes; it will be a gift and a legacy, "a window into your soul" that loved ones will cherish.

What to Include

What you choose to include in your document will help determine the length of your ethical will. Describing life events, goals, values, and beliefs could require a lengthy will. This type of ethical will can offer rich insights and information that will be highly coveted by future generations. However, many individuals prefer to keep it short and simple, or to address specific topics such as "My Definition of True Success," "Why I Love You and Will Miss You," "What I Appreciate Most," "Mistakes I Have Learned From," "What Spirituality Means to Me," or "My Happiest and Funniest Moments." Consider including stories with deep personal meaning, your ancestral background, people or events that helped shape your life, familial obligations, favorite scripture passages, or even actions for which you would like to ask forgiveness.

After you have brainstormed, you may find it helpful to write each theme you plan to use in your ethical will at the top of a separate piece of paper, using the space below for an outline of details, anecdotes, and favorite sayings that support this theme. This will help you organize your ideas and make it easier to write a clear, cohesive, and meaningful ethical will.

Physical and Emotional Benefits

James W. Pennebaker, a Professor of Psychology at the University of Texas, has been at the forefront of recent studies that have documented the benefits of writing about emotionally significant and personally meaningful topics. For example, in one of Pennebaker's experiments (Pennebaker 1997), people who wrote about their deep feelings showed strikingly improved immune functions based on blood tests. Those who only jotted down trivialities failed to receive a boost in immune functioning. Six weeks after the journalists stopped writing, the findings still held—and those who expressed themselves in depth had made fewer doctor visits.

Dozens of similar studies have now been conducted by investigators around the world. Often in these experiments the focus of the writing is a traumatic or difficult-to-deal-with event. Collectively, the results indicate that from-the-heart writing can offer a variety of mental and emotional benefits as well as often providing small enhancements in physical well-being (Pennebaker 1997). It is logical to assume that the preparation of an ethical will may also offer similar benefits.

It Takes Courage

In composing an ethical will, you come face to face with your life and your mortality. You realize that we all live in the shadow of death, and that each day of life is a precious opportunity. Rabbi Jack Riemer speaks to this challenge:

An ethical will is not an easy thing to write. In doing so, one confronts oneself. One must look inward to see what are the essential truths one has learned in a lifetime, face up to one's failures, and consider what are the things that really count. Thus an individual learns a great deal about himself or herself when writing an ethical will.

(Riemer & Stampfer 1983)

It's Never Too Soon

Writing our ethical wills is not something we should put off. Death can be sudden, even for teenagers and younger children. Also, it's often best to write important material like this when we are fresh and unpressured by time. Starting early in life to write your ethical will can give you more time to record feelings from your heart as well as to interject pertinent historical facts.

Remember, too, that sometimes very late in life our mental and physical capacities diminish, making it difficult or even impossible to prepare an ethical will. An ethical will is a gift to both the giver and the receiver. It helps us clarify our values and put life in perspective. Writing an ethical will is a healthy, healing exercise. Don't put it off; it's never too soon. Look ahead on your calendar: Set aside some time to get away and be by yourself with pen and paper in hand.

Weigh Your Words Carefully

Carefully weigh your words before you decide to actually use them. Be aware of the potential damage ethical wills could produce if wielded as a weapon from the grave to control and chastise the recipient. Such abuse of a rich tradition could be damaging. Remember, once you die, you cannot take back anything you say. Of course, it will be up to you to decide the best time to share your ethical will. If you choose to present it before your death, you may want to consider leaving a second will to be read upon your death. Likewise, you should update the will whenever you feel the need.

Examples of Ethical Wills

Following are two examples of brief ethical wills. Please note the wide variety of sentiments and ideas that can be expressed using this means.

Dear Anna, Peter and Eddie,

Although I have recently been diagnosed as a man in "tip-top condition" by Dr. Lewis, I am nonetheless reminded that time is still passing, and in a couple of years I will have to retire from commercial farming. Don't worry; I'm leaving farming with little in the way of regrets. It has provided your mother and me with enough money to retire.

While tobacco and dairy farming gave my grandfather, father, and me a solid, respectable way to care for our families, I know each of you has other plans for your future. I want to say that I am not disappointed in any of my children for choosing other ways of life. You have each made me proud in your own way.

I am a quiet man, and I know I have never offered much in the way of spiritual guidance. However, I hope that my manner of living has served as a living example of my own moral code.

As you know, this family has had its roots here at Otter Creek since your great-grandpa Jack settled it way back in 1667, I certainly don't expect you to keep the farm; I realize that even little Eddie will follow his big brother and sister to the city. My only request is that the house and the 15 surrounding acres be preserved as a family vacation spot. I want you to bring your children to relax, fish, swim, and have fun pursuing life's simple things, but most importantly, to stick together as a family.

I love you all,

Dad

Dear Kids,

I won't take up much of your time. I know I wasn't around much while you were growing up, so why should I preach to you now?

My wish is that you do not make the mistake of staying in a job that consumes your life, especially if the job offers you nothing more than financial security. You will just end up stressed out, emotionally drained, and most importantly, ten to twenty years of your life will be behind you, used up, never to be relived.

Obi, please continue to pursue your interests in community service and acting; Abdul, I hope you stick with the violin and music which bring you so much happiness. If you both focus on things that are important to you, failures may come, but they will be fewer.

Don't let yourselves be easily discouraged. If you gauge your achievements on those of others, you will most likely be disappointed. Stand on your own merit and accomplishments. "Trust me on this one; I know from experience.

I will always be proud of both of you. Stay true to yourselves and give your best effort. As you know, I have left you both money to cover your college education. Use this time to study things that interest you. Don't try to live up to the expectations of others as I did. Pursue your chosen path, and use your college education to get you started.

Love always,

Mom

References

Flashman, M., R. Flashman, and S. Quick. *Ethical Wills—Passing on Values Important to You.* Lexington: University of Kentucky Cooperative Extension Service Press, 1998.

Frankl, V. (1962). *Man's Search for Meaning.* Boston Beacon Press: Quoted in Justice, B. *Who Gets Sick: Thinking and Health* (Houston Peak Press, 1987), 205.

Pennebaker, J. *Opening Up: The Healing Power of Expressing Emotions.* New York: Guilford Press, 1997.

Riemer, J., and N. Stampfer. *Ethical Wills: A Modern Jewish Treasury.* New York: Schocken Books, 1983.

Riemer, J., and N. Stampfer. *So That Your Values Live On: Ethical Wills and How to Prepare Them.* Woodstock, VT: Jewish Lights Publishing, 1991, xvii.

Sobel (MD), D., and R. Ornstein. *The Healthy Mind Healthy Body Handbook.* New York: Patient Education Media, Inc., 1996, 40.

Tiller, E. *Ethical Wills: Spiritual Bequests,* Wisdom Newsletter from Community Ministries, Baptist Senior Adult Ministries, Washington, D.C., 1996.

Composing a Life Story

Mary Catherine Bateson

Mary Catherine Bateson *(1939–) is a writer and cultural anthropologist. She has been a faculty member at many colleges and universities, including Harvard University and Amherst College, and an administrator at several institutions, including the Institute for Intercultural Studies, where she was president. She is now a visiting scholar at the Sloan Center on Aging and Work at Boston College. Composing a life story, she says, has three complementary meanings and we can compose our life stories in various ways.*

This essay is the edited and retitled transcript of a talk on my book *Composing a Life* given at a Common Boundary Conference in the early 1990s, later published as a book on the "power of stories to transform and heal." This piece reflects on the uses of memoir and how telling one's story plays a role in composing a life, for future possibilities are always understood in relation to an interpretation of the past. I have included it here as a bridge connecting what I have written about my parents to what I have written more generally about the shapes of lives and how they can be studied.

—MCB, 2004

There are three meanings that "composing a life," as a phrase, has to me. Two of those meanings compare living to different arts, in that I see the way people live their lives as, in itself, an artistic process. An artist takes ingredients that may seem incompatible, and organizes them into a whole that is not only workable, but finally pleasing and true, even beautiful. As you get up in the morning, as you make decisions, as you spend money, make friends, make commitments, you are creating a piece of art called your life. The word *compose* helps me look at two aspects of that process.

Very often in the visual arts, you put together components to find a way that they fit together and balance each other in space. You make a visual composition of form and color. One thing that you do in composing a life is to put together disparate elements that need to be in some kind of balance, like a still life with tools, fruit, and musical instruments. This sense of balance is something that women have been especially aware of in recent years because they cannot solve the problem of composing the different elements of their lives simply by making them separate, as men have.

Of course, less and less are men able to compartmentalize their lives. For a long time it was possible for men to think in terms of a line between the public and the private. A man would go to the workplace, and then, at a certain point, he would switch that part of the day off and go home to a world where the atmosphere was different. He could switch gears from one aspect of his life to the other.

But it hasn't been possible for women to separate their commitments in quite the same way. It is one thing in the traditional nuclear family for the husband to go to the office and stop thinking about his family during the day because he has left his wife in charge. It is quite a different thing for both parents to go off and feel that they can completely forget what is happening with the family. Many women have the sense that the combining of different areas in their lives is a problem that is with them all the time.

What this has meant is that women have lived their lives experiencing multiple simultaneous demands from multiple directions. Increasingly men are also living that way. So thinking about how people manage this is becoming more and more important. One way to approach the situation is to think of how a painter composes a painting: by synchronously putting elements together and finding a pattern in how they fit.

But of course *compose* has another meaning in music. Music is an art in which you create something that happens *over time*, that goes through various transitions. Examining your life in this way, you have to look at the change that occurs within a lifetime—discontinuities, transitions, and growth of various sorts—and the artistic unity, like that of a symphony with very different movements, that can characterize a life.

In addition to these two meanings of composing a life—one that relates to the visual arts and the other that relates to music—I want to emphasize a third meaning, one that has to do with the ways in which you compose your own *versions* of your life. I'm referring to the stories you make about your life, the stories you tell first to yourself and then to other people, the stories you use as lenses for interpreting experience as it comes along. What I want to say is that you can play with, compose, multiple versions of a life.

There are advantages in having access to multiple versions of your life story. I am not referring to a true version versus a false version, or to one that works in a given therapeutic context as opposed to others, or to one that will sell to *People* magazine as opposed to ones that won't. I am referring to the freedom that comes not only from owning your memory and your life story but also from knowing that you make creative choices in how you look at your life.

In the postmodern environment in which we live, it is easy to say that no version is fixed, no version is completely true. I want to push beyond that awareness and encourage you to think about the creative responsibility involved in the fact that there are different ways to tell your stories. It's not that one is true and another is not true. It's a matter of emphasis and context. For example, one of the things that people do at meetings is to introduce themselves. I was at a conference recently where, in the course of two days, I introduced myself three times in different breakout groups. One person who had been there all three times came up to me and said, "You know, you said something completely different every time." Of course I did. The contexts were different.

Imagine the choices you have in saying things about yourself and about other people. These are real choices, but they are made in the presence of a set of conventions. Think of a self-introduction as a literary genre. There are things you include and things you don't. Those decisions are related to who you're talking to and where you are, as well as who you're talking about.

You can do the same with versions of your life history. For instance, most people can tell a version that emphasizes the continuities in their lives to make a single story that goes in a clear direction. But the same people can also tell their life stories as if they were following on this statement: "After lots of surprises and choices, or interruptions and disappointments, I have arrived someplace I could never have anticipated." Every one of us has a preference for one of these versions, but if we try, we can produce both. My guess is that there are a lot of people reading this who think of themselves as growing and developing and moving on smoothly. That's part of the intellectual context many of us are in. But some of us experience our lives as discontinuous, interrupted processes.

For example, one version of my life story goes like this: I already thought of myself as a writer when I was in high school, and there hasn't been a year since college that I haven't published something. Now I spend half the year writing full-time and half the year writing and teaching. Many of my students are future writers.

That's one version of me. The other version goes like this: I planned in high school to be a poet. But I gave up writing poetry in college. The only writing I did for years was academic publish-or-perish writing. When I became unemployed because of the Iranian revolution, shortly after my mother died, I dealt with unemployment by starting to write a memoir. I suddenly found that I could write nonfiction. Now I'm considering switching again and writing a novel.

Both of these are true stories. But they are very different stories.

One person told me there had been so much discontinuity in her life that it wasn't hard to think of a discontinuous version, but it was painful to tell it. I think that's a problem many people have. Because our society has preferred continuous versions of stories, discontinuities seem to indicate that something is wrong with you. A discontinuous story becomes a very difficult story to claim.

I would say that the most important effect of my recent book *Composing a Life* has been to give people who feel that they've been bumped from one thing to another, with no thread of continuity, a way of positively interpreting their experience. You might be uncomfortable with your life if it has been like *The Perils of Pauline,* yet many of us have lives like that. One strategy for working with that kind of life is to make a story that *interprets change as continuity.* One of my favorites was someone who said, "My life is like surfing, with one wave coming after another." He unified his whole life with that single simile.

The choice you make affects what you can do next. Often people use the choice of emphasizing either continuity or discontinuity as a way of preparing for the next step. They interpret the present in a way that helps them construct a particular future.

One of the most striking examples here is the way people talk about divorce. Some people approach a divorce by emphasizing what was wrong with the marriage all along: "Finally we got a divorce. But it's been awful for twenty years." I think some of the anger that develops in divorce situations comes from a need to re-create a continuity. But then there are some who don't need to create continuity by tracing the problem back. They emphasize the discontinuity and view the problem as absolutely new. Perhaps they would tend to focus on loss in that situation rather than anger.

When I started *Composing a Life,* the issue I wanted to explore was discontinuity. Part of my interest was based on two events in my own life. One was that I had just gone through the experience of losing, in a rather painful way, a job I cared about. I had been forced to change jobs before, because of my husband changing jobs, and I had had to adapt to that situation. So what I set out to do was to look at a group of women who had been through a lot of transitions and who were able to cope with the changes. I was asking the question "How on earth does one survive this kind of interruption?"

The other circumstance that made me focus on the issue of discontinuity had to do with my experiences in Iran. At the time of the Iranian revolution, my husband and I had been living and working there for seven years. We, and a great many of our friends, had to make fresh starts; many Iranians became refugees. The way they interpreted their situation was absolutely critical to their adjustment. I could see very clearly, among them, that there were those who came into the refugee situation with a sense that they had skills and adaptive patterns they could transfer to the new situation. They were emphasizing continuity. Other people came into the refugee situation feeling that their lives had ended and they had to start from zero. You could see that the choices people made about how to interpret the continuities and discontinuities in their lives had great implications for the way they approached the future.

Much of coping with discontinuity has to do with discovering threads of continuity. You cannot adjust to change unless you can recognize some analogy between your old situation and your new situation. Without that analogy you cannot transfer learning. You cannot apply skills. If you can recognize a problem that you've solved before, in however different a guise, you have a much greater chance of solving that problem in the new situation. That recognition is critical to the transfer of learning.

It can be very difficult to recognize the ways in which one situation or event in your life is linked to others. When I was working on my memoir of my parents, *With a Daughter's Dye,* I found an example of this in my father's life. Some of you may know my father, Gregory Bateson, as a great anthropologist, a great thinker. But in the middle of his life, he went through a difficult period that lasted for some time. From year to year he didn't know whether he would have a salary, whether there would be anything to live on.

His career at that time must have seemed totally discontinuous. First he was a biologist. Then he got interested in anthropology and went to New Guinea. He made a couple of field trips that he never wrote up. Then to Bali. During World War II he wrote an analysis of propaganda films and worked in psychological warfare. Then he did a study of communication in psychotherapy. Then he worked on alcoholism and schizophrenia, and then on dolphins and octopuses. Somehow he turned into a philosopher.

One of the things that I realized while I was putting together the memoir is that only when he drew together a group of his articles—all written in very different contexts for very different audiences, with apparently different subject matter—to put them into the book called *Steps to an Ecology of Mind,* did it become clear to him that he had been working on the same kind of question all his life: The continuous thread through all of his work was an interest in the relationships between ideas.

The interruptions that forced him to change his research focus were absolutely critical to pushing him up the ladder of logical types, so that ultimately he could see continuity at a very abstract level. His insight, his understanding of what he had been working on all his life, was a result of a sometimes desperate search for a continuity beyond the discontinuities. So even when I was working on the memoir, I was picking at this question of continuity and discontinuity, and examining the incredible gains that can come from reconstruing a life history by combining both interpretations.

Of course, in composing any life story, there is a considerable weight of cultural pressure. Narratives have canonical forms. One of the stories that we, as a culture, respond to is the story in which the hero's or heroine's end is contained in the beginning. For example, there is a film about Henry Ford that I happened to watch recently on television. In one scene, he sees his first horseless carriage as a little boy and falls in love with it. In other words, you have an episode in childhood that prefigures all that is to come. Think about how many biographies you have read in which the baby who grew up to be a great violinist loved lullabies, or loved listening to the radio: stories about talent that was visible from the very beginning.

One of my favorite examples is a story from the life of St. Teresa of Avila, a Counter-Reformation saint. When she was a child, part of Spain was still controlled by the Moors: part of the country was Catholic, and part was Muslim. When she was ten or so, she set out, with her younger brother, for the territory controlled by the Moors in order to be martyred and go to heaven. This becomes an appropriate story to prefigure a life of self-sacrifice and dedication to God. Many biographies and autobiographies have this pattern.

Another popular form is one that we can think of as the conversion narrative. It's a simple plot. Lives that in reality have a lot of zigzags in them get reconstrued into before-and-after narratives with one major discontinuity. One very interesting example is the *Confessions of St. Augustine,* which tells the story of his life before and after his conversion to Christianity. The narrative structure requires that he depict himself before conversion as a terrible sinner, that he devalue all he did before he was converted, and that he dredge up sins to talk about so he can describe a total turnaround.

As I read this book today, what strikes me is that St. Augustine after his conversion to Christianity was not that different from St. Augustine before his conversion to Christianity. He pursued a reasonable, intellectual life. He was a seeker. He experimented with different things. After his conversion, it is true, he disowned his mistress, who had borne him a son, an act that is construed, in this story, as a sign of virtue. But he continued to be, as he is throughout the narrative, profoundly self-centered. The universe was apparently organized around bringing him to God, and other people were very peripheral. In that sense, you can follow the same story throughout the book.

A more complicated conversion story is *The Autobiography of Malcolm X.* Much of the book tells of how Malcolm X, who had been a small-time crook, was converted in prison to the Nation of Islam, Elijah Muhammad's American Black Muslim movement. About two-thirds of the book is written as a conventional conversion narrative: "I was deep in sin and then I was saved by Elijah Muhammad."

But then another big discontinuity occurs. Malcolm X becomes disillusioned with the corruption within the Nation of Islam and isolated by the politics around Elijah Muhammad. He separates from them, making a pilgrimage to Mecca and converting to orthodox Islam, and starts his own Muslim organization in the

United States. So in this book you have the image of somebody who developed an interpretation of his life to support the validity of one particular message of salvation and then had to flip over into another one. It's an extraordinarily interesting and unusual story because the conversion happens not once but twice.

One very common example of the uses of the conversion story shows up in Twelve-Step programs. Twelve-Step programs essentially convey the message that if you can construe your life in such a way as to support a turnaround, we will help you construct a new life. But you have to define yourself, as St. Augustine had to define himself, as a sinner, or as Malcolm X had to define himself for his second conversion, as having been duped. An emphasis on a turnaround becomes the condition for moving on to the next stage.

The conversion narrative can be a very empowering way of telling your story, because it allows you to make a fresh start. The more continuous story, in which the end is prefigured in the beginning, is powerful in different ways. But what I want to emphasize are the advantages of choosing a particular interpretation at a particular time, and the even greater advantage *of* using *multiple* interpretations.

The availability of multiple interpretations of a life story is particularly important in how the generations communicate with each other. When we, as parents, talk to our children about our lives, there is a great temptation to edit out the discontinuities, to reshape our histories so that they look more coherent than they are. But when we tell stories to our children with the zigzags edited out, it causes problems for many of those children. A lot of young people have great difficulty committing themselves to a relationship or to a career because of the feeling that once they do, they're trapped for a long, long time. They feel they've got to get on the right "track" because, after all, this is a long and terrifying commitment. I think it is very liberating for college students when an older person says to them, "Your first job after college need not be the beginning of an ascending curve that's going to take you through your life. It can be a zigzag. You might be doing something different in five years." That's something young people need to hear: that the continuous story, where the whole of a person's life is prefigured very early on, is often a cultural creation, not a reflection of life as it is really lived.

The ways in which we interpret our life stories have a great effect on how our children come to define their own identities. An example of this occurred in my own life when my daughter was about to become a teenager. She said to me, "Gee, Mom, it must be awfully hard on you and Daddy that I'm not interested in any of the things you're interested in." I said, "What do you mean?" She said, "Well, you're professors. You write books about social science. I'm an actress. I care about theater." I said a secret prayer because it was clearly a very tricky moment. Maybe she needed to believe in that discontinuity. Maybe it was worrying her and she needed to get away from that discontinuity.

But what I said to her was "Well, to be a social scientist, to be an anthropologist, you have to be a good observer of human behavior. You have to try and understand how people think and why they behave as they do. It strikes me that that's pretty important for a good actor." She has been telling that story ever since because it gave her permission to pursue what she deeply wanted to pursue without feeling she was betraying me and her father. But it also gave her permission to use anything she might pick up from us by giving her a way of construing the cross-generational relationship as a continuity.

As parents, we also need to be flexible in how we construe our children's lives. Recently, I was in Israel visiting on several kibbutzim. Many of the older people on the kibbutzim are in distress about the fact that their children do not want to "follow in their footsteps." Their children want to travel. They want to live in the city. They want to go to the university. Some of them even want to leave Israel, to emigrate.

I started having a series of conversations with the older people in which I would say, "Tell me about your parents. Were they farmers? Did they live on a kibbutz?" People would say things like "Oh no. My father was a tailor in Poland. He lived in the city," Then I would ask how their parents felt when they became socialists and Zionists and came to Israel. In many cases the answer was "They were appalled." Sometimes the answer was "They were thrilled that I was doing something they never could have done."

What the parents I was talking to did not realize was that their children were indeed following in their footsteps. Their children were doing exactly as they had done: leaving the location, lifestyle, and convictions of their parents and going out to do something new in a new place.

The continuity and the discontinuity are at different logical levels in each of these examples. If you can be aware of those different levels simultaneously, you can have an advantage in coping with your life. Otherwise, it may happen that when you are trying to achieve continuity, you actually create the opposite effect. You may be looking for continuity in the wrong place.

If you create continuity by freezing some superficial variable, the result, very often, is to create deep change. This is something my father used to talk about in relation to evolutionary theory. He used the example of a tightrope walker. The tightrope walker is walking along a high wire, carrying a very light bamboo rod. To keep his balance, he continually moves the rod. He keeps changing the angle of the rod to maintain a constancy, his balance in space. If you froze the rod, what would happen to him? He would fall off. In other words, the superficial variation has the function of maintaining the deeper continuity. In evolution, the deeper continuity is survival. For the tightrope walker, it's staying on the high wire.

I found an interesting example recently of a group of people who were able to maintain a deep continuity in their lives through many superficial changes. They were members of an order of Catholic nuns between the ages of fifty-five and sixty-five whom I was invited to address at a convention. They had all joined the order before the reforms of Vatican II. When they joined, nuns lived in convents. They wore black habits and white headdresses. They never had friendships. They were told what to do in every way.

Then came the reform of the religious orders. It is well known that at that time many nuns left their orders. Some of them left because they felt there was too much change; others, because they felt there wasn't enough. But the interesting thing to me was the question of who stayed.

Among the people I talked to, it was clear to me that those who stayed were those who were able to ride the changes and to adapt. At some fundamental level, they were able to bridge all the superficial changes and to say, "My commitment is the same commitment that brought me here in the first place." They were people with an extraordinary capacity to *translate*. The people who were fixated on the habit or the details of ritual couldn't stay when they lost those things.

It's worth giving some thought to what kinds of things deserve to be held steady and what kinds of things it's most adaptive to vary. I think you can argue that one way of looking at addiction is that the addict is trying to keep something steady, a certain level of intoxication, that is, in fact, producing profound and worsening change. An addiction is a constancy of the wrong kind.

When you are able to see multiple levels of change and consistency, you are empowered to make your own decisions, I think this is true of diversity in general. I want to offer one final example from my own life. People who have one famous, successful parent are often locked into the problem of whether or not they succeed in living up to the model of that person. One of the things I gained by having two famous and very different parents is the freedom to be myself.

For a long time, I thought that my interests had nothing to do with theirs. When I went to college, I was fascinated with linguistics. I read the work of Edward Sapir and Benjamin Whorf and decided that linguistics was going to be my life's work. Nobody had told me that linguistics as done by Whorf and Sapir is a branch of anthropology. So I walked, as a total innocent, into the family business. But I opened up a branch in a new neighborhood.

Moral Imagination and Management Decision Making

Patricia H. Werhane and Brian Moriarty

Patricia H. Werhane *is the Wicklander Chair of Business Ethics in the department of philosophy and executive director of the Institute for Business and Professional Ethics at DePaul University. She is also a senior fellow at the Olsson Center for Applied Ethics in the Darden School at the University of Virginia. Professor Werhane is the author or editor of over twenty books about business ethics.*

Brian Moriarty *(1968–) is director at the Business Roundtable Institute for Corporate Ethics at University of Virginia's Darden School of Business. He also teaches management communication in the Darden School. He has been recognized as one of the Top 100 Thought Leaders in Trustworthy Business Behavior by Trust Across America. His research focuses on the relationship of narrative to perception, performance excellence, and organizational action.*

Introduction

During periods of large-scale corporate scandals, it is easy to forget that business is essentially a moral enterprise—it is about working together to create value. We find it easy to focus most of our attention on the specific persons involved in wrongdoing, proclaiming these "few bad apples" to be the sole cause of corporate malfeasance, while failing to investigate carefully better ways to make decisions.

There are, however, two key problems with this approach. First, we find ourselves stuck with only a partial story that acknowledges the symptoms (e.g., various frauds and scandals) but neglects accurately diagnosing and treating their root cause.

Second, we see this perpetuates the error of viewing economics and ethics as two distinct forms of discourse in describing management and corporate practices. This "separation thesis" forces false dilemmas onto business practitioners, creating the illusion that doing well and doing good are often incompatible.

Neither widespread ignorance of ethical theory, nor a lack of moral reasoning skills, nor a deficiency in regulatory law is sufficient in explaining why ordinary, decent, intelligent employees sometimes engage in questionable activities or why the activities sometimes are encouraged or even instigated by the climate or culture of the companies they manage.

If we really hope to account for moral success and failure in business, we need to recognize and appreciate the vital role of moral imagination that managers use in everyday decision making, along with available options they disregard or fail to recognize.

A Definition of Moral Imagination

Successful companies are usually hotbeds of imagination—especially with regard to the innovation of products, services, and operations that are required for successfully competing in the marketplace.

Concerns over a lack of imagination in business, however, have little to do with the overall quantity of imagination and much more to do with the quality of imagination being exercised regularly in the workplace. Why do successful companies often ignore the ethical dimensions of their processes, decisions, and actions?

The problem is not a one-time weakness of will but something more akin to moral amnesia—a habitual inability to remember or learn from one's own and others' past mistakes and a failure to transfer that knowledge when fresh challenges arise.

Concerns over a lack of imagination in business, however, have little to do with the overall quantity of imagination and much more to do with the quality of imagination being exercised regularly in the workplace.

Moral imagination includes an awareness of the various dimensions embedded in a particular situation—in particular, the moral and ethical ones. It entails the ability to understand one's situation from a number of perspectives. Moral imagination enables managers to recognize a set of options that may not be obvious from within the overarching organizational framework; evaluate these options from a moral point of view; and actualize them.

Moral imagination is the ability to discover and evaluate possibilities within a particular set of circumstances by questioning and expanding one's operative mental framework. In managerial moral decision making, moral imagination entails perceiving the norms, social roles, and relationships entwined in any situation.

Developing moral imagination requires a heightened awareness of contextual moral dilemmas and the active engagement of additional perspectives toward these dilemmas that enables managers to reframe them and discover better, economically viable and morally justifiable solutions.

Moral imagination is the ability to discover and evaluate possibilities within a particular set of circumstances by questioning and expanding one's operative mental framework.

The concept of moral imagination is found at the root of our free enterprise system. Scottish economist and philosopher Adam Smith writes: "When I sympathize, I place myself in another's situation, not because of how that situation feels to me or might affect me, but rather as if I were that person. I project myself into another's experience . . ."As Smith indicates, moral imagination is about putting ourselves into the shoes of the various stakeholders in order to develop a strategy for aligning them in practice in ways that are mutually beneficial.

Moral imagination differs from other forms of free reflection because it is grounded in practice and distinguished by the following three characteristics:

1. Beginning not with the general but with a particular situation;
2. Entailing the ability to disengage from one's primary framework or to extend or adapt that framework in a meaningful way;
3. Dealing not merely with fantasies but with possibilities or ideals that are viable and actualizable. Such possibilities have a normative or prescriptive character; they are concerned with what one *ought* to do.

Narratives and frameworks are tools that we share that help us interpret our environment and understand our role within a community. They are interpretive lenses that enable us to work together toward common goals, and they provide us with a point of view—a grounds upon which we can reason, make decisions, and form judgments.

Rhinoceros Armor: Narrative and Frameworks

When one narrative becomes dominant, we appeal to that story for reinforcement of the facts, assuming it represents what actually happened even though it may have distorting effects.

It is morally important to understand the constructive nature and limits of narratives. Such is illustrated by Dennis Gioia's report of his activities as recall coordinator at the Ford Motor Company during the Pinto era.

Between 1973 and 1975, Gioia was in charge of recalling defective automobiles at Ford. He had always thought of himself as an extremely moral and socially responsible person. Yet, when Gioia became intimately familiar with problems related to the Pinto—specifically, that they were catching on fire in low-speed accidents, resulting in injuries and deaths—he did not advocate ordering a recall. In fact, he drove a Pinto and even sold one to his sister.

Gioia eventually came to view his decision not to recall the Pinto as a moral failure—a failure to think outside his prevailing background narrative or script at the point of decision. "My own schematized (scripted) knowledge influenced me to perceive recall issues in terms of the prevailing decision environment and to unconsciously overlook key features of the Pinto case," Gioia said, "mainly because they did not fit an existing script."[1] While personal morality was very important to Gioia, he admits that the framing narrative of his workplace "did not include ethical dimensions."[2] The moral mistake here was that there were other, better choices—albeit ones outside the purview of Gioia's framing narrative—he could have made.

Background narratives provide us with frameworks for understanding the world and our place in it. We are not simply the characters in these narratives; we are also their authors. It is important to recognize that we have a role both in making adjustments to our narrative frameworks and in trying to connect our stories to those within other groups. When we mistakenly view our narrative frameworks as static, we not only risk moral laziness, but we also may miss opportunities to reshape in very positive ways our narratives and roles therein.

Narratives can confuse, bias, and invent what we take to be data, facts, or even truths. This same lens, like the eyepiece of a telescope, which allows us to view a particular element in our field of vision with precision, can also prevent us from seeing other things up close.

Sometimes managers confuse reality with what they want it to be. Sometimes individuals lack a sense of the variety of possibilities and the moral consequences of their decisions as well as the ability to imagine a wider range of possible issues, consequences, and solutions. Sometimes managers and institutions become trapped in their historical framework or a framework perpetuated by their organization, corporate culture, or tradition. Even if managers are only vaguely aware of their particular framework, it can drive their decision making to preclude taking into account moral concerns. A powerful and pervasive framework sometimes allows or even encourages managers to overestimate their powers and abilities.

A point of view can become etched indelibly in our brain even though it actually misrepresents experienced phenomena. Art historian E. H. Gombrich pointed out that sixteenth-century artist Albrecht Durer's depiction of a rhino with a heavy coat of armor served as a model rendering of the animal in natural history books until the eighteenth century, though rhinos do not exhibit armor. Similarly, an early 1598 engraving depicting a whale with ears served as a model for numerous whale images as depicted by later artists; however, whales are earless.[3]

Sometimes managers confuse reality with what they want it to be.

Narratives or mental models can function as specific framing scripts or mini-belief systems in specific kinds of situations or within the culture of institutions such as corporations. When a single story serves as the prototype, it can mold new information to fit within its framework thus shaping the facts. As was the case of Gioia and the Ford Pinto, this can occur even if other valid, yet contradictory, interpretations exist or other equally verifiable facts contradict the prototype narrative.

O-Rings and Ice Water

All companies have narratives—mission statements, principles, and core values—that communicate the identity and purpose of the firm to its stakeholders, especially the employees. A story that defines a firm's purpose, mission, and values can empower managers to search for and identify new opportunities that fit within the company's moral framework and handle unforeseen crises.

Having a narrative that is alive within the organization before a crisis hits can help managers avoid disaster. For example, most people are familiar with the Johnson & Johnson (J&J) Tylenol case. In 1982, after a number of poisoning incidents involving Tylenol capsules, J&J CEO James Burke, in consultation with his top managers, withdrew Tylenol capsules from the market even though the company was not at fault for the poisonings.

Having a narrative that is alive within the organization before a crisis hits can help managers avoid disaster.

When Burke and his leadership team made the difficult decision to pull Tylenol capsules off store shelves, most experts did not believe that the company would ever recapture its share of the pain medication market—although this did eventually happen. Given the company's credo, which states in its first lines, "We believe our first responsibility is to doctors, nurses and patients, to mothers and to all others who use our products and services," Burke and his leadership team, however, described their decision, which lost J&J an estimated $500 million, as a "no brainer."[4]

The Tylenol story illustrates how a framing narrative can become a positive driving force for moral imagination. J&J executives made decisions that were not obvious and could even be viewed as violating the precepts of good marketing practices. Likewise, they insisted that their customers' safety should be the primary decision driver, questioning their legal counsel who was afraid that this action would be perceived as an admission of guilt.

The ability of J&J executives to use moral imagination in the midst of a severe crisis was no accident—on the contrary, it was largely the result of the firm's long-standing commitment to the moral development of its employees. What is of critical importance, yet sometimes overlooked in the Tylenol case, is that J&J had been holding an ongoing series of "challenge meetings," where individuals at all levels in the company were encouraged to speak up if they felt the company was not living the values embodied in the credo. These challenge meetings served as a moral exercise for J&J employees and managers, who became accustomed to putting themselves in the shoes of their stakeholders. When the Tylenol crisis hit, imagining the perspective of a customer was indeed a "no brainer" because it was already an established habit and part of the organizational culture.

We must note that narratives should be somewhat flexible and open to new interpretations and situations if they are to help a company thrive over the long term. A senior executive participating in an Institute ethics seminar claimed that his company had for many years a great reputation for ethical business practice—one that was firmly woven into the company's history. When evidence of some financial malfeasance began to appear at the firm, senior managers were not prepared and did not react as quickly as they could have because they were so accustomed to resting upon the company's history. "No one believed something like this could happen here," the executive said.

Any leader who thinks her organization is immune to moral and ethical problems stands upon thin ground. Moral disasters can happen even if there is no intent to do harm by any of the parties involved—a fact that is illuminated by the Challenger case.

The Challenger space shuttle was a joint project of NASA and a number of highly regarded subcontractors including Morton Thiokol, a corporation created by the merger of two reputable companies. Before 1986, there had been only one accident during the history of NASAs spaceflights, and 24 previous launches of space shuttles constructed almost identically to the Challenger had proceeded without problems. Despite NASA's fine safety record and Thiokol's expertise in space travel, on January 28, 1986, which was the 25th mission of the space shuttle program, the Challenger exploded within 60 seconds of liftoff.[5] Everyone on board was killed, including the first schoolteacher to journey into space.

The Challenger explosion has been traced to the failure of the O-rings—the seals in the connecting joint between the two segments of the rocket booster—to seal one of the boosters. According to testimony given to the Rogers Commission, the group appointed to investigate the disaster, from the very beginning of the rocket booster's development, Morton Thiokol engineers had worried about the flexibility and the strength of the O-ring sealing mechanism. Roger Boisjoly, Morton Thiokol's leading expert on booster seals, sent memos to his superiors at Thiokol warning of the weakness of the O-ring configuration.

Following the seventeenth successful shuttle flight, Larry Mulloy, the manager of the solid rocket booster project for NASA at the Marshall Space Center described evidence of erosion to both the primary and the secondary O-rings as "accepted and indeed expected—and no longer considered an anomaly." After numerous successful launches, NASA officials may have begun to think that the agency was invincible and that the space shuttle was a perfect, even risk-free vehicle. The consequences of accepting this narrative are obvious.

Moral disasters can happen even if there is no intent to do harm by any of the parties involved—a fact that is illuminated by the Challenger case.

This aura of confidence was not the sole factor, however, that led to the Challenger disaster. Another problem involved the ways in which different parties framed risk measurement, resulting in radically different perceptions of the dangers of the space shuttles.

Richard Feynman, a Nobel Prize physicist and member of the Rogers Commission, interviewed a number of NASA officials, engineers, and managers after the explosion and found that their various estimates of the probability of booster failure ranged from as high as 1 in 10 to as low as 1 in 10,000.

The project managers and the engineers had different frameworks for understanding and assessing risk. No one in either group, however, realized that the words they were using had very different meanings and implications for members of the other group.

Due to these misunderstandings, critical information was misinterpreted. On the night before the launch, engineers were asked to prove that the O-rings would fail at temperatures below 50 degrees. Engineers typically interpret lack of proof that something will fail as evidence of a greater risk. In this case, the managers interpreted the engineers' inability to prove on short notice that the O-rings would fail in low temperatures as an increased likelihood of success. Without realizing it, the engineers and managers were talking in circles.

While the engineers neglected to answer the question about O-ring failure from a managerial perspective, the managers similarly failed to understand the engineers' silence as a reason for serious concern about launch safety; neither realized its failure to communicate.

Both groups suffered from what philosopher Michael Davis has termed "microscopic vision"—focusing on a narrow range of phenomena or data without imagining how others might understand the same data differently. This failure to communicate was made explicit when Richard Feynman dropped an O-ring into a glass of ice water during the Rogers Commission hearings. The O-ring cracked.

Social Roles

One useful function that narratives and frameworks provide to the process of value creation is a division of responsibility. Everyone in an organization has a role or number of roles that define various relationships between individuals, individuals and organizations, layers of the organization, and organizations themselves. For example, a person employed as a customer service representative may be assigned certain responsibilities related to customer satisfaction. This employee reports to a manager who in turn is responsible for oversight of an entire team. Likewise, the customer service division of the firm has a specified relationship with the sales department and with the leadership of the firm.

Roles carry with them expectations, rights and duties, norms, and ideals that are either explicit or implicit. Sometimes these rights and duties are legally or contractually defined. Most people adhere to these expectations most of the time, which permits an amount of predictability to human behavior.

Ordinarily there are good moral reasons for acting according to a role's demands or ideals. For example, a father who ignores his children or a manager who does not take seriously her fiduciary responsibilities to her company under most circumstances is judged to be negligent and immoral—both by the standards of role morality and judgment of a common sense perspective.[6] There are, however, cases where roles themselves can become morally problematic.

In the Challenger disaster, all people involved were well meaning and acting within the normative expectations of their roles. Despite their good intentions and concerns about the risk associated with O-rings, the engineers at Morton Thiokol who protested the launch internally did not "blow the whistle" to top management at Thiokol or NASA before the launch took place. Perhaps it is because the engineers viewed their role as providers of data, lacking power as final decision makers. Social roles provide a degree of predictability to human behavior within an organization, but a rigid understanding of roles limits habits of behavior in ways that fail to empower employees and managers to deal effectively with unanticipated situations or crises.

Another problem with social roles—one that is of special significance for managers—is how they can structure authority within organizations. Many managers conceive of good leadership as being primarily about motivating employees to do what they want them to do. Sometimes obedience to authority is part of the problem. The truth, as based on widely-cited human behavior research conducted by Yale Professor Stanley Milgram, is that individuals will often carry out instructions that are absurd, immoral, dangerous, or life-threatening when given by a person in authority.

This phenomenon is as relevant today in organizations as it was previously in Milgram's research lab. Obedience on the part of middle managers enabled the $11 billion fraud at WorldCom, the largest in corporate history. To her credit, Betty Vinson, a senior manager in WorldCom's accounting division, initially refused to follow orders when she was asked to make improper accounting adjustments—in the amount of $828 million—in order to help the company leaders convince Wall Street investors and analysts that it had met the quarterly earnings numbers these executives had predicted.[7] In the financial quarters following the initial fraud, Vinson, who was concerned about jeopardizing the financial well-being of her family should she leave her position at WorldCom, eventually complied with these directives. Over the next two years, Vinson and dozens of other WorldCom employees repeatedly created fraudulent accounting records, even though they knew it was a dishonest and absurd way of doing business. Scott Sullivan, WorldCom's CFO and a chief architect of the fraud, tried to assuage employee anxiety related to this activity by saying that, "nothing they had done was illegal and that he would assume all responsibility."[8] While Sullivan may have been credited with such sweeping authority within WorldCom's culture, his illusory power to take responsibility for the actions of others evaporated before both the law and public sentiment. When the fraud became public, prosecutors failed to accept Vinson's assertion that she was only following orders, and rather than risk indictment, she ended up negotiating a guilty plea as a co-conspirator in the fraud.[9]

Leaders often fail to recognize that employee obedience usually has little to do with their own brilliance, values, experience, or ability to lead—it is primarily due to their position of recognized authority. The problem is not simply the phenomenon of obedience to authority; it is also an issue of leadership. Leaders can become so involved in their roles and accompanying expectations that their decisions reflect what they perceive to be their own role responsibilities. When this happens, leaders may fail to examine how their directives are being interpreted and implemented several layers down within the organization.

... individuals will often carry out instructions that are absurd, immoral, dangerous, or life-threatening when given by a person in authority.

The truth is that employee obedience can sometimes destroy a company. At Enron and WorldCom, employees ordered to "hit the numbers" did so—even at the expense of the truth and ultimately—at the expense of their firms and all of their stakeholders.

Moral Imagination as a Window to a Better Framework

Crises may be unavoidable, but disaster is not. In the unfortunate cases of the Ford Pinto, the Challenger, and WorldCom, better choices were available. The managers in these organizations—ordinary, decent people—however, were unpracticed in the habit of moral imagination, which could have led to alternate solutions.

Moral imagination enables one to assess a situation, evaluate the present and new possibilities, and create decisions that are not narrowly embedded in a restricted context or confined by a certain point of view. Typically, this means stepping back from one's role in an organization and using imagination to consider a situation from an unfamiliar perspective.

In April 2007, WellPoint—a U.S.-based health benefits company with over 34 million members, whose stated mission is "to improve the lives of the people we serve and the health of our communities"—decided to take the unprecedented step of linking employee compensation to success in improving the health of its members.[10] In order to assess the health of its members, WellPoint developed a set of metrics based on a combination of national standards and company-devised indicators. Metrics for customers with diabetes, for example, will "help to measure if they are getting necessary eye exams, maintaining their blood sugar level to reduce complications and having their blood pressure level controlled."[11]

The logic behind this initiative is to actively engage all employees in the primary purpose of the firm, which is to improve the health of those it serves. Whether or not this act of moral imagination proves successful in the long term, aligning employees with activities more traditionally associated with the role of physicians should be viewed as a reasonable business decision. Health benefits firms that fail to positively impact the health of their members will cease to exist, and WellPoint's initiative may help insulate the firm from such a risk.

Sometimes moral imagination can enable firms to in effect reinvent their own products. Since its launch in June 2005, web-based mapping application Google Earth has gained over 200 million subscribers.[12] Most visitors use the sight recreationally to zoom in and out on detailed satellite images of the earth. In April 2007, however, Google transformed perceptions of its already-popular application by deciding to form a joint initiative with The U.S. Holocaust Memorial Museum. The venture, the Genocide Prevention Mapping Initiative, highlights the ongoing genocide in the Darfur region of Western Sudan with the social aim of increasing public awareness of—and sympathy for—the plight of the victims.

Visitors to Google Earth who focus the tool on the Darfur region encounter various graphic symbols that link to up-to-date information on the crisis, including "video footage, photographs, and eyewitness testimony." An image of "red flames brings up a place that has been destroyed; yellow-and-red flames show a village only partially damaged."[13] As explained by John Prendergast, a senior advisor for the International crisis group, the crisis in Darfur "is David versus

Goliath, and Google Earth just gave David a stone for his slingshot."[14] In this imaginative act, which exceeds typical expectations of a business, Google demonstrated leadership by expanding the range and type of value creation initially envisioned for its own product.

Creative moral imagination helps us to project beyond the constraints of particular narrative frameworks, roles, or biases. While moral imagination is a critical first step, it cannot in itself transform a crisis into a success. Just because we imagine a certain moral possibility does not mean that it is our best path or that it is even achievable in actuality.

For this reason, moral imagination must go hand-in-hand with practical moral reasoning, which enables a manager to contextualize potential scenarios and decisions in terms of values, principles, and moral norms. Moral imagination is most likely to be employed successfully by purpose-driven organizations having values statements alive within their culture.

… moral imagination must go hand-in-hand with practical moral reasoning which enables a manager to contextualize potential scenarios and decisions in terms of values, principles, and moral norms.

From its founding in 1999 through the first six weeks of 2007, JetBlue Airways had experienced a meteoric rise, garnering a multitude of loyal customers based largely upon a reputation for exemplifying the firm's core value of "bringing humanity back to air travel and making the experience of flying happier and easier."[15]

The discount airline was heralded as much for its friendly service and passenger amenities as it was for its inexpensive flights.[16] In *BusinessWeek's* first customer service ranking of global firms, JetBlue was listed at number four—based on survey data gathered in 2006—rated higher than customer satisfaction stalwarts like Nordstrom at number five and UPS at number eight.[17] By the time the magazine was published on March 5, 2007, however, *BusinessWeek* had decided to remove JetBlue from its rankings list due to a recent headline-grabbing customer service disaster at the airline.[18]

JetBlue's operations infrastructure and personnel training, which had proved sufficient under normal conditions, failed to respond and adapt adequately to challenges resulting from an ice storm that crippled much of the Eastern United States on February 14, 2007. The storm "left a large portion of the airline's 11,000 pilots and flight attendants far from where they needed to be to operate the planes, and JetBlue lacked the staff to find them and tell them where to go."[19] This operations disaster caused some customers to be stranded in planes on the tarmac for up to 10 hours and led to the cancellation of roughly 1,000 flights within the next four days.[20]

As one well-known ethics expert, Rushworth M. Kidder, was quick to point out, "stranding tens of thousands of passengers, many of them parents with children, starting long-planned vacations during the President Day school holidays . . . isn't just a business failure; it's a moral calamity."[21] It is a moral calamity precisely because JetBlue lacked the moral imagination to prepare for a scenario that was not only predictable, but arguably, inevitable. No one knows with certainty when and where a devastating storm will hit, but sooner or later transportation companies serving large areas are bound to face such a crisis.

While JetBlue's lack of disaster preparation prior to the storm demonstrates a culpable lack of imagination, the firm's response after the disaster is an exemplary case of moral imagination in action. JetBlue's CEO and founder, David Neeleman, immediately issued public apologies via a video on the company Web site and on YouTube, via an email sent to all customers, and via other public forums such as late night talk shows and numerous interviews with print, broadcast, and Web media. Neeleman admitted that he was "humiliated and mortified" by his company's failure to handle the crisis, and he promised the airline would act quickly to build the operational capacity to handle future crises. He also promised to compensate customers who experienced delays due to a "controllable irregularity."[22]

While JetBlue's lack of disaster preparation prior to the storm demonstrates a culpable lack of imagination, the firm's response after the disaster is an exemplary case of moral imagination in action.

Neeleman's words were embodied by company action on several fronts, some of which exhibited moral imagination, as JetBlue developed innovative responses to a new environment where they were attempting to win back customer trust. Christopher Kercher, a JetBlue passenger stranded during the ice storm describes one aspect of this exceptional response:

> Not only did the airline move quickly to apologize, accept full responsibility, and proactively introduce a passenger's bill of rights (all effectively communicated by e-mail from CEO David Neeleman), but they actually had someone call me to apologize. When I wasn't available, they even e-mailed me to find out when would be the best time to speak with me.

> When they reached me, the caller was not some outsourced telemarketer working from a script. Instead, she actually asked me for my opinion of what went wrong and how they could fix it. She engaged me in a dialogue about the steps the airline was considering and sought my opinion on whether the measures would be enough. She thanked me for my help and patience and asked me to give the airline a second chance. They got it.[23]

Just six days after the ice storm, JetBlue fulfilled Neeleman's promise by issuing a cutting edge customer bill of rights that agrees to compensate passengers who experience lengthy delays.[24] Neeleman's stated goal in voluntarily making his firm responsible for compensating postponed passengers was to create a policy "more aggressive than any airline lobbyist would let congress do."[25]

As with Christopher Kercher, initial reactions to JetBlue's imaginative response—which included a much improved operational performance when the next major winter storm hit only a month after the February 14 disaster—were highly positive. Within two week after the disaster, a significant number of investment firms had "upgraded Jetblue's shares to a 'buy,'" and 80% of the visitors who responded to a poll on BusinessWeek's Web site said they would have opted to keep the airline at number four in the magazine's customer service rankings.[26]

While Google's active moral imagination resulted in a new use for their product and JetBlue's exercises of moral imagination led to innovations in organizational structure and policies, employing moral imagination can also have a positive impact on product quality and trust. Actions taken by *The New York Times* in the wake of the Jayson Blair scandal exemplify this latter concept.

For the last century *The New York Times*—sometimes referred to as the "Gray Lady" for its accurate and objective reporting—has enjoyed a reputation as one of the world's most respected source of news information.

On May 11, 2003 a front-page, 7,561-word story in the *Times* reported that:

> A staff reporter for *The New York Times* committed frequent acts of journalistic fraud while covering significant news events in recent months, an investigation by *Times* journalists has found. The widespread fabrication and plagiarism represent a profound betrayal of trust and a low point in the 152-year history of the newspaper.
>
> The reporter, Jayson Blair, 27, misled readers and *Times* colleagues with dispatches that purported to be from Maryland, Texas and other states, when often he was far away, in New York. He fabricated comments. He concocted scenes. He lifted material from other newspapers and wire services. He selected details from photographs to create the impression he had been somewhere or seen someone, when he had not.[27]

In all, Blair was found to have fabricated at least 36 of the 73 articles he authored during his tenure at the *Times*. It is important to note, however, that despite the *Times's* thorough investigation and lengthy reporting on the Blair scandal, it was not the newspaper that broke the story.

The *Times* was scooped by the *San Antonio Express-News* whose editor, Robert Rivard sent an e-mail to Howell Raines and Managing Editor Gerald Boyd on April 29, 2003, requesting that they "acknowledge publicly that the *Times* wrongfully appropriated reporter Macarena Hernandez's work."[28] When this accusation against the *Times* and one of its reporters, Jayson Blair, became public the following day, other newspapers began to issue additional complaints about Blair's unacknowledged purloining of their stories.

Publisher Arthur Sulzberger, whose family has owned and managed the paper since 1896, fired the chief editor Howell Raines in the wake of this scandal—less than two years after he had taken the helm.[29] In July 2003, Sulzberger replaced Raines with former managing editor Bill Keller who had been passed over in favor of Raines two years earlier, largely because Raines was viewed by Sulzberger as being more innovative.[30]

Keller proved to be more of a revolutionary leader than anyone had anticipated. Within the *Times* he made so many executive changes that after his first 18 months, "two-thirds of all newsroom workers . . . [reported] to a new boss."[31]

Perhaps Keller's most daring innovation, however, was to appoint Daniel Okrent, a former editor at *Life* and *Time* magazines, to an 18-month, non-renewable term as the first public editor of the *Times*.[32] Okrent's role demanded that he maintain an external perspective on the *Times* while serving as the "designated representative of the newspaper's readers."[33]

In his role as public editor or ombudsman, Okrent did not report to management—essentially, he could not be fired—he was given full access to the newsroom and "an unfettered opportunity to address readers' comments about the *Times's* coverage, to raise questions of his own, and to write about such matters in commentaries that would be published in the newspaper as often as he saw fit."[34] For the first time in its history, *The New York Times* would regularly include stories not reviewed by any of its editors.

The reason for placing Okrent in this newly created post was not just to restore the trust of the paper's readers, it was also part of an effort to repair problems that had become endemic in the culture of the newsroom. The *Times's* initial inquiry on the Blair scandal outlines multiple "signs of trouble" that were available to the *Times* upper management before disaster struck. A number of reporters and editors who had grown concerned over the regularity of errors in Blair's stories reported their "misgivings about [his] reporting skills, maturity and behavior" to newsroom administrators, including a terse email from metropolitan editor John Landman stating: "We have to stop Jayson from writing for the *Times*. Right now."[35]

It was also common knowledge among fellow reporters that Blair improperly used his expense account and company vehicles for personal activities.[36] Given the long list of warning signs, why did the *Times* fail to take the actions necessary to protect its most valuable asset, the trust of its readers? None of the newsroom administrators stood to benefit from Blair's misdeeds—in fact, many of them were seriously harmed by them.

A strong culture of professional ethics and values was present at *The New York Times* leading up to the Blair scandal—however, as Howell Raines had noted, the

Times also suffered from a "defining myth of effortless superiority."[37] This myth or narrative—based upon the *Times's* history of excellence and seemingly validated by a slew of Pulitzers—made it difficult for managers to see that the type of journalistic fraud committed by Blair could actually take place within their culture.

While strong organizational cultures are a good defense against most ethical failings, the Achilles heel is their susceptibility to what psychologists term groupthink—"a strong concurrence-seeking tendency that interferes with effective decision making."[38] In particular, groupthink fosters the illusion that an organization lacks certain vulnerabilities or is inherently more moral than others.[39] What was missing at the *Times* was a highly developed moral imagination that would have enabled managers to critique and correct the sense of superiority that prevented the paper from making effective decisions to halt a tiny blaze of misdeeds before they became an inferno.

Keller's decision to give a critic unrestricted access and a regular, unedited column in the Times could not have been easy for staff reporters to accept. As Harold Evans, former editor of the *Sunday Times of London* has noted, "It is hardly inspirational to be identified in a column in one's own paper as variously 'nasty,' 'arrogant,' 'unfair,' 'dysfunctional,' 'ideological,' 'credulous,' 'condescending'"— all terms which Okrent used during his tenure.[40]

Despite these difficulties, Evans acknowledges that if a public editor had been in place during Howell Raines's tenure, "it is quite likely that . . . he would have detected significant tremors before the earthquakes . . . . The fault lines were there before Raines took over."[41] The morally imaginative step of giving one's critics a voice—and a very public soapbox—helped to break the enchantment of the *Times's* myth of invincible superiority, not only restoring trust in the current paper, but also helping to ensure that future problems would not go unchecked as they did in the case of Jayson Blair.

Creative moral imagination helps managers criticize their own and others' points of view and generate adequate alternatives.

Creative imagination facilitates the ability to envision and actualize novel possibilities through a fresh point of view or conceptual scheme. Creative moral imagination helps managers criticize their own and others' points of view and generate adequate alternatives. Ed Keller and David Neeleman freed their imaginations from traditional mindsets in order to see that other options were in fact available.

Moral decision making is a dynamic process, one which calls for an imaginative response by managers encountering new situations that do not easily fit within an existing narrative or framework. Moral judgments are not always clear—more often than not they are a result of a delicate balance of context, evaluations of the situation, and the presence or absence of imagination.

The moral decision-making process is seldom complete, since moral judgments are at best partial or temporary solutions. These solutions are, however, also starting points or models for future sets of decisions. Each new set of decisions is an opportunity for moral growth, an occasion to further develop a moral imagination that perceives the nuances of a situation, challenges the framework or narrative in which the event is embedded, and imagines how that situation and other situations might be different.

Nothing short of a very active free-playing imagination will enable us to distance ourselves from our scripts, roles, or narratives to envision new and better possibilities. Moral imagination entails an ability to consider a situation from the perspectives of various stakeholders—a facility that can help managers avoid the ethical trap of confusing reality with what they want it to be. Leaders will better prepare their organizations for the unanticipated situations they will inevitably face by expanding the notion of managerial responsibility to include moral imagination as a cultural practice and value.

Implications and Take-Aways for Managers

Moral imagination can be taught and developed inside cubicles as well as in the board room. It should be a key factor in developing the next generation of corporate leaders.

While the role and circumstance of corporations differ, most firms would recognize serious benefits from developing and "routinizing" the exercise of moral imagination in the daily work routine of their employees. Moral imagination is not just about avoiding disasters—it is about creating value through new products, services, processes, and organizations. Because of this close alignment to innovation, moral imagination could financially benefit companies facing the challenge of organic growth.

Four Key Issues:

Managers interested in fostering moral imagination may use the following key issues and accompanying recommendations as starting points.

1. Failure to speak a common language

Different professions or areas within the same organization may exhibit very different ways of framing issues. The Challenger disaster happened in part because Thiokol's managers failed to understand the engineers' definition of risk; one of the senior managers overrode the engineers protest; and Thiokol signed off on the launch.

Recommendation:

Organizations—particularly large global ones—need to include individuals who understand and can translate multiple frameworks. In order to make good decisions, firms must develop common systems that facilitate interaction between the various narratives and mental models.

2. Obedience to authority

Sometimes obedience to authority contributes to moral disaster. Individuals, when given a set of instructions by a person in authority, will often carry out these instructions, even when they are absurd, immoral, dangerous, or life-threatening.[42]

Recommendation:

A) Creating a culture of pushback—like Johnson & Johnson's challenge meetings—can be an effective method for leaders. This does not happen organically; it must be built in from the top of the organization. A tone must exist at the top that actively seeks out and listens to internal voices of dissent.

B) Shared responsibility can be achieved when individuals author and participate in their own history and narratives. No matter a person's place in an organization, each person is responsible for helping to build or change the culture. If something is disturbing about a company, individuals should envision how they can become change agents.

3. The lesser of two evils

When faced with a difficult choice, we often may feel forced to choose between the lesser of two evils, figuring that the moral response is to choose the option that does the least harm.

Recommendation:

It is precisely when it seems there is no good option among our available choices that we should think outside our current role and framework and imagine what a good choice or a better story might look like. The real choice is not simply between the lesser of two evils, but between accepting this framework, turning a blind eye to other possibilities and to our own responsibility, or imagining and searching for a better answer.

4. Groupthink

Groupthink occurs when a community narrative is so powerful that it remains unquestioned. It can lead to illusions of invulnerability or moral superiority, which create organizational blind spots, crippling an individual's ability to make good decisions.

Recommendation:

A) Internalizing critics may be the best safeguard for organizational integrity. If external critics are breaking "bad news" about the company, it may be too late to fix any problems. External perspectives are key to avoiding groupthink.

Communications and public relations personnel serve an important, ethical role by listening to and engaging stakeholders outside the firm. Whenever it takes a publicly visible crisis to make a firm sensitive to ethics issues within a company, it must be viewed as a cultural and management failure.

B) Reaping the benefits of diversity with regard to race, gender, cultural background, and personality/modes of thinking and expressing one's self is of great value. These differences, when recognized, can help an organization to develop internal leaders who can criticize the organization.

C) Consulting other leaders outside the firm is a great benefit to those in leadership positions. It provides insight and an opportunity for conversation about difficult ethics issues. Likewise, the Business Roundtable Institute for Corporate Ethics's CEO Ethics Seminars operate on the principle that the corner office can be a lonely place—especially with regard to ethics issues—and that there is great benefit to be had from leaders of different firms engaging in conversations about ethical issues with one another.

Notes

1. Dennis Gioia, "Pinto Fires and Personal Ethics: A script Analysis of Missed Opportunities," *Journal of Business Ethics* 11 (1992): 385.

2. Gioia, 385.

3. E. H. Gombrich, Art and Illusion, (Princeton: Princeton University Press, 1961), 80–82.

4. Wendy K. Smith, and Richard S. Tedlow, "James Burke: A Career in American Business," Harvard University Graduate School of Business Case #9-389-1771989 (Boston: Harvard Business School Press, 1989).

5. Patricia H. Werhane, "Engineers and Management: The Challenge of the Challenger Incident," *Journal of Business Ethics* 10, (1991): 605–615.

6. Judith Andre, "Role Morality as a Complex Instance of Ordinary Morality," *American Philosophical Quarterly* 28, (1991): 73–80.

7. Susan Pulliam, "Over the Line: A Staffer Ordered To Commit Fraud Balked, Then Caved—Pushed by WorldCom Bosses, Accountant Betty Vinson Helped Cook the Books—A Confession at the Marriott," *The Wall Street Journal*, 23 June 2003, sec. A1.

8. Pulliam, A1.

9. Pulliam, A1.

10. Wellpoint website: http://www.wellpoint.com/business/about_mission.asp. Wellpoint company news release, "WellPoint is Nation's First Health Benefits Company to Measure the Health of its Members" (April 4, 2007): http://phx.corporate-ir.net/phoenix.zhtml?c=130104&p=irol-newsArticle_ general&t=Regular&id=981192&.

11. Wellpoint company news release (April 4, 2007).

12. Nora Boustany, "Museum, Google Zoom In on Darfur," *Washington Post*, 14 April 2007, sec. A10, http://www.washingtonpost.com/wp-dyn/content/article/2007/04/13/AR2007041302189_pf.html.

13. Boustany, A1.

14. Quoted in Boutsany, A1.

15. David Neeleman, "An Apology from JetBlue Airways email message to customers," February 22, 2007.

16. JetBlue website: http://www.jetblue.com/about/ourcompany/history/about_our history.html.

17. Jenna McGregor, "Special Report: Customer Service Champs," *BusinessWeek*, (5 March 2007): 54–58.

18. McGregor, 58.

19. Jeff Bailey, "Chief 'Mortified' by JetBlue Crisis," *The New York Times*, 19 February 2007, sec. 1.

20. Bailey, 2007.

21. Rushworth M. Kidder, "Ice, JetBlue, and the Collapse of Prudence," *Ethics Newsline*, 20 February 2007, (www.globalethics.org/newsline/).

22. David Neeleman quoted by Bailey, 2007; JetBlue Airways Customer Bill of Rights, http://www.jetblue.com/about/ourcompany/promise/index.html.

23. Christopher Kercher, "Readers Report," *BusinessWeek*, (26 March 2007).

24. JetBlue News Release. "JetBlue Announces the JetBlue Customer Bill of Rights," Feb. 20, 2007, http://investor.jetblue.com/phoenix.zhtml?c=131045&p=irol-newsArticle&ID=965052&highlight.

25. Neeleman as quoted by Bailey, 2007.

26. Terry Keenan, "JetBlue Damage Control," FOX News, (27 February 2007); http://www.foxnews.com/story/0,2933,255101,00.html; and Robert Trigaux, "Service is Knowing How to Say You're Sorry," *St. Petersburg Times*.

27. Dan Barry, David Barstow, Jonathan D. Glater, Adam Liptak, and Jacques Steinberg, "Times Reporter Who Resigned Leaves Long Trail of Deception," *The New York Times*, 11 May 2003, sec. 1.

28. T. A. Badger, "San Antonio Express-News Claims New York Times Reporter Appropriated Material," Associated Press, 30 April 2003.

29. Anthony Bianco, John Rossant, and Lauren Gard, "The Future of The New York Times; Publisher Arthur Sulzberger Jr. Has His Hands Full: Weaker Earnings. A Changing Media World. A Scandal's Aftermath. He Also Has an Ambitious Business Plan," *BusinessWeek* 3916, no. 64 (17 January 2005).

30. Bianco et al., 2005.

31. Bianco et al., 2005.

32. "Interview: Journalist Daniel Okrent talks about being the first ombudsman of The New York Times," *Fresh Air*, 17 May 2006.

33. Jacques Steinberg, "The Times Chooses Veteran of Magazines and Publishing as Its First Public Editor," *The New York Times*, 27 October 2003.

34. Steinberg, 2003.

35. Dan Barry, David Barstow, Jonathan D. Glater, Adam Liptak, and Jacques Steinberg, "Times Reporter Who Resigned Leaves Long Trail of Deception," *The New York Times*, 11 May 2003, sec. 1.

36. Barry et al., 2003.

37. Howell Raines as quoted by Bianco et al., 2005.

38. Forsyth as cited in Arnold P. Goldstein, *The Psychology of Group Aggression*, (Chichester, England: John Wiley & Sons, 2002), 32.

39. Goldstein, 34,

40. Harold Evans, "Eye on The Times: Book Review of Public Editor #1: The Collected Columns (With Reflections, Reconsiderations, and Even a Few Retractions) of the First Ombudsman of The New York Times, by Daniel Okrent," *The New York Times*, 18 June 2006.

41. Evans, 2006.

42. S. Milgram, *Obedience to Authority* (New York: Harper Collins, 1974).

Chapter 2

Moral Development Theory

Indoctrination Versus Relativity in Value Education

Lawrence Kohlberg

Lawrence Kohlberg (1927–1987) was one of the most preeminent psychologists of the 20th century. His stage theory of moral development, which was inspired by the work of Jean Piaget, continues to be influential today. Kohlberg held teaching positions at Yale, the University of Chicago, and at Harvard University, where he established the Center for Moral Development and Education. Among his most important writings are "Stage and Sequence: The Cognitive-Developmental Approach to Socialization" (1969), The Meaning and Measure of Moral Development *(1981),* The Philosophy of Moral Development *(1981),* The Psychology of Moral Development *(1984),* and Child Psychology and Childhood Education: A Cognitive-Developmental View *(1987). Kohlberg also initiated moral development curricula in schools and prisons. His theory became the basis for the Defining Issues Test (D1T), which was developed by lames Rest in the early 1980s, to identify a person's level of moral development.*

The first point I want to make is that the problem raised by my title, "Indoctrination Versus Relativity in Value Education," requires coming to grips with morality and moral education. I hope I will be able to make moral education a somewhat less forbidding term by presenting my own approach to it. My basic task, however, is not to convince you of my approach to moral education but to convince you that the only way to solve the problems of relativity and indoctrination in value education is to formulate a notion of *moral development* that is justified philosophically and psychologically.

Although *moral education* has a forbidding sound to teachers, they constantly practice it. They tell children what to do, make evaluations of children's behavior, and direct children's relations in the classrooms. Sometimes teachers do these things without being aware that they are engaging in moral education, but the children are aware of it. For example, my second-grade son told me that he did not want to be one of the bad boys. Asked "Who were the bad boys?" he replied,

56

"The ones who don't put their books back where they belong and get yelled at." His teacher would have been surprised to know that her concerns with classroom management defined for her children what she and her school thought were basic moral values or that she was engaged in value indoctrination.

Most teachers are aware that they are teaching values, like it or not, and are very concerned as to whether this teaching is unjustified indoctrination. In particular, they are uncertain as to whether their own moral opinions should be presented as "moral truths," whether they should be expressed merely as personal opinion or should be omitted from classroom discussion entirely. As an example, an experienced junior high school teacher told us,

> My class deals with morality and right and wrong quite a bit. I don't expect all of them to agree with me; each has to satisfy himself according to his own convictions, as long as he is sincere and thinks he is pursuing what is right. I often discuss cheating this way but I always get *defeated*, because they still argue cheating is all right. After you accept the idea that kids have the right to build a position with logical arguments, you have to accept what they come out with, even though you drive at it ten times a year and they still come out with the same conclusion.

This teacher's confusion is apparent. She believes everyone should "have his own ideas," and yet she is most unhappy if this leads to a point where some of these ideas include the notion that "it's all right to cheat." In other words, she is smack up against the problem of relativity of values in moral education. Using this teacher as an example, I will attempt to demonstrate that moral education can be free from the charge of cultural relativity and arbitrary indoctrination that inhibits her when she talks about cheating.

Cop-Out Solutions to the Relativity Problem

To begin with, I want to reject a few cop-outs or false solutions sometimes suggested as solving the relativity problem. One is to call moral education *socialization*. Sociologists have sometimes claimed that moralization in the interests of classroom management and maintenance of the school as a social system is a hidden curriculum; that it performs hidden services in helping children adapt to society (Jackson, 1968). They have argued that, since praise and blame on the part of teachers is a necessary aspect of the socialization process, the teacher does not have to consider the psychological and philosophic issues of moral education. In learning to conform to the teacher's expectations and the school rules, children are becoming socialized, they are internalizing the norms and standards of society. I argue in Chapter 2 why this approach is a cop-out. In practice, it means that we call the teacher's yelling at her students for not putting their books away *socialization*. To label it *socialization* does not legitimate it as valid education, nor does it remove the charge of arbitrary indoctrination from it. Basically, this sociological argument implies that respect for social authority is a moral good in itself. Stated in different terms, the notion that it is valid for the teacher to have an unreflective hidden curriculum is based on the notion that the teacher is the agent of the state, the church, or the social system, rather than being a free moral agent dealing with children who are free moral agents. The notion that the teacher is the agent of the state is taken for granted in some educational systems, such as that of the Soviets. However, the moral curriculum is not hidden in Soviet education; it is done explicitly and well as straight indoctrination (Bronfenbrenner, 1968). For the moment, I will not argue what is wrong with indoctrination but will assume that it is incompatible with the conceptions of civil liberties that are central not only to American democracy but to any just social system.

Let us turn now to the second cop-out. This is to rely on vaguely positive and honorific-sounding terms such as "moral values" or "moral and spiritual values." We can see in the following statements how a program called "Teaching Children Values in the Upper Elementary School" (Carr and Wellenberg, 1966) relies on a vague usage of "moral and spiritual values":

> Many of our national leaders have expressed anxiety about an increasing lack of concern for personal moral and spiritual values. Throughout history, nations have sought value systems to help people live congenially. The Golden Rule and the Ten Commandments are examples of such value systems. Each pupil needs to acquire a foundation of sound values to help him act correctly and make proper choices between right and wrong, truth and untruth. The teacher can develop a sound value system in the following ways:
>
> 1. Be a good example.
> 2. Help young people to assess conflict situations and to gain insight into the development of constructive values and attitudes. Situations arise daily in which pupils can receive praise that will reinforce behavior that exemplified desired values.
> 3. Show young people how to make generalizations concerning experience through evaluation and expression of desirable values.
> 4. Help students acquire an understanding of the importance of values that society considers worthwhile.
> 5. Aid children to uphold and use positive values when confronted by adverse pressure from peers.

The problem, however, is to define these "positive values." We may agree that "positive values" are desirable, but the term conceals the fact that teachers, children, and societies have different ideas as to what constitutes "positive values." Although Carr and Wellenberg cite the Ten Commandments and the Golden Rule as "value systems sought by nations," they also could have used the code of the Hitler or of the communist youth as examples of "value systems sought by nations."

I raise the issue of the "relativity of values" in this context because the words *moral, positive,* and *values* are interpreted by each teacher in a different way, depending on the teacher's own values and standards.

This becomes clear when we consider our third cop-out. This is the cop-out of defining moral values in terms of what I call a "bag of virtues." By a "bag of virtues," I mean a set of personality traits generally considered to be positive. Defining the aims of moral education in terms of a set of "virtues" is as old as Aristotle, who said, "Virtue . . . [is] of two kinds, intellectual and moral. . . . [The moral] virtues we get by first exercising them . . . we become just by doing just acts, temperate by doing temperate acts, brave by doing brave acts."

The attraction of such an approach is evident. Although it is true that people often cannot agree on details of right and wrong or even on fundamental moral principles, we all think such "traits" as honesty and responsibility are good things. By adding enough traits to the virtue bag, we eventually get a list that contains something to suit everyone.

This approach to moral education was widely prevalent in the public schools in the 1920s and 1930s and was called "character education." The educators and psychologists, such as Havighurst and Taba (1949), who developed these approaches defined character as the sum total of a set of "those traits of personality which are subject to the moral sanctions of society."

One difficulty with this approach to moral character is that everyone has his own bag. However, the problem runs deeper than the composition of a given list of virtues and vices. Although it may be true that the notion of teaching virtues, such as honesty or integrity, arouses little controversy, it is also true that a vague consensus on the goodness of these virtues conceals a great deal of actual disagreement over their definitions. What is one person's "integrity" is another person's "stubbornness," what is one person's honesty in "expressing your true feelings" is another person's insensitivity to the feelings of others. This is evident in controversial fields of adult behavior. Student protesters view their behavior as reflecting the virtues of altruism, idealism, awareness, and courage. Those in opposition regard the same behavior as reflecting the vices of irresponsibility and disrespect for "law and order." Although this difficulty can be recognized clearly in college education, it is easier for teachers of younger children to think that their judgments in terms of the bag of virtues are objective and independent of their own value biases. However, a parent will not agree that a child's specific failure to obey an "unreasonable" request by the teacher was wrong, even if the teacher calls the act "uncooperative," as some teachers are prone to do.

I have summarized three cop-outs from the relativity problem and rejected them. Socialization, teaching positive values, and developing a bag of virtues all leave the teacher where she was—stuck with her own personal value standards and biases to be imposed on her students. There is one last cop-out to the relativity problem. That is to lie back and enjoy it or encourage it. In the new social studies, this is called *value clarification*.

As summarized by Engel (in Simon, 1971, p. 902), this position holds that:

> In the consideration of values, there is no single correct answer, but value clarification is supremely important. One must contrast value clarification and value inculcation. Inculcation suggests that the learner has limited control and hence limited responsibility in the development of his own values. He needs to be told what values are or what he should value.
>
> This is not to suggest, however, that nothing is ever inculcated. As a matter of fact, in order to clarify values, at least one principle needs to be adopted by all concerned. Perhaps the only way the principle can be adopted is through some procedure which might best be termed *inculcation*. That principle might be stated as follows: in the consideration of values there is no single correct answer. More specifically it might be said that the adequate posture both for students and teachers in clarifying values is openness.

Although the basic premise of this value clarification approach is that "everyone has his own values," it is further advocated that children can and should learn (1) to be more aware of their own values and how they relate to their decisions, (2) to make their values consistent and to order them in hierarchies for decisions, (3) to be more aware of the divergencies between their value hierarchies and those of others, and (4) to learn to tolerate these divergencies. In other words, although values are regarded as arbitrary and relative, there may be universal, rational strategies for making decisions that maximize these values. Part of this rational strategy is to recognize that values are relative. Within this set of premises, it is quite logical to teach that values are relative as part of the overall program.

An elaboration of this approach can be found in *Decision Making: A Guide for Teachers Who Would Help Preadolescent Children Become Imaginative and Responsible Decision Makers* (Dodder and Dodder, 1968). In a portion of this book, modern social scientific perspectives are used to develop a curriculum unit entitled "Why Don't We All Make the Same Decisions?" A set of classroom materials and activities are then presented to demonstrate to children the following propositions: (1) we don't all make the same decisions because our values are different; (2) our values tend to originate outside ourselves; (3) our values are different because each of us has been influenced by different important others; and (4) our values are different because each of us has been influenced by a different cultural environment.

The teacher is told to have the children discuss moral dilemmas in such a way as to reveal those different values. As an example, one child might make a moral decision in terms of avoiding punishment, another in terms of the welfare of other people, another in terms of certain rules, another in terms of getting the most for himself. The children are then to be encouraged to discuss their values with each other and to recognize that everyone has different values. Whether or not "the welfare of others" is a more adequate value than "avoiding punishment" is not an issue to be raised by the teacher. Rather, the teacher is instructed to teach only that "our values are different."

Indeed, acceptance of the idea that *all* values are relative does, logically, lead to the conclusion that the teacher should not attempt to teach *any* particular moral values. This leaves the teacher in the quandary of our teacher who could not successfully argue against cheating. The students of a teacher who has been successful in communicating moral relativism will believe, like the teacher, that "everyone has his own bag" and that "everyone should keep doing his thing." If one of these students has learned his relativity lesson, when he is caught cheating he will argue that he did nothing wrong. The basis of his argument will be that his own hierarchy of values, which may be different from that of the teacher, made it right for him to cheat. Although recognizing that other people believe that cheating is wrong, he himself holds the "value" that one should cheat when the opportunity presents itself. If teachers want to be consistent and retain their relativistic beliefs, they would have to concede.

Now I am not criticizing the value clarification approach itself. It is a basic and valuable component of the new social studies curricula, as I have discussed (1973). My point is, rather, that value clarification is not a sufficient solution to the relativity problem. Furthermore, the actual teaching of relativism is itself an indoctrination or teaching of a fixed belief, a belief that we are going to show is not true scientifically or philosophically (see Chapter 4).

A Typological Scheme on the Stages of Moral Thought

In other words, I am happy to report that I can propose a solution to the relativity problem that has plagued philosophers for three thousand years. I can say this with due modesty because it did not depend on being smart. It only happened that my colleagues and I were the first people in history to do detailed cross-cultural studies on the development of moral thinking.

The following dilemma should clarify the issue:

The Heinz Dilemma

> In Europe, a woman was near death from a very bad disease, a special kind of cancer. There was one drug that the doctors thought might save her. It was a form of radium that a druggist in the same town had recently discovered. The drug was expensive to make, but the druggist was charging ten times what the drug cost him to make. He paid $200 for the radium and charged $2,000 for a small dose of the drug. The sick woman's husband, Heinz, went to everyone he knew to borrow the money, but he could get together only about $1,000, which was half of what it cost. He told the druggist that his wife was dying and asked him to sell it cheaper or let him pay later. But the druggist said, "No, I

discovered the drug and I'm going to make money from it." Heinz got desperate and broke into the man's store to steal the drug for his wife.

Should the husband have done that? Was it right or wrong? Is your decision that it is right (or wrong) objectively right, is it morally universal, or is it your personal opinion? If you think it is morally right to steal the drug, you must face the fact that it is legally wrong. What is the basis of your view that it is morally right, then, more than your personal opinion? Is it anything that can be agreed on? If you think so, let me report the results of a National Opinion Research Survey on the question, asked of a representative sample of adult Americans. Seventy-five percent said it was wrong to steal, though most said they might do it.

Can one take anything but a relativist position on the question? By a relativist position, I mean a position like that of Bob, a high school senior. He said, "There's a million ways to look at it. Heinz had a moral decision to make. Was it worse to steal or let his wife die? In my mind, I can either condemn him or condone him. In this case, I think it was fine. But possibly the druggist was working on a capitalist morality of supply and demand."

I went on to ask Bob, "Would it be wrong if he didn't steal it?"

Bob replied, "It depends on how he is oriented morally. If he thinks it's worse to steal than to let his wife die, then it would be wrong what he did. It's all relative; what I would do is steal the drug. I can't say that's right or wrong or that it's what everyone should do."

But even if you agree with Bob's relativism you may not want to go as far as he did. He started the interview by wondering if he could answer because he "questioned the whole terminology, the whole moral bag." He continued, "But then I'm also an incredible moralist, a real puritan in some sense and moods. My moral judgment and the way I perceive things morally changes very much when my mood changes. When I'm in a cynical mood, I take a cynical view of morals, but still, whether I like it or not, I'm terribly moral in the way I look at things. But I'm not too comfortable with it." Bob's moral perspective was well expressed in the late Joe Gould's poem called "My Religion." Brief and to the point, the poem said, "In winter I'm a Buddhist, in the summer I'm a nudist."

Now, Bob's relativism rests on a confusion. The confusion is that between relativity as the social science fact that different people *do* have different moral values and relativity as the philosophic claim that people *ought* to have different moral values, that no moral values are justified for all people.

To illustrate, I quote a not atypical response of one of my graduate students to the same moral dilemma. She said, "I think he should steal it because if there is any such thing as a universal human value, it is the value of life, and that would justify it."

I then asked her, "Is there any such thing as a universal human value?" and she answered, "No, all values are relative to your culture."

She began by claiming that one ought to act in terms of the universal value of human life, implying that human life is a universal value in the sense that it is logical and desirable for all people to respect all human life, that one can demonstrate to other people that it is logical and desirable to act in this way. If she were clear in her thinking, she would see that the fact that all people do not always act in terms of this value does not contradict the claim that all people ought to always act in accordance with it. Because she made this confusion, she ended in total confusion.

What I am going to claim is that if we distinguish the issues of universality as fact and the possibility of universal moral ideals we get a positive answer to both questions. As far as facts go, I claim just the opposite of what Dodder and Dodder (1968) claimed to be basic social science truths. I claim that

1. We often make different decisions and yet have the same basic moral values.
2. Our values tend to originate inside ourselves as we process our social experience.
3. In every culture and subculture of the world, both the same basic moral values and the same steps toward moral maturity are found. Although social environments directly produce different specific beliefs (for example, smoking is wrong, eating pork is wrong), they do not engender different basic moral principles (for example, "consider the welfare of others," "treat other people equally," and so on).
4. Basic values are different largely because we are at different levels of maturity in thinking about basic moral and social issues and concepts. Exposure to others more mature than ourselves helps stimulate maturity in our own value process.

All parents know that the basic values of their children do not come from the outside, from the parents, although many wish they did. For example, at the age of four my son joined the pacifist and vegetarian movement and refused to eat meat because, he said, it is bad to kill animals. In spite of his parents' attempts to dissuade him by arguing about the difference between justified and unjustified killing, he remained a vegetarian for six months. However, he did recognize that some forms of killing were "legitimate." One night I read to him from a book about Eskimo life that included a description of a seal-killing expedition. While listening to the story, he became very angry and said, "You know, there is one kind of meat I would eat, Eskimo meat. It's bad to kill animals so it's all right to eat Eskimos."

This episode illustrates (1) that children often generate their own moral values and maintain them in the face of cultural training, and (2) that these values have universal roots. Every child believes it is bad to kill because regard for the lives of others or pain at death is a natural empathic response, although it is not necessarily universally and consistently maintained. In this example, the value of life led both to vegetarianism and to the desire to kill Eskimos. This latter desire comes also from a universal value tendency: a belief in justice or reciprocity here expressed in terms of revenge or punishment (at higher levels, the belief that those who infringe on the rights of others cannot expect their own rights to be respected).

I quoted my son's response because it is shockingly different from the way you think and yet it has universal elements you will recognize. What is the shocking difference between my son's way of thinking and your own? If you are a psychoanalyst, you will start thinking about oral cannibalistic fantasies and defenses against them and all that. However, that is not, really what the difference is at all. You do not have to be cannibalistic to wonder why it is right for humans to kill and eat animals but it is not right for animals or humans to kill and eat humans. The response really shows that my son was a philosopher, like every young child: he wondered about things that most grown-ups take for granted. If you want to study children, however, you have to be a bit of a philosopher yourself and ask the moral philosopher's question: "Why is it all right to kill and eat animals but not humans?" I wonder how many of you can give a good answer. In any case, Piaget started the modern study of child development by recognizing that the child, like the adult philosopher, was puzzled by the basic questions of life: by the meaning of space, time, causality, life, death, right and wrong, and so on. What he found was that the child asked all the great philosophic questions but answered them in a very different way from the adults. This way was so different that Piaget called the difference a difference in stage or quality of thinking, rather than a difference in amount of knowledge or accuracy of thinking. The difference in thinking between you and my son, then, is basically a difference in stage.

My own work on morality started from Piaget's notions of stages and Piaget's notion that the child was a philosopher. Inspired by Jean Piaget's (1948) pioneering effort to apply a structural approach to moral development, I have gradually elaborated over the years a typological scheme describing general stages of moral thought that can be defined independently of the specific content of particular moral decisions or actions. We studied seventy-five American boys from early adolescence on. These youths were continually presented with hypothetical moral dilemmas, all deliberately philosophical, some found in medieval works of casuistry. On the basis of their reasoning about these dilemmas at a given age, we constructed the typology of definite and universal levels of development in moral thought.

The typology contains three distinct levels of moral thinking, and within each of these levels are two related stages. These levels and stages may be considered separate moral philosophies, distinct views of the social-moral world.

We can speak of the children as having their own morality or series of moralities. Adults seldom listen to children's moralizing. If children throw back a few adult cliches and behave themselves, most parents—and many anthropologists and psychologists as well—think that the children have adopted or internalized the appropriate parental standards.

Actually, as soon as we talk with children about morality we find that they have many ways of making judgments that are not "internalized" from the outside and that do not come in any direct and obvious way from parents, teachers, or even peers.

The preconventional level is the first of three levels of moral thinking; the second level is conventional; and the third is postconventional or autonomous. Although preconventional children are often "well behaved" and responsive to cultural labels of good and bad, they interpret these labels in terms of their physical consequences (punishment, reward, exchange of favors) or in terms of the physical power of those who enunciate the rules and labels of good and bad.

This level is usually occupied by children aged four to ten, a fact well known to sensitive observers of children. The capacity of "properly behaved" children of this age to engage in cruel behavior when there are holes in the power structure is sometimes noted as tragic (*Lord of the Flies* and *High Wind in Jamaica*), sometimes as comic (Lucy in *Peanuts*).

The second or conventional level also can be described as *conformist*—but that is perhaps too smug a term. Maintaining the expectations and rules of the individual's family, group, or nation is perceived as valuable in its own right. There is a concern not only with conforming to the individual's social order but in maintaining, supporting, and justifying this order.

The postconventional level is characterized by a major thrust toward autonomous moral principles that have validity and application apart from authority of the groups or people who hold them and apart from the individual's identification with those people or groups.

Within each of these three levels, there are two discernible stages. The following paragraphs explain the dual moral stages of each level just described.

Definition of Moral Stages

Preconventional Level

At this level, the child is responsive to cultural rules and labels of good and bad, right or wrong, but interprets these labels in terms of either the physical or the hedonistic consequences of action (punishment, reward, exchange of favors) or in terms of the physical power of those who enunciate the rules and labels. The level is divided into the following two stages:

Stage 1. The Punishment and Obedience Orientation

The physical consequences of action determine its goodness or badness regardless of the human meaning or value of these consequences. Avoidance of punishment and unquestioning deference to power are valued in their own right.

Stage 2. The Instrumental Relativist Orientation

Right action consists of that which instrumentally satisfies one's needs and occasionally the needs of others. Human relations are viewed in terms like those of the marketplace. Elements of fairness, reciprocity, and equal sharing are present, but they are always interpreted in a physical, pragmatic way. Reciprocity is a matter of "You scratch my back and I'll scratch yours."

Conventional Level

At this level, maintaining the expectations of the individual's family, group, or nation is perceived as valuable in its own right, regardless of immediate and obvious consequences. The attitude is not only one of conformity to personal expectations and social order, but of loyalty to it, of actively maintaining, supporting, and justifying the order and of identifying with the people or group involved in it. At this level, there are the following two stages:

Stage 3. The Interpersonal Concordance or "Good Boy–Nice Girl" Orientation

Good behavior is that which pleases or helps others and is approved by them. There is much conformity to stereotypical images of what is majority or "natural" behavior. Behavior is frequently judged by intention—the judgment "he means well" becomes important for the first time. One earns approval by being "nice."

Stage 4. Society Maintaining Orientation

There is an orientation toward authority, fixed rules, and the maintenance of the social order. Right behavior consists of doing one's duty, showing respect for authority, and maintaining the given social order for its own sake.

Postconventional, Autonomous, or Principled Level

At this level, there is a clear effort to define moral values and principles that have validity and application apart from the authority of the groups or people holding these principles and apart from the individual's own identification with these groups. This level again has two stages:

Stage 5. The Social Contract Orientation

Right action tends to be defined in terms of general individual rights and in terms of standards that have been critically examined and agreed on by the whole society. There is a clear awareness of the relativism of personal values and opinions and a corresponding emphasis on procedural rules for reaching consensus. Aside from what is constitutionally and democratically agreed on, the right is a matter of personal "values" and "opinion." The result is an emphasis on the "legal point of view," but with an emphasis on the possibility of changing law in terms of rational considerations of social utility (rather than freezing it in terms of Stage 4 "law and order"). Outside the legal realm, free agreement and contract are the binding elements of obligation. This is the "official" morality of the American government and Constitution.

Stage 6. The Universal Ethical Principle Orientation

Right is defined by the decision of conscience in accord with self-chosen ethical principles appealing to logical comprehensiveness, universality, and consistency. These principles are abstract and ethical (the Golden Rule, the categorical imperative); they are not concrete moral rules such as the Ten Commandments. At heart, these are universal principles of justice, of the reciprocity and equality of human rights, and of respect for the dignity of human beings as individuals.

To understand what these stages mean concretely, let us look at them with regard to two of twenty-five basic moral concepts or aspects used to form the dilemmas we used in our research. One such aspect, for instance, is "motive given for rule obedience or moral action." In this instance, the six stages look like this:

1. Obey rules to avoid punishment.
2. Conform to obtain rewards, have favors returned, and so on.
3. Conform to avoid disapproval and dislike by others.
4. Conform to avoid censure by legitimate authorities and resultant guilt.
5. Conform to maintain the respect of the impartial spectator judging in terms of community welfare.
6. Conform to avoid self-condemnation.

In another of these twenty-five moral aspects, the value of human life, the six stages can be defined thus:

1. The value of human life is confused with the value of physical objects and is based on the social status or physical attributes of the possessor.
2. The value of human life is seen as instrumental to the satisfaction of the needs of its possessor or of other people.
3. The value of human life is based on the empathy and affection of family members and others toward its possessor.
4. Life is conceived as sacred in terms of its place in a categorical moral or religious order of rights and duties.
5. Life is valued both in terms of its relation to community welfare and in terms of life being a universal human right.
6. Human life is sacred—a universal human value of respect for the individual.

I have called this scheme a *typology*. This is because about 67 percent of most people's thinking is at a single stage, regardless of the moral dilemma involved. We call our types *stages* because they seem to represent an invariant developmental sequence. "True" stages come one at a time and always in the same order.

In our stages, all movement is forward in sequence and does not skip steps. Children may move through these stages at varying speeds, of course, and may be found half in and half out of a particular stage. Individuals may stop at any given stage and at any age, but if they continue to move, they must move in accord with these steps. Moral reasoning of the conventional kind or Stages 3–4, never occurs before the preconventional Stage 1 and Stage 2 thought has taken place. No adult in Stage 4 has gone through Stage 5, but all Stage 5 adults have gone through Stage 4.

Although the evidence is not complete, my study strongly suggests that moral change fits the stage pattern just described.

As a single example of our findings of stage sequence, take the progress of two boys on the aspect "the value of human life." The first boy, Tommy, who had suggested that one should perhaps steal for an important person, is asked, "Is it better to save the life of one important person or a lot of unimportant people?" At age ten, he answers, "All the people that aren't important because one man just has one house, maybe a lot of furniture, but a whole bunch of people have an awful lot of furniture, and some of these poor people might have a lot of money and it doesn't look it."

Clearly Tommy is Stage 1: he confuses the value of a human being with the value of the property he possesses. Three years later (age thirteen), Tommy's conceptions of life's values are most clearly elicited by the question "Should the doctor 'mercy kill' a fatally ill woman requesting death because of her pain?" He answers, "Maybe it would be good to put her out of pain, she'd be better off that way. But the husband wouldn't want it, it's not like an animal. If a pet dies you can get along without it—it isn't something you really need. Well, you can get a new wife, but it's not really the same."

Here his answer is Stage 2: the value of the woman's life is partly contingent on its instrumental value to her husband, who cannot replace her as easily as he can a pet.

Three years later still (age sixteen), Tommy's conception of life's value is elicited by the same question, to which he replies, "It might be best for her, but her husband—it's human life—not like an animal; it just doesn't have the same relationship that a human being does to a family. You can become attached to a dog, but nothing like a human, you know."

Now Tommy has moved from a Stage 2 instrumental view of the woman's value to a Stage 3 view based on the husband's distinctively human emphathy and love for someone in his family. Equally clearly, it lacks any basis for a universal human value of the woman's life, which would hold if she had no husband or if her husband did not love her. Tommy, then, has moved step by step through three stages during the age ten to sixteen. Although bright (IQ 120), he is a slow developer in moral judgment.

Let us take another boy, Richard, to show us sequential movement through the remaining three steps. At age thirteen, Richard said about the mercy killing, "If she requests it, it's really up to her. She is in such terrible pain, just the same as people are always putting animals out of their pain," and in general showed a mixture of Stage 2 and Stage 3 responses concerning the value of life. At sixteen, he said, "I don't know. In one way, it's murder, it's not right or privilege of man to decide who shall live and who should die. God put life into everybody on earth and you're taking away something from that person that came directly from God, and you're destroying something that is very sacred, it's in a way part of God and it's almost destroying a part of God when you kill a person. There's something of God in everyone."

Here Richard clearly displays a Stage 4 concept of life as sacred in terms of its place in a categorical moral or religious order. The value of human life is universal; it is true for all humans. It still, however, depends on something else—on respect for God and God's authority; it is not an autonomous human value. Presumably if God told Richard to murder, as God commanded Abraham to murder Isaac, he would do so.

At age twenty, Richard said to the same question, "There are more and more people in the medical profession who think it is a hardship on everyone, the person, the family, when you know they are going to die. When a person is kept alive by an artificial lung or kidney, it's more like being a vegetable than being a human. If it's her own choice, I think there are certain rights and privileges that go along with being a human being. I am a human being, and I have certain desires for life, and I think everybody else does too. You have a world of which you are the center, and everybody else does too, and in that sense we're all equal."

Richard's response is clearly Stage 5, in that the value of life is defined in terms of equal and universal human rights in a context of relativity ("You have a world of which you are the center, and in that sense we're all equal") and of concern for utility or welfare consequences.

At twenty-four, Richard says, "A human life, whoever it is, takes precedence over any other moral or legal value. A human life has inherent value whether or not it is valued by a particular individual. The worth of the individual human being is central where the principles of justice and love are normative for all human relationships."

This young man is at Stage 6 in seeing the value of human life as absolute in representing a universal and equal respect for the human as an individual. He has moved step by step through a sequence culminating in a definition of human life as centrally valuable rather than derived from or dependent on social or divine authority.

In a genuine and culturally universal sense, these steps lead toward an increased morality of value judgment, where morality is considered as a form of judging, as it has been in a philosophic tradition running from the analyses of Kant to those of the modern analytic or "ordinary language" philosophers. At Stage 6 people have disentangled judgments of—or language about—human life from status and property values (Stage 1); from its uses to others (Stage 2); from interpersonal affection (Stage 3); and so on; they have a means of moral judgment that is universal and impersonal. Stage 6 people answer in moral words such as *duty* or *morally right* and use them in a way implying universality, ideals and impersonality. They think and speak in phrases such as "regardless of who it was" or "I would do it in spite of punishment."

Universal Invariant Sequence of Moral Development

When I first decided to explore moral development in other cultures, I was told by anthropologist friends that I would have to throw away my culture-bound moral concepts and stories and start from scratch learning a whole new set of values for each new culture. My first try consisted of a brace of villages, one Atayal (Malaysian aboriginal) and the other Taiwanese.

My guide was a young Chinese ethnographer who had written an account of the moral and religious patterns of the Atayal and Taiwanese villages. Taiwanese boys in the ten to thirteen age group were asked about a story involving theft of food: A man's wife is starving to death but the store owner would not give the man any food unless he could pay, and he cannot. Should he break in and steal some food? Why? Many of the boys said, "He should steal the food for his wife because if she dies he'll have to pay for her funeral, and that costs a lot."

My guide was amused by these responses, but I was relieved: they were, of course, "classic" Stage 2 responses. In the Atayal village, funerals were not such a big thing, so the Stage 2 boys said, "He should steal the food because he needs his wife to cook for him."

This means that we have to consult our anthropologists to know what content Stage 2 children will include in instrumental exchange calculations, or what Stage 4 adults will identify as the proper social order. But one certainly does not have to start from scratch. What made my guide laugh was the difference in from between the children's Stage 2 thought and his own, a difference definable independently of particular cultures.

Figures 2.1 and 2.2 indicate the cultural universality of the sequence of stages we have found. Figure 1.1 presents the age trends for middle-class urban boys in the United States, Taiwan, and Mexico. At age ten in each country, the order of use of each stage is the same as the order of its difficulty or maturity.

In the United States, by age sixteen the order is the reverse, from the highest to the lowest, except that Stage 6 is still little used. At age thirteen, the good-boy middle stage (Stage 3) is most used.

The results in Mexico and Taiwan are the same, except that development is a little slower. The most conspicuous feature is that, at the age of sixteen, Stage 5 thinking is much more salient in the United States than in Mexico or Taiwan. Nevertheless, it is present in the other countries, so we know that this is not purely an American democratic construct.

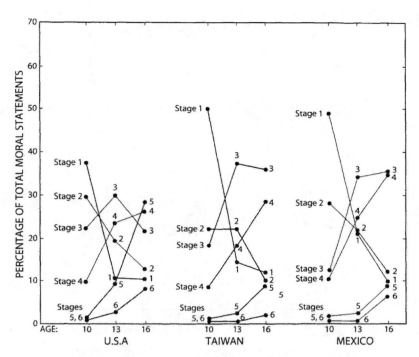

Figure 2.1. Moral development of middle-class urban boys in the United States, Taiwan, and Mexico. At age ten, the stages are used according to difficulty. At age thirteen, Stage 3 is most used by all three groups. At age sixteen, U.S. boys have reversed the order of age ten stages (with the exception of 6). In Taiwan and Mexico, conventional (3–4) stages prevail at age sixteen, with Stage 5 also little used (Kohlberg, 1968a).

Figure 2.2 shows strikingly similar results from two isolated villages, one in Yucatan, one in Turkey. Although conventional moral thought increases steadily from ages ten to sixteen, it still has not achieved a clear ascendancy over preconventional thought.

Trends for lower-class urban groups are intermediate in the rate of development between those for the middle-class and for the village boys. In the three divergent cultures that I studied, middle-class children were found to be more advanced in moral judgment than matched lower-class children. This was not due to the fact that the middle-class children heavily favored some one type of thought that could be seen as corresponding to the prevailing middle-class pattern. Instead, middle-class and working-class children move through the same sequences, but the middle-class children move faster and farther.

This sequence is not dependent on a particular religion or on any religion at all in the usual sense. I found no important differences in the development of moral thinking among Catholics, Protestants, Jews, Buddhists, Moslems, and atheists.

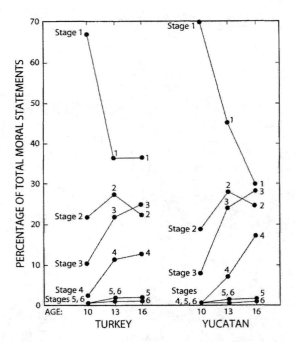

Figure 2.2. Two isolated villages, one in Turkey, the other in Yucatan, show similar patterns in moral thinking. There is no reversal of order, and conventional (stages 3–4) thought does not gain a clear ascendancy over preconventional stages at age sixteen (Kohlberg, 1968a).

In summary, the nature of our sequence is not significantly affected by widely varying social, cultural, or religious conditions. The only thing that is affected is the rate at which individuals progress through this sequence.

Why should there be such a universal invariant sequence of development? In answering this question, we need first to analyze these developing social concepts in terms of their internal logical structure. At each stage, the same basic moral concept or aspect is defined, but at each higher stage this definition is more differentiated, more integrated, and more general or universal. When one's concept of human life moves from Stage 1 to Stage 2, the value of life becomes more differentiated from the value of property, more integrated (the value of life enters an organizational hierarchy where it is "higher" than property so that one steals property in order to save life), and more universalized (the life of any sentient being is valuable regardless of status or property). The same advance is true at each stage in the hierarchy. Each step of development, then, is a better cognitive organization than the one before it, one that takes account of everything present in the previous stage but making new distinctions and organizes them into a more comprehensive or more equilibrated structure. The fact that this is the case has been demonstrated by a series of studies indicating that children and adolescents comprehend all stages up to their own, but not more than one stage beyond their own (Rest, 1973) And, importantly, they prefer this next stage.

Moral thought, then, seems to behave like all other kinds of thought. Progress through the moral levels and stages is characterized by increasing differentiation and increasing integration, and hence is the same kind of progress that scientific theory represents. Like acceptable scientific theory—or like any theory or structure of knowledge—moral thought may be considered partially to generate its own data as it goes along, or at least to expand so as to contain in a balanced, self-consistent way a wider and wider experiential field. The raw data in the case of our ethical philosophies may be considered as conflicts between roles, or values, or as the social order in which people live.

The social worlds of all people seem to contain the same basic structures. All the societies we have studied have the same basic institutions—family, economy, law, government. In addition, however, all societies are alike because they are societies—systems of defined complementary roles. In order to play a social role in the family, school, or society, children must implicitly take the role of others toward themselves and toward others in the group. These role-taking tendencies form the basis of all social institutions. They represent various patternings of shared or complementary expectations.

In the preconventional and conventional levels (Stages 1-4), moral content or value is largely accidental or culture bound. Anything from "honesty" to "courage in battle" can be the central value. But in the higher postconventional levels, Socrates, Lincoln. Thoreau, and Martin Luther King tend to speak without confusion of tongues, as it were. This is because the ideal principles of any social structure are basically alike, if only because there simply are not that many principles that are articulate, comprehensive, and integrated enough to be satisfying to the human intellect. And most of these principles have gone by the name of justice.

I have discussed at some length the culturally universal sequences of stages of moral judgment. I have not entirely clarified how such a sequence helps to resolve relativistic questioning of moral principles, a task taken up in our Chapter 4, "From *Is* to *Ought*." It is easier to clarify how such a sequence helps resolve the dilemma of relativity versus indoctrination in values education. The sequence provides us with a concept of moral development that can be stimulated by education without indoctrination and yet that helps to move student judgment toward more adequate principles.

The way to stimulate stage growth is to pose real or hypothetical dilemmas to students in such a way as to arouse disagreement and uncertainty as to what is right. The teacher's primary role is to present such dilemmas and to ask Socratic questions that arouse student reasoning and focus student listening on one another's reasons.

I noted research by Rest (1973) showing that students prefer the highest stage of reasoning they comprehend but that they do not comprehend more than one stage above their own. As a result, assimilation of reasoning occurs primarily when it is the next stage up from the student's level. Developmental moral discussion thus arouses cognitive-moral conflict and exposes students to reasoning by other students at the next stage above their own.

Using this approach, Blatt and Kohlberg (1975) were able to stimulate one-third of experimental classes of students to advance one stage in a time period in which control classes remained unchanged in moral stage. One year later, the experimental classes retained their relative advance over the control classes.

The developmental approach, first experimentally elaborated by Blatt, is one that any thoughtful classroom teacher may practice. Unlike values clarification, its assumptions are not relativistic but, rather, are based on universal goals and principles. It asks the student for reasons, on the assumption that some reasons are more adequate than others.

The approach differs from indoctrinative approaches because it tries to move student's thinking in a direction that is natural for the student rather than moving the student in the direction of accepting the teacher's moral assumptions. It avoids preaching or didacticism linked to the teacher's authority.

As I have characterized developmental moral education, it is neither an indoctinative or relativistic classroom discussion process. When we shift from a curriculum of moral discussion to the "hidden curriculum" of the classroom, a further set of philosophic and educational issues are raised. In my opinion, the resolution, of these problems rests on creating a democratic classroom in which issues of fairness are settled by discussion and a democratic vote.

New Maps of Development: New Visions of Maturity

Carol Gilligan

Carol Gilligan *(1936–) was born in New York City, the only child of a lawyer and a nursery school teacher. After beginning her teaching career at Harvard University, she joined the faculty of New York University in 2002. As a psychologist and feminist, Gilligan has written prolifically on the moral development of women. Her most well-known work,* In a Different Voice *(1982), was described by Harvard University Press as "the little book that started a revolution." In this paper from the* American Journal of Orthopsychiatry, *Gilligan elaborates on her view of moral development, situates her work in the broader context of related inquiry, and illustrates her perspective with case studies of two children addressing a morally ambiguous situation.*

That development is the aim of a liberal education seems clear until we begin to ask what is a liberal education and what constitutes development. The current spirit of reappraisal in the field of education stems in part from the fact that some old promises have failed and new practices must be found if the vision of education for freedom and for democracy is to be realized or sustained. But this current reappraisal in the field of education finds its parallel in the field of developmental psychology where a similar reassessment is taking place, a reassessment that began in the early 1970s when developmental psychologists began to question the adulthood that formerly they had taken for granted and when the exclusion of women from the research samples from which developmental theories were generated began to be noticed as a serious omission and one that pointed to the exclusion of other groups as well. Thus, if the changing population of students, particularly the larger number of adults and especially of adult women entering postsecondary education, has raised a series of questions about the aims of education and the nature of educational practice, the study of adulthood and of women has generated a new set of questions for theorists of human development.

To ask whether current developmental theories can be applied to understanding or assessing the lives of people who differ from those upon whose experience these theories were based is only to introduce a problem of far greater magnitude, the adequacy of current theories themselves. The answer to the initial question is in one sense clear, given that these theories are used repeatedly in assessing the development of different groups. But the question asked in such assessment is how much like the original group is the different group being assessed. For example, if the criteria for development are derived from studies of males and these criteria are then used to measure the development of females, the question being asked is how much like men do women develop. The assumption underlying this approach is that there is a universal standard of development and a single scale of measurement along which differences found can be aligned as higher and lower, better and worse. Yet, the initial exclusion of women displays the fallacy of this assumption and indicates a recognition of difference, pointing to the problem I wish to address. While I will use the experience of women to demonstrate how the group left out in the construction of theory calls attention to what is missing in its account, my interest lies not only in women and the perspective they add to the narrative of growth but also in the problem that differences post for a liberal educational philosophy that strives toward an ideal of equality and for a developmental psychology that posits a universal and invariant sequence of growth. In joining the subjects of morality and women, I focus specifically on the questions of value inherent in education and in developmental psychology, and indicate how the lives of women call into question current maps of development and inform a new vision of human growth.

The repeated marking of women's experience as, in Freud's terms, "a dark continent for psychology"[5] raises a question as to what has shadowed the understanding of women's lives. Since women in fact do not live on a continent apart from men but instead repeatedly engage with them in the activities of everyday life, the mystery deepens and the suggestion emerges that theory may be blinding observation. While the disparity between women's experience and the representation of human development, noted throughout the psychological literature, has generally been seen to signify a problem in women's development, the failure of women to fit existing models of human growth may point to a problem in the representation, a limitation in the conception of the human condition, an omission of certain truths about life. The nature of these truths and their implications for understanding development and thinking about education are the subjects of this paper.

Construction of Relationships and the Concept of Morality

Evidence of sex differences in the findings of psychological research comes mainly from studies that reveal the way in which men and women construct the relation between self and others. While the differences observed in women's experience and understanding of relationships have posed a problem of interpretation that recurs throughout the literature on psychoanalysis and personality psychology, this problem emerges with particular clarity in the field of moral judgment research. Since moral judgments pertain to conflicts in the relation of self to others, a difference in the construction of that relationship would lead to a difference in the conception of the moral domain. This difference would be manifest in the way in which moral problems are seen, in the questions asked which then serve to guide the judgment and resolution of moral dilemmas. While the failure to perceive this difference has led psychologists to apply constructs derived from research on men to the interpretation of women's experience and thought, the recognition of this difference points to the limitation of this approach. If women's moral judgments reflect a different understanding of social relationships, then they may point to a line of social development whose presence in both sexes is currently obscured.

Theories of Moral Development

This discussion of moral development takes place against the background of a field where, beginning with Freud's theory that tied superego formation to castration anxiety, extending through Piaget's study of boys' conceptions of the rules of their games, and culminating in Kohlberg's derivation of six stages of moral development from research on adolescent males, the line of development has been shaped by the pattern of male experience and thought. The continual reliance on male experience to build the model of moral growth has been coupled with a continuity in the conception of morality itself. Freud's observation that "the first requisite of civilization is justice, the assurance that a rule once made will not be broken in favour of an "individual,"[4] extends through Piaget's conception of morality as consisting in respect for rules[16] and into Kohlberg's claim that justice is the most adequate of moral ideals.[12] The imagery that runs through this equation of morality with justice depicts a world comprised of separate individuals whose claims fundamentally conflict but who find in morality a mode of regulating conflict by agreement that allows the development of life lived in common.

The notion that moral development witnesses the replacement of the rule of brute force with the rule of law, bringing isolated and endangered individuals into a tempered connection with one another, then leads to the observation that women, less aggressive and thus less preoccupied with rules, are as a result less morally developed. The recurrent observations of sex differences that mark the literature on moral development are striking not only in their concurrence but in their reiterative elaboration of a single theme. Whether expressed in the general statement that women show less sense of justice than men[5] or in the particular notation that girls, in contrast to boys, think it better to give back fewer blows than one has received,[16] the direction of these differences is always the same, pointing in women to a greater sense of connection, a concern with relationships more than with rules. But this observation then yields to the paradoxical conclusion that women's preoccupation with relationships constitutes an impediment to the progress of their moral development.

The Moral Judgments of Two Eleven-Year-Olds

To illustrate how a difference in the understanding of relationships leads to a difference in the conceptions of morality and of self, I begin with the moral judgments of two 11-year-old children, a boy and a girl who see in the same dilemma two very different moral problems. Demonstrating how brightly current theory illuminates the line and the logic of the boy's thought while casting scant light on that of the girl, I will show how the girl's judgments reflect a fundamentally different approach. I have chosen for the purposes of this discussion a girl whose moral judgments elude current categories of developmental assessment, in order to highlight the problem of interpretation rather than to exemplify sex differences per se. My aim is to show how, by adding a new line of interpretation, it becomes possible to see development where previously development was not discerned and to consider differences in the understanding of relationships without lining up these differences on a scale from better to worse.

The two children—Amy and Jake—were in the same sixth grade class at school and participated in a study[8] designed to explore different conceptions of morality and self. The sample selected for study was chosen to focus the variables of gender and age while maximizing developmental potential by holding constant, at a high level, the factors of intelligence, education, and social class that have been associated with moral development, at least as measured by existing scales. The children in question were both bright and articulate and at least in their 11-year-old aspirations, resisted easy categories of sex-role stereotyping since Amy aspired to become a scientist while Jake preferred English to math. Yet their moral judgments seemed initially to confirm previous findings of differences between the sexes, suggesting that the edge girls have on moral development during the early school years gives way at puberty with the ascendance of formal logical thought in boys.

The dilemma these children were asked to resolve was one in the series devised by Kohlberg to measure moral development in adolescence by presenting a conflict between moral norms and exploring the logic of its resolution. In this particular dilemma, a man named Heinz considers whether or not to steal a drug, which he cannot afford to buy, in order to save the life of his wife. In the standard format of Kohlberg's interviewing procedure, the description of the dilemma itself—Heinz's predicament, the wife's disease, the druggist's refusal to lower his price—is followed by the question, should Heinz steal the drug? Then the reasons for and against stealing are explored through a series of further questions, conceived as probes and designed to reveal the underlying structure of moral thought.

Jake

Jake, at 11, is clear from the outset that Heinz should steal the drug. Constructing the dilemma as Kohlberg did as a conflict between the values of property and life, he discerns the logical priority of life and uses that logic to justify his choice:

> For one thing, a human life is worth more than money, and if the druggist only makes $1000, he is still going to live, but if Heinz doesn't steal the drug, his wife is going to die. [*Why is life worth more than money?*] Because the druggist can get a thousand dollars later from rich people with cancer, but Heinz can't get his wife again. [*Why not?*] Because people are all different, and so you couldn't get Heinz's wife again.

Asked if Heinz should steal the drug if he does not love his wife, Jake replies that he should, saying that not only is there "a difference between hating and killing," but also, if Heinz were caught, "the judge would probably think it was the right thing to do." Asked about the fact that, in stealing, Heinz would be breaking the law, he says that "the laws have mistakes and you can't go writing up a law for everything that you can imagine."

Thus, while taking the law into account and recognizing its function in maintaining social order (the judge, he says, "should give Heinz the lightest possible sentence"), he also sees the law as man-made and therefore subject to error and change. Yet his judgment that Heinz should steal the drug, like his view of the law as having mistakes, rests on the assumption of agreement, a societal consensus around moral values that allows one to know and expect others will recognize "the right thing to do."

Fascinated by the power of logic, this 11-year-old boy locates truth in math which, he says, is "the only thing that is totally logical." Considering the moral dilemma to be "sort of like a math problem with humans," he sets it up as an equation and proceeds to work out the solution. Since his solution is rationally derived, he assumes that anyone following reason would arrive at the same conclusion and thus that a judge would also consider stealing to be the right thing for Heinz to do. Yet he is also aware of the limits of logic; asked whether there is a right answer to moral problems, he says that "there can only be right and wrong in judgment," since the parameters of action are variable and complex. Illustrating how actions undertaken with the best of intentions can eventuate in the most disastrous of consequences, he says

> . . . like if you give an old lady your seat on the trolley, if you are in a trolley crash and that seat goes through the window, it might be that reason that the old lady dies.

Theories of developmental psychology illuminate well the position of this child, standing at the jucture of childhood and adolescence, at what Piaget described as the pinnacle of childhood intelligence, and beginning through thought to discover a wider universe of possibility. The moment of preadolescence is caught by the conjunction of formal operational thought with a description of self still anchored in the factual parameters of his childhood world, his age, his town, his father's occupation, the substance of his likes, dislikes, and beliefs. Yet as his self-description radiates the self-confidence of a child who has arrived, in Erikson's terms, at a favorable balance of industry over inferiority—competent, sure of himself, and knowing well the rules of the game—so his emergent capacity for formal thought, his ability to think about thinking and to reason things out in a logical way, frees him from dependence on authority and allows him to find solutions to problems by himself.

This emergent autonomy then charts the trajectory that Kohlberg's six stages of moral development trace, a three-level progression from an egocentric understanding of fairness based on individual need (stages one and two), to a conception of fairness anchored in the shared conventions of societal agreement (stages three and four), and finally to a principled understanding of fairness that rests on the free-standing logic of equality and reciprocity (stages five and six). While Jake's judgments at 11 are scored as conventional on Kohlberg's scale, a mixture of stages three and four, his ability to bring deductive logic to bear on the solution of moral dilemmas, to differentiate morality from law, and to see how laws can be considered to have mistakes, points toward the principled conception of justice that Kohlberg equates with moral maturity.

Amy

In contrast, Amy's response to the dilemma conveys a very different impression, an image of development stunted by a failure of logic, an inability to think for herself. Asked if Heinz should steal the drug, she replies in a way that seems evasive and unsure:

> Well, I don't think so. I think there might be other ways besides stealing it, like if he could borrow the money or make a loan or something, but he really shouldn't steal the drug, but his wife shouldn't die either.

Asked why he should not steal the drug, she considers neither property nor law but rather the effect that theft could have on the relationship between Heinz and his wife. If he stole the drug, she explains,

> . . . he might save his wife then, but if he did, he might have to go to jail, and then his wife might get sicker again, and he couldn't get more of the drug, and it might not be good. So, they should really just talk it out and find some other way to make the money.

Seeing in the dilemma not a math problem with humans but a narrative of relationships that extends over time, she envisions the wife's continuing need for her husband and the husband's continuing concern for his wife and seeks to respond to the druggist's need in a way that would sustain rather than sever connection. As she ties the wife's survival to the preservation of relationships, so she considers the value of her life in a context of relationships, saying that it would be wrong to let her die because, "if she died, it hurts a lot of people and it hurts her." Since her moral judgment is grounded in the belief that "if somebody has something that would keep somebody alive, then it's not right not to give it to them," she considers the problem in the dilemma to arise not from the druggist's assertion of rights but from his failure of response.

While the interviewer proceeds with the series of questions that follow Kohlberg's construction of the dilemma, Amy's answers remain essentially unchanged, the various probes serving neither to elucidate nor to modify her initial response. Whether or not Heinz loves his wife, he still shouldn't steal or let her die; if it were a stranger dying instead, she says that "if the stranger didn't have anybody near or anyone she knew," then Heinz should try to save her life but he shouldn't steal the drug. But as the interviewer conveys through the repetition of questions that the answers she has given are not heard or not right, Amy's confidence begins to diminish and her replies become more constrained and unsure. Asked again why Heinz should not steal the drug, she simply repeats, "Because it's not right." Asked again to explain why, she states again that theft would not be a good solution, adding lamely, that, "if he took it, he might not know how to give it to his wife, and so his wife might still die." Failing to see the dilemma as a self-contained problem in moral logic, she does not discern the internal structure of its resolution; as she constructs the problem differently herself, Kohlberg's conception completely evades her.

Instead, seeing a world comprised of relationships rather than of people standing alone, a world that coheres through human connection rather than through systems of rules, she finds the puzzle in the dilemma to lie in the failure of the druggist to respond to the wife. Saying that "it is not right for someone to die when their life could be saved," she assumes that if the druggist were to see the consequences of his refusal to lower his price, he would realize that "he should just give it to the wife and then have the husband pay back the money later." Thus she considers the solution to the dilemma to lie in making the wife's condition more salient to the druggist or, that failing, in appealing to others who are in a position to help.

Just as Jake is confident the judge would agree that stealing is the right thing for Heinz to do, so Amy is confident that, "if Heinz and the druggist had talked it out long enough, they could reach something besides stealing." As he considers the law to "have mistakes," so she sees this drama as a mistake, believing that "the world should just share things more and then people wouldn't have to steal." Both children thus recognize the need for agreement but see it as mediated in different ways: he impersonally through systems of logic and law, she personally through communication in relationship. As he relies on the conventions of logic to deduce the solution to this dilemma, assuming these conventions to be shared, so she relies on a process of communication, assuming connection and believing that her voice will be heard. Yet while his assumptions about agreement are confirmed by the convergence in logic between his answers and the questions posed, her assumptions are belied by the failure in communication, the interviewer's inability to understand her response.

Measuring Moral Development: Assessing Diverse Perceptions

While the frustration of the interview with Amy is apparent in the repetition of questions and its ultimate circularity, the problem of interpretation arises when it comes to assessing her development. Considered in the light of Kohlberg's conception of the stages and sequence of moral development, her moral judgments are a full stage lower in moral maturity than those of the boy. Scored as a mixture of stages two and three, they seem to reveal a feeling of powerlessness in the world, an inability to think systematically about the concepts of morality or law, a reluctance to challenge authority or to examine the logic of received moral truths, a failure even to conceive of acting directly to save a life or to consider that such action, if taken, could possibly have an effect. As her reliance on relationships seems to reveal a continuing dependence and vulnerability, so her belief in communication as the mode through which to resolve moral dilemmas appears naive and cognitively immature.

Yet her description of herself conveys a markedly different impression. Once again, the hallmarks of the preadolescent child depict a child secure in her sense of herself, confident in the substance of her beliefs, and sure of her ability to do something of value in the world. Describing herself at 11 as "growing and changing," Amy says that she "sees some things differently now, just because I know myself really well now, and I know a lot more about the world." Yet the world she knows is a different world from that refracted by Kohlberg's construction of Heinz's dilemma. Her world is a world of relationships and psychological truths, where an awareness of the connection between people gives rise to a recognition of responsibility for one another, a perception of the need for response. Seen in this light, her view of morality as arising from the recognition of relationship, her belief in communication as the mode of conflict resolution, and her conviction that the solution to the dilemma will follow from its compelling representation seem far from naive or cognitively immature; rather, her judgments contain the insights central to an ethic of care, just as Jake's judgments reflect the logic of the justice approach. Her incipient awareness of the "method of truth," central to nonviolent conflict resolution, and her belief in the restorative activity of care, lead her to see the actors in the dilemma arrayed not as opponents in a contest of rights but as members of a network of relationships on whose continuation they all depend. Consequently her solution to the dilemma lies in activating the network by communication, securing the inclusion of the wife by strengthening rather than severing connection.

But the different logic of Amy's response calls attention to a problem in the interpretation of the interview itself. Conceived as an interrogation, it appears as a dialogue that takes on moral dimensions of its own, pertaining to the interviewer's uses of power and to the manifestations of respect. With this shift in the conception of the interview, it immediately becomes clear that the interviewer's problem in hearing Amy's response stems from the fact that Amy is answering a different question from the one the interviewer thought had been posed. Amy is considering not *whether* Heinz should act in this situation (*Should* Heinz steal the drug?) but rather *how* Heinz should act in response to his awareness of his wife's need (Should Heinz *steal* the drug?). The interviewer takes the mode of action for granted, presuming it to be a matter of fact. Amy assumes the necessity for action and considers what form it should take. In the interviewer's failure to imagine a response not dreamt of in Kohlberg's moral philosophy lies the failure to hear Amy's question and to see the logic in her response, to discern that what from one perspective appears to be an evasion of the dilemma signifies in other terms a recognition of the problem and a search for a more adequate solution.

Thus in Kohlberg's dilemma these two children see two very different moral problems—Jake a conflict between life and property that can be resolved by logical deduction, Amy a fracture of human relationship that must be mended with its own thread. Asking different questions that arise from different conceptions of the moral domain, they arrive at answers that fundamentally diverge, and the arrangement of these answers as successive stages on a scale of increasing moral maturity calibrated by the logic of the boy's response misses the different truth revealed in the judgment of the girl. To the question, "What does he see that she does not?", Kohlberg's theory provides a ready response, manifest in the scoring of his judgments a full stage higher than hers in moral maturity; to the questions, "What does she see that he does not?", Kohlberg's theory has nothing to say. Since most of her responses fall through the sieve of Kohlberg's scoring system, her responses appear from his perspective to lie outside the moral domain.

Yet just as Jake reveals a sophisticated understanding of the logic of justification, so Amy is equally sophisticated in her understanding of the nature of choice. Saying that "if both the roads went in totally separate ways, if you pick one, you'll never know what would happen if you went the other way," she explains that "that's the chance you have to take, and like I said, it's just really a guess." To illustrate her point "in a simple way," she describes how, in choosing to spend the summer at camp, she

. . . will never know what would have happened if I had stayed here, and if something goes wrong at camp. I'll never know if I stayed here if it would have been better. There's really no way around it because there's no way you can do both at once, so you've got to decide, but you'll never know.

In this way, these two 11-year-old children, both highly intelligent, though perceptive about life in different ways, display different modes of moral under-standing, different ways of thinking about conflict and choice. Jake, in resolving the dilemma, follows the construction that Kohlberg has posed. Relying on theft to avoid confrontation and turning to the law to mediate the dispute, he transposes a hierarchy of power into a hierarchy of values by recasting a conflict between people into a conflict of claims. Thus abstracting the moral problem from the interpersonal situation, he finds in the logic of fairness an objective means of deciding who will win the dispute. But this hierarchical ordering, with its imagery of winning and losing and the potential for violence which it contains, gives way in Amy's construction of the dilemma to a network of connection, a network sustained by a process of communication. With this shift, the moral problem changes from one of unfair domination, the imposition of property over life, to one of unnecessary exclusion, the failure of the druggist to respond to the wife.

This shift in the formulation of the moral problem and the concomitant change in the imagery of relationships are illustrated as well by the responses of two eight-year-olds who participated in the same study[8] and were asked to describe a situation in which they weren't sure of the right thing to do:

JEFFREY (age 8): When I really want to go to my friends and my mother is clean-ing the cellar, I think about my friends, and then I think about my mother, and then I think about the right thing to do. *[But how do you know it's the right thing to do?]* Because some things go before other things.

KAREN (age 8): I have a lot of friends, and I can't always play with all of them, so everybody's going to have to take a turn, because they're all my friends. But like if someone's all alone, I'll play with them. *[What kind of things do you think about when you are trying to make that deci-sion?]* Um, someone all alone, loneliness.

While Jeffrey sets up a hierarchical ordering in thinking about the conflict between desire and duty, Karen describes a network of relationships that includes all of her friends. Both children deal with the issues of exclusion and priority cre-ated by choice, but while Jeffrey thinks about what goes first, Karen focuses on who is left out.

Moral Judgment and Self-Descriptions

In illustrating a difference in children's thinking about moral conflict and choice, I have described two views that are complementary rather than sequential or opposed. In doing so, I go against the bias of developmental theory toward ordering differences in a hierarchical mode. This correspondence between the order of developmental theory and that manifest in the boys' responses contrasts with the disparity between the structure of theory and that manifest in the thought of the girls. Yet, in neither comparison does one child's thought appear as precursor of the other's position. Thus, questions arise about the relation between these perspectives; what is the significance of these differences, and how do these two modes of thinking connect? To pursue these questions, I return to the eleven-year-olds and consider the way they describe themselves.

> *[How would you describe yourself to yourself?]*

JAKE: Perfect, That's my conceited side. What do you want—any way that I choose to describe myself?

AMY: You mean my character? *[What do you think?]* Well, I don't know. I'd describe myself as, well, what do you mean?

[If you had to describe the person you are in a way that you yourself would know it was you, what would you say?]

JAKE: I'd start off with eleven years old. Jake [last name]. I'd have to add that I live in [town] because that is a big part of me, and also that my father is a doctor because I think that does change me a little bit, and that I don't believe in crime, except for when your name is Heinz . . . that I think school is boring because I think that kind of changes your character a little bit. I don't sort of know how to describe myself, because I don't know how to read my personality. *[If you had to describe the way you actually would describe yourself, what would you say?]* I like corny jokes. I don't really like to get down to work, but I can do all the stuff in school. Every single problem that I have seen in school I have been able to do, except for ones that take knowledge, and after I do the reading, I have been able to do them, but sometimes I don't want to waste my time on easy homework. And also I'm crazy about sports. I think, unlike a lot of people, that the world still has hope.... Most people that I know I like, and I have the good life, pretty much as good as any I have seen, and I am tall for my age.

AMY: Well, I'd say that I was someone who likes school and studying, and that's what I want to do with my life. I want to be some kind of a scientist or something, and I want to do things, and I want to help people. And I think that's what kind of person I am, or what kind of person I try to be. And that's probably how I'd describe myself. And I want to do something to help other people. *[Why is that?]* Well, because I think that this world has a lot of problems, and I think that everybody should try to help somebody else in some way, and the way I'm choosing is through science.

In the voice of the 11-year-old boy, a familiar form of self-definition appears, resonating to the schoolbook inscription of the young Stephen Daedalus ("himself, his name and where he was")[10] and echoing the descriptions that appear in *Our Town*,[18] laying out across the coordinates of time and space a hierarchical order in which to define one's place. Describing himself as distinct by locating his particular position in the world, Jake sets himself apart from that world by his abilities, his beliefs, and his height. Although Amy also enumerates her likes, her wants, and her beliefs, she locates herself in relation to the world, describing herself through actions that bring her into connection with others, elaborating ties through her ability to provide help. To Jake's ideal of perfection against which he measures the worth of himself, Amy counterposes an ideal of care against which she measures the worth of her activity. While she places herself in relation to the world and chooses to help others through science, he places the world in relation to himself as it defines his character, his position, and the quality of life.

Conclusions

As the voices of these children illuminate two modes of self-description and two modes of moral judgment, so they illustrate how readily we hear the voice that speaks of justice and of separation and the difficulty we encounter in listening to the voice that speaks of care and connection. Listening through developmental theories and through the structures of our educational and social system, we are attuned to a hierarchical ordering that represents development as a progress of separation, a chronicle of individual success. In contrast, the understanding of development as a progress of human relationships, a narrative of expanding connection, is an unimagined representation. The image of network or web thus seems more readily to connote entrapment rather than an alternative and nonhierarchical vision of human connection.

This central limitation in the representation of development is most clearly apparent in recent portrayals of adult life, where the insistent focus on self and on work provides scanty representation of an adulthood spent in the activities of relationship and care. The tendency to chart the unfamiliar waters of adult development with the familiar markers of adolescent separation and growth leads to an equation of development with separation; it results in a failure to represent the reality of connection both in love and in work. Levinson,[13] patterning the stages of adult development on the seasons of a man's life, defined the developmental process explicitly as one of individuation, yet reported his distress at the absence of friendships in men's lives. Vaillant,[17] deriving his account of adaptation to life from the lives of the men who took part in the Grant study, noted that the question these men found most difficult to answer was, "Can you describe your wife?" In this light, the observation that women's embeddedness in lives of relationship, their orientation to interdependence, their subordination of achievement to care, and their conflicts over competitive success leave them personally at risk in mid-life, though generally construed as a problem in women's development, seems more a commentary on our society and on the representation of development itself.

In suggesting that the consideration of women's lives and of adulthood calls attention to the need for an expansion in the mapping of human development, I have pointed to a distinction between two modes of self-definition and two modes of moral judgment and indicated how these modes reflect different ways of imagining relationships. That these modes are tied to different experiences may explain their empirical association with gender, though that association is by no means absolute. That they reflect different forms of thought—one relying on a formal logic whose development Piaget has described, the other on a narrative and contextual mode of thought whose development remains to be traced—indicates the implication of this distinction for psychological assessment and education.

The experiences of inequality and of interdependence are embedded in the cycle of life, universal because inherent in the relationship of parent and child. These experiences of inequality and interdependence give rise to the ethics of justice and care, the ideals of human relationship—the vision that self and other will be treated as of equal worth, that despite differences in power, things will be fair; the vision that everyone will be responded to and included, that no one will be left alone or hurt. The adolescent, capable of envisioning the ideal, reflects on the childhood experiences of powerlessness and vulnerability and conceives a Utopian world laid out along the coordinates of justice and care. This ability to conceive the hypothetical and to construct contrary-to-fact hypotheses has led the adolescent to be proclaimed a "philosopher,"[11] a "metaphysician par excellence."[9] But the representation of the adolescent's moral philosophy in the literature of developmental psychology has been limited to the portrayal of changes in the conception of justice that supports the adolescent's claim to equality and the separation of other and self. My own work[7] has expanded this description by identifying two different moral languages, the language of rights that protects separation and the language of responsibilities that sustains connection. In dialogue, these languages not only create the ongoing tension of moral discourse, but also reveal how the dynamics of separation and attachment in the process of identity formation relate to the themes of justice and care in moral growth. This expanded representation of identity and moral development allows a more complex rendering of differences, and points to the need to understand and foster the development of both modes.

The old promise of a liberal education, of an education that frees individuals from blinding constraints and engenders a questioning of assumptions formerly taken for granted remains a compelling vision. But among the prevailing assumptions that need to be questioned are the assumptions about human development. The lives of women, in pointing to an uncharted path of human growth and one that leads to a less violent mode of life, are particularly compelling at this time in history and thus deserve particular attention. The failure to attend to the voices of women and the difficulty in hearing what they say when they speak has compromised women's development and education, leading them to doubt the veracity of their perceptions and to question the truth of their experience. This problem becomes acute for women in adolescence, when thought becomes reflective and the problem of interpretation thus enters the stream of development itself. But the failure to represent women's experience also contributes to the presentation of competitive relationships and hierarchical modes of social organization as the natural ordering of life. For this reason, the consideration of women's lives brings to the conception of development a much needed corrective, stressing the importance of narrative modes of thought and pointing to the contextual nature of psychological truths and the reality of interdependence in human life.

The process of selection that has shadowed this vision can be seen in Kohlberg's reading of Martin Luther King's letter from the Birmingham jail,[11] since Kohlberg extracted King's justification for breaking the law in the name of justice but omitted the way in which King's vision of justice was embedded in a vision of human connection. Replying to the clergy who criticized his action, King not only offered a justification of his action but also defended the necessity for action, anchoring that necessity in the realization of interdependence:

> I am in Birmingham because injustice is here. I cannot sit idly by in Atlanta and not be concerned about what happens in Birmingham. Injustice anywhere is a threat to justice everywhere. We are caught in an inescapable network of mutality, tied in a single garment of destiny. Whatever affects one directly, affects all indirectly.

Thus, like Bonhoeffer,[1] who stated that action comes "not from thought but from a readiness for responsibility," King tied his responsiveness to a caring that arises from an understanding of the connection between people's lives, a connection not forged by systems of rules but by a perception of the fact of relationship, a connection not freely contracted but built into the very fabric of life.

The ideals of a liberal democratic society—of freedom and equality—have been mirrored in the developmental vision of autonomy, the image of the educated man thinking for himself, the image of the ideal moral agent acting alone on the basis of his principles, blinding himself with a Rawlsian "veil of ignorance," playing a solitary Kohlbergian game of "moral musical chairs." Yet the developmental psychologists who dared, with Erikson,[3] to "ask what is an adult," immediately began to see the limitations of this vision. Erikson himself has come increasingly to talk about the activity of caretaking and to identify caring as the virtue and strength of maturity.[2] When integrated into a developmental understanding, this insight should spur the search for the antecedents of this strength in childhood and in adolescence. Kohlberg,[13] turning to consider adulthood, tied adult development to the experiences of "sustained responsibility for the welfare of others" and of the irreversible consequences of choice. The resonance of these themes of maturity to the voice of the 11-year-old girl calls into question current assumptions about the sequence of development and suggests a different path of growth.

The story of moral development, as it is presently told, traces the history of human development through shifts in the hierarchy of power relationships, implying that the dissolution of this hierarchy into an order of equality represents the ideal vision of things. But the conception of relationships in terms of hierarchies implies separation as the moral ideal—for everyone to stand alone, independent, self-sufficient, connected to others by the abstractions of logical thought. There is, then, a need to represent in the mapping of development a nonhierarchical image of human connection, and to embody in the vision of maturity the reality of interdependence. This alternate vision of the web of connection is the recognition of relationship that prevents aggression and gives rise to the understanding that generates response.

References

Bonhoeffer, D. 1953. *Letters and Papers from Prison*. Macmillan, New York.

Erikson, E. 1976. "Reflections on Dr. Borg's Life Cycle." Daedalus 105; 1–29.

Erikson, E. 1970. "Reflections on the dissent of contemporary youth." Daedalus 99:154–176.

Freud, S. 1929. "Civilization and its discontents." In Standard Edition of *The Complete Psychological Works of Sigmund Freud*, Vol. XXI. J. Strachey, ed. Hogarth Press, London (1961).

Freud, S. 1926. "The question of lay analysis." In Standard Edition of *The Complete Psychological Works of Sigmund Freud*, Vol. XX. J. Straehey, ed. Hogarth Press, London (1961).

Freud, S. 1925. "Some physical consequences of the anatomical distinction between the sexes." In Standard Edition of *The Complete Psychological Works of Sigmund Freud*, Vol. XIX. J. Straehey, ed. Hogarth Press, London (1961).

Gilligan, C. 1982. *In a Different Voice: Psychological Theory and Women's Development*, Harvard University Press, Cambridge, Mass.

Gilligan, C. Langdale. S. and Lyons N. 1982. "The Contribution of Women's Thought to Developmental Theory: The Elimination of Sex-Bias in Moral Development Theory and Research." Final report to the National Institute of Education, Washington, D.C.

Inhelder, B. and Piaget. J. 1958. *The Growth of Logical Thinking from Childhood to Adolescence*. Basic Books, New York.

Joyce, J. 1916. *A Portrait of the Artist as a Young Man.* Viking Press, New York (1956. p. 15).

King, M., Jr. 1964. *Why We Can't Wait.* Harper and Row, New York.

Kohlberg, L. 1981. *The Philosophy of Moral Development.* Harper and Row, San Francisco.

Kohlberg, L. 1973. "Continuities and discontinuities in childhood and adult moral development revisited." In *Life-Span Developmental Psychology: Personality and Socialization.* P. Bakes and K. Schaie, eds. Academic Press, New York.

Kohlberg, L. and Gilligan C. 1971. *The Adolescent as a Philosopher: The Discovery of the Self in a Post-Conventional World.* Daedalus, 100:1051–1086.

Levinson, D. 1978. *The Seasons of a Man's Life.* Knopf, New York.

Piaget, J. 1932. *The Moral Judgment of the Child.* Free Press, New York (1965).

Vaillant, G. 1977. *Adaptation to Life.* Little Brown, Boston.

Wilder, T. 1938. *Our Town.* Coward McCann, New York.

Marooned on Gilligan's Island: Are Women Morally Superior to Men?

Katha Pollitt

Katha Pollitt *(1949–) writes widely on feminism. Her writings have appeared in* The New Yorker, Harpers's Magazine, Ms. Magazine, *the* New York Times, *and* The Nation, *for which she is a regular columnist. Her book* Subject To Debate: Sense and Dissents on Women, Politics, and Culture *is a collection of her* Nation *columns. She is also the author of* Reasonable Creatures: Essays on Women and Feminism *(1994) and* Virginity or Death!: And Other Social and Political Issues of Our Time *(2006). Pollitt won a National Book Critics Award in 1983 for her poetry* Antarctic Traveller.

Some years ago, I was invited by the wife of a well-known writer to sign a women's peace petition. It made the points such documents usually make: that women, as mothers, caregivers and nurturers, have a special awareness of the precariousness of human life, see through jingoism and Cold War rhetoric and would prefer nations to work out their difficulties peacefully so that the military budget could be diverted to schools and hospitals and housing. It had the literary tone such documents usually have, as well—at once superior and plaintive, as if the authors didn't know whether they were bragging or begging. We are wiser than you poor deluded menfolk, was the subtext, so will you please-please-please listen to your moms?

To sign or not to sign? Of course, I was all for peace. But was I for peace *as a woman?* I wasn't a mother then—I wasn't even an aunt. Did my lack of nurturing credentials make my grasp of the horrors of war and the folly of the arms race only theoretical, like a white person's understanding of racism? Were mothers the natural leaders of the peace movement, to whose judgment nonmothers, male and female, must defer, because after all we couldn't *know,* couldn't *feel* that tenderness toward fragile human life that a woman who had borne and raised children had experienced? On the other hand, I was indeed a woman. Was motherhood with its special wisdom somehow deep inside me, to be called upon when needed, like my uterus?

91

Complicating matters in a way relevant to this essay was my response to the famous writer's wife herself. Here was a woman in her fifties, her child-raising long behind her. Was motherhood the only banner under which she could gain a foothold on civic life? Perhaps so. Her only other public identity was that of a wife, and wifehood, even to a famous man, isn't much to claim credit for these days. ("To think I spent all those years ironing his underpants!" she once burst out to a mutual friend.) Motherhood was what she had in the work-and-accomplishment department, so it was understandable that she try to maximize its moral status. But I was not in her situation: I was a writer, a single woman. By sending me a petition from which I was excluded even as I was invited to add my name, perhaps she was telling me that by leading a nondomestic life I had abandoned the moral high ground, was "acting like a man," but could redeem myself by acknowledging the moral preeminence of the class of women I refused to join.

The ascription of particular virtues—compassion, patience, common sense, nonviolence—to mothers, and the tendency to conflate "mothers" with "women," has a long history in the peace movement, but it goes way beyond issues of war and peace. At present it permeates discussions of just about every field, from management training to theology. Indeed, although the media like to caricature feminism as denying the existence of sexual differences, for the women's movement and its opponents alike "difference" is where the action is. Thus, business writers wonder if women's nurturing, intuitive qualities will make them better executives. Educators suggest that female students suffer in classrooms that emphasize competition over cooperation. Women politicians tout their playground-honed negotiating skills, their egoless devotion to public service, their gender-based commitment to fairness and caring. A variety of political causes—environmentalism, animal rights, even vegetarianism—are promoted as logical extensions of women's putative peacefulness, closeness to nature, horror of aggression and concern for others' health. (Indeed, to some extent these causes are arenas in which women fight one another over definitions of femininity, which is why debates over disposable diapers and over the wearing of fur—both rather minor sources of harm, even if their opponents are right— loom so large and are so acrimonious.) In the arts, we hear a lot about what women's "real" subjects, methods and materials ought to be. Painting is male. Rhyme is male. Plot is male. Perhaps, say the Lacanian feminists, even logic and language are male. What is female? Nature. Blood. Milk. Communal gatherings. The moon. Quilts.

Haven't we been here before? Indeed we have. Woman as sharer and carer, woman as earth mother, woman as guardian of all the small rituals that knit together a family and a community, woman as beneath, above or beyond such manly concerns as law, reason, abstract ideas—these images are as old as time. Open defenders of male supremacy have always used them to declare women flatly inferior to men; covert ones use them to place women on a pedestal as too good for this naughty world. Thus, in the *Eumenides,* Aeschylus celebrated law as the defeat by males of primitive female principles of bloodguilt and vengeance, while the Ayatollah Khomeini thought women should be barred from judgeships because they were too tenderhearted. Different rationale, same outcome: Women, because of their indifference to an impersonal moral order, cannot be full participants in civic life.

There exists an equally ancient line of thought, however, that uses femininity to posit a subversive challenge to the social order: Think of Sophocles' Antigone, who resists tyranny out of love and piety, or Aristophanes' Lysistrata, the original women's-strike-for-peace-nik, or Shakespeare's unworldly, loving innocents: Desdemona, Cordelia. For reasons of power, money and persistent social structures, the vision of the morally superior woman can never overcome the dominant ethos in reality but exists alongside it as a kind of permanent wish or hope: If only powerful and powerless could change places, and the meek inherit the earth! Thus, it is perpetually being rediscovered, dressed in fashionable clothes and presented, despite its antiquity, as a radical new idea.

In the 1950s, which we think of as the glory days of traditional sex roles, the anthropologist Ashley Montagu argued in "The Natural Superiority of Women" that females had it all over males in every way that counted, including the possession of two X chromosomes that made them stabler, saner and healthier than men, with their X and Y. Montagu's essay, originally published in *The Saturday Review* and later expanded into a book, is witty and high-spirited and, interestingly, anticipates the current feminist challenge to male-defined categories. (He notes, for example, that while men are stronger than women in the furniture-moving sense, women are stronger than men when faced with extreme physical hardship and tests of endurance; so when we say that men are stronger than women, we are equating strength with what men have.) But the fundamental thrust of Montagu's, essay was to confirm traditional gender roles while revising the way we value them. Having proved to his own satisfaction that women could scale the artistic and intellectual heights, he argued that most would (that is, should) refrain, because women's true genius was "humanness," and their real mission was to "humanize" men before men blew up the world. And that, he left no doubt, was a full-time job.

Contemporary proponents of "difference feminism" advance a variation on the same argument, without Montagu's puckish humor. Instead of his whimsical chromosomal explanation, we get, for example, the psychoanalytic one proposed by Nancy Chodorow in *The Reproduction of Mothering:* Daughters define themselves by relating to their mothers, the primary love object of all children, and are therefore empathic, relationship-oriented, nonhierarchical and interested in forging consensus; sons must separate from their mothers, and are therefore individualistic, competitive, resistant to connection with others and focused on abstract rules and rights. Chodorow's theory has become a kind of mantra of difference feminism, endlessly cited as if it explained phenomena we all agree are universal, though this is far from the case. The central question Chodorow poses— Why are women the primary caregivers of children?—could not even be asked before the advent of modern birth control, and can be answered without resorting to psychology. Historically, women have taken care of children because high fertility and lack of other options left most of them no choice. Those rich enough to avoid personally raising their children often did, as Rousseau observed to his horror.

Popularizers of Chodorow water down and sentimentalize her thesis. They embrace her proposition that traditional mothering produces "relational" women and "autonomous" men but forget her less, congenial argument that it also results in sexual inequality, misogyny and hostility between mothers and daughters, who, like sons, desire independence but have a much harder time achieving it. Unlike her followers, Chodorow does not romanticize mothering: "Exclusive single parenting is bad for mother and child alike," she concludes; in a tragic paradox, female "caring," "intimacy" and "nurturance" do not soften but *produce* aggressive, competitive, hypermasculine men.

The relational woman and autonomous man described in psychoanalytic terms by Chodorow have become stock figures in other areas of social science as well. Thus, in her immensely influential book, *In a Different Voice,* the educational psychologist Carol Gilligan argues that the sexes make moral decisions according to separate criteria: Women employ an "ethic of care," men an "ethic of rights." The sociolinguist Deborah Tannen, in the best-selling *You Just Don't Understand,* analyzes male-female conversation as "cross-cultural communication" by people from different backgrounds: the single-sex world of children's play in which girls cooperate and boys compete. While these two writers differ in important ways— Tannen, writing at a more popular level, is by far the clearer thinker and the one more interested in analyzing actual human interactions in daily life, about which she is often quite shrewd—they share important liabilities, too. Both largely confine their observations to the white middle class—especially Gilligan, much of whose elaborate theory of gendered ethics rests on interviews with a handful of Harvard-Radcliffe undergraduates—and seem unaware that this limits the applicability of their data. (In their 1992 book, *Meeting at the Crossroads,* Gilligan and her coauthor, Lyn Mikel Brown, make a similar mistake. Their whole theory of "loss of relationship" as the central trauma of female adolescence rests on interviews with students at one posh single-sex private school.) Both massage their findings to fit their theories: Gilligan's male and female responses are actually quite similar to each other, as experimenters have subsequently shown by removing the names and asking subjects to try to sort the answers by gender; Tannen is quick to attribute blatant rudeness or sexism in male speech to anxiety, helplessness, fear of loss of face—to anything, indeed, but rudeness and sexism. Both look only at what people say, not what they do. For Tannen this isn't a decisive objection because speech is her subject, although it limits the extent to which her findings can be applied to other areas of behavior; for Gilligan, it is a major obstacle, unless you believe, as she apparently does, that the way people say they would resolve far-fetched hypothetical dilemmas—Should a poor man steal drugs to save his dying wife?—tells us how they reason in real-life situations or, more important, how they act.

But the biggest problem with all these accounts of gender difference is that they credit the differences they find to universal features of male and female development rather than to the economic and social positions men and women hold, or to the actual power differences between individual men and women. In *The Mismeasure of Woman,* her trenchant and witty attack on contemporary theories of gender difference, Carol Tavris points out that much of what can be said about women applies as well to poor people, who also tend to focus more on family and relationships and less on work and self-advancement; to behave deferentially with those more socially powerful; and to appear to others more emotional and "intuitive" than rational and logical in their thinking. Then, too, there is the question of whether the difference theorists are measuring anything beyond their own willingness to think in stereotypes. If Chodorow is right, relational women and autonomous men should be the norm, but are they? Or is it just that women and men use different language, have different social styles, offer different explanations for similar behavior? Certainly, it is easy to find in one's own acquaintance, as well as in the world at large, men and women who don't fit the models. Difference feminists like to attribute ruthlessness, coldness and hyperrationality in successful women—Margaret Thatcher is the standard example to the fact that men control the networks of power and permit only women like themselves to rise. But I've met plenty of rigid, insensitive, aggressive women who are stay-at-home mothers and secretaries and nurses. And I know plenty of sweet, unambitious men whose main satisfactions lie in their social, domestic and romantic lives, although not all of them would admit this to an inquiring social scientist. We tend to tell strangers what we think will make us sound good. I myself, to my utter amazement, informed a telephone pollster that I exercised regularly, a barefaced lie. How much more difficult to describe truthfully one's moral and ethical values even if one knew what they were, which, as Socrates demonstrated at length, almost no one does.

So why are Gilligan and Tannen the toasts of feminist social science, endlessly cited and discussed in academia, and out of it too, in gender-sensitivity sessions

in the business world and even, following the Anita Hill-Clarence Thomas hearings, in Congress? The success of the difference theorists proves yet again that
social science is one part science and nine parts social. They say what people want
to hear: Women really are different, in just the ways we always thought. Women
embrace Gilligan and Tannen because they offer flattering accounts of traits for
which they have historically been castigated. Men like them because, while they
urge understanding and respect for "female" values and behaviors, they also let
men off the hook: Men have power, wealth and control of social resources because
women don't really want them. The pernicious tendencies of difference feminism
are perfectly illustrated by the Sears sex discrimination case, in which Rosalind
Rosenberg, a professor of women's history at Barnard College, testified for Sears
that female employees held lower-paying salaried jobs while men worked selling
big-ticket items on commission because women preferred low-risk, noncompeti-
tive positions that did not interfere with family responsibilities. Sears won its case.

While early-childhood development is the point of departure for most of the
difference feminists, it is possible to construct a theory of gendered ethics on other
grounds. The most interesting attempt I've seen is by the pacifist philosopher
Sara Ruddick. Although not widely known outside academic circles, her *Maternal
Thinking* makes an argument that can be found in such mainstream sources as the
columns of Anna Quindlen in *The New York Times.* For Ruddick it is not psychosex-
ual development that produces the Gilliganian virtues but intimate involvement
in child-raising, the hands-on work of mothering. Men too can be mothers if they
do the work that women do. (And women can be Fathers—a word Ruddick uses,
complete with arrogant capital letter, for distant, uninvolved authority-figure parents.) Mothers are patient, peace-loving, attentive to emotional context and so on,
because those are the qualities you need to get the job done, the way accountants
are precise, lawyers argumentative, writers self-centered. Thus mothers constitute
a logical constituency—for pacifist and antiwar politics, and, by extension, a "caring" domestic agenda.

But what is the job of mothering? Ruddick defines "maternal practice"
as meeting three demands: preservation, growth and social acceptability. She
acknowledges the enormously varying manifestations of these demands, but she
doesn't incorporate into her theory the qualifications, limits and contradictions
she notes—perhaps because to do so would reveal these demands as so flexible as
to be practically empty terms.

Almost anything mothers do can be explained under one of these rubrics,
however cruel, dangerous, unfair or authoritarian—the genital mutilation of African and Arab girls, the foot-binding of prerevolutionary Chinese ones, the sacrifice

of some children to increase the resources available for others, as in the killing or malnourishing of female infants in India and China today. In this country, many mothers who commit what is legally child abuse *think* they are merely disciplining their kids in the good old-fashioned way.

As long as the practices are culturally acceptable (and sometimes even when they're not), the mothers who perform them think of themselves as good parents. But if all these behaviors count as mothering, how can mothering have a necessary connection with any single belief about anything, let alone how to stop war, or any single set of personality traits, let alone nonviolent ones?

We should not be surprised that motherhood does not produce uniform beliefs and behaviors: It is, after all, not a job; it has no standard of admission, and almost nobody gets fired. Motherhood is open to any woman who can have a baby or adopt one. *Not* to be a mother is a decision; becoming one requires merely that a woman accede, perhaps only for as long as it takes to get pregnant, to thousands of years of cumulative social pressure. After that, she's on her own; she can soothe her child's nightmares or let him cry in the dark. Nothing intrinsic to child-raising will tell her what is the better choice for her child (each has been the favored practice at different times). Although Ruddick starts off by looking closely at maternal practice, when that practice contradicts her own ideas about good mothering it is filed away as an exception, a distortion imposed by Fathers or poverty or some other outside force. But if you add up all the exceptions, you are left with a rather small group of people—women like Ruddick herself, enlightened, up-to-date, educated, upper-middle-class liberals.

And not even all of them. Consider the issue of physical punishment. Ruddick argues that experience teaches mothers that violence is useless; it only creates anger, deception and more violence. Negotiation is the mother's way of resolving disputes and encouraging good behavior. As Ann Crittenden put it in *The Nation* during the Gulf War: "One learns, in theory and in practice, to try to resolve conflict in ways that do not involve the sheer imposition of will or brute force. One learns that violence just doesn't work." Crittenden would have a hard time explaining all those moms in uniform who participated in Operation Desert Storm—but then she'd have a hard time explaining all those mothers screaming at their kids in the supermarket, too.

As it happens, I agree that violence is a bad way to teach, and I made a decision never, no matter what, to spank my daughter. But mothers who do not hit their children, or permit their husbands to do so, are as rare as conscientious objectors in wartime. According to one survey, 78 percent approve of an occasional "good, hard spanking"—because they think violence is an effective way of teaching, because they think that hitting children isn't really violence, because they just lose it. Even *Parenting* found that more than a third of its readers hit their kids. And *Parenting's* audience is not only far more educated, affluent and liberal than the general population, it consists entirely of people who care what experts think about child development—and contemporary experts revile corporal punishment. Interestingly, the moms who hit tended to be the ones who fretted the most about raising their children well. Mothers who think too much?

Like old-style socialists finding "proletarian virtue" in the working class, Ruddick claims to be describing what mothers do, but all too often she is really prescribing what she thinks they ought-to do. "When their children flourish, almost all mothers have a sense of well-being." Hasn't she ever heard of postpartum depression? Of mothers who belittle their children's accomplishments and resent their growing independence? "What mother wouldn't want the power to keep her children healthy . . . to create hospitals, schools, jobs, day care, and work schedules that serve her maternal work?" Notice how neatly the modest and commonsensical wish for a healthy child balloons into the hotly contested and by no means universal wish of mothers for day-care and flextime. Notice, too, how Ruddick moves from a mother's desire for social institutions that serve *her* children to an assumption that this desire translates into wanting comparable care for *all* children. But mothers feature prominently in local struggles against busing, mergers of rich and poor schools and the opening in their neighborhoods of group homes for foster children, boarder babies and the retarded. Why? The true reasons may be property values and racism, but what these mothers often say is that they are simply protecting their kids. Ruddick seems to think Maternal Thinking leads naturally to Sweden; in the United States it is equally likely to lead to Fortress Suburbia.

As Gilligan does with all women, Ruddick scrutinizes mothers for what she expects to find, and sure enough, there it is. But why look to mothers for her peaceful constituency in the first place? Why not health professionals, who spend their lives saving lives? Or historians, who know how rarely war yields a benefit remotely commensurate with its cost in human misery? Or, I don't know, gardeners, blamelessly tending their innocent flowers? You can read almost any kind of work as affirming life and conferring wisdom. Ruddick chooses mothering because she's already decided that women possess the Gilliganian virtues and she wants a non-essentialist peg to hang them on, so that men can acquire them, too. A disinterested observer scouring the world for labor that encourages humane values would never pick child-raising: It's too quirky, too embedded in repellent cultural norms, too hot.

Despite its intellectual flabbiness, differences feminism is deeply appealing to many women. Why? For one thing, it seems to explain some important phenomena: that women—and this is a cross-cultural truth—commit very little criminal violence compared with men; that women fill the ranks of the so-called caring professions; that women are much less likely than men to abandon their children. Difference feminists want to give women credit for these good behaviors by raising them from the level of instinct or passivity—the Camille Paglia vision of femininity—to the level of moral choice and principled decision. Who can blame women for embracing theories that tell them the sacrifices they make on behalf of domesticity and children are legitimate, moral, even noble? By stressing the mentality of nurturance—the *ethic* of caring, maternal *thinking*—Gilligan and Ruddick challenge the ancient division of humanity into rational males and irrational females. They offer women a way to argue that their views have equal status with those of men and to resist the customary marginalization of their voices in public debate. Doubtless many women have felt emboldened by Gilliganian accounts of moral difference: Speaking in a different voice is, after all, a big step up from silence.

The vision of women as sharers and carers is tempting in another way, too. Despite much media blather about the popularity of the victim position, most people want to believe they act out of free will and choice. The uncomfortable truth that women have all too little of either is a difficult hurdle for feminists. Acknowledging the systematic oppression of women seems to deprive them of existential freedom, to turn them into puppets, slaves and Stepford wives. Deny it, and you can't make change. By arguing that the traditional qualities, tasks and ways of life of women are as important, valuable and serious as those of men (if not more so), Gilligan and others let women feel that nothing needs to change except the social valuation accorded to what they are already doing. It's a rationale for the status quo, which is why men like it, and a burst of grateful applause, which is why women like it. Men keep the power, but since power is bad, so much the worse for them.

Another rather curious appeal of difference feminism is that it offers a way for women to define themselves as independent of men. In a culture that sees women almost entirely in relation to men, this is no small achievement. Sex, for example—the enormous amount of female energy, money and time spent on beauty and fashion and romance, on attracting men and keeping them, on placating male power, strategizing ways around it or making it serve one's own ends—plays a minute role in these theories. You would never guess from Gilligan or Ruddick that men, individually and collectively, are signal beneficiaries of female nurturance, much less that this goes far to explain why society encourages nurturance in women. No, it is always children whom women are described as fostering and sacrificing for, or the community, or even other women—not husbands or lovers. It's as though wives cook dinner only for their kids, leaving the husband to raid the fridge on his own. And no doubt many a woman, quietly smoldering at her mate's refusal to share domestic labor, persuades herself that she is serving only her children, or her own preferences, rather than confront the inequality of her marriage.

The peaceful mother and the relational woman are a kinder, gentler, leftish version of "family values," and both are modern versions of the separate-spheres ideology of the Victorians. In the nineteenth century, too, some women tried to turn the ideology of sexual difference on its head and expand the moral claims of motherhood to include the public realm. Middle-class women became social reformers, abolitionists, temperance advocates, settlement workers and even took paying jobs in the "helping professions"—nursing, social work, teaching—which were perceived as extensions of women's domestic role although practiced mostly by single women. These women did not deny that their sex fitted them for the home, but argued that domesticity did not end at the front door of the house, or confine itself to dusting (or telling the housemaid to dust). Even the vote could be cast as an extension of domesticity: Women, being more moral than men, would purify the government of vice and corruption, end war and make America safe for family life. (The persistence of this metaphor came home to me when I attended a Women's Action Coalition demonstration during the 1992 Democratic National Convention. There—along with WAC's funny and ferocious all-in-black drum corps and contingents of hip downtown artists brandishing Barbara Kruger posters and shouting slogans like "We're Women! We're Angry! We're Not Going Shopping!"—was a trio of street performers with housecoats and kerchiefs over black catsuits and spiky hair, pushing brooms: Women will clean up government!)

The separate-spheres ideology had obvious advantages for middle-class women in an era when they were formally barred from higher education, political power and most jobs that paid a living wage. But its defects are equally obvious. It defined all women by a single standard, and one developed by a sexist society. It offered women no way to enter jobs that could not be defined as extensions of their domestic roles—you could be a math teacher but not a mathematician, a secretary but not a sea captain—and no way to challenge any but the grossest abuses of male privilege. Difference feminists are making a similar bid for power on behalf of women today, and are caught in similar contradictions. Once again, women are defined by their family roles. Child-raising is seen as woman's glory and joy and opportunity for self-transcendence, while Dad naps on the couch. Women who do not fit the stereotype are castigated as unfeminine—nurses nurture, doctors do not—and domestic labor is romanticized and sold to women as a badge of moral worth.

For all the many current explanations of perceived moral difference between the sexes, one hears remarkably little about the material basis of the family. Yet the motherhood and womanhood being valorized cannot be considered apart from questions of power, privilege and money. There is a reason a non-earning woman can proudly call herself a "wife and mother" and a non-earning man is just unemployed: The traditional female role, with its attendant real or imagined traits and values, implies a male income. Middle-class women go to great lengths to separate themselves from this uncomfortable fact. One often hears married mothers defend their decision to stay at home by heaping scorn on paid employment—caricatured as making widgets or pushing papers or dressing for success—-and the difference feminists, too, like to distinguish between altruistic, poorly paid female jobs and the nasty, profitable ones performed by men. In *Prisoners of Men's Dreams*, Suzanne Gordon comes close to blaming the modest status of jobs like nursing and flight attending on women's entry into jobs like medicine and piloting, as if before the women's movement those female-dominated occupations were respected and rewarded. (Nurses should be glad the field no longer has a huge captive labor pool of women: The nursing shortage has led to dramatic improvements in pay, benefits and responsibility. Now nurses earn a man-size income, and men are applying to nursing school in record numbers— exactly what Gordon wants.) It's all very well for some women to condemn others for "acting like men"—i.e., being ambitious, assertive, interested in money and position. But if their husbands did not "act like men," where would they be? Jean Bethke Elshtain, who strenuously resists the notion of gendered ethics, nevertheless bemoans the loss to their communities when women leave volunteering and informal mutual support networks for paid employment. But money must come from somewhere; if women leave to men the job of earning the family income (an option fewer and fewer families can afford), they will be economically dependent on their husbands, a situation that, besides carrying obvious risks in an age of frequent divorce, weakens their bargaining position in the family and insures that men will largely control major decisions affecting family life.

Difference theorists would like to separate out the aspects of traditional womanhood that they approve of and speak only of those. But the parts they like (caring, nurturing, intimacy) are inseparable from the parts they don't like (economic dependence and the subordination of women within the family). The difference theorists try to get around this by positing a world that contains two cultures—a female world of love and ritual and a male world of getting and spending and killing—which mysteriously share a single planet. That vision is expressed neatly in a recent pop-psychology title, *Men Are From Mars, Women Are From Venus*. It would be truer to say men are from Illinois and women are from Indiana—different, sure, but not in ways that have much ethical consequence.

The truth is, there is only one culture, and it shapes each sex in distinct but mutually dependent ways in order to reproduce itself. To the extent that the stereotypes are true, women have the "relational" domestic qualities *because* men have the "autonomous" qualities required to survive and prosper in modern capitalism. She needs a wage earner (even if she has a job, thanks to job discrimination), and he needs someone to mind his children, hold his hand and have his emotions for him. This—not, as Gordon imagines, some treason to her sex—explains why women who move into male sectors act very much like men: If they didn't, they'd find themselves back home in a jiffy. The same necessities and pressures affect them as affect the men who hold those jobs. Because we are in a transition period, in which many women were raised with modest expectations and much emphasis on the need to please others, social scientists who look for it can find traces of empathy, caring and so on in some women who have risen in the world of work and power. But when they tell us that women doctors will transform American medicine, or women executives will transform the corporate world, they are looking backward, not forward. If women really do enter the workforce on equal terms with men—if they become 50 percent of all lawyers, politicians, car dealers and prison guards—they may be less sexist (although the example of Soviet doctors, a majority of them female, is not inspiring to those who know about the brutal gynecological customs prevailing in the former U.S.S.R.). And they may bring with them a distinct set of manners, a separate social style. But they won't be, in some general way, more honest, kind, egalitarian, empathic or indifferent to profit. To argue otherwise is to believe that the reason factory owners bust unions, doctors refuse Medicaid patients and New York City school custodians don't mop the floors is because they are men.

The ultimate paradox of difference feminism is that it has come to the fore at a moment when the lives of the sexes are becoming less distinct than they ever have been in the West. Look at the decline of single-sex education (researchers may tout the benefits of all-female schools and colleges, but girls overwhelmingly choose coeducation); the growth of female athletics; the virtual abolition of virginity as a requirement for girls; the equalization of college-attendance rates of males and females; the explosion of employment for married women and mothers even of small children; the crossing of workplace gender lines by both females and males; the cultural pressure on men to be warm and active fathers, to do at least some housework, to choose mates who are their equals in education and income potential.

It's fashionable these days to talk about the backlash against equality feminism—I talk this way myself when I'm feeling blue—but equality feminism has scored amazing successes. It has transformed women's expectations in every area of their lives. However, it has not yet transformed society to meet those expectations. The workplace still discriminates. On the home front few men practice egalitarianism, although many preach it; single mothers—and given the high divorce rate, every mother is potentially a single mother—lead incredibly difficult lives.

In this social context, difference feminism is essentially a way for women both to take advantage of equality feminism's success and to accommodate themselves to its limits. It appeals to particular kinds of women—those in the "helping professions" or the home, for example, rather than those who want to be bomber pilots or neurosurgeons or electricians. At the popular level, it encourages women who feel disadvantaged or demeaned by equality to direct their anger against women who have benefited from it by thinking of them as gender traitors and of themselves as suffering for their virtue—thus the hostility of some nurses toward female doctors, and of some stay-at-home mothers toward employed mothers.

For its academic proponents, the appeal lies elsewhere: Difference feminism is a way to carve out a safe space in the face of academia's resistance to female advancement. It works much like multiculturalism, making an end run around a static and discriminatory employment structure by creating an intellectual niche that can be filled only by members of the discriminated-against group. And like other forms of multiculturalism, it looks everywhere for its explanatory force— biology, psychology, sociology, cultural identity— *except* economics. The difference feminists cannot say that the differences between men and women are the result of their relative economic positions, because to say that would be to move the whole discussion out of the realm of psychology and feel-good cultural pride and into the realm of a tough political struggle over the distribution of resources and justice and money.

Although it is couched in the language of praise, difference feminism is demeaning to women. It asks that women be admitted into public life and public discourse not because they have a right to be there but because they will improve them. Even if this were true, and not the wishful thinking I believe it to be, why should the task of moral and social transformation be laid on women's doorstep and not on everyone's—or, for that matter, on men's, by the you-broke-it-you-fix-it principle? Peace, the environment, a more humane workplace, economic justice, social support for children—these are issues that affect us all and are everyone's responsibility. By promising to assume that responsibility, difference feminists lay the groundwork for excluding women again, as soon as it becomes clear that the promise cannot be kept.

No one asks that other oppressed groups win their freedom by claiming to be extra-good. And no other oppressed group thinks it must make such a claim in order to be accommodated fully and across the board by society. For blacks and other racial minorities, it is enough to want to earn a living, exercise one's talents, get a fair hearing in the public forum. Only for women is simple justice an insufficient argument. It is as though women don't really believe they are entitled to full citizenship unless they can make a special claim to virtue. Why isn't being human enough?

In the end, I didn't sign that peace petition, although I was sorry to disappoint a woman I liked, and although I am very much for peace. I decided to wait for a petition that welcomed my signature as a person, an American, a citizen implicated, against my will, in war and the war economy. I still think I did the right thing.

Two Moralities? A Critical Discussion of an Ethic of Care and Responsibility versus an Ethic of Rights and Justice

Gertrud Nunner-Winkler

Gertrud Nunner-Winkler *is a prolific researcher in the field of moral development, especially in the areas of moral motivation and changes in identity and gender roles. She was formally trained as a sociologist and has been a research fellow or leader at various Max Planck Institutes in Germany since 1971. In 1990, Nunner-Winkler took a faculty position at the Ludwig-Maximilians University in Munich. She is currently the leader of the working group at the Max Planck Institute for Human Cognitive and Neurosciences in Munich. Nunner-Winkler is one of the editors of* Advances in Psychology: Morality in Context *(2005).*

Gilligan has recently claimed that there are two contrasting approaches to morality: an ethic of care and responsibility and an ethic of justice and rights (1977, 1983; see also Murphy & Gilligan 1980; Gilligan, Langdale & Lyons 1982). The first approach, more typical for females, corresponds to the experience of the self as part of relationships, as "connected self; moral judgments consider specific details of concrete situations and are guided by an interest in minimizing the overall harm done. The justice orientation, more characteristic of males, on the other hand, is an expression of an autonomous, independent, "individuated" self; moral judgments follow principles defining rights and duties without "due" consideration of specific circumstances and costs implied. Gilligan accuses Lawrence Kohlberg of stating the justice orientation as the only valid moral orientation, thus neglecting the contribution of the other approach to morality.

In this essay I shall try to reinterpret Gilligan's position. First, differences noted between the "male" and the "female" approach, as far as they are moral, I take to be differences not in ethical position but in emphasis of one against the other of two types of moral duties. Second, the consideration of situational particularities does not discriminate between the two moral orientations. Third, a considerable part of the sex-specific differences are not moral differences: Gilligan's description of an ethic of care and responsibility includes questions concerning the conception of the good life that do not belong to morality proper. In the last part of the essay I shall attempt to derive several hypotheses about sex-specific moral preferences formulated in terms of theoretical distinctions introduced in the first part and shall test them against empirical data collected in a study on adolescent development.

The Distinction between Perfect and Imperfect Duties

For theoretical clarification I consider a distinction that was introduced by Kant in his *Metaphysik der Sitten* (1797/1977) and later elaborated especially by B. Gert in his *The Moral Rules* (1973), namely, the distinction between perfect and imperfect duties. Perfect duties are *negative* duties, that is duties of omission (e.g., do not kill, do not cheat, etc.); imperfect duties are *positive* duties, duties of commission, which, however, do not prescribe specific acts but only formulate a maxim to guide action (e.g., practice charity). This maxim thus delineates a broad set of recommendable courses of action some of which the actor realizes by, at the same time, applying pragmatic rules and taking into account concrete conditions, such as individual preferences, contingencies of location in space and time, and so on.

Perfect duties, because they require only *not* to act, can, at least in nonconflictual cases, be followed strictly by everybody at any time and location and with regard to everybody (Gert 1973). Imperfect duties, on the other hand, can never be observed completely: it is impossible to practice charity all the time and with regard to everybody. Positive maxims do not define limits of their application, do not specify which and how many good deeds have to be performed and whom they are to benefit so that the maxim can be said to have been followed. Due to this latitude, the following of maxims requires what Kant calls power of judgment *(Urteilskraft)*. The asymmetry between perfect and imperfect duties is also reflected in the differential reactions to transgression. The failure to meet perfect duties is considered a vice *(Laster)*, the failure to meet imperfect duties is lack of virtue *(Untugend)*.

The Ethic of Care and Responsibility as an Ethic of Imperfect Duties; The Ethic of Rights and Justice as an Ethic of Perfect Duties

The characteristics Gilligan (1977) enumerates show the ethic of care and responsibility to be primarily an orientation to imperfect duties, the ethic of rights and justice to be primarily an orientation to perfect duties. Thus, the most eminent goals of the ethic of care are the wish to care for and help others, to meet obligations and responsibilities, a concern for others and feelings of compassion, a responsibility to discern and alleviate trouble in this world (511). This orientation to imperfect duties finds its most concise expression in one woman's statement in an interview: "Is it right to spend money on a pair of shoes, when I have a pair of shoes and other people are shoeless?" (510). The very form this reflection takes, the interrogative, is proof of its being derived from an imperfect duty, namely, the principle of charity, which does not define its own form of application, its own limits, and the degree to which it is binding.

The ethic of rights and justice, on the other hand, is depicted as being mainly concerned with rights of individuals and their protection, that is, ways of ensuring that rights of individuals will not be interfered with by others. Such rights, it seems, are conceived to be invulnerable, absolute rights valid at all times and places and for all persons; they are conceived as rights corresponding to perfect duties. No one would deny that both kinds of duties are considered part of one morality, the unity of which is constituted through adherence to some universalizing procedure. How, then, is Gilligan's claim that it is still a question of contrasting moral approaches to be understood. I think it can be interpreted to mean that females (1) feel more obliged to fulfill imperfect duties than males; and (2) in cases of conflict will more likely opt for the fulfillment of imperfect duties, whereas males will insist more rigidly on having the perfect duties respected. The first part of the statement, I think, is more adequately construed as a difference in moral action and moral character and not as a difference in ethical position, for the latitude of imperfect duties per definition requires that individuals make use of their moral understanding to derive concrete action decisions. This kind of difference in interpersonal orientation parallels the distinction between diffuse and specific role relationships that Talcott Parsons (1964, 65ff., 153ff.) notes: in diffuse relationships, that is, relations between relatives, friends, neighbors, it is assumed that one may ask for any kind of support, and the burden of proof rests with the role partner who withholds help. In specific relationships, on the contrary, the kind of help that may legitimately be asked for is clearly specified and limited, and the burden of proof rests with the partner demanding support. The hypothesized sex-difference in orientation might thus be a consequence of the fact that traditionally females are much more exclusively involved in diffuse relationships than are men and therefore feel bound to meet any need arising, whereas men are much more used to specific relationships and tend first to question the other person's "right to demand help." This hypothesis I shall take up in the last part of the essay.

The interpretation that in cases of conflict females opt for fulfilling imperfect duties, and males perfect duties, implies a difference in ethical positions insofar as females might be assumed to reverse the male order of priority of perfect over imperfect duties. Yet this interpretation is implausible, for Gilligan ascribes to the ethic of care an orientation to contextual particularities—"It is the reconstruction of a moral dilemma in its contextual particularity which allows an understanding . . . and thus engages the compassion and tolerance considered previously to qualify the feminine sense of justice" (1977, 511)— which is incompatible with an a priori strict ordering of one set of rules over the other. In fact, it is precisely this consideration of contextual particularities that Gilligan sees as lacking in the ethic of rights and justice—"Kohlberg retains his conception that principles of justice are context free" (1983, 83). This differential awareness of situational specifics marks one of the main differences between the two ethics.

The plausibility of this implied equation between an orientation to imperfect duties and to contextual particularity, respectively, to perfect duties and their contextual independence will be discussed in the following passages. I want to show that this equation holds true only for a very specific aspect of Kant's moral position that is shared by scarcely anyone, namely, that perfect duties allow no exceptions. It does not hold true for Kohlberg, even though he presents his construction of rights in such a misleading way that it does provoke the kind of criticism Gilligan voices.

The Role of Situation-specific Knowledge in Moral Judgment

In the nonconflictual case, the following of perfect duties presupposes scarcely any knowledge of situational specifics. As all that is required is not to act in a specified way at any time or location and with regard to everybody, all one needs to know are some general empirical facts valid for all situations (e.g., what substances are poisonous, giving strong enough poisons to a human being will kill him or her, etc.) or at best some narrowly limited specific facts (e.g., if that person does not receive a specific medicine now, he or she will die) or truth-values for specific statements (e.g., it is true that x happened). Yet the range of concrete facts one might need to know is clearly confinable and can deductively be determined: only those facts are relevant that pertain immediately to the rule in question; that is, for the rule "do not kill," relevant facts are all potential risks to life; for the rule "do not lie," only the empirical truth of statements asked is relevant.

Imperfect duties, on the other hand, require situation-specific knowledge, for they demand contextually situated decisions in regard to when and where to act and in regard to whom. Thus, Gilligan's proposition that the ethic of care takes situational details into account, whereas the ethic of rights does not, seems plausible: imperfect duties require by their logical characteristics a concrete specification that perfect duties do not. Yet the picture gets more complicated as soon as one considers cases where duties collide. Only if one assumes that there are rules without exceptions can there be any moral judgments that can be made without taking note of situational specifics. This actually is Kant's position. Kant (1959) maintains that perfect duties enjoy absolute priority over imperfect duties, that is, allow for no exceptions. Thus, he explicitly states that even if lying to a murderer might save a friend's life, it cannot be justified, for "truthfulness . . . is a *perfect duty valid under all circumstances*" (205).[1]

This position is extreme, however, and is shared by scarcely anyone. In modern discussion the justifiability of exceptions to rules is widely accepted. It finds a clear expression in the differentiation between actual duties and prima facie duties that W. D. Ross (1930, 8-31, 61f.) introduced: rules are valid only prima facie, that is, under normal circumstances, when there are no other moral considerations that bear on the decision. In Gert's (1973) exposition, the "except" clause plays the same role. Thus, Gilligan's claim that the ethic of care is oriented to situational particularities that the ethic of rights will neglect is valid only at first sight. For even to observe perfect duties requires—if exceptions are deemed justifiable—that the question of consequences of different courses of action in a specific situation has to be examined: for it might well be that the imperfect duty to prevent harm may in a concrete case legitimately override obligations following from a perfect duty. Therefore I think one cannot very well hold context orientation to be a feature that constitutes contrasting approaches to morality. Context orientation is a prerequisite for *all actual moral judgments.*

One problem still remains open: how moral decision is to be reached in such cases of conflicting duties. Moral choice in dilemmas is based on a process of reflection on the potential universalizability of the specific solution, found by taking all particulars of the concrete situation into account. It is this compatibility of universalism with an orientation to situational particularities that has often been overlooked. Hare makes this point very lucidly in his distinction between universality and generality: "The thesis of universalizability does not require moral judgments to be made on the basis of highly general moral principles. . . . Moral development . . . consists in the main in making our moral principles more and more specific by writing into them exceptions and qualifications to cover kinds of cases of which we have had experience" (1963, 40).

It may very well be true that people will come up with different solutions: People will differ in the weight they will give to various considerations. As Gert puts it: "One man might publicly advocate killing one man in order to save ten others.... Another man might not publicly advocate violation in this situation. He might feel that a significant decrease in the protection from violations of the rule plus general anxiety due to added uncertainty more than offsets the possible benefit" (1973, 99). This is true because "evils are ranked in too many diverse ways" (ibid., 126). It might also be true that sex-specific differences in the ranking of evils might show up; thus, for instance, I would assume, in accordance with the hypothesis put forward earlier, that females might weigh consequences on the level of the social system as less grave than consequences on the level of interpersonal relations. Yet this could be taken to be a sex-specific filling in of a latitude that is conceded within the limits of morality, whereby morality is understood as constituted through an obligation to some universalizing procedure, that is, to impartiality.

One minor point may still be noted pertaining to the question of methodology. Gilligan tends to see Kohlberg's use of hypothetical dilemma as another indication of the abstraction of moral problems from the "contingencies of human social existence" she criticizes in him:

> While the analytic logic of justice is consonant with rational social and ethical theories and can be traced through the resolution of hypothetical dilemmas, the ethic of care depends on the contextual understanding of relationships. . . . While the analytic logic of justice can be traced through the deductive resolution of *hypothetical* dilemmas and the understanding of systems of rules, the ethic of care is manifested through the understanding of *actual* situations of moral conflict and choice. (1983, 9–10)

I think this is a misunderstanding. If exceptions are allowed, concrete circumstances have to be taken into account in solving a moral conflict—be it a hypothetical or an actual conflict. There is a difference, namely, that in actual dilemmas one can never be sure whether facts are correctly perceived. Yet this difference lies on the level of empirical truth of descriptive statements, not on the level of normative judgment.

Kohlberg's Position

The main criticism Gilligan directs against Kohlberg is that he neglects situational particularities in making moral judgments: "Kohlberg built a theory of moral development on a unitary moral conception of fairness and justice. . . . Thus the social concept of moral decision was replaced by the structures of formal thought which provided a rational system for decision that was autonomous and *independent of time and place*" (1983, 7). Kohlberg's "principles of justice [are] *context-free* and [can] generate *objectively right* solutions to moral problems" (Murphy & Gilligan 1980, 83). Yet by the logic of his own moral convictions Kohlberg by necessity must orient his moral judgments to concrete situational circumstances. This is because in a conflict between perfect and imperfect duties he not only maintains—unlike Kant—that the perfect duty *may* be violated, but almost requires that it *must* be violated; that is, Kohlberg adopts a radical female position, however ironic this may sound. Thus, for instance, in the Heinz dilemma the issue is whether Heinz may break into the druggist's store to steal a drug to save his wife's life. In terms of the distinctions introduced earlier, the Heinz dilemma depicts a conflict between a perfect duty (not to steal) and an imperfect duty (to prevent evil, namely, the death of the sick woman). Kant would have denied that Heinz may break into the store: if one may not lie in order to save a life, one may not steal either. Kant (1959) gives another example that proves the same point: a man has been entrusted with a large sum of money. The owner dies without the heirs knowing anything of the deposit. The man, a charitable and philanthropic person, lost all his fortune without any fault of his own; his wife and children are starving. The heirs, however, are unkind, rich, and wasteful, and "it were just as well that the additional wealth were to be thrown into the ocean" (1959, 82). Even in this extreme situation the man may not keep the money to feed his wife and children, for "it is wrong, it contradicts duty" (82)—that is, it is wrong under all circumstances, context free.

Kohlberg, quite on the contrary, demands that Heinz steal the drug "because the right to life supersedes or transcends the right to property" (Colby, Gibbs, Kohlberg, et al. 1979, 80). This justification rests on the assumption of a clear hierarchy of differentially binding duties and obligations. Yet whereas in Kant the hierarchical ordering of duties is based on their formal characteristics (perfect duties, as they are negative duties, which can be followed and are to be followed under all circumstances and with regard to everybody, are superordinate to imperfect duties, which only formulate maxims that can never be completely followed), Kohlberg seems to posit the hierarchy of rights by content: "There is a hierarchy of rights and values. Stealing is justified as serving a universal right to or value of life which is prior to laws" (ibid.). Because of its utmost priority, this universal right to life is henceforth treated as if it were a perfect right corresponding to a perfect duty in Kant's sense: it is a right that must be granted universally; that is, it implies seemingly perfect duties regardless of concrete circumstances or of personal ties. Thus, for Kohlberg it is as much a duty to steal for a stranger as it is to steal for one's own wife: "It would be right to steal for a stranger because the right to life should be accorded universally to all men whose lives can be saved regardless of personal ties" (ibid., 82). The problem with this position is that "saving life" by its structural characteristics is an imperfect duty, which does not specify its own limits: a universally accorded right to life implies the universal duty to save "all men whose lives can be saved regardless of personal ties," even if that would require violation of property rights. Thus we all are not only required to give away all the money we own but also justified—in fact, maybe even obliged—to rob all banks as well as all members of our society who own more than they need to feed themselves, so as to be able to save the starving children in the third world, whose sad fate is well known to all of us.[2]

I assume Kohlberg would not support such a revolutionary Robin Hood strategy. If this were correct, it follows that, for Kohlberg as well, decisions in moral dilemmas hinge on concrete circumstances: thus, it may be justifiable to rob for one's own wife or even a stranger one has met, but it may be less justifiable to rob with the intent to send the money to India. Yet in Kohlberg's own justifications, the factual dependency of moral judgments on a consideration of concrete circumstances is veiled; thus, Gilligan rightly denounces the neglect of situational contingencies on Kohlberg's part. This neglect, though, I take—in contrast to Gilligan—not to be characteristic of a certain type of morality, the morality of rights and justice; rather, it is because Kohlberg has not clearly recognized the logical structure of imperfect duties. This can be seen from the misleading formulation he uses. He speaks of a universal right to life, which seems to imply a universal, hence perfect, duty to save life. Perfect duties, however, can be formulated only in the negative: All one can say is that every human being has a right not to be killed, disabled, deprived of freedom by others.

Morality versus Questions of the Good Life

Thus far only part of Gilligan's position has been discussed: the assumption that an orientation to care can be juxtaposed to an orientation to rights, whereby only the former takes situational particularities into account, whereas the latter denies their relevance. The second half of this assumption has been refuted: consideration of concrete situational details is indispensable for *all* moral judgments (if exceptions are allowed). The first part has been reformulated: females feel more obliged to fulfill imperfect duties of charity, whereas males adhere more strictly to the perfect duties of noninterference, although both types of duty belong to morality.

Yet Gilligan's conceptualization of the two approaches to morality is more encompassing than has hitherto been stated. Gilligan sees them as emanating from different experiences of the self in the world: "The principle of nonviolence and an ethic of care . . . informs the world of the connected self, the principle of fairness and an ethic of justice . . . informs the world of the separate self (Gilligan, Langdale & Lyons 1982, 42–43). The experience of the self in the world is itself a process of development, described for the ethic of care as the unfolding of the concept of responsibility. I think that in this conceptualization of the "connected self and of stages of responsibility, moral orientation and development is mixed with aspects of ego development and with questions of the good life. To substantiate this claim I will analyze two examples. In the first, concerning ways of conflict resolution in child's play, "social connectedness" is interpreted by Gilligan, Langdale and Lyons as the basis of a specific moral orientation, although it might well be simply an expression of specific ego interests. The second example concerns reflections about life plans at pregnancy; in the decision of this issue questions of the good life are confounded with moral problems.

In the first example, two six-year-olds respond to the dilemma "created when, in playing with a friend, they discover that they and their friend want to play a different game." Characteristic of the little girl are the following statements: *"We don't have a real fight"* and *"we agree what we should do"* and *"we should play one . . ., then the other"*; while the little boy starts out by stating: "I wanted to stay outside—he wanted to go in" and ends with the statement *"I would do what I want—he would do what he wants."* The italicized statements are pointed out by the authors as especially good exemplifications of the contrasting principles of care versus fairness. As long as it is so described, however, this dilemma is not a moral dilemma, but the inner conflict of an individual choosing among his or her own conflicting needs. Each child has two desires: the desire to play a specific game and the desire to play with a specific friend. The little girl forgoes the chance to play the preferred game (at least for some time) yet in return maintains the chance to play with the friend. The little boy, on the other hand, proves to be more interested in playing the preferred game, though be it alone, than in playing with his friend. Thus far each child may have chosen among different needs that proved not to be simultaneously satisfiable. There is nothing moral about this choice: it is well known that females are more interested in relationships and males more in things (objects).[3] Neither one nor the other of these preferences is morally more recommendable. Gilligan might consider this very construction of the dilemma to be a male version, while she sees it as a moral dilemma, that is, not as an intraindividual choice among one's own conflicting needs but as an interindividual choice between satisfying one's own needs or the needs of others. Yet I do not think that it really is a moral question. Adequately satisfying each other's needs is what a good relationship means. If a relationship is not good, that is, if both partners cannot find satisfaction and enrichment in sharing alter's interests, separating and searching for a more congenial partner might-so long as no other considerations must be considered, such as marriage and children-be better than a permanent pseudomoral adoption to alien interests.

Once the friendship dilemma comes to be seen as a moral dilemma of conflicting needs of ego and alter, however, the central issue of imperfect duties arises immediately: how far to go in fulfilling the needs of alter. It is this issue around which Gilligan presents the female moral development as revolving. Different levels of the conceptualization of responsibility formulate different answers: on the first level, responsibility centers on the self and on relationships that are self-serving; on the second level, responsibility orients to the needs of others such that the satisfaction of one's own needs is considered selfish, and self-sacrifice is deemed as "good"; on the last level, the focus of responsibility is shifted to the relationship itself, the stability of which is comprehended as depending on the fulfillment of the needs of self and other. This developmental sequence, although it answers a central problem of imperfect duties, is too narrowly conceived as moral development: it is a more encompassing learning process; it is a process of the development of self as an autonomous person, as a competent actor. Thus, on the third level the insight is developed that the second-level understanding of goodness as self-sacrifice is a welcome device to avoid taking upon oneself the responsibility for one's own actions. And it is only on the third level that the individual can clearly recognize his or her own needs and interests and separate them from externally obtruded ones, and becomes willing to assume the responsibility for the consequences that the following of one's own needs may entail. This competence is a prerequisite for all life choices (career, partner, worldview, political conviction, etc.), of which moral decisions make up only one part.

Gilligan, I think, unduly treats this general process of ego development as moral development and treats as moral choices what in reality are decisions about ways of life. This can be seen very clearly in the way Gilligan (1977) presents her interviews on abortion. The women questioned answer not the issue of whether an abortion is morally justifiable but rather questions of the "good life": namely, "What kind of person do I want to be?" "What kind of life do I want to lead?" This claim may seem unjustified, for most of the women do start off the discussion with formulating moral considerations, such as, "I don't believe in abortion. Who can say when life begins" (1977, 497), or even "It is taking a life" (499). Yet in fact these considerations do not enter the decision process; the question of abortion is dealt with as a choice between different ways of life. This can be seen if one examines the kind of reasons that are put forward by the same woman who considers abortion as taking life. Among the reasons she lists for having an abortion are the fear of losing a good job, losing independence, difficulties in handling the relationship with the father of the child; among the reasons against having an abortion she mentions enjoying more home life, being admired by others for bringing up a child alone; having less feelings of guilt. Another woman is quoted as comprehending through pregnancy her own "inner conflict between the wish to be a college president and to be making pottery and flowers, having kids and staying home" (1977, 508).

I do not want to deny that morally relevant considerations do sometimes enter into the question of life choice. Thus, for instance, the woman quoted earlier hesitates about a professional career for fear of losing her compassion on the way up. Yet most considerations mentioned concern morally neutral ego goals, such as a desire for a fulfilling occupation or the desire to avoid internal conflicts of priority between family and job, and the decision seems mainly to involve a morally neutral balancing out of different ego interests.

To summarize, I tend to think that not all the differences Gilligan sees as constitutive for two contrasting approaches to morality are really differences in moral orientation. Social connectedness is largely a result of greater social- than task-oriented interests; stages of responsibility describe a process of disentangling self from conformity expectations, which is a general process of ego development inasmuch as conformity expectations extend to many nonmoral issues. It may still be true that females feel more obliged than males to fulfill imperfect duties, to answer to concrete needs of others, even at their own costs. It also seems plausible that this characteristic is, as Gilligan suggests, a consequence of women's greater social involvement. It might also be, however, merely a consequence of an inability to recognize and stand up to one's own needs, that is, a consequence of lack of ego strength, of an inability to say no. If this is true, the status of a "female" approach to morality would be very ambiguous, indeed.

Some Data Concerning Sex Differences in Moral Judgment

In this last section I employ the data Rainer Doebert and I have collected. We interviewed 112 male and female adolescents in the age range of sixteen to twenty-two years and of different socioeconomic backgrounds. The interview covered intensity of adolescent crisis, moral judgment, coping, and defense styles, parental patterns of conflict resolution and child rearing, political socialization, and so on. It was not designed specifically to test sex-specific morality, yet some of the results may serve to test the following hypotheses derived from the assumptions of an ethic of care and responsibility:

1. Females feel more bound by imperfect duties than do males; that is, in a conflict between a perfect and an imperfect duty females will more likely opt for transgression of the perfect duty.
2. In moral decisions females will take more situational details into account.

To test these hypotheses, a subsample of ninety-eight subjects was drawn from the original study, that matched male and female subjects on educational background and, as far as possible, on age as well. The subjects are distributed as shown in Table 2.1.

Table 2.1: Distribution of the sample over the variable age, education, and sex

Variable	Male			Female		
Education	High	Medium	Low	High	Medium	Low
Number of subjects	15	16	17	15	17	17
Average age	18.5	17.1	16.2	19	16.8	16.5

To test the first hypothesis, three different morally relevant decisions will be used. The first concerns the decision in Kohlberg's mercy-killing dilemma: A woman who is incurably ill and suffers unbearable pain asks the doctor for an extra dose of morphine to make her die. Should the doctor give it to her or refuse it? This story depicts a conflict between a perfect duty, do not kill, and an imperfect duty, relieve pain. The action decision was classified into four categories:

1. The doctor should give the drug, notwithstanding the law, because the woman suffers so much and should be allowed to decide for herself (active mercy-killing).
2. The doctor should not give the drug, because the law is legitimate; at most he may stop excessive medical support (passive mercy-killing).
3. The doctor should not give the drug so as not to risk punishment.
4. Undecided: the doctor should, because of pain, yet should not, because of punishment.

The subjects' responses are distributed over these four categories as is shown in Table 2.2.

The data show that in this dilemma females do not feel more bound by the imperfect duty to relieve pain. If anything at all, females more eagerly seek to avoid punishment. This finding might be taken as proof of the female tendency to consider consequences in making moral decisions, yet the moral ambiguity of this tendency is that it is not specified how consequences for the different persons involved are to be balanced. Any procedure balancing costs to ego versus benefits to alter would, I assume, have to make use of some universalizing procedure.

In the second morally relevant decision, subjects were asked to pass a moral judgment on the following action: A person talks an old-age pensioner into ordering a useless journal. The judgment could take the following form: I find this action very bad (for a score of 3), pretty bad (2), not particularly bad (1). From the "female" point of view, this action might be interpreted as exploitation of a weak or poor elderly person by a skillful salesperson who simply tries to maximize his or her own profits at all costs. From the "male" point of view, one might defend this action as a legitimate pursuit of business interests, based on the assumption that all market partners can take care of themselves and look out for their own interests. Thus, one might expect females to condemn this action more than males. This is not the case, however: The average evaluation of this action by males and females is identical; both find it pretty bad (for the average score of 2.0).

Table 2.2: Distribution of answers to the mercy-killing dilemma

Response	Male	Female
Doctor should—pain	30	24
Doctor should not—law	7	8
Doctor should not—punishment	11	14
Undecided	1	3

For the third morally relevant decision, the same format (with a scale of 1–3) was used for an evaluation of the following action: A person does not want to lend some money to a friend and therefore pretends not to have any money. Again, females might be expected to deny help less readily when asked for it, and therefore to condemn this action more strongly. Again, the data do not bear out this expectation: males and females alike judge this action as not particularly bad (for the average scores—males 1.4, females 1.3).

To test the hypothesis that in moral decisions females will take more situational details into account, responses to the following dilemma (taken from Gleser & Ihilevich 1969) depicting an interpersonal conflict were analyzed. "You live with your aunt and uncle, who have taken care of you since your parents were killed in an accident when you were only five years old. One stormy night you have a date with a friend, but your aunt and uncle will not let you go out because it is late and the weather is bad. You are about to leave anyhow when your uncle issues the order: 'You stay at home because I said so.'" No situational details were considered to have been taken into account in responses such as these: "I'd go anyhow"; "That's none of his business"; "I'd be furious and leave." Situational details were considered to have been taken into account in these: "I would go, if the date was very important to me, if not, I'd stay"; "If I'd accepted them as parents, I would stay, because I respect them"; "It depends how they handle conflicts in other situations—if they forbid everything, I'd go"; "If we were meeting in a group and it was only 8 o'clock, I'd go; if we were meeting alone and it was 10 o'clock I'd stay at home."

Of the subjects, fourteen of the males and twelve of the females considered concrete situational particularities when making their decisions on how to act in this interpersonal conflict. Those taking situational details into account are slightly older (.35 years) and of higher socioeconomic background (of the lowest educational level, only 16 percent, of the two higher levels, 42 percent consider concrete circumstances).

Certainly one could not hold the analysis of these few data to be an adequate test of sex differences in moral judgment. Still, it should be noted that the data presented do not lend support to the assumption that females (at least in the age range tested) observe imperfect duties more closely than do males or give more consideration to contextual particularities.

Notes

1. Cf. "It cannot be that opposing rules are simultaneously obliging: if it is [strict] duty to act according to one rule, then it is not only not duty to act according to a contrary one, but it is even undutiful. Thus a collision of duties and obligations is unthinkable. It can be, though, that two reasons of obligations collide. . . . [In that case] it is not the stronger obligation but the stronger reason of obligation that dominates" (Kant 1797/1977, 330).

2. Gilligan, Langdale & Lyons 1982 also points out this difficulty in Kohlberg (pp. 52–53, interim report).

3. This difference in interests also is reflected in career choices. In our study, for example, 27 percent of girls but only 5 percent of boys mentioned "contact with other people" as one of the most important criteria in selecting among different careers. On the other hand, 25 percent of the boys and only 12 percent of the girls report specific factual interests that they want to follow up in a career, such as interest in cars and in natural sciences.

Survival of the Kindest

Dacher Keltner

Dacher Keltner is a professor of psychology at the University of California at Berkeley where he studies the social functions of emotions, specifically how individual differences in positive emotions shape an individual's relationships, physical environment and sources of pleasure. He also does work on power, social perception, behavior, and morality. He is the director of the Greater Good Science Center and co-editor of the Greater Good *magazine (greatergood.berkeley.edu). The following reading comes from a chapter of his 2009 book* Born to Be Good: The Science of a Meaningful Life.

In November 1943, S. L. A. "Slam" Marshall, a U.S. Army lieutenant colonel, arrived with American troops on the beaches of Makin Island to fight the Japanese. After four days of bloody, chaotic combat, the Americans secured the island. In the ensuing calm, Marshall was asked to interview several soldiers to clarify some specifics of the four-day battle, with medals, heroic claims, and rights to wartime stories at stake. Marshall subsequently interviewed hundreds of soldiers who fought in Europe and the Pacific during World War II, often immediately after engagement. In 1947, he published the results from these interviews in *Men Against Fire: The Problem of Battle Command.*

His interviews yielded an astonishing finding: Only 15 percent of World War II riflemen had fired at the enemy during combat. Often soldiers refused to fire at the enemy with superior officers barking commands nearby and bullets zipping past their heads. In the wake of this revelatory finding, the army radically changed how it prepared soldiers to kill. Infantry training exercises played down the notion that shooting kills humans. Soldiers were taught to shoot at nonhuman targets—trees, hills, bushes, cars, hovels, huts. The effects were dramatic. According to army estimates, 90 percent of soldiers in the Vietnam War fired at their enemies.

If Charles Darwin and his close intellectual peers—Thomas Henry Huxley and Alfred Russel Wallace—were to discuss this finding with Charlie Rose or on C-SPAN—that in the heat of battle soldiers most typically refused to harm fellow human beings in spite of their self-preservation being on the line—they would reach contrasting conclusions. For Alfred Russel Wallace, a codiscoverer of the theory of evolution by natural selection, this concern for the welfare of others would be taken as evidence of how God has shaped human beings' more benevolent tendencies. Wallace argued that while the body was shaped by natural selection, our mental faculties, and most notably our capacity for good, were created by "an unseen universe of the Spirit" (p. 354). It was some kind of spiritual force that kept soldiers from pulling the trigger to end the lives of enemies.

T. H. Huxley, progeny of one of England's well-known intellectual families, was evolutionary theory's fiercest early advocate and public spokesman. In Oxford and Cambridge circles he was nicknamed Darwin's bulldog. He would have readily attributed Marshall's findings to the constructive forces of culture. In Huxley's view, human nature is aggressive and competitive, forged by evolution in a violent, selfish struggle for existence. Altruistic actions oriented toward benefiting the welfare of others—soldiers refusing to harm, daily civilities of public life, kindness toward strangers—must be cultivated by education and training. Cultural forces arise to counteract the base instincts that evolution has produced at the core of human nature.

Darwin would have reached yet a different conclusion, parting ways with his two colleagues. Had he been able to do so, he might have placed Marshall's empirical gem in his first book on humans, *Descent of Man,* published twelve years after the *On the Origin of Species.* In *Descent,* Darwin argued that the social instincts—instincts toward sympathy, play, belonging in groups, caring for offspring, reciprocating acts of generosity, and worrying about the regard of others—are part of human nature. In Darwin's typically modest but provocative prose:

> The following proposition seems to me in a high degree probable—namely, that any animal whatever, endowed with well-marked social instincts, the parental and filial affections being here included, would inevitably acquire a moral sense or conscience, as soon as its intellectual powers had become as well, or nearly as well developed, as in man. For, firstly, the social instincts lead an animal to take pleasure in the society of its fellows, to feel a certain amount of sympathy with them, and to perform various services for them. The services may be of a definite and evidently instinctive nature; or there may be only a wish and readiness, as with most of the higher social animals, to aid their fellows in certain general ways. But these feelings and services are by no means extended to all the individuals of the same species, only to those of the same association. . . . after the power of language had been acquired, and the wishes of the community could be expressed, the common opinion how each member ought to act for the public good, would naturally become in a paramount degree the guide to action. But it should be borne in mind that however great weight we may attribute to public opinion, our regard for the approbation and disapprobation of our fellows depends on sympathy, which, as we shall see, forms an essential

part of the social instinct, and is indeed its foundation-stone. Lastly, habit in the individual would ultimately play a very important part in guiding the conduct of each member; for the social instinct, together with sympathy, is, like any other instinct, greatly strengthened by habit, and so consequently would be obedience to the wishes and judgment of the community.

Our moral capacities, Darwin reasoned, are rooted in sympathy. These capacities are constrained by association or familial relatedness (anticipating what would come to be called, nearly 100 years later, kin selection theory). They are strengthened by habit and social practice. Later, in explaining acts of altruism, Darwin makes an even stronger claim:

Such actions as the above appear to be the simple result of the greater strength of the social or maternal instincts than that of any other instinct or motive; for they are performed too instantaneously for reflection, or for pleasure or pain to be felt at the time; though, if prevented by any cause, distress or even misery might be felt. In a timid man, on the other hand, the instinct of self-preservation, might be so strong, that he would be unable to force himself to run any such risk perhaps not even for his own child.

Our evolved tendencies toward goodness. Darwin proposed, are performed with the automatic, well-honed speed of other reflexes—the flinch of the body at a loud, unexpected sound, the grasping reflex of the young infant. They are stronger than those toward self-preservation, the default orientation of timid men. Darwin's early formulations of the social instincts of humans were clearly tilted toward a positive *jen* ratio, where the good is stronger than the bad.

Cro-Magnon Field Notes

There are many books I would love to read but, alas, never will: the autobiography of Jesus; a stream-of-consciousness narrative of Virginia Woolf's last thoughts as she plunged into the River Ouse, weighed down by heavy rocks tucked into her coat pockets. As alluring as those certain best sellers would be, at the top of my list would be the field notes of a Cro-Magnon anthropologist, who would have had the wherewithal to travel through Africa, Europe, and Asia to characterize the social life of our most immediate hominid predecessors some 30,000 to 50,000 years ago.

A detailed portrayal of the day in the life of our hominid predecessors would shed light on our environment of evolutionary adaptedness (EEA). The EEA is an abstract description of the social and physical environment in which the human species evolved. It is within this environment that certain genetically based traits— for example, to avoid foods with foul odors that signal decay, to respond with charm and sexual readiness when a female is ovulating—led to greater success in the games of survival and reproduction, and became encoded into the human genome, while others led to increased probabilities of fatality and cold shoulders from potential mates, and quickly to the scrap heap of evolution.

These Cro-Magnon field notes would flesh out Darwin's early evolutionary analysis of our moral capacities. A clear picture of early hominid social life would tell us of the recurring social contexts that reduce the chances of genes making it to the next generation—the perils of escalated aggression between males, the prevalence of infidelity and strategic cuckoldry, the reduced likelihood of offspring surviving if fathers are not engaged. We would also read of the social tendencies that increase the chances of gene replication—the sharing of food or caring for offspring, social strategies that allow females and males to rise in social hierarchies, thereby gaining preferential access to resources and mates. Knowing these social facets of the EEA would then lay a platform for understanding the deeper origins of where the blush of embarrassment comes from, why we can communicate pro-social emotions like gratitude or compassion by one-second touches to a stranger's arm, how devoted love is represented in the flow of certain neuropeptides in the bloodstream.

Absent these Cro-Magnon field notes, we can turn to several kinds of evidence, and a Darwinian capacity for going beyond the information given, to envisage our EEA. We can turn to studies of our closest primate relatives, chimpanzees and bonobos in particular— with whom the human species shared a common ancestor some seven to eight million years ago. Here similarities in social existence—caregiving or hierarchical organization, for example—tell us about basic primate social tendencies and the organization of the pro-social branches of the nervous system. Differences—for example in pair bonding patterns—uncover likely sources of the specifics of human design, and new dimensions to our emotional life.

We can turn to the scanty archaeological record of human ancestry. Here exciting debates are clarifying the meaning of piles of animal bones near ancient hearths, shifts in skeletal structure in the predecessors of *Homo sapiens,* and the first attempts at visual art and music. From these debates we are learning some basic facts about our hominid predecessors.

Finally, we can rely on the detailed observations of contemporary hunter-gatherer societies in remote places in the Amazon, Africa, and New Guinea. These rich descriptions of hunter-gatherer social life—studies of the !Kung San of southern Africa, for example—provide hints into what day-to-day life might have been like for our hunter-gatherer predecessors tens of thousands of years ago.

If we had those Cro-Magnon field notes, we would read that our hominid predecessors spent most of their minutes alive in the presence of other group members, living in close proximity in thirty-to seventy-five-person groups. Division of labor was pronounced: Females served as the primary gatherers of food and caretakers of infants during the extended period of immaturity, traveling less than males, who would have devoted much of their time to the tasks of hunting—flaking stones for weapons, carving spears, tracking game, sharing information about migration patterns and moments of prey vulnerability. Our Cro-Magnon writer, though, would have to have taken note of the relative similarity in size of females and males (the average difference in size between modern human males and females is about 15 percent; in the hominid species that preceded our immediate predecessor, males were about 50 percent bigger than females) and the competition between males for access to mates that would have produced this leveling off of size differences between the sexes.

Several chapters would reveal the darker side of our hominid predecessors, and the origins of the disturbing tendencies of contemporary humans. Here the Cro-Magnon anthropologist would have ample data to write about the regularity of male-on-male violence. There would be extensive observations about warlike behavior, and raids on other groups that might give rise to murder and rape. The regularity of strategic infanticide would emerge as a theme.

At the same time, our Cro-Magnon anthropologist would write specific chapters about social dimensions of the lives of our hominid predecessors that would illuminate the origins of emotions like embarrassment, compassion, love, and awe, and our early capacity for *jen*.

Take Care or Die

The first chapter of the Cro-Magnon field notes would be devoted to the prevalence of caregiving, a hallmark feature of higher primates. As Frans de Waal has observed, chimpanzees and bonobos often become wildly distressed when witnessing harm to other group members. Chimps and bonobos routinely protect conspecifics born blind. They shift their play, resource allocations, and physical navigation of the environment when interacting with fellow primates crippled by physical abnormalities. They, like us, are attuned to harm and vulnerability, and tailor their actions accordingly.

Caregiving is all the more pressing an adaptation in hominids, thanks to shifts in the composition of our predecessors' social groups. Studies of our predecessors' bones reveal that for the first time in primate history, our predecessors were often living into old age, up to the age of sixty. These first older primates, wise with information about food sources, how to care for offspring, and climate patterns, likely required care from younger members of the group.

Even a more pervasive and pressing fount of caregiving was the radical dependence of our hominid predecessors' offspring. Our hominid predecessors evolved bigger brains: *Homo erectus* had brains about 1,000 cc, which is 50 percent bigger than those of their immediate predecessors, *Homo habilis*. The females evolved narrower pelvises, which emerged to support upright walking as our predecessors descended from arboreal life to become bipedal omnivores on the

African savannah. As a result, early hominids were born premature, to squeeze through the narrower pelvis region. They entered the world with big brains but few physical survival skills. They had a longer period of dependency than those of their primate predecessors, and required more care, so much so that our hominid social organization had to shift radically, as did our nervous systems.

In his review of hunter-gatherer social life in The *Tangled Wing,* Melvin Konner notes the pervasiveness of intensive infant care. This care was typically provided by mothers, but also by engaging fathers, younger female relatives (aunts, sisters), and younger children. Such care might seem indulgent to our modern, Benjamin Spock-trained sensitivities, but in hunter-gatherer culture, it was a given. Thus, Konner observes that the !Kung infant is

> carried in a sling at the mother's side, held vertically in continuous skin-to-skin contact. Reflexes such as crawling movements in the legs, the use of the arms to move and free the head, and grasping responses in the hands allow the infant to adjust to the mother's movements and avoid smothering in her skin and clothing. These movements also signal the infant's changes of state, teaching the mother to anticipate its waking, hunger, or defecation. The hip position lets infants see the mother's social world, the objects hung around the neck, any work in her hands, and the breast. Mutual gaze with the mother is easy, and when she is standing the infant's face is just at the eye level of keenly interested ten- to twelve-year olds, who frequently initiate brief, intense, face-to-face inter-actions. When not in the sling, infants are passed from hand to hand around a fire for similar interactions with adults and children. They are kissed on their faces, bellies, and genitals, sung to, bounced, entertained, encouraged, and addressed at length in conversational tones before they can understand words.
>
> The mother indulges the infant's dependency completely in the first year and the second year resists it only slightly. Nursing is continual, four times an hour throughout the day on average, triggered by any slightly fretful signs. Close contact for the first two years allows for a much more fine-grained responsive-ness by the mother than can be attained in a culture where mother and infant are often apart.

Caregiving is a way of life in humans, and has been wired into our nervous system in the forms of emotions, such as sympathy and filial love.

Face to Face

A second feature of early humans' social EEA is that it was almost continually face-to-face. Don't be misled by the hours you spend alone, commuting, on the Internet, on your cell phone, or fingering your BlackBerry while eating in your car. The amount of time we spend alone is a radical aberration for our species (and a source of many contemporary social and physical ills). Early humans required one another to accomplish the basic tasks of survival and reproduction. They did so in highly coordinated, face-to-face interactions. Cooperative child rearing, where relatives and friends traded off duties, was central to quotidian life, as hinted at in Konner's quotation above.

Studies of archaeological sites reveal consistent evidence of cooperative hunting for meat—a critical part of early hominid diet. Relative to many of the animals early humans hunted—bison, elephants, rhinoceroses—our predecessors were weak and slow of foot, and lacking in the fangs, claws, speed, and strength seen in other predators. Early hominid strength was found in coordination and cooperation. For example, at Mauran, in the French Pyrenees, a massive accumulation of bison bones near a river, thought to be 50,000 years old, suggests that teams of Neanderthals banded together to force herds of bison off cliff edges, to fall to their deaths.

The continual coordination required of early human social life coevolved with morphological changes that gave rise to our remarkable capacity to communicate, which is unlike that of any other species in terms of precision, flexibility, sensitivity, and band width. Unlike our primate relatives, the human face has relatively little obscuring hair (which most likely was lost in the hot African savannah, for purposes of cooling), making it a beacon of social messages. And our facial anatomy includes more facial muscles than those of our primate relatives, in particular around the eyes allowing for a much richer vocabulary of expressive behavior originating in the face.

The evolving capacity to communicate is even more pronounced in the human voice. With emerging bipedalism in our hominid predecessors, the human vocal apparatus evolved dramatically. Compared to our primate predecessors, the human vocal tract is elongated. As a result, the tongue has greater range of movement at the back near the larynx, allowing for the capacity to produce a remarkable variety of sounds. Some of the great apes, for example, have an extremely limited repertoire of vocalizations, which reduces to a few grunts. Humans, in contrast, can exhort, punish, threaten, tease, comfort, soothe, flirt, and seduce with the voice.

Our evolving capabilities to communicate co-evolved with our broader capacity for culture, our tendency to produce artifacts, to imitate, to represent and spread information across time and space with language. As charming as chimps and bonobos are, careful studies of their social existence find little evidence of anything remotely resembling culture—a point many have recently made in suggesting that the human capacity for imitation, symbolic language, memory, and coordination is radically different from that of our primate relatives. In humans our basic emotional tendencies can quickly spread to others, through mimicry, imitation, and communication. The spread of emotions like compassion, love, and awe becomes the basis for social ritual and ethical guidelines, and binds individuals into cooperative groups.

Cro-Magnon CEOS

Our Cro-Magnon anthropologist would readily discern a third feature of early human social life—that it is hierarchical. Every moment of early hominid social life, from who sleeps with whom to who eats what to who touches whom, was stratified. In contemporary humans, individuals fall into social hierarchies with remarkable ease. In research with my colleague Cameron Anderson, we have found that hallmates, within one week of having moved into college dormitories, are nearly unanimous in singling out those whom they report to be of high status, having respect, prominence and influence in their emergent groups. They likewise readily agree in their judgments of who occupies the lower rungs of the totem pole. Differences in status quickly emerge in younger children (down to two years old, where status hierarchies have been observed on the seemingly egalitarian circle rugs of preschools). And don't be fooled by gender-based assumptions: The concern for status is not just a male thing. Female adults attain comparable levels of status with just as much alacrity and effect. This is echoed in recent studies by Frans de Waal and others, who have documented clear hierarchies in female chimpanzee life. Primate social life is hierarchical, in large part because hierarchies enable group members to decide how to allocate resources with speed and minimal conflict.

Yet the hierarchical social organization of higher primates and early humans differs dramatically from that of other species. In higher primates and humans, lower-status individuals can readily form alliances, most typically dyadic coalitions, which potentially negate many advantages that higher-status individuals might enjoy in physical size or power. In addition, humans developed several forms of social communication—for example, gossip—by which low-status individuals can comment upon and determine the status of other group members. The emergence of coalitions and alliances in group life, and the capacity for low-status individuals to comment on the reputations of those in power, placed new demands upon high-power individuals. Their power would come to rest increasingly upon the ability to engage socially and advance the interests of the group.

Frans de Waal has found in his groundbreaking studies of primate politics that with the rise of the capacity of lower-status individuals to form coalitions, "alpha" males and females must rely on social intelligence to acquire and retain their privileged positions. Pure intimidation displays—chest pounding, random fang-bearing charges, throwing stones, and din making—are and were still stock-in-trade for alpha chimps and bonobos and our human predecessors, but new skills were required. Higher-status primates spend a great deal of their day smoothing over the rough edges of their group's social existence. They are the ones who are likely to mediate conflicts, for example by bringing adversaries into physical contact with one another and encouraging grooming activities that reduce conflict. They are the ones who make sure that more equitable allocations of resources occur.

My own research with humans paints a similar picture. We have studied who quickly rises in male and female hierarchies in groups of children and young adults. We find that it is not the domineering, muscle-flexing, fear-inspiring, backstabbing types who gain elevated status in the eyes of their peers (apologies to Machiavelli). Instead, it is the socially intelligent individuals who advance the interests of other group members (in the service of their own self-interest) who rise in social hierarchies. Power goes to those who are socially engaged. It is the young adults and children who brim with social energy, who bring people together, who can tell a good joke or tease in ways that playfully identify inappropriate actions, or soothe another in distress, who end up at the top. The literature on socially rejected children finds that bullies, who resort to aggression, throwing their weight around, and raw forms of intimidation and dominance, in point of fact, are outcasts and low in the social hierarchy. Power and status are inevitable facets of hominid social life but are founded on social intelligence more than Social Darwinism.

The Perpetual Conflict of Being

Lest you suspect that our Cro-Magnon anthropologist suffers from a Pollyanaish view of her own kind—a universal bias of most human groups—it is wise to consider her fourth generalization. Here she would observe that almost every waking second of early hominid social life is pervaded by continual and often painful conflict.

There would be discussion of obvious within-sex conflicts, for example, over mates and resources. Early hominid social organization increasingly came to revolve around the competition between males for access to females. The same applies to females, who, as Darwin long ago surmised, adorn and beautify themselves in an arms race of beauty to attract resource-rich mates.

This logic of competing interests extends to parent-offspring relations, as Sarah Blaffer Hrdy brilliantly shows in *Mother Nature*. Offspring make competing demands upon parents. As a result, parents are required to make strategic and often disarmingly utilitarian judgments about which offspring to devote resources to, and, in extreme circumstances such as famine (or in today's political climate, civil war), which to abandon.

This parent-offspring conflict even extends to mother-fetus relations, as Harvard evolutionary biologist David Haig has demonstrated at the genetic and physiological levels. Many of the pathologies of human pregnancy—hypertension and diabetes, for example—have been newly understood from the perspective of the fetus's making self-serving demands upon the mother's supply of nutrients, at considerable cost to the mother.

Siblings are not safe from perpetual, and occasionally mortal, conflict. I remember late one night preparing for a lecture on family dynamics and moral development, having just put my daughters, Natalie, then 4, and Serafina, then 2, to bed. As they peacefully slept in their splayed-out positions, as if dropped out of space onto their beds next to one another, I encountered a fact that left me in shoulder-slumping laughter and tears. In an observational study of American families, four-and two-year-old siblings were observed to engage in conflicts—eye poking, name calling, hair pulling, toy grabbing, arm biting, cheek scratching— every eleven minutes of waking existence.

This kind of sibling conflict, Frank Sulloway reveals in *Born to Rebel*, is expected, based on evolutionary theory. Siblings share, on average, 50 percent of their genes, and compete over numerous resources, from the protection and affection of parents to food to mates—particularly when resources are scarce. Sibling conflict is frequent, widespread, and, on occasion, deadly. Sibling sand sharks devour one another prior to birth in the oviducts of the mother, until one well-fed shark emerges. Once a blue-footed boobie drops below 80 percent of its body weight, its siblings exclude it from the nest, and at times will peck it to death. Infant hyenas are born with large canine teeth, which they often turn to deadly effect upon their newly born siblings.

Conflict is synonymous with human social life. Yet early hominid conflict differed from that of many other species: It was met with evolved capacities to reconcile. This essential insight can be traced back to the observations of Jane Goodall and Frans de Waal, who documented how our primate relatives reconcile after aggressive encounters. Prior to Goodall and de Waal's work, the prevailing wisdom, developed by ethologist Konrad Lorenz, was that following an aggressive encounter, aggressors moved away from each other as far as possible. This view might make sense for solitary species, like the golden hamster, who flee upon attack, or territorial species, like many birds, who rely on birdsong to create invisible but audible property lines to avoid deadly conflicts.

For many mammals, though, these options—fleeing the group or solitary territorial arrangements—do not make evolutionary sense. Our hominid predecessors were dependent upon one another to defend against predators, hunt, reproduce, and ensure that offspring reached the age of viability and reproduction. Individuals who were better able to negotiate conflicts almost certainly fared better in the tasks of survival and gene replication. Recent studies have found that wolves who have been kicked out of their group for excessive aggression and an inability to play are less likely to reproduce and more likely to die. Many physiological difficulties associated with human isolation—namely, increased stress, weaker responses to disease, and even shorter lives—suggest that our survival depends on healthy, stable bonds with others. Conflict is costly and painful but better than the alternative—a solitary existence of fending for oneself. Out of the perpetual conflict that runs through human social life emerged a rich array of capacities that short-circuit or defuse conflict—appeasement displays; forgiveness, play, teasing, and laughter.

Fragile Monogamy and the New Dad

Finally, our Cro-Magnon anthropologist would have to devote a surprisingly chaste chapter to the bawdy politics of our primate predecessors. Their sexual organization differs from that of our closest primate relatives, and makes us resemble the local Towhee or warbler flitting about rather than baboons or chimpanzees. We are relative prudes compared to these primate relatives. Once a female chimpanzee is sexually mature at age fifteen, she advertises her sexual receptiveness by a large pink patch of sexual skin, and for a ten-day period during a thirty-six-day menstrual cycle, she copulates several dozen times a day, with all or most of the adult males in her social group. Aggression and jockeying for access to female chimpanzees during these periods become all-consuming for male chimpanzees. Females raise offspring largely on their own; males contribute to the community but not to individual offspring, and males don't know which offspring they have fathered.

Then there are the bonobos, now recognized as a separate species from chimpanzees, and widely envied by humans yearning for the next sexual revolution. Bonobo females are sexually active for about five years before they become fertile, and copulate freely with many of the adult males in their immediate social group. Female and male homosexual relations are common. Younger males often engage in sexual activity with older females in what looks life sexual initiation play. Sexual contact among the bonobos is the basis of friendships, conflict reduction, and play.

The monogamous tendencies documented by our Cro-Magnon anthropologist, by contrast, are unusual for higher primates. They have never been observed, except in hominids, in species where the sexes mix in large groups without territorial boundaries. This sexual organization had several important implications. Females evolved to become sexually active throughout their menstrual cycles. Males and females could maintain exclusive sexual interest in each other. For example, in a survey of world cultures, monogamy was recognized as official policy in only 16 percent of 853 societies sampled, but sexual monogamy was the most common sexual pattern. Males evolved to know who their offspring were and to provide resources and care to them.

Our Cro-Magnon anthropologist, then, would conclude that the social environment of the EEA would be defined by an acute tendency to care, by highly coordinated, face-to-face social exchanges, by the need to reconcile and the flattening of social hierarchies, by perpetually negotiated conflicts of interests, and by the emergence of the tendency toward sexual monogamy. It is these properties of our early social existence that gave rise to the moral emotions, of interest to Darwin but long ignored by the science of emotion that he inspired. Compassion, embarrassment, awe, love, and gratitude emerged in the recurring social interactions of early hominid social life: the attending to vulnerable offspring, the playful exchanges between kith and kin, the status moves and negotiations, the courtships and flirtations between current and potential sexual partners. These emotions were wired into the body and our social life through processes of natural and sexual selection. They evolved into the language of human social life, the species-characteristic patterns of parent-offspring relations, relations between mates and allies, dominant and subordinate members of hierarchies, and in mating relationships. These emotions became our ethical guides to help us fold into stable, cooperative communities. They operated according to three general principles, revealed in a tournament that pitted the brightest mathematicians and computer hacks against one another in an attempt to discover what strategies prevail in the survival of the fittest.

The Wisdom of Tit-for-Tat and the Great Shift

In *The Evolution of Cooperation* Robert Axelrod asks the following question: How might cooperation emerge in competitive environments governed by the ruthless pursuit of self-interest? How might compassion, awe, love, and gratitude, powerfully oriented toward enhancing the welfare of others, take hold within social communities governed by the pursuit of self-interest, in such a fashion that they would become favored by natural selection and encoded into our genes and nervous system?

Axelrod himself was taken aback by striking acts of cooperation that confound assumptions about self-preservation and self-interest. In the trenches of World War I, for example, British and French soldiers were separated from their enemies, the Germans, by a few hundred yards of burned-out, treeless, muddy no-man's-land. Brutal assaults by one side were typically met with equally fierce, lethal attacks by the other. And, yet, in these nightmarish patches of annihilation, cooperation emerged. The two sides flew certain special flags, signaling nonconfrontation. They made verbal agreements not to shoot at each other. They evolved patterns of firing their weapons in purely symbolic, harmless ways, to signal nonlethal intent. All of these cooperative strategies allowed the soldiers to eat meals peacefully and to enjoy long periods of nonengagement. On special occasions, the warring sides even fraternized with one another. In fact, cooperation became so pervasive that commanding generals had to intervene, demanding a return to deadly combat.

From historical anecdote Axelrod turned to the prisoner's dilemma game (see table below) to answer his question about the evolution of cooperation. He conducted a tournament in which players—cold war strategists, psychologists, prize-winning mathematicians, computer specialists, and other aficionados of the game—were invited to submit computer programs that specified what choice to make on a certain round of the prisoner's dilemma game, given what had happened in previous rounds. In Axelrod's first tournament, fourteen different strategies were submitted. Each was subsequently pitted against the others for 200 rounds. Here the game really mirrors human social life. Individuals with different strategic approaches went toe-to-toe with one another, much as bullies and altruists do on the grammar-school playground, Machiavellians and kindhearted colleagues do at work, hawks and doves do in foreign policy debate, and presumably our hominid predecessors—genetically prone, through random mutation, to cooperate or compete—did. Who prevailed?

The Prisoner's Dilemma Game (PDG)

		Partner's action cooperate	Compete
Your Action	Cooperate	5,5	0,8
	Compete	8,0	2,2

In the PDG, participants are required to make a simple choice: to cooperate or compete with one another. If both participants cooperate, they do well (in our example, they each receive $5). If one competes while the other cooperates, the competitor thrives at the expense of the cooperator (in our example receiving $8 to the cooperator's zilch). If both compete, they each get $2. From the perspective of maximizing self-interest, the rational thing to do is to compete. The rub, though, is that, as in arms races, the use of shared resources, intimate life, and business partnerships, the mutual pursuit of self-interest leads to worse joint outcomes.

A tit-for-tat strategy was submitted by Anatol Rapaport. It is disarmingly simple: It cooperates on the first round with every opponent. Then it reciprocates whatever the opponent did in the previous round. An opponent's cooperation is rewarded with immediate cooperation. The tit-for-tat was not blindly cooperative, however: it met an opponent's competition with competition. Defection was punished with immediate defection.

Axelrod held a second tournament that attracted the eager submission of sixty-two strategies. All of the entrants knew the results of the first round—namely, that tit-for-tat had won. All had the opportunity to return to their blackboard, to adjust their mathematical algorithms and carry out further computer simulations, and to devise a strategy that could unseat the tit-for-tat. In this second tournament, once again the tit-for-tat prevailed. The tit-for-tat did not prevail, it is important to note, against all strategies. For example, your more sinister mind might have anticipated that a strategy that starts out competitively and always competes will have the upper hand against the tit-for-tat, because it establishes an advantage in the first round (of course, this strategy scores few points, and suffers profoundly, against other purely competitive strategies). Overall, however, tit-for-tat, so simple and cooperative in its *jen*-like design, achieved the highest outcomes against the society of different strategies in the tournament.

Why tit-for-tat? Three principles underlie the tit-for-tat and also underlie emotions like compassion, embarrassment, love, and awe, which promote the meaningful life. A first is what might be called cost-benefit reversal. Giving to others is costly. Devoting resources to others—food, affection, mating opportunities, protection—entails costs to the self. In the long run, generosity risks dangerous exploitation if it is directed at others who do not reciprocate in kind. The costs of giving constrain the tendency toward cooperation.

Built into the human organism, therefore, must be a set of mechanisms that reverse the cost-benefit analysis of giving. These mechanisms might prioritize the gains of others over those of the self, and transform others' gains into one's own. The tit-for-tat instantiates this principle of cost-benefit reversal. Its default setting is to cooperate, to benefit the other as well as the self. It is not envious; the tit-for-tat does not shift strategy as its partner's gains mount. And it forgives; it is willing to cooperate at the first cooperative action of its partner, even after long runs of mean-spirited defection.

The emotions that promote the meaningful life are organized according to an interest in the welfare of others. Compassion shifts the mind in ways that increase the likelihood of taking pleasure in the improved welfare of others. Awe shifts the very contents of our self-definition, away from the emphasis on personal desires and preferences and toward that which connects us to others. Neurochemicals (oxytocin) and regions of the nervous system related to these emotions promote trust and long-term devotion. We have been designed to care about things other than the gratification of desire and the maximizing of self-interest.

A second principle is what we might call the principle of reliable identification. This is clearly evident in the tit-for-tat—it is easy to read. There is no trickery to it, no Machivellian dissembling, no strategic misinformation. It would likely take only five to ten rounds against the tit-for-tat to make confident predictions about its future moves. Contrary to what you see on cable poker tournaments (where stone faces and inscrutability are the demeanor of the day), in the emergence of cooperative bonds transparency of benevolent intent is the wiser course. Cooperation is more likely to emerge and prosper when cooperative individuals can selectively interact with other good-natured individuals.

The implication is clear: Cooperation, kindness, and virtue are embodied in observable acts—facial muscle movements, brief vocalizations, ways of moving the hands or positioning the body, patterns of gaze activity—that are signals detectable to the ordinary eye. These outward signals of virtue, it further stands to reason, have involuntary elements that are not likely to be faked, and are likely to be put to use as people form intuitions about whom to trust and love and sacrifice for. This central premise—that for cooperation and goodness to emerge there must be outward signs of trustworthiness and cooperation—shapes the very design of the nonverbal signs of compassion, gratitude, and love. As science has begun to map the pro-social emotions in the body, new facial displays of embarrassment, shame, compassion, awe, love, and desire have been discovered. Studies of new modalities of communication, such as touch, have revealed that we can communicate gratitude, compassion, and love with a brief touch to the forearm. We are wired to detect benevolent intent in others in the moment-to-moment flow of the microinteractions of our daily living.

Finally, the tit-for-tat evokes cooperation in others—the principle of contagious cooperation. The tendency to cooperate and give can be readily exploited by individuals who are competitive and self-serving; nice guys do finish last in certain contexts. Kind individuals fare better, however, if they are able to evoke pro-social tendencies in others, thus prompting cooperative exchange. To the extent that goodness evokes beneficent responses in others, it should flourish.

Compassion, embarrassment, and awe are contagious at many different levels. Perceiving a person's smile, even below subliminal awareness, prompts the perceiver to feel good and to show shifts away from fight-flight physiology. Perhaps more remarkable are the feelings evoked in hearing of others' kindness—the swelling in the chest, goose-bumps, and occasional tearing. Jonathan Haidt has called this state elevation, and he argues that we're wired to be inspired by hearing the good acts of others. Through touch, cooperation and kindness can spread across people and physical space within seconds. The emotions that promote the meaningful life are powerfully contagious, which increases their chance for propagation, and their encoding into our nervous systems and their ritualization into cultural practice.

We have now set the stage for our examination of emotions that promote high *jen* ratios and the meaningful life. We have reviewed the intellectual backdrop in which this work has taken place, which has assumed that emotions are disruptive, base tendencies, part of a human nature largely oriented toward the gratification of desire. We have considered the specifics of emotions that have been discovered in the past thirty years. We have learned that emotions serve as commitment devices, are embodied in our bodies, and shape moral judgment in systematic fashion. And in this past chapter we have sketched what kind of evolutionary environment might have given rise to emotions like compassion or gratitude, and what general principles these emotions abide by. We will now turn to scientific studies that illuminate this new swath of human design, and that will lend credence to Darwin's insight about the origins of human goodness: that it is rooted in our emotion, and that these social instincts may be stronger than those "of any other instinct or motive."

Chapter 3

Ethical Relativism

The Escape from Positivism

Kwame Appiah

Kwame Anthony Appiah *(1954–) was born in London and raised in Ghana. Appiah's uncle was king of the Ashanti and his grandfather was British Chancellor of the Exchequer. He earned his B.A. and PhD from Clare College, Cambridge University. In addition to Cambridge, he has held appointments at Yale, Cornell, Duke, Harvard, and Princeton, where he now serves in the Philosophy Department and the University Center for Human Values. His work has been wide ranging, including contributions in semantics and ethics. His current interests range over African and African-American intellectual history and literary studies, ethics and philosophy of mind and language; and he has also taught regularly about African traditional religions; but his major current work has to do (a) with the philosophical foundations of liberalism and (b) with questions of method in arriving at knowledge about values. He has published numerous books including* The Ethics of Identity *(2005),* Cosmopolitanism: Ethics in a World of Strangers *(2006), and* Experiments in Ethics *(2008). He has also published three novels.*

Professional Relativism

Cultural anthropologists are great enthusiasts for other cultures. That is, after all, their business. Once, not so long ago, before everybody in the world was within hearing distance of a radio, before Michael Jackson was famous on the steppes of Inner Mongolia and Pele was known along the banks of the Congo River, an anthropologist could set out from Europe or North America for places that had never before seen the "white man." There, at the ground zero of ethnography, the moment of first contact, he or she could come face to face with people who were completely unknown. Their gods, their food, their language, their dance, their music, their carving, their medicines, their family lives, their rituals of peace and war, their jokes and the stories they told their children: all could be wonderfully, fascinatingly strange. Ethnographers spent long days and hard nights in the rain forest or the desert or the tundra, battling fever or frostbite, struggling against loneliness as they tried to make sense of people who were, naturally, equally puzzled by them. And then, after disappearing from "civilization" for a year or two, they would come back with an account of these strangers, bearing (along with a collection of pottery, carvings, or weapons for the museum) a story about how their culture fit together.

For all this to be worthwhile, that story had to be news. So, naturally, the ethnographer didn't usually come back with a report whose one-sentence summary was: they are pretty much like us. And yet, of course, they had to be. They did, after all, mostly have gods, food, language, dance, music, carving, medicines, family lives, rituals, jokes, and children's tales. They smiled, slept, had sex and children, wept, and, in the end, died. And it was possible for this total stranger, the anthropologist, who was, nevertheless, a fellow human being, to make progress with their language and religion, their habits—things that every adult member of the society had had a couple of decades to work on—in a year or two. Without those similarities, how could cultural anthropology be possible?

Now, you might think that anthropologists, whose lives begin with this intellectual curiosity about other peoples, are bound to be cosmopolitans. Not so. While they do share, by necessity, a cosmopolitan curiosity about strangers, many anthropologists mistrust talk about universal morality, and spend a great deal of time urging us not to intervene in the lives of other societies; if they think we have a responsibility, it is to leave well enough alone.

One reason for this skepticism about intervention is simply historical. Much well-intentioned intervention in the past has undermined old ways of life without replacing them with better ones; and, of course, much intervention was not well intentioned. The history of empire—Persian, Macedonian, Roman Mongol, Hun, Mughal, Ottoman, Dutch, French, British, American—has many unhappy moments. But there are even broader reasons for the anthropologists' skepticism. What we outsiders see as failings in other societies often make a good deal more sense to the ethnographer who has lived among them. The ethnographer has, after all, set out to make sense of "his" people. And even if there is as much mischief as insight in the old maxim *"Tout comprendre, c'est tout pardonner"*—to understand all is to forgive all—it does reflect a genuine human tendency. We often *do* forgive, once we understand. Anthropologists are likely, as a result, to find many outside interventions ignorant and uninformed. We think female circumcision, or female genital cutting, as many anthropologists prefer to call it, a disgusting mutilation that deprives women of the full pleasures of sexual experience. They know young women who look forward to the rite, think that it allows them to display courage, declare it makes their sexual organs more beautiful, and insist that they enjoy sex enormously. They will point out that our society encourages all kinds of physical alterations of human bodies—from tattoos and ear (and now tongue, nose,

and umbilicus) piercing to male circumcision to rhinoplasty to breast augmenta-
tion—and that each of these practices, like all bodily alterations, has some medical
risks. They will show us that the medical risks allegedly associated with female
genital cutting—scarring, infections leading to infertility, fatal septicemia—have
been wildly exaggerated; that they are, perhaps, just rationalizations for what is
simply revulsion against an unfamiliar practice. In contrast to us, they feel, they
have escaped the prejudices of their backgrounds, in part through the intellectual
discipline of fieldwork, living intimately with strangers. And many of them are
inclined to think that words like "right" and "wrong" make sense only relative to
particular customs, conventions, cultures.

Certainly the basic suspicion that moral claims just reflect local preferences is
age-old. In book three of Herodotus's *Histories*, we read that when Darius

> was king of Persia, he summoned the Greeks who happened to be present at
> his court, and asked them what they would take to eat the dead bodies of their
> fathers. They replied that they would not do it for any money in the world.
> Later, in the presence of the Greeks, and through an interpreter, so that they
> could understand what was said, he asked some Indians, of the tribe called Cal-
> latiae, who do in fact eat their parents' dead bodies, what they would take to
> burn them. They uttered a cry of horror and forbade him to mention such a
> dreadful thing. One can see by this what custom can do, and Pindar, in my opin-
> ion, was right when he called it "king of all."

One of Tolstoy's stories is about a Chechen warlord called Hadji Murat, who
tells a Russian officer one of his people's traditional sayings: "'A dog asked a donkey to eat with him and gave him meat, the donkey asked the dog and gave him
hay: they both went hungry.' He smiled. 'Every people finds its own ways good.'"

And doubtless there is something salutary about the ethnographic inclination
to pause over our own abominations and taboos. In the 1906 classic *Folkways*, the
anthropologist William G. Sumner tells of a chief of the Miranhas, in the Amazon, who is baffled that Europeans regard cannibalism as an abomination: "It is
all a matter of habit. When I have killed an enemy, it is better to eat him than to
let him go to waste. Big game is rare because it does not lay eggs like turtles. The
bad thing is not being eaten, but death." Sumner, who coined the term "ethnocen-
trism," was not himself recommending cannibalism. But he clearly had sympathy
for the chief's account: *chacun a son gout.*

Or, in the words of Burton's fictive Sufi,

> What works me weal that call I "good,"
>   What harms and hurts I hold as "ill":
> They change with place, they shift with race;
>   And, in the veriest span of Time,
> Each Vice has won a Virtue's crown;
>   All good was banned as Sin or Crime.

Yet the modern doctrines of relativism—the approach that cultural anthropologists often subscribe to—go beyond the old skeptical traditions. A lingering suspicion that a lot of what we take to be right and wrong is simply a matter of local custom has hardened, in the modern age, into a scientific certainty that talk of objective moral "truths" is just a conceptual error.

The Exile of Value

What grounds modern relativism is a scientific worldview that makes a sharp distinction between *facts* and *values*. John Maynard Keynes used to say that those who claimed that they were just talking common sense were often simply in the grip of an old theory. This distinction between facts and values is now commonsense, but behind it is a philosophical theory that goes back at least to the early Enlightenment. Its origins have sometimes been traced to the eighteenth-century Scottish philosopher David Hume, whose cosmopolitan engagement with the variety of human societies I mentioned in the last chapter. As it happens, I doubt that Hume would have endorsed this theory (or, indeed, that he invented it), but something very like this view was certainly current in the twentieth-century heyday of a philosophical movement called logical positivism, so I'm going to call it Positivism. The picture took a while to develop, but here it is, in a simplified, final version.

It is never easy to sketch a philosophical position, least of all to the satisfaction of those who claim it as their own. So I should make it plain that I am not trying to characterize the view of this or that philosopher, however influential, but rather a picture of the world, elaborated by many philosophers over the last few centuries in the West, that has now so penetrated the educated common sense of our civilization that it can be hard to persuade people that it *is* a picture and not just a bunch of self-evident truths. That would not matter, of course, if the picture never got in the way of our understanding the world. But, as we shall see, the Positivist picture *can* get in the way; in particular, it often gets in the way of the cosmopolitan project, when it leads people to overestimate some obstacles to cross-cultural understanding while underestimating others.

What people do, Positivism holds, is driven by two fundamentally different kinds of psychological states. Beliefs—the first kind—are supposed to reflect how the world is. Desires, by contrast, reflect how we'd like it to be. As the philosopher Elizabeth Anscombe once put it, beliefs and desires have different "directions of fit": beliefs are meant to fit the world; the world is meant to fit desires. So beliefs can be true or false, reasonable or unreasonable. Desires, on the other hand, are satisfied or unsatisfied.

Beliefs are supposed to be formed on the basis of evidence, and there are principles of reasoning that determine what it is rational to believe on the basis of what evidence. Desires are just facts about us. In an earlier philosophical language, indeed, these desires would have been called "passions," from a Latin root meaning something you suffer, or undergo (a meaning still left to us in talk of the Passion of Christ). Because passions are just things that happen to us, no evidence determines which ones are right. All desires, in fact, are just like matters of taste; and, as the saying goes, there's no accounting for those. When we act, we use our beliefs about the world to figure out how to get what we desire. Reason, as Hume famously said, is "the slave of the passions." If our passion is for apples, we go to where our beliefs suggest the apples are. And, once we go looking for the apples we're after, we'll find out whether our beliefs were right.

Because beliefs are about the world, and there's only one world, they can be either right or wrong, and we can criticize other people's beliefs for being unreasonable or simply false. But desires can't be right or wrong, in this sense. Desires are simply not responses to the world; they're aimed at changing it, not at reflecting how it is.

There's a complication to the story, because much of what we ordinarily desire has beliefs, so to speak, built into it. Like you, I want money; but only because of what it can get me. If I didn't believe that money could get me other stuff that I wanted, I wouldn't want it any more. So my desire for money (I'd rather not call it a passion, if you don't mind) is *conditional*; it would disappear, if I discovered—as I might in some apocalyptic scenario—not only that money can't buy me love (this I have known since my first Beatles concert), but that it couldn't buy me anything at all. Desires that are conditional in this way can be rationally criticized by criticizing the underlying beliefs. I want an apple. You tell me I'm allergic and it will make me sick. I say: I don't mind being sick, if I can just have that delicious taste. You tell me that this apple won't have that delicious taste. I say: Find me something that will. You say: The only things that have that taste will kill you. I say: So be it. It will be worth it. I die happy. It looks as if nothing in the world can stop me from wanting that taste. On the Positivist picture, this is the only way desires can be criticized: by criticizing beliefs they presuppose. Once you remove the conditional element from the specification of a desire, you get to what we might call your *basic desires*. And since these depend on *no* assumptions about how the world is, you can't criticize them for getting the world wrong. So the fundamental point remains.

Hume himself drew the distinction, in a famous passage, between judgments about how things are and judgments about how things ought to be. Normative judgments naturally come with views about what one ought to think, do, or feel. And the Positivist picture is often thought to be Humean in part because Hume insisted that the distinction between "is" and "ought" was, as he said, "of the last consequence." Like desires, *oughts* are intrinsically action guiding, in a way that *is* isn't. And so, in the familiar slogan, "you can't get an ought from an is." Since we are often tempted to move from what is to what ought to be, this move, like many moves philosophers think illicit, has a disparaging name: we call it the *naturalistic fallacy*.

Such a distinction between the way beliefs and desires work in action is the key to this picture of how human beings work. Desires—or, more precisely, basic desires—set the ends we aim for; beliefs specify the means for getting to them. Since these desires can't be wrong or right, you can criticize only the means people adopt, not their ends. Finally, the Positivist identifies the truths that beliefs aim at with the facts. If you believe something and your belief is true, it gets one of the facts in the world right.

If that's what facts are on the Positivist view, what are values? You could say that, strictly speaking, the Positivist thinks there aren't any values. Not, at least in the world. "The world," the young Ludwig Wittgenstein said, "is the totality of facts." After all, have you ever seen a value out there in the world? As the philosopher John L. Mackie used to argue, values, if there were any, would be very strange entities. ("Queer" was the word he used: and his argument that there aren't really any values in the world he called "the argument from queerness.") The world can force us to believe in *things,* because if we don't they'll bump into us anyhow, get in our way. But reality can't force us to desire anything. Where, after all, would one look in the world for the wrongness of a basic desire? What science would demonstrate it? A science might be able to explain why you desire something. It couldn't explain that you should—or shouldn't—desire it.

Talk of values, then, is really a way of talking about certain of our desires. Which ones? Well, when we appeal to what we take to be universal values in our discussions with one another—the value of art or of democracy or of philosophy—we're talking about things we want everyone to want. If exposure to art is valuable, then, roughly, we'd like everyone to want to experience it. If we say democracy is valuable, then, roughly again, we want everyone to want to live in a democracy. We might say, as *façon de parler,* that someone who wants everyone to want X "believes that X is valuable," but that is still just, in reality, a way of talking about a complex desire. Again, some values will subsist upon certain facts. I could value universal vaccination for smallpox, because I wanted to make everyone safer—but give up this "value" once I learned that smallpox had been eradicated. If a value reflects unconditional desires, however, since these basic desires can't be criticized, values can't either. I value kindness. I want to be kind. I want me to want to be kind. I want all of you to want to be kind. As a matter of fact, I want *you* to want everyone to want to be kind. But I don't want this because I believe that all these kindnesses will lead to something else. I value kindness intrinsically, unconditionally. Even if you showed me that some acts of kindness would have effects I didn't want, that wouldn't persuade me to give up kindness as a value. It would only show me that kindness can sometimes conflict with other things I care about.

It may be that there are basic desires like this that everyone has. So it may turn out that there are things that everyone values. Those values will be *empirically* universal. Still, on the Positivist view, there's no rational basis on which to establish that they're correct.

If you accept that all this is a fair, if sketchy, version of a philosophical account that has been extremely influential for at least the last two and a half centuries in the West, you'll see that many of the consequences of thinking in this way are recognizable parts of our common sense. There are facts and there are values. *Check.* Unlike values, facts—the things that make beliefs true and false—are the natural inhabitants of the world, the things that scientists can study or that we can explore with our own senses. *Check.* So, if people in other places have different basic desires from people around here—and so have different values—that's not something that we can rationally criticize. No appeal to reasons can correct them. *Check.* And if no appeal to reasons can correct them, then trying to change their minds must involve appeal to something other than reason: which is to say, to something unreasonable. There seems no alternative to relativism about fundamental values. *Checkmate.*

I don't know how sensible this picture of human reasoning seems to you, but it grabbed the imaginations of many students of other cultures. That's why the great anthropologist Melville Herskovits once wrote, "There is no way to play this game of making judgments across cultures except with loaded dice." Yet it has implications that are inconsistent with what most of us believe. A Tormentor who wanted everyone to want to cause innocent people pain, we might say, takes the infliction of pointless suffering to be a value. We'd also want to say that he was wrong. Do we have to content ourselves with the Positivist view that our judgment *just* reflects our desires, as the Tormentor's reflects his?

Positivist Problems

There are various moves critics of Positivism have proposed in response to such challenges. One is, so to speak, to go on the offensive. There are lots of facts that one can't point to and lots of beliefs that we don't have evidence for (if that means evidence from experience, from seeing, hearing, tasting, smelling, touching). If every true belief corresponds to a fact, then isn't it a fact that one and one make two? Where exactly is *that* fact? And what's the *evidence* that bachelors can't be married? However many unmarried bachelors you find, that won't show you that bachelors *can't* be married. So far as I know, no one has ever found a pine tree with exactly fifty-seven cones painted purple and gold. Still, nobody thinks there couldn't be one. For that matter, who could deny that, as Socrates insisted, all men are mortal? So where is *that* fact?

The Positivist picture, in short, seems to generalize too quickly from one kind of belief: beliefs about the properties of particular concrete things that you can see, hear, touch, smell, or feel. What are we to say about beliefs about universals (all human beings), about possibilities and impossibilities (married bachelors), and about abstract objects (the number two)? The Positivist seems to be suggesting that if we can't answer the question "Where is that fact?" or meet the command "Show me the evidence," then there can't be any true beliefs about that subject matter. Every true belief corresponds to a fact "out there" in the world, the

Positivist claims. But then we'd have to abandon belief not only in values but also in possibilities, numbers, universal truths, and, one suspects, a whole lot more. A theory that sounded plausible to begin with now looks as if it comes with a pretty high price tag. It's not that the Positivists don't have theories about numbers and universals and possibilities. It's that once you grasp that you have to tell a lot of different stories about different kinds of truths, the idea that observable facts are what truths correspond to looks a good deal less obvious.

There is another fundamental puzzle for the Positivist. The Positivist thinks that you can criticize beliefs and actions as unreasonable. Okay. Is it a *fact* that they're unreasonable? If it is, then can't we ask about *that* fact what the Positivist asked when we claimed that causing innocent people pain was wrong? Where is it? Where, for example, is the *fact* that it's unreasonable to believe that something that looks green is actually red? And what evidence supports the claim that it's unreasonable to believe that something's green when it looks red? Someone who thinks this is reasonable is hardly going to be persuaded by our showing him red-looking things and insisting they are red. These questions look just as hard for the Positivist as the ones he posed to us.

If, on the other hand, it isn't a *fact* that certain beliefs are unreasonable, then, presumably, it's a *value*. (For the Positivist, those are the only options.) So to say, "It's unreasonable to believe that what looks green is red," just means that you want everybody to want not to think that what looks green is red. And if it's a basic value, then it can't be critically evaluated. The Positivist has no rational objection to make to people who make this preposterous assertion. But surely people who think red-looking things are green aren't just pursuing an "alternative lifestyle" with its own values. They're irrational, and they ought not to think that way.

There's a disconnect, too, between the Positivist creed and the relativist counsel that we ought not to intercede in other societies on behalf of our own values. For on the Positivist account, to value something is, roughly, to want everyone to want it. And if that's the case, then values are, in a certain way, naturally imperialist. So the whole strategy of arguing for toleration of other cultures on the basis of Positivism seems self-contradictory. How can you argue rationally that other people's basic value choices should be tolerated on the basis of a view that says that there are no rational arguments for such basic choices? Positivism doesn't motivate intervention; but it doesn't motivate nonintervention, either. (One may be reminded of an old story from the days of colonial India. A British officer who was trying to stop a suttee was told by an Indian man, "It's our custom to burn a widow on her husband's funeral pyre." To which the officer replied, "And it's our custom to execute murderers.")

Some relativists confuse two different senses in which judgments can be *sub-jective*. The view that moral judgments express desires means that they are, in one sense, subjective. Which judgments you will agree to depends on what desires you have, which is a feature of you. But, in this sense, factual judgments are subjective also. Which ones you will accept depends on what beliefs you have, which is similarly a feature of you. From the fact that beliefs are subjective in this way, therefore, it does not follow that they are subjective in the sense that you are *entitled* to make any judgments you like. Indeed, to go from the first claim to the second is to make one of those moves from "is" to "ought" that furrowed Hume's brow. It's to commit the naturalistic fallacy. So even on the Positivist view there is no route from the subjectivity of value judgments to a defense of toleration. Toleration is just another value.

Values Reclaimed

What's an alternative to the Positivist picture of values? Values guide our acts, our thoughts, and our feelings. These are our *responses* to values. Because you recognize the value of great art, you go to museums and to concert halls and read books. Because you see the value of courtesy, you try to understand the conventions of each society that you live in so that you can avoid giving offense. You act as you do because you respond to the values that guide you. And values shape thought and feeling as well. Truth and reason, values you recognize, shape (but, alas, do not determine) your beliefs. Because you respond, with the instinct of a cosmopolitan, to the value of elegance of verbal expression, you take pleasure in Akan proverbs, Oscar Wilde's plays, Basho's haiku verses, Nietzsche's philosophy. Your respect for wit doesn't just lead you to these works; it shapes how you respond to them. Just so, valuing kindness leads you to admire some gentle souls, and leaves you irritated by other thoughtless ones. It's true that when you think of, say, kindness, as a universal value, you want everybody to want to be kind. And, since you want them to agree with you, you also want *them* to want everybody to want everybody to be kind. But perhaps the Positivist has the story exactly the wrong way round. Perhaps you want people to want each other to be kind *because you recognize the value of kindness*. You want people to agree with you because people who agree with you will be kind and encourage kindness in others. The same thing is true about everything you hold to be a universal value, a basic human good: your valuing it is a judgment that we all have a good reason to do or to think or to feel certain things in certain contexts, and so, also, have reason to encourage these acts and thoughts and feelings in others.

How, in fact, do people learn that it is good to be kind? Is it by being treated kindly and noticing that they like it? Or by being cruelly treated and disliking it? That doesn't seem quite right: kindness isn't like chocolate, where you find whether you have a taste for it by giving it a try. Rather, the idea that it's a good seems to be part of the very concept. Learning what kindness is means learning, among other things, that it's good. We'd suspect that someone who denied that kindness was good—or that cruelty was bad—didn't really understand what it was. The concept itself is value-laden, and therefore action guiding.

The Positivist will no doubt ask us what we will do about the ones who think cruelty good. And I think the right answer is that we should do with them what we should do with people who think that red things are green. Faced with the Tormentor who genuinely thinks it good to be cruel, the Positivist has just the options we have. Change the Tormentor's mind. Keep out of his way. Keep him out of ours.

Disagreements of this fundamental sort are actually quite unusual. You have probably never met someone who sincerely admits to thinking that it's just fine to be cruel to ordinary innocent human beings. There are people who think that it is okay to be cruel to animals. There are people who favor cruelty to wicked people. There are people who don't recognize what they are doing is cruel. And there are people who think that cruelty can be justified by other considerations. Many people think torture can be a necessary evil to uncover terrorist plots. Still, it is, exactly, as a necessary *evil*, a bad thing done in the service of a greater good. Defending particular acts of cruelty in this way means that you recognize the value of avoiding cruelty if you can.

The deepest problem with Positivism, however, is not in its conclusions. It is in its starting point. I began, as I think one must if one is to make the Positivist story believable, with a single person, acting on her own beliefs and desires. Starting from there, one has to give an account of values that begins with what it is for me—this single person—to regard something as valuable. But to understand how values work, you must see them not as guiding us as individuals on our own but as guiding people who are trying to share their lives.

The philosopher Hilary Putnam famously argued that, as he once put it, "Meanings ain't in the head." You can talk about elm trees, even if you personally couldn't tell an elm from a beech; you can talk about electrons, even if you couldn't give a very good account of what they are. And the reason you can use these words—and *mean* something by them—is that other people in your language community do have the relevant expertise. There are physicists who are experts on electronics, naturalists who know all about elms. Our use of factual terms like these depends upon these social circumstances. What I mean doesn't depend only on what's in my brain.

We go astray, similarly, when we think of a moral vocabulary as the possession of a solitary individual. If meanings ain't in the head, neither are morals. The concept of kindness, or cruelty, enshrines a kind of social consensus. An individual who decides that kindness is bad and cruelty good is acting like Lewis Carroll's Humpty-Dumpty, for whom a word "means just what I choose it to mean—neither more, nor less." The language of values is, after all, language. And the key insight of modern philosophical reflection on language is that language is, first and foremost, a public thing, something we share. Like all vocabulary, evaluative language is primarily a tool we use to talk to one another, not an instrument for talking to ourselves. You know what you call someone who uses language mostly to talk to himself? Crazy.

Our language of values is one of the central ways we coordinate our lives with one another. We appeal to values when we are trying to get things done *together*. Suppose we are discussing a movie. You say that it expresses a cynical view of human nature. This is not just an invitation to me to accept a fact about the film's picture of the characters and their motivations; it is also an attempt to shape how I feel. Seeing it that way, I am more likely, for example, to resist my first emotional responses, my sympathy, say, with certain characters. If I hold on to those feelings, I might want to resist your characterization. Not cynical, I might say; pessimistic, for sure, but also deeply humane. *Cynical, humane, pessimistic:* these are part of the vocabulary of value. And, as I say, they are meant to shape our responses.

Why, you might ask, should we care how other people think and feel about stories? Why do we talk about them in this language of value? One answer is just that it is part of being human. People tell stories and discuss them in every culture, and we know they have done so back as far as the record goes. The *Iliad* and the *Odyssey*, the *Epic of Gilgamesh*, the *Tale of Genji*, the Ananse stories I grew up with in Asante, weren't just read or recited: they were discussed, evaluated, referred to in everyday life. We wouldn't recognize a community as human if it had no stories, if its people had no narrative imagination. So one answer to the question why we do it is: it's just one of the things that humans do.

But a deeper answer is that evaluating stories together is one of the central human ways of learning to align our responses to the world. And that alignment of responses is, in turn, one of the ways we maintain the social fabric, the texture of our relationships. The 2004 Afghan film *Osama*, which tells the story of the life of a girl under the Taliban, shows us women and girls driven out of public life to hide in the shadows, as murderous and moralizing mullahs seek to impose a vision of gender they claim to derive from Islam. It shows us the waste of human talent: Osama's mother is a doctor who cannot practice. It shows us, too, that there are women who find small ways of resisting, and men who are forced into acts of courage as well as moments of dishonesty to help them. And it reminds us, at the end, when Osama is handed over to be the latest of four unwilling wives of an elderly mullah, that what makes oppression possible is that there are people who profit as well as people who suffer. Robbing Peter to pay Paul, as George Bernard Shaw observed shrewdly, is a policy that will, at least, guarantee you the vigorous support of Paul.

Our response to this film, when we discuss it with one another, reinforces our common understanding, and the values we share. *Murderous, waste, courage, dishonesty, oppression:* these are value terms, meant to shape our responses to the movie. And if the story it tells is truly representative, our discussion of it will help us decide not only what we feel about the characters but how we should act in the world. Talk about *Osama* can help us think about whether it was right for so many of the nations of the world to unite to remove the Taliban regime. It helps us, too, to think about other kinds of oppression, other places for courage, other wasted opportunities. It keeps our vocabulary of evaluation honed, ready to do its work in our lives. And that work, as I say, is first to help us act together.

You could insist on a technical use of the word "reason" to mean something like "calculation," which is what it seems to mean when modern Positivists use it. And then it would be fine to say that when people talk in these ways they are not, strictly speaking, reasoning together. But in the English we speak every day, it is natural to call what we do when we seek, through a conversation rich in the language of value, to shape each other's thoughts and sentiments and deeds, "offering reasons."

Folktales, drama, opera, novels, short stories; biographies, histories, ethnographies; fiction or nonfiction; painting, music, sculpture, and dance: every human civilization has ways to reveal to us values we had not previously recognized or undermine our commitment to values that we had settled into. Armed with these terms, fortified with a shared language of value, we can often guide one another, in the cosmopolitan spirit, to shared responses; and when we cannot agree, the understanding that our responses are shaped by some of the same vocabulary can make it easier to agree to disagree. All this is part of the truth about human life. And it is a part of the truth that Positivism makes it very hard to see.

For if relativism about ethics and morality were true, then, at the end of many discussions, we would each have to end up saying, "From where I stand, I am right. From where you stand, you are right." And there would be nothing further to say. From our different perspectives, we would be living effectively in different worlds. And without a shared world, what is there to discuss? People often recommend relativism because they think it will lead to tolerance. But if we cannot learn from one another what it is right to think and feel and do, then conversation between us will be pointless. Relativism of that sort isn't a way to encourage conversation; it's just a reason to fall silent.

Chapter 4

Religion and Ethics

Religion, Morality, and Conscience

John Arthur

John Arthur *(1946–2007) was an accomplished teacher and scholar in the areas of social ethics, political philosophy, and philosophy of law. He earned a PhD in philosophy from Vanderbilt University and taught at a number of universities, including the State University of New York at Binghamton, where he spent eighteen years. In the following piece, Arthur explores several ways religion has been claimed to be necessary for morality. Specifically, he examines whether religion is necessary for (1) giving us the motivation to behave morally, (2) enabling us to discern which actions are morally required and which are forbidden, and (3) the very existence of an objective right and wrong.*

What is morality? Does it need religion in some way? Or is it purely social? In this essay, John Arthur first discusses, and rejects, three ways morality has been thought to depend on religion: that without religious motivation people could not be expected to do the right thing; that religion is necessary to provide guidance to people in their search for the correct course of action; and that religion is essential for there even to be a right and wrong. Arthur then considers another conception of morality, suggested by John Dewey, which claims "morality is social." He concludes with some brief comments on the importance of these reflections for moral deliberation and for education. John Arthur is professor of philosophy and director of the Program in Philosophy, Politics, and Law at Binghamton University.

My first and prime concern in this paper is to explore the connections, if any, between morality and religion. I will argue that although there are a variety of ways the two can be connected, in fact religion is not necessary for morality. Despite the lack of any logical or other necessary connection, I will claim, there remain important respects in which the two are related. In the concluding section I will discuss the notion of moral conscience, and then look briefly at the various respects in which morality is "social" and the implications of that idea for moral education. First, however, I want to say something about the subjects: Just what are we referring to when we speak of morality and of religion?

1. Morality And Religion

A useful way to approach the first question—the nature of morality—is to ask what it would mean for a society to exist without a social moral code. How would such people think and behave? What would that society look like? First, it seems clear that such people would never feel guilt or resentment. For example, the notions that I ought to remember my parents' anniversary, that he has a moral responsibility to help care for his children after the divorce, that she has a right to equal pay for equal work, and that discrimination on the basis of race is unfair would be absent in such a society. Notions of duty, rights, and obligations would not be present, except perhaps in the legal sense; concepts of justice and fairness would also be foreign to these people. In short, people would have no tendency to evaluate or criticize the behavior of others, nor to feel remorse about their own behavior. Children would not be taught to be ashamed when they steal or hurt others, nor would they be allowed to complain when others treat them badly. (People might, however, feel regret at a decision that didn't turn out as they had hoped; but that would only be because their expectations were frustrated, not because they feel guilty.)

Such a society lacks a moral code. What, then, of religion? Is it possible that a society such as the one I have described would have religious beliefs? It seems clear that it is possible. Suppose every day these same people file into their place of worship to pay homage to God (they may believe in many gods or in one all-powerful creator of heaven and earth). Often they can be heard praying to God for help in dealing with their problems and thanking Him for their good fortune. Frequently they give sacrifices to God, sometimes in the form of money spent to build beautiful temples and churches, other times by performing actions they believe God would approve, such as helping those in need. These practices might also be institutionalized, in the sense that certain people are assigned important leadership roles. Specific texts might also be taken as authoritative, indicating the ways God has acted in history and His role in their lives or the lives of their ancestors.

To have a moral code, then, is to tend to evaluate (perhaps without even expressing it) the behavior of others and to feel guilt at certain actions when we perform them. Religion, on the other hand, involves beliefs in supernatural power(s) that created and perhaps also control nature, the tendency to worship and pray to those supernatural forces or beings, and the presence of organizational structures and authoritative texts. The practices of morality and religion are thus importantly different. One involves our attitudes toward various forms of behavior (lying and killing, for example), typically expressed using the notions of rules, rights, and obligations. The other, religion, typically involves prayer, worship, beliefs about the supernatural, institutional forms, and authoritative texts.

We come, then, to the central question: What is the connection, if any, between a society's moral code and its religious practices and beliefs? Many people have felt that morality is in some way dependent on religion or religious truths. But what sort of "dependence" might there be? In what follows, I distinguish various ways in which one might claim that religion is necessary for morality, arguing against those who claim morality depends in some way on religion. I will also suggest, however, some other important ways in which the two are related, concluding with a brief discussion of conscience and moral education.

2. Religious Motivation And Guidance

One possible role which religion might play in morality relates to motives people have. Religion, it is often said, is necessary so that people will DO right. Typically, the argument begins with the important point that doing what is right often has costs: refusing to shoplift or cheat can mean people go without some good or fail a test; returning a billfold means they don't get the contents. Religion is therefore said to be necessary in that it provides motivation to do the right thing. God rewards those who follow His commands by providing for them a place in heaven or by ensuring that they prosper and are happy on earth. He also punishes those who violate the moral law. Others emphasize less self-interested ways in which religious motives may encourage people to act rightly. Since God is the creator of the universe and has ordained that His plan should be followed, they point out, it is important to live one's life in accord with this divinely ordained plan. Only by living a moral life, it is said, can people live in harmony with the larger, divinely created order.

The first claim, then, is that religion is necessary to provide moral motivation. The problem with that argument, however, is that religious motives are far from the only ones people have. For most of us, a decision to do the right thing (if that is our decision) is made for a variety of reasons: "What if I get caught? What if somebody sees me—what will he or she think? How will I feel afterwards? Will I regret it?" Or maybe the thought of cheating just doesn't arise. We were raised to be a decent person, and that's what we are—period. Behaving fairly and treating others well is more important than whatever we might gain from stealing or cheating, let alone seriously harming another person. So it seems clear that many motives for doing the right thing have nothing whatsoever to do with religion. Most of us, in fact, do worry about getting caught, being blamed, and being looked down on by others. We also may do what is right just because it's right, or because we don't want to hurt others or embarrass family and friends. To say that we need religion to act morally is mistaken; indeed, it seems to me that many of us, when it really gets down to it, don't give much of a thought to religion when making moral decisions. All those other reasons are the ones that we tend to consider, or else we just don't consider cheating and stealing at all. So far, then, there seems to be no reason to suppose that people can't be moral yet irreligious at the same time.

A second argument that is available for those who think religion is necessary to morality, however, focuses on moral guidance and knowledge rather than on people's motives. However much people may want to do the right thing, according to this view, we cannot ever know for certain what is right without the guidance of religious teaching. Human understanding is simply inadequate to this difficult and controversial task; morality involves immensely complex problems, and so we must consult religious revelation for help.

Again, however, this argument fails. First, consider how much we would need to know about religion and revelation in order for religion to provide moral guidance. Besides being aware that there is a God, we'd also have to think about which of the many religions is true. How can anybody be sure his or her religion is the right one? But even if we assume that Judeo-Christian God is the real one, we still need to find out just what it is He wants us to do, which means we must think about revelation.

Revelation comes in at least two forms, and not even all Christians agree on which is the best way to understand revelation. Some hold that revelation occurs when God tells us what he wants by providing us with His words: The Ten Commandments are an example. Many even believe, as evangelist Billy Graham once said, that the entire Bible was written by God using thirty-nine secretaries. Others, however, doubt that the "word of God" refers literally to the words God has spoken, but believe instead that the Bible is an historical document, written by human beings, of the events or occasions in which God revealed himself. It is an especially important document, of course, but nothing more than that. So on this second view, revelation is not understood as *statements* made by God but rather as His *acts,* such as leading His people from Egypt, testing Job, and sending His son as an example of the ideal life. The Bible is not itself revelation, it's the historical account of revelatory actions.

If we are to use revelation as a moral guide, then, we must first know what is to count as revelation—words given us by God, historical events, or both? But even supposing that we could somehow answer those questions, the problems of relying on revelation are still not over since we still must interpret that revelation. Some feel, for example, that the Bible justifies various forms of killing, including war and capital punishment, on the basis of such statements as "An eye for an eye." Others, emphasizing such sayings as "Judge not lest ye be judged" and "Thou shalt not kill," believe the Bible demands absolute pacifism. How are we to know which interpretation is correct? It is likely, of course, that the answer people give to such religious questions will be influenced in part at least by their own moral beliefs; if capital punishment is thought to be unjust, for example, then an interpreter will seek to read the Bible in a way that is consistent with that moral truth. That is not, however, a happy conclusion for those wishing to rest morality on revelation, for it means that their understanding of what God has revealed is itself dependent on their prior moral views. Rather than revelation serving as a guide for morality, morality is serving as a guide for how we interpret revelation.

So my general conclusion is that far from providing a short-cut to moral understanding, looking to revelation for guidance often creates more questions and problems. It seems wiser under the circumstances to address complex moral problems like abortion, capital punishment, and affirmative action directly, considering the pros and cons of each side, rather than to seek answers through the much more controversial and difficult route of revelation.

3. The Divine Command Theory

It may seem, however, that we have still not really gotten to the heart of the matter. Even if religion is not necessary for moral motivation or guidance, it is often claimed, religion is necessary in another more fundamental sense. According to this view, religion is necessary for morality because without God there could BE no right or wrong. God, in other words, provides the foundation or bedrock on which morality is grounded. This idea was expressed by Bishop R. C. Mortimer:

> God made us and all the world. Because of that He has an absolute claim on our obedience . . . From [this] it follows that a thing is not right simply because we think it is. It is right because God commands it.[1]

What Bishop Mortimer has in mind can be seen by comparing moral rules with legal ones. Legal statutes, we know, are created by legislatures; if the state assembly of New York had not passed a law limiting the speed people can travel, then there would be no such legal obligation. Without the statutory enactments, such a law simply would not exist. Mortimer's view, the *divine command theory*, would mean that God has the same sort of relation to moral law as the legislature has to statutes it enacts: without God's commands there would be no moral rules, just as without a legislature there would be no statutes.

Defenders of the divine command theory often add to this a further claim, that only by assuming God sits at the foundation of morality can we explain the objective difference between right and wrong. This point was forcefully argued by F. C. Copleston in a 1948 British Broadcasting Corporation radio debate with Bertrand Russell.

> COPLESTON: . . . The validity of such an interpretation of man's conduct depends on the recognition of God's existence, obviously. . . . Let's take a look at the Commandant of the [Nazi] concentration camp at Belsen. That appears to you as undesirable and evil and to me too. To Adolph Hitler we suppose it appeared as something good and desirable. I suppose you'd have to admit that for Hitler it was good and for you it is evil.
>
> RUSSELL: No, I shouldn't go so far as that. I mean, I think people can make mistakes in that as they can in other things. If you have jaundice you see things yellow that are not yellow. You're making a mistake.

COPLESTON: Yes, one can make mistakes, but can you make a mistake if it's simply a question of reference to a feeling or emotion? Surely Hitler would be the only possible judge of what appealed to his emotions.

RUSSELL: . . . You can say various things about that; among others, that if that sort of thing makes that sort of appeal to Hitler's emotions, then Hitler makes quite a different appeal to my emotions.

COPLESTON: Granted. But there's no objective criterion outside feeling then for condemning the conduct of the Commandant of Belsen, in your view. . . . The human being's idea of the content of the moral law depends certainly to a large extent on education and environment, and a man has to use his reason in assessing the validity of the actual moral ideas of his social group. But the possibility of criticizing the accepted moral code presupposes that there is an objective standard, that there is an ideal moral order, which imposes itself. . . . It implies the existence of a real foundation of God.[2]

Against those who, like Bertrand Russell, seek to ground morality in feelings and attitudes, Copleston argues that there must be a more solid foundation if we are to be able to claim truly that the Nazis were evil. God, according to Copleston, is able to provide the objective basis for the distinction, which we all know to exist, between right and wrong. Without divine commands at the root of human obligations, we would have no real reason for condemning the behavior of anybody, even Nazis. Morality, Copleston thinks, would then be nothing more than an expression of personal feeling.

To begin assessing the divine command theory, let's first consider this last point. Is it really true that only the commands of God can provide an objective basis for moral judgments? Certainly many philosophers have felt that morality rests on its own perfectly sound footing, be it reason, human nature, or natural sentiments. It seems wrong to conclude, automatically, that morality cannot rest on anything but religion. And it is also possible that morality doesn't have any foundation or basis at all, so that its claims should be ignored in favor of whatever serves our own self-interest.

In addition to these problems with Copleston's argument, the divine command theory faces other problems as well. First, we would need to say much more about the relationship between morality and divine commands. Certainly the expressions "is commanded by God" and "is morally required" do not *mean* the same thing. People and even whole societies can use moral concepts without understanding them to make any reference to God. And while it is true that God (or any other moral being for that matter) would tend to want others to do the right thing, this hardly shows that being right and being commanded by God are the same thing. Parents want their children to do the right thing, too, but that doesn't mean parents, or anybody else, can make a thing right just by commanding it!

I think that, in fact, theists should reject the divine command theory. One reason is what it implies. Suppose we were to grant (just for the sake of argument) that the divine command theory is correct, so that actions are right just because they are commanded by God. The same, of course, can be said about those deeds that we believe are wrong. If God hadn't commanded us not to do them, they would not be wrong.

But now notice this consequence of the divine command theory. Since God is all-powerful, and since right is determined solely by His commands, is it not possible that He might change the rules and make what we now think of as wrong into right? It would seem that according to the divine command theory the answer is "yes": it is theoretically possible that tomorrow God would decree that virtues such as kindness and courage have become vices while actions that show cruelty and cowardice will henceforth be the right actions. (Recall the analogy with a legislature and the power it has to change law.) So now rather than it being right for people to help each other out and prevent innocent people from suffering unnecessarily, it would be right (God having changed His mind) to create as much pain among innocent children as we possibly can! To adopt the divine command theory therefore commits its advocate to the seemingly absurd position that even the greatest atrocities might be not only acceptable but morally required if God were to command them.

Plato made a similar point in the dialogue *Euthyphro*. Socrates is asking Euthyphro what it is that makes the virtue of holiness a virtue, just as we have been asking what makes kindness and courage virtues. Euthyphro has suggested that holiness is just whatever all the gods love.

SOCRATES: Well, then, Euthyphro, what do we say about holiness? Is it not loved by all the gods, according to your definition?

EUTHYPHRO: Yes.

SOCRATES: Because it is holy, or for some other reason?

EUTHYPHRO: No, because it is holy.

SOCRATES: Then it is loved by the gods because it is holy: it is not holy because it is loved by them?

EUTHYPHRO: It seems so.

SOCRATES: . . . Then holiness is not what is pleasing to the gods, and what is pleasing to the gods is not holy as you say, Euthyphro. They are different things.

EUTHYPHRO: And why, Socrates?

SOCRATES: Because we are agreed that the gods love holiness because it is holy: and that it is not holy because they love it.[3]

This raises an interesting question. Why, having claimed at first that virtues are merely what is loved (or commanded) by the gods, would Euthyphro contradict this and agree that the gods love holiness *because* it's holy, rather than the reverse? One likely possibility is that Euthyphro believes that whenever the gods love something, they do so with good reason, not without justification and arbitrarily. To deny this and say that it is merely the gods' love that makes holiness a virtue would mean that the gods have no basis for their attitudes, that they are arbitrary in what they love. Yet—and this is the crucial point—it's far from clear that a religious person would want to say that God is arbitrary in that way. If we say that it is simply God's loving something that makes it right, then what sense would it make to say God wants us to do right? All that could mean, it seems, is that God wants us to do what He wants us to do; He would have no reason for wanting it. Similarly, "God is good" would mean little more than "God does what He pleases." The divine command theory therefore leads us to the results that God is morally arbitrary, and that His wishing us to do good or even God's being just mean nothing more than that God does what He does and wants whatever He wants. Religious people who reject that consequence would also, I am suggesting, have reason to reject the divine command theory itself, seeking a different understanding of morality.

This now raises another problem, however. If God approves kindness because it is a virtue and hates the Nazis because they were evil, then it seems that God discovers morality rather than inventing it. So haven't we then identified a limitation on God's power, since He now, being a good God, must love kindness and command us not to be cruel? Without the divine command theory, in other words, what is left of God's omnipotence?

But why, we may ask, is such a limitation on God unacceptable? It is not at all clear that God really can do anything at all. Can God, for example, destroy Himself? Or make a rock so heavy that He cannot lift it? Or create a universe which was never created by Him? Many have thought that God cannot do these things, but also that His inability to do them does not constitute a serious limitation on His power since these are things that cannot be done at all: to do them would violate the laws of logic. Christianity's most influential theologian, Thomas Aquinas, wrote in this regard that "whatever implies contradiction does not come within the scope of divine omnipotence, because it cannot have the aspect of possibility. Hence it is more appropriate to say that such things cannot be done than that God cannot do them."[4]

How, then, ought we to understand God's relationship to morality if we reject the divine command theory? Can religious people consistently maintain their faith in God the Creator and yet deny that what is right is right because He commands it? I think the answer to this is "yes." Making cruelty good is not like making a universe that wasn't made, of course. It's a moral limit on God rather than a logical one. But why suppose that God's limits are only logical?

One final point about this. Even if we agree that God loves justice or kindness because of their nature, not arbitrarily, there still remains a sense in which God could change morality even having rejected the divine command theory. That's because if we assume, plausibly, I think, that morality depends in part on how we reason, what we desire and need, and the circumstances in which we find ourselves, then morality will still be under God's control since God could have constructed us or our environment very differently. Suppose, for instance, that he created us so that we couldn't be hurt by others or didn't care about freedom. Or perhaps our natural environment were created differently, so that all we have to do is ask and anything we want is given to us. If God had created either nature or us that way, then it seems likely our morality might also be different in important ways from the one we now think correct. In that sense, then, morality depends on God whether or not one supports the divine command theory.

4. "Morality Is Social"

I have argued here that religion is not necessary in providing moral motivation or guidance, and that the religious person should not subscribe to the divine command theory's claim that God is necessary for there to be morality. In this last section, I want first to look briefly at how religion and morality sometimes *do* influence each other. Then I will consider briefly the important ways in which morality might correctly be thought to be "social."

Nothing I have said so far means that morality and religion are independent of each other. But in what ways are they related, assuming I am correct in claiming morality does not *depend* on religion? First, of course, we should note the historical influence religions have had on the development of morality as well as on politics and law. Many of the important leaders of the abolitionist and civil rights movements were religious leaders, as are many current members of the pro-life movement. The relationship is not, however, onesided: morality has also influenced religion, as the current debate within the Catholic [C]hurch over the role of women, abortion, and other social issues shows. In reality, then, it seems clear that the practices of morality and religion have historically each exerted an influence on the other.

But just as the two have shaped each other historically, so, too, do they interact at the personal level. I have already suggested how people's understanding of revelation, for instance, is often shaped by morality as they seek the best interpretations of revealed texts. Whether trying to understand a work of art, a legal statute, or a religious text, interpreters regularly seek to understand them in the best light—to make them as good as they can be, which requires that they bring moral judgment to the task of religious interpretation and understanding.

The relationship can go the other direction as well, however, as people's moral views are shaped by their religious training and their current religious beliefs. These relationships are often complex, hidden even from ourselves, but it does seem clear that our views on important moral issues, from sexual morality and war to welfare and capital punishment, are often influenced by our religious outlook. So not only are religious and moral practices and understandings historically linked, but for many religious people the relationship extends to the personal level—to their understanding of moral obligations as well as their sense of who they are and their vision of who they wish to be.

Morality, then, is influenced by religion (as is religion by morality), but morality's social character extends deeper even than that, I want to argue. First, of course, the existence of morality assumes that we possess a socially acquired language within which we think about our choices and which alternatives we ought to follow. Second, morality is social in that it governs relationships among people, defining our responsibilities to others and theirs to us. Morality provides the standards we rely on in gauging our interactions with family, lovers, friends, fellow citizens, and even strangers. Third, morality is social in the sense that we are, in fact, subject to criticism by others for our actions. We discuss with others what we should do, and often hear from them concerning whether our decisions were acceptable. Blame and praise are a central feature of morality.

While not disputing any of this, John Dewey has suggested another important sense in which morality is social. Consider the following comments about the origins of morality and conscience taken from an article be titled "Morality Is Social":

> In language and imagination we rehearse the responses of others just as we dramatically enact other consequences. We foreknow how others will act, and the foreknowledge is the beginning of judgment passed on action. We know *with* them; there is conscience. An assembly is formed within our breast which discusses and appraises proposed and performed acts. The community without becomes a forum and tribunal within, a judgment-seat of charges, assessments and exculpations. Our thoughts of our own actions are saturated with the ideas that others entertain about them. . . Explicit recognition of this fact is a prerequisite of improvement in moral education. . . . Reflection is morally indispensable.[5]

So in addition to the three points I already mentioned, Dewey also wants to make another, and in some ways more important suggestion about morality's social character. This fourth idea depends on appreciating the fact that to think from the moral point of view, as opposed to the selfish one, for instance, demands that we reject our private, subjective perspective in favor of the perspective of others, envisioning how they might respond to various choices we might make. Far from being private and unrelated to others, moral conscience is in that sense "public." To consider a decision from the moral perspective requires envisioning what Dewey terms an "assembly of others" that is "formed within our breast." In that way, conscience cannot even be distinguished from the social: conscience invariably brings with it, or constitutes, the perspective of the other. "Is this right?" and "What would this look like were I to have to defend it to others?" are not separate questions.[6]

It is important not to confuse Dewey's point here, however. He is *not* saying that what is right is finally to be determined by the reactions of actually existing other people, or even by the reaction of society as a whole. To the contrary, what is right, and accords with the true dictates of conscience, might in fact not meet the approval of others. Conscience is "social" not in the sense that morality is determined by surveying what others in society think. Understood as the voice of an "assembly" of others within each of us, conscience cannot be reduced to the expected reaction of any existing individual or group. But what then does Dewey mean? The answer is that the assembly Dewey is describing is not an actual one but instead an hypothetical, "ideal" one; the actual "community without" is transformed into a "forum and tribunal within, a judgment seat of charges, assessments and exculpations." Only through the powers of imagination can we exercise our moral powers, envisioning with the powers of judgment what conscience requires.

Morality is therefore *inherently* social, in a variety of ways. It depends on socially learned language, is learned from interactions with others, and governs our interactions with others in society. But it also demands, as Dewey put it, that we know "with" others, envisioning for ourselves what their points of view would require along with our own. Conscience demands we occupy the positions of others.

Viewed in this light, God might play a role in moral reflection and conscience. That is because it is unlikely a religious person would wish to exclude God from the "forum and tribunal" that constitutes conscience. Rather, for the religious person conscience would almost certainly include the imagined reaction of God along with the reactions of others who might be affected by the action. So it seems that for a religious person morality and God's will cannot be separated, though the connection between them is not as envisioned by the divine command theory.

This leads to my final point, about moral education. If Dewey is correct, then it seems clear there is an important sense in which morality not only can be taught but must be. Besides early moral training, moral thinking depends on our ability to imagine others' reactions and to imaginatively put ourselves into their shoes. "What would somebody (including, perhaps, God) think if this got out?" expresses more than a concern with being embarrassed or punished; it is also the voice of conscience and indeed of morality itself. But that would mean, thinking of education, that listening to others, reading about what others think and do, and reflecting within ourselves about our actions and whether we could defend them to others are part of the practice of morality itself. Morality cannot exist without the broader, social perspective introduced by others, and this social nature ties it, in that way, with education and with public discussion, both actual and imagined.

"Private" moral reflection taking place independently of the social world would be no moral reflection at all; and moral education is not only possible, but essential.

Notes

1. R. C. Mortimer, *Christian Ethics* (London: Hutchinson's University Library, 1950), pp. 7–8.

2. This debate was broadcast on the Third Program of the British Broadcasting Corporation in 1948.

3. Plato, *Euthyphro*, trans. H. N. Fowler (Cambridge, MA: Harvard University Press, 1947).

4. Thomas Aquinas, *Summa Theologica*, Part I, Q. 25. Art. 3.

5. John Dewey, "Morality Is Social," in *The Moral Writings of John Dewey*, rev. ed., ed. James Gouinlock (Amherst, NY: Prometheus Books, 1994), pp. 182–4.

6. Obligations to animals raise an interesting problem for this conception of morality. It is wrong to torture animals only because other *people* could be expected to disapprove? Or is it that the animal itself would disapprove? Or, perhaps, that duties to animals rest on sympathy and compassion while human moral relations are more like Dewey describes, resting on morality's inherently social nature and on the dictates of conscience viewed as an assembly of others?

Euthyphro

Plato

Euthyphro *(c. 399 BCE) is one of the early works of the Classical Greek philosopher* **Plato** *(427–347 BCE). Plato, who was one of the most important philosophers of the ancient world, help set down the foundations of Western philosophy. His writings are mostly presented as dialogues between his mentor Socrates and various other characters. These dialogues are philosophical discussion though which various concepts or problems are explored. In* Euthyphro's*, Socrates questions the eponymous interlocutor about the nature of piety or holiness but fails to come to a satisfying conclusion. This dialogue contains a question that has affected discussions of religion and morality ever since: "Is piety loved by the gods because it is pious, or is it pious because it is loved by the gods?"*

Translated by Benjamin Jowett

PERSONS OF THE DIALOGUE: Socrates, Euthyphro

SCENE: The Porch of the King Archon.

EUTHYPHRO: Why have you left the Lyceum, Socrates? and what are you doing in the Porch of the King Archon? Surely you cannot be concerned in a suit before the King, like myself?

SOCRATES: Not in a suit, Euthyphro; impeachment is the word which the Athenians use.

EUTHYPHRO: What! I suppose that some one has been prosecuting you, for I cannot believe that you are the prosecutor of another.

SOCRATES: Certainly not.

EUTHYPHRO: Then some one else has been prosecuting you?

SOCRATES:	Yes.
EUTHYPHRO:	And who is he?
SOCRATES:	A young man who is little known, Euthyphro; and I hardly know him: his name is Meletus, and he is of the deme of Pitthis. Perhaps you may remember his appearance; he has a beak, and long straight hair, and a beard which is ill grown.
EUTHYPHRO:	No, I do not remember him, Socrates. But what is the charge which he brings against you?
SOCRATES:	What is the charge? Well, a very serious charge, which shows a good deal of character in the young man, and for which he is certainly not to be despised. He says he knows how the youth are corrupted and who are their corruptors. I fancy that he must be a wise man, and seeing that I am the reverse of a wise man, he has found me out, and is going to accuse me of corrupting his young friends. And of this our mother the state is to be the judge. Of all our political men he is the only one who seems to me to begin in the right way, with the cultivation of virtue in youth; like a good husbandman, he makes the young shoots his first care, and clears away us who are the destroyers of them. This is only the first step; he will afterwards attend to the elder branches; and if he goes on as he has begun, he will be a very great public benefactor.
EUTHYPHRO:	I hope that he may; but I rather fear, Socrates, that the opposite will turn out to be the truth. My opinion is that in attacking you he is simply aiming a blow at the foundation of the state. But in what way does he say that you corrupt the young?
SOCRATES:	He brings a wonderful accusation against me, which at first hearing excites surprise: he says that I am a poet or maker of gods, and that I invent new gods and deny the existence of old ones; this is the ground of his indictment.
EUTHYPHRO:	I understand, Socrates; he means to attack you about the familiar sign which occasionally, as you say, comes to you. He thinks that you are a neologian, and he is going to have you up before the court for this. He knows that such a charge is readily received by the world, as I myself know too well; for when I speak in the assembly about divine things, and foretell the future to them, they laugh at me and think me a madman. Yet every word that I say is true. But they are jealous of us all; and we must be brave and go at them.
SOCRATES:	Their laughter, friend Euthyphro, is not a matter of much consequence. For a man may be thought wise; but the Athenians, I suspect, do not much trouble themselves about him until he begins to impart his wisdom to others, and then for some reason or other, perhaps, as you say, from jealousy, they are angry.

EUTHYPHRO:	I am never likely to try their temper in this way.
SOCRATES:	I dare say not, for you are reserved in your behaviour, and seldom impart your wisdom. But I have a benevolent habit of pouring out myself to everybody, and would even pay for a listener, and I am afraid that the Athenians may think me too talkative. Now if, as I was saying, they would only laugh at me, as you say that they laugh at you, the time might pass gaily enough in the court; but perhaps they may be in earnest, and then what the end will be you soothsayers only can predict.
EUTHYPHRO:	I dare say that the affair will end in nothing, Socrates, and that you will win your cause; and I think that I shall win my own.
SOCRATES:	And what is your suit, Euthyphro? are you the pursuer or the defendant?
EUTHYPHRO:	I am the pursuer.
SOCRATES:	Of whom?
EUTHYPHRO:	You will think me mad when I tell you.
SOCRATES:	Why, has the fugitive wings?
EUTHYPHRO:	Nay, he is not very volatile at his time of life.
SOCRATES:	Who is he?
EUTHYPHRO:	My father.
SOCRATES:	Your father! my good man?
EUTHYPHRO:	Yes.
SOCRATES:	And of what is he accused?
EUTHYPHRO:	Of murder, Socrates.
SOCRATES:	By the powers, Euthyphro! how little does the common herd know of the nature of right and truth. A man must be an extraordinary man, and have made great strides in wisdom, before he could have seen his way to bring such an action.
EUTHYPHRO:	Indeed, Socrates, he must.
SOCRATES:	I suppose that the man whom your father murdered was one of your relatives—clearly he was; for if he had been a stranger you would never have thought of prosecuting him.
EUTHYPHRO:	I am amused, Socrates, at your making a distinction between one who is a relation and one who is not a relation; for surely the pollution is the same in either case, if you knowingly associate with the murderer when you ought to clear yourself and him by proceeding against him. The real question is whether the murdered man has been justly slain. If justly, then your duty is to let the matter alone;

but if unjustly, then even if the murderer lives under the same roof with you and eats at the same table, proceed against him. Now the man who is dead was a poor dependent of mine who worked for us as a field labourer on our farm in Naxos, and one day in a fit of drunken passion he got into a quarrel with one of our domestic servants and slew him. My father bound him hand and foot and threw him into a ditch, and then sent to Athens to ask of a diviner what he should do with him. Meanwhile he never attended to him and took no care about him, for he regarded him as a murderer; and thought that no great harm would be done even if he did die. Now this was just what happened. For such was the effect of cold and hunger and chains upon him, that before the messenger returned from the diviner, he was dead. And my father and family are angry with me for taking the part of the murderer and prosecuting my father. They say that he did not kill him, and that if he did, the dead man was but a murderer, and I ought not to take any notice, for that a son is impious who prosecutes a father. Which shows, Socrates, how little they know what the gods think about piety and impiety.

SOCRATES: Good heavens, Euthyphro! and is your knowledge of religion and of things pious and impious so very exact, that, supposing the circumstances to be as you state them, you are not afraid lest you too may be doing an impious thing in bringing an action against your father?

EUTHYPHRO: The best of Euthyphro, and that which distinguishes him, Socrates, from other men, is his exact knowledge of all such matters. What should I be good for without it?

SOCRATES: Rare friend! I think that I cannot do better than be your disciple. Then before the trial with Meletus comes on I shall challenge him, and say that I have always had a great interest in religious questions, and now, as he charges me with rash imaginations and innovations in religion, I have become your disciple. You, Meletus, as I shall say to him, acknowledge Euthyphro to be a great theologian, and sound in his opinions; and if you approve of him you ought to approve of me, and not have me into court; but if you disapprove, you should begin by indicting him who is my teacher, and who will be the ruin, not of the young, but of the old; that is to say, of myself whom he instructs, and of his old father whom he admonishes and chastises. And if Meletus refuses to listen to me, but will go on, and will not shift the indictment from me to you, I cannot do better than repeat this challenge in the court.

EUTHYPHRO: Yes, indeed, Socrates; and if he attempts to indict me I am mistaken if I do not find a flaw in him; the court shall have a great deal more to say to him than to me.

SOCRATES: And I, my dear friend, knowing this, am desirous of becoming your disciple. For I observe that no one appears to notice you—not even this Meletus; but his sharp eyes have found me out at once, and he has indicted me for impiety. And therefore, I adjure you to tell me the nature of piety and impiety, which you said that you knew so well, and of murder, and of other offences against the gods. What are they? Is not piety in every action always the same? and impiety, again—is it not always the opposite of piety, and also the same with itself, having, as impiety, one notion which includes whatever is impious?

EUTHYPHRO: To be sure, Socrates.

SOCRATES: And what is piety, and what is impiety?

EUTHYPHRO: Piety is doing as I am doing; that is to say, prosecuting any one who is guilty of murder, sacrilege, or of any similar crime—whether he be your father or mother, or whoever he may be—that makes no difference; and not to prosecute them is impiety. And please to consider, Socrates, what a notable proof I will give you of the truth of my words, a proof which I have already given to others:—of the principle, I mean, that the impious, whoever he may be, ought not to go unpunished. For do not men regard Zeus as the best and most righteous of the gods?—and yet admit that he bound his father (Cronos) because he wickedly devoured his sons, and that he too had punished his own father (Uranus) for a similar reason, in a nameless manner. And yet when I proceed against my father, they are angry with me. So inconsistent are they in their way of talking when the gods are concerned, and when I am concerned.

SOCRATES: May not this be the reason, Euthyphro, why I am charged with impiety—that I cannot away with these stories about the gods? and therefore I suppose that people think me wrong. But, as you who are well informed about them approve of them, I cannot do better than assent to your superior wisdom. What else can I say, confessing as I do, that I know nothing about them? Tell me, for the love of Zeus, whether you really believe that they are true.

EUTHYPHRO: Yes, Socrates; and things more wonderful still, of which the world is in ignorance.

SOCRATES: And do you really believe that the gods fought with one another, and had dire quarrels, battles, and the like, as the poets say, and as you may see represented in the works of great artists? The temples are full of them; and notably the robe of Athene, which is carried up to the Acropolis at the great Panathenaea, is embroidered with them. Are all these tales of the gods true, Euthyphro?

EUTHYPHRO: Yes, Socrates; and, as I was saying, I can tell you, if you would like to hear them, many other things about the gods which would quite amaze you.

SOCRATES: I dare say; and you shall tell me them at some other time when I have leisure. But just at present I would rather hear from you a more precise answer, which you have not as yet given, my friend, to the question, What is "piety"? When asked, you only replied, Doing as you do, charging your father with murder.

EUTHYPHRO: And what I said was true, Socrates.

SOCRATES: No doubt, Euthyphro; but you would admit that there are many other pious acts?

EUTHYPHRO: There are.

SOCRATES: Remember that I did not ask you to give me two or three examples of piety, but to explain the general idea which makes all pious things to be pious. Do you not recollect that there was one idea which made the impious impious, and the pious pious?

EUTHYPHRO: I remember.

SOCRATES: Tell me what is the nature of this idea, and then I shall have a standard to which I may look, and by which I may measure actions, whether yours or those of any one else, and then I shall be able to say that such and such an action is pious, such another impious.

EUTHYPHRO: I will tell you, if you like.

SOCRATES: I should very much like.

EUTHYPHRO: Piety, then, is that which is dear to the gods, and impiety is that which is not dear to them.

SOCRATES: Very good, Euthyphro; you have now given me the sort of answer which I wanted. But whether what you say is true or not I cannot as yet tell, although I make no doubt that you will prove the truth of your words.

EUTHYPHRO: Of course.

SOCRATES: Come, then, and let us examine what we are saying. That thing or person which is dear to the gods is pious, and that thing or person which is hateful to the gods is impious, these two being the extreme opposites of one another. Was not that said?

EUTHYPHRO: It was.

SOCRATES: And well said?

EUTHYPHRO: Yes, Socrates, I thought so; it was certainly said.

SOCRATES:	And further, Euthyphro, the gods were admitted to have enmities and hatreds and differences?
EUTHYPHRO:	Yes, that was also said.
SOCRATES:	And what sort of difference creates enmity and anger? Suppose for example that you and I, my good friend, differ about a number; do differences of this sort make us enemies and set us at variance with one another? Do we not go at once to arithmetic, and put an end to them by a sum?
EUTHYPHRO:	True.
SOCRATES:	Or suppose that we differ about magnitudes, do we not quickly end the differences by measuring?
EUTHYPHRO:	Very true.
SOCRATES:	And we end a controversy about heavy and light by resorting to a weighing machine?
EUTHYPHRO:	To be sure.
SOCRATES:	But what differences are there which cannot be thus decided, and which therefore make us angry and set us at enmity with one another? I dare say the answer does not occur to you at the moment, and therefore I will suggest that these enmities arise when the matters of difference are the just and unjust, good and evil, honourable and dishonourable. Are not these the points about which men differ, and about which when we are unable satisfactorily to decide our differences, you and I and all of us quarrel, when we do quarrel?
EUTHYPHRO:	Yes, Socrates, the nature of the differences about which we quarrel is such as you describe.
SOCRATES:	And the quarrels of the gods, noble Euthyphro, when they occur, are of a like nature?
EUTHYPHRO:	Certainly they are.
SOCRATES:	They have differences of opinion, as you say, about good and evil, just and unjust, honourable and dishonourable: there would have been no quarrels among them, if there had been no such differences— would there now?
EUTHYPHRO:	You are quite right.
SOCRATES:	Does not every man love that which he deems noble and just and good, and hate the opposite of them?
EUTHYPHRO:	Very true.
SOCRATES:	But, as you say, people regard the same things, some as just and others as unjust,—about these they dispute; and so there arise wars and fightings among them.

EUTHYPHRO: Very true.

SOCRATES: Then the same things are hated by the gods and loved by the gods, and are both hateful and dear to them?

EUTHYPHRO: True.

SOCRATES: And upon this view the same things, Euthyphro, will be pious and also impious?

EUTHYPHRO: So I should suppose.

SOCRATES: Then, my friend, I remark with surprise that you have not answered the question which I asked. For I certainly did not ask you to tell me what action is both pious and impious: but now it would seem that what is loved by the gods is also hated by them. And therefore, Euthyphro, in thus chastising your father you may very likely be doing what is agreeable to Zeus but disagreeable to Cronos or Uranus, and what is acceptable to Hephaestus but unacceptable to Here, and there may be other gods who have similar differences of opinion.

EUTHYPHRO: But I believe, Socrates, that all the gods would be agreed as to the propriety of punishing a murderer: there would be no difference of opinion about that.

SOCRATES: Well, but speaking of men, Euthyphro, did you ever hear any one arguing that a murderer or any sort of evil-doer ought to be let off?

EUTHYPHRO: I should rather say that these are the questions which they are always arguing, especially in courts of law: they commit all sorts of crimes, and there is nothing which they will not do or say in their own defence.

SOCRATES: But do they admit their guilt, Euthyphro, and yet say that they ought not to be punished?

EUTHYPHRO: No; they do not.

SOCRATES: Then there are some things which they do not venture to say and do: for they do not venture to argue that the guilty are to be unpunished, but they deny their guilt, do they not?

EUTHYPHRO: Yes.

SOCRATES: Then they do not argue that the evil-doer should not be punished, but they argue about the fact of who the evil-doer is, and what he did and when?

EUTHYPHRO: True.

SOCRATES: And the gods are in the same case, if as you assert they quarrel about just and unjust, and some of them say while others deny that injustice is done among them. For surely neither God nor man will ever venture to say that the doer of injustice is not to be punished?

EUTHYPHRO: That is true, Socrates, in the main.

SOCRATES: But they join issue about the particulars—gods and men alike; and, if they dispute at all, they dispute about some act which is called in question, and which by some is affirmed to be just, by others to be unjust. Is not that true?

EUTHYPHRO: Quite true.

SOCRATES: Well then, my dear friend Euthyphro, do tell me, for my better instruction and information, what proof have you that in the opinion of all the gods a servant who is guilty of murder, and is put in chains by the master of the dead man, and dies because he is put in chains before he who bound him can learn from the interpreters of the gods what he ought to do with him, dies unjustly; and that on behalf of such an one a son ought to proceed against his father and accuse him of murder. How would you show that all the gods absolutely agree in approving of his act? Prove to me that they do, and I will applaud your wisdom as long as I live.

EUTHYPHRO: It will be a difficult task; but I could make the matter very dear indeed to you.

SOCRATES: I understand; you mean to say that I am not so quick of apprehension as the judges: for to them you will be sure to prove that the act is unjust, and hateful to the gods.

EUTHYPHRO: Yes indeed, Socrates; at least if they will listen to me.

SOCRATES: But they will be sure to listen if they find that you are a good speaker. There was a notion that came into my mind while you were speaking; I said to myself: "Well, and what if Euthyphro does prove to me that all the gods regarded the death of the serf as unjust, how do I know anything more of the nature of piety and impiety? for granting that this action may be hateful to the gods, still piety and impiety are not adequately defined by these distinctions, for that which is hateful to the gods has been shown to be also pleasing and dear to them." And therefore, Euthyphro, I do not ask you to prove this; I will suppose, if you like, that all the gods condemn and abominate such an action. But I will amend the definition so far as to say that what all the gods hate is impious, and what they love pious or holy; and what some of them love and others hate is both or neither. Shall this be our definition of piety and impiety?

EUTHYPHRO: Why not, Socrates?

SOCRATES: Why not! certainly, as far as I am concerned, Euthyphro, there is no reason why not. But whether this admission will greatly assist you in the task of instructing me as you promised, is a matter for you to consider.

EUTHYPHRO: Yes, I should say that what all the gods love is pious and holy, and the opposite which they all hate, impious.

SOCRATES: Ought we to enquire into the truth of this, Euthyphro, or simply to accept the mere statement on our own authority and that of others? What do you say?

EUTHYPHRO: We should enquire; and I believe that the statement will stand the test of enquiry.

SOCRATES: We shall know better, my good friend, in a little while. The point which I should first wish to understand is whether the pious or holy is beloved by the gods because it is holy, or holy because it is beloved of the gods.

EUTHYPHRO: I do not understand your meaning, Socrates.

SOCRATES: I will endeavour to explain: we, speak of carrying and we speak of being carried, of leading and being led, seeing and being seen. You know that in all such cases there is a difference, and you know also in what the difference lies?

EUTHYPHRO: I think that I understand.

SOCRATES: And is not that which is beloved distinct from that which loves?

EUTHYPHRO: Certainly.

SOCRATES: Well; and now tell me, is that which is carried in this state of carrying because it is carried, or for some other reason?

EUTHYPHRO: No; that is the reason.

SOCRATES: And the same is true of what is led and of what is seen?

EUTHYPHRO: True.

SOCRATES: And a thing is not seen because it is visible, but conversely, visible because it is seen; nor is a thing led because it is in the state of being led, or carried because it is in the state of being carried, but the converse of this. And now I think, Euthyphro, that my meaning will be intelligible; and my meaning is, that any state of action or passion implies previous action or passion. It does not become because it is becoming, but it is in a state of becoming because it becomes; neither does it suffer because it is in a state of suffering, but it is in a state of suffering because it suffers. Do you not agree?

EUTHYPHRO: Yes.

SOCRATES: Is not that which is loved in some state either of becoming or suffering?

EUTHYPHRO:	Yes.
SOCRATES:	And the same holds as in the previous instances; the state of being loved follows the act of being loved, and not the act the state.
EUTHYPHRO:	Certainly.
SOCRATES:	And what do you say of piety, Euthyphro: is not piety, according to your definition, loved by all the gods?
EUTHYPHRO:	Yes.
SOCRATES:	Because it is pious or holy, or for some other reason?
EUTHYPHRO:	No, that is the reason.
SOCRATES:	It is loved because it is holy, not holy because it is loved?
EUTHYPHRO:	Yes.
SOCRATES:	And that which is dear to the gods is loved by them, and is in a state to be loved of them because it is loved of them?
EUTHYPHRO:	Certainly.
SOCRATES:	Then that which is dear to the gods, Euthyphro, is not holy, nor is that which is holy loved of God, as you affirm; but they are two different things.
EUTHYPHRO:	How do you mean, Socrates?
SOCRATES:	I mean to say that the holy has been acknowledged by us to be loved of God because it is holy, not to be holy because it is loved.
EUTHYPHRO:	Yes.
SOCRATES:	But that which is dear to the gods is dear to them because it is loved by them, not loved by them because it is dear to them.
EUTHYPHRO:	True.
SOCRATES:	But, friend Euthyphro, if that which is holy is the same with that which is dear to God, and is loved because it is holy, then that which is dear to God would have been loved as being dear to God; but if that which is dear to God is dear to him because loved by him, then that which is holy would have been holy because loved by him. But now you see that the reverse is the case, and that they are quite different from one another. For one (theophiles) is of a kind to be loved cause it is loved, and the other (osion) is loved because it is of a kind to be loved. Thus you appear to me, Euthyphro, when I ask you what is the essence of holiness, to offer an attribute only, and not the essence—the attribute of being loved by all the gods. But you still refuse to explain to me the nature of holiness. And therefore, if you please, I will ask you not to hide your treasure, but to tell me once more what holiness or piety really is, whether dear to the gods or

not (for that is a matter about which we will not quarrel) and what is
impiety?

EUTHYPHRO: I really do not know, Socrates, how to express what I mean. For
somehow or other our arguments, on whatever ground we rest
them, seem to turn round and walk away from us.

SOCRATES: Your words, Euthyphro, are like the handiwork of my ancestor
Daedalus; and if I were the sayer or propounder of them, you might
say that my arguments walk away and will not remain fixed where
they are placed because I am a descendant of his. But now, since
these notions are your own, you must find some other gibe, for they
certainly, as you yourself allow, show an inclination to be on the
move.

EUTHYPHRO: Nay, Socrates, I shall still say that you are the Daedalus who sets
arguments in motion; not I, certainly, but you make them move or go
round, for they would never have stirred, as far as I am concerned.

SOCRATES: Then I must be a greater than Daedalus: for whereas he only made
his own inventions to move, I move those of other people as well.
And the beauty of it is, that I would rather not. For I would give the
wisdom of Daedalus, and the wealth of Tantalus, to be able to detain
them and keep them fixed. But enough of this. As I perceive that you
are lazy, I will myself endeavor to show you how you might instruct
me in the nature of piety; and I hope that you will not grudge your
labour. Tell me, then—Is not that which is pious necessarily just?

EUTHYPHRO: Yes.

SOCRATES: And is, then, all which is just pious? or, is that which is pious all just,
but that which is just, only in part and not all, pious?

EUTHYPHRO: I do not understand you, Socrates.

SOCRATES: And yet I know that you are as much wiser than I am, as you are
younger. But, as I was saying, revered friend, the abundance of your
wisdom makes you lazy. Please to exert yourself, for there is no real
difficulty in understanding me. What I mean I may explain by an
illustration of what I do not mean. The poet (Stasinus) sings—

'Of Zeus, the author and creator of all these things, You will not tell:
for where there is fear there is also reverence.'

Now I disagree with this poet. Shall I tell you in what respect?

EUTHYPHRO: By all means.

SOCRATES: I should not say that where there is fear there is also reverence; for
I am sure that many persons fear poverty and disease, and the like
evils, but I do not perceive that they reverence the objects of their fear.

EUTHYPHRO: Very true.

SOCRATES: But where reverence is, there is fear; for he who has a feeling of reverence and shame about the commission of any action, fears and is afraid of an ill reputation.

EUTHYPHRO: No doubt.

SOCRATES: Then we are wrong in saying that where there is fear there is also reverence; and we should say, where there is reverence there is also fear. But there is not always reverence where there is fear; for fear is a more extended notion, and reverence is a part of fear, just as the odd is a part of number, and number is a more extended notion than the odd. I suppose that you follow me now?

EUTHYPHRO: Quite well.

SOCRATES: That was the sort of question which I meant to raise when I asked whether the just is always the pious, or the pious always the just; and whether there may not be justice where there is not piety; for justice is the more extended notion of which piety is only a part. Do you dissent?

EUTHYPHRO: No, I think that you are quite right.

SOCRATES: Then, if piety is a part of justice, I suppose that we should enquire what part? If you had pursued the enquiry in the previous cases; for instance, if you had asked me what is an even number, and what part of number the even is, I should have had no difficulty in replying, a number which represents a figure having two equal sides. Do you not agree?

EUTHYPHRO: Yes, I quite agree.

SOCRATES: In like manner, I want you to tell me what part of justice is piety or holiness, that I may be able to tell Meletus not to do me injustice, or indict me for impiety, as I am now adequately instructed by you in the nature of piety or holiness, and their opposites.

EUTHYPHRO: Piety or holiness, Socrates, appears to me to be that part of justice which attends to the gods, as there is the other part of justice which attends to men.

SOCRATES: That is good, Euthyphro; yet still there is a little point about which I should like to have further information, What is the meaning of 'attention'? For attention can hardly be used in the same sense when applied to the gods as when applied to other things. For instance, horses are said to require attention, and not every person is able to attend to them, but only a person skilled in horsemanship. Is it not so?

EUTHYPHRO: Certainly.

SOCRATES: I should suppose that the art of horsemanship is the art of attending to horses?

EUTHYPHRO:	Yes.
SOCRATES:	Nor is every one qualified to attend to dogs, but only the huntsman?
EUTHYPHRO:	True.
SOCRATES:	And I should also conceive that the art of the huntsman is the art of attending to dogs?
EUTHYPHRO:	Yes.
SOCRATES:	As the art of the ox herd is the art of attending to oxen?
EUTHYPHRO:	Very true.
SOCRATES:	In like manner holiness or piety is the art of attending to the gods?—that would be your meaning, Euthyphro?
EUTHYPHRO:	Yes.
SOCRATES:	And is not attention always designed for the good or benefit of that to which the attention is given? As in the case of horses, you may observe that when attended to by the horseman's art they are benefited and improved, are they not?
EUTHYPHRO:	True.
SOCRATES:	As the dogs are benefited by the huntsman's art, and the oxen by the art of the ox herd, and all other things are tended or attended for their good and not for their hurt?
EUTHYPHRO:	Certainly, not for their hurt.
SOCRATES:	But for their good?
EUTHYPHRO:	Of course.
SOCRATES:	And does piety or holiness, which has been defined to be the art of attending to the gods, benefit or improve them? Would you say that when you do a holy act you make any of the gods better?
EUTHYPHRO:	No, no; that was certainly not what I meant.
SOCRATES:	And I, Euthyphro, never supposed that you did. I asked you the question about the nature of the attention, because I thought that you did not.
EUTHYPHRO:	You do me justice, Socrates; that is not the sort of attention which I mean.
SOCRATES:	Good: but I must still ask what is this attention to the gods which is called piety?
EUTHYPHRO:	It is such, Socrates, as servants show to their masters.
SOCRATES:	I understand—a sort of ministration to the gods.
EUTHYPHRO:	Exactly.

SOCRATES: Medicine is also a sort of ministration or service, having in view the attainment of some object—would you not say of health?

EUTHYPHRO: I should.

SOCRATES: Again, there is an art which ministers to the ship-builder with a view to the attainment of some result?

EUTHYPHRO: Yes, Socrates, with a view to the building of a ship.

SOCRATES: As there is an art which ministers to the housebuilder with a view to the building of a house?

EUTHYPHRO: Yes.

SOCRATES: And now tell me, my good friend, about the art which ministers to the gods: what work does that help to accomplish? For you must surely know if, as you say, you are of all men living the one who is best instructed in religion.

EUTHYPHRO: And I speak the truth, Socrates.

SOCRATES: Tell me then, oh tell me—what is that fair work which the gods do by the help of our ministrations?

EUTHYPHRO: Many and fair, Socrates, are the works which they do.

SOCRATES: Why, my friend, and so are those of a general. But the chief of them is easily told. Would you not say that victory in war is the chief of them?

EUTHYPHRO: Certainly.

SOCRATES: Many and fair, too, are the works of the husbandman, if I am not mistaken; but his chief work is the production of food from the earth?

EUTHYPHRO: Exactly.

SOCRATES: And of the many and fair things done by the gods, which is the chief or principal one?

EUTHYPHRO: I have told you already, Socrates, that to learn all these things accurately will be very tiresome. Let me simply say that piety or holiness is learning, how to please the gods in word and deed, by prayers and sacrifices. Such piety is the salvation of families and states, just as the impious, which is unpleasing to the gods, is their ruin and destruction.

SOCRATES: I think that you could have answered in much fewer words the chief question which I asked, Euthyphro, if you had chosen. But I see plainly that you are not disposed to instruct me—dearly not: else why, when we reached the point, did you turn aside? Had you only answered me I should have truly learned of you by this time the nature of piety. Now, as the asker of a question is necessarily dependent on the answerer, whither he leads I must follow; and can only ask again, what is the pious, and what is piety? Do you mean that they are a sort of science of praying and sacrificing?

EUTHYPHRO: Yes, I do.

SOCRATES: And sacrificing is giving to the gods, and prayer is asking of the gods?

EUTHYPHRO: Yes, Socrates.

SOCRATES: Upon this view, then piety is a science of asking and giving?

EUTHYPHRO: You understand me capitally, Socrates.

SOCRATES: Yes, my friend; the reason is that I am a votary of your science, and give my mind to it, and therefore nothing which you say will be thrown away upon me. Please then to tell me, what is the nature of this service to the gods? Do you mean that we prefer requests and give gifts to them?

EUTHYPHRO: Yes, I do.

SOCRATES: Is not the right way of asking to ask of them what we want?

EUTHYPHRO: Certainly.

SOCRATES: And the right way of giving is to give to them in return what they want of us. There would be no meaning in an art which gives to any one that which he does not want.

EUTHYPHRO: Very true, Socrates.

SOCRATES: Then piety, Euthyphro, is an art which gods and men have of doing business with one another?

EUTHYPHRO: That is an expression which you may use, if you like.

SOCRATES: But I have no particular liking for anything but the truth. I wish, however, that you would tell me what benefit accrues to the gods from our gifts. There is no doubt about what they give to us; for there is no good thing which they do not give; but how we can give any good thing to them in return is far from being equally clear. If they give everything and we give nothing, that must be an affair of business in which we have very greatly the advantage of them.

EUTHYPHRO: And do you imagine, Socrates, that any benefit accrues to the gods from our gifts?

SOCRATES: But if not, Euthyphro, what is the meaning of gifts which are conferred by us upon the gods?

EUTHYPHRO: What else, but tributes of honour; and, as I was just now saying, what pleases them?

SOCRATES: Piety, then, is pleasing to the gods, but not beneficial or dear to them?

EUTHYPHRO: I should say that nothing could be dearer.

SOCRATES: Then once more the assertion is repeated that piety is dear to the gods?

EUTHYPHRO: Certainly.

SOCRATES: And when you say this, can you wonder at your words not standing firm, but walking away? Will you accuse me of being the Daedalus who makes them walk away, not perceiving that there is another and far greater artist than Daedalus who makes them go round in a circle, and he is yourself; for the argument, as you will perceive, comes round to the same point. Were we not saying that the holy or pious was not the same with that which is loved of the gods? Have you forgotten?

EUTHYPHRO: I quite remember.

SOCRATES: And are you not saying that what is loved of the gods is holy; and is not this the same as what is dear to them—do you see?

EUTHYPHRO: True.

SOCRATES: Then either we were wrong in former assertion; or, if we were right then, we are wrong now.

EUTHYPHRO: One of the two must be true.

SOCRATES: Then we must begin again and ask, What is piety? That is an enquiry which I shall never be weary of pursuing as far as in me lies; and I entreat you not to scorn me, but to apply your mind to the utmost, and tell me the truth. For, if any man knows, you are he; and therefore I must detain you, like Proteus, until you tell. If you had not certainly known the nature of piety and impiety, I am confident that you would never, on behalf of a serf, have charged your aged father with murder. You would not have run such a risk of doing wrong in the sight of the gods, and you would have had too much respect for the opinions of men. I am sure, therefore, that you know the nature of piety and impiety. Speak out then, my dear Euthyphro, and do not hide your knowledge.

EUTHYPHRO: Another time, Socrates; for I am in a hurry, and must go now.

SOCRATES: Alas! my companion, and will you leave me in despair? I was hoping that you would instruct me in the nature of piety and impiety; and then I might have cleared myself of Meletus and his indictment. I would have told him that I had been enlightened by Euthyphro, and had given up rash innovations and speculations, in which I indulged only through ignorance, and that now I am about to lead a better life.

The Law of Human Nature

C. S. Lewis

C. S. Lewis *(1897–1963) was a professor of medieval literature at Oxford University and the University of Cambridge for most of his adult life. As a member of the "Inklings" with J. R. R. Tolkien, he composed the* Chronicles of Narnia *for children and wrote books on Christian apologetics for adults. A former atheist, he was asked by the BBC to give five-minute radio addresses on his understanding of the Christian faith. The following selection is the first five addresses in what was later entitled* Mere Christianity.

Every one has heard people quarrelling. Sometimes it sounds funny and some-times it sounds merely unpleasant; but however it sounds, I believe we can learn something very important from listening to the kinds of things they say. They say things like this: "How'd you like it if anyone did the same to you?"—"That's my seat, I was there first"—"Leave him alone, he isn't doing you any harm"—"Why should you shove in first?"—"Give me a bit of your orange, I gave you a bit of mine"—"Come on, you promised." People say things like that every day, edu-cated people as well as uneducated, and children as well as grown-ups.

Now what interests me about all these remarks is that the man who makes them is not merely saying that the other man's behaviour does not happen to please him. He is appealing to some kind of standard of behaviour which he expects the other man to know about. And the other man very seldom replies: "To hell with your standard." Nearly always he tries to make out that what he has been doing does not really go against the standard, or that if it does there is some special excuse. He pretends there is some special reason in this particular case why the person who took the seat first should not keep it, or that things were quite dif-ferent when he was given the bit of orange, or that something has turned up which lets him off keeping his promise. It looks, in fact, very much as if both parties had in mind some kind of Law or Rule of fair play or decent behaviour or morality or whatever you like to call it, about which they really agreed. And they have. If they had not, they might, of course, fight like animals, but they could not *quarrel* in the human sense of the word. Quarrelling means trying to show that the other man is in the wrong. And there would be no sense in trying to do that unless you and he had some sort of agreement as to what Right and Wrong are; just as there would be no sense in saying that a footballer had committed a foul unless there was some agreement about the rules of football.

Now this Law or Rule about Right and Wrong used to be called the Law of Nature. Nowadays, when we talk of the "laws of nature" we usually mean things like gravitation, or heredity, or the laws of chemistry. But when the older thinkers called the Law of Right and Wrong "the Law of Nature," they really meant the Law of *Human* Nature. The idea was that, just as all bodies are governed by the law of gravitation and organisms by biological laws, so the creature called man also had *his* law—with this great difference, that a body could not choose whether it obeyed the law of gravitation or not, but a man could choose either to obey the Law of Human Nature or to disobey it.

We may put this in another way. Each man is at every moment subjected to several sets of law but there is only one of these which he is free to disobey. As a body, he is subjected to gravitation and cannot disobey it; if you leave him unsupported in mid-air, he has no more choice about falling than a stone has. As an organism, he is subjected to various biological laws which he cannot disobey any more than an animal can. That is, he cannot disobey those laws which he shares with other things; but the law which is peculiar to his human nature, the law he does not share with animals or vegetables or inorganic things, is the one he can disobey if he chooses.

This law was called the Law of Nature because people thought that every one knew it by nature and did not need to be taught it. They did not mean, of course, that you might not find an odd individual here and there who did not know it, just as you find a few people who are colour-blind or have no ear for a tune. But taking the race as a whole, they thought that the human idea of decent behaviour was obvious to every one. And I believe they were right. If they were not, then all the things we said about the war were non-sense. What was the sense in saying the enemy were in the wrong unless Right is a real thing which the Nazis at bottom knew as well as we did and ought to have practiced? If they had no notion of what we mean by right, then, though we might still have had to fight them, we could no more have blamed them for that than for the colour of their hair.

I know that some people say the idea of a Law of Nature or decent behaviour known to all men is unsound, because different civilisations and different ages have had quite different moralities.

But this is not true. There have been differences between their moralities, but these have never amounted to anything like a total difference. If anyone will take the trouble to compare the moral teaching of, say, the ancient Egyptians, Babylonians, Hindus, Chinese, Greeks and Romans, what will really strike him will be how very like they are to each other and to our own. Some of the evidence for this I have put together in the appendix of another book called *The Abolition of Man;* but for our present purpose I need only ask the reader to think what a totally different morality would mean. Think of a country where people were admired for running away in battle, or where a man felt proud of doublecrossing all the people who had been kindest to him. You might just as well try to imagine a country where two and two made five. Men have differed as regards what people you ought to be unselfish to—whether it was only your own family, or your fellow countrymen, or everyone. But they have always agreed that you ought not to put yourself first. Selfishness has never been admired. Men have differed as to whether you should have one wife or four. But they have always agreed that you must not simply have any woman you liked.

But the most remarkable thing is this. Whenever you find a man who says he does not believe in a real Right and Wrong, you will find the same man going back on this a moment later. He may break his promise to you, but if you try breaking one to him he will be complaining "It's not fair" before you can say Jack Robinson. A nation may say treaties do not matter; but then, next minute, they spoil their case by saying that the particular treaty they want to break was an unfair one. But if treaties do not matter, and if there is no such thing as Right and Wrong—in other words, if there is no Law of Nature—what is the difference between a fair treaty and an unfair one? Have they not let the cat out of the bag and shown that, whatever they say, they really know the Law of Nature just like anyone else?

It seems, then, we are forced to believe in a real Right and Wrong. People may be sometimes mistaken about them, just as people sometimes get their sums wrong; but they are not a matter of mere taste and opinion any more than the multiplication table. Now if we are agreed about that, I go on to my next point, which is this. None of us are really keeping the Law of Nature. If there are any exceptions among you, I apologize to them. They had much better read some other work, for nothing I am going to say concerns them. And now, turning to the ordinary human beings who are left:

I hope you will not misunderstand what I am going to say. I am not preaching, and Heaven knows I do not pretend to be better than anyone else. I am only trying to call attention to a fact; the fact that this year, or this month, or more likely, this very day, we have failed to practice ourselves the kind of behaviour we expect from other people. There may be all sorts of excuses for us. That time you were so unfair to the children was when you were very tired. That slightly shady business about the money—the one you have almost forgotten—came when you were very hard up. And what you promised to do for old So-and-so and have never done— well, you never would have promised if you had known how frightfully busy you were going to be. And as for your behaviour to your wife (or husband) or sister (or brother) if I knew how irritating they could be, I would not wonder at it—and who the dickens am I, anyway? I am just the same. That is to say, I do not succeed in keeping the Law of Nature very well, and the moment anyone tells me I am not keeping it, there starts up in my mind a string of excuses as long as your arm. The question at the moment is not whether they are good excuses. The point is that they are one more proof of how deeply, whether we like it or not, we believe in the Law of Nature. If we do not believe in decent behaviour, why should we be so anxious to make excuses for not having behaved decently? The truth is, we believe in decency so much—we feel the Rule of Law pressing on us so—that we cannot bear to face the fact that we are breaking it, and consequently we try to shift the responsibility. For you notice that it is only for our bad behaviour that we find all these explanations. It is only our bad temper that we put down to being tired or worried or hungry; we put our good temper down to ourselves.

These, then, are the two points I wanted to make. First, that human beings, all over the earth, have this curious idea that they ought to behave in a certain way, and cannot really get rid of it. Secondly, that they do not in fact behave in that way. They know the Law of Nature; they break it. These two facts are the foundation of all clear thinking about ourselves and the universe we live in.

Some Objections

If they are the foundation, I had better stop to make that foundation firm before I go on. Some of the letters I have had show that a good many people find it difficult to understand just what this Law of Human Nature, or Moral Law, or Rule of Decent Behaviour is.

For example, some people wrote to me saying, "Isn't what you call the Moral Law simply our herd instinct and hasn't it been developed just like all our other instinct?" Now I do not deny that we may have a herd instinct: but that is not what I mean by the Moral Law. We all know what it feels like to be prompted by instinct—by mother love, or sexual instinct, or the instinct for food. It means that you feel a strong want or desire to act in a certain way. And, of course, we sometimes do feel just that sort of desire to help another person: and no doubt that desire is due to the herd instinct. But feeling a desire to help is quite different from feeling that you ought to help whether you want to or not. Supposing you hear a cry for help from a man in danger. You will probably feel two desires—one a desire to give help (due to your herd instinct), the other a desire to keep out of danger (due to the instinct for self-preservation). But you will find inside you, in addition to these two impulses, a third thing which tells you that you ought to follow the impulse to help, and suppress the impulse to run away. Now this thing that judges between two instincts, that decides which should be encouraged, cannot itself be either of them. You might as well say the sheet of music which tells you, at a given moment, to play one note on the piano and not another, is itself one of the notes on the keyboard. The Moral Law tells us the tune we have to play: our instincts are merely the keys.

Another way of seeing that the Moral Law is not simply one of our instincts is this. If two instincts are in conflict, and there is nothing in a creature's mind except those two instincts, obviously the stronger of the two must win. But at those moments when we are most conscious of the Moral Law, it usually seems to be telling us to side with the weaker of the two impulses. You probably *want* to be safe much more than you want to help the man who is drowning: but the Moral Law tells you to help him all the same. And surely it often tells us to try to make the right impulse stronger than it naturally is? I mean, we often feel it our duty to stimulate the herd instinct, by waking up our imaginations and arousing our pity and so on, so as to get up enough steam for doing the right thing. But clearly we are not acting *from* instinct when we set about making an instinct stronger than it is. The thing that says to you, "Your herd instinct is asleep. Wake it up," cannot itself *be* the herd instinct. The thing that tells you which note on the piano needs to be played louder cannot itself be that note.

Here is a third way of seeing it. If the Moral Law was one of our instincts, we ought to be able to point to some one impulse inside us which was always what we call "good," always in agreement with the rule of right behaviour. But you cannot. There is none of our impulses which the Moral Law may not sometimes tell us to suppress, and none which it may not sometimes tell us to encourage. It is a mistake to think that some of our impulses—say mother love or patriotism—are good, and others, like sex or the fighting instinct, are bad. All we mean is that the occasions on which the fighting instinct or the sexual desire need to be restrained are rather more frequent than those for restraining mother love or patriotism. But there are situations in which it is the duty of a married man to encourage his sexual impulse and of a soldier to encourage the fighting instinct. There are also occasions on which a mother's love for her own children or a man's love for his own country have to be suppressed or they will lead to unfairness towards other people's children or countries. Strictly speaking, there are no such things as good and bad impulses. Think once again of a piano. It has not got two kinds of notes on it, the "right" notes and the "wrong" ones. Every single note is right at one time and wrong at another. The Moral Law is not any one instinct or any set of instincts: it is something which makes a kind of tune (the tune we call goodness or right conduct) by directing the instincts.

By the way, this point is of great practical consequence. The most dangerous thing you can do is to take any one impulse of your own nature and set it up as the thing you ought to follow at all costs. There is not one of them which will not make us into devils if we set it up as an absolute guide. You might think love of humanity in general was safe, but it is not. If you leave out justice you will find yourself breaking agreements and faking evidence in trials "for the sake of humanity," and become in the end a cruel and treacherous man.

Other people wrote to me saying, "Isn't what you call the Moral Law just a social convention, something that is put into us by education?" I think there is a misunderstanding here. The people who ask that question are usually taking it for granted that if we have learned a thing from parents and teachers, then that thing must be merely a human invention. But, of course, that is not so. We all learned the multiplication table at school. A child who grew up alone on a desert island would not know it. But surely it does not follow that the multiplication table is simply a human convention, something human beings have made up for themselves and might have made different if they had liked? I fully agree that we learn the Rule of Decent Behaviour from parents and teachers, and friends and books, as we learn everything else. But some of the things we learn are mere conventions which might have been different—we learn to keep to the left of the road, but it might just as well have been the rule to keep to the right—and others of them, like mathematics, are real truths. The question is to which class the Law of Human Nature belongs.

There are two reasons for saying it belongs to the same class as mathematics. The first is, as I said in the first chapter, that though there are differences between the moral ideas of one time or country and those of another, the differences are not really very great—not nearly so great as most people imagine—and you can recognize the same law running through them all: whereas mere conventions, like the rule of the road or the kind of clothes people wear, may differ to any extent. The other reason is this. When you think about these differences between the morality of one people and another, do you think that the morality of one people is ever better or worse than that of another? Have any of the changes been improvements? If not, then of course there could never be any moral progress. Progress means not just changing, but changing for the better. If no set of moral ideas were truer or better than any other, there would be no sense in preferring civilised morality to savage morality, or Christian morality to Nazi morality. In fact, of course, we all do believe that some moralities are better than others. We do believe that some of the people who tried to change the moral ideas of their own age were what we would call Reformers or Pioneers— people who understood morality better than their neighbours did. Very well then. The moment you say that one set of moral ideas can be better than another, you are, in fact, measuring them both by a standard, saying that one of them conforms to that standard more nearly than the other. But the standard that measures two things is something different from either. You are, in fact, comparing them both with some Real Morality, admitting that there is such a thing as a real Right, independent of what people think, and that some people's ideas get nearer to that real Right than others. Or put in this way. If your moral ideas can be truer, and those of the Nazis less true, there must be something— some Real Morality—for them to be true about. The reason why your idea of New York can be truer or less true than mine is that New York is a real place, existing quite apart from what either of us thinks. If when each of us said "New York" each meant merely. "The town I am imagining in my own head," how could one of us have truer ideas than the other? There would be no question of truth or falsehood at all. In the same way, if the Rule of Decent Behaviour meant simply "whatever each nation happens to approve," there would be no sense in saying that any one nation had ever been more correct in its approval than any other; no sense in saying that the world could ever grow morally better or morally worse.

I conclude then, that though the differences between people's ideas of Decent Behaviour often make you suspect that there is no real natural Law of Behaviour at all, yet the things we are bound to think about these differences really prove just the opposite. But one word before I end. I have met people who exaggerate the differences, because they have not distinguished between differences of belief about facts. For example, one man said to me, "Three hundred years ago people in England were putting witches to death. Was that what you call the Rule of Human Nature or Right Conduct?" But surely the reason we do not execute witches is that we do not believe there are such things. If we did—if we really thought that there were people going about who had sold themselves to the devil and received supernatural powers from him in return and were using these powers to kill their neighbours or drive them mad or bring bad weather, surely we would all agree that if anyone deserved the death penalty, then these filthy quislings did. There is no difference of moral principle here: the difference is simply about matter of fact. It may be a great advance in knowledge not to believe in witches: there is no moral advance in not executing them when you do not think they are there. You would not call a man humane for ceasing to set mousetraps if he did so because he believed there were no mice in the house.

The Reality of the Law

I now go back to what I said at the end of the first chapter, that there were two odd things about the human race. First, that they were haunted by the idea of a sort of behaviour they ought to practise, what you might call fair play, or decency, or morality, or the Law of Nature. Second, that they did not in fact do so. Now some of you may wonder why I called this odd. It may seem to you the most natural thing in the world. In particular, you may have thought I was rather hard on the human race. After all, you may say, what I call breaking the Law of Right and Wrong or of Nature, only means that people are not perfect. And why on earth should I expect them to be? That would be a good answer if what I was trying to do was to fix the exact amount of blame which is due to us for not behaving as we expect others to behave. But that is not my job at all. I am not concerned at present with blame; I am trying to find out truth. And from that point of view the very idea of something being imperfect, of its not being what it ought to be, has certain consequences.

If you take a thing like a stone or a tree, it is what it is and there seems no sense in saying it ought to have been otherwise. Of course you may say a stone is "the wrong shape" if you want to use it for a rockery, or that a tree is a bad tree because it does not give you as much shade as you expected. But all you mean is that the stone or tree does not happen to be convenient for some purpose of your own. You are not, except as a joke, blaming them for that. You really know, that, given the weather and the soil, the tree could not have been any different. What we, from our point of view, call a "bad" tree is obeying the laws of its nature just as much as a "good" one.

Now have you noticed what follows? It follows that what we usually call the laws of nature—the way weather works on a tree for example—may not really be *laws* in the strict sense, but only in a manner of speaking. When you say that falling stones always obey the law of gravitation, is not this much the same as saying that the law only means "what stones always do"? You do not really think that when a stone is let go, it suddenly remembers that it is under orders to fall to the ground. You only mean that, in fact, it does fall. In other words, you cannot be sure that there is anything over and above the facts themselves, any law about what ought to happen, as distinct from what does happen. The laws of nature, as applied to stones or trees, may only mean "what Nature, in fact, does." But if you turn to the Law of Human Nature, the Law of Decent Behavior, it is a different matter. That law certainly does not mean "what human beings, in fact, do"; for as I said before, many of them do not obey this law at all, and none of them obey it completely. The law of gravity tells you what stones do if you drop them; but the Law of Human Nature tells you what human beings ought to do and do not. In other words, when you are dealing with humans, something else comes in above and beyond the actual facts. You have the facts (how men do behave) and you also have something else (how they ought to behave). In the rest of the universe there need not be anything but the facts. Electrons and molecules behave in a certain way, and certain results follow, and that may be the whole story.* But men behave in a certain way and that is not the whole story, for all the time you know that they ought to behave differently.

Now this is really so peculiar that one is tempted to try to explain it away. For instance, we might try to make out that when you say a man ought not to act as he does, you only mean the same as when you say that a stone is the wrong shape; namely, that what he is doing happens to be inconvenient to you. But that is simply untrue. A man occupying the corner seat in the train because he got there first, and a man who slipped into it while my back was turned and removed my bag, are both equally inconvenient. But I blame the second man and do not blame the first. I am not angry—except perhaps for a moment before I come to my senses—with a

---

* I do not think it *is* the whole story, as you will see later. I mean that, as far as the argument has gone up to date, it *may* be.

man who trips me up by accident; I am angry with a man who tries to trip me up even if he does not succeed. Yet the first has hurt me and the second has not. Sometimes the behaviour which I call bad is not inconvenient to me at all, but the very opposite. In war, each side may find a traitor on the other side very useful. But though they use him and pay him they regard him as human vermin. So you cannot say that what we call decent behaviour in others is simply the behaviour that happens to be useful to us. And as for decent behaviour in ourselves, I suppose it is pretty obvious that it does not mean the behaviour that pays. It means things like being content with thirty shillings when you might have got three pounds, doing school work honestly when it would be easy to cheat, leaving a girl alone when you would like to make love to her, staying in dangerous places when you could go somewhere safer, keeping promises you would rather not keep, and telling the truth even when it makes you look a fool.

Some people say that though decent conduct does not mean what pays each particular person at a particular moment, still, it means what pays the human race as a whole; and that consequently there is no mystery about it. Human beings, after all, have some sense; they see that you cannot have real safety or happiness except in a society where every one plays fair, and it is because they see this that they try to behave decently. Now, of course, it is perfectly true that safety and happiness can only come from individuals, classes, and nations being honest and fair and kind to each other. It is one of the most important truths in the world. But as an explanation of why we feel as we do about Right and Wrong it just misses the point. If we ask: "Why ought I to be unselfish?" and you reply "Because it is good for society," we may then ask, "Why should I care what's good for society except when it happens to pay *me* personally?" and then you will have to say, "Because you ought to be unselfish"—which simply brings us back to where we started. You are saying what is true, but you are not getting any further. If a man asked what was the point of playing football, it would not be much good saying "in order to score goals," for trying to score goals is the game itself, not the reason for the game, and you would really only be saying that football was football—which is true, but not worth saying. In the same way, if a man asks what is the point of behaving decently, it is no good replying, "in order to benefit society," for trying to benefit society, in other words being unselfish (for "society" after all only means "other people"), is one of the things decent behaviour consists in; all you are really saying is that decent behaviour is decent behaviour. You would have said just as much if you had stopped at the statement, "Men ought to be unselfish."

And that is where I do stop. Men ought to be unselfish, ought to be fair. Not that men are unselfish, nor that they like being unselfish, but that they ought to be. The Moral Law, or Law of Human Nature, is not simply a fact about human behaviour in the same way as the Law of Gravitation is, or may be, simply a fact about how heavy objects behave. On the other hand, it is not a mere fancy, for we cannot get rid of the idea, and most of the things we say and think about men would be reduced to nonsense if we did. And it is not simply a statement about how we should like men to behave for our own convenience; for the behaviour we call bad or unfair is not exactly the same as the behaviour we find inconvenient, and may even be the opposite. Consequently, this Rule of Right and Wrong, or Law of Human Nature, or whatever you call it, must somehow or other be a real thing—a thing that is really there, not made up by ourselves. And yet it is not a fact in the ordinary sense, in the same way as our actual behaviour is a fact. It begins to look as if we shall have to admit that there is more than one kind of reality; that, in this particular case, there is something above and beyond the ordinary facts of men's behaviour, and yet quite definitely real—a real law, which none of us made, but which we find pressing on us.

What Lies Behind the Law

Let us sum up what we have reached so far. In the case of stones and trees and things of that sort, what we call the Laws of Nature may not be anything except a way of speaking. When you say that nature is governed by certain laws, this may only mean that nature does, in fact, behave in a certain way. The so-called laws may not be anything real—anything above and beyond the actual facts which we observe. But in the case of Man, we saw that this will not do. The Law of Human Nature, or Right and Wrong, must be something above and beyond the actual facts of human behaviour. In this case, besides the actual facts, you have something else—a real law which we did not invent and which we know we ought to obey.

I now want to consider what this tells us about the universe we live in. Ever since men were able to think, they have been wondering what this universe really is and how it came to be there. And, very roughly, two views have been held. First, there is what is called the materialist view. People who take that view think that matter and space just happen to exist, and always have existed, nobody knows why; and that the matter, behaving in certain fixed ways, has just happened, by a sort of fluke, to produce creatures like ourselves who are able to think. By one chance in a thousand something hit our sun and made it produce the planets; and by another thousandth chance the chemicals necessary for life, and the right temperature, occurred on one of these planets, and so some of the matter on this earth came alive; and then, by a very long series of chances, the living creatures developed into things like us. The other view is the religious view.** According to it, what is behind the universe is more like a mind than it is like anything else we know. That is to say, it is conscious, and has purposes, and prefers one thing to another. And on this view it made the universe, partly for purposes we do not know, but partly, at any rate, in order to produce creatures like itself—I mean, like

---

** See Note at the end of this chapter.

itself to the extent of having minds. Please do not think that one of these views was held a long time ago and that the other has gradually taken its place. Wherever there have been thinking men both views turn up. And note this too. You cannot find out which view is the right one by science in the ordinary sense. Science works by experiments. It watches how things behave. Every scientific statement in the long run, however complicated it looks, really means something like, "I pointed the telescope to such and such a part of the sky at 2:20 A.M. on January 15th and saw so-and-so," or, "I put some of this stuff in a pot and heated it to such-and-such a temperature and it did so-and-so." Do not think I am saying anything against science: I am only saying what its job is. And the more scientific a man is, the more (I believe) he would agree with me that this is the job of science—and a very useful and necessary job it is too. But why anything comes to be there at all, and whether there is anything behind the things science observes—something of a different kind—this is not a scientific question. If there is "Something Behind," then either it will have to remain altogether unknown to men or else make itself known in some different way. The statement that there is any such thing, and the statement that there is no such thing, are neither of them statements that science can make. And real scientists do not usually make them. It is usually the journalists and popular novelists who have picked up a few odds and ends of half-baked science from textbooks who go in for them. After all, it is really a matter of common sense. Supposing science ever became complete so that it knew every single thing in the whole universe. Is it not plain that the questions, "Why is there a universe?" "Why does it go on as it does?" "Has it any meaning?" would remain just as they were?

Now the position would be quite hopeless but for this. There is one thing, and only one, in the whole universe which we know more about than we could learn from external observation. That one thing is Man. We do not merely observe men we *are* men. In this case we have, so to speak, inside information; we are in the know. And because of that, we know that men find themselves under a moral law, which they did not make, and cannot quite forget even when they try, and which they know they ought to obey. Notice the following point. Anyone studying Man from the outside as we study electricity or cabbages, not knowing our language and consequently not able to get any inside knowledge from us, but merely observing what we did, would never get the slightest evidence that we had this moral law. How could he? For his observations would only show what we did, and the moral law is about what we ought to do. In the same way, if there were anything above or behind the observed facts in the case of stones or the weather, we, by studying them from outside, could never hope to discover it.

The position of the question, then, is like this. We want to know whether the universe simply happens to be what it is for no reason or whether there is a power behind it that makes it what it is. Since that power, if it exists, would be not one of the observed facts but a reality which makes them, no mere observation of the facts can find it. There is only one case in which we can know whether there is anything more, namely our own case, and in that one case we find there is. Or put it the other way round. If there was a controlling power outside the universe, it could not show itself to us as one of the facts inside the universe—no more than the architect of a house could actually be a wall or staircase or fireplace in that house. The only way in which we could expect it to show itself would be inside ourselves as an influence or a command trying to get us to behave in a certain way. And that is just what we do find inside ourselves. Surely this ought to arouse our suspicions? In the only case where you can expect to get an answer, the answer turns out to be Yes; and in the other cases, where you do not get an answer, you see why you do not. Suppose someone asked me, when I see a man in a blue uniform going down the street leaving little paper packets at each house, why I suppose that they contain letters? I should reply, "Because whenever he leaves a similar little packet for me I find it does contain a letter." And if he then objected, "But you've never seen all these letters which you think the other people are getting," I should say, "Of course not, and I shouldn't expect to, because they're not addressed to me. I'm explaining the packets I'm not allowed to open by the ones I am allowed to open." It is the same about this question. The only packet I am allowed to open is Man. When I do, especially when I open that particular man called Myself, I find that I do not exist on my own, that I am under a law; that somebody or something wants me to behave in a certain way. I do not, of course, think that if I could get inside a stone or a tree I should find exactly the same thing, just as I do not think all the other people in the street get the same letters as I do. I should expect, for instance, to find that the stone had to obey the law of gravity—that whereas the sender of the letters merely tells me to obey the law of my human nature, He compels the stone to obey the laws of its stony nature. But I should expect to find that there was, so to speak, a sender of letters in both cases, a Power behind the facts, a Director, a Guide.

Do not think I am going faster than I really am. I am not yet within a hundred miles of the God of Christian theology. All I have got to is a Something which is directing the universe, and which appears in me as a law urging me to do right and making me feel responsible and uncomfortable when I do wrong. I think we have to assume it is more like a mind than it is like anything else we know—because after all the only other thing we know is matter and you can hardly imagine a bit of matter giving instructions. But, of course, it need not be very like a mind, still less like a person. In the next chapter we shall see if we can find out anything more about it. But one word of warning. There has been a great deal of soft soap talked about God for the last hundred years. That is not what I am offering. You can cut all that out.

NOTE.—In order to keep this section short enough when it was given on the air, I mentioned only the Materialist view and the Religious view. But to be complete I ought to mention the Inbetween view called Life-Force philosophy, or Creative Evolution, or Emergent Evolution. The wittiest expositions of it come in the works of Bernard Shaw, but the most profound ones in those of Bergson. People who hold this view say that the small variations by which life on this planet "evolved" from the lowest forms to Man were not due to chance but to the "striving" or "purposiveness" of a Life-Force. When people say this we must ask them whether by Life-Force they mean something with a mind or not. If they do, then "a mind bringing life into existence and leading it to perfection" is really a God, and their view is thus identical with the Religious. If they do not, then what is the sense in saying that something without a mind "strives" or has "purposes"? This seems to me fatal to their view. One reason why many people find Creative Evolution so attractive is that it gives one much of the emotional comfort of believing in God and none of the less pleasant consequences. When you are feeling fit and the sun is shining and you do not want to believe that the whole universe is a mere mechanical dance of atoms, it is nice to be able to think of this great mysterious Force rolling on through the centuries and carrying you on its crest. If, on the other hand, you want to do something rather shabby, the Life-Force, being only a blind force, with no morals and no mind, will never interfere with you like that troublesome God we learned about when we were children. The Life-Force is a sort of tame God. You can switch it on when you want, but it will not bother you. All the thrills of religion and none of the cost. Is the Life-Force the greatest achievement of wishful thinking the world has yet seen?

We Have Cause to Be Uneasy

I ended my last Chapter with the idea that in the Moral Law somebody or something from beyond the material universe was actually getting at us. And I expect when I reached that point some of you felt a certain annoyance. You may even have thought that 1 had played a trick on you—that I had been carefully wrapping up to look like philosophy what turns out to be one more "religious jaw." You may have felt you were ready to listen to me as long as you thought I had anything new to say; but if it turns out to be only religion, well, the world has tried that and "you cannot put the clock back. If anyone is feeling that way I should like to say three things to him.

First, as to putting the clock back. Would you think I was joking if I said that you can put a clock back, and that if the clock is wrong it is often a very sensible thing to do? But I would rather get away from that whole idea of clocks. We all want progress. But progress means getting nearer to the place where you want to be. And if you have taken a wrong turning, then to go forward does not get you any nearer. If you are on the wrong road, progress means doing an about-turn and walking back to the right road; and in that case the man who turns back soonest is the most progressive man. We have all seen this when doing arithmetic. When I have started a sum the wrong way, the sooner I admit this and go back and start over again, the faster I shall get on. There is nothing progressive about being pig-headed and refusing to admit a mistake. And I think if you look at the present state of the world, it is pretty plain that humanity has been making some big mistake. We are on the wrong road. And if that is so, we must go back. Going back is the quickest way on.

Then, secondly, this has not yet turned exactly into a "religious jaw." We have not yet got as far as the God of any actual religion, still less the God of that particular religion called Christianity. We have only got as far as a Somebody or Something behind the Moral Law. We are not taking anything from the Bible or the Churches, we are trying to see what we can find out about this Somebody on our own steam. And I want to make it quite clear that what we find out on our own steam is something that gives us a shock. We have two bits of evidence about the Somebody. One is the universe He has made. If we used that as our only clue, then I think we should have to conclude that He was a great artist (for the universe is a very beautiful place), but also that He is quite merciless and no friend to man (for the universe is a very dangerous and terrifying place). The other bit of evidence is that Moral Law which He has put into our minds. And this is a better bit of evidence than the other, because it is inside information. You find out more about God from the Moral Law than from the universe in general just as you find out more about a man by listening to his conversation than by looking at a house he has built. Now, from this second bit of evidence we conclude that the Being behind the universe is intensely interested in right conduct—in fair play, unselfishness, courage, good faith, honesty and truthfulness. In that sense we should agree with the account given by Christianity and some other religions, that God is "good." But do not let us go too fast here. The Moral Law does not give us any grounds for thinking that God is "good" in the sense of being indulgent, or soft, or sympa-thetic. There is nothing indulgent about the Moral Law. It is as hard as nails. It tells you to do the straight thing and it does not seem to care how painful, or danger-ous, or difficult it is to do. If God is like the Moral Law, then He is not soft. It is no use, at this stage, saying that what you mean by a "good" God is a God who can forgive. You are going too quickly. Only a Person can forgive. And we have not yet got as far as a personal God—only as far as a power, behind the Moral Law, and more like a mind than it is like anything else. But it may still be very unlike a Person. If it is pure impersonal mind, there may be no sense in asking it to make allowances for you or let you off, just as there is no sense in asking the multiplica-tion table to let you off when you do your sums wrong. You are bound to get the wrong answer. And it is no use either saying that if there is a God of that sort—an impersonal absolute goodness—then you do not like Him and are not going to bother about Him. For the trouble is that one part of you is on His side and really agrees with His disapproval of human greed and trickery and exploitation. You may want Him to make an exception in your own case, to let you off this one time; but you know at bottom that unless the power behind the world really and unalterably detests that sort of behaviour, then He cannot to be good. On the other hand, we know that if there does exist an absolute goodness it must hate most of what we do. That is the terrible fix we are in. If the universe is not governed by an absolute goodness, then all our efforts are in the long run hopeless. But if it is, then we are making ourselves enemies to that goodness every day, and are not in the least likely to do any better tomorrow, and so our case is hopeless again. We cannot do without it, and we cannot do with it. God is the only comfort, He is also the supreme terror: the thing we most need and the thing we most want to hide from. He is our only possible ally, and we have made ourselves His enemies. Some people talk as if meeting the gaze of absolute goodness would be fun. They need to think again. They are still only playing with religion. Goodness is either the great safety or the great danger—according to the way you react to it. And we have reacted the wrong way.

Now my third point. When I chose to get to my real subject in this roundabout way, I was not trying to play any kind of trick on you. I had a different reason. My reason was that Christianity simply does not make sense until you have faced the sort of facts I have been describing. Christianity tells people to repent and promises them forgiveness. It therefore has nothing (as far as I know) to say to people who do not know they have done anything to repent of and who do not feel that they need any forgiveness. It is after you have realised that there is a real Moral Law, and a Power behind the law, and that you have broken that law and put yourself wrong with that Power—it is after all this, and not a moment sooner, that Christianity begins to talk. When you know you are sick, you will listen to the doctor. When you have realised that our position is nearly desperate you will begin to understand what the Christians are talking about. They offer an explanation of how we got into our present state of both hating goodness and loving it. They offer an explanation of how God can be this impersonal mind at the back of the Moral Law and yet also a Person. They tell you how the demands of this law, which you and I cannot meet, have been met on our behalf, how God Himself becomes a man to save man from the disapproval of God. It is an old story and if you want to go into it you will no doubt consult people who have more authority to talk about it than I have. All I am doing is to ask people to face the facts—to understand the questions which Christianity claims to answer. And they are very terrifying facts. I wish it was possible to say something more agreeable. But I must say what I think true. Of course, I quite agree that the Christian religion is, in the long run, a thing of unspeakable comfort. But it does not begin in comfort; it begins in the dismay I have been describing, and it is no use at all trying to go on to that comfort without first going through that dismay. In religion, as in war and everything else, comfort is the one thing you cannot get by looking for it. If you look for truth, you may find comfort in the end: If you look for comfort you will not get either comfort or truth—only soft soap and wishful thinking to begin with and, in the end, despair. Most of us have got over the prewar wishful thinking about international politics. It is time we did the same about religion.

Worshiping in Ignorance

Stephen R. Prothero

Stephen R. Prothero *is a professor of religion at Boston University. He is the author of numerous books including* Religious Literacy: What Americans Need to Know. *In his latest book,* God is Not One, *Prothero argues that "religion is not merely a private affair. It matters socially, economically, politically, and militarily. Religion may or may not move mountains, but it is one of the prime movers in politics worldwide." In this selection, Prothero suggests that most Americans are ignorant of the most basic tenets of many religions and that religious literacy is necessary for civic engagement.*

For the past two years, I have given students in my introductory religious-studies course at Boston University a religious-literacy quiz. I ask them to list the four Gospels, Roman Catholicism's seven sacraments, and the Ten Commandments. I ask them to name the holy book of Islam. They do not fare well.

In their quizzes, they inform me that Ramadan is a Jewish holiday, that Revelation is one of the first five books of the Hebrew Bible, and that Paul led the Israelites on the Exodus out of Egypt. This year I had a Hindu student who couldn't name one Hindu scripture, a Baptist student who didn't know that "Blessed are the poor in spirit" is a Bible quote, and Catholic students unfamiliar with the golden rule. Over the past two years, only 17 percent of my students passed the quiz.

"Cultural literacy" has been hotly debated ever since E. D. Hirsch Jr.'s best seller of that name injected the desideratum into the culture wars in 1987. Today religious illiteracy is at least as pervasive as cultural illiteracy, and certainly more dangerous. Religious illiteracy is more dangerous because religion is the most volatile constituent of culture. Religion has been, in addition to one of the greatest forces for good in world history, one of the greatest forces for evil.

Nonetheless, Americans remain profoundly ignorant about their own religions and those of others. According to recent polls, most American adults cannot name even one of the four Gospels, and many high-school seniors think that Sodom and Gomorrah were husband and wife. A few years ago, no one in Jay Leno's *The*

Tonight Show audience could name any of the Twelve Apostles, but everyone was able to shout out the four Beatles.

One might imagine that religious illiteracy is nothing more than a religious problem—a challenge for ministers, priests, rabbis, and imams. But in the United States today, presidents quote from the Bible during their inauguration speeches, members of Congress cite the "Good Samaritan" story in debates over immigration legislation, and politicians of all stripes invoke the Book of Genesis in debates over the environment. So religious ignorance is a civic problem, too.

In an era when the public square is, rightly or wrongly, awash in religious rhetoric, can one really participate fully in public life without knowing something about Christianity and the world's other major religions? Is it possible to decide whether intelligent design is "religious" or "scientific" without some knowledge of religion as well as science? Is it possible to determine whether the effort to yoke Christianity and "family values" makes sense without knowing what sort of "family man" Jesus was? Is it possible to adjudicate between President Bush's description of Islam as a religion of peace and the conviction of many televangelists that Islam is a religion of war, without some basic information about Muhammad and the Quran?

Unfortunately, U.S. citizens today lack this basic religious literacy. As a result, many Americans are too easily swayed by demagogues. Few of us are able to challenge claims made by politicians or pundits about Islam's place in the war on terrorism, or about what the Bible says concerning homosexuality. This ignorance imperils our public life, putting citizens in the thrall of talking heads and effectively transferring power from the Third Estate (the people) to the Fourth (the press).

Over the past few months, Harvard faculty members and administrators considered whether to require a religious-studies course of all Harvard undergraduates. In December the university announced that it had dropped the proposed "reason and faith" requirement. In the process, Harvard dropped the ball. Since September 11, 2001, religion has become an increasingly visible topic on college campuses. Enrollments are up sharply in religious-studies courses at my university. But most colleges—Harvard included—continue to chum out graduates who do not know the first thing about either Christianity or Islam, the Bible or the Quran. That isn't just a shame—it is a scandal.

Rather than follow Harvard's lead and turn a blind eye to our crisis of religious ignorance, American colleges should be addressing this problem by doing what Harvard failed to do: requiring a religious-studies course of all undergraduates.

Since the 1960s, the academic study of religion has found a home at many private and public colleges and universities in the United States. Programs and departments in religious studies at roughly 800 campuses offer a major, and courses on the Bible and world religions count toward general-education requirements at most of those colleges. Religious-studies courses are required of all students in most Catholic and evangelical-Protestant institutions. Yet the vast majority of public and nonsectarian private colleges do not require a single course in the subject. So every year, colleges award bachelor's degrees to millions of students who cannot name the first book of the Bible, who think that Jesus parted the Red Sea and Moses agonized in the Garden of Gethsemane, who know nothing about what Islam teaches about war and peace, and who cannot name one salient difference between Hinduism and Buddhism.

Think of the ripple effect if recipients of B.A. degrees in communications—our future journalists, newscasters, television producers, and film directors—knew something about the world's religions. Or if college graduates going into politics or business were even mildly conversant with the Quran.

Thinkers who argue for greater attention to religion in public life are often assumed to have a theological agenda. Such assumptions are often correct. My goal, however, is civic. I do not want to make American colleges or American undergraduates more religious. My brief for religious literacy proceeds on purely secular grounds, on the theory that Americans are not equipped for citizenship (or, for that matter, cocktail-party conversation) without a basic understanding of Christianity and the world's other religions. The college courses I support would teach about religion, not proselytize for it.

In recent years, George M. Marsden, a historian at the University of Notre Dame, and Warren A. Nord, a lecturer in philosophy at the University of North Carolina at Chapel Hill, have argued for the return of "normative religious teaching" to American colleges and universities. They want professors not only to describe religious traditions but also to weigh in on their vices and virtues. Each of these scholars has also argued that it is essential for students to learn "religious perspectives" in disciplines other than religious studies—to study theological critiques of classical economics and "religious interpretations of history." "There should be room," writes Nord, for both objective analysis of religion and *"normative* reflection on religion."

What Marsden and Nord seem to want is to make colleges and universities (or pockets of them) into religious places once again—to resurrect the big questions of God, creation, and sin not only in departments of religion but also in courses in philosophy and economics and history and political science. My proposal is more modest and less controversial. I simply want to persuade the lords of American higher education to stop trivializing this subject. There is no reason not to expect from America's future leaders at least minimal religious literacy.

Literacy of this sort could be cultivated in a wide variety of courses. The most obvious is a world-religions course that covers, at a minimum, Judaism, Christianity, Islam, Buddhism, Hinduism, and the religions of China. During such a course, students would learn the basic symbols, beliefs, practices, and narratives of those religions. At the end, they would be better equipped to understand what is at stake today for Muslims, Christians, and Jews in Jerusalem; for Hindus and Muslims in Kashmir; and for Hindus and Buddhists in Sri Lanka.

Cynics might reply that this is too little, too late—that our collective amnesia about religion is too far advanced. If, as the French sociologist Danièle Hervieu-Léger has argued, religion is a chain of memory, then Americans have broken the chain. Perhaps that is the case. But I believe otherwise. In fact, I am convinced that American higher education is ripe for change.

Over the course of American history, ignorance about religion has been fueled by a series of moral commitments to religious tolerance that had the effect of obscuring the differences between religious traditions. In the aftermath of the Second Great Awakening, in the early 19th century, Americans obscured the differences between Protestant denominations in order to cooperate on abolitionism, women's rights, and other social reforms. During the religious revival that followed World War II, they obscured the differences between Christianity and Judaism in order to fight atheistic communism. More recently they have overlooked, in the name of the Abrahamic tradition, the differences among Muslims, Christians, and Jews, while Americans of the "spiritual but not religious" variety have overlooked, in the name of compassion, the differences between Buddhism and Christianity, Hinduism and Judaism.

But a countervailing impulse now seems to be at play—a recovery of particularity in both academe and American culture writ large. The melting pot is now widely seen as a myth. We are, as the Catholic writer Michael Novak put it, "unmeltable ethnics." But we aren't proud just of our Irishness or our Africanness, of being brown or red. We are proud as well of our Coptic Orthodoxy and our Tibetan Buddhism, our Orthodox Judaism and our evangelical Protestantism. Recent immigrants from India to the United States report few pressures to give up Hinduism; in fact, Hindus typically become more religious, not less, upon moving here. Even conservative-Christian critiques of the "naked public square" are often framed in terms of this new devotion to particularity. And born-again Christians are increasingly coming out of the closet as students and professors who have accepted Jesus as Savior and Lord.

There is doubtless a widening gap in the United States between what we actually know about religion and what we ought to know. But there is also a determination to narrow that gap—a sense of shame, or guilt at least, about our forgetfulness, about breaking the chains of memory that once bound our ancestors to one another, and to the particular religious traditions they held dear. Catholic laments over bygone Catholic literacy are routine, as are evangelical laments over the fall into biblical illiteracy and Jewish hand-wringing over Jewish illiteracy.

When it comes to religion, we have had good reasons for this collective amnesia. More often than not, it was tolerance—first for other Protestants, then for Catholics and Jews, and most recently for Muslims, Buddhists, and Hindus—that drove us to jettison theology for morality, to trade in the doctrines and stories of our religious traditions for the promise of social order. There are surely many Americans today who are delighted to have the not-so-golden age of bitter sectarian disputes about infant baptism and holy communion behind us, who are convinced that nothing good can come of learning about how theologians reckon the number of angels dancing on the head of a pin. But the costs of perpetuating religious ignorance are too high in a world in which faith moves, if not mountains, then elections and armies. It does nothing for the secular left to remain ignorant of the religious right, or vice versa. And it puts the United States at risk to remain ignorant as a society of the beliefs and practices of Confucians in North Korea, Hindus in India, and Muslims in Iran.

In debates about the fate of the Middle East, the propriety of gay marriage, and the politics of Islam, the stakes are too high to defer to politicians and pundits. Given the ubiquity of religious discourse in American public life, and the public power of religion at home and abroad, we Americans—whether liberals or conservatives, believers or unbelievers—need to learn about evangelicalism and Islam for ourselves, to see for ourselves what the Bible says about family values, homosexuality, war, and capital punishment, and to be aware of what Islam says about those things, too.

Each of the world's great religions has wrestled for centuries with the foundational questions of life and death and whatever (if anything) lies beyond. Each has developed sophisticated theologies for making sense of other religions, for regulating war, for fighting injustice. But we as a nation are forgetting those hard-won theologies, replacing them in many cases with bromides that only an advertising hack could be proud of—bromides, it should be noted, that are themselves ripe for replacement whenever a sexier advertising pitch comes along. Moreover, the politicians and pundits eager to exploit those bromides for partisan purposes— to turn God, Jesus, and Muhammad into pawns in their political and military games—are legion.

From this nation's beginnings, it has been widely understood that the success of the American experiment rests on an educated citizenry. Today it is simply irresponsible to use the word "educated" to describe college graduates who are ignorant of the ancient creeds, stories, and rituals that continue to motivate the beliefs and behaviors of the overwhelming majority of the world's population. In a world as robustly religious as ours, it is foolish to imagine that such graduates are equipped to participate fully in the politics of the nation or the affairs of the world.

It is now commonplace in the United States to outsource computer programming and customer-service work to developing nations. But democracy cannot be outsourced. To continue to defer to television's talkocracy on matters as important as the political theology of Islam, the biblical view of marriage, or what Jesus would do about the environment is to recuse ourselves from democracy itself. The alternative is to "get" religion—to cultivate in our college students basic literacy about the world's religions.

Moving forward on the problem of religious illiteracy will require compromise on both the secular left and the religious right. In *Divided by God* (Farrar, Straus and Giroux, 2005), the New York University law professor Noah Feldman charts a creative middle path between "values evangelicals" and "legal secularists." On the broader question of religion in the public square, he proposes a compromise that allows for more leeway on public displays of religion but stricter controls over the flow of state funds to religious institutions.

Setting aside the merits of this particular effort to reunite a nation "divided by God" into blues and reds, Feldman is right to sense a desire for reconciliation. Most Americans are weary of the culture wars, which owe their continued existence almost entirely to partisan politicians and pundits—in other words, to that minuscule portion of the population that owes its livelihood and celebrity to biased bickering. No one wants to revive the Bible wars of 19th-century public schools, yet the vast majority of Americans want their children to learn more about religion. To take one example, a required world-religions course for ninth graders in the highly diverse school district of Modesto, Calif, has caused little controversy and won districtwide support not only from teachers and administrators but also from parents. Only two or three students out of 3,000 assigned to the course each year choose to opt out of the requirement.

Progress on this score will take compromise, too. The secular left will need to yield on the dogma that religion has no place in the public square. The religious right will need to give up its desire to use our nation's classrooms for proselytizing purposes. The middle path here is instruction that takes believers seriously but refuses to plump either for or against what they believe, that leaves responsibility for inculcating faith where it rightly belongs: in homes and religious congregations. But this middle path is not complicit in the conspiracy of silence that has kept Americans religiously illiterate for generations. It gives both religion and American undergraduates their due.

Religious Ideas: Should They Be Critically Engaged or Given a Pass?

David A. Hollinger

David Hollinger *is currently the Preston Hotchkis Professor of History at the University of California, Berkeley. His works include his widely used source book,* The American Intellectual Tradition *(2006) and* Cosmopolitanism and Solidarity: Studies in Ethnoracial, Religious, and Professional Affiliation in the United States *(2006), as well as many articles and papers which focus on the intellectual history of America. His works cover a wide range including science, cosmopolitanism, diversity and religion and its role in the American intellectual process. He received his PhD from the University of California, Berkeley, and is currently President Elect of the Organization of American Historians.*

Would the democratic public culture of the United States be well served by a robust, critical discussion of religious ideas? Or do principles of ethical propriety and political prudence encourage us instead to ignore each other's ideas about religion, however silly they may seem?

Two recent developments give point to these questions.

One is a striking increase in the number and intensity of demands for a greater role for religion in public affairs, and for more "flexible" and "realistic" approaches to the constitutional separation of church and state.[1] Faith-based initiatives are widely supported by leaders of both political parties. The very idea of a distinctly secular public sphere is said to entail a bias against religion. Republicans tend to favor more religion in public life than do many leading Democrats, but the latter scramble to assure their constituents that they, too, learned a lot from the nuns when they were in parochial school, or that they still attend services at a church or synagogue. The leaders of the Air Force Academy have not believed it a violation of the church-state separation to place heavy and repeated pressure on cadets and faculty to attend Protestant and Catholic religious services regularly and to decorate the ostensibly secular campus with banners proclaiming the Air Force of the

United States to be "Christ's Warriors." Only a lawsuit led the academy's leaders to somewhat modify their practices, as has been pointed out in Ray Suarez's *The Holy Vote*.[2] If religious ideas are going to be more widely accepted as legitimate justifications for public policy, shouldn't those ideas be assessed according the same rules that apply in the public debate of other ideas?

The second development is the sudden appearance of, and extensive public attention given to, what the press likes to call "the new atheism."[3] The books of four polemical atheists—Richard Dawkins, Daniel Dennett, Sam Harris, and Christopher Hitchens—are roundly condemned in one forum after another for their arrogance, ignorance, and sweeping rejection of all religion. Can these writers not distinguish between Methodists and morons? Reviewers and bloggers mock the new atheists for failing to appreciate the intellectual sophistication of the average Episcopalian.[4] The price of credibility, it seems, is respect for at least some kinds of religion and for a higher standard of civility than other discourses demand. The religion of one's neighbors may be the last stronghold of the old Sunday school maxim, "If you can't say something good about a person, don't say anything at all." Does the buzz-saw now carving up the books written by the new atheists indicate that a vigorous, public debate about religious ideas is a mistake, after all?

Let's begin with what it means to give religious ideas a "pass." I have in mind the *convention of protecting religious ideas from the same kind of critical scrutiny to which we commonly subject ideas about almost everything else.* The new atheists are getting so much attention partly because they are flouting this convention. The convention is deeply rooted in American culture. When Al Gore—one of the most highly educated of liberal democratic politicians, and one whose favorite book is Thomas Kuhn's *Structure of Scientific Revolutions*—claims to resolve life's tough problems by asking "What Would Jesus Do," he can count on the respectful silence of those who doubt the guidance actually provided by this principle of applied ethics. Nobody with a modicum of tact asks Gore if he has examined his religious ideas with the same scrutiny he has applied to claims and counterclaims about global warming, or to competing theories of how science makes progress.

The discussion of other topics really is different. If someone says women cannot do first-rate science, or that African Americans are just not as smart as Korean Americans, or that homosexuality is a choice rather than a condition, or that taxation is essentially a form of theft, or that the Americans won World War II with minimal help from the Soviets, it is okay to challenge the speaker with evidence and reasoning. Responding in this argumentative manner is less okay if someone says that his or her support for Israel is based on what God has said in the Bible, or that Jesus Christ will come to earth soon, or that some good thing happened because God answered someone's prayers. Religion, wrote Richard Rorty in a widely quoted essay of 1994, is often a "conversation-stopper."[5] When someone starts going on about "The Rapture," the prescribed behavior is to politely change the subject, or to indulge the speaker as one might a child or an aged relative. In the case of The Rapture, the implications for one's fellow citizens may be uncertain, but to invoke a religious justification for a public policy issue is to discourage an opponent from actually debating it.

This convention of giving religious ideas a pass has impressive foundations, and not only in the virtues of decency and humility. These foundations reside also in a constitutional tradition that does indeed treat religious ideas as a distinct category. These foundations are embedded, further, in a history of religious diversity that renders silence a good way to keep the peace. Protestant ancestors of my own were murdered by Catholic terrorists who were surely convinced that these killings were responsive to God's will. The privatization of religion has been integral to the creation and maintenance of a public sphere in which persons of any and all religious orientations, including nonbelief, can function together.

If religious ideas were genuinely trivial from a civic standpoint, playing no appreciable role in how people dealt with anyone other than themselves and their immediate families and their voluntary associations, religion could be more comfortably ignored. But we are nowadays constantly told that religious ideas are a legitimate and vibrant ground for action in the public square and should not be suppressed. This assertion is frequently bolstered by a historical narrative emphasizing the wholesome effects of religion on American politics. Anyone who worries that religion might be counterprogressive is instantly reminded of the importance of religion to Martin Luther King, Jr., and to the role of religious ideas in propelling the civil rights movement. But even when King's supporters among the most liberal of the white Protestants and Catholics are added to his base among the Black churches, the total amounts to a small minority of Christians in the United States at that time. Most white Protestants and Catholics were dubious about, if not actually opposed to civil rights agitation prior to about 1964.[6] The most intensely Christian segment of white America during the 1950s and 1960s was the segregationist south. The religion-is-good-for-America narrative proudly invokes the Social Gospel, which largely failed in its effort to advance social and economic equality, but has little to say about the role of religious ideas in bringing about Prohibition, which for more than a decade succeeded. Gaines M. Foster's *Moral Reconstruction* shows the triumph of Prohibition to be the culmination of decades of religiously connected political activity remarkably like that we see around us today.[7]

This popular but seriously imbalanced account of the history of religion-and-politics facilitates today's discourse, in which we are awash with treatises and manifestos claiming that post-World War II interpretations of the church-state separation function to suppress religious faith by preventing its free exercise in the design and execution of public policy. To keep religion out of public life, we are told, is to trivialize religion. How unfair, indeed how absurd it is that the faithful are asked to "check their religion at the door." Among the legions who invoke this phrase is Congressman Mark Souder of Ohio:

> To ask me to check my Christian beliefs at the public door is to ask me to expel the Holy Spirit from my life when I serve as a congressman, and that I will not do. Either I am a Christian or I am not. Either I reflect His glory or I do not.[8]

Yet there is a formidable theoretical tradition that defends the checking of one's religion at the door. The late John Rawls and his followers, including Joshua Cohen and Martha Minnow, have argued that participants in a shared democratic polity owe it to one another to conduct the business of that polity within premises that are particular to that polity and not to any of the yet more sectarian persuasions that may be present within it.[9] In this view, checking one's religion at the door, in the sense of declining to use it as a justification for actions in which one asks others of different religious orientations to join, is not a bias, nor an inappropriate restraint on free exercise. Rather, it is a mark of democratic commitment and a sign of solidarity with co-citizens in a diverse society. In this view, if absolutists like Souder are unable to accept a domain in which their religious faith is less all-defining, they should stay out of politics. This is exactly what Souder's Mennonite forebears did: they stayed out of public affairs because, like Souder, they believed "radical discipleship" applied 24/7 in every setting. But today, Souder cries foul if the faithful are discouraged from bringing their unmitigated religious witness into the Congress of the United States.

But some politicians see the appeal of the distinguished tradition of democratic theory represented by Rawls. Senator Barack Obama, who professes Christian faith as fervently as Souder does, has endorsed the Rawlsian view explicitly in speeches widely hailed for the element of religious testimony they embody and defend. Obama does encourage Americans to be upfront about their religious motives. But he offers a qualification not often quoted. Like a good philosopher, the senator understands the distinction between motivation and warrant.

> Democracy demands that the religiously motivated translate their concerns into universal, rather than religion-specific, values. Democracy requires that their proposals be subject to argument, and amenable to reason. *I may be opposed to abortion for religious reasons, but if I seek to pass a law banning the practice, I cannot simply point to the teachings of my church or evoke God's will. I have to explain why abortion violates some principle that is accessible to people of all faiths, including those with no faith at all.* . . . Politics depends on our ability to persuade each other of common aims based on a common reality. It involves the compromise, the art of what's possible. At some fundamental level, religion does not allow for compromise. It's the art of the impossible. If God has spoken, then followers are expected to live up to God's edicts, regardless of the consequences. To base one's life on such uncompromising commitments may be sublime, but to base our policy making on such commitments would be a dangerous thing.[10]

Obama's example can give courage to those wanting to defend a strong, autonomous sphere of civil government without infringing on the constitutionally protected free exercise of religion. Civic patriotism has been unfashionable on the liberal Left since the late 1960s on account of the efforts made in its name to discourage cultural diversity and to stifle criticism of American foreign and domestic policy. But its renewal in the present context could encourage pride in the church-state separation and celebrate a distinctive civic sphere in which persons of many religious orientations, including persons who count themselves as nonbelievers in any religion, can be full participants in their distinctive capacity as Americans. It might be too crude to brand as "un-American" those who try to bring church and state closer together, but civic patriotism can at once support a secular public sphere and a private religious one.

Yet even if a renewal of civic patriotism were to persuade everyone that a secular public sphere is not in itself a threat to the constitutional right of free exercise of religion, the religious culture of citizens would obviously continue to affect what happened in the secular sphere of public affairs. Religious ideas, even if not put forth as justifications for public policy, do constitute a vital matrix for political culture. Scholars assume this when they study almost any society in the world. Beliefs about the nature of the world and of human beings, whatever the content of such ideas, are understood to be important. Historians and social scientists trying to understand the political and economic order of any society take belief systems into account. Often, these belief systems are religious. Are we going to proceed differently with the United States of our own time? Are basic ideas about the universe assumed to be both constitutive and performative in Victorian England, Nazi Germany, Confucian China, Inca Peru, Maratha India, Soviet Russia, Ancient Athens, Asante Africa, the Crow Nation of nineteenth-century Montana, and Puritan New England but *not* in the United States today? Can we defend a version of American exceptionalism according to which belief systems are functional everywhere else but not here? Do we not all have a stake in what our fellow citizens take to be true about the world?

The religious ideas of masses of Americans have been shielded from the aspects of modern thought that have led so many scientists and social scientists away from religion.[11] Perhaps critical debate would encourage popular faiths more consistent with modern standards of plausibility, more resistant to the manipulation of politicians belonging to any party, and more accepting of the wisdom in the sharp separation between church and state. Where, after all did we get liberal religion? We got it out of orthodox religion. Especially did the great biblical scholars of the eighteenth and nineteenth century provide the cognitive context for a variety of liberalized religious faiths, including the capacity of many Christians to absorb the Darwinian revolution in science. Religious dialogue has been vital to the intellectual and political history of the North Atlantic West for centuries, until twentieth-century secularists complacently assumed religion was on the way out and ceased to engage it critically.

The absence of sustained, public scrutiny of religious ideas in our time has created a vacuum filled with easy God talk. Politicians are not the only ones skilled in this idiom, but President George W. Bush certainly exemplifies it when he assures the world that his policies in Iraq correspond to God's will. How different was the voice of Lincoln, who never joined a church, but whose God talk was anything but easy. Lincoln invoked the deity in a spirit of humility. In his Second Inaugural Address of 1865, Lincoln cautiously alluded to "those divine attributes which the believers in a Living God always ascribe to him," speculated about what such an omniscient God's will might be, and stopped well short of expressing confidence that, as president, he could be sure that God was on his side.

In Lincoln's time, religious ideas were less often given a pass. In much of nineteenth-century America religious ideas were critically debated, sometimes with a touch of ridicule, even as the church-state separation was defended. An example is the antebellum debates over slavery. The bible, proslavery theologians and politicians reasonably argued, had no problem with slavery. These proslavery Christians insisted that abolitionists just did not know their Bible and were projecting their own secular ideas on the sacred text. Leviticus, Exodus, Ephesians, and First Timothy were routinely cited as biblical warrant for the acceptance of slavery, and abolitionists were hard pressed to find scriptural warrant for their side even in the gospels and in the letters of Paul.[12] When proslavery Americans established their own government—the Confederate States of America—they put God right into their constitution, a step that dramatically set their political order apart from that of the United States itself.

But beyond the slavery debates, the nineteenth-century Americans who discussed issues of public policy understood full well that no matter how the church-state separation was construed, the kind of society in which they lived depended in part on the basic view of the world accepted by their fellow citizens. The great feminist Elizabeth Cady Stanton issued what she called *The Woman's Bible* in the 1890s, in which she openly renounced passages of scripture she found offensive to women, and there were a lot of them. Stanton understood, just as the canon-revisers in our English departments of the 1980s understood, that the books people read had something to do with what kind of people they became and what kinds of political culture they would create; Stanton went after the Bible with a vengeance, the New Testament as well as the Old, and scolded the authors of the ancient texts like a confident schoolmistress correcting the spelling mistakes of the class dunce. She ridiculed the male theologians and preachers of her own time who continued to reinforce the scriptures whole, rather than reading them with modern, enlightened understandings of the gender distinction.[13]

Not everyone appreciated this. Stanton's religious writings were felt by many other feminists to be ethically inappropriate and, more important, politically imprudent. Upon her death in 1902 Stanton's memory was largely erased by the American feminist movement and not recovered until the 1960s. Stanton's place in the movement was obscured with a new celebration of the more conventional Susan B. Anthony.

Stanton's contemporary, Robert Ingersoll, the agnostic whose performances as a lyceum speaker made him a household name and a constant foil for preachers, also went after specific religious ideas with a critical sprit. But at least his generation—Ingersoll died in 1900—was familiar with some of the same objections to Christianity that, when raised in our own time by Sam Harris, seem unconscionably rude. Ingersoll had many critics, but Ingersoll and his enemies were at least part of the same conversation, and one in which religious ideas were taken seriously by secular intellectuals as well as by the faithful.

During the twentieth century unbelieving intellectuals too often assumed, complacently, that religion was in the process of dying out and that religious ideas therefore did not need attention. The British philosopher Bertrand Russell's writings of the 1910s and 1920s were among the last to make a big production of attacking Christianity for its intellectual deficiencies, but American secular intellectuals often found Russell's fussing about religion quaintly anachronistic. He displayed the mark of a true Victorian, it was often said in the 1940s and 1950s: Russell still thought that to reject belief in God was an act of great moral courage.[14]

The new atheists echo many of Russell's complaints, but unlike Russell's confident contemporaries they do not take for granted religion's eventual demise. Rather, they treat it as a serious and dangerous enemy of civilization. But if anyone is complacent in the current controversy over the new atheism, it is those who dismiss the writings of Dawkins, Dennett, Harris, and Hitchens too rapidly. The value of bringing evidence and reasoning to a discussion of religious ideas is lost when we jump on the obvious failings of these writers and ignore the power of the basic Enlightenment critique of religious obscurantism that their books embody.

Refuting Sam Harris has become rather like refuting Samuel Huntington: almost any academic can do it, and when you finish you congratulate yourself for your cleverness and move on to something else. But if Huntington is wrong to characterize Mexican Americans as uniquely subversive of the traditional, immigrant-based social order of the United States, the questions he raises about immigration and assimilation and the cultural foundations of democracy are far from silly, and deserve better answers than most of Huntington's critics provide.[15] So, too, with Harris.

Part of the problem is that Harris connects his critique of religion to a naturalistic metaphysics more specific than his mission requires. This portentous turn is also taken by Dennett and Dawkins, whose philosophical reach has struck many informed readers as extending well beyond the grasp of the evolutionary biology on which it is ostensibly based. The biologist H. Allen Orr, who is no apologist for religion, has been particularly convincing in showing the limits of the scientific foundation for the new atheism.[16] But there is more to the problem than simply espousing a metaphysics that even many agnostics and atheists do not feel compelled to accept.

Harris has no sense of history, and no understanding of the traditional role of religious argumentation in promoting liberalized versions of faith. Harris buries his rasping, potentially valuable critique of genuinely obscurantist ideas beneath undiscerning attacks on people he calls "religious moderates." Both *The End of Faith* and *Letter to a Christian Elation* reject the liberal Protestants, liberal Catholics, liberal Muslims, and so on, who could be Harris's strategic allies. Reviewer after reviewer has treated Harris's books as not worth systematic refutation because the author can't tell the difference between Jerry Falwell and Peter Gomes, and can't distinguish between the Muslim fanatics who attacked the World Trade Center and the liberal Muslims written about in Jytte Klausen's *The Islamic Challenge*.[17] Harris accuses religious moderates of serving as covers for more outrageously irrational versions of the faith. Yet these religious moderates are, like him, inheritors of the best features of the Enlightenment, and are thus his natural allies. Harris reveals no understanding of the historical circumstances that have led many highly intelligent and well-educated people to espouse religious faith, or of the range of ideas that have passed as religious. The popular novel by Marilynne Robinson *Gilead* explores a liberal religious culture with strong roots in the United States, yet Harris is altogether oblivious to the character of this culture.[18] Harris's logic is similar to that of the communist international's theory of social fascism as advanced in the early 1930s, when social democrats in Germany, the United States, and other nations were said to be functionally indistinguishable from fascists simply because they had not renounced bourgeois reform in order to side with the communists.

But the social democrats fought back. They did not leave the political arena to the communists and the fascists. What will happen now?

It remains to be seen what kind of political and cultural alliance can develop between secularists who are more patient with religious liberals than the New Atheists are and religious liberals themselves. And this is where the issue of giving religious ideas a "pass" has become especially difficult. Political liberals of secular orientation tend to give religious ideas a pass because they hope thereby to achieve issue-specific alliances with faith-affirming Americans on the environment, health care, foreign policy, taxation, and so on.[19] Why mess things up by embarrassing the faithful and demanding that they repudiate more resoundingly their more conservative coreligionists? In the meantime, religious liberals are under constant attack from their conservative coreligionists for being on a slippery slope to secularism and are thus reluctant to break ranks with more conservative believers to an extent that secularists would find productive. Hence these religious liberals, too, prefer to seek issue-specific alliances with secular liberals and leave potentially divisive religious argumentation aside.

This continued avoidance of actual debate about religious issues seems to me viable only if religious liberals and secular liberals can advance a civic patriotism that would celebrate a distinctly secular public sphere along the lines advocated by Rawls and Obama. The need to engage religious ideas diminishes somewhat if those ideas are understood, in keeping with modern church-state separationist doctrine, to be inappropriate justifications for public policy. There is a lot to be said for letting each other alone. But in the absence of such an agreement—repudiating the views of Congressman Souder and comparable defenders of politics as a form of religious witness—the case for a robust, public debate of religious issues seems to me hard to refute. If the New Atheists are too sweeping in their rejections, the rest of us need not be.

Notes

This piece has profited from conversations with several colleagues and friends, especially Carol J. Clover, John Connelly, E. J. Dionne, Robert Post, and Alan Wolfe. Several sentences are drawn from my "Among the Believers," *Harper's*, November 2004.

1. A convenient point of access to this discussion is E. J. Dionne, Jr., Jean Bethke Elshtain, and Kayla M. Drogosz, eds., *One Electorate Under God? A Dialogue on Religion and American Politics* (Washington, D.C., 2004).

2. Ray Suarez, *The Holy Vote: The Politics of Faith in America* (New York, 2006), 73–90.

3. Anthony Gottlieb, "Atheists with Attitude," *New Yorker*, May 21, 2007, is one of the more discerning overviews of "the new atheism." Another is David Aikman, "The Atheist Onslaught," *Implications*, May 25, 2007, http://www.ttf.org/index/journal/detail/the-atheist-onslaught/. The works most at issue are the following: Richard Dawkins, *The God Delusion* (Boston, 2006); Christopher Hitchens, *God Is Not Great* (New York, 2007); Sam Harris, *The End of Faith: Religion, Terror, and the Future of Reason* (New York, 2005); Sam Harris, *Letter to a Christian Nation* (New York, 2006); Daniel Dennett, *Breaking the Spell: Religion as a Natural Phenomenon* (New York, 2006).

4. A widely discussed example is Terry Eagleton's review of Dawkins: "Lunging, Flailing, Mispunching," *London Review of Books*, October 19, 2006.

5. Richard Rorty, "Religion as Conversation-Stopper," *Common Knowledge* (Spring 1994): 1–6.

6. Historians have recently begun to correct this widespread misunderstanding about the history of religion and politics in mid-twentieth-century America. For an example of the new scholarship on "the theology of segregation," see Jane Dailey, "Sex, Segregation, and the Sacred after *Brown*," *Journal of American History* (June 2004).

7. Gaines M. Foster, *Moral Reconstruction: Christian Lobbyists and the Federal Legislation of Morality, 1865–1920* (Chapel Hill, NC, 2002).

8. Mark Souder, "A Conservative Christian's View on Public Life," in Dionne, Elshtain, and Drogosz, *One Electorate*, 21.

9. John Rawls, "The Idea of Public Reason Revisited," *University of Chicago Law Review* (Summer 1997): 765–807. See also Martha Minnow, "Governing Religion," in Dionne, Elshtain, and Drogosz, *One Electorate,* 144–49, and Joshua Cohen's Tanner Lectures as delivered at the University of California, Berkeley, April 2007.

10. Barack Obama, "Call to Renewal," Keynote Address, June 28, 2006, accessible at Barack Obama: U.S. Senator for Illinois, http://obama.senate.gov/speech/060628-call_to_renewal/. Emphasis added.

11. Ample evidence shows that, as a general rule, the greater the amount of scientifically warranted knowledge people acquire about the world, the less able they are to accept traditional religious beliefs. There are dramatic exceptions to this general rule: I have not the slightest doubt that some of the most learned and wise people in the world retain religious beliefs of one kind or another. For a helpful summary and analysis of the many studies of religious belief by various occupational and educational groups, especially scientists who have been elected to academies, see Benjamin Beit-Hallahmi, "Atheists: A Psychological Profile," in Michael Martin, ed., *The Cambridge Companion to Atheism* (New York, 2006), 300–18.

12. An excellent intellectual history of the debates over slavery is found in Elizabeth Fox-Genovese and Eugene Genovese, *The Mind of the Master Class: History and Faith in the Southern Slaveholder's Worldview* (New York, 2005). esp. 505–27. The Genoveses demonstrate commandingly that the proslavery writers had superior scriptural warrant for their position that slavery was not a sin, but that the abolitionists were on stronger ground in attacking the specifically racial basis for slavery as it existed in the United States in their time.

13. For an account of the writing and contemporary impact of this important work, rarely discussed today, see Kathi Kern, *Mrs. Stanton's Bible* (Ithaca, 2002).

14. See especially Bertrand Russell, *Why I Am Not a Christian* (London, 1927).

15. Samuel Huntington, *Who Are We? The Challenges to America's National Identity* (New York, 2004).

16. See esp. "A Mission to Convert," *New York Review of Books,* January 11, 2007 (directed primarily at Dawkins), and "A Religion for Darwinians?' *New York Review of Books,* August 16, 2007 (contrasting the approach of the new atheists to the more scientifically and philosophically cautious book of Philip Kitcher, *Living With Darwin: Evolution, Design, and the Future of Faith* [New York, 2007]).

17. Jytte Klausen, *The Islamic Challenge: Politics and Religion in Western Europe* (Oxford, 2005).

18. Marilynne Robinson, *Gilead* (New York, 2004).

19. A comment by Congressman Souder can remind us of the dangers in accepting religious justifications on an issue-specific basis. Souder observes that nobody objects to his using Christian values as a basis for his votes on environmental protection and on the protection of women and children from abuse, but suddenly when he wants to "speak out against homosexual marriages, pornography, abortion, gambling, or evolution across species" on the basis if his religious faith, he is criticized for bringing religion into politics; Souder, "Conservative Christian," 21. Surely, Souder is on to something: if secular liberals refrain from criticizing a theological warrant for policies they embrace, must these secular liberals not also accept the legitimacy of a theological warrant for opposition to same-sex marriage and to the teaching of evolution in public schools?

On "Moralistic Therapeutic Deism" as U.S. Teenagers' Actual, Tacit, De Facto Religious Faith[1]

Christian Smith

Christian Smith (1960–) *is the William R. Kenan, Jr. Professor of Sociology and Director of the Center for the Study of Religion and Society and the Center for Social Research at the University of Notre Dame. His work addresses the relationship between religion and culture. His ideas about "moralistic therapeutic deism," were introduced in his book (co-written with Melinda Lundquist Denton)* Soul Searching: The Religious and Spiritual Lives of American Teenagers *(2005).*

My book *Soul Searching: The Religious and Spiritual Lives of American Teenagers,* coauthored with Melinda Lundquist Denton, follows over hundreds of pages a variety of topical trains of thought and sometimes pursued diversions and digressions. But what does the bigger picture of the religious and spiritual lives of U.S. teenagers look like when we stand back and try to put it all together? When we get past what we discovered about adolescent inarticulacy regarding religion, systematically sort through the myriad stories and statements about religious faith and practice, and pull apart and piece back together what seem to be the key ideas and relevant issues, what did we conclude?

Here we resummarize our observations in venturing a general thesis about teenage religion and spirituality in the United States. We advance this thesis somewhat tentatively, as less than a conclusive fact but more than mere conjecture. Namely, we suggest that the de facto dominant religion among contemporary teenagers in the United States is what we might call "Moralistic Therapeutic Deism." The creed of this religion, as codified from what emerged from our interviews with U.S. teenagers, sounds something like this:

1. A God exists who created and orders the world and watches over human life on earth.
2. God wants people to be good, nice, and fair to each other, as taught in the Bible and by most world religions.
3. The central goal of life is to be happy and to feel good about oneself.
4. God does not need to be particularly involved in one's life except when he is needed to resolve a problem.
5. Good people go to heaven when they die.

Such a de facto creed is particularly evident among mainline Protestant and Catholic youth but is also more than a little visible among black and conservative Protestants, Jewish teens, other religious types of teenagers, and even many "non-religious" teenagers in the United States.

Note that no teenagers would actually use the terminology "Moralistic Thera-peutic Deist" to describe themselves. That is *our* summarizing term. And very few teenagers would lay out the five points of its creed as clearly and concisely as we have just done. But when one sifts through and digests hundreds of discussions with U.S. teenagers about religion, God, faith, prayer, and other spiritual practices, what seems to emerge as the dominant, de facto religious viewpoint turns out to be some version of this faith. We could literally fill another chapter of this book with more quotes from teen interviews illustrating Moralistic Therapeutic Deism and exploring its nuances and variants. Given space limitations, however, suffice it here to examine merely a few more representative quotes depicting this reli-gion's core components.

First, Moralistic Therapeutic Deism is about inculcating a moralistic approach to life. It believes that central to living a good and happy life is being a good, moral person. That means being nice, kind, pleasant, respectful, and responsible; work-ing on self-improvement; taking care of one's health; and doing one's best to be successful. One seventeen-year-old white Mormon boy from Utah said this very clearly: "I believe in, well, my whole religion is where you try to be good and, ah, if you're not good then you should just try to get better, that's all." Being moral in this faith means being the kind of person who other people will like, fulfill-ing one's personal potential, and not being socially disruptive or interpersonally obnoxious. As more than one teenager summarized morality for us: "Just don't be an asshole, that's all." Such a moral vision is inclusive of most religions, which are presumed ultimately to stand for equivalent moral views. Thus, a nonreligious white girl from Maryland said,

> Morals play a large part in religion; morals are good if they're healthy for society. Like Christianity, which is all I know, the values you get from like the Ten Com-mandments. I think every religion is important in its own respect. You know, if you're Muslim, then Islam is the way for you. If you're Jewish, well, that's great

too. If you're Christian, well, good for you. It's just whatever makes you feel good about you.

Feeling good about oneself is thus also an essential aspect of living a moral life, according to this dominant de facto teenage religious faith.[2] Which leads to our next point.

Moralistic Therapeutic Deism is also about providing therapeutic benefits to its adherents.[3] This is not a religion of repentance from sin, of keeping the Sabbath, of living as a servant of a sovereign divine, of steadfastly saying one's prayers, of faithfully observing high holy days, of building character through suffering, of basking in God's love and grace, of spending oneself in gratitude and love for the cause of social justice, etc. Rather, what appears to be the actual dominant religion among U.S. teenagers is centrally about feeling good, happy, secure, at peace. It is about attaining subjective well-being, being able to resolve problems, and getting along amiably with other people. One fifteen-year-old Hispanic conservative Protestant girl from Florida expressed the therapeutic benefits of her faith in these terms: "God is like someone who is always there for you; I don't know, it's like God is God. He's just like somebody that'll always help you go through whatever you're going through. When I became a Christian I was just praying, and it always made me feel better." Making a similar point, though drawing it out from a different religious tradition, this fourteen-year-old white Jewish girl from Washington describes what her faith is all about in this way: "I guess for me Judaism is more about how you live your life. Part of the guidelines are like how to live and I guess be happy with who you are, cause if you're out there helping someone, you're gonna feel good about yourself, you know?" Thus, service to others can be one means to feeling good about oneself. Other personal religious practices can also serve that therapeutic end, as this fifteen-year-old Asian Buddhist girl from Alabama observed, "When I pray, it makes me feel good afterward." Similarly, one fifteen-year-old white conservative Protestant girl from Illinois explained: "Religion is very important, because when you have no one else to talk to about stuff, you can just get it off your chest, you just talk [to God]. It's good." And this fourteen-year-old East Indian Hindu girl from California said of her religious practices, "I don't know, they just really help me feel good." It is thus no wonder that so many religious and nonreligious teenagers are so positive about religion. For the faith many of them have in mind effectively helps to achieve a primary life goal: to feel good and happy about oneself and one's life. It is also no wonder that most teens are so religiously inarticulate. As long as one is happy, why bother with being able to talk about the belief content of one's faith?

Finally, Moralistic Therapeutic Deism is about belief in a particular kind of God, one who exists, created the world, and defines our general moral order, but not one who is particularly personally involved in our affairs—especially affairs in which we would prefer not to have God involved. Most of the time, the God of this faith keeps a safe distance. He is often described by teens as "watching over everything from above" and "the creator of everything and is just up there now controlling everything." As one fifteen-year-old Arabic Muslim boy from California put it:

> God is like an entity that decides when, if, he wants to intervene with a lot of things. To me God is pretty much like intervention, like extreme luck. Say you're $50 away from something and you find $50 on the floor, then that's probably God's intervention or something like that. But other than that it just seems like he's monitoring. He just kind of stays back and watches, like he's watching a play, like he's a producer. He makes the play all possible and then he watches it, and if there's something he doesn't like, he changes it.

For many teens—as with adults—God sometimes does get involved in people's lives, but usually only when they call upon him, which is usually when they have some trouble or problem or bad feeling that they want resolved. In this sense, the Deism here is revised from its classical eighteenth-century version by the Therapeutic qualifier, making the distant God selectively available for taking care of needs. As this fourteen-year-old white mainline Protestant boy from Colorado said, "I believe there's a God, so sometimes when I'm in trouble or in danger, then I'll start thinking about that." Like the Deistic God of the eighteenth-century philosophers, the God of contemporary teenage Moralistic Therapeutic Deism is primarily a divine Creator and Law-Giver. He designed the universe and establishes moral law and order. But this God is not Trinitarian, he did not speak through the Torah or the prophets of Israel, was never resurrected from the dead, and does not fill and transform people through his Spirit. This God is not demanding. He actually can't be, since his job is to solve our problems and make people feel good. In short, God is something like a combination Divine Butler and Cosmic Therapist—he is always on call, takes care of any problems that arise, professionally helps his people to feel better about themselves, and does not become too personally involved in the process. As one fourteen-year-old white Catholic boy from Pennsylvania responded to our inquiry about why religion matters, "Cause God made us and if you ask him for something I believe he gives it to you. Yeah, he hasn't let me down yet. [So what is God like?] God is a spirit that grants you anything you want, but not anything bad." Similarly, this seventeen-year-old conservative Protestant girl from Florida told us, "God's all around you, all the time. He believes in forgiving people and whatnot, and he's there to guide us, for somebody to talk to and help us through our problems. Of course, he doesn't talk back." This last statement is perhaps doubly telling: God, being distant, does not directly verbally answer prayers, according to this girl, but he also does not offer any challenging comebacks to or arguments about our requests. Perhaps the worst the God of Moralistic Therapeutic Deism can do is to simply fail to provide his promised therapeutic blessings, in which case those who believe in him are entitled to be grumpy. Thus, one sixteen-year-old white mainline Protestant boy from Texas complained with some sarcasm in his interview that, "Well, God is almighty, I guess [yawns]. But I think he's on vacation right now because of all the crap that's happening in the world, cause it wasn't like this back when he was famous." Likewise, this fourteen-year-old white conservative Protestant boy from Ohio told us that, "God is an overall ruler who controls everything, so like, if I'm depressed or something and things aren't going my way, I blame it on him. I don't know why." But few teens we talked to end up blaming God for failing them, since Moralistic Therapeutic Deism usually seems to be effective in delivering its promised benefits to its many teenage believers in the United States.

We want to be very clear about our thesis here. We are not saying that all U.S. teens are adherents of Moralistic Therapeutic Deism. Some teens are simply disengaged from anything religious or spiritual, and other teens embrace substantive religious beliefs and practices that effectively repudiate those of this revisionist faith. Some teens do appear to be truly very serious about their religious faith in ways that seem faithful to the authoritative or orthodox claims of the faith traditions they profess. We are also not saying than anyone has founded an official religion by the name of Moralistic Therapeutic Deism, nor that most U.S. teenagers have abandoned their religious denominations and congregations to practice it elsewhere or under another name. Rather, it seems that the latter is simply colonizing many established religious traditions and congregations in the United States, that it is merely becoming the new spirit living within the old body. Its typical embrace and practice is de facto, functional, practical, and tacit—not formal or acknowledged as a distinctive religion. Furthermore, we are not suggesting that Moralistic Therapeutic Deism is a religious faith limited to teenage adherents in the United States. To the contrary, it seems that it is also a widespread, popular faith among very many U.S. adults. Our religiously conventional adolescents seem to be merely absorbing and reflecting religiously what the adult world is routinely modeling for and inculcating in its youth.

Moreover, we are not suggesting that Moralistic Therapeutic Deism is a religion that teenagers (and adults) adopt and practice wholesale or not at all. Instead, the elements of its creed are normally assimilated by degrees, in parts, admixed with elements of more traditional religious faiths. Indeed, this religious creed appears in this way to operate as a parasitic faith. It cannot sustain its own integral, independent life. Rather it must attach itself like an incubus to established historical religious traditions, feeding on their doctrines and sensibilities, and expanding by mutating their theological substance to resemble its own distinctive image. This helps to explain why millions of U.S. teenagers and adults are not self-declared, card-carrying, organizationally gathered Moralistic Therapeutic Deists. This religion generally does not and cannot stand on its own. So its adherents must be Christian Moralistic Therapeutic Deists, Jewish Moralistic Therapeutic Deists, Mormon Moralistic Therapeutic Deists, and even Nonreligious Moralistic Therapeutic Deists. These may be either devout followers or mere nominal believers of their respective traditional faiths. But they often have some connection to an established historical faith tradition that this alternative faith feeds upon and gradually co-opts if not devours. Believers in each larger tradition practice their own versions of this otherwise common parasitic religion. The Jewish version, for instance, may emphasize the ethical living aspect of the creed, while the Methodist version stresses the getting-to-heaven part. Each then can think of themselves as belonging to the specific religious tradition they name as their own—Catholic, Baptist, Jewish, Mormon, whatever—while simultaneously sharing the cross-cutting, core beliefs of their de facto common Moralistic Therapeutic Deist faith. In effect, these believers get to enjoy whatever particulars of their own faith heritages appeal to them, while also reaping the benefits of this shared, harmonizing, interfaith religion. This helps to explain the noticeable lack of religious conflict between teenagers of apparently different faiths. For, in fact, we suggest that many of them actually share the same deeper religious faith: Moralistic Therapeutic Deism. What is there to have conflict about?

One way to gauge people's interest in different matters is to track their language use. What do people talk about? How often do they use different kinds of key words and phrases? The idea behind this approach is that people's discourse roughly reflects their concerns and interests. We used this method as one means of assessing U.S. teenagers' relative orientations to religious and therapeutic concerns. We systematically counted in our interview transcripts the number of teenagers who made reference to specific subjects or phrases of interest. We found, first, that relatively few U.S. teenagers made reference in their interviews to a variety of historically central religious and theological ideas. The following list shows the number of teenagers who explicitly mentioned these concepts in their interviews:

47—personally sinning or being a sinner
13—obeying God or the church
12—religious repentance or repenting from wrongdoing
9—expressing love for God
8—righteousness, divine or human
7—resurrection or rising again of Jesus
6—giving glory to or glorifying God
6—salvation
5—resurrection of the dead on the Last Day
5—the kingdom of God (2 Christian, 3 Mormon)
5—keeping Sabbath (of 18 Jewish interviews)[4]
4—discipleship or being a religious disciple
4—God as Trinity

4—keeping Kosher (of 18 Jewish interviews)[5]
3—the grace of God
3—the Bible as holy
3—honoring God in life
3—loving one's neighbor
3—observing high holy days (of 18 Jewish interviews)
2—God as holy or reflecting holiness
2—the justice of God
0—self-discipline
0—working for social justice
0—justification or being justified
0—sanctification or being sanctified

When teenagers talked in their interviews about "grace," they were usually talking about the television show *Will and Grace,* not about God's grace. When teenagers discussed "honor," they were almost always talking about taking honors courses or making the honor role at school, very rarely about honoring God with their lives. When teens mentioned being "justified," they almost always meant having a reason for doing something behaviorally questionable, not having their relationship with God made right.

For comparison with these tallies on religious terms, we also counted the number of teens who made reference to the key therapeutic ideas of feeling happy, good, better, and fulfilled. What we found—as shown in the following list—is that U.S. teenagers were much more likely to talk in terms broadly related to therapeutic concerns than in the religious terms examined above:

112—personally feeling, being, getting, or being made happy
99—feeling good about oneself or life
92—feeling better about oneself or life
26—being or feeling personally satisfied or enjoying life satisfaction
21—being or feeling personally fulfilled

Note that these are not total number of times that teenagers used a word or phrase, but simply the number of teens who used them. In fact, our interviewed teenagers used the single, specific phrase to "feel happy," for instance, more than two thousand times. In short, our teen interview transcripts reveal clearly that the language that dominates U.S. adolescent interests and thinking about life—including religious and spiritual life—is primarily about personally feeling good and being happy. That is what defines the dominant epistemological framework and evaluative standard for most contemporary U.S. teenagers—and probably for most of their baby-boomer parents. This, we think, has major implications for religious faiths seriously attempting to pass on the established beliefs and practices of their historical traditions.

What we are theorizing here, in other words, is the very real existence of a shared American religion that is analogous to the American civil religion that Robert Bellah astutely described in 1967,[6] yet which operates at an entirely different level than civil religion. It is not uncommon for people to think of the United States as comprising a variety of diverse religions that coexist more or less harmoniously: Protestant, Catholic, Jew, Freewill Baptist, Irish Catholic, Conservative Judaism, Reformed Presbyterian, Latter-day Saint, and so on. But the reality is actually more complicated than that. "Religion" in the United States separates itself out and operates at multiple levels in different ways. American religion is most obvious at the level of formal organizations, the plane on which denominations, seminaries, religious congregations, publishing houses, and other religious organizations operate. But religion also often operates distinctively at a level "below" the organizational plane, at the level of individual belief and practice. Here religious faith is often eclectic, idiosyncratic, and syncretistic, inconsistently—from the perspective of most organized religious traditions, at least—mixing together elements as diverse as belief in infant baptism, interest in horoscope predictions, and the collection of religious kitsch. This is the dimension that some scholars have called "lived religion" or "popular religion."[7] Beyond these two levels, Bellah's major contribution in 1967 was to reveal civil religion operating in the United States at yet another level—"above" the plane of formal religious organizations. Bellah very insightfully showed how religious symbols and discourse—appropriated and abstracted from the Judeo-Christian tradition—are mobilized at a national civic level for purposes of national order, unity, and purpose.

What we are suggesting here in our observations about Moralistic Therapeutic Deism is that, to understand the fullness of "religion" in the United States, we need to come to see yet another level or plane of religious life or practice operating in this social order (as shown in figure 2 on page 169 *of Soul Searching*). At the "bottom" exists the eclectic, idiosyncratic, and discretely syncretistic faiths operating at the level of individual religion. "Higher up" abides the more coherent, systematized faiths operating on the plane of organizational religion. Even "higher" exists the nationally unifying political faith of American civil religion. But situated between the individual level at the "bottom" level and the organized religions and civil religion on planes above that, there operates yet another distinct level of religion in the United States—the widely shared, interfaith religion of Moralistic Therapeutic Deism. Like American civil religion, Moralistic Therapeutic Deism appropriates, abstracts, and revises doctrinal elements from mostly Christianity and Judaism for its own purpose. But it does so in a "downward," apolitical direction. Its social function is not to unify and give purpose to the nation at the level of civic affairs. Rather, it functions to foster subjective well-being in its believers and to lubricate interpersonal relationships in the local public sphere. Moralistic Therapeutic Deism exists, with God's aid, to help people succeed in life, to make them feel good, and to help them get along with others—who otherwise are differ-ent—in school, at work, on the team, and in other routine areas of life.

Finally, to suggest that "religion" in the United States operates complexly and distinctly on different levels, however, does not mean that those levels never inter-act or influence each other. They do. Purely individual beliefs, for instance, are shaped in part by the teachings of organized religion—as well as by horoscopes, advice columns, talk show hosts, and so on. American civil religion is affected both by liberal religious activism and by the Religious Right operating at the level of formal religious organization. The same observation about interlevel interaction and influence is also true of Moralistic Therapeutic Deism. It helps to organize and harmonize individual religious beliefs "below" it. It also both feeds upon and shapes—one might say infects—the religious doctrines and practices at the organi-zational and institutional level "above" it. In addition it mirrors and may very well interface with American civil religion at the highest level by providing the nations inhabitants a parallel and complementary common, unifying, functional faith that operates at a more apolitical, private, and interpersonal level of human life. The cultural influence of Moralistic Therapeutic Deism may also be nudging Ameri-can civil religion in a "softer," more inclusive, ecumenical, and multireligious direction. "What is conservative becomes more "compassionate," what is liberal becomes more "bleeding heart" and "inclusive," and what is remotely particular-istic is increasingly universalized. All can then together hold hands and declare in unison, "Each person decides for himself/herself!" And those who believe that only the born again who are justified by the spilled blood of Jesus Christ go to heaven, or that the Angel Moroni really did appear to Joseph Smith with a new and commanding revelation, or that God's chosen people really must faithfully observe his laws are suspect. The flock of sheep is diversified and expanded, but certain goats remain part of the picture nonetheless.[8]

Adults in the United States over the last many decades have recurrently emphasized that which separates teenagers from grown-ups, highlighting things that make each of them different and seemingly unable to relate to each other. But, as reported in our book, *Soul Searching,* our conversations with ordinary teenag-ers around the country made the contrary clear to us, that in most cases teenage religion and spirituality in the United States are much better understood as largely reflecting the world of adult religion, especially parental religion, and are in strong continuity with it. Few teenagers today are rejecting or reacting against the adult religion into which they are being socialized. Rather, most are living out their religious lives in very conventional and accommodating ways. The religion and spirituality of most teenagers actually strike us as very powerfully reflecting the contours, priorities, expectations, and structures of the larger adult world into which adolescents are being socialized. In many ways, religion is simply happily absorbed by youth, largely, one might say, "by osmosis"—as one sixteen-year-old white Catholic boy from Pennsylvania stated so well: "Yeah, religion affects my life a lot, but you just really don't think about it as much. It just comes natural I guess after a while."

However, it appears that only a minority of U.S. teenagers are naturally absorbing by osmosis the traditional substantive content and character of the religious traditions to which they claim to belong. For, it appears to us, another popular religious faith—Moralistic Therapeutic Deism—is colonizing many historical religious traditions and, almost without anyone noticing, converting believers in the old faiths to its alternative religious vision of divinely underwritten personal happiness and interpersonal niceness. Exactly how this process is affecting American Judaism and Mormonism we refrain from further commenting on, since these faiths and cultures are not our primary fields of expertise. Other more accomplished scholars in those areas will have to examine and evaluate these possibilities in greater depth. But we can say that we have come with some confidence to believe that a significant part of "Christianity" in the United States is actually only tenuously connected to the actual historical Christian tradition,[9] but has rather substantially morphed into Christianity's misbegotten step-cousin, Christian Moralistic Therapeutic Deism. This has happened in the minds and hearts of many individual believers and, it also appears, within the structures of at least some Christian organizations and institutions. The language—and therefore experience—of Trinity, holiness, sin, grace, justification, sanctification, church, Eucharist, and heaven and hell appear, among most Christian teenagers in the United States at the very least, to be being supplanted by the language of happiness, niceness, and an earned heavenly reward. It is not so much that Christianity in the United States is being secularized. Rather more subtly, either Christianity is at least degenerating into a pathetic version of itself or, more significantly, Christianity is actively being colonized and displaced by a quite different religious faith.

Notes

1. This paper is a version of "Summary Interpretation: Moralistic Therapeutic Deism," from *Soul Searching: The Religious and Spiritual Lives of American Teenagers* by Christian Smith with Melinda Lundquist Denton, copyright © 2005 by Oxford University Press, Inc. Used by permission of Oxford University Press.

2. There is a strong connect between this vision of morality and the "emotivism" described by Alasdair MacIntyre in *After Virtue* (Notre Dame, IN: University of Notre Dame Press, 1982).

3. For more on the therapeutic in culture, see James Nolan, *The Therapeutic State: Justifying Government at Century's End* (New York: New York University Press, 1998); Philip Rieff, *The Triumph of the Therapeutic* (Chicago: University of Chicago Press, 1966); Christopher Lasch, *The Culture of Narcissism* (New York: Warner Books, 1979); James Hunter, *The Death of Character: Moral Education in an Age without Good or Evil* (New York: Basic Books, 2000); Joel Shuman and Keith Meador, *Heal Thyself: Spirituality, Medicine, and the Distortion of Christianity* (Oxford: Oxford University Press, 2003); Andrew Polsky, *The Rise of the Therapeutic State* (Princeton: Princeton University Press, 1991); John S. Rice, *A Disease of One's Own: Psychotherapy, Addiction, and the Emergence of Co-Dependency* (New Brunswick, NJ: Transaction Publishers, 1996); Ronald Dworkin, *The Rise of the Imperial Self* (Lanham, MD: Rowman & Littlefield, 1996); Robert Bellah, et al., *Habits of the Heart* (Berkeley: University of California Press, 1985); Daniel Bell, *The Cultural Contradictions of Capitalism* (New York: Basic Books, 1976); Daniel Yankelovich, *New Rules: Searching for Self Fulfillment in a World Turned Upside Down* (New York: Bantam Books, 1981); James Nolan, *Reinventing Justice: The American Drug Court Movement* (Princeton: Princeton University Press, 2003).

4. Four other Jewish teenagers mentioned Sabbath specifically to say that they do not keep or observe the Sabbath.

5. Three Jewish teens mentioned keeping Kosher to say that they do not.

6. Robert Bellah, "Civil Religion in America," *Daedalus* (Winter 1967): 1–21.

7. See, for example, David Hall, *Lived Religion in America* (Princeton: Princeton University Press, 1997); Erling Jorstad, *Popular Religion in America* (Westport, CT: Greenwood Press, 1993).

8. For an explanation about how such status differentiations and cultural constructions of difference are essential to the making of human identities, see Christian Smith et al., *American Evangelicalism: Embattled and Thriving* (Chicago: University of Chicago Press, 1998).

9. As specified by numerous, defining historical creeds and confessions, including the Apostles' Creed, the Nicene Creed, the Chalcedonian Creed, the Athanasian Creed, Canons of the Council of Orange, the Belgic Confession, the Westminster Confessions, the Heidelberg Catechism, the Augsburg Confession, the Canons of Dort, the Scots Confession, the Thirty Nine Articles of the Church of England, the First London Confession of Faith, the Schleitheim Articles, the Articles of Religion of the Methodist Church, Documents of the Second Vatican Council, the Catechism of the Catholic Church, and so on.

Chapter 5

Philosophy and Ethics

Why Not Lie?[1]

Elizabeth Kamarck Minnich

Elizabeth Kamarck Minnich *(1943–) is a senior scholar at the Association of American Colleges and Universities in the Office of Diversity, Equity, and Global Initiatives. She earned her MA and PhD in Philosophy from the Graduate Faculty of Political and Social Science, The New School for Social Research in New York, where she worked closely with Hannah Arendt. Dr. Minnich has held administrative and faculty positions at Union Institute and University, Barnard College, Hollins College, Sarah Lawrence College, Brooklyn College, and Scripps College, among others. Her book* Transforming Knowledge *(1990, 2005) examines how we define knowledge and how we think about moral and political questions.*

I think we should start by being honest about lying. The prohibition against it is a peculiar one; it doesn't feel like others with which we are familiar. The moral-social taboos against things like stealing, hitting people, getting drunk, sleeping around are both serious and humorous. There are a lot of jokes about them: "Everything I like is either immoral, illegal or fattening" admits openly that we would really like to be able to indulge sometimes. Much of the behavior we have taboos against is tempting behavior, and we recognize that. What is forbidden, or anyway supposed to be kept carefully under control, is the stuff of fantasies.

But who has fantasies about indulging in a binge of lying? Who even admits that it is tempting to lie? There doesn't seem to be any fun in lying, any release. The question we don't even need to ask about most of the other forbidden or restricted indulgences—Why would you want to do it anyway?—does need to be asked about lying. After all, if we need to tell ourselves individually and collectively that we shouldn't lie, there must be a reason why we might lie if we weren't prohibited from doing so.

Let's think about it. What am I doing when I lie? What does it feel like? Often I feel at least slightly defiant—defiant, nervous, and watchful: I've just broken the rules. Will they catch me? In a moment, I go from being *with* people to being, if only a bit, *against* them.

There is a truth I am refusing to tell, an admission I am refusing to make, a situation with which I am refusing to deal. I am making my own, strictly private decision to do what *I* want, despite any other claims on me.

Lying frees me from something I do not like, something that frightens me, that demands something of me I do not want to give. I lie when a situation has become messy, to get myself out of a trap. I lie when I want things to go differently, when I do not like the way things are developing. I lie when I want to look better than I am, to create a different image of myself. I lie to protect, to free, to promote myself—or someone or some purpose I have adopted. Sometimes I lie for fun, to show that I am not bound by the facts of the matter.

But however and whenever I do it, I am, when I lie, refusing to honor the expectations of other people and accept my obligation to submit to the demands of reality. I am setting myself against, and over, other people.

It is important to notice and take seriously something so obvious that we overlook its significance: You and I are able to lie. That we can lie at all means that we can free ourselves from reality, from obligations to acknowledge what is, the past, other people. It means that we have a special power, a secret special power, one that is really ours alone and depends solely on us. If anyone else knows that we use it, it is made useless. There is a real excitement in knowing that we have such a power.

I can lie. I can assert myself in the very face of pressures from others. I can get myself out of something complex and sticky. I can get something done quickly that would otherwise take a lot of time and effort. It is in my power to make things come out differently.

So there *is* a great temptation in lying. It is the temptation to stop submitting—to reality, to obligations I bear to other people, to the past, to all the taboos I have internalized.

Lying gives us an almost magical sense of our own power and freedom. In that, it is like imagination, like creativity, like play. Our admiration for creative people and our willingness temporarily to suspend normal standards for human behavior when it comes to artists show how important it is to us to know that we can, sometimes at least, be free of the thousands of thin, strong ropes that hold us in the real socially respectable, oh-so-responsible adult world. Artists break all kinds of rules, those of perception and those of morality, for us. And we accept it, we admire it—as long as the artistry, the playing with reality, is openly admitted. We love a magician; we do not want to be able to see through the tricks; but we do need to know, nevertheless, that there are tricks involved.

We are delighted to be released from reality and obligations, but only if the release at the same time honors them. We do not want anyone to do magic without admitting it.

Lying is unadmitted magic. It is both very tempting and very frightening because it proves that we need not accept things as they are . . . or so, at least, it seems. Everyday, over and over, we choose to withhold from ourselves a power and a freedom we could have. We could lie; we don't. The temptation is not a sometime thing. It is always there. No wonder we are so serious about lying, we rarely joke about it. If the prohibition against lying were not so strong, we—and, what's worse, others—could lie all the time.

But what, after all, is so wrong about that? If we have magic, why can't we use it? Consider three different kinds of lying, divided by the kind of expectations refused, by whom we lie to, rather than by the kind of statement made. I can lie to myself; I can lie to those with whom I live and share a set of meanings; and I can lie in public, to those I do not even know. There are *personal, social* and *political* lies.

That I can lie to myself is really rather odd, since in that case I am myself both deceiver and deceived. Not only can I choose to lie, I can choose to be lied to. If I do not want to remember something, if something has become more complex than I like, if I do not want to hold myself to an obligation I have made, I can simplify, I can persuade myself I didn't really promise, and I can do so without admitting to myself that I am doing it.

What makes that possible? Clearly, there are at least two of me, a deceiver as well as a deceived. I learn from the possibility of self-deception something I can also learn (but not so strikingly) by thinking about thinking. We are not only conscious but self-conscious creatures. We not only think, we can think about thinking. We not only see, we see ourselves seeing. Socrates spoke of thinking as a dialogue with oneself. When I think, I am not simply following the stream of my consciousness: I interrupt myself. I say, "No, that's not right," "But what about . . ." "That doesn't make sense." I converse with myself through my other voices, as if I always lived with friends who are ready to talk with me even when I am absolutely alone.

In a different vein, Freud wrote about the super ego, the internalized prohibitions we have from our parents and our society that keep watch over us even in their absence. Conscience is the still, small voice that tells us someone may be watching. We have the voices of others in us, and our relationship to those voices can be as varied as our relationships with other people.

When I lie to myself, I risk shutting off future conversations with my own other voices. I am trying to make things simple, to free myself from self-consciousness by choosing one voice over others. Lying is rather like snapping back to early childhood when self and world, self and self, are still undifferentiated. It is indeed burdensome always to have people talking to you, correcting you, reminding you even when no one else is there. The self-deceiver has tried to shut those voices up. In the moment I deceive myself, I feel as if I am freeing myself from all the complex interweaving with my past, my world, the people I have known. Lying, even to myself, feels defiant, like a re-claiming of my own power and freedom.

But what happens when I have silenced some of my other selves? It becomes necessary to keep them silenced. If I persist in this stubborn repression, I may finally lose the ability to think. If I have shut off the voice of my memory, I lose all I have learned from the past. If I shut off my learned sense of the complexity of a situation, I also shut off the chance of understanding it. If I shut off my reminders, my internal friends and critics, I become less powerful and free. I need those other voices; they help me make sense in a world in which meaning is a shared reality. One definition of madness is being closed into a private meaning system: Madness is a private language, a monologue.

I have worked with schizophrenics whose problem is not that they do not make sense but that they make sense only to themselves, only by their own very strict and private meaning system. That is extreme, but it is on a continuum with self-deception. I may feel as if I assert my power when I defiantly deceive my other selves, but I risk losing it. The emperor who has lost the ability to see himself except as he wants is extremely vulnerable. There is always a child in the crowd to say, "The emperor is naked." In an attempt to protect our lie to ourselves, we are pushed either to withdraw further and further, or to dominate more and more, to go crazy or to become a tyrant. Whichever direction we move, flight or fight, we have lost our freedom simply to be—with ourselves, with others, in the world.

So one critical reason not to lie to ourselves is not an external one or even, in the usual sense, a moral one. It is that you cannot think well when there are things you cannot allow yourself to think about, and you cannot communicate with others when you have stopped being able to communicate with yourself. Making sense is a social act; it requires that crowd of other voices we all have in us. It requires that we be our own friends. Self-deception destroys that friendship and makes us, finally, alone.

What about lying to others with whom I live? The social lie is very familiar and often very tempting. One of the serious prices we pay for growing up is that we become increasingly responsible to and for other people. As that responsibility grows, it becomes tempting to cut through its complexity, its stickiness, and take the easy way. What is a little lie on occasion, after all? I can even lie out of care for others, and surely then I do them no damage.

The problem is that when I tell a social lie I decide, by myself and in secret, what needs to be said. I change other people's reality without their permission. My intentions may be all for the best: I may be a Peter Pan, spinning out an alternative, magical world that is ever so much nicer than the real one. But in doing so, I am, like Peter Pan, stealing from those to whom I lie the choice of their own relation to reality, to me, to themselves. In however small a way, I am substituting my world for their world, for our world. And in so doing, I am putting myself above them, making them dependent on me. The longer the lie continues, the more I must compound it, protect it, protect myself from being found out. That means that the person to whom I lied, perhaps even out of some kind of care for them, becomes, first, subject to me and then, finally, a kind of enemy of mine—all without knowing it.

Because a lie must be secret, because it is the result of my taking power over reality into my own hands, it is anti-social and inegalitarian. Just as the person who lies to herself or himself becomes increasingly isolated, needs to retreat or to dominate to protect the lie, the person who lies to others becomes also an outsider. The freedom from obligation, the power to make things go right we took without admitting it, again turns into its opposite. We end having to scuttle around re-interpreting reality, compounding the lie, cheating on relationships with others who still think we are *with* rather than *against*—or over—them. Telling a social lie is rather like trying to direct a play when the actors haven't agreed to be in your play. We have to get them to do what we want without being able to tell them to do it. We have to manipulate them.

It is, finally, more egalitarian and more free and powerful to remain within the binding, constricting web of social relations than to isolate oneself by taking reality into one's own hands, cutting oneself off from open, genuine relations with others. However wonderful Peter Pan's world, the children will one day choose to return to their own nursery and get on with growing up.

To lie is to cut off the present from its entanglements with the past, the simple from its complicated context, and, most important of all, to cut ourselves off from the only world we have—the world we share with others. For a moment of secret defiance, of self-assertive freedom, we give up too much. The temptation of the lie is like the temptation of the genii in the bottle. Why not rub the bottle and let the genii, who is bound by no human restraint, fix things for us? Once released, the genii may not go back into the bottle. Reality does indeed depend on us, but not for its existence. It is in our power to deny it or to shape it, but not to make or destroy it.

It is our effort to stay open to the truth, to our world as it is and as it is understood and lived in by other people, that both limits and empowers us.

But, of course, what the truth is is itself an exceedingly difficult question. And when we come to consider political lies, it becomes even more difficult. Political lies are different from personal or social ones because political truth is different.

"Truth" usually means correspondence or coherence; that is, what I say is true if it corresponds to something real, to a situation, a fact, a thing or if it is consistent within a given system. The statement, "the ball is red," is true if the ball is indeed red. The statement, "2 + 2 = 4," is true not because two things added to any two other things will always make four things (two gases added to two matches may make an explosion) but because I have correctly followed the rules of addition. My statement is coherent within a system. For both of these kinds of truth, what matters is that my statement check out with a given state of affairs or a given system of thought. Truth is, in effect, merely the result of properly relaxing one thing/statement with something else. I don't mean to imply that juxtaposing a thought against a thing or following the rules of a system is simple. Not at all. But the situation is in many ways even more complicated when we consider political truths.

When I speak politically, I am not simply reporting or communicating. I am acting; I am trying to do something. What I say, how I say it, when and to whom I say it will have consequences. Having an effect, letting loose consequences is what it means to be political, to be out in public as an actor. The head of the Federal Reserve can say at home that she thinks there will be a significant drop in interest rates within the next week, and what matters is that she say what she really thinks is the case. But if she says publicly that interest rates are about to drop, her words have a different reality. They will quite possibly have such a dramatic effect on what happens that it will become necessary *not* to lower the interest rates. Will she then have lied? No, of course not, and it would be foolish to hold it against her that she said one thing and then, in response to a genuinely changed situation, helped to make something else happen.

Words are acts in politics and should not be judged solely against pre-existing states of affairs or other statements. To so judge them would be to refuse to take account of the equal reality of consequences, of change, and of the political necessity to remain flexible and open to new situations. A truth-teller in public who did not realize that words have effects and become themselves new factors in the reality of which we must take account could very soon seriously harm the public.

We know somehow that this is true, but we do not often think about and take seriously what it means. It means that an ethics of truth in politics must be different in some important respects from an ethic of truth for the private or merely social individuals.

In private morality we put a high value on motivation. If someone lies, we are willing to consider why she or he lied, and we judge a good intention less harshly. But intentions *are* private, and precede acts. In public, what is private and what precedes the act may matter in making it an appropriate or effective act, but are not so relevant for judging it. The best intentions in the world cannot make a disastrous political act one we should judge leniently, and the worst intentions cannot change good consequences. We may *like* a well-intentioned politician better than a mean one, but when we judge them as politicians, it is the consequences of their acts that matter. If we lose sight of that, we become very poor judges and very poor defenders of the public realm.

When we speak in public, we act, and when we act, we take on a responsibility for how we act and for its consequences that goes way beyond our responsibility to ourselves and to whatever we are reporting on, speaking about. In public, how we say what we say matters greatly, as does when we say it and to whom. We are not being noble and exceedingly moral when we disregard everything but the truth of what we say. Quite the contrary. We are being foolish and arrogant and very possibly politically dangerous. When we speak to others as we do when we are attempting to act, we must take account of them, of who they are, how they will hear us, what will happen when we say what we say. Adjusting to our audience while maintaining strict regard for our purposes is not shifty or dishonest but responsible to other people and to the reality we are helping to make.

But because truth in politics is not just reporting, because reality is in effect in our care when we act, we are not therefore free to do whatever we want. Despite its differences from private and social truth, political truth does have some real similarities. Any kind of lie is an assertion of my own power and freedom, my ability to choose not to honor the claims of pre-existent reality or the expectations of others. Politically, to choose myself over others, to give myself license to change reality *in secret* is to run the risk of becoming powerless (or creating the need for domination) as it is in the private world.

It is even more evident politically than privately that we are cheating on our relations to other people when we lie. When we lie, we cut ourselves off from the people we are trying to act with because we cannot admit to them what is really going on, and, what is worse, we have to hide it from them. We cheat on the public when we lie politically, and once we have betrayed it, we are suddenly against, not with, others. Instead of speaking to persuade others, we must begin speaking to manipulate them. And manipulation in politics is the first step towards the use of force. In my social relations, even if I am a manipulator, I must stay open and responsive to those I manipulate to be successful. I must make the actors in the play do what I want by getting them to do it as if they had chosen it; that is, I must understand them well enough to know how to move them. That means that I must maintain at least some closeness to them, some openness. But the political figure who has taken the secret power given by lying can, if successful, attain a position from which it is no longer necessary to manipulate. He or she may gain control of the sources of violence of the state—the police, the army, the laws that must be obeyed whether or not people are persuaded (or manipulated) into agreeing with them.

The power of the political lie is a foreshadowing of the efficacy of violence. Both are temptations to those who are trying to do something in public because both promise, as lies characteristically do, quick and easy solutions. Violence is also a genii that may not return to the bottle. Like the lie, violence requires constant reenforcement. An unpersuaded person will do what I want as long as I have a gun at hand, but that requires me to keep the gun there. A lie will be effective as long as it is not proven to be a lie, but that requires me to keep adjusting reality so that the secret is kept.

If I speak openly and thoughtfully to people, if I include them in the thinking that persuaded me, if I can understand them well enough to speak so that they really understand me, we may be able to reach agreement. And people who have been persuaded that something is the right thing to do will do it whether or not I am there, whether or not I have visible, immediate control over them. The most effective long-range political tool is not violence but persuasion. Persuasion takes longer and demands more at first, but makes what follows easier.

If I lie to myself, I risk losing the ability to think (which requires that I be my own friend), and consequently the ability to be with and make sense to others. If I lie to others, I risk losing the ability to be with them as an equal, because I must either hide from or manipulate them. If I lie politically, I risk losing the ability to persuade people and to keep them with me working willingly. I risk being pushed toward violence to make public reality conform to my private view.

Where we deal with other people, the quick, easy solution backfires. Politically, this limit on my choice of a personal, secret power is especially significant because in being political I am choosing to emerge from my privacy.

Simply to be in the world with others as myself takes constant effort and attention—and real courage. It requires openness and vulnerability—to my own other voices; to new and entirely different voices; to change as well as continuity, to a reality that I effect and for which I am responsible but that I do not make and cannot fully control. No wonder that lying appears as an immense temptation. Why not have done with all this interaction, this complexity, and make my own world? But that "why not" is treacherous. It contains, "Why not create my own social world—why not create a cult, a sect, a Never-Neverland?" "Why not make people do what I want—why not become a tyrant?"

It can also mean, "Why not drop out?" If I rid myself of the deep temptation to exercise my magic, to impose my secretly chosen shape on reality, I may well then want simply to stay out of the way of others who have perhaps succumbed to the same temptation. In politics, that temptation is all too familiar. To opt out of the public realm where differences and conflict are always present simply because we are not all alike and because the future does depend on our efforts is the decision most of us make. We are predominantly private creatures these days—not by nature but because of the way our polity and our economy and our society have developed. The protection of "happiness" that in our tradition goes with "life" and "liberty" seems now to mean the preservation of *private* pleasure, and it sometimes seems odd that it is included in our political documents at all. The excitement and self-realization that come from appearing in public, creating a character for ourselves that is not dependent on intimacy, having a real effect on the way the future develops are rare experiences and are not usually what we have in mind when we think about being happy. We suspect people who *do* take pleasure in acting, in being public and political. Judging from standards for morality appropriate to the private realm, we have a strong inclination to judge those who are political. "She is a power seeker," we say—as if wanting power were in itself a bad thing.

But without power, we are not necessarily noble or good or moral. We are, simply, powerless. And being powerless is by no means necessarily conducive to being good. Those who do not have access to the public, to the places and processes by which power is created and used, are not free from but subject to those who do exercise power.

The popular assumption that "power corrupts" is a dangerous one grounded in one of the most basic of modern political lies. Accepting it has serious consequences. For one thing, it leads us to assume that those who have power are necessarily corrupt—which leads directly to exempting them from any further judgment. After all, if all political people are corrupt, why bother developing or applying any standards of behavior to them? And if we believe that power corrupts, the best of us will avoid it—which leaves it for the worst among us. But most importantly of all, the belief that power corrupts deceives us into thinking that power is something we should not even want to have.

Power does not isolate us or make us need to dominate other people, to use force against them. We only need to *force* people to do what we, in opposition to them, want if we do *not* have power. It is a clear mark of the loss of power when a person or a government must resort to secrecy, to lies, or to violence. Power springs up wherever people act together. Power is public; it results from the recognition of others, from their acceptance of a commonality of interest. A powerful person is someone followed by choice. A leader is created by followers; power is created by and based on trust. We have power as long as we are together, as long as we are responsible, visibly and openly, for our acts. It is when we cheat on the public, when we lose our sensitivity to those we work with, when we start pursuing our own rather than our shared purposes that we begin to need substitutes for power such as lies and violence. The totalitarian ruler who must use terror and all its immense machinery to make people obey is utterly without power. The spokesperson of the people, who gives voice to a clear and shared understanding, has immense power.

It is powerlessness that corrupts, that isolates and lessens people, that removes them from the constant correction of friction with other people, that can drive them to use means that are utterly destructive of human community. Power grows with being shared. The more of us there are, the more powerful we are; the more we seek genuine power, the more we must remain open to others, receptive to them, expressive of their interests.

The choice to avoid acting publicly, which, like the choice to lie, seems the easy way out ends by being harder and more costly. There is no private power, no private freedom any more than there is a private truth, a private system of meaning.

What about the social world? Can I opt out of responsibility for our shared, non-political reality, for the ways we live together that are rarely debated or chosen in public? All societies have shared sets of beliefs that are re-enforced by shaming, social ostracism, denial of access to status just as states have rules for action re-enforced by laws, police, armies. To opt our of concern for the creation and maintenance of our social order and beliefs can have just as severe implications as opting out of the creation of the laws and political structures that shape our lives. In fact, since our shared belief systems shape the way we understand our world, a lack of social responsibility has political and personal consequences. The prejudices of a society underlie its political structure; they *can* come into conflict with it and even be corrected by it as well as enforced by it, but like a subterranean stream, they are always there, stubborn and persistent and often unaffected by our efforts to bring them to the surface.

Some of those belief systems are based on and maintained by lies. They do not correspond to reality, and they conflict with other key systems of meaning. When we lie, we attempt to make reality; when we hold prejudices, we attempt to make reality fit our beliefs. To be prejudiced is precisely to hold onto a belief in the face of evidence that contradicts it. As the lie forces an individual to retreat from or try to dominate those to whom the lie is told, a prejudice forces us to retreat from or try to dominate those against whom it is held.

Think of the complicated prejudices and consequent desperate efforts to change reality that surround the social myth of the "natural" inferiority of women. One half of the human race is supposed to be less than the other half in almost every respect: A "true" man is supposed to be smarter, stronger, better than all women at almost everything. He is even supposed to be taller than all women. That some women are smarter, stronger, taller than some men isn't allowed to change that "should." Men look for women who are less than they are—younger, shorter, less educated, less trained, earning less money. They receive sympathy from others if 'their' woman begins to earn more, goes ahead and gets more education, works hard and wins a promotion that makes her out-rank them.

Let me make it explicit: One sure mark of a lie, personal, social or political, is not just that it doesn't correspond to reality, our usual definition of a lie, but that there is effort put into making reality correspond to it. Lies are our effort to make things go the way we want them to. And lies in general and prejudices in particular depend on but misjudge the fact that reality is dependent on us. We *can* make it go the way we want . . . up to a point. In society, as in politics, a lie that goes too far, that is too opposed to the complexity that is reality, leads to isolation or violence.

Where ghettoization and/or violence (they go together) characterize the history and infect the range of experience of a whole group of people, it is a sure sign that a social lie exists—and that it is one that serves some other group well. The behavior of women, as of black people and other oppressed groups, is shaped and controlled by the threat of violence, a threat carried out often enough to be effective. A woman who does not act as if she is weak and dependent, who does not place herself under the protection of a man, is "asking to be raped." She must not go out alone at night; she must not live alone; she cannot even list her full name in the telephone book lest the world know that a woman is on her own; she must not reveal her sexuality. Women who are dependent on and weaker than men are so because it is the only safe way to be, not because they are so naturally. The truth has been forced to conform to prejudice for so long that we do not even know which is which anymore. And we expend an extraordinary amount of energy maintaining our belief systems, bringing people up "right" so that the lie will not be contradicted, punishing those who stubbornly violate it.

Finally, we are thrown back on ourselves. Only individual openness to experiences that contradict our belief systems can free us to seek a truer relation to ourselves, to each other, to our world. If I am able to lie to myself, I am also able to go along with social and political lies, and to do so peacefully. And all of us do so all the time. We become very good at compartmentalizing, locking off one set of beliefs, one kind of experience from others so that we do not have to check it against reality—or against our own principles. Most of us grant ourselves exemptions in some areas of our lives, and it is those exemptions that make us complicit in the lies that we like to *say* we abhor.

Many an otherwise good man is not at all good to the woman who lives with him. He rests from his battles with the world at home, and needs her to make him feel better about himself, to comfort and care for him. He would be infuriated and deeply betrayed if she were to ask him to remain as fully conscious of who he is and how he acts in the privacy of "his" home as he is out in the world. It is, I believe, because it is so very hard to hold ourselves open to experience, to check ourselves so that we do not grant ourselves exemptions, that sexism is one of the most stubborn of social prejudices. It not only hits close to home: it is precisely at home that it hits hardest. Those who have a commitment to being liberal, open-minded and up-to-date seem to need a rest in their private lives. So, to women as to other groups that suffer from being made to prove prejudices true, it can come to seem easier to be with those who are conspicuously prejudiced than with those who, because of a commitment to being "good," need constant shoring up. The self-deceiver demands a lot of those around him. He needs for his lies to be protected, to be cushioned from experiences that would make him face himself. The fury of a good person confronted with evidence that he or she has made an exception for himself—that she has made an exception for herself—is often extreme. To those who are no longer willing to act as if a lie were true, it begins to seem safer to be with those whose fury is predictable. We know, then, where the struggle is and what will trigger it. It is easier to be treated as an enemy than to be feared as a potential betrayer.

While we allow ourselves to compartmentalize, to avoid checking our beliefs against experience and our own principles, we remain vulnerable to the lies of others. To stand against a political lie, to refuse to participate in a social lie, it is necessary first to see it clearly, and then to have the strength to be your own friend. If it is hard to live with another person who refuses to go along with your need to be shored up, to have respite from your own principles, it is even harder in the long run to live with yourself if you cannot talk back to yourself.

Reality is indeed complex. It is not just of the present but has also a past that pushes it toward a probable but never necessary future. It is simultaneously resistant to our efforts, even capable of taking its revenge on our attempts to alter it, *and* dependent on us. We *can* think and act as if it is simple; we *can* exercise our secret power to free ourselves; we *can* deceive ourselves and others; and we discover, when we do so, that what seems the easy way out is rarely so. The final punishment for exercising our secret power, for making the wish to control reality, is that it come true.

Lying makes reality harder to bear, not easier, because it makes us solely responsible for it. Fortunately, there are other ways to ease the burden that tempts us to lie. *Forgiveness* keeps us from being tied to the past, and *promises* help us shape the future. Forgiveness recognizes that we can't change reality however desperately we may want to, and yet allows us to go on. It frees us from the past. Promises recognize that we can and do choose and affect reality. They help us control the future. Together, forgiveness and promises take into account both the stubborn persistence of reality and its dependence on us. And they do so without setting us against other people. We need other people to forgive us, and we need to make promises to and with other people. For both, we need a good, strong, clear and open relationship to others. In contrast to that of lying, the power of forgiveness and of promises is not private and is lessened if it is secret.

And in the present, when I must choose whether to lie or not, there is compassion to help me deal with the burden of situations I would love to get out of without doing the violence to them that is a lie. There is also creativity, the counterpart of the lie that doesn't cut us off from what is true but makes us open to it and to ourselves so that we can take reality and, without doing violence to it, transform it.

Because we do not realize how great the temptation to lie is, and how constantly with us, we counter it only by exhorting people to tell the truth—as if that were not itself complicated and difficult, and as if the desire to lie were easily suppressed. Political truth is changing and elusive, and political truth-telling must be done with full recognition of the responsibility it entails for the consequences of action. Social truth and social truth-telling can conflict with the deepest, most emotionally-held belief-systems that bind a society and can therefore open us up to vicious retaliation. Personal truth and truth-telling require that we be constantly aware of ourselves and of all our own other voices, that we live intimately with ourselves as our own friend—our own most caring self and most severe critic. If we try to tell ourselves the truth, we open ourselves up to guilt, that painful reminder that we are indeed free, that we could always have done otherwise and that, because we are free, we are responsible. That is a very heavy burden indeed, and there is a lot of support from others for our efforts to avoid feeling guilty.

Truth, because it is complex, time-bound, multi-faceted and rarely clear, requires constant effort and is not in our control. But it is in our keeping. It is up to us to choose to remain our own friend, and the friend of others, and that, finally, is what makes this not just a world we share with others, a human world, but a humane world.

Note

1. Throughout this reflective thought piece, this essay, I am thinking with my mentor, Hannah Arendt, in mind (and, as those who know her and/or philosophy will of course recognize, with Plato, Kant, Heidegger, and Jaspers, key among Arendt's own thinking friends, as well as Dewey and Wittgenstein). I owe far more to Arendt than any specific citation properly conveys—hence this single, over-loaded endnote—but among texts, reference should be made particularly to *The Human Condition*—cf. especially Section V, "Action." Along with some of my reflections on power, the brief comments on promises and forgiveness (which Arendt, herself thinking there especially with Jesus, Nietzsche, and perhaps Augustine, urged us to take more seriously politically) are grounded there (sections 33 & 34). *Hannah Arendt, The Human Condition,* 2nd Edition; Univ. of Chicago Press, Chicago & London: 1958

How to Be a Good Person: According to Aristotle

Eleanor Wittrup

Eleanor Wittrup *teaches philosophy at University of the Pacific. She has a masters degree in Theological Studies from Harvard University. She earned her PhD at the University of California–San Diego where she studied ethics and moral psychology. She was elected to the Board of Directors of the Coastside County Water District in 1999 and served for two years. She teaches mainly history of philosophy and ethics.*

Virtue and Vice Defined

Aristotle says that we are excellent people when we do the right thing at the right time in the right way for the right reason. Most people don't find this terribly helpful as a guide to solving difficult moral problems. The crux of the problem is this: what the right thing is depends on the circumstances—and what the right thing is for you to do will often depend on who you are, what you can do, and what the particulars of the situation are. If we want to become the sort of people who can reliably do the right thing, even in very difficult, upsetting, and confusing circumstances, we have to develop our moral and intellectual virtues.

"Virtue" Means "Excellence"

For Aristotle, adaptability and flexibility are at the core of what makes a person an excellent human being. We are used to thinking about this kind of excellence only in relation to specific activities. For example, a person who is virtuous with respect to playing the piano is a "virtuoso." A person who is excellent at fixing cars is a virtuoso mechanic. A person who is excellent at fixing teeth is a virtuoso dentist. What we mean when we say someone is excellent (AKA an "expert") at something is that he can be counted on to do the right thing at the right time in the right way for the right reasons in that area. What the right thing is depends on a number of factors, but the expert is an expert because he is knowledgeable enough to recognize what the right thing is and capable of actually doing it. To be a virtuous person is just to be excellent at being a human being. What human beings *do* is to adapt their actions to a given situation in order to bring about the best possible outcome.

To be an excellent person is not just being good at being yourself. Because we are human beings and human beings are social animals, we have to be good members of our community as well. (Aristotle says "political" but I'll explain that later.) A human being who doesn't need other human beings is either a beast or a god, says Aristotle. So being a virtuous human being is more like being a virtuoso piano player with an opera company than it is like being a virtuoso solo pianist. Of course if you really are a virtuoso, the necessities of playing with the opera will not present a huge problem, just an interesting and fun bunch of challenges. You can practice on your own, but if you never got to play with others your life would be sad and unfulfilling.

Doing the right thing is not simple. Most people who try hard to be good human beings find that it is complicated. The three major limitations we run up against are: our emotional limitations, our intellectual limitations, and the limits and demands of the society in which we find ourselves. Aristotle is concerned with each of these areas. To cultivate virtue we have to cultivate the moral virtues (our emotional dispositions), our intellectual virtues (our knowledge and ability to critically and imaginatively reason), and to support, encourage, and defend a just society. I'll explain each of these as we go.

Moral Virtue: The Doctrine of the Mean

Aristotle defines a moral virtue as, "a disposition lying in the mean." What is a disposition? A disposition is something that only makes sense over a period of time; it cannot be defined in terms of a single act or a momentary state. To say that a kind of plastic is brittle is not to say that it is now lying in shards on the ground, or that it is a rectangular stick. To say that the plastic is brittle is to name its disposition, that is, to say how it is likely to behave under stress, namely that it will shatter. We talk about people's dispositions all the time when we say things like "He's short tempered, he gets mad at everything" or "She's fearless, I've never seen her afraid of anything." We think about people we know in terms of their character, how they tend to react and respond to the world around them. We tend to think of character, the kind of emotional reactions people automatically have, as relatively fixed. Aristotle thought of emotional reactions as things that could be trained.

An aside on terminology: *"Virtue" and "vice" are words which have, over the years, drifted in their meanings. This creates confusion for people when they first read Aristotle.*

Virtue: *While "virtue" still means "a morally good aspect of character" to us, it no longer has the general meaning of "specific excellence of a thing." In Aristotle's time, people thought of themselves much less as independent individuals, and much more as integral members of an organic whole. In our time we tend to think of ourselves as independent agents, as forces of nature in our own right. Aristotle thought of us as much more like the organs or parts of a body, each with its own specific function but all relying on the operations of the others. In extreme circumstances a body part might need to be sacrificed (a finger or a toe, or even a spleen) but only in dire circumstances when the survival of the whole is at stake. Virtue isn't about rigidly following rules, but about flexibly adapting to the needs of the circumstances for the good of the whole.*

Vice: *The meaning of "vice" has changed significantly since Aristotle's time. When we think of vice now we think of specific behaviors, such as gambling, prostitution, alcoholism, and addictions of various sorts. Older people, or people raised in some religious traditions also tend to think of vices as specific emotional bad habits along the lines of the seven deadly sins: sloth, envy, lust, greed, rage, pride, and gluttony. Aristotle meant something more general. For Aristotle "vice" is a general term that denotes a limitation in our ability to respond. In the context of the moral virtues it meant something more like what we mean by "neurosis" today: a sort of dysfunctional automatic emotional response. When we say someone is "vicious" we mean he is cruel and violent. In earlier times to label someone "vicious" just meant that they were subject to one of any number of habitual moral or intellectual failings.*

Aristotle says that moral virtues are "dispositions lying in the mean." Each virtue has two corresponding vices: one is having the disposition too strongly (to an excess), and the other is having the disposition too weakly. So if we take the example of courage, having too much is called foolhardiness or fearlessness, which means that you are disposed to do dangerous things for stupid reasons, or for no reason at all. It is not rational to do something that could cause you grave harm for trivial reasons, so this is not a good disposition to have. The foolhardy person is, in fact, unlikely to pass up an opportunity to do something dangerous. At the other end of the spectrum of courage we have cowardice, which means that you are disposed to avoid slight dangers, even if there is overwhelmingly good reason to do it. A cowardly person can't muster the will to do a dangerous thing even if his life depends on it. Courage, by contrast, is the disposition to do dangerous things when it makes sense, to walk away when the risk is not worth the reward, and to rush into danger when it is necessary. So the courageous person has access to the full range of human responses, while the foolhardy or cowardly person only has access to their end of the spectrum. Notice that the courageous person is not fearless, but is fearful in the right amount without being immobilized by it.

The metaphor of a sound mixing board may help you understand how moral dispositions work. Emotional dispositions are a lot like where you set the sound levels on a board. If you set them to one side, the sound can be very loud, but not very soft, on the other end of the board, very soft, but not very loud. The level doesn't absolutely determine that sound, but it constrains it. An emotional disposition is like that. It sets the range of the emotional response. Take the case of anger. If you are short tempered, lots of things can make you angry. Some things can make you very, very angry, even send you into a rage. Quietly letting things go is not really something you do. Your "level" of this emotion is turned up pretty high. If the level is set too low, your response might range from "Something happened?" to being mildly annoyed, but total rage will not be in your repertoire, no matter what happens. In one case the disposition is "in excess"; in the other it is "deficient." These are both vices. They are vices because they limit the range of your responses. If your disposition was "moderate"—or the channel on the board was set in the middle—then you would have access to the whole range of possible emotions. You could also think of this as having a good center of balance emotionally.

Because so many people who teach and study Aristotle get confused about this point, I am going to say it one more time: Virtuous people are capable of any and every possible response. Virtue allows people to respond by walking away, carefully planning a moderately risky course of action and executing it, or rushing into danger depending on what is the best response to the situation in which they find themselves. It is hard to predict what a virtuous person will do. Vicious people, by contrast, are limited to their stereotypic responses, running away in the case of the coward, doing stupidly dangerous things in the case of the foolhardy. The actions of a person in the grip of a vice are easy to predict. Virtuous people are capable of passively letting an injury go, of giving a mild rebuke, of making a stern warning or of going into a deadly rage, depending on the circumstances and if it is the best thing to do. People in the grip of a vice have a limited number of options. The passive person rarely objects to any injury except the most egregious, and then only relatively mildly or with strong but ineffective anger. The short-tempered person takes offense even at accidental slights or injuries, and can do great damage to others and relationships by going into a rage. The short-tempered person has a difficult time letting things go.

Clearly, in most of our lives the responses toward the middle of the dispositional spectrum are most often useful. For most of us, almost all the time, the responses at the extremes are only rarely if ever useful, so we mostly don't practice or experience them.

We have as many virtues (and twice as many possible vices) as we have emotional responses. Other moral theories focus on intention (Kantian deontology), and results (utilitarianism), while Aristotle focuses on action. Aristotle organized his exposition of the virtues around the main external areas of action. He locates the virtues in relation to their corresponding vices of excess and deficiency. His list includes the following virtues with their excessive vice and deficient vice:

Virtue	Excess Vice	Deficient Vice
Generosity	Spendthrift	Stinginess
Magnificence	Vulgarity	Cheapness
High-mindedness	Excessive pride	Mealy-mouthed
Friendliness	Obsequiousness	Ornery
Courage	Foolhardiness	Cowardice
Temperance	Self-indulgent	Insensible
Liberality	Over spending	Penny pinching
Magnanimity	Vain	Self-effacing
Proper ambition	Empty vanity	Unambitious
Patience/good temper	Short tempered	Lack of spirit
Truthfulness	Boastful/oversharing	Dishonest
Wittiness	Buffoon	Boorish
Modesty	Shy	Shameless
Indignation	Envy	Spiteful

The ancient Greek approach to understanding virtue was quite different from ours, so it may be more useful to think of virtues according to our most common shared values:

Virtue	Excess	Deficient
Honesty	Over-sharing	Lying/deceptive
Respect	Brown-nosing	Contemptuous
Responsibility	Hyper-responsible	Irresponsible
Courage	Thrill-seeking	Timid
Compassion	Emotional vampire	Cold-hearted
Fair	Self-sacrificing	Self-centered
Leadership	Bossiness	Passivity
Solidarity/Community	Bigotry	Egocentric

In practice, the important point is not so much which scheme you choose, because the individual virtues are all tied together in practice. Aristotle claims that to truly have one virtue you have to have them all (which is called "the Doctrine of the Unity of the Virtues"). This makes sense if you think about how difficult it would be to be really just, or loyal, or even friendly if you were a terrible coward. You might want to do the right thing, but you wouldn't be able to bring yourself to do it.

Many of us have had the experience of intending to do something or say something, and then . . . just being unable to do it. My most dramatic "fail" in this arena was when I was skiing. I was out with friends who were much better skiers than I was, and we went down a run that had a narrow bit that went over a small cliff. The most adventurous would simply go over it and land below. If you didn't want to go over the cliff (which I most certainly didn't since I would not be able to land safely) you had to turn and go through a chute to get to the lower part of the slope. The chute was short and no problem for me, but it required a left turn (my bad side) that I hadn't anticipated and the slope was quite steep. So, I stopped. I looked around. I determined that I had plenty of space to make the turn and the chute without going over the cliff. I planted my pole and willed myself to go and . . . nothing. This was very strange. I tried again, "one, two, three, GO!" I told myself. "Nope," replied my body. Okay, I was not going to be able to get myself to do this. "Just do a kick turn!" yelled my friend from down slope. "Right," I thought, "I can just stand here and turn my skis in the other direction and go from there." This was a sensible and conservative solution to the problem. My body did not agree. Try as I might my downhill leg was not going to come up and flip around. In the end I (embarrassingly) sat down, lay on my back and swung my skis around, and then stood back up. My friends were highly amused. I was not pleased. My physical courage that day simply failed me, preventing me from doing what I meant to do. I failed due to a vice. I experienced what Aristotle calls "akrasia" in Greek, or "weakness of the will."

Most people have had the experience of working themselves up to have a hard conversation with someone they care about, and then, when in the presence of the person and fully intending to say their piece, had something else entirely come out of their mouths, or being unable to say anything at all. It is most discouraging. It is the result of a vice. Our dispositions, when they are not moderate, limit our actions. Cultivating virtue is a process by which we remove or alter those limitations.[1]

To go back to our sound mixing board metaphor, it is like there are limiting cords that connect all of the individual slides, so the channels can't quite get to the middle position if one is way out to the end. At the same time, the closer the majority of the channels get to the center (the mean) the more pressure they exert on the extreme (vice) to move toward the center (virtue.)

Moral Virtues Continued: Calibrating Our Emotional Responses

How do we become virtuous? Clearly, some people live their lives as slaves to their vices; in modern terms we think of these as addictions, compulsions, and neuroses. Babies are born with particular temperaments that are modified over time. For example, some very young children tend toward aggression such as impulsively biting other people when they feel threatened or frustrated. By the end of first grade, while these children still sometimes feel like biting someone, almost none of them do it. By college, none of them bite, nor do they even feel like biting. How does this happen? No one is born with all the moral virtues. We have to develop virtue through practice. And we need an environment that supports the practice of developing virtue.

Contrary to our usual way of thinking, our emotional responses are not fixed. While they are involuntary in the individual case, (you cannot just *will* yourself to be happy about your best friend marrying a questionable character) they are plastic or able to be shaped over time. Our dispositions are reset, our automatic emotional responses shaped, in two ways: first by external feedback, second by deciding to shape our own responses by "faking it 'til we make it." When we are born we come into the world with certain dispositions—some babies are easily angered, some are timid, some are outgoing. These basic dispositions are then shaped, made stronger or weaker by how the people who care for us respond to us. If a baby finds her needs are met more quickly and effectively when she gets very angry, she will develop the habit of getting angry easily. In Aristotle's terms her disposition toward anger will slide toward the short-tempered end of the spectrum. Parents "train" babies, almost always unintentionally and unconsciously, reshaping their innate emotional dispositions by responding to some and ignoring others. As we get older our caretakers shape our emotional responses by insisting on certain behaviors; that is, we are required to act grateful long before gratitude takes hold in our hearts. We are required to act forgiving before we learn to genuinely forgive. Our parents and teachers help us to "fake it" until we "make it." Whatever dispositions we are born with—short-tempered, even-tempered, or passive—the people who surround us when we are children profoundly shape what we become in adulthood by encouraging or discouraging our behavior and reactions as we go through life.

When we get old enough to understand the world and start to recognize our own limitations, we can shape our own responses by acting as if we have the virtue until that response becomes "second nature." We can choose to "fake it 'til we make it" by ourselves. In this way, our moral character is under our control. At any particular moment we do not have complete control over the feelings that come up—that process is automatic. But we can and do train those feelings over time; so they are in our control over time, and thus in our control. As with all habits, moral character is easier to shape when you are young and the habits are still relatively new. It is harder to shape moral character when you are older; the longer you have had a habit, the more effort it takes to change it. Make no mistake, however; it can be changed. This is why we are responsible for our moral virtues and vices as adults, but not so much as children. Once we develop a virtue it is easy or at least natural to do the right thing, and it is satisfying to do it. Why, after all, wouldn't you want to do the right thing, at the right time, in the right way, for the right reason? And the more challenging the situation, the more fun it is to do it. When people say, "virtue is its own reward" this is what they mean—that being virtuous is just being the sort of person for whom doing the right thing is fun and satisfying.

Aristotle names three stages in our moral development; incontinence, continence, and virtue. Incontinence is when you know the right thing to do, but can't manage to do it. Continence is when you know the right thing to do, but you struggle to do it. Virtue is when you know the right thing to do and it is the easy and natural thing to do. Most of my students have played Tetris. The process of learning to play Tetris is a good model for learning to be virtuous. The aim of the game and the process of rotating shapes are very simple and easily understood, but at first you make mistakes. You know the right thing to do (mostly) but can't do it, or can't do it fast enough. With practice, you start to develop some rules and strategies about how to handle particular shapes, and manipulating them becomes more automatic. If you play long enough you can get to the point where you know what to do and can do it well enough that the game becomes boring if it is not sped up. At this level the challenge is to get into the "zone" and just respond to the situation as it comes as fast as it changes. Notice that as long as you are trying and improving the game remains fun. If the game didn't ever get more difficult than level one, it would become boring very quickly. In the same way, vices make life boring, since you make the same mistakes and get the same (bad) results over and over. Virtue and developing virtue keeps life interesting and challenging.

Doing the right thing is one challenge, but knowing what the right thing is involves not just moral virtue, but intellectual virtue.

Human Nature: The Parts of the Soul[2]

Most people today think of human beings as either bodies with souls, or just bodies who think. Aristotle had a very different model. It will be much easier to understand what the moral and intellectual virtues are and how they are supposed to work together if we understand the basic model that Aristotle was working with. According to Aristotle, people have three souls with five functions. (Stick with me here.) He believed that every living thing was alive because it had some kind of a soul. Different kinds of souls create different functions, and so you can tell what kinds of soul a living thing has by looking at what they do. It is a bit hard to explain this in his terms, because we know so much more about biology than

Aristotle did. Remember, he is creating his theory before any of the modern bio-logical sciences were even thought of. The microscope had yet to be invented, so no one has any idea about cells or bacteria or any level of organization below what can be seen with the naked eye.

The simplest and most common soul is the vegetative soul. This is the kind of soul that every living thing has—it makes it possible to grow and reproduce, to heal injuries and take in and use nutrients. All plants have this kind of soul. All animals have it too, even very simple ones, but they have other kind(s) of souls as well.

The next kind of soul is the sensitive soul, which has two functions. The sensitive soul enables us to sense or perceive our environment and to move around. A being with a sensitive soul is repelled and attracted by things and can initiate motion in response to these impulses. The living things that have both vegetative and sensitive souls range from beings such as sea anemonies and venus fly traps to fish and rabbits and whales and humans. The sensitive soul creates the capacity for motion as well as response. Our desires, how we are attracted or repelled by things in our environment determines the action dispositions we have toward them.

After the sensitive soul comes the rational soul. A rational soul gives an animal flexibility in how it responds to the problem of getting what it needs to survive. The rational soul also has two potential functions; it enables us to solve problems (practical reason and skill) and to imagine better outcomes (contemplation). The rational soul can be present in greater and lesser degrees. If you have more of a rational soul, you have a greater range of capacities for solving problems. Those of us with the most rational soul are not only capable of solving very difficult problems; we also discover new problems to solve. Animals with less rational souls solve their problems by trial and error. Animals with more rational souls are capable of more creativity and flexibility in their attempts to solve problems. We would say that all mammals and some reptiles and a few invertebrates (octopi) have rational souls. Because some animals have more rational souls than others, some animals are better at solving problems than others. Rats are much better at solving problems than guinea pigs or rabbits—because they have more rational souls. We could say that crows have a more rational soul than sparrows, because they can figure out novel ways to get what they want. Human beings have more rational souls than any other animal. Having the greatest rational souls gives us the capacity to do qualitatively different kinds of problem solving than other animals. Non-human animals are limited in their responses to the world by their instinctive needs. Different rational animals need different things and have different abilities, and their solutions are limited to getting what they naturally need to survive and prosper. Dogs can figure out how to open the cabinet door to get the kibble, but cannot untangle themselves when they get their leash wrapped around a tree. Rats can figure out how to get cheese in a maze, but not how to escape from their captors. Human beings have so great a rational soul that we can do qualitatively different things. Please take note of the fact that the rational soul depends on the operation of the sensitive and vegetative souls. In the case of most animals the range of operation of the rational soul is limited by the needs of the other two souls. Human beings are fundamentally different than other animals because we have so great a rational soul that it is no longer limited by the necessities of our sensitive and vegetative souls, and our rational soul can regulate or deregulate our desires and actions (sensitive soul.)

Human beings have a very extensive rational soul (Aristotle thought some classes of people have a greater share than others.) This makes us "cleverer" or "smarter" than other animals. Specifically it motivates us to imagine the world better than we find it. Our rational soul gives us the ability to imagine solutions to our problems, that is, to manipulate objects in the world in our heads without doing it in practice. This capacity for imagination also gives us the ability to devise entirely new solutions and approaches to solutions. It also, and less helpfully, gives us the ability to devise new and unnecessary problems. Thus, the rational soul not only creates opportunities unique to human beings, it creates dangers unique to us as well.

The highest expression of the rational soul, and the one *only* human beings have (and only some human beings in Aristotle's view) is contemplation. Once we have lived long enough to learn how and why the world is the way it is, we can then contemplate the world we know and imagine how it might be better. Contemplation requires all the intellectual virtues, and trying to implement the imagined improvements requires all the virtues, moral and intellectual. But what are those intellectual virtues?

Intellectual Virtue

Suppose you have developed your dispositions to the point that they are all well within the range of moderate—so you have acquired a full set of moral virtues. Your actions are no longer determined by emotional habits or compulsions. How should you choose/govern your actions now? Action should be governed by reason. To be a virtuous person we must not be driven by our emotions, because to do so is putting the cart before the horse. A virtuous person governs her actions by reason and her emotions arise in accord with a correct understanding of the situation and its necessities. The trouble is that life is complicated, and the right thing to do is often unclear. To figure out what you should do in any given situation you will need intellectual virtues. You will need to be able to use reason effectively to figure out the right thing to do. Just like all skills, the more you reason and the more you understand about the world, the easier and more obvious solutions become.

The right thing to do must be right in several ways. It must be based on accurate knowledge and understanding of the situation. It must aim at a realistic and desirable outcome. The outcome must be realistically achievable given the resources available, one's own abilities, and the likely actions of others involved. Reason is what makes us able to make these calls.

While it may seem obvious what we mean by "reason," Aristotle means something very specific. Aristotle starts with the idea that there is basic material "stuff" which is relatively undifferentiated in itself (i.e., a very general idea of "matter" without elements). What gives the various living and non-living things their particular characteristics and dispositions is how they participate in patterns. Reason enables us to recognize and respond to the patterns. It is important to stress that what is most important when we try to understand the world is not the particulars but the patterns that the particular things and events fit into.

Aristotle divides knowledge into knowledge of things that change (animals, plants, weather, metal, land, water, etc.) and knowledge of things that don't change (mathematics, logic, moral principles). There are two categories of how we understand things that change: in the context of making or fabricating things, and in the context of acting (which is not aimed at fabricating a specific product). There are also two categories of things that don't change: the patterns or forms of thought, and objects in the world (think astronomy, but remember that Aristotle thought of the heavens as glass spheres around the earth—not as the cosmos as we understand it). Aristotle gives different names to the excellence of thinking about each of these areas.

We understand things that change when we understand the pattern of how they change. As we understand more and more about the deep structure (ecology, geology, biology, chemistry, physics) of how and why things change we can deliberate about what is going to happen next and what we could do about it. Aristotle would be very impressed with our understanding of the forces that govern change in the physical world, and how diverse and pervasive our efforts at fabrication have become. Today, we live in an almost entirely artificial/manufactured world. He would also be impressed with how much progress we are making in understanding how to act to create conditions in which all human beings have the opportunity to flourish physically, emotionally, and mentally. He would also be impressed with the growth in knowledge of things that don't change. Geometry was advanced mathematics when Aristotle wrote. Now it is taught to school children. Formal logic is a sophisticated technical discipline. Advances in cognitive science are making good on his hopes for discovering deep patterns of thought.

Aristotle says that the intellectual virtues must be taught to us for us to learn them well. It is unrealistic to expect us to spontaneously develop them on our own. Intellectual virtues, and our ability to pass them down through generations, are a particularly human achievement. Aristotle identified five varieties of intellectual virtue. We do not think of intellectual life and thought in this way any more, so I will use the names he gives them in Greek. The five kinds of intellectual virtue are: *techne, nous, phronesis, sophia,* and *episteme.* They are all important for ethics, but on a day to day level most of us just work with *techne.* When we confront difficult moral problems, we use *phronesis.* Big questions about the meaning of life and what is ultimately valuable can be answered only by *sophia.*

The first and most basic are skills or what he calls *techne. Techne* is the specialized knowledge that craftsmen have about making *things.* The knowledge of carpentry, horse-training, metal-working, masonry, weaving, cooking, and all the particular technical arts are instances of *techne.* Highly developed *techne* is what we think of as practical expertise.[3] It is sometimes tempting for people getting advanced degrees to minimize the importance and complexity of *techne.* I advise such people to spend a weekend trying to install baseboard and crown molding in a room of their house, or hang wallpaper. These tasks seem like they should be pretty straightforward, but doing them well is difficult and doing them well and quickly is an art. *Techne* combined with trade and friendship make up the foundation of civilization and to a large degree makes possible the opportunity to develop the other intellectual virtues. This kind of knowledge can be deep and complex, but it is not necessarily scientific in our modern sense. It is possible to be a master of *techne* without a deep theory of what one is doing. For example, master sword makers have been making Samurai swords for centuries, long before anyone knew modern theories of chemistry or metallurgy. The product of their traditional methods still routinely exceeds anything that metallurgists and machinists create.

Another example is the musician who has an expert "feel" for the music but doesn't know any music theory. My brother played in a band for years with a guy named Buck, who was a great guitarist. When my brother came back from college with a head full of music theory and sat down with Buck (and their guitars) to talk about it, Buck rapidly picked up the meaning of the terms and "got" the truth of the theory. He started out with only *techne* but since he was an expert, rapidly recognized the truth of the theory with *nous.* Having a body of knowledge about how to make a particular kind of thing, combined with expertise in making those things are what is necessary for *techne.* To understand why the techniques a master uses work requires *nous* and *episteme.*

Nous is the ability to perceive necessary rational truths. *Nous* is important because we must be able to recognize logical and mathematical truths to be able to reason about what we should do and how we should act. *Nous* is especially important because it enables us to "get it" and recognize the necessity of a conclusion when someone tells us what their reasoning is. At its most basic level, *nous* "gets" what numbers are. Numbers are basic forms or patterns. There is no "thing" that is two. There are symbols for the number (2 and II) and there are sets of two items, but what is "two" itself? "Two" is an idea; it is recognized by *nous. Nous* also enables us to "get" logical and mathematical proofs. Here is a basic form/pattern of proof:

> If A is greater that B,
> And B is greater than C,
> Then A is greater than C.

Notice that it doesn't matter what A, B, and C are (they could be anything from beads to planets); if the first two statements are true then the last one *must necessarily* be true. How do you know that? *Nous* recognizes the necessity of the reasoning.

Some people have very good *nous* and are quick to recognize these necessary formal truths (patterns.) Mathematicians and musicians typically have sharp *nous*. For other people it takes more attention and effort to "see" the patterns. When my brother described music theory to his friend Buck, Buck immediately "saw" the patterns my brother was describing and recognized their implications as necessary and true. *Nous* did not build the theory that my brother was telling Buck; that was done (over centuries) by people using *episteme. Nous* is the ability to recognize first principles and logical forms when we see them.

Episteme is the ability to manipulate ideas according to the rules of logic. Aristotle divides the world into things that change and things that don't change, and *episteme* is how we think about things that don't change, such as numbers and sets. *Episteme* enables us to make inferences and draw conclusions, to go beyond what we knew to figure out what else might be true based on what we already know. If I give you a series of numbers and ask you to continue them, you use *episteme* to continue them (and *nous* to recognize if your answer is correct or not.) For example if I started this series:

> 3, 6, 9, 12, 15, 18 . . .

And if you continued the series ten or twelve items out,[4] you would be using *episteme*. If I told you that all the members of a set can be divided by two, and I told you that 12 is a member of that set, you would easily be able to predict that twelve is divisible by two, even if you didn't know what "twelve" and "two" were. Whenever you do math or a proof in geometry you are using *episteme*, the ability to manipulate the patterns.

Phronesis is what we use when we reason about things that change, specifically actions. It is the crucial aspect of reason when we are concerned with acting well. People with good *phronesis* are practically wise; they are people who choose to act in ways that improve themselves, the people around them, and the society they live in. They are realistic and have a "feel" for how people act. They understand the patterns that govern human behavior. In modern times we might say they were good "practical behavioral psychologists." People who work well with others and are good at managing others have cultivated excellence in *phronesis*. When we make something well we are exercising *techne;* when we determine the best things to make, we are using *phronesis*. When we discover the basic principles of biology or chemistry we are using *episteme*; when we put that knowledge to good and beneficial use we are using *phronesis*.

Sophia is reason that contemplates and appreciates the highest things. The eternal truths and unchanging objects in the world are the domain of *sophia*. People who reflect on the eternal truths, like moral laws, the laws of physics and astronomy, are lovers of *sophia*. When we combine and embody excellence in all these areas we become truly virtuous people; we become virtuosi at life.

Politics and the Healthy Society

Aristotle says that human beings are "political animals." This is a bit confusing to modern readers because he means something different by "political" than we do. When we think of politics, we think of politicians or of backbiting and scheming co-workers. This is not at all what Aristotle meant. A "polis" in Greek just means a "city-state." So a political animal is one that naturally creates and lives in a city, just like beavers live in families in dens in dams that they construct, and bees live in organized hierarchies in hives that they construct. Like other animals. we are naturally social—we live in groups of others, and require nurturing by our own kind when we are young. Like other animals, we shape our habitat by altering it and building homes. Unlike other animals, our associations with others are not exclusively familial or based on reproductive groups. And unlike other animals, we organize ourselves in a way that makes us dependent on the activities of non-family others for our physical comfort and survival.

Political animals are essentially different than other animals in that we organize ourselves into complex, economically interdependent, non-familial groups that raise our physical standard of living through trade. In his book "The Politics," Aristotle tells a story about how a polis comes to be that is helpful for understanding just what a polis is.

The most basic unit of human organization is the nuclear family: a mother, a father, and their offspring. Over time, as the children grow up and find their own mates and have children, these family groupings form themselves into extended families that live in villages. At this level of social organization people have somewhat specialized skills, but mostly everyone can do everything that is required for survival. When people have disputes, they generally look to their parents to resolve them as children, and to elders, grandparents, or eldest aunts and uncles, to resolve them in larger more extended groups.

If the extended family grows beyond the carrying capacity of their local environment, it will split, and some members will go off and form their own independent familial grouping. When several of these groups live in an area they form a clan or a tribe. Because different physical locations offer different resources, the tribes begin to specialize and trade with each other. If one group lives near a marsh where there is good basket making material, and the other lives near clay deposits, the one group will make baskets and the other will make pots and they will trade. Two things are important to notice about this dynamic: first, they naturally find it convenient to develop particular skills, which raises the overall quality of their goods; and second, this dynamic makes everyone better off than they were before, since now they have pots and baskets and both are better than they would have been if they only had one or the other. Disputes inevitably arise, and in these very extended family groups or clans the natural approach to resolving them—appealing to the judgments of elders—still is the usual course. The details of how people organize their familial and social relations vary from group to group, culture to culture. So some people believe that who your father is is more important that who your mother is, others believe that who your mother is is more important. For Aristotle's story these details don't matter very much. The important points are that these groups grow, settle in geographical territories, specialize their labor, and trade.

As these groups grow and spread out, they inevitably come into contact with people they are not related to. Regular trade networks and friendships with people from other clans form the basis of the polis. A polis is a stable, complex network of regular trade and friendship between people who are from different clans. Aristotle says that people naturally (over time) create this kind of social organization. This kind of organization takes the specialization of production a step further than the clans do since it covers a much larger geographical area and so can take advantage of more diversity of natural resources. Thus, people in the polis are much richer and have much more stable economic lives than people who can only draw on smaller and less complex social organizations. The trend toward specialization increases, and productivity increases along with it until it creates a surplus. Now there is enough that the society can afford for some people to not work directly on subsistence activities. There is some breathing room to develop arts and music and philosophy. Make no mistake, arts and music and philosophy are present at all levels of social organization, but only in the polis are there sufficient social resources to support individuals who devote themselves exclusively to such pursuits. It is only in the polis that a person might have the opportunity to develop their full range of human virtues.

This opportunity comes at a cost, however, and the price is this: members of the polis must regard themselves as primarily parts of a larger and more valuable whole, and not primarily as independent individuals with rights that can supersede or override the good of the whole. While this may seem like a radical view to us now, for Aristotle it seemed perfectly clear that the whole was both greater and more valuable than any of the individual parts. In a just and healthy society, people are not often called upon to sacrifice their lives for the good of the whole, but it does happen from time to time. In a just and healthy society, people routinely make the small sacrifices that support and enrich the society as a whole: paying taxes, obeying inconvenient laws, serving on juries and committees, etc.[5]

This new and more prosperous organization based on non-clan trade and friendship creates a new and difficult problem: how will disputes be resolved without disrupting the wider network of trade and friendship? There is no shared pool of elders to draw on, and the elders are very likely to decide any issue with a strong bias to members of their own group. What to do? Aristotle says there are three basic arrangements—rule by one person (kingship/tyranny), rule by a few people (aristocracy/oligarchy), and rule by the many (democracy/timocracy). Each way can succeed or fail. Unhappily, the arrangement that is best when it succeeds is worst when it fails; a good king is the best arrangement, and a tyrant is the worst.[6]

In a stable and established polis, it now becomes possible for some people to develop not only moral virtues, but also intellectual virtues. People in this new environment can develop their talents and their characters to a far higher degree than they can in poorer societies. There is leisure to specialize, and stability to preserve what past generations have learned.

What happens in an unhealthy polis? Let's take a modern example. Suppose you lived in a modern tyranny where the government had made a law against having a satellite dish because they didn't want their people to know how other societies live and think. A number of modern tyrannies had exactly this policy when satellite dishes were large and hard to hide. Then satellite dishes got small, inexpensive, and relatively easy to hide. A lot more people got satellite dishes to watch TV. The problem is that kids watch cartoons and then go to school and talk about what they've watched with their friends. But if an informer hears that a kid has been watching a cartoon that is *only* available on satellite, then the family gets investigated and punished. So families must teach their children to lie to their friends, their teachers, and everyone else. But training small children to lie quickly makes them good at it, and they are going to use this new skill in all kinds of situations, not just the ones the parents want. In a decade or so you end up with a population that habitually lies. It is difficult to build a healthy functional society on the basis of lying. It is important that citizens (and friends and family members) be able to tell the hard truths instead of the easy lies in order to live good lives.

How to Solve Moral Problems: Using Reason to Determine the Right Thing to Do

There is no point in trying to teach ethics to young people, or so Aristotle says. I disagree with him about that. His reason is that ethics (the science of how we should act in a polis) requires extensive knowledge of "things that change" and young people don't have the breadth of experience necessary to have a working understanding of social and cultural dynamics. While I have some sympathy with this view,[7] I don't think his observation about the knowledge base of young people is entirely warranted any more.

The reasons Aristotle gives for not teaching young people ethics are that they don't understand why institutions and cultures are the way they are and how they work, and they don't understand how the natural world works, they don't understand formal reasoning, they lack enough stories to guide them, and they don't have a good feel for how human nature works. Clearly, these things are not nearly as true of young people today as they were then. To begin with, the average fourth grader knows more about animal ethology, biology, and ecology than Aristotle himself did, and with far more accuracy. They also have more instruction in formal reasoning, aka mathematics. Today geometry is typically taught in high school, but in Aristotle's time it was cutting edge advanced mathematics and the Pythagorean theorem was still a closely guarded secret of the Pythagorean cult. Calculus, trigonometry and analytic geometry, formal logic, and statistics had yet to be invented. Now a twelve-year-old baseball fanatic can typically do basic statistical calculations in his head while eating a hot dog. Thirteen-year-olds can go to calculus summer camp. Because of television, movies, and novels we know far more and more diverse stories than children in the distant past. We also have access to two millennia of well recorded multi-cultural history and the social sciences, which (when done correctly) can offer a great many hard won insights into how and why institutions and cultures work the way they do. In Aristotle's time education like this was expensive and scarce. It is now common and essentially free. Human nature is still a bit of a tough nut, but we have made huge progress in the last hundred years, figuring out learning disabilities, mental illness, and the science of motivation, and we seem to be making more and more rapid progress.

We should be careful to observe that simply having all this information and potential understanding at our fingertips does not make us wise or inherently increase our understanding any more than having a garage full of great tools and plans makes us great carpenters. We must still do the work of learning how to use all the tools we have, and develop the skills and wisdom (*techne* and *phronesis*) to put them into action. We can learn to use the tools faster, however, when we don't have to invent the tools as we go along. At the same time we ought to keep in mind that we can do more harm too.

When we find ourselves in a difficult or confusing situation we first check to see what our emotions are telling us. Then we reason (according to the intellectual virtues) to cross check our "gut reaction." When we have time, we consider the situation from four points of view: First, we should carefully and critically investigate the situation so that our knowledge of it is reliable and complete. Next, drawing on the stories we know and the knowledge we have about how things generally go, we should imagine what the possible and most likely outcome(s) are. We should then evaluate the possible outcomes against what we understand to be the best and highest standard. Then we should assess what course of action we are capable of and have the resources to pursue, paying particular attention to ones that push us out of our comfort zone (thereby helping us develop virtue). Next, we should consider what supports the development of virtue in the other people involved. Finally we must consider how our actions support or undermine the social institutions and cultural norms that make our society stable and healthy. In a pinch we could just ask ourselves, what would a virtuous person do in this situation?

According to Aristotle we should aim to be the best (most excellent/virtuous) person we can be. And we must support our friends and others developing their virtues. We do this so that we can live in and pass on a healthy society to our children and grandchildren. It is difficult to know in any particular situation what the absolute best thing is to do. And the fact is that even if we did know what that was, we couldn't do it. But among the options that are not the absolute best there are clearly better and worse options, and our job is to do the very best we can, at least partly in the hope that we will do better in the future. To act virtuously we must take the long view; we must be willing to trade short-term discomfort for long-term gain. Pleasure and pain cannot be the deciding factors for us because human beings need more than simply enjoying pleasures and avoiding pain. Our greatest satisfactions come from pursuing aims that are counted among the highest and ultimate goals.

When we are confused about what to do and we are in a difficult situation, the right thing to do will often be something that is a challenge for us. It will be something that calls on others to act well. It will be something that supports (or at least doesn't undermine) the social structures and institutions that nurture our communities and the individuals in them. It may be something that will help to improve our communities, and give individuals opportunities to develop more virtues. At a minimum we must aim at this kind of outcome. Learning to effectively pursue virtue (and its lived experience, *eudaimonia* most often translated as "happiness") takes a long time. Like all skills, we get better and faster the more often and more consciously we practice.

Why Would Anyone Want to Cultivate Virtue?

The simple answer to this question is that everyone (whether they consciously know it right this minute or not) wants to *eudaimon*. This greek word is most often translated as "happiness," but what we mean by happiness is not what Aristotle had in mind. We tend to think of happiness as "Disneyland happiness" a kind of enjoyable, unremitting pleasantness of bright colors, diverting activity, and amusement. But happiness that revolves around and depends on pleasure is not what Aristotle had in mind. Life is often difficult and inevitably painful. If we want to live well, and be good friends and live in a healthy society, we must be able to endure difficult times and muster our courage and resources to do difficult things in the face of adversity, and (here is the tough part) ideally we should be able to have some fun doing it.[8] This might seem like a strange notion at first—what does fun have to do with adversity? For the person who is in the grip of a number of vices: nothing. Adversity for such a person is always and inevitably painful. But a virtuous person is not at the mercy of pleasure and pain. *Eudaimon*, in Greek, translates literally as "possessed by a good spirit." Good spirited people regard pleasure and pain like the weather: something that may make one's plans easier or harder to accomplish, and more or less comfortable, but not as dictating what can and cannot be done. So even in the face of discomfort or pain (physical, emotional, spiritual, social, etc.) a virtuous person can do what is necessary.

This might sound like virtuous people have less fun than people with vices, but precisely the opposite is true. Here is a little thought experiment. Let us take two situations that we normally regard as "good" and "bad." For the virtuous (or *eudaimon*) person both are in fact good, but for the person in the grip of vice both are bad, and the "good" situation is actually *worse* than the "bad" situation. Suppose a person who has a vice, say an addiction to cocaine, or an excessive need for approval, gets rich and famous. Being rich and famous is generally considered a better situation than being poor and unknown. But if you are addicted to cocaine and you are rich and need to surround yourself with people who approve of you, you are much more likely to indulge that addiction and possibly die from it than you would be if you were poor and surrounded by people of various opinions. So, in fact, being rich makes you worse off because it eliminates or minimizes the external forces forcing you to get better. Being rich enables you to indulge your vices and make them worse. Being poor, on the other hand, creates a lot of problems for the indulgence of these vices. You will rapidly run out of money. Addicts are not very good people to have around so you will rapidly run out of friends. Should you try to use your friends and loved ones to get money to support your habit, you will make yourself unpopular. You will, in short, have a lot of external incentives to get better, to diminish your vices and cultivate your virtues. This is, clearly, painful in the short run, but leads to better outcomes in the long run. A similar analysis can be done for most any vice. So for the person in the grip of vice fame and fortune are worse than being poor and unknown. It is not much fun.

For a person of virtue, however, the situation is reversed. Fame and fortune will not undermine their virtue, but will provide a different set of resources for them to pursue the good, possibly (but not inevitably) making them better off than they were when poor and unknown. But poverty and anonymity are not particular handicaps to the *eudaimon* person, they just present a different situation. It might even be *more* fun than being rich and famous. Think about it this way: which is more fun, playing a game you are already very very good at and are not challenged by, or playing a new and challenging game right at the edge of your ability? Playing a game (think "go fish") that is too easy is boring. Playing a game that is too hard is frustrating and discouraging. The best situation is to have a game to play that is challenging but winnable with effort. This is the nature of fun. And there is satisfaction in playing a game to the best of your ability when you are challenged—win or lose. But winning a game of "go fish" against a couple of first graders is not satisfying in the same way, if at all.

Thus, there is little or no satisfaction in a life ruled by vice, whether the person has good fortune or bad. But there is always a great deal of satisfaction in a life of virtue, no matter what the world dumps on us. It is, I find, difficult for people today to imagine being "good at life" in the way Aristotle has in mind. We tend to think a person can be really good at one or two specialized skills and then just "o.k." at everything else. But Aristotle thought about life as a whole: about what it takes to live a satisfying life no matter what happens. What would it be like to be the sort of person who can get a kick out of the curveballs thrown by fate? Who sees adversity as a kind of a challenge to see what they can do? Who wakes up in the morning feeling competent to deal with whatever the day brings? Surely everyone would rather be that person than the addict who wakes up (after sleeping badly) and is driven to pursue their next fix.

So why should you want to pursue virtue? Because *eudaimon* people have the best and most fun and satisfying lives, no matter when or where or in what circumstances they live.

Notes

1. Two familiar ways of talking about how we cultivate virtue come from education and developmental psychology. We cultivate virtue when we behave in ways that are at the edges of our dispositional range. Professional educators call this the "zone of proximal development." Behavioral psychologists call it "operating outside your comfort zone" in the "zone of optimal performance."

2. Disclaimer: I am going to explain this using modern terms to make it more easily understandable for current students. Aristotle was thinking about this long before modern biology, psychology, and ethology. Many of the technical distinctions we take for granted were not available to him as they hadn't been discovered yet. For example, no one had made the distinction between mammals and reptiles, so they thought dolphins and whales were fish. We know a huge amount more about animals than Aristotle did, and a number of things he thought were just flat wrong. In light of the confusion this could create, I will explain these ideas using examples that are familiar to us, but that he couldn't or wouldn't have used.

3. It is interesting to observe that the hallmark of the products of highly developed *techne* is very often beauty or elegance.

4. 21, 24, 27, 30, 33, 36, 39 . . .

5. It is helpful to remember that the definition of making a "sacrifice" is "trading the lesser good for the greater." If one trades a greater good for a lesser that is not a sacrifice, it is just a bad bargain.

6. Democracy is the best version of the worst arrangement. The reason Aristotle gives for this judgment is that in a democracy people tend to be more concerned with their own advantage and benefit and forget that they are part of a larger whole, so the habits and attitudes that hold a society together tend to fall apart, and the society grows steadily more dysfunctional. In its degenerate form rule by the many turns into rule by the wealthy (timocracy) who get fewer and fewer as they use their political advantage for financial gain, until the many rally behind a charismatic leader and revolt, ordinarily making the leader a tyrant. It is not a pretty picture. Since Aristotle wrote people have developed a "hedge" against the degeneration of the forms of government: the rule of law. There was no independent judiciary in Ancient Greece, nor was there a separation of powers. The legislature was the judiciary as well, the executive was very weak (unless it was a strong king/tyrant), and there were no constitutional protections to limit the actions of the rulers.

7. This opinion is widely shared, and is captured by this widely repeated quotation, "When I was a boy of fourteen, my father was so ignorant I could hardly stand to have the old man around. But when I got to be twenty-one, I was astonished by how much he'd learned in seven years."—Mark Twain

8. This is not an argument that Aristotle gives explicitly, but it is implied by most of what he says, and was the common view in his day. I have formulated it as Boethius does in the last book of *The Consolation of Philosophy*.

The Kantian Perspective:
Fairness and Justice

Russ Shafer-Landau

Russ Shafer-Landau earned a PhD in philosophy from the University of Arizona in 1992 and is currently a professor of philosophy at the University of Wisconsin at Madison. In the following two chapters from his philosophy primer, Fundamentals of Ethics, *he explains and assesses part of Immanuel Kant's moral philosophy. Kant (Germany, 1724–1804) is undoubtedly one of the most prolific and influential philosophers the world has known. As Shafer-Landau explains, Kant attempted to offer criteria for distinguishing moral from immoral actions; and, importantly, these criteria focused on something other than the consequences of the actions, which makes Kant a vigorous opponent of utilitarianism. Shafer-Landau's first chapter focuses on what is known as Kant's "principle of universalizability," and the second chapter focuses on Kant's "principle of humanity."*

Imagine a person who reasons as follows: I should keep my money rather than pay it out in taxes, because if I keep it, I'll be able to afford a wonderful vacation for myself and my family. And no one is actually going to suffer if I pocket the money, since it's only a few thousand dollars that we're talking about. There's no way that money could bring as much happiness in the government's hands as it could in mine.

Suppose he is right about that. He spends the money on his vacation. He and his family have a terrific time. He is never caught.

Still, he has done something wrong. So has the person who cheats on her exams and gets away with it. So has the person who gleefully speeds down the emergency lane and escapes the traffic jam that the rest of us are stuck in. So has the person whose campaign of dirty tricks has gotten him securely into office.

Despite any good results that may arise from their actions, these people did wrong—or so we think. And the explanation of their immorality is simple. What they did was unfair. They took advantage of the system. They broke the rules that work to everyone's benefit. They violated the rights of others. No matter how much personal gain such actions bring, they are still wrong, because they are unfair and unjust.

Immanuel Kant (1724–1804) thought this way, and was very likely the most brilliant philosopher ever to have done so. He remains perhaps the most important voice of opposition to utilitarianism and its claim that the ultimate point of morality is to improve well-being rather than do justice.

Consistency and Fairness

There is a natural way to understand what is wrong about the actions in the examples just given. In each case, people are making exceptions of themselves. Their success depends on violating rules that most other people are following. This is a kind of inconsistency—of playing by one set of rules while insisting that others obey a different set.

People are inconsistent to the extent that they treat similar cases differently. There's nothing special about the tax cheat or the dirty politician that licenses their actions. They acted as if they had a unique privilege and were exempt from the rules that everyone must follow. But there has to be something unusual about a person, or her situation, in order to gain that sort of privilege. That you can get away with making an exception of your-self doesn't mean that it is right to do so.

Our deep opposition to unfairness, and the corresponding importance we assign to consistency, is shown in some very familiar tests for immorality. The two most popular tests each take the form of a question:

1. What if everyone did that?
2. How would you like it if I did that to you?

When we ask such questions—in the face of a bully, a liar, or a double-crosser—we are trying to get the person to see that he is acting unfairly, making an exception of himself, living by a set of rules that work only because others are not doing what he is doing. These basic moral challenges are designed to reveal the inconsistency, and so the immorality, of that person's behavior.

Consider the first question: What if everyone did that? This question is really shorthand for the following test: *If disastrous results would occur if everyone did X, then X is immoral.* If everyone used the emergency lanes in traffic jams, then ambulances and fire trucks would often fail to provide needed help, leaving many to die. If everyone cheated on their taxes, society would crumble. If every candidate resorted to dirty tricks, then the entire political system would become corrupted. The test works easily and well for these cases.

But the test fails for other cases, and so it cannot serve as a reliable way to learn the morality of actions. Consider a common argument against homosexual sex: If everyone did that, disaster would soon follow, for the human race would quickly die out. Even if this were true, that wouldn't show that homosexual sex is immoral. Why not? Well, consider those who have decided to remain celibate—perhaps they are priests, or committed lifelong bachelors who believe that one shouldn't have sex without being married. What if everyone did *that*—i.e., refrained from having sex? The same results would follow. But that doesn't show that celibacy is immoral.

The real problem for this test, apart from the fact that it sometimes delivers mistaken verdicts, is that it makes the morality of an action depend on how it is described. Suppose the sexual relations of a gay couple were described as their having consensual, enjoyable sex. In that case, their actions would pass the test. But that undermines the test, because it shows that the test yields contradictory results. The very same action is said to be both morally wrong and morally acceptable, depending only on how it is described. Without any independent guidance on how to select one description over another, this test cannot do the job it was supposed to do—namely, identify which acts are immoral.

What about the other test, the one that asks: How would you like it if I did that to you? This is a direct application of the **golden rule**, which tells you to treat others as you would like to be treated. The golden rule is the classic test of morality. Clearly, it is meant to be a test of consistency. If you wouldn't want to be slandered or exploited, then don't do such things to others. If you do them anyway, you are acting inconsistently, hence unfairly, and therefore immorally.

Getting people to imagine what it would be like to switch places with their intended victims is often a very effective way to convey a moral message. That is why films and literature are often such powerful tools of moral education. But imaginatively filling someone else's shoes, and asking yourself whether you'd accept being treated in a certain way, is actually an unreliable test of morality. The golden rule cannot be correct.

Kant himself identified the basic reason for this. The golden rule makes morality depend on a person's desires. Most of us don't like to be hit. And so the golden rule forbids us from hitting others. So far, so good. But what about masochists who enjoy being hit? The golden rule allows them to go around hitting others. That's bad. The morality of hitting people shouldn't depend on whether you like to take a beating every now and then.

Consider a related problem, that of the fanatic. Fanatics are principled people. It's just that their principles are ones that we find frightening and revolting. Some fanatics are so wedded to their cause, so strong-willed and self-disciplined, that they would accept the suffering that they want to impose on their victims, were the role of victim and persecutor reversed. True, few Nazis, for instance, would really accept a march to the gas chamber were they to discover their Jewish ancestry. Most Nazis, like most fanatics generally, are opportunists of bad faith, ones with very limited empathy and only a feeble ability to imagine themselves in someone else's place. If roles really were reversed, they'd much more likely beg for mercy and abandon their genocidal principles. But some would not. There are true believers out there who are willing to suffer any harm in the name of their chosen cause. The golden rule licenses their extremism because it makes the morality of an action depend entirely on what you want and what you are willing to put up with.

The golden rule also fails to give us guidance on **self-regarding actions**— i.e., those that concern only oneself. That's not a problem for most people these days, since it's now unusual to think that we owe moral duties to ourselves. But in Kant's time, self-regarding duties were widely endorsed, and many people still think, for instance, that there is something immoral about suicide or about letting one's talents go to waste, even if no one else is harmed in the process.

Because the golden rule sometimes gives the wrong answer to moral questions, it cannot be the ultimate test of morality. Something else must explain why it works, when it does. Kant thought he had the answer.

The Principle of Universalizability

Kant, like most of us, felt the appeal of the two tests just discussed. He agreed that common sense is deeply committed to the importance of fairness and consistency, something that these two tests were trying, but not quite succeeding, in capturing. His aim was to identify the ultimate principle of morality, one that would explain the attraction of the two tests while correcting for their shortcomings.

He thought he had found it in the following standard, the **principle of universalizability**:

An act is morally acceptable if and only if its maxim is universalizable.

To understand what this means, we need to understand two things: what a **maxim** is, and what it is for a maxim to be **universalizable**.

A maxim is simply the principle of action you give yourself when you are about to do something. For instance, if you send a regular check to Oxfam, your maxim might be: contribute fifty dollars per month to Oxfam to help alleviate hunger. A maxim has two parts. It states what you are about to do, and why you are about to do it. You dictate your own maxims. These are the rules you live by.

Kant thought that every action has a maxim. Of course we don't always formulate these maxims clearly to ourselves prior to acting, but at some level, whenever we act, we intend to do something, and we have a reason for doing it. A maxim is nothing but a record of that intention and its underlying reason. Maxims are what we cite when we try to explain to others why we act as we do.

If we lack a maxim, then we aren't really acting at all. We could be moving our bodies, as we do when we sneeze or roll across the bed in our sleep. But the absence of a maxim in these cases shows that these are mere bodily movements, rather than genuine actions.

Kant thought that an action's Tightness depends on its maxim. And this leads directly to a very important implication. For Kant, the morality of our actions has nothing to do with results. It has everything to do with our intentions and reasons for action, those that are embedded within the principles we live by. This is a clear break with consequentialism.

Indeed, we can imagine two people doing the same thing, but for different reasons. That means that they will have different maxims. And even if their actions bring about identical results, one of the actions may be right and the other wrong, since only one of the maxims may be morally acceptable. This is something that act consequentialists cannot accept.

It might be, for instance, that I keep my promise to you because I think it's right to do so. But I might also keep my promise to you because I want you to develop such a trust in me that you leave me your fortune in your will. Assume that the way I keep my promise in both cases is the same. And assume that the results are the same in both cases as well. Then the utilitarian thinks that the morality of my action cannot change between the two cases. But since my maxim is different in these cases, Kant thinks that the morality of these two actions might be different. It all depends, as we'll shortly see, on whether these maxims are universalizable.

Many people agree with Kant's view that the morality of our actions depends not on their results, but on our maxims. For this supports our thought that those who set out to do evil are acting immorally, even if, through sheer chance, they manage to do good. It also justifies the claim that people who live by noble principles are acting morally, even when some unforeseeable accident intervenes, and their action brings only bad results.

Kant had a deep reason for making the morality of an action depend on its maxim, rather than its results. That reason (discussed in detail in the next chapter) is this: it is crucial that the morality of our actions depends entirely on what is within our control. We *can* control which maxims will govern our actions. We decide for ourselves what we intend to do. Even in cases where my options are severely limited, as when a thug has a gun at my head, it is up to me to decide which choice to make.

By contrast, the results of our actions are often out of our hands. We can't always control them. And it is unfair to assign credit or blame for things we can't control. That is why we have an insanity defense. That is why we don't prosecute animals for the damage they sometimes cause. That is why we don't condemn infants for any harm they do.

So the morality of actions depends on their maxims. But how, precisely? Not every maxim is going to be a good one. We need a way to sort out the good maxims from the bad. That's where universalizability comes in.

How can we tell whether a maxim is universalizable? Here is a three-part test:

1. Formulate your maxim clearly—state what you intend to do, and why you intend to do it.
2. Imagine a world in which everyone supports and acts on your maxim.
3. Then ask: Can the goal of my action be achieved in such a world?

If the answer to this last question is *yes,* then the maxim is universalizable, and the action is morally acceptable. If the answer is *no,* then the maxim is not universalizable, and the action it calls for is immoral.

This should strike a familiar note. The test of a maxim's universalizability clearly echoes the rule consequentialist's test for optimific social rules (see the previous chapter), and the *What if everyone did that?* test. Indeed, Kant has us ask a version of that question in the second step of this three-part test. But unlike these other tests, Kant doesn't ask about whether people would be much better off in the imagined world, or about whether disaster would strike there. Instead, he asks about whether we could achieve our own goals in that world. But what is so important about that?

The importance, for Kant, is that this three-part test serves as the real way to determine whether we are being consistent and fair. If our maxim is universalizable, then we are pursuing actions for reasons that everyone could stand behind. We are not making exceptions of ourselves. Our goals are ones that everyone *could* support, even if, in the real world, some are dead set against them. If they can be, this shows that we are living by fair rules. Were we making an exception of ourselves, our maxims wouldn't be universalizable.

Consider the tax cheat again. The only reason he can get what he is aiming for (a lovely vacation) is because enough others are not adopting his maxim. The same goes for the careless driver who speeds down the emergency lane.

Kant sought to make this point with an example of his own. (I am embellishing a bit, but the essence of the example is Kant's.) Suppose that I am a compulsive gambler who is constantly in debt. One night I go to the tables to recoup my losses, only to dig myself further in the hole. The casino boss is having his men drop by tonight to collect. I can either pay them or have my kneecaps broken. I know which one I'd prefer.

The problem is, I don't have the money, the bank won't lend me any more, and I don't have one to turn to but you. (No one else trusts me any longer to repay my debts). Since you are aware of any my reputation, I know that the only way to get the money is by lying to you. So, I beg and plead and promise you, by all I hold dear, that I will repay you—all the while having no intention of doing so. I have just made what Kant calls a *lying promise.*

It seems clear that what I am about to do is immoral. And that is true even if, through a minor miracle, I then feel so much guilt that I repent of my ways, transform myself, and make the lie turn out for the best in the end. The morality of the action doesn't depend on its results, but on its maxim. And my maxim here is not universalizable. So my action is immoral, as Kant says, and as we believe.

Here's why. Suppose my maxim is: lie to a friend, in order to escape from being hurt. And suppose everyone acts on this maxim. They lie whenever they think that it is necessary to avoid some personal harm. In that situation, no one would trust the promises of others. And without that trust, people could not achieve the goals they are aiming for with their promises. In a world where no one believed the promises of others, I'd never be able to get money from you with my promise. And so the purpose of my promise would be defeated. And so my maxim is not universalizable. I am making an exception of myself, and am treating you unfairly. My action is therefore immoral.

Morality and Rationality

Kant claimed that when we act on a maxim that can't be universalized, we are contradicting ourselves. We are being inconsistent. We are assuming that it is acceptable to act in a certain way, even though our purposes could not be achieved if others acted in that very same way. When we make an exception of ourselves, we are acting as if we were more important than anyone else, and going on as if we were exempt from rules that others must obey. But we are not more important than others, and we are not exempt from these requirements.

It follows that when we behave immorally, we are reasoning badly. We are making mistaken assumptions—that we are more important than other people, that the rules applying to them do not apply to us. Those mistakes, and the inconsistent, contradictory reasoning behind them, show that *immoral conduct is irrational.*

That is a very striking claim, and one that most of us hope is true. We want to be able to convict rapists or terrorists of irrationality, of ignoring their strongest reasons. We want to be able to truthfully say that there were excellent reasons for them to do good and to avoid evil. Kant believed that we could do this.

But how could Kant be right? Consider the ruthless contract killer who knows precisely what he wants, knows exactly how to get it, and executes his plan without fail. Morality doesn't enter into his calculations. He knows that what he is doing is immoral, but that doesn't faze him. It seems that such a person is reasoning flawlessly. How could we convict him of irrationality?

Let's call this the *Amoralist's Challenge.* The **amoralist** is someone who believes in right and wrong but doesn't care about morality at all. The amoralist has the same attitude to moral rules as I do to the rules of professional cricket—yes, they really exist, but they have no bearing on my life at all. Obedience to these rules is completely optional. If I am interested in playing the game, then I'll follow the rules. If not, then there is no reason to do so.

The Amoralist's Challenge supports this view in the following way:

1. People have a reason to do something only if doing it will get them what they care about.
2. Doing their moral duty sometimes fails to get people what they care about.
3. Therefore, people sometimes lack any reason to do their moral duty.
4. If people lack any reason to do their moral duty, then violating their moral duty can be perfectly rational.
5. Therefore, it can be perfectly rational for people to violate their moral duty.

The success of this argument would undermine the thought that morality, all by itself, supplies us with good reason to do as it says. It would also refute Kant's claim that immoral actions are always irrational.

Kant thought that you act irrationally when you act contrary to your strongest reasons. And he thought that when moral reasons apply to a given situation, they are always the strongest reasons. Moral reasons defeat the importance of any other kind of consideration. If morality requires you to do something, then that is what you must do—even if you don't want to do it, even if you'll suffer for doing it, and even if the results of doing it are generally disastrous. When you act immorally, you are acting irrationally.

Kant admits that the ruthless contract killer, like so many other successful criminals, did, in a sense, reason perfectly well. He followed what Kant called **hypothetical imperatives**. Specifically, these imperatives (commands) are commands of reason. They command us to do whatever is needed in order to get what we care about. Hypothetical imperatives tell us how to achieve our goals. They require us, on pain of irrationality, to do certain things, but only because such actions will get us what we want.

For instance, if my goal is to lose twenty pounds (as it often is), then reason requires me to forgo that pint of luscious coffee ice cream. If I want to get that Wall Street job, then reason requires that I line up a good summer internship. Reason demands that I look both ways at a busy intersection if I want to remain alive. These rational commands apply to me because of what I care about. I am irrational if I disregard them or act in a way that frustrates them.

But what if I decide that I don't care about weight loss or the benefits that weight loss can bring? What if I don't care about a Wall Street job? What if I want to die rather than live? In that case, I am no longer rationally required to pass on the ice cream, get the internship, or look both ways before crossing the street. These commands of reason are precarious. Their existence depends entirely on what I want. When my desires change, these rational requirements change or disappear.

Many people think that all rational requirements are like this—that they are all hypothetical imperatives. That's precisely what the first premise of the Amoralist's Challenge states: all of our reasons for action depend on what we care about.

Kant saw the implications of this argument very clearly, and knew that he had to challenge that first premise. In his jargon, what we need is to show how there can be such a thing as a **categorical imperative**. This is also a command of reason. But unlike hypothetical imperatives, categorical imperatives are rational requirements that do *not* depend on what we care about. They are requirements of reason that apply to everyone who possesses reason—i.e., everyone able to reflect on the wisdom of her actions, and able to use such reflections to guide her actions. Categorical imperatives command us to do things whether we want to or not, with the result that if we ignore or disobey them, we are acting contrary to reason—i.e., irrationally.

Kant thought that *all moral duties are categorical imperatives.* They apply to us just because we are rational beings. We must obey them even if we don't want to, and even if moral obedience gets us nothing that we care about.

One lesson Kant took from his consideration of the golden rule is that the basic rules of morality do not depend on our desires. If they did, then moral rules would fail to apply to everyone, since our desires can differ from person to person. This would make morality too variable, and make it possible for people to escape from their moral duty just by changing what they want. Kant thought that he was defending common sense when he claimed that morality is, in this sense, universal—that everyone who can reason must obey its commands.

If moral duties really are categorical imperatives, then we act rationally so long as we act morally, and we act irrationally if we disregard the demands of morality. Is that sort of view defensible? Can we really justify the claim that it is rational for everyone to act morally—even if we know that, for some people, moral conduct will only undermine their goals?

Kant thought he could do this. Consider his *Argument for the Irrationality of Immorality:*

1. If you are rational, then you are consistent.
2. If you are consistent, then you obey the principle of universalizability.
3. If you obey the principle of universalizability, then you act morally.
4. Therefore, if you are rational, then you act morally.
5. Therefore, if you act immorally, then you are irrational.

Its does seem that rationality requires consistency, as the first premise asserts. And, as we have discussed, the principle of universalizability is a demand of consistency. So, while more could certainly be said about these first two premises, let us take them for granted here and focus on the third. This is the claim that obedience to the principle of universalizability guarantees that our conduct is moral.

Its location in this argument tells us that the principle of universalizability is a crucial element in Kant's reply to the Amoralist's Challenge. He needs to successfully defend the principle in order to secure the claim that rational people are moral people, and immoral people are irrational. Can he do it?

Assessing the Principle of Universalizability

Unfortunately, the principle of universalizability fails as a general test for the morality of our actions. Look at premise 3 of Kant's Argument for the Irrationality of Immorality. It says that a maxim's universalizability is a guarantee of an action's Tightness. That is false. We can act on universalizable maxims and still do wrong.

The principle of universalizability seems to be a very attractive way of pointing out how unfairness and inconsistency lead to immorality. So, for instance, when a thief robs a bank in order to gain riches, Kant can show why his action is immoral. If everyone acted on that maxim, there would be no money in the bank to steal, and the thief's goal could not be achieved. But what if the thief had robbed the bank in order to cripple it and put it out of business? If everyone acted that way, then the thief's goal *could* be achieved. So the principle of universalizability fails to condemn the robbery. And yet such an act is surely wrong.

Suppose that someone wants nothing more than to have a picture-perfect lawn. His basic maxim is to do whatever it takes to preserve the beauty of his grass. This would be strange, but that is no strike against his plans. The real thorn in this guy's side is the mail carrier, who always trots across the lovely yard on his way to delivering the mail. He has been warned, repeatedly, to use the sidewalk—to no avail. So the homeowner decides to take matters into his own hands. The next time the mailman tramples his lawn, the homeowner pulls out a gun and kills him.

That's clearly the wrong thing to do. But this man's maxim is universalizable. It tells him to take whatever steps are necessary (including killing) in order to preserve the beauty of his lawn. What if everyone were to act upon this maxim? Could the homeowner's goal be met? Undoubtedly. And so, if the principle of universalizability is true, this is no murder; it is justifiable killing. That has to cast serious doubt on the principle.

This unlikely example is just an instance of a general problem, one that we have seen before. Recall the case of the fanatic that arose in discussion of the *What if everyone did that?* test. The goals of fanatics are ones that can often be met in a world in which everyone shares their aims. Fanatics (such as the lawn fanatic) need not make exceptions of themselves. The murderous aims of any number of groups could easily be achieved in a world in which everyone supported them. Thus fanatics can be consistent in the relevant sense: their guiding principles could be fulfilled if everyone else were to adopt them.

I think this shows that the principle of universalizability fails to give us an adequate test of fairness. For we can follow its advice while still singling out individuals or groups for discriminatory treatment. There can be consistent Nazis, after all. It doesn't follow that their policies are fair or morally acceptable.

Integrity

While utilitarians think of benevolence (the steady commitment to do good for others) as the central moral virtue, Kant touts integrity. Having integrity is living in harmony with the principles you believe in. It is the virtue of consistency. Integrity requires that you resist making an exception of yourself. It demands that you follow your principles even when doing so comes at a real cost. Kant is surely right that there is something admirable about integrity.

But integrity is not the only moral virtue, and it isn't even the most important one. The example of the fanatic reveals this. We may be absolutely dedicated to our principles, but if those principles are deeply flawed, it would be better, morally speaking, for us to have less integrity. That's surely what we want of the Nazi commandant or the dedicated terrorist. It would be better were they less principled people. We want them to be more flexible, and more open to the possibility that their guiding ideals are mistaken. When Huck Finn beats himself up for continuing to hide Jim, the escaped slave who accompanies him down the Mississippi, we applaud Huck's lack of integrity. A Huck with greater integrity is also one who would betray Jim's location. We want Huck to be less than fully conscientious, since that will mean Jim's freedom.

Integrity is worthy of our admiration only when it is tied to morally legitimate principles. The problem, as we have seen, is that people of integrity may still be doing wrong. Refusing to make an exception of myself is no guarantee that my principles are morally acceptable. It's not that consistency is worthless. But it fails as a general test for the morality of the principles we live by.

Kant on Absolute Moral Duties

Kant thought that certain sorts of actions are never permitted. Lying is one of them. In a much-discussed case, that of the inquiring murderer, Kant has us imagine a man bent on killing. This man knocks at your door and asks if you know the location of his intended victim. You do. Should you reveal it? If you do, your information is almost certainly going to lead to murder.

Kant thought you had two decent choices. Ideally, you'd just say nothing. That wouldn't help the murderer, and it wouldn't involve lying. But what if this isn't an option? What if you have to say something? In that case, you have to tell the truth—because you must never lie, under any circumstances.

I think that this is the wrong answer, and the interesting thing is that Kant's own theory does not require him to give it. Kant himself was so convinced of the absolute immorality of lying that he misapplied him own theory.

Kant never provided an argument for the claim that the moral rules that prohibit such things as lying and killing are absolute (i.e., never permissibly broken).
The closest he came to supplying such an argument was in his belief that moral
considerations are more important than anything else. In any conflict between
moral duty and other demands—say, those of the law, self-interest, or tradition—
morality wins.

Still, it doesn't follow that moral duties are absolute. For even if they always
outweigh other kinds of considerations, moral duties might conflict *with other
moral duties*. And if they do, they can't all be absolute. Some of them must give
way to others.

And can't moral duties conflict with each other? It seems, for instance, that
there is a duty to avoid hurting people's feelings, a duty to preserve national
security, a duty not to start a panic, and a duty to protect innocent people from
dangerous attackers. It also seems that fulfilling these duties will sometimes
require us to lie, and that there is a moral duty not to do so. Perhaps none of these
are really moral duties. Or perhaps, implausibly, we'd never need to lie in order to
respect these duties. But much more likely is the thought that these are real duties,
and that they really can conflict with another genuine duty—the duty not to lie.

But if that is so, then these duties cannot all be absolute. For if they were, then
contradiction would ensue. Suppose, for instance, that the president is under an
absolute duty to preserve national security. But if the only way to do that is to lie,
and if lying is always wrong, then lying in this case would be both right (because
it preserved national security) and wrong (because it was a lie). And this is a contradiction. So if moral duties can conflict—and it certainly seems they can—then
they cannot all be absolute.[1]

This does not spell disaster for Kant. He does not need to defend the existence of absolute moral duties. His philosophy can, for instance, justify lying to the
inquiring murderer. Kant's hatred of lying made him overlook a crucial element of
his own view—namely, that the morality of action depends on one's maxim. He just
assumed that anyone who lied would be operating with a maxim like this: tell a lie
so as to gain some benefit. That maxim is not universalizable. In a world in which
everyone did this, no one would trust the words of others, and people would be
unable to secure any of the goals they were trying to achieve through lying.

But why think that Kant's maxim is the only one you could have in such a
situation? A maxim is a principle that you give yourself. No one forces it on you.
You decide what you are about to do, and why you are about to do it. For instance,
suppose I used this maxim to justify lying to the inquiring murderer: say what you
need to say in order to prevent the murder of an innocent person. I think that this
maxim is universalizable. If everyone adopted this maxim, there would not be a
general breakdown of trust and communication. People would still believe one

another. The goal I am aiming for—to save an innocent person's life—could be achieved if this maxim were shared by everyone.

The maxim that tells me to lie to the inquiring murderer may be quite different from yours or anyone else's. And since, for Kant, the morality of an action depends on its maxim, we can't determine whether an act is right or wrong until we know its maxim. There is only way for Kant to absolutely ban a type of action. And that is to be sure in advance that every maxim that allows it fails to be universalizable. It is hard to see how we could ever know that.

This is all to the good, since it opens up the possibility that lying to the inquiring murderer is morally okay. Of course, if Kant is right, then we would have to have a universalizable maxim that permits this. But nothing Kant ever said should make us think that this is impossible. Contrary to Kant's personal view, we don't have to regard all (or perhaps any) moral duties as absolute.

Note

1. For much more discussion of absolute duties, conflicts among them, and the nature of contradiction, please see chapter 15, pp. 211–212.

The Kantian Perspective: Autonomy and Respect

Russ Shafer-Landau

Is there anything wrong with slavery?

This probably sounds like an idiotic question. Of course slavery is wrong. So let me rephrase my question: Is there anything wrong, in and of itself, with enslaving other people? In practice, slavery has always created much more harm than good. But what if that were not the case? What if the members of a slave society—slaves as well as masters—were, on the whole, wealthier, better educated, healthier, and better satisfied with their lives than most members of a free society? And what if the abolition of slavery was sure to undercut these greater benefits? In those circumstances, would slavery still be wrong?

This thought experiment was put to readers by an important twentieth-century moral philosopher, Richard Hare. In his article "What Is Wrong with Slavery,"[1] Hare defended the utilitarian view that denied that anything in intrinsically wrong with slavery. Everything depends on the actual results of a slave system; is the imagined example, Hare had to admit that the slave society, since it created greater overall benefits, was the morally superior option. This despite the fact that Hare was, for all practical purposes, once a slave himself. As a British soldier in World War II, he was captured by Japanese forces and interned in a camp that effectively enslaved its inmates.

Hare emphasized that his views did not license any slave system as actually practiced. He presented the story as a way to show that there is nothing intrinsically wrong with slavery. The utilitarian says that the morality of slavery, like that of any other practice, depends entirely on its results. In the picture Hare paints, slavery can be morally acceptable.

Many will recoil at this verdict. They will feel that slavery can never be morally right, because it grossly violates people's autonomy. Slavery allows people to be treated as mere things—objects without any rights, of no intrinsic importance.

This is precisely the Kantian objection to slavery. Morality requires us always to treat human beings with the dignity they deserve. Slavery is inherently disrespectful. No one deserves such treatment. That is what explains why slavery is wrong.

Intuitively, this makes good sense. But it requires a bit of work to unpack it. We need to better understand why treating people as they deserve is so important, and what it means, specifically, to say that we deserve dignity and respect.

The Principle of Humanity

In the course of his work, Kant identified a number of different candidates for the role of ultimate moral principle. He thought that they each ended up requiring and forbidding precisely the same things, thought most philosophers see important differences in these principles, and think that they sometimes issue different recommendations. While the principle of universalizability clearly emphasizes the moral importance of fairness, another of Kant's formulations directs our attention to the respect and dignity that serve as the basis of our moral treatment of others. This formulation is widely known as the **principle of humanity:**

> Always treat a human being (yourself included) as an end, and never as a mere means.

To understand this principle, we need to get clear about three things: humanity, ends, and means.

When Kant spoke of *humanity*, he was not thinking of all members of the species Homo sapiens. Rather, he was (for reasons that will soon become clear) referring to all rational and autonomous beings. Perhaps there are aliens, or some other mammals, who are rational and autonomous. If so, then they count as human beings for purposes of Kant's principle.

Treating someone *as an end* is treating her with the respect she deserves. Treating someone *as a means* is dealing with her so that she helps you achieve one of your goals. This may be perfectly okay. I do this, for instance, when I hire a plumber to fix a broken water pipe in my kitchen. In an innocent sense, I am using him—he is needed to get me what I want (a functioning sink, in this case). Yet if I greet him at the door, give him any assistance he asks for, and then pay him as he leaves, I am also treating him with respect, and so, in Kantian terms, I am also treating him as an end.

But what if, while the plumber is checking the leak, I remove a wrench from his toolkit and whack him over the head with it? He's out cold—excellent. I then snugly fit his head into the space where the pipe has corroded, thus temporarily stopping the leak. While he's unconscious, I rush off to the hardware store and buy a cheap bit of PVC pipe. The plumber wakes up just as I am returning from the store. I scold him for falling asleep on the job, and usher him out the door with a curt good riddance. Then I proceed to fix the leak myself, saving myself a hefty fee.

What has happened in this ridiculous scenario is that I've used the plumber literally as a thing, as a piece of pipe. He might as well have been an inanimate object. I failed to treat him in a way that recognized any of his distinctively human features. That's why I have treated him *as a mere means.*

While it often happens that people do treat one another both as an end and as a means, one can't treat people both as an end and as a *mere* means. Treating someone as an end implies a degree of respect that is absent when treating someone as a mere means.

Most of us think that there is something about humanity that lends us dignity and makes us worthy of respect. Most of us also think that human beings are worthy of greater respect than anything else in creation. Humans are more important than monkeys or sharks or daffodils or amoebas. Is this a defensible position, or is it just a self-interested prejudice?

Kant had an answer. He claimed that we are each rational and autonomous, and that these traits are what justify our special moral status. These two powers make us worthy of respect. Being rational, as we have seen, involves using our reason to tell us how to achieve our goals and to determine whether we can pursue them in a morally acceptable way. It takes a lot of brainpower to be able to formulate your goals, to imagine a world where everyone pursues them as you do, and then to ask about the consistency of your actions. Human beings are the only species on earth that can engage in such complex reasoning.

Being autonomous literally means being a self-legislator. Autonomous people are those who decide for themselves which principles are going to govern their life. You are an autonomous person. You possess the ultimate responsibility for the choices you make, the goals you aim for, and the manner in which you pursue them. You are not a slave to your passions; you can resist temptation, check your animalistic urges, and decide for yourself whether to indulge them. You are not absolutely forced to act as you do, but are free to choose your own path.

Kant thought that our rationality and autonomy made each of us literally priceless. Despite the work of actuaries and juries in wrongful death suits, you cannot really put a dollar figure on a human life. Unlike mere objects, human beings are not replaceable one for another. The assumption that we are infinitely valuable explains our feelings of agonized loss at the death of a loved one. If we had to choose between the destruction of the most beautiful are object in the world and the killing of a human being, we should choose the former. No matter how valuable the object, the value of a human life exceeds it by an infinite amount.

The Importance of Rationality and Autonomy

Kant argues that rationality and autonomy support the dignity of each human being, and that everyone is owed a level of respect because of these traits. This makes excellent sense of a number of deeply held moral beliefs. Here are the most important of them.

1. It explains, in the first place, the immorality of a fanatic's actions. Such people don't regard human life as infinitely precious, but rather treat their despised opponents as mere obstacles to the achievement of their goals. The principle of humanity forbids such behavior, even when it is consistently undertaken, and thus allows us to address the most severe problem facing the principle of universalizability.

2. The importance of autonomy explains why slavery and rape are always immoral. Slavery treats the oppressed without regard for their own goals and hopes. Rape is treating another human being solely as a source of one's own gratification, as if the victim had no legitimate say in the matter. These are the most extreme examples of duress and coercion. They are immoral because of their complete denial of the victim's autonomy. As such, these crimes are perhaps the clearest cases of treating other people as mere means.

3. The principle of humanity easily explains our outrage at paternalism. To be paternalistic is to assume the rights and privileges of a parent—toward another adult. Paternalism has us limit the liberty of others, for their own good, against their will. It is treating autonomous individuals as children, as if we, and not they, were best suited to making the crucial decisions of their lives. It is paternalistic, for instance, if a roommate sells your TV set because he is worried about your spending too much time watching *Seinfeld* reruns and too little time on your homework. Or imagine a classmate who thinks that your boyfriend is bad for you, and so writes him a nasty note and forges your signature, hoping that he'll break off your relationship. Anyone who has experienced paternalistic treatment knows how infuriating it can be. And the reason is simple: We are autonomous and rational, and the ability to create our own life plan entitles us to do so. We ought to be free to make a life for ourselves, even if, as is sometimes the case, we make a mess of things.

4. Our autonomy is what justifies the attitude of never abandoning hope in people. The chances that a very hard-hearted man will change his outlook may be very small, but the probability never reduces to zero. No matter how badly he was raised, or how badly he has lived his life, he is still autonomous, and so can always choose to better himself. It is usually naive to expect such a transformation. Changing your character and habits is hardly easy. But the possibility of redemption is always there, and that is only because we are free to determine the principles that will guide our lives.

5. Many people believe in universal human rights. These are moral rights that protect every human being from certain kinds of treatment and entitle each of us to a minimum of respect, just because we are human. Kant can explain

why we have such rights. We have them because of our rationality and autonomy. These two traits are the basis for living a meaningful life. If you doubt this, just imagine a life without them. It is a life fit for an insect, or a plant. What endows our life with preciousness is our ability to reason and choose for ourselves how we are going to live it. Every person is rational and autonomous to some degree, and every person needs these powers protected in order to have the sorts of experiences, engage in the kinds of activities, and support the sorts of relationships that make life worth living. Human rights protect these powers at a very fundamental level.

6.   Our autonomy is what explains our practices of holding one another accountable for our deeds and misdeeds. Because we are not robots, but rather free and rational human beings, we are morally responsible for our choices and actions. We are fit for praise and blame, and that is because our conduct is up to us. We don't blame sharks or falcons for killing their prey; neither do we condemn a wilted orchid or a nasty-smelling ginkgo tree. Plants and animals deserve neither credit nor blame, and this is because their lives are not autonomous ones.

7.   Relatedly, most people believe that punishment, rather than conditioning, is the appropriate response to serious wrongdoers. When dogs "misbe-have," we don't try to reason with them. We try to condition them to change their behavior through a set of rewards and punishments. They don't deserve to be punished when they break our rules, and that is because they lack the power to change their behavior by reasoning about it. By contrast, humans do sometimes deserve to be punished, precisely because they could have chosen to act well, but decided to act badly instead. People also deserve not to be manipulated into becoming obe-dient citizens. If we want criminals to behave differently, we must still respect their autonomy. The importance of autonomy explains why it is so objectionable to brain-wash people, or to drug or torture them into doing what we want.

The Good Will and Moral Worth

Kant's insistence on the importance of rationality and autonomy led him to a view of intrinsic value that is very different from that of consequentialists. The struc-ture of consequentialist thought is simple. Identify what is worth pursuing for its own sake; your moral duty is to maximize this value. Kant rejected this picture in every way.

Kant rejected the idea that happiness (or well-being in any form) is the ulti-mate value. Happiness has *no* value, he said, if it is experienced as a result of wrongdoing. (The enjoyment that a sadistic killer brings to his task does not add value to his crime, but only makes it worse.) And the same goes for other possible values. Wealth can be misused; so can power, and health, and understanding, and bravery. None of these is unconditionally valuable—none is valuable in every context. There is only one thing that is valuable, no matter what—only one thing whose presence in any situation is bound to add value to it. That one thing is the **good will.**

The good will has two parts. It is the ability to reliably know what your duty is, and a steady commitment to doing your duty for its own sake. The good will works in a familiar way: we see what we are morally required to do, and we do it for that very reason. No calculations of costs and benefits, no worries about what impression we might be making, what enemies we might be gaining, what riches might be in store for us. Once we understand where our duty lies, we do it straightaway.

Kant had some very interesting ideas about how the good will worked. Two of these ideas are especially important; Kant thought, first, that acting from the good will is the only way that actions can be truly praiseworthy. (Kant referred to such actions as those that possessed **moral worth.**) He also thought that acting from such a motive is entirely an exercise of reason.

Consider the first point. Kant has us imagine two shopkeepers, each of whom does his duty by giving his customers the correct change. But the first does this only because he fears that if he were to cheat them, word would get out and he would lose business in the long run. He does his duty, but there is nothing morally worthy about his behavior.

The second store owner does the very same thing, but for completely different reasons. He treats his customers fairly because he thinks that cheating people is wrong, and he is committed to living up to the highest moral standards. This motivation earns the second shopkeeper the greatest praise. According to Kant, his actions and character display a worth that (like the value of humanity) is literally priceless. He is not for sale; he cannot be bought.

Kant's second point, about the importance of reason in motivating worthy conduct, is fairly complex. He thought that reason, operating alone and in the absence of any desires or emotions, could do double duty. It could reveal your moral duty, and it could motivate you to obey it.

To have a good will is, first of all, to know where your duty lies. Reason alone can tell you this. We can know what is morally required of us without the help of our feelings and emotions. When we determine whether a maxim is universalizable or think about whether a proposed action will respect the humanity in others, we don't need to want or feel anything at all. We just need to carefully follow the three-step test for a maxim's universalizability, or to reflect on the importance of autonomy. We can reason our way to moral knowledge. Indeed, neither our wants nor our emotions play any essential role in moral discovery. For Kant, we must be able to determine what is right and wrong by rational thinking alone, without the aid of desires or feelings.

That's because Kant saw these as unreliable moral guides. Compassion can lead you to wrongly help an escaping criminal; the courage of a terrorist can make his actions worse; anger can cloud impartial judgment. Our emotions often lead us astray, says Kant. They need to be guided by sound principles before we can trust them. Without such guidance, we *might* end up doing our duty, but that would be just a matter of luck.[2]

Further, and importantly, Kant thought that moral wisdom should be available to everyone, regardless of his or her emotional makeup. All of us are rational. We each have the power to reason well, even if we often fail to use this power as we should. But our emotions are not always under our control, and they will differ from person to person. If a specific emotional makeup is needed to gain moral wisdom, then such wisdom might be out of reach for many of us. Kant thought that such a view is elitist and a denial of the fundamental equality of all human beings.

Knowing what you are required to do is one thing; actually doing it is another. Here Kant also downgraded desires and emotions in favor of reason. He denied the claim, made famous by Hume, that our motivations always depend on our desires. Hume thought that beliefs alone could never move us, and that we must want something before we will ever act. By contrast, Kant thought that we could do things even if we didn't want to do them, and even if we didn't think they'd get us anything we wanted. When acting from the good will, we are acting solely from an understanding of what is morally required of us, not from any desire or emotion. If our action is to have moral worth, then this understanding, all by itself, must be enough to motivate us.

Anticipating Freud by a hundred years, Kant argued that our motivations are hardly transparent. In fact, we can never be sure that we have *ever* acted from a good will. Still, even if we can't be sure that our actions have ever earned moral worth, we *can* know what standard we should aim for.

Kant went so far as to write that dutiful actions motivated by emotions or desires lack any moral worth. Those whose generous nature causes them to lend a helping hand are to receive no credit. Aid workers whose compassion or whose love of their work leads them to do what they do are not to be praised for their good deeds. But those who overcome a complete lack of interest and nonetheless offer help, not because they want to but just because it is their duty to do so, will receive full moral credit.

There are two ways to interpret Kant's message here. The first says that the presence of emotions is enough to rob an action of moral worth. The second is more charitable. It says that actions done solely from desire or emotion cannot possess moral worth, but that some cases of mixed motives—cases in which the good will moves us to act, though helped along by an emotional push—can yet have moral worth. Kant scholars are still conflicted as to which interpretation best captures his intentions.

Five Problems with the Principle of Humanity

Despite its many attractions, the principle of humanity, and the emphasis on rationality and autonomy that underlies it, are not trouble-free. There are five especially serious worries about the principle:

1. The notion of treating someone as an end is vague, and so the principle is difficult to apply.
2. The principle fails to give us good advice about how to determine what people deserve.
3. The principle assumes that we are genuinely autonomous, but that assumption may be false.
4. The principle assumes that the morality of our actions depends only on what we can autonomously control, but the existence of **moral luck** calls this into question.
5. The principle cannot explain why those who lack rationality and autonomy are deserving of respect.

Let's consider each of these problems in turn.

Vagueness

Unlike the three-step process used to apply the principle of universalizability, there is no straightforward test that tells us how to apply the principle of humanity. It tells us to treat humanity as an end—i.e., with the respect that people deserve. It's sometimes crystal clear whether the principle is being honored. No one doubts, for instance, that the principle is violated by treating a plumber as a piece of pipe or shooting a trespasser for trampling the lawn. But the vagueness of the notion of treating someone as an end often makes it difficult to know whether our actions are morally acceptable. Do we respect celebrities by telling the truth about their private lives—even when this is damaging to their reputations? Is it disrespectful to enemy soldiers to set land mines at our borders? Are we failing to give due respect to famine victims if we spend money on a new TV rather than giving money to an aid agency?

We can't know the answer to these questions without a better understanding of what it is to treat someone as an end. Without a more precise test of when we are respecting others and treating them as they deserve (i.e., as their rationality and autonomy demands), the principle of humanity fails to give us the guidance that we expect from an ultimate moral principle.

Determining Just Deserts

The second concern is about whether it is always appropriate to give people what they deserve. Kant certainly thought so. Recall his thinking, from the last chapter, about the prime importance of doing justice. Doing justice involves giving people their just deserts—even if this is not going to benefit anyone. Sometimes this seems clearly right. A murderer ought to be punished, even if a governor's pardon will make more people happier. An employee ought to get paid for her work, even if her employer could do more good by giving her salary to charity. But there are also problems, as we'll see.

Kant has a partial reply to the problem of vagueness, mentioned earlier. He offers us a test for what *wrongdoers* deserve. That isn't the whole story, of course, since we also want to know how to apply the principle of humanity in cases where blame and punishment are not an issue. But even in contexts of condemnation, Kant's test—the famous **lex talionis,** or eye-for-an-eye principle—is fraught with difficulties. And so we are left with problems. In some cases, we don't know how to apply the principle of humanity, because it is unclear what treating a person as an end really amounts to. In other cases, it *is* clear— but also pretty clearly mistaken.

Lex talionis (the law of retaliation) tells us to treat criminals as they have treated their victims. Kant claimed that such punishment treats a criminal as an end—i.e., with the respect he deserves—because it treats him as a rational and autonomous person. Punishment is justified, for Kant, only if criminals are autonomous, and so able to freely choose their maxims. Those who are insane, for instance, are not fit for punishment. Punishment also presupposes that criminals are rational, in the sense of trying to act on principles that they can consistently intend everyone else to act on. A criminal's rationality permits us to turn his principles back on him, and do to him what he did to his victim. That is just what lex talionis requires.

Punishment that is administered as lex advises can be deeply satisfying. It can get criminals to see things from their victims' perspective, and so open their eyes to the true nature of the damage they have done. Further, punishment in line with lex seems perfectly just, since the criminal can't rightly complain of being mistreated. As Kant says, we would laugh at a criminal who protested against a punishment that harmed him exactly as he harmed his victim. Lastly, in the difficult matter of determining how to punish criminals, lex often gives us concrete, practical advice. What to do with a murderer, for instance? Kant counsels us to avoid the "serpent-windings" of utilitarianism and banish all thoughts of whether the death penalty is going to reduce the murder rate. A murderer deserves to die— lex says so. Therefore, morality requires his execution.

These attractions can explain lex's broad appeal. Despite the wide-spread enthusiasm, however, lex talionis is fatally flawed. Three reasons explain its failure.

1.   First, *lex* cannot explain why criminals who intentionally hurt their victims should be punished more than those who accidentally cause the same harm. Lex tells us to set the punishment by reference to the suffering of the victim. But victims can suffer the same harm, whether the perpetrator has carefully planned to cause it or has caused it by accident. If I am recklessly practicing archery in

my backyard and unintentionally skewer my neighbor, I deserve less punishment than a cold-blooded murderer. Or so we think. Lex does not allow for that, since the victims in both cases have suffered the same harm.

We could say that what criminals deserve is determined not only by the harm they have done, but also by how blameworthy they are in bringing it about. So a hired killer should be punished more than a reckless archer, because the murderer displays a kind of moral corruption that the archer lacks. This does give us the right answer—the callous killer *should* be punished more. But it comes at the cost of abandoning lex.

For we are no longer required to treat the criminal as he treated his victim. If an assassin deserves to be executed, then those who kill, but are less guilty than an assassin, should receive a lighter sentence than death. That undermines the letter and spirit of *lex talionis*, since these less-guilty killers will not be harmed just as they have harmed their victims. And it also removes one of the great virtues of lex talionis—that of offering precise guidance on how much criminals should be punished.

2. A second problem with lex is that it cannot tell us what many criminals deserve. This is most obvious in crimes that lack victims. Suppose an assassin attempts (but fails) to kill his victim, and the victim never discovers this. No harm, no foul? Suppose that someone leaves a bar well and truly drunk, and then manages to drive home without hurting anyone. Still, she deserves to be punished, but since there is no victim, lex offers no basis for punishment.

Other crimes may have victims, and yet lex offers no advice about their punishment. What to do with a hijacker or a counterfeiter? A kidnapper? Someone who transports stolen mattresses across state lines? The idea of treating these people just as they've treated their victims makes little sense.

3. Lastly, the guidance that lex provides, when it does prescribe a punishment, is sometimes deeply immoral. It's a sad truth: Any horror you can imagine people doing to one another has probably already been done. People have raped and tortured others, have burned whole families as they slept in their homes, have severed their limbs, tossed acid in their faces, and thrown handcuffed victims out of airplanes and helicopters. Does morality really require that we do such things to the criminals who committed such deeds? Surely we don't want official torturers, rapists, and arsonists on the state payroll. Legal punishment is the state's business, and we insist that the state meet certain minimum moral standards. A state that rapes its rapists is failing, miserably.

These three problems show that lex cannot be the whole story about justice, because lex sometimes fails to give advice when it is needed, and sometimes gives bad advice. That means that when lex gets it right, it does so because its recommendations agree with those given by some more basic principle of justice. Homework: discover that basic principle.

In any event, most of us think that giving people the punishment they deserve sometimes has to take a backseat to other moral concerns. Our practice of allowing for parole, plea bargains, executive clemency, suspended sentences, and pardons attests to that. Each of these can be seen as an exercise in mercy—in treating people more kindly than they deserve. And mercy is a virtue. Kant's position requires that we never indulge in merciful treatment of criminals.

Suppose that maintaining a system of punishment required so much money that we had to drastically sacrifice funds for schooling, for health programs, and for national defense. In that case, perhaps we should punish criminals a bit less than they deserve, so as to save resources to meet these other social needs.

Suppose that punishing criminals as they deserve were to *increase* the crime rate rather than reduce it. Most would think this an excellent reason to lighten punishments.

Justice is very important. But these considerations should make us wonder whether Kant was right to think that justice must always be done, no matter its costs.

Are We Autonomous?

A third concern about the principle of humanity is that it is based largely on a questionable assumption—namely, that we are autonomous, that we are free to choose which principles to live by, and able to govern our actions by our choices. I do believe that I am autonomous. And so do you. We all do. But our confidence may be misplaced. *The Argument Against Autonomy* explains why:

1. Either our choices are necessitated or they are not.
2. If they are necessitated, then they are out of our control, and so we lack autonomy.
3. If they are not necessitated, then they are random, and so we lack autonomy.
4. Therefore, we lack autonomy.

Suppose our choices are necessitated—suppose, in other words, that we are determined to choose as we do. But how could that be? After all, don't you at this very moment have a choice about whether to put this book down or whether to continue reading? The choice is up to you. So long as your free choices are dictating your actions, you are autonomous.

But consider: Is anything influencing your choice? Of course. You choose to continue reading at least partly because you want to, because you believe you are able to, because you have no more appealing options, and because no one is forcing you to choose something else. *Given* all of these influences (and others, no doubt), it seems that you were bound to choose as you did.

True, it's not as if you are fated to keep reading *no matter what*. Rather, the idea is that you are destined to keep reading given your circumstances and your mind-set (you beliefs, desires, aims, etc.).

But the causes of your choice (your beliefs, desires, etc.) are also caused. These further causes don't spring up from nothing. You chose to keep reading partly because you wanted to. And you wanted to keep reading because (perhaps) you have been assigned this chapter and want to do well in the course you are taking. But your desire to do well in the course also has an explanation. It was caused by other desires and beliefs of yours, which, in turn, were caused by other factors, and so on, and so on. Ultimately, our choices can be traced to causes over which we lack control—causes such as our genetic inheritance, our parental upbringing, and a variety of social influences. If we choose as we do because of factors that ultimately are out of our control, then our choices are ultimately out of our control. And so, if our choices are necessitated to be what they are, then we are not autonomous.

Now suppose that our choices are not necessitated. Suppose that nothing really determined that you were going to choose to continue reading, for instance. You just chose to do so. If that were the case, wouldn't that show that you chose freely?

No. If nothing causes us to choose as we do, then our choices seem completely random. Randomness undermines control, and hence undercuts autonomy.

Suppose I'm walking down the hall and see someone thrust out her arm and hit a bystander. Did she choose to hit him? Yes. Why? No reason. No cause. No explanation. It was just one of those things, completely out of the blue, unaccountable. But if that is really so—if nothing at all is causing her choice—then it seems that she isn't in command of her choices. They are something that happen to her, a passing fit of some sort, rather than something we can credit or blame her for. Her choices are out of her control.

Thus either way we go—whether our choices are necessitated or not—it seems that we lack autonomy. *If* that is so, the fundamental Kantian basis of our dignity, and the source of our duty to respect others, is undermined.

Of course many philosophers (and almost all non-philosophers) think that something is wrong with this argument. Its logic is watertight, so if there is an error, it must be in one of the three premises. Premise 1 is pretty clearly true. So the problem, if there is one, must lie in premise 2 or 3. Philosophers who think that we really do have autonomy have split on which premise to attack. Their work has been fruitful. (It has certainly multiplied—the issues of freedom and determinism nowadays form an entire subfield within philosophy.) So perhaps the pessimistic conclusion of this argument is false. But only a great deal more philosophy can show it so.

Moral Luck

Perhaps there is a flaw in the Argument Against Autonomy. I hope so. Let's indulge this hope for now and assume that we *are* genuinely autonomous. Even so, there are reasons to doubt that the morality of actions really depends on our autonomous choice.

Kant believes that we are rightly praised or blamed only for what we can control. That's why autonomy is so important. For autonomy *is* control—over our choices, and over our actions. Yet factors outside of our control apparently affect the morality of our conduct. If that is true, then autonomy may not play the central role in morality that Kant thinks it does.

The results of our actions are not fully within our control. And therefore they are morally irrelevant, from Kant's point of view. That is one of the main reasons that he so strongly opposes utilitarianism. And yet the results of our actions often *do* seem to make a moral difference.

Consider a good parent who, in a moment of extreme frustration, shakes her baby to jolt it out of a crying jag. Ordinarily, there is no lasting harm, the incident is forgotten, and we don't change our view of the mother's virtues. But babies sometimes die from such treatment. When they do, we judge the killer much more harshly than we do other parents—most of whom have shaken their babies at least once or twice, but have luckily done so without any permanent damage.

I sometimes find myself effectively driving on auto pilot. I've drifted over into the oncoming lane; I've failed to see a pedestrian at a crosswalk; I missed a passing car in my side mirror. In each case it was pure luck that my inattention didn't cause a (possibly fatal) accident. Many people are not so lucky. When their negligence results in someone's death, they are blamed far more than I have ever been. Yet they may be no worse a driver (or a person) than I am.

You probably know someone who is petty, vindictive, and coldly unsympathetic to the needs of others. A strict rule follower, someone who likes to pander to authority. Calculating and smart. This is the sort of person who can make office life pure hell. In decent circumstances, that is the worst he can do. Yet if he finds himself a citizen of an authoritarian regime, such a man can take the reins of a torture unit or a concentration camp and manage it with ruthless efficiency. It is simply a matter of luck that he is living in a peaceful society, rather than Germany in the 1940s, South Africa in the 1980s, or North Korea today. In different circumstances, we might well have charged him with complicity in torture or murder.

These are all examples of **moral luck**—cases in which the morality of an action or a decision depends on factors outside of our control. If Kant is right, moral luck cannot exist. And he may be right. But if he is, then we have to revise our moral views in each of these cases, and many others. A drag race down country lanes is fondly remembered—unless it leads to a paralyzing accident. The risky investment is harshly condemned if it forces bankruptcy, but celebrated if it establishes a family fortune. A revolutionary is a hero if his side wins, a despised traitor if it doesn't.

There is a tension at the heart of our moral thinking. We don't blame babies for any harm they cause. Adults who have been hypnotized or those who have been slipped an LSD tab are also immune from blame. Kant explained this perfectly: Such people lack autonomy. They aren't in full control of their actions. But if Kant is right, and control is essential for moral responsibility, then we must abandon all of the moral judgments recorded in the previous paragraphs. It isn't an easy choice to make.

The Scope of the Moral Community

The final concern has to do with the scope of the moral community. Kant's emphasis on rationality and autonomy forces us to draw the lines of this community very narrowly. We are in. Infants aren't. The severely mentally ill and mentally retarded are out. So too are all nonhuman animals and animal species, and all plants and ecosystems. They all lack rationality and autonomy. By Kant's lights, they therefore have no intrinsic moral importance. We owe them no moral concern, and so, it seems, we can treat them any way we want.

We can express this worry in the Argument Against Animals:

1. If the principle of humanity is true, then animals have no rights.
2. If animals lack rights, then it is morally acceptable to torture them.
3. Therefore, if the principle of humanity is true, then it is morally acceptable to torture animals.
4. It isn't.
5. Therefore, the principle of humanity is false.

Though this argument focuses on animals, we could easily amend it to apply to infants, the severely mentally retarded, etc. Kant's views exclude all of them from the moral community. But since Kant himself focused only on the case of animals, let's follow his lead. We can discuss the other cases as needed.

Kant thought that it is wrong to torture or otherwise mistreat animals. So he accepts the fourth premise of the argument. He also accepts its first premise. He thought that rights require autonomy, that animals lack it, and that they therefore lack rights. As he saw it, the second premise is the one that has to go.

Kant offered two arguments for rejecting the second premise. Both of them fail.

He first claimed that harming animals will harden our hearts, and so make it likely that we will mistreat our fellow human beings. Since that really would be immoral, we must not harm animals.

Kant's predictions about how we might be led to harm our fellow human beings are quite shaky. Most of us are easily able to make distinctions in our treatment of members of different groups. Abusive bosses usually treat their superiors with respect. Ruthless prison guards can be loving parents. Doctors who are condescending to their patients and nurses are often quite decent to their fellow doctors. So mistreating one group needn't lead to mistreating others.

Further, if Kant is right, we humans really do possess infinitely greater moral importance than animals. Anyone who takes that message to heart would resist harming his fellow humans—even if he felt comfortable hurting animals.

Kant faces a problem even if his predictions are right. For the reasoning he is employing here is pure consequentialism. Don't torture animals, because that will have terrible results (it will lead to the mistreatment of humans). But as we have seen, Kant bases his theory on the view that results are irrelevant to the morality of actions. So this reply will not do.

He has a second. I own a desk. It obviously isn't rational or autonomous. And yet no matter how much someone wanted to take a hammer to it, it would be wrong to do so. Not because the vandal would be wronging the desk, but because he would be wronging me. The desk has no rights. But I do. And these must be honored. And so, even though my three cats, for instance, have no rights, it would be immoral to hurt them, since in doing so, my rights (as their owner) would be violated.

There are two basic difficulties with this view. First, it offers no moral protections to wild animals. And second, domesticated animals will have no moral protection against their owners. If I decided to destroy my desk, just for the fun of it, I'd be doing nothing wrong. And since the Kantian view sees animals as morally on a par with my possessions, it can't explain why it would be wrong of me to destroy my animals simply because I wanted to.

That isn't the only bad news. Remember, this problem applies not only to animals but also to all human beings who lack rationality and autonomy. True, most of them (infants, the senile, the temporarily comatose, etc.) are loved by others. And so Kant might be able to claim that our rights (i.e., the rights of those who love such human beings) would be violated if anyone were to harm them. But what of the most piteous of humanity—the unloved, abandoned human beings who lack autonomy? Kant's theory gives them the same status as an unowned desk or animal. They are disposable and may be treated as we like. Kant thus excludes the most vulnerable among us from membership in the moral community.

Conclusion

Kant's ethical views are rich and suggestive. They are extremely important in their own right, but it can also be quite helpful to contrast them with the consequentialist outlook that is so popular in political and economic circles these days. As we have seen, Kant's opposition to consequentialism was deep and thorough. These are the main points of disagreement:

1. Kant denied that benevolence is the central moral virtue, and thought instead that justice and integrity occupied that role.

2. Kant regarded many of the basic moral rules as absolute, and so insisted that it was never acceptable to break them—even if breaking them led to better results.

3. Kant denied that the morality of actions could depend on results or other factors outside of one's control, and claimed instead that they depend solely on what we can be held responsible for—our maxims and our free actions.

4. In a related point, Kant rejected the exclusive emphasis on the future and an action's results in determining what is right and wrong, and instead made past actions, and their just deserts, a central basis for moral evaluation.

5. According to consequentialists, all it takes to be a member of the moral community is a minimal level of well-being; Kant thought instead that autonomy and rationality determined moral status.

6. Kant denied that happiness or well-being is always valuable in its own right, and instead believed that the good will—the steady commitment to do one's duty for its own sake—is the only thing that is valuable in all situations.

Many of the shortcomings of consequentialism are nicely handled by the Kantian theory. But consequentialists are pleased to return the favor: the Kantian theory isn't without its own problems, and many of those are neatly addressed by consequentialism. Let's now have a look at another important contender, the social contract theory, whose defenders hope to secure many of the benefits of these two ethical outlooks, while escaping the problems that confront them.

Notes

1. *Philosophy and Public Affairs* 8 (1979): 103–21.

2. This thought is perfectly illustrated by a catty remark quoted in a biography of Napoleon's sister, Pauline. She was notoriously pampered and unfaithful, an irresponsible spendthrift with a full sense of entitlement. She was sometimes capable of bravery and generosity. But this was unpredictable, and for the most part she behaved very badly. Later in life, a former acquaintance gave the following account: "Although she was the most beautiful person one could imagine, she was also the most unreasonable. . . . talking inconsequentially, laughing at nothing and at everything, she contradicted the most serious people and put out her tongue at her sister-in-law when Josephine wasn't looking. . . . *she had no principles and was likely to do the right thing only by caprice.*" (My italics.) As quoted in Flora Fraser, *Pauline Bonaparte: Venus of Empire* (Alfred A. Knopf, 2009), p. 25.

Chapter 6

Psychology and Ethics

Selective Moral Disengagement in the Exercise of Moral Agency

Albert Bandura

Albert Bandura (1925–) is among the most well-known and often cited scholars in the field of psychology. Since 1953, Bandura has spent his entire career at Stanford University. He is perhaps best known for his social cognitive theory (a.k.a., social learning theory), but his later work on self-efficacy and moral disengagement has garnered broad attention. The following paper provides a recent examination by Bandura of the mechanisms and dangers of moral disengagement. At issue is why, and under what circumstances, individuals choose to act, or not act, as moral agents. Bandura goes on to discuss the long-term social implications of abandoning humanistic principles.

This article addresses the important but neglected issue of selective moral disengagement in the exercise of moral agency. In a recent book entitled, *Everybody Does It*, Thomas Gabor (1994) documents the pervasiveness of moral disengagement by people of all statuses in all walks of life. Psychological theories of morality have traditionally focused heavily on the formal character of moral reasoning to the neglect of moral conduct. People suffer from the wrongs done to them regardless of how perpetrators justify their inhumane actions. The regulation of humane conduct involves much more than moral reasoning. A complete theory of moral agency must link moral knowledge and reasoning to moral conduct. This requires an agentic theory of morality rather than one confined mainly to cognitions about morality. In the social cognitive theory of the moral self (Bandura, 1986, 1991), moral reasoning is linked to moral action through affective self-regulatory mechanisms by which moral agency is exercised. The moral self is thus embedded in a broader socio-cognitive self theory encompassing self-organising, proactive, self-reflective and self-regulative mechanisms (Bandura, 2001). These self-referent processes provide the motivational as well as the cognitive regulators of moral conduct.

In the development of a moral self, individuals adopt standards of right and wrong that serve as guides and deterrents for conduct. In this self-regulatory process, people monitor their conduct and the conditions under which it occurs, judge it in relation to their moral standards and perceived circumstances, and regulate their actions by the consequences they apply to themselves. They do things that give them satisfaction and a sense of self-worth. They refrain from behaving in ways that violate their moral standards because such conduct will bring self-condemnation. The constraint of negative self-sanctions for conduct that violates one's moral standards and the support of positive self-sanctions for conduct faithful to personal moral standards operate anticipatorily. In the face of situational inducements to behave in inhumane ways, people can choose to behave otherwise by exerting self-influence. Self-sanctions keep conduct in line with internal standards. It is through the ongoing exercise of evaluative self-influence that moral conduct is motivated and regulated. Morality is thus rooted in a self-reactive selfhood, rather than in dispassionate abstract reasoning.

The self-regulation of morality is not entirely an intrapsychic matter as rationalist theories might lead one to believe. People do not operate as autonomous moral agents, impervious to the social realities in which they are enmeshed. Social cognitive theory adopts an interactionist perspective to morality. Moral actions are the product of the reciprocal interplay of cognitive, affective and social influences.

Mechanisms of Moral Disengagement

Moral standards do not function as fixed internal regulators of conduct. Self-regulatory mechanisms do not operate unless they are activated. There are many psychosocial manoeuvres by which moral self-sanctions can be disengaged from inhumane conduct. Selective activation and disengagement of self-sanctions permits different types of conduct by people with the same moral standards.

Figure 1 shows the points in the process of moral control at which moral self-censure can be disengaged from reprehensible conduct. The disengagement may centre on redefining harmful conduct as honourable by moral justification, exonerating social comparison and sanitising language. It may focus on agency of action so that perpetrators can minimise their role in causing harm by diffusion and displacement of responsibility. It may involve minimising or distorting the harm that flows from detrimental actions; and the disengagement may include dehumanising and blaming the victims of the maltreatment.

The sections that follow analyse how each of these types of moral disengagement function in the perpetration of inhumanities.

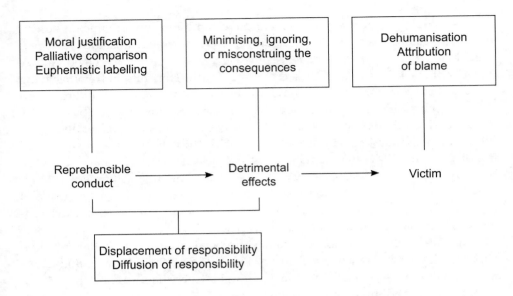

Figure 1-1 Mechanism through which moral self-sanctions are selectively activated and disengaged from detrimental behaviour at different points in the self-regulatory process (Bandura, 1986).

Moral Justification

One set of disengagement practices operates on the reconstruction of the behaviour itself. People do not usually engage in harmful conduct until they have justified, to themselves, the morality of their actions. In this process of moral justification, pernicious conduct is made personally and socially acceptable by portraying it as serving socially worthy or moral purposes. People then can act on a moral imperative and preserve their view of themselves as moral agents while inflicting harm on others.

Rapid radical shifts in destructive behaviour through moral justification are most strikingly revealed in military pursuits. The conversion of socialised people into dedicated fighters is achieved not by altering their personality structures, aggressive drives or moral standards. Rather, it is accomplished by cognitively redefining the morality of killing so that it can be done free from self-censure. Through moral justification of violent means, people see themselves as fighting ruthless oppressors, protecting their cherished values, preserving world peace, saving humanity from subjugation or honouring their country's commitments. Moral justifications sanctify the violent means. Voltaire put it well when he said, "Those who can make you believe absurdities, can make you commit atrocities."

Over the centuries, much destructive conduct has been perpetrated by ordinary, decent people in the name of righteous ideologies, religious principles and nationalistic imperatives (Rapoport & Alexander, 1982; Kramer, 1990; Reich, 1990). Adversaries sanctify their militant actions, but condemn those of their antagonists as barbarity masquerading under a mask of outrageous moral reasoning. Each side feels morally superior to the other.

The politicisation of religion has a long-blooded history. In holy terror, perpetrators twist theology so they see themselves as doing God's will. Pope Urban launched the Crusades with the following impassioned moral proclamation: "I address those present, I proclaim it, to those absent. Christ commands it. For all those going thither, there will be remission of sins if they come to the end of this fettered life." He then dehumanises and beastialises the Muslim enemies: "What a disgrace if a race so despicable, degenerate, and enslaved by demons, should overcome a people endowed with faith in Almighty God and resplendent in the name of Christ! Let those who once fought against brothers and relatives now rightfully fight against the barbarians under the guidance of the Lord."

Islamic extremists mount their jihad, construed as self-defence against tyrannical, decadent infidels who despoil and seek to enslave the Muslim) world. Bin Laden ennobled his global terrorism as serving a holy imperative. "We will continue this course because it is part of our religion and because Allah, praise and glory be to him, ordered us to carry out jihad so that the word of Allah may remain exalted to the heights." Through the jihad they are carrying out Allah's will as a "religious duty". The prime agency for the holy terror is displaced to Allah. Bin Laden beastialises the American enemy as "lowly people" perpetrating acts that "the most ravenous of animals would not descend to". Terrorism is sanitised as "The winds of faith have come" to eradicate the "debauched" oppressors. His followers see themselves as holy warriors who gain a blessed eternal life through their martyrdom.

Rabin's assassin was similarly acting on a divine mandate using the rabbinical pursuer's decree as moral justification. Those who give over their people and land to the enemy must be killed. As he explained the killing to prevent transfer of land to Palestinian control: "Maybe physically, I acted alone but what pulled the trigger was not only my finger but the finger of this whole nation which, for 2,000 years, yearned for this land and dreamed of it." Paul Hill, the Presbyterian minister, also justified the killing of a doctor and his elderly assistant outside the abortion clinic as carrying out God's will: "God's law positively requires us to defend helpless people. God has used people, who are willing to die for their cause to save human life. I'm willing to do that."

Euphemistic Labelling

Language shapes thought patterns on which actions are based. Activities can take on different appearances depending on what they are called. Euphemistic language is used widely to make harmful conduct respectable and to reduce personal responsibility for it (Lutz, 1987). Euphemising is an injurious weapon. People behave much more cruelly when assaultive actions are given a sanitised label than when they are called aggression (Diener *et al.*, 1975).

In an insightful analysis of the language of non-responsibility, Gambino (1973) identified the different varieties of euphemisms. One form relies on *sanitising language*. Through the power of sanitised language, even killing a human being loses much of its repugnancy. Soldiers "waste" people rather than kill them. Bombing missions are described as "servicing the target", in the likeness of a public utility. The attacks become "clean, surgical strikes", arousing imagery of curative activities. The civilians the bombs kill are linguistically converted to "collateral damage".

In an effort to sanitise State executions, a United States senator proclaimed that, "Capital punishment is our society's recognition of the sanctity of human life." This memorable verbal sanitisation won him the uncoveted, third-place award in the national Doublespeak competition.

Sanitising euphemisms are also used extensively in unpleasant activities that people perform from time to time. In the language of some government agencies, people are not fired, they are given a "career alternative enhancement" as though they were receiving a promotion. Being disfellowshipped is getting oneself fired by the Baptists. In the Watergate hearings, lies became "a different version of the facts". An "involuntary conversion of a 727" is a plain old airplane crash. The television industry produces and markets some of the most brutal forms of human cruelty under the sanitised labels of "action and adventure" programming. The nuclear power industry has created its own specialised set of euphemisms for the injurious effects of nuclear mishaps. An explosion becomes an "energetic disassembly", and a reactor accident is a "normal aberration".

The *agentless passive voice* serves as another exonerative tool. It creates the appearance that reprehensible acts are the work of nameless forces, rather then people (Bolinger, 1982). It is as though people are moved mechanically but are not really the agents of their own acts. Even inanimate objects are sometimes turned into agents. Here is a driver explaining to police how he managed to demolish a telephone pole, "The telephone pole was approaching. I was attempting to swerve out of its way, when it struck my front end."

The specialised jargon of a legitimate enterprise is also misused to lend respectability to an illegitimate one. In the vocabulary of the law breakers in Nixon's administration, criminal conspiracy became a "game plan", and the conspirators were "team players", like the best of sportsmen. They elevated word corruption to new heights in the service of criminal conduct.

Advantageous Comparison

How behaviour is viewed is coloured by what it is compared against. By exploiting the contrast principle reprehensible acts can be made righteous. Terrorists see their behaviour as acts of selfless martyrdom by comparing them with widespread cruelties inflicted on the people with whom they identify (Bandura, 1990). The more flagrant the contrasting inhumanities, the more likely it is that one's own destructive conduct will appear benevolent. For example, the massive destruction in Vietnam was minimised by portraying the American military intervention as saving the populace from Communist enslavement. Expedient historical comparison also serves self-exonerating purposes. Apologists for the lawlessness of political figures they support point to transgressions by rival administrations as vindications. Adapters of violent means are quick to point out that democracies, such as those of France and the United States, were achieved through violence against oppressive rule.

Exonerating comparison relies heavily on moral justification by utilitarian standards. The task of making violence morally acceptable from a utilitarian perspective is facilitated by two sets of judgements. First, non-violent options are judged to be ineffective to achieve desired changes. This removes them from consideration. Secondly, utilitarian analyses affirm that one's injurious actions will prevent more human suffering than they cause.

The utilitarian calculus is quite slippery in specific applications, however. The future contains many uncertainties and human judgement is subject to a lot of biases. As a result, calculations of long-term human costs and benefits are often suspect. There is much subjectivity in estimating the gravity of potential threats.

Cognitive restructuring of harmful conduct through moral justifications, sanitising language and exonerating comparisons is the most effective set of psychological mechanisms for disengaging moral control. Investing harmful conduct with high moral purpose not only eliminates self-censure so destructive acts can be performed without personal distress and moral questions. Sanctification engages self-approval in the service of destructive exploits. What was once morally condemnable becomes a source of self-valuation. Functionaries work hard to become proficient at them and take pride in their destructive accomplishments.

Displacement of Responsibility

Moral control operates most strongly when people acknowledge that they are contributors to harmful outcomes. The second set of disengagement practises operates by obscuring or minimising the agentive role in the harm one causes. People will behave in ways they normally repudiate if a legitimate authority accepts responsibility for the effects of their conduct (Milgram, 1974; Diener, 1977). Under displaced responsibility, they view their actions as stemming from the dictates of authorities rather than being personally responsible for them. Because they are not the actual agent of their actions, they are spared self-condemning reactions.

Self-exemption from gross inhumanities by displacement of responsibility is revealed most gruesomely in socially sanctioned mass executions. Nazi prison commandants and their staffs divested themselves of personal responsibility for their unprecedented inhumanities (Andrus, 1969). They claimed they were simply carrying out orders.

Self-exonerating obedience to horrific orders is similarly evident in military atrocities, such as the My Lai massacre (Kelman, 1973).

In psychological studies of disengagement of moral control by displacement of responsibility, authorities explicitly authorise injurious actions and hold themselves responsible for the harm caused by their followers. For example, Milgram (1974) induced people to escalate their level of punitiveness by commanding them to do so and telling them that he took full responsibility for the consequences of their actions. The greater the legitimisation and closeness of authority issuing injurious commands, the higher the obedient aggression.

The sanctioning of pernicious conduct in everyday life differs in two important ways from Milgram's authorising system. Responsibility is rarely assumed that openly. Only obtuse authorities would leave themselves accusable of authorising destructive acts. They usually invite and support harmful conduct in insidious ways by surreptitious sanctioning systems for personal and social reasons. Sanctioning by indirection shields them from social condemnation should things go awry. It also enables them to protect against loss of self-respect for authorising human cruelty that leaves blood on their hands.

Authorities act in ways that keep themselves intentionally uninformed. As a Secretary of State instructed a presidential adviser in the Iran affair, "Just tell me what I need to know". Authorities do not go looking for evidence of wrongdoing. Obvious questions that would reveal incriminating information remain unasked, so that officials do not find out what they do not want to know. Implicit agreements and insulating social arrangements are created that leave the higher echelons unblamable.

When harmful practices are publicised, they are officially dismissed as only isolated incidents arising from misunderstanding of what had been authorised. Efforts are made to limit any blame to subordinates, who are portrayed as misguided or overzealous. Investigators who go looking for evident incriminating records of authorisation display naivete about the insidious ways that pernicious practices are sanctioned and carried out. One finds arrangements of non-responsibility rather than incriminating traces of smoking guns.

There is another basic difference in the authorising system from the one created by Milgram. Perpetration of inhumanities requires obedient functionaries. They do not cast off all responsibility for their behaviour as if they were mindless extensions of others. If they disowned all responsibility, they would be quite unreliable, performing their duties only when commanded to do so. It requires a strong sense of responsibility to be a good functionary. One must, therefore, distinguish between two levels of responsibility: a strong sense of duty to one's superiors, and account-ability for the effects of one's actions. The best functionaries are those who honour their obligations to authorities but feel no personal responsibility for the harm they cause.

Goldhagen (1996) builds a strong case that many of the perpetrators in the German genocide infantry were more than willing executioners. Cultural hatreds create low thresholds for the disengagement of moral self-sanctions. Inhumanities toward human beings cast in disliked categories become not only permissible but righteous.

Diffusion of Responsibility

The exercise of moral control is also weakened when personal agency is obscured by diffusing responsibility for detrimental behaviour. Kelman (1973) documents the different ways in which personal agency gets obscured by social diffusion of responsibility. Responsibility can be diffused by division of labour. Subdivided tasks seem harmless in themselves. People shift their attention from the meaning of what they are doing to the details of their specific job.

Group decision-making is another common practice that enables otherwise considerate people to behave inhumanely. Where everyone is responsible no one really feels responsible. Collective action, which provides anonymity, is still another expedient for weakening moral control. Any harm done by a group can always be attributed largely to the behaviour of others. People act more cruelly under group responsibility than when they hold themselves personally accountable for their actions (Bandura *et al.*, 1975; Zimbardo, 1995).

Disregard or Distortion of Consequences

To be able to perpetrate inhumanities requires more than absolving personal responsibility. Other ways of weakening moral control operate by minimising, disregarding or distorting the effects of one's action. When people pursue activities that harm others, they avoid facing the harm they cause or minimise it. If minimisation does not work, the evidence of harm can be discredited. As long as the harmful results of one's conduct are ignored, minimised, distorted or disbelieved there is little reason for self-censure to be activated.

It is easier to harm others when their suffering is not visible and when destructive actions are physically and temporally remote from their injurious effects. Our death technologies have become highly lethal and depersonalised. We are now in the era of faceless electronic warfare, in which mass destruction is delivered remotely with deadly accuracy by computer and laser-controlled systems.

When people can see and hear the suffering they cause, vicariously aroused distress and self-censure serve as self-restrainers (Bandura, 1992). In studies of obedient aggression, people are less compliant to the injurious commands of authorities as the victims' pain becomes more evident and personalised (Milgram, 1974). Even a high sense of personal responsibility for the effects of one's actions is a weak restrainer of injurious conduct when aggressors do not see the harm they inflict on their victims (Tilker, 1970).

A Pulitzer Prize was awarded for a powerful photograph that captured the anguished cries of a little girl whose clothes were burned off by the napalm bombing of her village in Vietnam. This single humanisation of inflicted destruction probably did more to turn the American public against the war than the countless reports filed by journalists. The military now bans cameras and journalists from battlefield areas to block disturbing images of death and destruction that can erode public support for resolving international disputes by military means.

Most organisations involve hierarchical chains of command in which superiors formulate plans and intermediaries transmit them to functionaries who then carry them out. The further removed individuals are from the destructive end results, the weaker is the restraining power of injurious effects. Disengagement of moral control is easiest for the intermediaries in a hierarchical system—they neither bear responsibility for the decisions nor do they carry them out and face the harm being inflicted (Kilham & Mann, 1974).

Dehumanisation

The final set of disengagement practices operates on the recipients of detrimental acts. The strength of moral self-censure depends on how the perpetrators regard the people they mistreat. To perceive another as human activates empathetic reactions through perceived similarity (Bandura, 1992). The joys and suffering of those with whom one identifies are more vicariously arousing than are those of strangers or those divested of human qualities. It is difficult to mistreat humanised people without risking personal distress and self-condemnation.

Self-censure for cruel conduct can be disengaged or blunted by stripping people of human qualities. Once dehumanised, they are no longer viewed as persons with feelings, hopes and concerns but as sub-human objects. They are portrayed as mindless "savages", "gooks" and other despicable wretches (Ivie, 1980; Keen, 1986). If dispossessing one's foes of humanness does not weaken self-censure, it can be eliminated by attributing demonic or bestial qualities to them. They become "satanic fiends", "degenerates" and other bestial creatures. It is easier to brutalise people when they are viewed as low animal forms, as when Greek torturers referred to their victims as "worms" (Gibson & Haritos-Fatouros, 1986). During wartime, nations cast their enemies in the most dehumanised, demonic and bestial images to make it easier to kill them.

In studies of the perniciousness of dehumanisation, people who are given punitive power treat dehumanised individuals more ruthlessly than those who have
been invested with human qualities (Bandura *et al.*, 1975). Combining diffused
responsibility with dehumanisation greatly escalates the level of punitiveness. The
combined effect of personalising responsibility and humanising others together
has powerful self-restraining effect.

The process of dehumanisation is an essential ingredient in the perpetration of
inhumanities. Primo Levi (1989) asked a Nazi camp commandant why they went
to extreme lengths to degrade their victims, whom they were going to kill anyway. The commandant chillingly explained that it was not a matter of purposeless
cruelty. The victims had to be degraded to subhuman objects so that those who
operated the gas chambers would be less burdened by distress.

Many conditions of contemporary life are conducive to impersonalisation and
dehumanisation (Bernard *et al.*, 1965). Bureaucratisation, automation, urbanisation
and high mobility lead people to relate to each other in anonymous, impersonal
ways. In addition, social practises that divide people into ingroup and outgroup
members produce human estrangement that fosters dehumanisation. Strangers
can be more easily depersonalised than can acquaintances.

The findings from research on moral disengagement are in accord with the historical chronicle of human atrocities. It requires conducive social conditions rather
than monstrous people to produce atrocious deeds. Given appropriate social conditions, decent, ordinary people can do extraordinarily cruel things.

Power of Humanisation

Psychological research tends to emphasise how easy it is to bring out the worst in
people through dehumanisation and other self-exonerating means. The sensational
negative findings receive the greatest attention. For example, Milgram's (1974)
research on obedient aggression is cited widely as evidence that good people can
be talked into performing cruel deeds. What is rarely noted is the equally striking
evidence that most people refuse to behave cruelly, even with strong authoritarian
commands, toward humanised others (Bandura *et al.*, 1975), and when they have
to inflict pain directly rather than remotely (Milgram, 1974).

The emphasis on obedient aggression is understandable considering the prevalence of people's inhumanities to one another; but the power of humanisation to
counteract cruel conduct also has important social implications, the affirmation of
common humanity can bring out the best in others.

Attribution of Blame

Blaming one's adversaries or circumstances is another expedient that serves
self-exonerating purposes. People view themselves as faultless victims driven to
injurious conduct by forcible provocation. Violent conduct becomes a justifiable

defensive reaction to belligerent provocations. Victims get blamed for bringing suffering on themselves. Self-exoneration is also achievable by viewing one's harmful conduct as forced by compelling circumstances rather than as a personal decision. By fixing the blame on others or on compelling circumstances one's own injurious actions are excusable but one can even feel self-righteous in the process.

Justified abuse can have more devastating human consequences than acknowledged cruelty. Mistreatment that is not clothed in righteousness makes the perpetrator rather than the victim blameworthy; but when victims are convincingly blamed for their plight, they may eventually come to believe the degrading characterisations of themselves (Hallie, 1971). Exonerated inhumanity is, thus, more likely to instill self-contempt in victims than inhumanity that does not attempt to justify itself. Seeing victims suffer maltreatment for which they are held partially responsible leads observers to derogate them (Lerner & Miller, 1978). The devaluation and indignation aroused by ascribed culpability provides further moral justification for even greater maltreatment.

Transformative Power of Progressive Moral Disengagement

Disengagement practises will not instantly transform considerate people into cruel ones. Rather, the change is achieved by progressive disengagement of self-censure. Initially, individuals perform mildly harmful acts they can tolerate with some discomfort. After their self-reproof has been diminished through repeated enactments, the level of ruthlessness increases, until eventually acts originally regarded as abhorrent can be performed with little anguish or self-censure. Inhumane practices become thoughtlessly routinised. The continuing interplay between moral thought, affect, action and its social reception is personally transformative. People may not even recognise the changes they have undergone as a moral self.

The transformative power of progressive moral disengagement is illustrated by a prison guard, who assisted in the execution of convicts by gassing. Putting people to death requires subdivision of the task to get someone to do it. The guard's role was limited to strapping the legs to the death chair. This spared him the image of executioner, "I never pulled the trigger. I wasn't the executioner", he explained.

Executioners require heavy use of euphemisms as well. The guard received $35 extra for each execution. In a linguistic rechristening of deathly gassing as benevolent caring he remarked "That was a lot of money for baby-sitting". He described the changes he had undergone over the course of 126 executions as follows: "It never bothered me when I was down at their legs strapping them in. But after I'd get home, I'd think about it. But then it would go away. And then, at last, it was just another job."

Under certain conditions, the exercise of institutional power changes the powerholders in ways that are conducive to dehumanisation. This typically occurs when authorities have coercive power over others and adequate safeguards for constraining the behaviour of powerholders are lacking. Powerholders come to devalue those over whom they wield control and have little desire to associate with them (Kipnis, 1974). In a simulated prison experiment (Haney *et al.*, 1973), even college students who had been chosen randomly to serve as either inmates or guards given unilateral power began to treat their charges in degrading, tyrannical ways as guards.

Sprinzak (1986, 1990) has shown that terrorists, whether on the political left or right, evolve gradually rather than set out to become radicals. The process of radicalisation involves a gradual disengagement of moral self-sanctions from violent conduct. It begins with prosocial efforts to change particular social policies and opposition to officials who are intent on keeping things as they are. Embittering failures to accomplish social change and hostile confrontations with authorities and police lead to growing disillusionment and alienation from the whole system. Escalative battles culminate in terrorists' efforts to destroy the system and its dehumanised rulers.

Dual Nature of Moral Agency

The exercise of moral agency has dual aspects—*inhibitive* and *proactive* (Bandura, 1999). The inhibitive form, is manifested in the power to refrain from behaving inhumanely. The proactive form of morality is expressed in the power to behave humanely. In this higher-order morality, people do good things as well as refrain from doing bad things. Rorty's (1993) analysis of the moral self in terms of a social-practice morality is another example of a theory that highlights proactive morality rooted in social obligation rather than just the morality of inhibition.

The My Lai massacre graphically illustrates the dual aspects of moral agency (Zganjar, 1998). An American platoon, led by Lt Calley, massacred 500 Vietnamese women, children and elderly men. Insightful analyses have documented how moral self-sanctions were disengaged from the brutal conduct (Kelman & Hamilton, 1989).

A ceremony, 30 years in coming, was recently held at the Vietnam Veteran's Memorial honouring extraordinary heroism of prosocial morality. The moral courage that was honoured, testifies to proactive morality through the remarkable power of humanisation. Thompson, a young helicopter pilot, swooped down over the village of My Lai on a search and destroy mission as the massacre was occurring. He spotted an injured girl, marked the spot with a smoke signal, and radioed for help.

Much to his horror, he saw a soldier flip her over and spray her with a round of fire. Upon seeing the human carnage in an irrigation ditch and soldiers firing into the bodies he realised that he was in the midst of a massacre.

He was moved to moral action by the sight of a terrified woman with a baby in her arms and a frightened child clinging to her leg. He explained his sense of common humanity, "These people were looking at me for help and there is no way I could turn my back on them."

He told a platoon officer to help him remove the remaining villagers. The officer replied, "The only help they'll get, is a hand grenade". Thompson moved his helicopter in the line of fire and commanded his gunner to fire on his approaching countrymen if they tried to harm the family. He radioed the accompanying gun-ships for help and together they airlifted the remaining dozen villagers to safety. He flew back to the irrigation ditch where they found and rescued a 2-year-old boy still clinging to his dead mother. Thompson described his empathetic human linkage: "I had a son at home about the same age".

Social psychology emphasises the power of the situation over the individual. In the case of proactive moral courage, the individual triumphs as a moral agent over compelling situational forces. Such moral heroism is most strikingly docu-mented in Holocaust rescuers who risked their lives under grave risks to save persecuted Jews from the death camps (Oliner & Oliner, 1988; Stein, 1988). The rescuers had no prior acquaintance with them and had nothing material or social to gain by doing so. Humanisation can rouse empathic sentiments and a strong sense of social obligation linked to evaluative self-sanctions that motivate humane actions on others' behalf at sacrifice of one's self-interest or even at one's own peril (Bandura, 1986). The rescuers viewed their behaviour as a human duty, rather than as extraordinary acts of heroism.

Conjoint Operation of Disengagement Mechanisms

The analysis thus far specified how the various mechanisms of moral disengage-ment operate individually to disengage moral self-sanctions. In the transactions of everyday life they operate together to promote inhumanities. This is well illus-trated in an American weapons dealer named Terpil (Thomas, 1982). He supplied despots with weapons, assassination equipment and the latest in terrorist technol-ogy. This case is especially informative because it reveals that those who trade in human destruction do not do it by themselves. They depend heavily on the collec-tive moral disengagement of reputable people managing respectable enterprises.

Terpil became a weapons merchant after he fell from grace at the Central Intel-ligence Agency. He masked his death operations in the euphemisms of a legitimate business fulfilling "consumer needs", under the sanitised name, "Intercontinental Technology".

To spare himself any self-censure for contributing to human atrocities, he avoided knowledge of the purposes to which his weapons would be put. "I don't ever want to know that", he said. When asked whether he was ever haunted by any thoughts about the suffering his deathly wares might cause, he explained that a weapons dealer cannot afford to think about human consequences, "If I really thought about the consequences all the time I certainly wouldn't have been in this business. You have to blank it off."

Probes for any signs of self-reproach, only brought self-exonerative comparisons. When asked if he felt any qualms about supplying torture equipment to Idi Amin, Terpil replied with justification by advantageous comparison. As he put it, "I'm sure that the people from Dow Chemical didn't think of the consequences of selling napalm. If they did, they wouldn't be working at the factory. I doubt very much if they'd feel any more responsible for the ultimate use than I did for my equipment."

When pressed about the atrocities committed at Amin's torture chambers, Terpil repeated his depersonalised view, "I do not get wrapped up emotionally with the country. I regard myself basically as neutral, and commercial." To give legitimacy to his "private practice", he claimed that he aided British and American covert operations abroad as well.

What began as a psychological analysis of the operator of a death industry ended in an international network of supporting legitimate enterprises run by upright folks. The merchandising of terrorism is not accomplished by a few unsavory individuals. It requires a worldwide network of reputable, high-level members of society who contribute to the deathly enterprise by fractionating the operation and diffusion of responsibility. One group manufactures the tools of destruction. Others amass the arsenals for legitimate sale. Others operate storage centres for them. Others procure export and import licences to move the deathly wares among different countries. Others obtain spurious end-user certificates that get the weaponry to embargoed nations through circuitous routes. Still others ship the lethal wares. And banks do a brisk business in laundered money.

The cogs in this worldwide network include weapons manufacturers, former government officials with political ties, ex-diplomatic, military and intelligence officers who provide valuable skills and contacts, weapons merchants and shippers operating legitimate businesses and bankers. By fractionating the enterprise, the contributors see themselves as decent, legitimate practitioners of their trade rather than as parties to a deathly operation.

Even producers of the television program *60 Minutes* contributed to Frank Terpil's coffers (San Francisco Chronicle, 1983). Terpil skipped bail to a foreign sanctuary after he was caught selling assassination equipment to an undercover FBI agent. He was tried in absentia. The District Attorney confronted the lead reporter of the programme about a payment of $12,000 to an intermediary for an interview with the fugitive, Terpil. The reporter pleaded innocence through various disengagement manoeuvres.

Edmund Burke's aphorism that, "The only thing necessary for the triumph of evil is for good men to do nothing" needs a companion adage under our technologically specialised realities: "The triumph of evil requires a lot of good people, doing a bit of it, in a morally disengaged way, with indifference to the human suffering they collectively cause."

Disengagement in Everyday Life

Moral disengagement mechanisms have been examined most extensively in military, and political violence. Such mechanisms do heavy duty in everyday situations in which decent people perform activities that bring them profits and other benefits at injurious costs to others. Self-exonerations are used to neutralise self-censure and to preserve self-esteem. Some industries cause harmful effects on a large scale. They resort to public-spirited vindications.

The products of the tobacco industry kill about 450,000 Americans annually (McGinnis & Foege, 1993). The aggressive marketing of cigarettes worldwide will produce a global epidemic of lung cancer killing millions. For years the tobacco industry disputed the view that nicotine is addictive and that smoking is a major contributor to lung cancer.

The vast supporting cast contributing to the promotion of this deadly product include talented chemists discovering ammonia as a means to increase the nicotine "kick" by speeding the body's absorption of nicotine (Meier, 1998a); inventive biotech researchers genetically engineering a tobacco seed that doubles the addictive nicotine content of tobacco plants (Meier, 1998b); creative advertisers targeting young age groups with merchandising and advertising schemes depicting smoking as a sign of youthful hipness, modernity, freedom and women's liberation (Lynch & Bonnie, 1994; Dedman, 1998); ingenious officials in a subsidiary of a major tobacco company engaging in an elaborate international cigarette smuggling operation to evade excise taxes (Drew, 1998); popular movie actors agreeing to smoke in their movies for a hefty fee; legislators with bountiful tobacco campaign contributions exempting nicotine from drug legislation even though it is the most addictive substance and passing preemption laws that block states from regulating tobacco products and their advertising (Public Citizen Health Research Group, 1993; Lynch & Bonnie, 1994); United States trade representatives threatening sanctions against countries that erect barriers against the importation of US cigarettes, and even a President firing his cabinet member presiding over the Department of Health, Education and Welfare for refusing to back off on the regulation of tobacco products. As indicated in the above examples and other analyses of industry-wide collective moral disengagement (Bandura, 1973; Bandura *et al.*, 2000), injurious corporate practices require a large network of otherwise considerate people performing jobs drawing on their expertise and social influence in the service of a detrimental enterprise.

Moral disengagement is an active player in daily life. Institutionalised discrimination of devalued subgroups in societies takes a heavy toll on its victims. It requires social justification, attributions of blame, dehumanisation, impersonalised agencies to carry out the discriminatory practices and inattention to the injurious effects they cause. Ideologies of male domination, dehumanisation, ascription of blame and distortion of injurious consequences play a heavy role in sexual abuse of women (Burt, 1980; Bandura, 1986; Sanday, 1997). We are currently extending our research to the role of moral disengagement in criminal pursuits, use of military force, capital punishment, child abuse and support of inequities that impoverish and demoralise the less advantaged members of affluent societies.

Impact of Moral Disengagement on Development Life Courses

Advances in the measurement of moral disengagement hold the promise of advancing understanding of how the disengagement aspect of morality develops and influences the courses lives take. Longitudinal analyses reveal that moral disengagement is already operating even in the early years of life (Bandura *et al.*, 1996). It contributes to social discordance in ways that are likely to lead down dissocial paths. High moral disengagers experience low guilt over injurious conduct. They are less prosocial. They are quick to resort to aggression and transgressive conduct. Gender differences in moral disengagement do not exist in the earlier years, but before long boys become more facile moral disengagers than do girls.

Moral development has typically been studied in terms of abstract principles of morality and measured under decontextualised and depersonalised circumstances. Adolescents who differ widely in delinquent conduct do not differ in abstract moral values (Elliott & Rinehart, 1995). Almost everyone is virtuous at the abstract level. It is in the ease of moral disengagement under the conditionals of life where the differences lie. Facile moral disengagers display higher levels of violence than those who bring moral self-reactions to bear on their conduct. This is true regardless of age, sex, race, ethnicity, socio-economic level and religious affiliation. Moral engagement against destructive means can be enhanced in children by peer modelling and espousal of peaceable solutions to human conflicts (McAlister *et al.*, 1999).

Reciprocal Interplay of Personal and Social Sanctions

Moral agency is socially situated and exercised in particularised ways depending on the life conditions under which people transact their affairs. Social cognitive theory, therefore, adopts an interactionist perspective to morality. Moral actions are the products of the reciprocal interplay of personal and social influences. Conflicts arise between self sanctions and social sanctions when individuals are punished socially for courses of action they regard as right and just. Principled dissenters and non-conformists often find themselves in this predicament. Some sacrifice their welfare for their convictions. People also commonly experience conflicts in which they are socially pressured to engage in conduct that violates their moral standards. Responses to such moral dilemmas are determined by the relative strength of self sanctions and social sanctions and the conditional application of moral standards.

Socio-structural theories and psychological theories are often regarded as rival conceptions of human behaviour or as representing different levels of causation. Human behaviour cannot be understood fully solely in terms of social structural factors or psychological factors. Social cognitive theory rejects a dualism between social structure and personal agency (Bandura, 1986, 1997). Socio-structural influences affect action via self-regulatory mechanisms operating through a set of sub-functions. Neither situational imperatives (Milgram, 1974) nor vile dispositions (Gillespie, 1971) provide a wholly adequate explanation of human malevolence. In social cognitive theory, both socio-structural and personal determinants operate interdependently within a unified causal structure in the perpetration of inhumanities.

Some of the moral disengagement practices, such as diffusion and displacement of responsibility, are built into the organisational and authority structures of societal systems. The ideological orientations of societies shape the form of moral justifications, sanction detrimental practices and influence who gets cast into devalued groups. These socio-structural practices create conditions conducive to moral disengagement, but people are producers as well as products of social systems. They have the agentic capabilities to change the nature of their social systems.

Concluding Remarks

The massive threats to human welfare stem mainly from deliberate acts of principle, rather than from unrestrained acts of impulse. As C. P. Snow insightfully observed. "More hideous crimes have been committed in the name of obedience, than in the name of rebellion." Principled resort to destructiveness is of greatest social concern but, ironically, it is the most ignored in psychological analyses of people's inhumanities toward each other.

Given many psychological devices for disengaging moral control, societies cannot rely entirely on individuals, however righteous their moral standards, to provide safeguards against human cruelty. Civilised life requires, in addition to humane personal codes, social systems that uphold compassionate behaviour and renounce cruelty.

Monolithic political systems, that exercise tight control over communication systems can more easily promote moral disengagement, than pluralistic systems that represent diverse perspectives, interests and concerns. Political diversity, and tolerance of dissent allow challenges to suspect moral appeals. Healthy scepticism toward moral pretensions puts a further check on the misuse of morality for inhumane purposes. To function humanely, societies must establish effective social safeguards against the misuse of institutional power for exploitive and destructive purposes. It should be made difficult for people to remove humanity from their conduct.

Acknowledgements

Preparation of this article and some of the cited research were facilitated by grants from the Grant Foundation and the Spencer Foundation.

Correspondence: Professor Albert Bandura, Department of Psychology, Stanford University, Stanford, CA 94305-2130, USA; Fax: +1 650 725 5699; E-mail: bandura@psych.stanford.edu.

References

Bandura, A. (1973) *Aggression: a social learning analysis* (Englewood Cliffs, NJ, Prentice-Hall).

Bandura, A. (1986) *Social Foundations of Thought and Action: a social cognitive theory* (Englewood Cliffs, NJ, Prentice-Hall).

Bandura, A. (1990) Mechanisms of moral disengagement, in: W. Reich (Ed.), *Origins of Terrorism: psychologies, ideologies, theologies, states of mind*, pp. 161–191 (Cambridge, Cambridge University Press).

Bandura, A. (1991) Social cognitive theory of moral thought and action, in: W. M. Kurtines & J. L. Gewirtz (Eds) *Handbook of Moral Behavior and Development: theory, research and applications*, Vol. 1, pp. 71–129 (Hillsdale, NJ, Erlbaum, 1990).

Bandura, A. (1992) Social cognitive theory of social referencing, in: S. Ffjnman (Ed.) *Social Referencing and the Social Construction of Reality in Infancy*, pp. 175–208 (New York, Plenum).

Bandura, A. (1997) *Self-efficacy: the exercise of control* (New York, Freeman).

Bandura, A. (1999) Moral disengagement in the perpetration of inhumanities, *Personality and Social Psychology Review* [Special Issue on Evil and Violence], 3, pp. 193–209.

Bandura, A. (2001) Social cognitive theory: an agentic perspective, *Annual Review of Psychology*, Vol. 52, pp. 1–26 (Palo Alto, Annual Reviews, Inc.).

Bandura, A., Barbaranelli, C., Caprara, G. V. & Pastorelli, C. (1996) Mechanisms of moral disengagement in the exercise of moral agency, *Journal of Personality and Social Psychology*, 71, pp. 364–374.

Bandura, A., Caprara, G. V. & Zsolnai, L. (2000) Corporate transgressions through moral disengagement, *Journal of Human Values*, 6, pp. 57–63.

Bandura, A., Underwood, B. & Fromson, M. E. (1975) Disinhibition of aggression through diffusion of responsibility and dehumanization of victims, *Journal of Research in Personality*, 9, pp. 253–269.

Bandura, V., Ottenberg, P. & Redl, F. (1965) Dehumanization: a composite psychological defense in relation to modern war, in: M. Schwebel (Ed.) *Behavioral Science and Human Survival*, pp. 64–82 (Palo Alto, CA, Science and Behavior Books).

Burt, M. R. (1980) Cultural myths and support for rape, *Journal of Personality and Social Psychology*, 38, pp. 217–230.

Bollinger, D. (1982) *Language: the loaded weapon* (London, Longman).

Dedman, B. (1998) Executive says he's uncertain about tobacco harm, *New York Times*, p. A16.

Diener, E. (1977) Deindividuation: causes and consequences, *Social Behavior and Personality,* 5, pp. 143–156.

Diener, E., Dineen, J., Endresen, K., Beaman, A. L. & Fraser, S. C. (1975) Effects of altered responsibility, cognitive set, and modeling on physical aggression and deindividuation, *Journal of Personality and Social Psychology,* 31, pp. 328–337.

Drew, C. (1998) RJR subsidiary pleads guilty to smuggling, *New York Times, p.* Al.

Elliott, D. S. & Rhinehart, M. (1995) *Moral disengagement, delinquent peers and delinquent behavior,* unpublished manuscript, Institute of Behavioral Science, University of Colorado.

Gabor, T. (1994) *Everybody Does It: crime by the public* (Toronto, University of Toronto Press).

Gambino, R. (1973) Watergate lingo: a language of non-responsibility, *Freedom at Issue,* 22, pp. 7–9, 15–17.

Gibson, J. T. & Haritos-Fatouros, M. (1986) The education of a torturer, *Psychology Today,* November, pp. 50–58.

Gillespie, W. H. (1971) Aggression and instinct theory, *International Journal of Psycho-analysis,* 52, pp. 155–160.

Goldhagen, D. J. (1996) *Hitler's Willing Executioners: ordinary Germans and the holocaust,* (New York, Knopf).

Hallie, P. P. (1971) Justification and rebellion, in: N. Sanford & C. Comstock (Eds) *Sanctions for Evil,* pp. 247–263 (San Francisco; Jossey-Bass).

Haney, C, Banks, W. C. & Zimbardo, P. G. (1973) Interpersonal dynamics in a simulated prison, *International Journal of Criminology & Penology,* 1, pp. 69–97.

Ivie, R. L. (1980) Images of savagery in American justifications for war, *Communication Monographs,* 47, pp. 270–294.

Keen, S. (1986) *Faces of the Enemy* (San Francisco, Harper & Row).

Kelman, H. C. (1973) Violence without moral restraint: reflections on the dehumanization of victims and victimizers, *Journal of Social Issues,* 29, pp. 25–61.

Kelman, H. C. & Hamilton, V. L. (1989) *Crimes of Obedience: toward a social psychology of authority and responsibility* (New Haven, CT, Yale University Press).

Kilham, W. & Mann, L. (1974) Level of destructive obedience as a function of transmitter and executant roles in the Milgram obedience paradigm, *Journal of Personality and Social Psychology,* 29, pp. 696–702.

Kipnis, D. (1974) The powerholders, in: J. T. Tedeschi (Ed.) *Perspectives on Social Power,* pp. 82–122 (Chicago, Aldine).

Kramer, M. (1990) The moral logic of Hizballah, in: W. Reich (Ed.) *Origins of Terrorism: psychologies, ideologies, theologies, states of mind,* pp. 131–157 (Cambridge, Cambridge University Press).

Lerner, M. J. & Miller, D. T. (1978) Just world research and the attribution process: looking back and ahead, *Psychological Bulletin,* 85, pp. 1030–1051.

Levi, P. (1987) *The Drowned and the Saved* (New York, Summit Books).

Lutz, W. D. (1987) Language, appearance, and reality doublespeak in 1984, in: PC. Boardman (Ed.) *The Legacy of Language—a tribute to Charlton Laird,* pp. 103–119 (Reno, NV, University of Nevada Press).

Lynch, B. S. & Bonnie, R. J. (Eds) (1994) *Growing Up Tobacco Free: preventing nicotine addiction in children and youths* (Washington, D.C., National Academy Press).

Mcalister, A. L., Ama, E., Barroro, C., Peters, R. J. & Kelder, S. (1999) *Promoting tolerance and moral engagement through peer counseling,* unpublished manuscript, University of Texas Health Science Center, Houston, TX.

Mcginnis, J. M. & Foege, W. H. (1993) Actual causes of death in the United States, *Journal of the American Medical Association,* 270, pp. 2207–2212.

Meier, B. (1998a) Cigarette maker manipulated nicotine, its records suggest, *New York Times,* p. 1, A16.

Meier, B. (1998b) U.S. brings its first charges in the tobacco investigation, *New York Times,* p. A17.

Milgram, S. (1974) *Obedience to Authority: an experimental view* (New York, Harper & Row).

Oliner, S. P. & Oliner, P. M. (1988) *The Altruistic Personality* (New York, Free Press).

Public Citizen Health Research Group (1993) The influence of tobacco money on the U.S. Congress, *Health Letter,* 9, pp. 1–7.

Rapoport, D. C. & Alexander, Y. (Eds) (1982) *The Morality of Terrorism: religious and secular justification* (Elmsford, NY, Pergamon Press).

Reich, W. (Ed.) (1990) *Origins of Terrorism: psychologies, ideologies, theologies, states of mind* (Cambridge, England, Cambridge University Press).

Rorty, A. O. (1993) What it takes to be good, in: G. Noam & T. E. Wren (Eds) *The Moral Self,* pp. 28–55. (Cambridge, MA, The MIT Press).

Sanday, P. R. (1997) The socio-cultural context of rape: a cross-cultural study, in: L. L. O'Toole & J. R. Schiffrnan (Eds) *Gender Violence: interdisciplinary perspectives,* pp. 52–66 (New York, New York University Press).

San Francisco Chronicle (1983) CBS reportedly paid two fugitives, September 22.

Sprinzak, E. (1986) *Fundamentalism, terrorism, and democracy: the case of the Gush Emunim underground,* paper presented at the Woodrow Wilson Center, Washington, DC.

Sprinzak, E. (1990) The psychopolitical formation of extreme left terrorism in a democracy: the case of the Weathermen, in: W. Reich (Ed.) *Origins of Terrorism: psychologies, ideologies, theologies, states of mind,* pp. 65–85 (Cambridge, England, Cambridge University Press).

Stein, A. (1988) *Quiet Heroes* (Toronto, Lester & Orpen Dennys).

Thomas, A. (1982) *Frank Terpil: confessions of a dangerous man* [film] (New York, Studio Film & Tape, Inc.).

Tilker, H. A. (1970) Socially responsible behavior as a function of observer responsibility and victim feedback, *Journal of Personality and Social Psychology,* 14, pp. 95–100.

Zganjar, L. (1998) Forgotten hero of Mai Lai to be honored after 30 years, *San Francisco Chronicle,* p. A9.

Zimbardo, P. G. (1995) The psychology of evil: a situationist perspective on recruiting good people to engage in anti-social acts, *Research in Social Psychology,* 11, pp. 125–133.

Investigating Social Dynamics: Power, Conformity, and Obedience

Philip Zimbardo

Philip Zimbardo *(1933–) is an internationally recognized researcher, teacher, and public figure in psychology. He has written over 300 publications, including* Shyness: What It Is, What To Do About It *(1977),* The Lucifer Effect: Understanding How Good People Turn Evil *(2008), and a popular introductory textbook in psychology titled* Psychology and Life, *which is now in its 19th edition. He is best known for his 1971 prison experiment at Stanford University, which investigated the psychological effects of being prisoners and prison guards (www.prisonexp.org). In 1990, he developed a series for PBS titled* Discovering Psychology, *which brought the field of psychology to the public. Zimbardo taught at Stanford for over forty years and is currently Professor Emeritus. He also is the Director of the Heroic Imagination Project, which he founded. The following reading is taken from his book* The Lucifer Effect.

I believe that in all men's lives at certain periods, and in many men's lives at all periods between infancy and extreme old age, one of the most dominant elements is the desire to be inside the local Ring and the terror of being left outside. . . . Of all the passions the passion for the Inner Ring is most skilful in making a man who is not yet a very bad man do very bad things.

—C. S. Lewis, "The Inner Ring" (1944)[1]

Motives and needs that ordinarily serve us well can lead us astray when they are aroused, amplified, or manipulated by situational forces that we fail to recognize as potent. This is why evil is so pervasive. Its temptation is just a small turn away, a slight detour on the path of life, a blur in our sideview mirror, leading to disaster.

In trying to understand the character transformations of the good young men in the Stanford Prison Experiment, I previously outlined a number of psychological processes that were pivotal in perverting their thoughts, feelings, perceptions, and actions. We saw how the basic need to belong, to associate with and be accepted

308

by others, so central to community building and family bonding, was diverted in the SPE into conformity with newly emergent norms that enabled the guards to abuse the prisoners.[2] We saw further that the basic motive for consistency between our private attitudes and public behavior allowed for dissonant commitments to be resolved and rationalized in violence against one's fellows.[3]

I will argue that the most dramatic instances of directed behavior change and "mind control" are not the consequence of exotic forms of influence, such as hypnosis, psychotropic drugs, or "brainwashing," but rather the systematic manipulation of the most mundane aspects of human nature over time in confining settings.[4]

It is in this sense, I believe what the English scholar C. S. Lewis proposed—that a powerful force in transforming human behavior, pushing people across the boundary between good and evil, comes from the basic desire to be "in" and not "out." If we think of social power as arrayed in a set of concentric circles from the most powerful central or inner ring moving outward to the least socially significant outer ring, we can appreciate his focus on the centripetal pull of that central circle. Lewis's "Inner Ring" is the elusive Camelot of acceptance into some special group, some privileged association, that confers instant status and enhanced identity. Its lure for most of us is obvious—who does not want to be a member of the "in-group"? Who does not want to know that she or he has been tried and found worthy of inclusion in, of ascendance into, a new, rarified realm of social acceptability?

Peer pressure has been identified as one social force that makes people, especially adolescents, do strange things—anything—to be accepted. However, the quest for the Inner Ring is nurtured from within. There is no peer-pressure power without that push from self-pressure for Them to want You. It makes people willing to suffer through painful, humiliating initiation rites in fraternities, cults, social clubs, or the military. It justifies for many suffering a lifelong existence climbing the corporate ladder.

This motivational force is doubly energized by what Lewis called the "terror of being left outside." This fear of rejection when one wants acceptance can cripple initiative and negate personal autonomy. It can turn social animals into shy introverts. The imagined threat of being cast into the out-group can lead some people to do virtually anything to avoid their terrifying rejection. Authorities can command total obedience not through punishments or rewards but by means of the double-edged weapon: the lure of acceptance coupled with the threat of rejection. So strong is this human motive that even strangers are empowered when they promise us a special place at their table of shared secrets—"just between you and me."[5]

A sordid example of these social dynamics came to light recently when a forty-year-old woman pleaded guilty to having sex with five high school boys and providing them and others with drugs and alcohol at weekly sex parties in her home for a full year. She told police that she had done it because she wanted to be a "cool mom." In her affidavit, this newly cool mom told investigators that she had never been popular with her classmates in high school, but orchestrating these parties enabled her to begin "feeling like one of the group."[6] Sadly, she caught the wrong Inner Ring.

Lewis goes on to describe the subtle process of initiation, the indoctrination of good people into a private Inner Ring that can have malevolent consequences, turning them into "scoundrels." I cite this passage at length because it is such an eloquent expression of how this basic human motive can be imperceptibly perverted by those with the power to admit or deny access to their Inner Ring. It will set the stage for our excursion into the experimental laboratories and field settings of social scientists who have investigated such phenomena in considerable depth.

> To nine out of ten of you the choice which could lead to scoundrelism will come, when it does come, in no very dramatic colors. Obviously bad men, obviously threatening or bribing, will almost certainly not appear. Over a drink or a cup of coffee, disguised as a triviality and sandwiched between two jokes, from the lips of a man, or woman, whom you have recently been getting to know rather better and whom you hope to know better still—just at the moment when you are most anxious not to appear crude, or naive or a prig—the hint will come. It will be the hint of something, which is not quite in accordance with the technical rules of fair play, something that the public, the ignorant, romantic public, would never understand. Something which even the outsiders in your own profession are apt to make a fuss about, but something, says your new friend, which "we"—and at the word "we" you try not to blush for mere pleasure—something "we always do." And you will be drawn in, if you are drawn in, not by desire for gain or ease, but simply because at that moment, when the cup was so near your lips, you cannot bear to be thrust back again into the cold outer would. It would be so terrible to see the other man's face—that genial, confidential, delightfully sophisticated face—turn suddenly cold an contemptuous, to know that you had been tried for the Inner Ring and rejected. And then, if you are drawn in, next week it will be something a little further from the rules, and next year something further still, but all in the jolliest, friendliest spirit. It may end in a crash, a scandal, and penal servitude; it may end in millions, a peerage and giving the prizes at your old school. But you will be a scoundrel.

Research Revelations of Situational Power

The Stanford Prison Experiment is a facet of the broad mosaic of research that reveals the power of social situations and the social construction of reality. We have seen how it focused on power relationships among individuals within an institutional setting. A variety of studies that preceded and followed it have illuminated many other aspects of human behavior that are shaped in unexpected ways by situational forces.

Groups can get us to do things we ordinarily might not do on our own, but their influence is often indirect, simply modeling the normative behavior that the group wants us to imitate and practice. In contrast, authority influence is more often direct and without subtlety: "You do what I tell you to do." But because the demand is so open and bold-faced, one can decide to disobey and not follow the leader. To see what I mean, consider this question: To what extent would a good, ordinary person resist against or comply with the demand of an authority figure that he harm, or even kill, an innocent stranger? This provocative question was put to experimental test in a controversial study on blind obedience to authority. It is a classic experiment about which you have probably heard because of its "shock-ing" effects, but there is much more of value embedded in its procedures that we will extract to aid in our quest to understand why good people can be induced to behave badly. We will review replications and extensions of this classic study and again ask the question posed of all such research: What is its external validity, what are real-world parallels to the laboratory demonstration of authority power?

Beware: Self-Serving Biases May Be at Work

Before we get into the details of this research, I must warn you of a bias you likely possess that might shield you from drawing the right conclusions from all you are about to read. Most of us construct self-enhancing, self-serving, egocentric biases that make us feel special—never ordinary, and certainly "above average."[7] Such cognitive biases serve a valuable function in boosting our self-esteem and pro-tecting against life's hard knocks. They enable us to explain away failures, take credit for our successes, and disown responsibility for bad decisions, perceiving our subjective world through rainbow prisms. For example, research shows that 86 percent of Australians rate their job performance as "above average," and 90 percent of American business managers rate their performance as superior to that of their average peer. (Pity that poor average dude.)

Yet these biases can be maladaptive as well by blinding us to our Similarity to others and distancing us from the reality that people just like us behave badly in certain toxic situations. Such biases also mean that we don't take basic precautions to avoid the undesired consequences of our behavior, assuming it won't happen to us. So we take sexual risks, driving risks, gambling risks, health risks, and more. In the extreme version of these biases, most people believe that they are less vulnerable to these self-serving biases than other people, even after being taught about them.[8]

That means when you read about the SPE or the many studies in this next section, you might well conclude that *you* would not do what the majority has done, that you would, of course, be the exception to the rule. That statistically unreasonable belief (since most of us share it) makes you even more vulnerable to situational forces precisely because you underestimate their power as you over-estimate yours. You are convinced that you would be the good guard, the defiant prisoner, the resistor, the dissident, the nonconformist, and, most of all, the Hero. Would that it were so, but heroes are a rare breed—some of whom we will meet in our final chapter.

So I invite you to suspend that bias for now and imagine that what the major-ity has done in these experiments is a fair base rate for you as well. At the very least, please consider that you can't be certain of whether or not you could be as readily seduced into doing what the average research participant has done in these studies—if you were in their shoes, under the same circumstances. I ask you to recall what Prisoner Clay–416, the sausage resister, said in his postexperimental interview with his tormenter, the "John Wayne" guard. When taunted with "What kind of guard would you have been if you were in my place?" he replied modestly, "I really don't know."

It is only through recognizing that we are all subject to the same dynamic forces in the human condition, that humility takes precedence over unfounded pride, that we can begin to acknowledge our vulnerability to situational forces. In this vein, recall John Donne's eloquent framing of our common interrelatedness and interdependence:

> All mankind is of one author, and is one volume; when one man dies, one chap-ter is not torn out of the book, but translated into a better language; and every chapter must be so translated. . . . As therefore the bell that rings to a sermon, calls not upon the preacher only, but upon the congregation to come: so this bell calls us all. . . . No man is an island, entire of itself . . . any man's death dimin-ishes me, because I am involved in mankind; and therefore never send to know for whom the bell tolls; it tolls for thee.
>
> (Meditations 27)

Classic Research on Conforming to Group Norms

One of the earliest studies on conformity, in 1935, was designed by a social psy-chologist from Turkey, Muzafer Sherif.[9] Sherif, a recent immigrant to the United States, believed that Americans in general tended to conform because their democ-racy emphasized mutually shared agreements. He devised an unusual means of demonstrating conformity of individuals to group standards in a novel setting.

Male college students were individually ushered into a totally dark room in which there was a stationary spot of light. Sherif knew that without any frame of reference, such a light appears to move about erratically, an illusion called the "autokinetic effect." A first, each of these subjects was asked individually to judge the movement of the light, Their judgments varied widely; some saw movement of a few inches, while others reported that the spot moved many feet. Each person soon established a range within which most of his reports would fall. Next, he was put into a group with several others. They gave estimates that varied widely, but in each group a norm "crystallized" wherein a range of judgments and an average-norm judgment emerged. After many trials, the other participants left, and the individual, now alone, was asked again to make estimates of the movement of the light—the test of his conformity to the new norm established in that group. His judgments now fell in this new group-sanctioned range, "departing significantly from his earlier personal range."

Sherif also used a confederate who was trained to give estimates that varied in their latitude from a small to a very large range. Sure enough, the naive subject's autokinetic experience mirrored that of the judgments of this devious confederate rather than sticking to his previously established personal perceptual standard.

Asch's Conformity Research: Getting into Line

Sherif's conformity effect was challenged in 1955 by another social psychologist, Solomon Asch,[10] who believed that Americans were actually more independent that Sherif's work had suggested. Asch believed that Americans could act autonomously, even when faced with a majority who saw the world differently from them. The problem with Sherif's test situation, he argued, was that it was so ambiguous, without any meaningful frame of reference or personal standard. When challenged by the alternative perception of the group, the individual had no real commitment to his original estimates so just went along. Real conformity required the group to challenge the basic perception and beliefs of the individual—to say that X was Y, when clearly that was not true. Under those circumstances. Asch predicted, relatively few would conform; most would be staunchly resistant to this extreme group pressure that was so transparently wrong.

What actually happened to people confronted with a social reality that conflicted with their basic perceptions of the world? To find out, let me put you into the seat of a typical research participant.

You are recruited for a study of visual perception that begins with judging the relative size of lines. You are shown cards with three lines of differing lengths and asked to state out loud which of the three is the same length as a comparison line on another card. One is shorter, one is longer, and one is exactly the same length as the comparison line. The task is a piece of cake for you. You make few mistakes, just like most others (less than 1 percent of the time). But you are not alone in this study; you are flanked by a bunch peers, seven of them, and you are number eight. At first, you answers are like theirs—all right on. But then unusual things start to happen. On some trials, each of them in turn reports seeing the long line as the same length as the medium line or the short line the same as the medium one. (Unknown to you, the other seven are members of Asch's research team who have been instructed to give incorrect answers unanimously on specific "critical" trials.) When it is your turn, they all look at you as you look at the card with the three lines. You are clearly seeing something different than they are, but do you say so? Do you stick to your guns and say what you know is right, or do you go along with what everyone else says is right? You face that same group pressure on twelve of the total eighteen trials where the group gives answers that are wrong, but they are accurate on the other six trials interspersed into the mix.

If you are like most of the 123 actual research participants in Asch's study, you would yield to the group about 70 percent of the time on some of those critical, wrong-judgment trials. Thirty percent of the original subjects conformed on the majority of trials, and only a quarter of them were able to maintain their independence throughout the testing. Some reported being aware of the differences between what they saw and the group consensus, but they felt it was easier to go along with the others. For others the discrepancy created a conflict that was resolved by coming to believe that the group was right and their perception was wrong! All those who yielded underestimated how much they had conformed, recalling yielding much less to the group pressure than had actually been the case. They remained independent—in their minds but not in their actions.

Follow-up studies showed that, when pitted against just one person giving an incorrect judgment, a participant exhibits some uneasiness but maintains independence. However, with a majority of three people opposed to him, errors rose to 32 percent. On a more optimistic note, however. Asch found one powerful way to promote independence. By giving the subject a partner whose views were in line with his, the power of the majority was greatly diminished. Peer support decreased errors to one fourth of what they had been when there was no partner— and this resistance effect endured even after the partner left.

One of the valuable additions to our understanding of why people conform comes from research that highlights two of the basic mechanisms that contribute to group conformity.[11] We conform first out of *informational needs:* other people often have ideas, views, perspectives, and knowledge that helps us to better navigate our world, especially through foreign shores and new ports. The second mechanism involves *normative needs:* other people are more likely to accept us when we agree with them than when we disagree, so we yield to their view of the world, driven by a powerful need to belong, to replace differences with similarities.

Conformity and Independence Light Up the Brain Differently

New technology, not available in Asch's day, offers intriguing insights into the role of the brain in social conformity. When people conform, are they rationally deciding to go along with the group out of normative needs, or are they actually changing their perceptions and accepting the validity of the new though erroneous information provided by the group? A recent Study utilized advanced brain-scanning technology to answer this question.[12] Researchers can now peer into the active brain as a person engages in various tasks by using a scanning device that detects which specific brain regions are energized as they carry out various mental tasks. The process is known as functional magnetic resonance imaging (FMRI). Understanding what mental functions various brain regions control tells us what it means when they are activated by any given experimental task.

Here's how the study worked. Imagine that you are one of thirty-two volunteers recruited for a study of perception. You have to mentally rotate images of three-dimensional objects to determine if the objects are the same as or different from a standard object. In the waiting room, you meet four other volunteers, with whom you begin to bond by practicing games on laptop computers, taking photos of one another, and chatting. (They are really actors—"confederates," as they are called in psychology—who will soon be faking their answers on the test trials so that they are in agreement with one another but not with the correct responses that you generate.) You are selected as the one to go into the scanner while the others outside look at the objects first as a group and then decide if they are the same or different. As in Asch's original experiment, the actors unanimously give wrong answers on some trials, correct answers on others, with occasional mixed group answers thrown in to make the test more believable. On each round, when it is you turn at bat, you are shown the answers given by the others. You have to decide if the objects are the same or different—as the group assessed them or as you saw them?

As in Asch's experiments, you (as the typical subject) would cave into group pressure, on average giving the group's wrong answers 41 percent of the time. When you yield to the group's erroneous judgment, your conformity would be seen in the brain scan as changes in selected regions of the brain's cortex dedicated to vision and spatial awareness (specifically, activity increases in the right intraparietal sulcus). Surprisingly, there would be no changes in areas of the forebrain that deal with monitoring conflicts, planning, and other higher-order mental activities. On the other hand, if you make independent judgments that go against the group, your brain would light up in the areas that are associated with emotional salience (the right amygdala and right caudate nucleus regions). This means that resistance creates an emotional burden for those who maintain their independence—autonomy comes at a psychic cost.

The lead author of this research, the neuroscientist Gregory Berns, concluded that "We like to think that seeing is believing, but the study's findings show that seeing is believing what the group tells you to believe." This means that other people's views, when crystallized into a group consensus, can actually affect how we perceive important aspects of the external world, thus calling into question the nature of truth itself. It is only by becoming aware of our vulnerability to social pressure that we can begin to build resistance to conformity when it is not in our best interest to yield to the mentality of the herd.

Minority Power to Impact the Majority

Juries can become "hung" when a dissenter gets support from at least one other person and together they challenge the dominant majority view. But can a small minority turn the majority around to create new norms using the same basic psychological principles that usually help to establish the majority view?

A research team of French psychologists put that question to an experimental test. In a color-naming task, if two confederates among groups of six female students consistently called, a blue light "green," almost a third of the naive majority subjects eventually followed their lead. However, the members of the majority did not given in to the consistent minority when they were gathered together. It was only later, when they were tested individually, that they responded as the minority had done, shifting their judgments by moving the boundary between blue and green toward the green of the color spectrum.[13]

Researchers have also studied minority influence in the context of simulated jury deliberations, where a disagreeing minority prevents unanimous acceptance of the majority point of view. The minority group was never well liked, and its persuasiveness, when it occurred, worked only gradually, over time. The vocal minority was most influential when it had four qualities: it persisted in affirming a consistent position, appeared confident, avoided seeming rigid and dogmatic, and was skilled in social influence. Eventually, the power of the many may be undercut by the persuasion of the dedicated few.

How do these qualities of a dissident minority—especially its persistence— help to sway the majority? Majority decisions tend to be made without engaging the systematic thought and critical thinking skills of the individuals in the group. Given the force of the group's normative power to shape the opinions of the followers who conform without thinking things through, they are often taken at face value. The persistent minority force the others to process the relevant information more mindfully.[14] Research shows that the decisions of a group as a whole are more thoughtful and creative when there is minority dissent than when it is absent.[15]

If a minority can win adherents to their side even when they are wrong, there is hope for minority with a valid cause. In society, the majority tends to be the defender of the status quo, while the force for innovation and change comes from the minority members or individuals either dissatisfied with the current system or able to visualize new and creative alternative ways of dealing with current problems. According to the French social theorist Serge Moscovici,[16] the conflict between the entrenched majority view and the dissident minority perspective is an essential precondition of innovation and revolution that can lead to positive social change. An individual is constantly engaged in a two-way exchange with society—adapting to its norms, roles, and status prescriptions but also acting upon society to reshape those norms.

Blind Obedience to Authority: Milgram's Shocking Research

"I was trying to think of a way to make Asch's conformity experiment more humanly significant. I was dissatisfied that the test of conformity was judgments about lines. I wondered whether groups could pressure a person into performing an act whose human import was more readily apparent; perhaps behaving aggressively toward another person, say by administering increasingly severe shocks to him. But to study the group effect . . . you'd have to know how the subject performed without any group pressure. At that instant, my thought shifted, zeroing in on this experimental control. Just how far would a person go under the experimenter's orders?"

These musings, from a former teaching and research assistant of Solomon Asch, started a remarkable series of studies by a social psychologist, Stanley Milgram, that have come to be known as investigations of "blind obedience to authority." His interest in the problem of obedience to authority came from deep personal concerns about how readily the Nazis had obediently killed Jews during the Holocaust.

"[My] laboratory paradigm . . . gave scientific expression to a more general concern about authority, a concern forced upon members of my generation, in particular upon Jews such as myself, by the atrocities of World War II. . . . The impact of the Holocaust on my own psyche energized my interest in obedience and shaped the particular form in which it was examined."[17]

I would like to re-create for you the situation faced by a typical volunteer in this research project, then go on to summarize the results, outline ten important lessons to be drawn from this research that can be generalized to other situations of behavioral transformations in everyday life, and then review extensions of this paradigm by providing a number of real-world parallels. (See the Notes for a description of my personal relationship with Stanley Milgram.[18])

Milgram's Obedience Paradigm

Imagine that you see the following advertisement in the Sunday newspaper and decide to apply. The original study involved only men, but women were used in a later study, so I invite all readers to participate in this imagined scenario.

Public Announcement

WE WILL PAY YOU $4.00 FOR
ONE HOUR OF YOUR TIME

Persons Needed for a Study of Memory

*We will pay five hundred New Haven men to help us complete a scientific study of memory and learning. The study is being done at Yale University.

*Each person who participates will be paid $4.00 (plus 50¢ carfare) for approximately I hour's time. We need you for only one hour: there are no further obligations. You may choose the time you would like to come (evenings, weekdays, or weekends).

*No special training, education, or experience is needed. We want:

Factory workers	Businessmen	Construction workers
City employees	Clerks	Salespeople
Laborers	Professional people	White-collar workers
Barbers	Telephone workers	Others

All persons must be between the ages of 20 and 50. High school and college students cannot be used.

*If you meet these qualifications, fill out the coupon below and mail it now to Professor Stanley Milgram. Department of Psychology, Yale University, New Haven. You will be notified later of the specific time and place of the study. We reserve the right to decline any application.

*You will be paid $4.00 (plus 50¢ carfare) as soon as you arrive at the laboratory.

To:
PROF. STANLEY MILGRAM, DEPARTMENT OF PSYCHOLOGY, YALE UNIVERSITY, NEW HAVEN, CONN. I want to take part in this study of memory and learning. I am between the ages of 20 and 50. I will be paid $4.00 (plus 50¢ carfare) if I participate.

A researcher whose serious demeanor and gray laboratory coat convey scientific importance greets you and another applicant at your arrival at a Yale University laboratory in Linsly-Chittenden Hall. You are here to help scientific psychology find ways to improve people's learning and memory through the use of punishment. He tells you why this new research may have important practical consequences. The task is straightforward: one of you will be the "teacher" who gives the "learner" a set of word pairings to memorize. During the test, the teacher gives each key word, and the learner must respond with the correct association. When right, the teacher gives a verbal reward, such as "Good" or "That's right." When wrong, the teacher is to press a lever on an impressive-looking shock apparatus that delivers an immediate shock to punish the error.

The shock generator has thirty switches, starting from a low level of 15 volts and increasing by 15 volts at each higher level. The experimenter tells you that every time the learner makes a mistake, you have to press the next higher voltage switch. The control panel indicates both the voltage level of each of the switches and a corresponding description of the level. The tenth level (150 volts) is "Strong Shock"; the 13th level (195 volts) is "Very Strong Shock"; the 17th level (255 volts) is "Intense Shock"; the 21st level (315 volts) is "Extremely Intense Shock"; the 25th level (375 volts) is "Danger, Severe Shock"; and at the 29th and 30th levels (435 and 450 volts) the control panel is simply marked with an ominous XXX (the pornography of ultimate pain and power).

You and another volunteer draw straws to see who will play each role; you are to be the teacher, and the other volunteer will be the learner. (The drawing is rigged, and the other volunteer is a confederate of the experimenter who always plays the learner.) He is a mild-mannered, middle-aged man whom you help escort to the next chamber. "Okay, now we are going to set up the learner so he can get some punishment," the researcher tells you both. The learner's arms are strapped down and an electrode is attached to his right wrist. The shock generator in the next room will deliver the shocks to the learner—if and when he makes any errors. The two of you communicate over the intercom, with the experimenter standing next to you. You get a sample shock of 45 volts, the third level, a slight tingly pain, so you now have a sense of what the shock levels mean. The experimenter then signals the start of your trial of the "memory improvement" study.

Initially, your pupil does well, but soon he begins making errors, and you start pressing the shock switches. He complains that the shocks are starting to hurt. You look at the experimenter, who nods to continue. As the shock levels increase in intensity, so do the learner's screams, saying he does not think he wants to continue. You hesitate and question whether you should go on, but the experimenter insists that you have no choice but to do so.

Now the learner begins complaining about his heart condition and you dissent, but the experimenter still insists that you continue. Errors galore; you plead with your pupil to concentrate to get the right associations, you don't want to hurt him with these very-high-level, intense shocks. But your concerns and motivational messages are to no avail. He gets the answers wrong again and again. As the shocks intensify, he shouts out, "I can't stand the pain, let me out of here!" Then he says to the experimenter, "You have no right to keep me here! Let me out!" Another level up, he screams, "I absolutely refuse to answer any more! Get me out of here! You can't hold me here! My heart's bothering me!"

Obviously you want nothing more to do with this experiment. You tell the experimenter that you refuse to continue. You are not the kind of person who harms other people in this way. You want out. But the experimenter continues to insist that you go on. He reminds you of the contract, of your agreement to participate fully. Moreover, he claims responsibility for the consequences of your shocking actions. After you press the 300-volt switch, you read the next keyword, but the learner doesn't answer. "He's not responding," you tell the experimenter. You want him to go into the other room and check on the learner to see if he is all right. The experimenter is impassive; he is not going to check on the learner. Instead he tells you, "If the learner doesn't answer in a reasonable time, about five seconds, consider it wrong," since errors of omission must be punished in the same way as errors of commission—that is a rule.

As you continue up to even more dangerous shock levels, there is no sound coming from your pupil's shock chamber. He may be unconscious or worse! You are really distressed and want to quit, but nothing you say works to get your exit from this unexpectedly distressing situation. You are told to follow the rules and keep posing the test items and shocking the errors.

Now try to imagine fully what your participation as the teacher would be. I am sure you are saying. "No way would I ever go all the way!" Obviously, you would have dissented, then disobeyed and just walked out. You would never sell out your morality for four bucks! But had you actually gone all the way to the last of the thirtieth shock levels, the experimenter would have insisted that you repeat that XXX switch two more times, for good measure! Now, that is really rubbing it in your face. Forget it, no sir, no way: you are out of there, right? So how far up the scale do you predict that *you* would you go before exiting? How far would the average person from this small city go in this situation?

The Outcome Predicted by Expert Judges

Milgram described his experiment to a group of forty psychiatrists and then asked them to estimate the percentage of American citizens who would go to each of the thirty levels in the experiment. On average, they predicted that less than 1 percent would go all the way to the end, that only sadists would engage in such sadistic behavior, and that most people would drop out at the tenth level of 150 volts. They could not have been more wrong! These experts on human behavior were totally wrong because, first, they ignored the situational determinants of behavior in the procedural description of the experiment. Second, their training in traditional psychiatry led them to rely too heavily on the dispositional perspective to understand unusual behavior and disregard situational factors. They were guilty of making the fundamental attribution error (FAE)!

The Shocking Truth

In fact, in Milgram's experiment, two of every three (65 percent) of the volunteers went all the way up the maximum shock level of 450 volts. The vast majority of people, the "teachers," shocked their "learner-victim" over and over again despite his increasingly desperate pleas to stop.

And now I invite you to venture another guess: What was the dropout rate after the shock level reached 330 volts—with only silence coming from the shock chamber, where the learner could reasonably be presumed to be unconscious? Who would go on at that point? Wouldn't every sensible person quit, drop out, refuse the experimenter's demands to go on shocking him?

Here is what one "teacher" reported about his reaction: "I didn't know what the hell was going on. I think, you know, maybe I'm killing this guy. I told the experimenter that I was not taking responsibility for going further. That's it." But when the experimenter reassured him that he would take the responsibility, the worried teacher obeyed and continued to the very end.[19]

And almost everyone who got that far did the same as this man. How is that possible? If they got that far, why did they continue on to the bitter end? One reason for this startling level of obedience may be related to the teacher's not knowing how to exit from the situation, rather than just blind obedience. Most participants dissented from time to time, saying they did not want to go on, but the experimenter did not let them out, continually coming up with reasons why they had to stay and prodding them to continue testing their suffering learner. Usually protests work and you can get out of unpleasant situations, but nothing you say affects this impervious experimenter, who insists that you must stay and continue to shock errors. You look at the shock panel and realize that the easiest exit lies at the end of the last shock lever. A few more lever presses is the fast way out, with no hassles from the experimenter and no further moans from the now-silent learner. Voila! 450 volts is the easy way out—achieving your freedom without directly confronting the authority figure or having to reconcile the suffering you have already caused with this additional pain to the victim. It is a simple matter of up and then out.

Variations on an Obedience Theme

Over the course of a year, Milgram carried out nineteen different experiments, each one a different variation of the basic paradigm of: experimenter/teacher/learner/memory testing/errors shocked. In each of these studies he varied one social psychological variable and observed its impact on the extent of obedience to the unjust authority's pressure to continue to shock the "learner-victim." In one study, he added women; in others he varied the physical proximity or remoteness of either the experimenter-teacher link or the teacher-learner link; had peers rebel or obey before the teacher had the chance to begin; and more.

In one set of experiments, Milgram wanted to show that his results were not due to the authority power of Yale University—which is what New Haven is all about. So he transplanted his laboratory to a run-down office building in downtown Bridgeport, Connecticut, and repeated the experiment as a project, ostensibly of a private research firm with no apparent connection to Yale. It made no difference; the participants fell under the same spell of this situational power.

The data clearly revealed the extreme pliability human nature: almost every-one could be totally obedient or almost everyone could resist authority pressures. It all depended on the situational variables they experienced. Milgram was able to demonstrate that compliance rates could soar to over 90 percent of people continu-ing the 450-volt maximum or be reduced to less than 10 percent—by introducing just one crucial variable into the compliance recipe.

Want maximum obedience? Make the subject a member of a "teaching team," in which the job of pulling the shock lever to punish the victim is given to another person (a confederate), while the subject assists with other parts of the proce-dure. Want people to resist authority pressures? Provide social models of peers who rebelled. Participants also refused to deliver the shocks if the learner said he wanted to be shocked; that's masochistic, and they are not sadists. They were also reluctant to give high levels of shock when the experimenter filled in as the learner. They were more likely to shock when the learner was remote than in proximity. In each of the other variations on this diverse range of ordinary American citizens, of widely varying ages and occupations and of both genders, it was possible to elicit low, medium, or high levels of compliant obedience with a flick of the situational switch—as if one were simply turning a "human nature dial" within their psyches. This large sample of a thousand ordinary citizens from such varied backgrounds makes the results of the Milgram obedience studies among the most generalizable in all the social sciences.

> When you think of the long and gloomy history of man, you will find far more hideous crimes have been committed in the name of obedience than have been committed in the name of rebellion.
>
> —C. P. Snow, "Either-Or" (1961)

Ten Lessons from the Milgram Studies: Creating Evil Traps for Good People

Let's outline some of the procedures in this research paradigm that seduced many ordinary citizens to engage in this apparently harmful behavior. In doing so, I want to draw parallels to compliance strategies used by "influence professionals" in real-world settings, such as salespeople, cult and military recruiters, media advertisers, and others.[20] There are ten methods we can extract from Milgram's paradigm for this purpose:

1. Prearranging some form of contractual obligation, verbal or written, to control the individual's behavior in pseudolegal fashion. (In Milgram's experiment, this was done by publicly agreeing to accept the tasks and the procedures.)

2. Giving participants meaningful roles to play ("teacher," "learner") that carry with them previously learned positive values and automatically activate response scripts.

3. Presenting basic rules to be followed that seem to make sense before their actual use but can then be used arbitrarily and impersonally to justify mindless compliance. Also, systems control people by making their rules vague and changing them as necessary but insisting that "rules are rules" and thus must be followed (as the researcher in the lab coat did in Milgram's experiment or the SPE guards did to force prisoner Clay–416 to eat the sausages).

4. Altering the semantics of the act, the actor, and the action (from "hurting victims" to "helping the experimenter," punishing the former for the lofty goal of scientific discovery)—replacing unpleasant reality with desirable rhetoric, gilding the frame so that the real picture is disguised. (We can see the same semantic framing at work in advertising, where, for example, bad-tasting mouthwash is framed as good for you because it kills germs and tastes like medicine is expected to taste.)

5. Creating opportunities for the diffusion of responsibility or abdication of responsibility for negative outcomes; others will be responsible, or the actor won't be held liable. (In Milgram's experiment, the authority figure said, when questioned by any "teacher," that he would take responsibility for anything that happened to the "learner")

6. Starting the path toward the ultimate evil act with a small, seemingly insignificant first step, the easy "foot in the door" that swings open subsequent greater compliance pressures, and leads down a slippery slope.[21] (In the obedience study, the initial shock was only a mild 15 volts.) This is also the operative principle in turning good kids into drug addicts, with that first little hit or sniff.

7. Having successively increasing steps on the pathway that are gradual, so that they are hardly noticeably different from one's most recent prior action. "Just a little bit more." (By increasing each level of aggression in gradual steps of only 15-volt increments, over the thirty switches, no new level of harm seemed like a noticeable difference from the prior level to Milgram's participants.)

8. Gradually changing the nature of the authority figure (the researcher, in Milgram's study) from initially "just" and reasonable to "unjust" and demanding, even irrational. This tactic elicits initial compliance and later confusion, since we expect consistency from authorities and friends. Not acknowledging that this transformation has occurred leads to mindless obedience (and it is part of many "date rape" scenarios and a reason why abused women stay with their abusing spouses).

9. Making the "exit costs" high and making the process of exiting difficult by allowing verbal dissent (which makes people feel better about themselves) while insisting on behavioral compliance.

10. Offering an ideology, or a big lie, to justify the use of any means to achieve the seemingly desirable, essential goal. (In Milgram's research this came in the form of providing an acceptable justification, or rationale, for engaging in the undesirable action, such as that science wants to help people improve their memory by judicious use of reward and punishment.) In social psychology experiments, this tactic is known as the "cover story" because it is a cover-up for the procedures that follow, which might be challenged because they do not make sense no their own. The real-world equivalent is known as a "ideology." Most nations rely on an ideology, typically, "threats to national security," before going to war or to suppress dissident political opposition. When citizens fear that their national security is being threatened, they become willing to surrender their basic freedoms to a government that offers them that exchange. Erich Fromm's classic analysis in *Escape from freedom* made us aware of this trade-off, which Hitler and other dictators have long used to gain and maintain power: namely, the claim that they will be able to provide security in exchange for citizens giving up their freedoms, which will give them the ability to control things better.[22]

Such procedures are utilized in varied influence situations where those in authority want others to do their bidding but know that few would engage in the "end game" without first being properly prepared psychologically to do the "unthinkable." In the future, when you are in a compromising position where your compliance is at stake, thinking back to these stepping-stones to mindless obedience many enable you to step back and not go all the way down the path—*their* path. A good way avoid crimes of obedience is to assert one's personal authority and always take full responsibility for one's actions.

Replications and Extensions of the Milgram Obedience Model

Because of its structural design and its detailed protocol, the basic Milgram obedience experiment encouraged replication by independent investigators in many countries. A recent comparative analysis was made of the rates of obedience in eight studies conducted in the United States and nine replications in European, African, and Asian countries. There were comparably high levels of compliance by research volunteers in these different studies and nations. The majority obedience effect of a mean 61 percent found in the U.S. replications was matched by the 66 percent obedience rate found across all the other national samples. The range of obedience went from a low 31 percent to a high of 91 percent in the U.S. studies, and from a low of 28 percent (Australia) to a high of 88 percent (south Africa) in the cross-national replications. There was also stability of obedience over decades of time as well as over place. There was no association between when study was done (between 1963 and 1985) and degree of obedience.[24]

Obedience to a Powerful Legitimate Authority

In the original obedience studies, the subjects conferred authority status on the person conducting the experiment because he was in an institutional setting and was dressed and acted like a serious scientist, even though he was only a high school biology teacher paid to play that role. His power came from being perceived as a representative of an authority system. (In Milgram's Bridgeport replication described earlier, the absence of the prestigious institutional setting of Yale reduced the obedience rate to 47.5 percent compared to 65 percent at Yale, although this drop was not a statistically significant one.) Several later studies showed how powerful the obedience effect can be when legitimate authorities exercise their power within their power domains.

When a college professor was the authority figure telling college student volunteers that their task was to train a puppy by conditioning its behavior using electric shocks, he elicited 75 percent obedience from them. In this experiment, both the "experimenter-teacher" and the "learner" were "authentic," That is, college students acted as the teacher, attempting to condition a cuddly little puppy, the learner, in a electrified apparatus. The puppy was supposed to learn a task, and shocks were given when it failed to respond correctly in a given time interval. As in Milgram's experiments, they had to deliver a series of thirty graded shocks, up to 450 volts in the training process. Each of the thirteen male and thirteen female subjects individually saw and heard the puppy squealing and jumping around the electrified grid as they pressed lever after lever. There was no doubt that they were hurting the puppy with each shock they administered. (Although the shock intensities were much lower than indicated by the voltage labels appearing on the shock box, they were still powerful enough to evoke clearly distressed reactions form the puppy with each successive press of the shock switches.)

As you might imagine, the students were clearly upset during the experiment. Some of the females cried, and the male students also expressed a lot of distress. Did they refuse to continue once they could see the suffering they were causing right before their eyes? For all too many, their personal distress did not lead be behavioral disobedience. About half of the males (54 percent) went all the way to 450 volts. The big surprise came from the women's high level of obedience. Despite their dissent and weeping, 100 percent of the female college students obeyed to the full extent possible in shocking the puppy as it tried to solve an insoluble task! A similar result was found in an unpublished study with adolescent high school girls. (The typical finding with human "victims," including Milgram's own findings, is that there are no male-female gender differences in obedience.[25])

Some critics of the obedience experiments tried to invalidate Milgram's findings by arguing that subjects quickly discover that the shocks are fake, and that is why they continue to give them to the very end.[26] This study, conducted back in 1972 (by psychologists Charles Sheridan and Richard King), removes any doubt that Milgram's high obedience rates could have resulted from subject's obedience reactions and a puppy's pain. Of further interest is the finding that half of the males who disobeyed lied to their teacher in reporting that the puppy had learned the insoluble task, a deceptive form of disobedience. When students in a comparable college class were asked to predict how far an average woman would go on this task, they estimated 0 percent—a far cry from 100 percent. (However, this faulty low estimate is reminiscent of the 1 percent figure given by the psychiatrists who assessed the Milgram paradigm.) Again this underscores one of my central arguments, that it is difficult for people to appreciate fully the power of situational forces acting on individual behavior when they are viewed outside the behavioral context.

Physician's Power over Nurses to Mistreat Patients

If the relationship between teachers and students is one of power-based authority, how much more so is that between physicians and nurses? How difficult is it, then, for a nurse to disobey an order from the powerful authority of the doctor—when she knows it is wrong? To find out, a team of doctors and nurses tested obedience in their authority system by determining whether nurses would follow or disobey an illegitimate request by an unknown physician in a real hospital setting.[27]

Each of twenty-two nurses individually received a call from a staff doctor who she had never met. He told her to administer a medication to a patient immediately, so that it would take effect by the time he arrived at the hospital. He would sign the drug order then. He ordered her to give his patient 20 milligrams of the drug "Astrogen." The label on the container of Astrogen indicated that 5 milliliters was usual and warned that 10 milliliters was the maximum dose. His order doubled that high dose.

The conflict created in the minds of each of these caregivers was whether to follow this order from an unfamiliar phone caller to administer an excessive dose of medicine or follow standard medical practice, which rejects such unauthorized orders. When this dilemma was presented as a hypothetical scenario to a dozen nurses in that hospital, ten said they would refuse to obey. However, when other nurses were put on the hot seat where they were faced with the physician's imminent arrival (and possible anger at being disobeyed), the nurses almost unanimously caved in and complied. All but one of twenty-two nurses put to the real test started to pour the medication (actually a placebo) to administer to the patient—before the researcher stopped them from doing so. That solitary disobedient nurse should have been given a raise and a hero's medal.

This dramatic effect is far from isolated. Equally high levels of blind obedience to doctors' almighty authority showed up in a recent survey of a large sample of registered nurses. Nearly half (46 percent) of the nurses reported that they could recall a time when they had in fact "carried out a physician's order that you felt could have had harmful consequences to the patient." These compliant nurses attributed less responsibility to themselves than they did to the physician when they followed an inappropriate command. In addition, they indicated that the primary basis of social power of physicians is their "legitimate power," the right to provide overall care to the patient.[28] They were just following what they construed as legitimate orders—but then the patient died. Thousands of hospitalized patients die needlessly each year due to a variety of staff mistakes, some of which, I assume, include such unquestioning obedience of nurses and tech aides to physicians' wrong orders.

Deadly Obedience to Authority

This potential for authority figures to exercise power over subordinates can have disastrous consequences in many domains of life. One such example is found in the dynamics of obedience in commercial airline cockpits, which have been shown to lead to many airline accidents. In a typical commercial airline cockpit, the captain is the central authority over a first officer and sometimes a flight engineer, and the might of that authority is enforced by organizational norms, the military background of most pilots, and flight rules that make the pilot directly responsible for operating the aircraft. Such authority can lead to flight errors when the crew feels forced to accept the "authority's definition of the situation," even when the authority is wrong.

An investigation of thirty-seven serious plane accidents where there were sufficient data from voice recorders revealed that in 81 percent of these cases, the first officer did not properly monitor or challenge the captain when he and made errors. Using a larger sample of seventy-five plane accidents as the context for evaluating destructive obedience, the author of this study concludes, "If we assume that both monitoring and challenging errors are due to excessive obedience, we may conclude that excessive obedience may cause as many as 25% of all airplane accidents."[29]

Administrative Obedience to Authority

In modern society people in positions of authority rarely punish others with physical violence as in the Milgram paradigm. What is more typical is, *mediated violence*, where authorities pass along orders to underlings who carry them out or the violence involves verbal abuse that undercuts the self-esteem and dignity of the powerless. Authorities often take actions that are punitive and whose consequences are not directly observable. For example, giving hostile feedback to someone that knowingly will disrupt their performance and adversely affect their chances of getting a job qualifies as a form of such socially mediated violence.

A team Dutch researchers assessed the extension of authority-based obedience to such a situation in a series of ingenious experiments involving twenty-five separate studies of nearly 500 participants from 1982 to 1985 at Utrecht University in the Netherlands.[30] In their "administrative obedience paradigm" the experimenter told the research participant, acting as administrator, to make a series of fifteen "stress remarks" to a job applicant (a trained accomplice) in the next room. Specifically, the subjects were instructed to administer a job selection test to the applicant—if he passed the test, he would get the job; if he failed, he would remain unemployed.

They were also instructed to disturb and stress the applicant while giving him the test. These fifteen graded remarks were critical of his test performance and also denigrated his personality, such as "That was really stupid of you." As the participant-administrators delivered these ever-more-hostile remarks, they "placed the applicant under such intense psychological strain that he did not perform satisfactorily and consequently failed to get the job." In addition, they were told by the researchers to continue despite any protests from the applicant. Any dissent by the participant-administrators was countered with up to four prods by the experimenter to continue the hostile remarks before they were finally permitted to stop if they were adamant. Finally, and most significantly, the subjects were informed that the ability to work under stress not *not* an essential job requirement, but the procedure had to be followed because it assisted the experimenter's research project, which was studying now stress affects test performance. Causing distress and hurting another person's job chances had no further use than the researcher's collection of some data. In the control condition, subjects could stop making the stress remarks at any point they chose.

When asked to predict whether they would make all the stress remarks under these circumstances, more than 90 percent of a separate set of comparable Dutch respondents said they would not comply. Again, the "outsider's view" was way off base: fully 91 percent of the subjects obeyed the authoritative experiment to the very end of the line. This same degree of extreme obedience held up even when personnel officers were used as the subjects despite their professional code of ethics for dealing with clients. Similarly high obedience was found when subjects were sent advance information several weeks before their appearance at the laboratory so that they had time to reflect on the nature of their potentially hostile role.

How might we generate *disobedience* in this setting? You can choose among several options: Have several peers rebel before the subject's turn, as in Milgram's study. Or notify the subject of his or her legal liability if the applicant-victim were harmed and sued the university. Or eliminate the authority pressure to go all the way, as in the control condition of this research—where no one fully obeyed.

Sexual Obedience to Authority: The Strip-Search Scam

"Strip-search scams" have been perpetrated in a number of fast-food restaurant chains throughout the United States. This phenomenon demonstrates the pervasiveness of obedience to an anonymous but seemingly important authority. The modus operandi is for an assistant store manager to be called to the phone by a male caller who indentifies himself as a police officer named, say, "Scott." He needs their urgent help with a case of employee theft at that restaurant. He insists on being called "Sir" in their conversation. Earlier he has gotten relevant inside information about store procedures and local details. He also knows how to solicit the information he wants through skillfully guided questions, as stage magicians and "mind readers" do. He is a good con man.

Ultimately Officer "Scott" solicits from the assistant manager the name of the attractive young new employee who, he says, has been stealing from the shop and is believed to have contraband on her now. He wants her to be isolated in the rear room and held until he or his men can pick her up. The employee is detained there and is given the option by the "Sir, Officer," who talks to her on the phone, of either being strip-searched then and there by a fellow employee or brought down to headquarters to be strip-searched there by the police. Invariably, she elects to be searched now since she knows she is innocent and has nothing to hide. The caller then instructs the assistant manager to strip search her; her anus and vagina are searched for stolen money or drugs. All the while the caller insists on being told in graphic detail what is happening, and all the while the video surveillance cameras are recording these remarkable events as they unfold. But this is only the beginning of a nightmare for the innocent young employee and a sexual and power turn-on for the caller-voyeur.

In a case in which I was an expert witness, this basic scenario then included having the frightened eighteen-year-old high school senior engage in a series of increasingly embarrassing and sexually degrading activities. The naked woman is told to jump up and down and to dance around. The assistant manager is told by the caller to get some older male employee to help confine the victim so she can go back to her duties in the restaurant. The scene degenerates into the caller insisting that the woman masturbate herself and have oral sex with the older male, who is supposedly containing her in the back room while the police are slowly wending their way to the restaurant. These sexual activities continue for several hours while they wait for the police to arrive, which of course never happens.

This bizarre authority influence in absentia seduces many people in that situation to violate store policy, and presumably their own ethical and moral principles, to sexually molest and humiliate an honest, churchgoing young employee. In the end, the store personnel are fired, some are charged with crimes, the store is sued, the victims are seriously distressed, and the perpetrator in this and similar hoaxes—a former corrections officer—is finally caught and convicted.

One reasonable reaction to learning about this hoax is to focus on the dispositions of the victim and her assailants, an naive, ignorant, gullible, weird individuals. However, when we learn that this scam has been carried out successfully in sixty-eight similar fast-food settings in thirty-two different states, in a half-dozen different restaurant chains, and with assistant managers of many restaurants around the country being conned, with both male and female victims, our analysis must shift away from simply blaming the victims to recognizing the power of situational forces involved in this scenario. So let us not underestimate the power of "authority" to generate obedience to an extent and of a kind that is hard to fathom.

Donna Summers, assistant manager at McDonald's in Mount Washington, Kentucky, fired for being deceived into participating in this authority phone hoax, expresses one of the main themes in our *Lucifer Effect* narrative about situational power. "You look back on it, and you say, I wouldn't a done it. But unless you're put in that situation, at that time, how do you know what you would do. You don't."[31]

In her book *Making Fast Food: From the Frying Pan into the Fryer*, the Canadian Sociologist Ester Reiter concludes that obedience to authority is the most valued trait in fast-food workers. "The assembly-line process very deliberately tries to take away any thought or discretion from workers. They are appendages to the machine," she said in a recent interview. Retired FBI special agent Dan Jablonski, a private detective who investigated some of these hoaxes, said, "You and I can sit here and judge these people and say they were blooming idiots. But they aren't trained to use common sense. They are trained to say and think, "Can I help you?""[32]

The Nazi Connection: Could it Happen in Your Town?

Recall that one of Milgram's motivations for initiating his research project was to understand how so many "good" German citizens could become involved in the brutal murder of millions of Jews. Rather than search for dispositional tendencies in the German national character to account for the evil of this genocide, he believed that features of the situation played a critical role; that obedience to authority was a "toxic trigger" for wanton murder. After completing his research, Milgram extended his scientific conclusions to a very dramatic prediction about the insidious and pervasive power of obedience to transform ordinary American citizens into Nazi death camp personnel: "If a system of death camps were set up in the United States of the sort we had seen in Nazi Germany, one would be able to find sufficient personnel for those camps in any medium-sized American town."[33]

Let us briefly consider this frightening prediction in light of five very different but fascinating inquiries into this Nazi connection with ordinary people willingly recruited to act against a declared "enemy of the state." The first two are classroom demonstrations by creative teachers with high school and grade school children. The third is by a former graduate student of mine who determined that American college students would indeed endorse the "final solution" if an authority figure provided sufficient justification for doing so. The last two directly studied Nazi SS and German policemen.

Creating Nazis in an American Classroom

Students in a Palo Alto, California, high school world history class were, like many of us, not able to comprehend the inhumanity of the Holocaust. How could such a racist and deadly social-political movement have thrived, and how could the average citizen have been ignorant of or indifferent to the suffering it imposed on fellow Jewish citizens? Their inventive teacher, Ron Jones, decided to modify his medium in order to make the message meaningful to these disbelievers. To do so, he switched from the usual didactic teaching method to an experiential learning mode.

He began by telling the class that they would simulate some aspects of the German experience in the coming week. Despite this forewarning, the role-playing "experiment" that took place over the next five days was a serious matter for the students and a shock for the teacher, not to mention the principal and the students' parents. Simulation and reality merged as these students created a totalitarian system of beliefs and coercive control that was all too much like that fashioned by Hitler's Nazi regime.[34]

First, Jones established new rigid classroom rules that had to be obeyed without question. All answers must be limited to three words or less and preceded by "Sir," as the student stood erect beside his or her desk. When no one challenged this and other arbitrary rules, the classroom atmosphere began to change. The more verbally fluent, intelligent students lost their positions of prominence as the less verbal, more physically assertive ones took over. The classroom movement was named "The Third Wave." A cupped-hand salute was introduced along with slogans that had to be shouted in unison on command. Each day there was a new powerful slogan: "Strength through discipline"; "Strength through community"; "Strength through action": and "Strength through pride." There would be one more reserved for later on. Secret handshakes indentified insiders, and critics had to be reported for "treason." Actions followed the slogans—making banners that were hung about the school, enlisting new members, teaching other students mandatory sitting postures, and so forth.

The original core of twenty history students soon swelled to more than a hundred eager new Third Wavers. The students then took over the assignment, making it their own. They issued special membership cards. Some of the brightest students were ordered out of class. The new authoritarian in-group was delighted and abused their former classmates as they were taken away.

Jones then confided to his followers that they were part of a nationwide movement to discover students who were willing to fight for political change. They
were "a select group of young people chosen to help in this cause," he told them.
A rally was scheduled for the next day at which a national presidential candidate was supposed to announce on TV the formation of a new Third Wave Youth
program. More than two hundred students filled the auditorium at Cubberly
High School in eager anticipation of this announcement. Exhilarated Wave members wearing white-shirted uniforms with homemade armbands posted banners
around the hall. While muscular students stood guard at the door, friends of the
teacher posing as reporters and photographers circulated among the mass of "true
believers." The TV was turned on, and everyone waited—and waited—for the
big announcement of their next collective goose steps forward. They shouted,
"Strength through discipline!"

Instead, the teacher projected a film of the Nuremberg rally; the history of the
Third Reich appeared in ghostly images. "Everyone must accept the blame—no
one can claim that they didn't in some way take part." That was the final frame
of the film and the end of the simulation. Jones explained the reason to all the
assembled students for this simulation which had gone way beyond his initial
intention. He told them that the new slogan for them should be "Strength through
understanding." Jones went on to conclude, "You have been manipulated. Shoved
by your own desires into the place you now find yourselves."

Ron Jones got into trouble with the administration because the parents of the
rejected classmates complained about their children being harassed and threatened
by the new regime. Nevertheless, he concluded that many of these youngsters had
learned a vital lesson by personally experiencing the ease with which their behavior could be so radically transformed by obeying a powerful authority within the
context of a fascistlike setting. In his later essay about the "experiment," Jones
noted that "In the four years I taught at Cubberly High School, no one ever admitted to attending the Third Wave rally. It was something we all wanted to forget."
(After leaving the school a few years later, Jones began working with special education students in San Francisco. A powerful docudrama of this simulated Nazi
experience, titled "The Wave," captured some of this transformation of good kids
into pseudo Hitler Youth.)[35]

Creating Little Elementary School Beasties: Brown Eyes
Versus Blue Eyes

The power of authorities is demonstrated not only in the extent to which they can
command obedience from followers, but also in the extent to which they can
define reality and alter habitual ways of thinking and acting. Case in point: Jane
Elliott, a popular third-grade schoolteacher in the small rural town of Riceville,

Iowa. Her challenge: how to teach white children from a small farm town with few minorities about the meaning of "brotherhood" and "tolerance." She decided to have them experience personally what it feels like to be an underdog and also the top dog, either the victim or the perpetrator of prejudice.[36]

This teacher arbitrarily designated on part of her class as superior to the other part, which was inferior—based only on their eye color. She began by informing her students that people with blue eyes were superior to those with brown eyes and gave a variety of supporting "evidence" to illustrate this truth, such as George Washington's having blue eyes and, closer to home, a student's father (who, the student had complained, had hit him) having brown eyes.

Starting immediately, said Ms. Elliott, the children with blue eyes would be the special "superior" ones and the brown-eyed ones would be the "inferior" group. The allegedly more intelligent blue-eyes were given special privileges, while the inferior brown-eyes had to obey rules that enforced their second-class status, including wearing a collar that enabled others to recognize their lowly status from a distance.

The previously friendly blue-eyed kids refused to play with the bad "brown-eyes," and they suggested that school officials should be notified that the brown-eyes might steal things. Soon fistfights erupted during recess, and one boy admitted hitting another "in the gut" because, "He called me brown-eyes, like being a black person, like a Negro." Within one day, the brown-eyed children began to do more poorly in their schoolwork and became depressed, sullen, and angry. They described themselves as "sad," "bad," "stupid," and "mean."

The next day was turnabout time. Mrs. Elliott told the class that she had been wrong—it was really the brown-eyed children who were superior and the blue-eyed ones who were inferior, and she provided specious new evidence to support this chromatic theory of good and evil. The blue-eyes now switched from their previously "happy," "good," "sweet," and "nice" self-labels to derogatory labels similar to those adopted the day before by the brown-eyes. Old friendship patterns between children temporarily dissolved and were replaced by hostility until this experiential project was ended and the children were carefully and fully debriefed and returned to their joy-filled classroom.

The teacher was amazed at the swift and total transformation of so many of her students whom she thought she knew so well. Mrs. Elliott concluded, "What had been marvelously cooperative, thoughtful children became nasty, vicious, discriminating little third-graders. . . . It was ghastly!"

Endorsing the Final Solution in Hawaii: Ridding the World of Misfits

Imagine that you are a college student at the University of Hawaii (Manoa campus) among 570 other students in any of several large evening school psychology classes. Tonight your teacher, with his Danish accent, alters his usual lecture to reveal a threat to national security being created by the population explosion (a hot topic in the early 1970s).[37] This authority describes the emerging threat to society posed by the rapidly increasing number of people who are physically and mentally unfit. The problem is convincingly presented as a high-minded scientific project, endorsed by scientists and planned for the benefit of humanity. You are then invited to help in "the application of scientific procedures to eliminate the mentally and emotionally unfit." The teacher further justifies the need to take action with an analogy to capital punishment as a deterrent against violent crime. He tells you that your opinions are being solicited because you and the others assembled here are intelligent and well educated and have high ethical values. It is flattering to think that you are in this select company. (Recall the lure of C. S. Lewis's: "Inner Ring.") In case there might be any lingering misgivings, he provides assurances that much careful research would be carried out before action of any kind would be taken with these misfit human creatures.

At this point, he wants only your opinions, recommendations, and personal views on a simple survey to be completed now by you and the rest of the students in the auditorium. You begin answering the questions because you have been persuaded that this is a new vital issue about which your voice matters. You diligently answer each of the seven questions and discover that there is a lot of uniformity between your answers and those of the rest of the group.

Ninety percent of you agree that there will always be some people more fit for survival than others.

Regarding killing of the unfit: 79 percent wanted one person to be responsible for the killing and another to carry out the act; 64 percent preferred anonymity for those who pressed the button with only one button causing death though many were pressed; 89 percent judged that painless drugs would be the most efficient and humane method of inducing death.

If required by law to assist, 89 percent wanted to be the one who assisted in the decisions, while 9 percent preferred to assist with the killings or both. Only 6 percent of the students *refused* to answer.

Most incredibly, fully 91 percent of all student respondents agreed with the conclusion that "under extreme circumstances it is entirely just to eliminate those judged most dangerous to the general welfare"!

Finally, a surprising 29 percent supported this "final solution" even if it had to be applied to their own families![38]

So these American college students (night school students and thus older than usual) were willing to endorse a deadly plan to kill off all others who were judged by some authorities to be less fit to live than they were—after only a brief presentation by their teacher-authority. Now we can see how ordinary, even intelligent Germans could readily endorse Hitler's "Final Solution" against the Jews, which was reinforced in many ways by their educational system and strengthened by systematic government propaganda.

Ordinary Men Indoctrinated into Extraordinary Killing

One of the clearest illustrations of my exploration of how ordinary people can be made to engage in evil deeds that are alien to their past history and moral values comes from a remarkable discovery by the historian Christopher Browning. He recounts that in March 1942 about 80 percent of all victims of the Holocaust were still alive, but a mere eleven months later about 80 percent were dead. In this short period of time, the *Endlosung* (Hitler's "Final Solution") was energized by means of an intense wave of mobile mass murder squads in Poland. This genocide required mobilization of a large-scale killing machine at the same time that able-bodied German soldiers were needed on the collapsing Russian front. Because most Polish Jews lived in small towns and not large cities, the question that Browning raised about the German high command was "where had they found the manpower during this pivotal year of the war for such an astounding logistical achievement in mass murder?"[39]

His answer came from archives of Nazi war crimes, which recorded the activities of Reserve Battalion 101, a unit about five hundred men from Hamburg, Germany. They were elderly family men, too old to be drafted into the Army; they came from working-class and lower-middle-class backgrounds, and they had no military police experience. They were raw recruits sent to Poland without warning of, or any training in, their secret mission—the total extermination of all Jews living in the remote villages of Poland. In just four months they shot to death at point-blank range at least 38,000 Jews and had another 45,000 deported to the concentration camp at Treblinka.

Initially their commander told them that this was a difficult mission that must be obeyed by the battalion. However, he added that any individual could refuse to execute these men, women, and children. The records indicated that at first about half the men refused and let the other police reservists engage in the mass murder. But over time, social modeling processes took over, as did guilt-induced persuasion by those reservists who had been doing the shooting, along with the usual group conformity pressures of "how would they be seen in the eyes of their comrades." By the end of their deadly journey, up to 90 percent of the men in Battalion 101 were blindly obedient to their battalion leader and were personally involved in the shootings. Many the them posed proudly for photographs of their up-close and personal killing of Jews. Like those who took photos of the prisoner abuse at Abu Ghraib Prison, these policemen posed in their "trophy photos" as proud destroyers of the Jewish menace.

Browning makes it clear that there was no special selection of these men, nor self-selection, nor self-interest of careerism that could account for these mass murders. Instead, they were as "ordinary" as can be imagined—until they were put into a novel situation in which they had "official" permission and encouragement to act sadistically against people who were arbitrarily labeled as the "enemy." What is most evident in Browning's penetrating analysis of these daily acts of human evil is that these ordinary men were part of a powerful authority system, a political police state with ideological justifications for destroying Jews and intense indoctrination of the moral imperatives of discipline and loyalty and duty to the state.

Interestingly, for the argument that I have been making that experimental research can have real-world relevance, Browning compared the underlying mechanisms operating in that far-off land at that distant time to the psychological processes at work in both the Milgram obedience studies and our Stanford Prison Experiment. The author goes on to note, "Zimbardo's spectrum of guard behavior bears an uncanny resemblance to the groupings that emerged within Reserve Police Battalion 101" (p. 168). He shows how some became sadistically "cruel and tough," enjoying the killing, whereas others were "tough, but fair" in "playing the rules," and a minority qualified as "good guards" who refused to kill and did small favors for the Jews.

The psychologist Ervin Staub (who as child survived the Nazi occupation of Hungary in a "protected house") concurs that most people under particular circumstances have a capacity for extreme violence and destruction of human life. From his attempt to understand the roots of evil in genocide and mass violence around the world, Staub has come to believe that "Evil that arises out of ordinary thinking and is committed by ordinary people is the norm, not the exception. . . . Great evil arises out of ordinary psychological processes that evolve, usually with a progression along the continuum of destruction." He highlights the significance of ordinary people being caught up in situations where they can learn to practice evil acts that are demanded by higher-level authority systems: "Being part of a system shapes views, rewards adherence to dominant views, and makes deviation psychologically demanding and difficult."[40]

Having lived through the horrors of Auschwitz, John Steiner (my dear friend and sociologist colleague) returned for decades to Germany to interview hundreds of former Nazi SS men, from privates to generals. He needed to know what had made these men embrace such unspeakable evil day in and day out. Steiner found that many of these men were high on the F-Scale measure of authoritarianism, which attracted them to the subculture of violence in the SS. He refers to them as "sleepers," people with certain traits that are latent and may never be expressed except when particular situations activate these violent tendencies. He concludes that "the situation tended to be the most immediate determinant of SS behavior," rousing "sleepers" into active killers. However, from his massive interview data Steiner also found that these men had led normal—violence-free—lives both before and after their violent years in the concentration camp setting.[41]

Steiner's extensive experience with many of the SS men at a personal and scholarly level led him to advance two important conclusions about institutional power and the role enactment of brutality: "Institutional support for roles of violence has apparently far more extensive effects that generally realized. When implicit, and especially explicit, social sanctions support such roles, people tend to be attracted to them who may not only derive satisfaction from the nature of their work but are quasiexecutioners in feeling as well as action."

Steiner goes on to describe how roles can trump character traits: "[It] has become evident that not everyone playing a brutal role has to have sadistic traits of character. Those who continued in roles originally not conducive to their personality often changed their values (i.e., had a tendency to adjust to what was expected of them in these roles). There were SS members who clearly identified with and enjoyed their positions. Finally there were those who were repulsed and sickened by what they were ordered to do. They tried to compensate by helping inmates whenever possible. (This writer's life was saved by SS personnel on several occasions.)"

It is important to acknowledge that the many hundreds of thousands of Germans who became perpetrators of evil during the Holocaust were not doing so simply because they were following the orders given by authorities. Obedience to an authority system that gave permission and reward for murdering Jews was built on a scaffold of intense anti-Semitism that existed in Germany and other European nations at that time. This prejudice was given direction and resolve by the German chain of command to ordinary Germans, who became "Hitler's willing executioners," in the analysis by the historian Daniel Goldhagen.[42]

Although it is important to note the motivating role of Germans' hatred of Jews, Goldhagen's analysis suffers from two flaws. First, historical evidence shows that from the early nineteenth century on there was less anti-Semitism in Germany than in neighboring countries such as France and Poland. He also errs in minimizing the influence of Hitler's authority system—a network that glorified racial fanaticism and the particular situations created by the authorities, like the concentration camps, which mechanized genocide. It was the interaction of personal variables of German citizens with situational opportunities provided by a System of fanatical prejudice that combined to empower so many to become willing or unwilling executioners for their state.

The Banality of Evil

In 1963, the social philosopher Hannah Arendt published what was to become a classic of our times, *Eichmann in Jerusalem; A Report on the Banality of Evil.* She provides a detailed analysis of the war crimes trial of Adolf Eichmann, the Nazi figure who personally arranged for the murder of millions of Jews. Eichmann's defense of his actions was similar to the testimony of other Nazi leaders: "I was only following orders." As Arendt put it, "[Eichmann] remembered perfectly well that the would have had a bad conscience only if he had not done what he had been ordered to do—to ship millions of men, women, and children to their death with great zeal and the most meticulous care" (p. 25).[43]

However, what is most striking in Arendt's account of Eichmann is all the ways in which he seemed absolutely ordinary:

> Half a dozen psychiatrists had certified him as "normal"—"More normal, at any rate, that I am after having examined him," one of them was said to have exclaimed, while another had found that his whole psychological outlook, his attitude toward his wife and children, mother and father, brothers, sisters, and friends, was "not only normal but most desirable" (pp. 25-26).

Through her analysis of Eichmann, Arendt reached her famous conclusion:

> The trouble with Eichmann was precisely that so many were like him, and that the many were neither perverted nor sadistic, that they were, and still are, terribly and terrifyingly normal. From the viewpoint of our legal institutions and our moral standards of judgment, this normality was much more terrifying than all the atrocities put together, for it implied . . . that this new type of criminal . . . commits his crimes under circumstances that make it well-nigh impossible for him to know or feel that he is doing wrong (p. 276).
>   It was as though in those last minutes [of Eichmann's life] he was summing up the lesson that this long course in human wickedness had taught us—the lesson of the fearsome, word-and-thought-defying banality of evil (p. 252).

Arendt's phrase "the banality of evil" continues to resonate because genocide has been unleashed around the world and torture and terrorism continue to be common features of our global landscape. We prefer to distance ourselves from such a fundamental truth, seeing the madness of evildoers and senseless violence of tyrants as dispositional characters within their personal makeup. Arendt's analysis was the first to deny this orientation by observing the fluidity with which social forces can prompt normal people to perform horrific acts.

Torturers and Executioners: Pathological Types or Situational Imperatives?

There is little doubt that the systematic torture by men of their fellow men and women represents one of the darkest sides of human nature. Surely, my colleagues and I reasoned, here was a place where dispositional evil would be manifest among torturers who did their daily dirty deeds for years in Brazil as policemen sanctioned by the government to get confessions by torturing "subversive" enemies of the state.

We began by focusing on the torturers, trying to understand both their psyches and the ways they were shaped by their circumstances, but we had to expand our analytical net to capture their comrades in arms who chose or were assigned to another branch of violence work: death squad executioners. They shared a "common enemy": men, women, and children who, though citizens of their state, even neighbors, were declared by "the System" to be threats to the country's national security—as socialists and Communists. Some had to be eliminated efficiently, while others, who might hold secret information, had to be made to yield it up by torture, confess to their treason, and then be killed.

In carrying out this mission, these torturers could rely in part on the "creative evil" embodied in torture devices and techniques that had been refined over centuries since the Inquisition by officials of the Catholic Church and later of many nation-states. However, they had to add a measure of improvisation when dealing with particular enemies to overcome their resistance and resiliency. Some of them claimed innocence, refused to acknowledge their culpability, or were tough enough not be intimidated by most coercive interrogation tactics. It took time and emerging insights into human weaknesses for these torturers to become adept at their craft. By contrast, the task of the death squads was easy. With hoods for anonymity, guns, and group support, they could dispatch their duty to country swiftly and impersonally: "just business." For torturer, the work could never be just business. Torture always involves a personal relationship; it is essential for the torturer to understand what kind of torture to employ, that intensity of torture to use on a certain person at a certain time. Wrong kind or too little—no confession. Too much—the victim dies before confessing. In either case, the torturer fails to deliver the goods and incurs the wrath of the senior officers. Learning to determine the right kind and degree of torture that yields up the desired information elicits abounding rewards and flowing praise from one's superiors.

What kind of men could do such deeds? Did they need to rely on sadistic impulses and a history of sociopathic life experiences to rip and tear the flesh of fellow beings day in and day out for years on end? Were these violence workers a breed apart from the rest of humanity, bad seeds, bad tree trunks, and bad flowers? Or is it conceivable that they could be ordinary people, programmed to carry out their deplorable acts by means of some identifiable and replicable training programs? Could we identify a set of external conditions, situational variables, that had contributed to the making of these torturers and killers? If their evil actions were not traceable to inner defects but rather attributable to outer forces acting on them—the political, economic, social, historical, and experiential components of their police training—we might be able to generalize across cultures and settings and discover some of the operative principles responsible for this remarkable human transformation.

The sociologist and Brazil expert Martha Huggins, the Greek psychologist and torture expert Mika Haritos-Fatouros, and I interviewed several dozen of these violence workers in depth at various venues in Brazil. (For a summary of our methods and detailed findings about these violence workers, see Huggins, Haritos-Fatouros, and Zimbardo).[44] Mika had done a similar, earlier study of torturers trained by the Greek military junta, and our results were largely congruent with hers.[45] We found that sadists are selected out of the training process by trainers because they are not controllable, get off on the pleasure of inflicting pain, and thus do not sustain the focus on the goal of extraction of confessions. Thus, from all the evidence we could muster, torturers and death squad executioners were not unusual or deviant in any way prior to practicing their new roles, nor were there any persisting deviant tendencies or pathologies among any of them in the years following their work as torturers and executioners. Their transformation was entirely explainable as being the consequence of a number of situational and systemic factors, such as the training they were given to play this new role; their group camaraderie; acceptance of the national security ideology; and their learned belief in socialists and Communists as enemies of their state. Other situational influences contributing to the new behavioral style included being made to feel special, above and better than their peers in public service by being awarded this special assignment; the secrecy of their duties being shared only with comrades in arms; and the constant pressure to produce results regardless of fatigue or personal problems.

We reported many detailed case studies that document the ordinariness of the men engaged in these most heinous of acts, sanctioned by their government, and secretly supported by the CIA at that point in the Cold War (1964–1985) against Soviet communism. The account *Torture in Brazil*, by members of the Catholic Archdiocese of Sao Paulo, provides detailed information of the extensive involvement of CIA agents in the torture training of Brazilian police.[46] Such information is consistent with all that is known of the systematic instruction in interrogation and torture offered at the "School of the Americas" to operatives from countries sharing a common enemy in Communism.[47]

However, my colleagues and I believe that such deeds are reproducible at any time in any nation when there is an obsession with threats to national security. Before the, fears and excesses engendered by the recent "war against terrorism," there was the nearly perpetual "war against crime" in many urban centers. In New York City's police department, that "war" spawned "the commandos of the NYPD." This insular police team was given free rein to hunt down alleged rapists, robbers, and muggers as local conditions dictated. They wore T-Shirts with their motto, "There is no hunting like the hunting of men." Their battle cry was "We own the night." Such a professionalized police culture was comparable to that of the Brazilian police-torturers we had studied. One of their notable atrocities was the murder of an African immigrant (Amadou Diallo, from Guinea), gunning him down with more than forty bullets while he tried to pull out his wallet to give them his ID.[48] Sometimes "bad shit happens," but usually there are identifiable situational and systemic forces operating to make it happen.

Suicide Bombers: Mindless Fanatics or Mindful Martyrs?

Amazingly, what holds true for these violence workers is comparable to the transformation of young Palestinians from students into suicide bombers intent on killing innocent Israeli civilians. Recent media accounts converge on the findings from more systematic analyses of the process of becoming a suicidal killer.[49]

Who adopts this fatalistic role? Is it poor, desperate, socially isolated, illiterate young people with no career and no future? Not at all. According to the results of a recent study of four hundred al-Qaeda members, three quarters of that sample came from the upper or middle class. This study by the forensic psychiatrist Marc Sageman also found other evidence of the normality and even superiority of these youths turned suicide bombers. The majority, 90 percent, came from caring, intact families. Two thirds had gone to college; two thirds were married; and most had children and jobs in science and engineering. "These are the best and brightest of their society in many ways," Sageman concludes.[50]

Anger, revenge, and outrage at perceived injustice are the motivational triggers for deciding to die for the cause. "People desire death when two fundamental needs are frustrated to the point of extinction," according to the psychologist Thomas Joiner in his treatise *Why People Die by Suicide*. The first need is one we have pointed to as central to conformity and social power, the need to belong with or connect to others. The second need is the need to feel effective with or to influence others.[51]

Ariel Merari, an Israeli psychologist who has studied this phenomenon extensively for many years, outlines the common steps on the path to these explosive deaths.[52] First, senior members of an extremist group identify young people who appear to have an intense patriotic fervor based on their declarations at a public rally against Israel or their support of some Islamic cause or Palestinian action. Next, they are invited to discuss how seriously they love their country and hate Israel. They are asked to commit to being trained. Those who do commit become part of a small secret cell of three to five youths. They learn the tricks of the trade from their elders: bomb making, disguise, and selecting and timing targets.

Finally, they make public their private commitment by making a videotape, declaring themselves to be "the living martyr" for Islam (*"al-shahid-al-hai"*). In one hand they hold the Koran, in the other a rifle; the insignia on their headband declares their new status. This video binds them to the final deed, because it is sent to their families. The recruits are also told the Big Lie that not only will they earn a place beside Allah, but their relatives will also be entitled to a high place in Heaven because of their martyrdom. The suicidal pie is sweetened with a sizable financial incentive, or a monthly pension, that goes to their family.

Their photo is emblazoned on posters that will be put on walls everywhere in the community the moment they succeed in their mission—to become inspirational models for the next round of suicide bombers. To stifle their concerns about the pain from wounds inflicted by exploding nails and other bomb parts, the recruits are assured that before the first drop of their blood touches the ground they will already be seated at the side of Allah, feeling no pain, only pleasure. The die is cast; their minds have been carefully prepared to do what is ordinarily unthinkable. Of course, the rhetoric of dehumanization serves to deny the humanity and innocence of their victims.

In these systematic ways a host of normal, angry young men and women become transformed into heroes and heroines. Their lethal actions model self-sacrifice and total commitment as true believers to the cause of the oppressed. That message is sent loud and clear to the next cadre of young suicide bombers in waiting.

We can see that this program utilizes a variety of social psychological and motivational principles to assist in turning collective hatred and general frenzy into a dedicated, seriously calculated program of indoctrination and training for individuals to become youthful living martyrs. It is neither mindless nor senseless, only a very different mind-set and with different sensibilities than we have been used to witnessing among young adults in most countries.

For his new film, *Suicide Killers,* the French filmmaker Pierre Rehov interviewed many Palestinians in Israeli jails who were caught before detonating their bombs or had abetted would-be attacks. His conclusion about them resonates with the analyses presented here: "Every single one of them tried to convince me it was the right thing to do for moralistic reasons. These aren't kids who want to do evil. These are kids who want to do good. . . . The result of this brainwashing was kids who were very good people inside (were) believing so much that they were doing something great."[53]

The suicide, the murder, of any young person is a gash in the fabric of the human family that we elders from every nation must unite to prevent. To encourage the sacrifice of youth for the sake of advancing the ideologies of the old must be considered a form of evil that transcends local politics and expedient strategies.

"Perfect 9/11 Soldiers" and "Ordinary British Lads" Are Bombing Us

Two final examples of the "ordinariness" of mass murderers are worth mentioning. The first comes from an in-depth study of the 9/11 hijackers, whose suicidal terrorist attacks in New York and Washington, D.C., resulted in the deaths of nearly three thousand innocent civilians. The second comes from the London police reports of suspected suicide bombers of London's Underground and a double-decker bus in June 2005 that resulted in scores of deaths and serious injuries.

The carefully researched portraits of several of the 9/11 terrorists by the reporter Terry McDermott in *Perfect Soldiers* underscores just how ordinary these men were in their everyday lives.[54] His research led McDermott to an ominous conclusion: "It is likely that there are a great many more men just like them" out there throughout the world. One review of this book takes us back to Arendt's banality-of-evil thesis, updated for our new era of global terrorism. *The New York Times'* reviewer Michiko Kakutani offers us a scary postscript: "*Perfect Soldiers* replaces the caricatures of outsize 'evil geniuses' and 'wild-eyed fanatics' with portraits of the 9/11 plotters as surprisingly mundane people, people who might easily be our neighbors or airplane seatmates."[55]

That frightening scenario was played out in the subsequent coordinated attacks on London's transit system by a team of suicide bombers, "mundane murderers," who anonymously rode a subway train or a bus. To their friends, relatives, and neighbors in the northern England city of Leeds, these young Muslim men were "ordinary British lads."[56] Nothing in their past history would mark them as dangerous; indeed, everything about them enabled these "ordinary lads" to fit in seamlessly in their town, at their jobs. One was a skilled cricket player who gave up drinking and women to lead a more devout life. Another was the son of a local businessman who ran a fish-and-chips shop. Another was a counselor who worked effectively with disabled children and had recently become a father and moved his family into a new home. Unlike the 9/11 hijackers, who had raised some suspicions as foreigners seeking flight training in the United States, these young men were homegrown, flying well below any police radar. "It's completely out of character for him. Someone must have brainwashed him and made him do it," reflected a friend of one of them.

"The most terrifying thing about suicide bombers is their sheer normality", concludes Andrew Silke, an expert on the subject.[57] He notes that in all the forensic examinations of the bodies of dead suicide bombers there have never been traces of alcohol or drugs. Their mission is undertaken with a clear mind and dedication.

And as we have seen, whenever there has been a student shooting in a school, as in Columbine High School in the United States, those who thought they knew the perpetrators typically report, "He was such a good kid, from a respectable family . . . you just can't believe he would do it." This harkens back to the point I raised in our first chapter—how well do we really know other people?—and its corollary—how well do we know ourselves to be certain of how we would behave in novel situations under intense situational pressures?

The Ultimate Test of Blind Obedience to Authority: Killing Your Children on Command

Our final extension of the social psychology of evil from artificial laboratory experiments to real-world contexts comes to us from the jungles of Guyana, where an American religious leader persuaded more than nine hundred of his followers to commit mass suicide or be killed by their relatives and friends on November 28, 1978. Jim Jones, the pastor of Peoples Temple congregations in San Francisco and Los Angeles, set out to create a socialist Utopia in this South American nation, where brotherhood and tolerance would be dominant over the materialism and racism he loathed in the United States. But over time and place Jones was transformed from the caring, spiritual "father" of this large Protestant congregation into and Angel of Death—a truly cosmic transformation of Luciferian proportions. For now I want only to establish the obedience to authority link between Milgram's basement laboratory in New Haven and this jungle—killing field.[58]

The dreams of the many poor members of the Peoples Temple for a new and better life in this alleged Utopia were demolished when Jones instituted extended forced labor, armed guards, total restriction of all civil liberties, semistarvation diets, and daily punishments amounting to torture for the slightest breach of any of his many rules. When concerned relatives convinced a congressman to inspect the compound, along with a media crew, Jones arranged for them to be murdered as they were leaving. He then gathered almost all of the members who were at the compound and gave a long speech in which he exhorted them all to take their lives by drinking poison, cyanide-laced Kool-Aid. Those who refused were forced to drink by the guards for shot trying to escape, but it appears as though most obeyed their leader.

Jones was surely an egomaniac; he had all of his speeches and proclamations, and even his torture sessions tape-recorded—including this last-hour suicide drill. In it Jones distorts reality, lies, pleads, makes false analogies, appeals to ideology and to transcendent future lives, and outright insists that they follow his orders, as his staff is efficiently distributing the deadly poison to the more than nine hundred members gathered around him. Some excerpts from that last hour convey a sense of the death-dealing tactics he used to induce total obedience an authority gone mad:

> Please get us some medication. It's simple. It's simple. There's no convulsions with it [of course there are, especially for the children]. . . . Don't be afraid to die. You'll see, there'll be a few people land out here. They'll torture some of our children here. They'll torture our people. They'll torture our seniors. We cannot have this. . . . Please, can we hasten? Can we hasten with that medication? You don't know what you've done. I tried. . . . Please. For God's sake, let's get on with it. We've lived—we've lived as no other people lived and loved. We've had as much of this world as you're gonna get. Let's just be done with it. Let's be done with the agony of it. [Applause.]. . . . Who wants to go with their child has a right to go with their child. I think it's humane. I want to go—I want to see you go, though. . . . It's not to be afeared. It is not to be feared. It is a friend. It's a friend . . . sitting there, show your love for one another. Let's get gone. Let's get gone. Let's get gone. [Children crying.]. . . . Lay down your life with dignity. Don't lay down with tears and agony. There's nothing to death. . . . it's just stepping over to another plane. Don't be this way. Stop this hysterics. . . . No way for us to die. We must die with some dignity. We must die with some dignity. We will have no choice. Now we have some choice. . . . Look children, it's just something to put you to rest. Oh, God. [Children crying.] . . . Mother, Mother, Mother, Mother, Mother, please. Mother, please, please, please. Don't—don't do this. Don't do this. Lay down your life with your child. [The full transcript is available online; see the Notes.[59]]

And they did, and they died for "Dad." The power of charismatic tyrannical leaders, like Jim Jones and Adolf Hitler, endures even after they do terrible things to their followers, and even after their demise. Whatever little good they may have done earlier somehow comes to dominate the legacy of their evil deeds in the minds of the faithful. Consider the example of a young man, Gary Scott, who followed his father into the Peoples Temple but was expelled for being disobedient. In his statement as he called the National Call-In following the broadcast of the NPR show "Father Cares: The Last of Jonestown," by James Reston, Jr., Gray describes how he was punished for an infraction of the rules. He was beaten, whipped, sexually abused, and forced to endure his worst fear of having a boa constrictor crawling all over him. But, more important, listen to the articulation of his enduring reaction to this torment. Does he hate Jim Jones? Not one bit. He has become a "true believer," a "faithful follower." Even though his father died in Jonestown at that poison fount, and he himself was brutally tortured and humiliated, Gary publically states that he still admires and even loves his "dad"—Jim Jones. Not even George Orwell's omnipotent *1984* party could honestly claim such a victory.

Now we need to go beyond conformity and authority obedience. Powerful as these are, they are only starters. In the confrontation of potential perpetrators and victims, like guard and prisoner, torturer and sufferer, suicide bomber and civilian victims, there are processes that operate to change the psychological makeup of one or the other. Deindividuation makes the perpetrator anonymous, thereby reducing personal accountability, responsibility, and self-monitoring. This allows perpetrators to act without conscience-inhibiting limits. Dehumanization takes away the humanity of potential victims, rendering them as animallike, or as nothing. We will also inquire about conditions that make bystanders to evil become passive observers and not active intruders, helpers, or whistle-blowing heroes. That slice of the evil of inaction is really a cornerstone of evil because it allows perpetrators to believe that others who knew what was going on accepted and approved it even if only by their silence.

A fitting conclusion to our investigation of the social dynamics of conformity and obedience comes from the Harvard psychologist Mahrzarin Banaji:

> What social psychology has given to an understanding of human nature is the discovery that forces larger than ourselves determine our mental life and our actions—chief among these forces [is] the power of the social situation.[60]

Notes

1. C. S. Lewis (1898–1963), professor of medieval and Renaissance English at Cambridge University, was also novelist, a writer of children's books, and a popular speaker on moral and religious issues. In his best-known book, *The Screwtape Letters* (1944), he impersonated a veteran devil in Hell that writes letters encouraging the efforts of a novice devil hard at work on Earth. "The Inner Ring" was the Memorial Lecture at King's College, University of London, delivered to the students in 1944.

2. R. F. Baumeister and M. R. Leary, "The Need to Belong: Desire for Interpersonal Attachments as a Fundamental Human Motivation," *Psychological Bulletin* 117 (1995): 427–529.

3. R. B. Cialdini, M. R. Trost, and J. T. Newsome, "Preference for Consistency: The Development of a Valid Measure and the Discovery of Surprising Behavioral Implications," *Journal of Personality and Social Psychology* 69 (1995): 318–28; Also see L. Festinger, *A Theory of Cognitive Dissonance* (Stanford, CA: Stanford University Press, 1957).

4. P. G. Zimbardo and S. A. Andersen, "Understanding Mind Control: Exotic and Mundane Mental Manipulations," in *Recovery from Cults,* ed. M. Langone, (New York: W. W. Norton, 1993); see also A. W. Scheflin and E. M. Opton, *Jr., The Mind Manipulators: A Non-Fiction Account* (New York: Paddington Press, 1978).

5. In addition to normative, social pressures to go along with others' views, there are rational forces at work because people can serve to provide valuable information and wisdom. M. Deutsch and H. B. Gerard, "A Study of Normative and Informational Social Influence upon Individual Judgement," *Journal of Abnormal and Social Psychology* 51 (1955): 629–36.

6. Associated Press (July 26, 2005), "'Cool Mom' Guilty of Sex with Schoolboys: She Said She Felt Like 'One of the Group.' "The report is of her sex and drug parties from October 2003 to October 2004 in the rural town of Golden, Colorado.

7. Self-serving, egocentric, and above-average biases have been investigated extensively. For a summary of the main effects across many different domains of application, see D. Myers, *Social Psychology* 8th ed. (New York: McGraw-Hill, 2005). pp. 66–77.

8. E. Pronin, J. Krager, K. Savitsky, and L. Ross, "You Don't know Me, but I Know You: The Illusion of Asymmetric Insight," *Journal of Personality and Social Psychology* 81 (2001): 639–56.

9. M. Sherif, "A Study of Some Social Factors in Perception," *Archives of Psychology* 27 (1935); pp. 210–11.

10. S. E. Asch, "Studies of Independence and Conformity: A Minority of One Against a Unanimous Majority," *Psychological Monograph* 70 (1951): whole no. 416; S. E. Asch, "Opinions and Social Pressure," *Scientific American,* November 1955. pp. 31–35.

11. M. Deutsch and H. B. Gerard (1995).

12. G. S. Berns, J. Chappelow, C. F. Zin, G. Pagnoni, M. E. Martin-Skurski, and J. Richards, "Neurobiological Correlates of Social Conformity an Independence During Mental Rotation," *Biological Psychiatry* 58 (August 1, 2005): 245–53; Sandra Blakeslee, "What Other People Say May Change What You See," *New York Times,* online: www.nytimes.com/2005/06/28/science/28brai.html, June 28, 2005.

13. S. Moscovici and C. Faucheux, "Social Influence, Conformity Bias, and the Study of Active Minorities," in *Advances in Experimental Social Psychology,* vol. 6, ed. L. Berkowitz (New York: Academic Press, 1978), pp. 149–202.

14. E. Langer, *Mindfulness.* (Reading, MA: Addison-Wesley, 1989).

15. C. J. Nemeth. "Differential Contributions to Majority and Minority Influence," *Psychological Review* 93 (1986): 23–32.

16. S. Moscovici. "Social Influence and Conformity," in *The Handbook of Social Psychology,* 3rd. ed., eds. G. Lindzey and E. Aronson (New York: Random House, 1985), pp. 347–412.

17. T. Blass, *Obedience to Authority: Current Perspectives on the Milgram Paradigm* (Mahwah. NJ: Erlbaum, 1999). p. 62.

18. In 1949, seated next to me in senior class at James Monroe High School in the Bronx. New York, was my classmate Stanley Milgram. We were both skinny kids full of ambition and a desire to make something of ourselves so that we might escape from life in the confines of our ghetto. Stanley was the little smart one whom we went to for authoritative answers. I was the tall popular one, the smiling guy other kids would go to for social advice. Even than we were budding situationists. I had just returned to Monroe High from a horrible year at North Hollywood High School, where I had been shunned and friendless (because, as I later learned, there was a rumor circulating that I was from a New York Sicilian Mafia family), to be chosen "Jimmy Monroe," the most popular boy in Monroe High School's senior class. Stanley and I discussed once how that transformation could have happened. We agreed that I had not changed but the situation was what had mattered. When we met years later, as Yale University in 1960, as beginning assistant professors, him starting out at Yale and me at NYU, it turned out that Stanley really wanted to be popular and I really wanted to be smart. So much for unfulfilled desires.

    I should also mention a recent discovery I made about another commonality that I shared with Stanley. I was the one who initially constructed a basement laboratory that was later modified to be the site in which Milgram's Yale obedience experiments were conducted (after he could no longer use the elegant interaction laboratory of sociologist O.K. Moore). I had done so a few years earlier for a study I did with Irving Sarnoff to test Freudian predictions about the differences between fear and anxiety in their effects on social affiliation. I fabricated a little lab in the basement of the building where we taught Introductory Psychology courses. It had the delightfully British name Linsly-Chittenden Hall. It is also interesting that both his experiments and the SPE were conducted in basements.

19. T. Blass, *The Man Who Shocked the World* (New York: Basic Books, 2004), p. 116.

20. See R. Cialdini, *Influence,* (New York: McGraw-Hill, 2001).

21. J. L. Freedman and S. C. Fraser, "Compliance Without Pressure: The Foot-in-the-Door Technique," *Journal of Personality and Social Psychology* 4 (1966): 195–202; also see S. J. Gilbert, "Another Look at the Milgram Obedience Studies: The Role of the Graduated Series of Shocks," *Personality and Social Psychology Bulletin* 4 (1981): 690–95.

22. E. Fromm, *Escape from Freedom* (New York: Holt, Rinehart and Winston, 1941). In the United States, the fear of threats to national security posed by terrorists, amplified by government officials, has led many citizens, the Pentagon, and national leaders to accept the torture of prisoners as a necessary method of eliciting information that could prevent further attacks. That reasoning, I will argue in chapter 15, contributed to the abuses by American guards at Abu Ghraib prison.

23. H. C. Kelman and V. L. Hamilton, *Crimes of Obedience: Toward a Social Psychology of Authority and Responsibility* (New Haven, CT: Yale University Press, 1989).

24. Blass, *The Man Who Shocked the World,* Appendix C, "The Stability of Obedience Across Time and Place."

25. C. L. Sheridan and R. G. King, "Obedience to Authority with an Authentic Victim," *Proceedings of the Annual Convention of the American Psychological Association,* vol. 7 (Part 1) 1972, pp. 165–66.

26. M. T. One and C. H. Holland, "One the Ecological Validity of Laboratory Deceptions," *International Journal of Psychiatry* 6 (1968) 282–93.

27. C. K. Hofling, E. Brotzman, S. Dalrymple, N. Graves, and C. M. Pierce, "An Experimental Study in Nurse-Physician Relationships," *Journal of Nervous and Mental Disease* 143 (1966): 171–80.

28. A. Kracknow and T. Blass, "When Nurses Obey or Defy Inappropriate Physician Orders: Attributional Differences," *Journal of Social Behavior and Personality* 10 (1995): 585–94.

29. E. Tarnow, "Self-Destructive Obedience in the Airplane Cockpit and the Concept of Obedience Optimization," *in obedience to Authority,* ed. T. Blass, pp. 111–23.

30. W. Meeus and Q. A. W. Raaijmakers, "Obedience in Modern Society: The Utrecht Studies," *Journal of Social Issues* 51 (1995): 155–76.

31. From *The Human Behavior Experiments,* transcript: Sundance Lock, May 9, 2006; Jig Saw Productions, p. 20. Transcript available on www.prisonexp.org/pdf/HBE-transcript.pdf.

32. These quotes and information about the strip-search hoaxes come from an informative article by Andrew Wolfson, "A Hoax Most Cruel," in *The Courier-Journal,* October 9 2004, available online at: www.courier-journal.com/apps/pbcs.dll/article?AID=/20051009/NEWS01/510090392/1008Hoax.

33. Quoted From a 1979 television interview in Robert V. Levine, "Milgram's Progress," *American Scientist Online,* July-August 2004. Originally in Blass, *Obedience to Authority,* pp. 35–36.

34. R. Jones, "The Third Wave," in *Experiencing Social Psychology,* ed. A. Pines and C. Masach (New York: Knopf 1978). pp. 144–52; also see the article that Ron Jones wrote about his Third Wave class exercise, available at: www.vaniercollege.qc.ca/Auxilliary/Psychology/Frank/Thirdwave.html.

35. "The Wave," television docudrama, directed by Alexander Grasshoff, 1981.

36. W. Peters, A *Class Divided Then and Now* (expanded ed.) (New Haven, CT: Yale University Press, 1985 [1971]). Peters was involved in the filming of both prizewinning documentaries, the ABC News documentary "The Eye of the Storm" (available from Guidance Associates, New York) and the follow-up PBS Frontline documentary "A Class Divided" (available online at www.pbs.org/sgbh/pages/frontline/shows/divided/etc/view.html).

37. H. H. Mansson, "Justifying the Final Solution," *Omega: The Journal of Death and Dying* 3 (1972): 79–87.

38. J. Carlson, "Extending the Final Solution to One's Family," unpublished report, University of Hawaii, Manoa, 1974.

39. C. R. Browning, *Ordinary Men: Reserve Police Battalion 101 and the Final Solution in Poland* (New York: HarperCollins, 1993), p. xvi.

40. E. Staub, *The Roots of Evil: The Origins of Genocide and Other Group Violence* (New York: Cambridge University Press, 1989), pp. 126–127.

41. J. M. Steiner, "The SS Yesterday and Today: A Sociopsychological View," in *Survivors, Victims, and Perpetrators: Essays on the Nazi Holocaust,* ed. J. E. Dinsdale (Washington, D.C.: Hemisphere Publishing Corporation, 1980), pp. 405–56; quotes on p. 433. Also see A. G. Miller, *The Obedience Experiments: A Case Study of Controversy in Social Science* (New York: Praeger, 1986).

42. D. J. Goldhagen, *Hitler's Willing Executioners* (New York: Knopf, 1999). Also see the review by Christopher Reed, "Ordinary German Killers," in *Harvard Magazine,* March–April 1999, p. 23.

43. H. Arendt, *Eichmann in Jerusalem: A Report on the Banality of Evil,* revised and enlarged edition (New York: Penguin Books, 1994), pp. 25, 26, 252, 276. Following quotes are from this source.

44. M. Huggins, M. Haritos-Fatouros, and P. G. Zimbardo, *Violence Workers: Police Torturers and Murders Reconstruct Brazilian Atrocities* (Berkeley: University of California Press, 2002).

45. M. Haritos-Fatouros, *The Psychological Origins of Institutionalized Torture* (London: Routledge, 2003).

46. Archdiocese of Sao Paulo, *Torture in Brazil* (New York: Vintage, 1998).

47. Official site for School of the Americas is www.ciponline.org/facts/soa.htm/; also see a critical site: www.soaw.org/new/.

48. F. Morales, "The Militarization of the Police," *Covert Action Quarterly* 67 (Spring–Summer 1999): 67.

49. See the body of literature on suicide bombers; among the sources recommended are: Ariel Merari, "Suicide Terrorism in the Context of the Israeli-Palestinian Conflict," Institute of Justice Conference, Washington, D.C., October 2004; Ariel Merari, "Israel Facing Terrorism," *Israel Affairs* 11 (2005): 223–37; Ariel Merari, "Suicidal Terrorism," in *Assessment, Treatment and Prevention of Suicidal Behavior,* eds. R. I. Yufit and D. Lester (New York: Wiley, 2005).

50. M. Sageman, "Understanding Terrorist Networks," November 1, 2004, available at www.fpri.org/enotes/20041101.middleeast.sageman.understandingterrornetworks.html. Also see M. Shermer, "Murdercide: Science Unravels the Myth of Suicide Bombers," *Scientific American,* January 2006, p. 33; A. B. Krueger, "Poverty Doesn't Create Terrorists," *The New York Times,* May 29, 2003.

51. T. Joiner, *Why People Die by Suicide.* Cambridge, MA: Harvard University Press, 2006; Scott Atran, "Genesis of Suicide Terrorism," *Science* 299 (2003): 1534–39; Mia M. Bloom, "Palestinian Suicide Bombing: Public Support, Market Share and Outbidding," *Political Science Quarterly* 119, no. 1 (2004): 61–88; Mia Bloom, *Dying to Kill: The Allure of Suicide Terrorism* (New York: Columbia University Press, 2005); Dipak K. Gupta and Kusum Mundra, "Suicide Bombing as a Strategic Weapon: An Empirical Investigation of Hamas and Islamic Jihad," *Terrorism and Political Violence* 17 (2005): 573–98; Shaul Kinmi and Shemuel Even, "Who Are the Palestinian Suicide Bombers?" *Terrorism and Political Violence* 16 (2005): 814–40; Ami Pedhahzur, "Toward an Analytical Model of Suicide Terrorism—A Comment," *Terrorism and Political Violence* 16 (2004): 841–44. Robert A. Pape, "The Strategic Logic of Suicide Terrorism." *American Political Science Review* 97 (2003): 343–61; Christopher Reuter, *My Life as a Weapon: A Modern History of Suicide Bombing* (Princeton, NJ: Princeton University Press, 2004): Andrew Silke, "The Role of Suicide in Politics, Conflict, and Terrorism," *Terrorism and Political Violence* 18 (2006): 35–46; Jeff Victoroff, "The Mind of the Terrorist: A Review and Critique of Psychological Approaches," *Journal of Conflict Resolution* 49, no. 1 (2005): 3–42.

52. A. Merari, "Psychological Aspects of Suicide Terrorism," in *Psychology of Terrorism*, eds. B. Bongar, L.M. Brown, L. Beutler, and P.G. Zimbardo (New York: Oxford University Press, 2006).

53. Jonathan Curiel, "The Mind of a Suicide Bomber," *San Francisco Chronicle* (October 22, 2006): p. El, 6: quote on p. E6.

54. T. McDermott, *Perfect Soldiers: The Hijackers: Who They Were, Why They Did It* (New York: HarperCollins, 2005).

55. M. Kakutani, "Ordinary but for the Evil They Wrought," the *New York Times*, May 20, 2005, p. B32.

56. Z. Coile, " 'Ordinary British Lads,' " *San Francisco Chronicle*, July 14, 2005, pp. Al, A10.

57. A. Silke, "Analysis: Ultimate Outrage," *The Times* (London), May 5, 2003.

58. I became connected to this experience through my acquaintance with the brother of one of the few people who had escaped the massacre, his sister, Diane Louie, and her boyfriend, Richard Clark. I offered them counseling when they returned to San Francisco and learned much from their firsthand horror accounts. Later, I became an expert witness for Larry Layton, accused of conspiracy to murder Congressman Ryan, and through him I became friends with his sister, Debbie Layton, another heroic resistor of Jim Jones's domination. We will learn more about them in our final chapter, where their heroism is discussed.

59. The transcript of Jones's last-hour speech on November 18, 1978, is known as the "Death Tape" (FBI no. Q042), and is available online free, courtesy of the Jonestown Institute in Oakland, California, as transcribed by Mary McCormick Maaga: http:// jonestown.sdsu.edu/Aboutjonestown/Tapes/Tapes/ Deathtape/Q042 .maaga. html.

60. M. Banaji, "Ordinary Prejudice," *Psychological Science Agenda* 8 (2001): 8–16; quote on p.15.

Resisting Situational Influences and Celebrating Heroism

Philip Zimbardo

> Every exit an entry somewhere else.
>
> —Tom Stoppard,
> *Rosencrantz and Guildenstern Are Dead*

We have come to the end of our journey through the dark places that imprison the minds of our fellow travelers. We have witnessed the conditions that reveal the brutal side of human nature and have been surprised by the ease and the extent to which good people can become so cruel to others. Our conceptual focus has been on trying to understand better how such transformations take place. Although evil can exist in any setting, we have looked most closely into its breeding ground in prisons and wars. They typically become crucibles, in which authority, power and dominance are blended and, when covered over by secrecy, suspend our humanity, and rob us of the qualities we humans value most: caring, kindness, cooperation, and love.

Much of our time was spent in the simulated prison that my colleagues and I created in the basement of Stanford University's Psychology Department. In just a few days and nights the virtual paradise that is Palo Alto, California, and Stanford University became a hellhole. Healthy young men developed pathological symptoms that reflected the extreme stress, frustration, and hopelessness they were experiencing as prisoners. Their counterparts, randomly assigned to the role of guards, repeatedly crossed the line from frivolously playing that role to seriously abusing "their prisoners." In less than a week, our little "experiment," our mock prison, receded into the background of our collective consciousness, to be replaced by a reality of prisoners, guards, and prison staff that seemed remarkably real to all. It was a prison run by psychologists rather than by the State.

The detailed scrutiny that I brought to the nature of these transformations, which have never before been fully elaborated, is aimed at bringing each reader as close as possible to that special place where we can pit person power against institutional power. I tried to convey a sense of the unfolding processes by which a host of seemingly minor situational variables, such as social roles, norms, and uniforms, came to have so powerful an impact on all those caught up in its system.

At a conceptual level, I have proposed that we give greater consideration and more weight to situational and systemic processes than we typically do when we are trying to account for aberrant behaviors and seeming personality changes. Human behavior is always subject to situational forces. This context is embedded within a larger, macrocosmic one, often a particular power system that is designed to maintain and sustain itself. Traditional analyses by most people, including those in legal, religious, and medical institutions, focus on the actor as the sole causal agent. Consequently, they minimize or disregard the impact of situational variables and systemic determinants that shape behavioral outcomes and transform actors.

Hopefully, the examples and supporting information in this book will challenge the rigid Fundamental Attribution Error that locates the inner qualities of people as the main source of their actions. We have added the need to recognize both the power of situations and the behavioral scaffolding provided by the System that crafts and upholds the social context.

We have journeyed from a make-believe prison to the nightmare reality that was Iraq's Abu Ghraib Prison. Surprising parallels emerged between the social psychological processes at work in both of those prisons, the mock one and the all-too-real one. In Abu Ghraib, our analytical spotlight focused on one young man, Staff Sergeant Ivan Chip Frederick, who made a dual transformation: From good soldier to bad prison guard and then to suffering prisoner. Our analysis revealed, just as in the Stanford Prison Experiment, the dispositional, situational, and systemic factors that played a crucial role in fostering the abuse and torture the Frederick and other military and civilian personnel heaped on the prisoners in their custody.

I moved then from my position as an impartial social science researcher to assume the role of a prosecutor. In doing so, exposed to you, readers-as-jurors, the crimes of the top brass in the military command and in the Bush administration that make them complicit in creating the conditions that in turn made possible such wide-ranging wanton abuse and torture throughout most U.S. Military prisons. As noted repeatedly, the view I have provided does not negate the responsibility of these MPs, nor their guilt; explanation and understanding do not excuse such misdeeds. Rather, understanding how the events happened and appreciating what were the situational forces operating on the soldiers can lead to proactive ways to modify the circumstances that elicit such unacceptable behavior. Punishing is not enough. "Bad systems" create "bad situations" create "bad apples" create "bad behaviors," even in good people.

For the last time, let's define Person, Situation, and System. The Person is an actor on the stage of life whose behavioral freedom is informed by his or her makeup—genetic, biological, physical, and psychological. The Situation is the behavioral context that has the power, through its reward and normative functions, to give meaning and indentify to the actor's roles and status. The System consists of the agents and agencies whose ideology, values, and power create situations and dictate the roles and expectations for approved behaviors of actors within its spheres of influence.

In this, the final phase of our journey, we will consider advice about how to prevent or combat negative situational forces that act upon all of us from time to time. We will explore how to resist influences that we neither want nor need but that rain upon us daily. We are not slaves to the power of situational forces. But we must learn methods of resisting and opposing them. In all the situations we have explored together, there were always a few, a minority, who stood firm. The time has come to try to expand their numbers by thinking about how they were able to resist.

If I have in some measure brought you to appreciate that under some circumstances *You* might behave in the ways that participants did in the research conditions outlined here and in the real prison of Abu Ghraib, I ask you to consider now, could you also accept a conception of *You* as a Hero? We will celebrate also the good in human nature, the heroes among us, and the heroic imagination in all of us.

Learning How to Resist Unwanted Influences

People with paranoid disorders have great difficulty in conforming to, complying with, or responding to a persuasive message, even when it is offered by their well-meaning therapists or loved ones. Their cynicism and distrust create an isolating barrier that shields them from involvement in most social encounters. Because they are adamantly resistant to social pressures, they provide an extreme model for immunity to influence, though obviously at great psychic cost. At the other end of the scale are the overly gullible, unconditionally trusting people who are easy marks for any and every scam artist.

Among them are the many people who fall prey to frauds, scams, and confidence games at some time in their lives. A full 12 percent of Americans are defrauded by con-artist criminals each year, sometimes losing their life savings. It is likely that this figure is shared by people in most nations. Although the majority of those defrauded are over fifty years old, at a time of life when wisdom should prevail, many people of all ages are regularly duped by tricksters in telemarketing, health care, and lottery scams.[1]

Remember the phony authority hoax perpetrated on an innocent teenager at a McDonald's restaurant that was described in chapter 12? Surely you asked yourself, "How could she and those adults duped by this caller be so stupid?" Well, this same hoax was effective in getting many other fast-food restaurant personnel to follow that false authority blindly. How many? Recall in a dozen different restaurant chains in nearly seventy different establishments, in thirty-two states![2]

We noted that one assistant manager in a McDonald's restaurant, who was totally duped by the phony caller-con man, asks us all, "Unless you are in that situation, at that time, how do you know what you would do? You don't know what you would do."[3]

The point is that instead of distancing ourselves from the individuals who were deceive by assuming negative dispositional attributes in them—stupidity, naivete—we need to understand why and how people like us were so completely seduced. Then we will be in a position to resist and to spread awareness of methods of resisting such hoaxes.

The Duality of Detachment Versus Saturation

A basis duality exists in the human condition of detachment versus saturation, of cynical suspicion versus engagement. Detaching ourselves from others in the fear to being "taken in" is an extreme defensive posture, but it is true that the more open we are to other people's persuasion, the more likely we are to be swayed by them. Nevertheless, open, passionate involvement with others is essential to human happiness. We want to feel strongly, to trust completely, to act spontaneously, and to feel connected to others. We want to be fully "saturated" in living. At least some of the time, we want to suspend our evaluative faculties and abandon our primitive fearful reserve. We want to dance with passion along with Zorba the Greek.

Yet, we must regularly asses the worth of our social involvements. The challenger for each of us is how best to oscillate between two poles, immersing fully and distancing appropriately. Knowing when to stay involved with others, when to support and be loyal to a cause or a relationship rather than dismissing it, is a delicate question that we all face regularly. We live in a world in which some people aim to use us. In that same world are others who genuinely want us to share what they believe are mutually positive goals. How to tell which is which? That is the question, dear Hamlet and dear Ophelia.

Before we begin to deal with specific means for combating mind-controlling influences, we must consider another possibility: the old illusion of *personal invulnerability*.[5] Them? Yes. Me? *No!* Our psychological journey should have convinced you to appreciate how the array of situational forces that we've highlighted can such in the majority of people. But not You, right? It is hard to extend the lessons we have learned from an intellectual assessment to affect our own codes of conduct. What is easily applied in the abstract to "those others" is not easily applied in the concrete to oneself. We are different. Just as no two fingerprints have identical patterns, no two people have identical genetic, developmental, and personality patterns.

Individual differences should be celebrated, but in the face of strong, common situational forces, individual differences shrink and are compressed. In such instances, behavioral scientists can predict what the majority of people will do knowing nothing about the particular people who comprise a group, only the nature of their behavioral context. It should be clear that not even the best psychology and predict how each and every individual will behave in a given situation; some degree of individual variance always exists that cannot be accounted for. Therefore, you may reject the lessons that we are about to learn as inapplicable to yourself; you are the special case, the special end of the tail of the normal distribution. However, know that you do so at the cost of being caught with our defenses down and your tail twisted.

My advice about that to do in case you encounter a "dirty, rotten scoundrel," disguised as a nice guy or a sweet old lady, has been accumulated over many decades from many personal experiences. As a scrawny, sickly kid trying to survive on the mean streets of my South Bronx ghetto, I had to learn basic street smarts; these consisted to figuring our quickly how certain people would be likely to act in certain situations. I god good enough at the skill to become a leader of the gang, the team, or the class. Then I was trained by an unscrupulous boss, a Fagin-like character in drag, on how to deceive Broadway theatergoers into checking their hats and costs when they did not want to and to manipulate them into paying tips to get them back, when tipping was not required. As her apprentice, I became experienced in selling expensive show programs when free versions were available and in overdosing kids with loads of candy and drinks if their parents were not chaperoning them to our candy counter. I was also trained to sell magazines door to door, eliciting pity from, and thereby sales to, sympathetic tenement dwellers. Later on, I studied formally the tactics police use to get confessions from suspects, that state-sanctioned torturers use to get anything they want from their victims, and that cult recruiters use in seducing the innocent into their dens. My scholarship extended to studying the mind control tactics used by the Soviets and the methods used by the Chinese Communists in the Korean War and in their massive national thought reform programs. I also studied our own homegrown mind manipulators in the CIA, the state-sponsored MKULTRA program,[6] and Jim Jones's lethal charismatic power over his religious followers (described in earlier chapters).

I have both counseled and learned from those who survived various cult experiences. In addition, I have engaged in a lifetime of investigative research on persuasion, compliance, dissonance, and group processes. My writing on some of these topics includes a training manual for peace activists during the Vietnam War, as well as several basic texts on attitude change and social influence.[7] These credentials are offered only to bolster the communicator credibility of the information provide next.

Promoting Altruism via the Virtuous Authority Experiment

Let us first imagine a "Reverse-Milgram" authority experiment. Our goal is to create a setting in which people will comply with demands that intensify over time *to do good*. The participants would be guided gradually to behave in ever-more-altruistic ways, slowly but surely moving further than they could have imagined toward ever-more-positive, prosocial actions. Instead of the paradigm arranged to facilitate a slow descent into evil, we could substitute a paradigm from a slow ascent into goodness. How could we formulate an experimental setting in which that was possible? Let us design such a thought experiment. To begin, imagine that we arrange for each participant a hierarchy of experiences or actions that range from slightly more positive acts than he or she is used to doing to ever-more-extreme "good" actions. The extremes of virtue push him or her upward all the way to engaging in actions that at first seemed unimaginable.

There might be a time-based dimension in the design for those busy citizens who do not practice virtue because they have convinced themselves that they just don't have time to spare for good deeds. The first "button" on the "Goodness Generator" might be to spend ten minutes writing a thank-you note to a friend or a get-well card to a colleague. The next level might demand twenty minutes of giving advice to a troubled child. Increasing the pressure in this paradigm might then entail the participant's agreeing to give thirty minutes of his time to read a story to a illiterate housekeeper. Then the altruism scale moves upward to spending an hour tutoring a needy student, then to babysitting for a few hours to allow a single parent to visit her sick mother, working for an evening in a soup kitchen, helping unemployed veterans, devoting part of a day to taking a group of orphaned children to the zoo, being available to talk with returning wounded veterans, and on and on upward, a step-by-step commitment to giving precious time every week to ever-more-worthy causes. Providing social models along the way who are already engaged in the requested task, or who take the initiative to ante up to the next level, should work to encourage obedience to virtuous authority, should it not? It's worth a try, especially since, as far as I know, nothing like this experiment has ever been done.

Ideally, our experiment in social goodness would end when the person was doing something that he or she could never have imagined doing before. Our goodness track could also include contributions to creating a healthy and sustainable environment that might go from minimal acts of conservation or recycling to ever more substantial activities, such as giving money, time, and personal involvement to "green" causes. I invite you to expand on this notion in a host of domains in which society would benefit as more citizens "went all the way"—doing good without any supporting ideology, for, as we know from dissonance theory, beliefs follow behavior. Get people to perform good actions, and they will generate the necessary underlying principles to justify them. Talmudic scholars are supposed to have preached not to require that people believe before they pray, only to do what is needed to get them to begin to pray; then they will come to believe in what and to whom they are praying.

Research Supports a Reverse-Milgram Altruism Effect

As noted, this reverse-Milgram experiment has never been done. Suppose we actually attempted to perform such an experiment in the laboratory or, better yet, in our homes and communities. Would it work? Could we use the power of authority and of the situation to produce virtue? Based on what I know about human beings and the principles of social influence. I am confident that we could do a better job of bringing about righteousness in our world, employing basic principles of social influence (see Notes for some references).[8]

The reverse-Milgram experiment described here combines three simple influence tactics that have been extensively studied and documented by social psychologists: the foot-in-the-door tactic, social modeling, and self-labeling of helpfulness. I've merely brought them together in one situation for promoting altruism. Moreover, researchers have found that these tactics can be used to promote all sorts of prosocial behavior—from donating one's hard-earned money to charity to increasing recycling and even to giving blood at the next Red Cross blood drive.

Our "slow ascent into goodness step by step" makes use of what social psychologists call the *"foot-in-the-door"* (FITD) tactic. This tactic begins by first asking someone to do a small request (which most people readily perform) and then later on to ask them to comply with a related but much bigger request (which was the actual goal all along)[9] The classic demonstration of this tactic was done more than forty years ago by Jonathan Freedman and Scott Fraser.[10] They asked suburbanites to put a big, ugly sign urging "Drive Carefully" in their nice suburban yard. Fewer than twenty percent of the homeowners did so. However, three fourths of the homeowners agreed to place that sign in their yards if two weeks earlier they had taken a small step and posted in their windows an unobtrusive three-inch sign urging safe driving. The same approach works with other pro-social behavior. For example, researchers have found that merely signing a petition leads to increased monetary support of the handicapped, filling out a brief questionnaire increases the willingness of people to donate their organs to others after death, conserving a small amount of energy induces homeowners to subsequently conserve more energy, and making a small public commitment increases the recycling of paper products.[11] What is more, this FITD effect can be enhanced by chaining together a series of increasingly larger requests, putting two feet in the door—just as in our reverse-Milgram experiment on promoting altruism.[12]

Our reverse-Milgram experiment would also employ *social models* to encourage prosocial behavior. In the SPE and Abu Ghraib Prison, there was an abundance of negative models that supported abusive behavior. Turning the power of social models around to enhance positive acts can be as effective in achieving the opposite, desirable outcome. Researchers have found that altruistic role models increase the likelihood that those around them will engage in positive, prosocial behavior. Here is just a sampling of findings: social role models have been shown to increase donations to the Salvation Army; to promote helping a stranger with a flat tire; to lower rates of aggression and promote nonviolent responses; to reduce littering; and to increase donating money to poor children and a willingness to share one's resources with others.[13] But one word of advice: Remember to practice what you preach. Models persuade far more effectively than words. For example, in one set of experiments, children were exposed to an adult model that preached either greed or charity to them in a persuasive sermon. However, that adult then went on to practice either greedy or charitable actions. The results showed that the children were more likely to do what the model did than what the model had said.[14]

The wisdom of the Talmudic scholars previously mentioned is consistent with another social influence principle underlying our reverse-Milgram experiment: Give someone an *indentify label* of the kind that you would like them to have as someone who will then do the action you want to elicit from them. When you tell a person that he or she is helpful, altruistic, and kind, that person is more likely to do helpful, altruistic, and kind behaviors for others. In the Stanford Prison Experiment, we randomly assigned young men to the roles of prisoner and guard, and they soon took on the manners and the behaviors of those roles. So, too, if we tell someone that he or she is a helpful person, he or she will take on the manners and actions consistent with that identity label. For example, researchers have found that telling someone that he or she is "a generous person" increases compliance with a request to make a large contribution to prevent multiple sclerosis; giving people feedback that they are kind makes them more likely to help someone who has dropped a large number of cards; and those given a salient identity as "blood donors" are more likely to continue to donate their own blood to a stranger whom they don't expect ever to know or meet.[15]

One of the great advantages of our species is the ability to explore and understand our social world and then to use what we know to make our lives better. Throughout this book, we have seen the power of the situation to produce evil. I now argue that we can take those same basic principles and use the power of the situation to produce virture. I fear for the future of humanity if my argument on this point is a failure or if I fail in making my argument acceptable to you. Might I suggest that you take small step today in carrying out the reverse-Milgram experiment in your own life? I think you are just the person to do it and to serve as a role model for others in transforming our world to one with a more positive future. If not you, then who?

A Ten-step Program to Resist Unwanted Influences

If we consider some of the social psychological principles that fostered the evils we saw during the course of our journey, then once again—as we have just done in constructing the Goodness Generator example—let us use variants of those principles to get people to accentuate the positive and eliminate the negative in their lives. Given the range of different types of influence, it would be necessary to tailor resistance to each type. Combating wrong dissonant commitments requires different tactics, from opposing compliance-gaining strategies used on us. Confronting persuasive speeches and powerful communicators forces us to use different principles that we need for dealing with those who would dehumanize us or deindividuate us. Ways of undercutting groupthink are also different from ways of modifying the impact of intense recruiters.

I have developed such a compendium for you; however, it offers more depth and specifics than is possible to deal with in this chapter. The solution is to make it all available to you free, online in the special website developed as a companion to this book: www.LuciferEffect.com. That way, you can read it at your leisure, take notes, check out the reference sources on which it is based, and contemplate scenarios in which you will put these resistance strategies into practice in your life. Also, after you have encountered a particular social influence tactic used on you or on others you know, you can turn to this handy guide for solution about what to do next time around to be in a better position to master that challenge.

Here is my ten-step program for resisting the impact of undesirable social influences and at the same time promoting personal resilience and civic virtue. It uses ideas that cut across various influence strategies and provides simple, effective modes of dealing with them. The key to resistances lies in development of the three Ss: self-awareness, situational sensitivity, and street smarts. You will see how they are central to many of these general strategies of resistance.

"I made a mistake!" Let's start out by encouraging admission of our mistakes, first to ourselves, then to others. Accept the dictum that to err is human. You have made an error in judgment; your decision was wrong. You had every reason to believe it was right when you made it, but now you know you were wrong. Say the six magic words. "I'm sorry", "I apologize"; "Forgive me." Say to yourself that you will learn from your mistakes, grow better from them. Don't continue to put your money, time, and resources into bad investments. Move on. Doing so openly reduces the need to justify or rationalize our mistakes and thereby to continue to give support to bad or immoral actions. Confession of error undercuts the motivation to reduce cognitive dissonance; dissonance evaporates when a reality check occurs." "Cutting bait" instead of resolutely "staying the course" when it is wrong has an immediate cost, but it always results in long-term gain. Consider how many years the Vietnam War continued long after top military and administration officials, such as Secretary of Defense Robert McNamara, knew that the war was wrong and could not be won.[16] How many thousands of lives were lost to such wrongheaded resistance, when acknowledging failure and error could have saved them? How much good could come to all of us were our political leaders able to admit their similar errors in Iraq? It is more than a political decision to "save face" by denying errors instead of saving soldiers' and civilian lives—it is a moral imperative.

"I am mindful." In many settings smart people do dumb things because they fail to attend to key features in the words or actions of influence agents and fail to notice obvious situational clues. Too often we function on automatic pilot, using outworn scripts that have worked for us in the past, never stopping to evaluate whether they are appropriate in the here and now.[17] Following the advice of the Harvard researcher Ellen Langer, we must transform our usual state of mindless inattention into "mindfulness," especially in new situations.[18] Don't hesitate to fire a wake-up shot to your cortex; when we are in familiar situations old habits continue to rule even though they have become obsolete or wrong. We need to be reminded not to live our lives on automatic pilot but always to take a Zen moment to reflection on the meaning of the immediate situation, to think before acting. Never go mindlessly into situations where angles and sensible people fear to tread. For the best results, add "critical thinking" to mindfulness in your resistance.[19] Ask for evidence to support assertions; demand that ideologies be sufficiently elaborated to allow you to separate rhetoric from substance. Try to determine whether the recommended means ever justify potentially harmful ends. Imagine endgame scenarios of the future consequences of any current practice. Reject simple solutions as quick fixes for complex personal or social problems. Support critical thinking from the earliest times in children's lives, alerting them to the deceptive TV ads, biased claims, and distorted perspectives being presented to them. Help them become wiser and warier knowledge consumers.[20]

"I am responsible." Talking responsibility for one's decisions and actions puts the actor in the driver's seat, for better or for worse. Allowing others to compromise their own responsibility, to diffuse it, makes them powerful backseat drivers and makes the car move recklessly ahead without a responsible driver. We become more resistant to undesirable social influence by always maintaining a sense of personal responsibility and by being willing to be held accountable for our actions. Obedience to authority is less blind to the extent that we are aware that diffusion of responsibility merely disguises our individual complicity in the conduct of questionable actions. Your conformity to antisocial group norms is undercut to the extent that you do not allow displacement of responsibility, when you refuse to spread responsibility around the gang, the frat, the shop, the battalion, or the corporation. Always imagine a future time when today's deed will be on trial and no one will accept your pleas of "only following orders," or "everyone else was doing it."

"I will assert my unique identity." Do not allow others to deindividuate you, to put you into a category, a box, a slot, to turn you into an object. Assert your individuality; politely state your name and your credentials, loud and clear. Insist on the same behavior in others. Make eye contact (remove all eye-concealing sunglasses), and offer information about yourself that reinforces your unique identity. Find common ground with dominant others in influence situations and use it to enhance similarities. Anonymity and secrecy conceal wrongdoing and undermine the human connection. They can become the breeding grounds that generate dehumanization, and, as we now know, dehumanization provides the killing ground for bullies, rapists, torturers, terrorists, and tyrants. Go a step beyond self-individuation. Work to change whatever social conditions make people feel anonymous. Instead, support practices that make other feel special, so that they too have a sense of personal value and self-worth. Never allow or practice negative stereotyping; words, labels, and jokes can be destructive, if they mock others.

"I respect just authority but rebel against unjust authority." In every situation, work to distinguish between those in authority who, because of their expertise, wisdom, seniority, or special status, deserve respect, and the unjust authority figures who demand our obedience without having any substance. Many who assume the mantel of authority are pseudo-leaders, false prophets, confidence men and women, self-promoters who should not be respected but rather disobeyed and openly exposed to critical evaluation. Parents, teachers, and religious leaders should play more active roles in teaching children this critical differentiation. They should be polite and courteous when such a stance is justified, yet be good, wise children by resisting those authorities who do not deserve their respect. Doing so will reduce our mindless obedience to self-proclaimed authorities whose priorities are not in our best interests.

"I want group acceptance, but value my independence." The lure of acceptance into a desired social group is more powerful than that of the mythical golden ring in *Lord of the Rings*. The power of that desire for acceptance will make some people do almost anything to be accepted and go to even further extremes to avoid rejection by the Group. We are indeed social animals, and usually our social connections benefit us and help us to achieve important goals that we could not achieve alone. However, there are times when conformity to a group norm is counterproductive to the social good. It is imperative to determine when to follow the norm and when to reject it. Ultimately, we live within our own minds, in solitary splendor, and therefore we must be willing and ready to declare our independence regardless of the social rejection it may elicit. It is not easy, especially for young people with a shaky self-image or adults whose self-image is isomorphic with that of their job. Pressures on them to be a "team player." to sacrifice personal morality for the good of the team, are nearly irresistible. What is required is that we step back, get outside opinions, and find new groups that will support our independence and promote our values. There will always be another, different, better group for us.

"I will be more frame-vigilant." Who makes the frame becomes the artist, or the con artist. The way issues are framed is often more influential than the persuasive arguments within their boundaries. Moreover, effective frames can seem not to be frames at all, just sound bites, visual images, slogans, and logos. They influence us without our being conscious of them, and they shape our orientation toward the ideas or issues they promote. For example, voters who favored reducing estate tax benefits for the rich were urged to vote against a "death tax"; the tax was exactly the same, but its defining term was different. We desire things that are framed as being "scarce," even when they are plentiful. We are averse to things that are framed as potential losses and prefer what is presented to us as a gain, even when the ratio of positive to negative prognoses is the same.[21] We don't want a 40 percent chance of losing X over Y, but we do want the 60 percent chance of gaining Y over X. The linguist George Lakoff clearly shows in his writings that it is crucial to be aware of frame power and to be vigilant in order to offset its insidious influence on our emotions, thoughts, and votes.[22]

"I will balance my time perspective." We can be led to do things that are not really what we believe in when we allow ourselves to become trapped in an expanded present moment. When we stop relying on our sense of past commitments and our sense of future liabilities, we open ourselves to situational temptations to engage in *Lord of the Flies* excesses. By not "going with the flow" when others around you are being abusive or out of control, you are relying on a temporal perspective that stretches beyond present-oriented hedonism or present-oriented fatalism. You are likely to engage in a cost-benefit analysis of your actions in terms of their future consequences. Or you many resist by being sufficiently conscious of a past time frame that contains your personal values and standards. By developing a balanced time perspective in which past, present, and future can be called into action depending on the situation and task at hand, you will be in a better position to act responsibly and wisely than when your time perspective is biased toward reliance on only one or two time frames. Situational power is weakened when past and future combine to contain the excesses of the present.[23] For example, research indicates that righteous Gentiles who helped to hide Dutch Jews from the Nazis did not engage in the kind of rationalizing their neighbors did in generating reasons for *not* helping. These heroes depended upon moral structures derived from their past and never lost sight of a future time when they would look back on this terrible situation and be forced to ask themselves whether they had done the right thing when they chose not to succumb to fear and social pressure.[24]

"I will not sacrifice personal or civic freedoms for the illusion of security." The need for security is a powerful determinant of human behavior. We can be manipulated into engaging in actions that are alien to us when faced with alleged threats to our security or the promise of security from danger. More often than not, influence peddlers gain power over us by offering a Faustian contract: You will be safe from harm if you will just surrender some of your freedom, either personal or civic, to that authority. The Mephistophelian tempter will argue that his power to save you depends upon all the people making small sacrifices of this little right or that small freedom. Reject that deal. Never sacrifice basic personal freedoms for the promise of security because the sacrifices are real and immediate and the security is a distant illusion. This is as true in traditional marital arrangements as it is in the commitment of good citizens to the interests of their nation when its leader promises personal safety and national security at the cost of a collective sacrifice of suspending laws, privacy, and freedoms. Erich Fromm's classic *Escape from Freedom* reminds us that this is the first step a fascist leader takes even in a nominally democratic society.

"I can oppose unjust systems." Individuals falter in the face of the intensity of the systems we have described: the military and prison systems as well as those of gangs, cuts, fraternities, corporations, and even dysfunctional families. But individual resistance in concert with that of others of the same mind and resolve can combine to make a difference. The next section in this chapter will portray individuals who changed systems by being willing to take the risk of blowing the whistle on corruption within them or by constructively working to change them. Resistance may involve physically removing one's self from a total situation in which all information, rewards, and punishments are controlled. It may involve challenging the groupthink mentality and being able to document all allegations of wrongdoing. It may involve getting help from other authorities, counselors, investigative reporters, or revolutionary compatriots. Systems have enormous power to resist change and withstand even righteous assault. Here is one place where individual acts of heroism to challenge unjust systems and their bad barrel makers are best performed by soliciting others to join one's cause. The system can redefine individual opposition as delusional, a pair of opponents as sharing a *folie a deux*. But with three no your side, you become a force of ideas to be reckoned with.

This ten-step program is really only a starter kit toward building individual resistance and communal resilience against undesirable influences and illegitimate attempts at persuasion. As mentioned, a fuller set of recommendations and relevant research-based references can be found on the Lucifer Effect website under *"Resisting influence Guide."*

Before moving to the final stop in our journey, celebrating heroes and heroism, I would like to add two final general recommendations. First, be discouraged form venal sins and small transgressions, such as cheating, lying, gossiping, spreading rumors, laughing at racist or sexist jokes, teasing, and bullying. They can become stepping-stones to more serious falls from grace. They serve as mini-facilitators for thinking and acting destructively against your fellow creatures. Second, moderate your in-group biases. That means accepting that your group is special but at the same time respecting the diversity that other groups offer. Fully appreciate the wonder of human variety and its variability. Assuming such a perspective will help you to reduce group biases that lead to derogating others, to prejudice and stereotyping, and to the evils of dehumanization.

Moral Reasoning:
Hints and Allegations

Joseph M. Paxton and Joshua D. Greene

Joseph M. Paxton is a PhD candidate in Psychology at Harvard University. He works on philosophically motivated empirical questions about moral reasoning and moral psychology.

Joshua D. Greene (1974–) is associate professor of psychology at Harvard University and director of Harvard's Moral Cognition Lab. His work integrates psychology, neuroscience, and moral philosophy. He and his colleagues have advanced a dual process theory of moral judgment that holds that the brain has competing moral subsystems, one generally disposed to deontological judgments and the other to utilitarian judgments.

ABSTRACT—Recent research in moral psychology highlights the role of emotion and intuition in moral judgment. In the wake of these findings, the role and significance of moral reasoning remain uncertain. In this article, we distinguish among different kinds of moral reasoning and review evidence suggesting that at least some kinds of moral reasoning play significant roles in moral judgment, including roles in abandoning moral intuitions in the absence of justifying reasons, applying both deontological and utilitarian moral principles, and counteracting automatic tendencies toward bias that would otherwise dominate behavior. We argue that little is known about the psychology of moral reasoning and that it may yet prove to be a potent social force.

1. Introduction

The following is based on a true story:

> Greg and Adam are high school buddies. Adam is a vegetarian. Greg is not. Both enjoy eating meat, but Adam has given it up after concluding that eating meat is morally wrong. Over many months, Adam and Greg argue about the ethics of eating meat. Adam agrees with Greg that hamburgers taste better than veggie burgers, but he argues that the additional enjoyment that we humans derive from eating meat is not enough to justify the suffering and ultimate death inflicted on animals such as cows. Greg is not easily convinced. He observes that eating meat is perfectly natural, pointing to his canine teeth. Adam replies that many things, such as wars of aggression, may be perfectly natural, but that such things are not necessarily right. Greg points out that the animals he eats owe their very existence to the demands of consumers such as himself. Adam replies that most animals raised for food live miserable lives and would be better off not existing. Through the course of many such discussions, Greg's mind is changed and he, too, becomes a vegetarian.

What is going on in this kind of exchange? For decades, the field of moral psychology emphasized the role of reasoning in moral judgment (Kohlberg, 1969; Smetana & Killen, 2006; Turiel, 1983), while more recent research (Greene, Sommerville, Nystrom, Darley, & Cohen, 2001; Haidt, 2001; Haidt, Koller, & Dias, 1993) emphasizes the power and prevalence of emotionally based moral intuition. There is a sense in which the above exchange must be a case of moral reasoning: Adam gave Greg reasons for becoming a vegetarian, and Greg changed his stated beliefs and behavior in response to those reasons. But there are two important ways in which the role of moral reasoning in this exchange remains uncertain. First, did Adam arrive at his current, pro-vegetarian stance because he was himself compelled by the arguments he gave, or are his arguments mere rationalizations for his preformed judgment? Second, independent of how Adam's attitudes were formed, did Adam change Greg's mind by modifying Greg's *intuitions* about eating meat? Or did Adam change Greg's mind by providing Greg with a reasoned argument that exerted an influence independent of, or even in spite of, Greg's intuitions? In more colloquial terms, did Adam change Greg's mind by appealing to his "heart" or his "head?" Is there a legitimate distinction between these two types of persuasion, and, if there is, what evidence is there concerning the reality, prevalence, and significance of each type of persuasion? In what follows we address these questions.

2. Two Theories of Moral Judgment

We begin with Haidt's (2001) highly influential framework for understanding moral psychology: the social intuitionist model (SIM). The SIM consists of a set

of causal "links" connecting three types of psychological process: intuition, judgment, and reasoning (Figure 1). The backbone of the SIM consists of two links.
The "intuitive judgment" link posits that one's judgments are driven primarily by
one's intuitions, while the "post-hoc reasoning" link posits (contrary to traditional
rationalist models) that one's reasoning is driven primarily by one's judgment,
rather than the other way around. These two links are supplemented by weaker
links that allow reasoning to, on occasion, exert a causal influence on judgment.
The "reasoned judgment" link allows one's reasoning to directly influence one's
judgment, while the "private reflection" link allows one's reasoning to influence
one's judgment by modifying one's intuitions. The "social" in the SIM comes from
two additional links: the "reasoned persuasion" link, by which one person's reasoning influences another's judgment by influencing that person's intuition, and
the "social persuasion" link, by which one's judgment, in the absence of explicit
attempts at reasoning, influences another's judgment by modifying that person's
intuition.

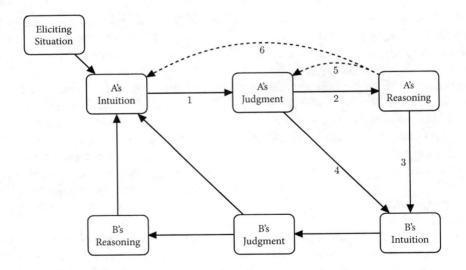

Figure 1. Haidt's (2001) social intuitionist model (SIM) consists of six links describing
causal connections among moral intuitions, moral judgments, and episodes of moral
reasoning: (1) intuitive judgment, (2) post-hoc reasoning, (3) reasoned persuasion,
(4) social persuasion, (5) reasoned judgment, and (6) private reflection. Dashed lines
indicate links that are rarely used.

Greene and colleagues (Greene, 2007; Greene, Morelli, Lowenberg, Nystrom,
& Cohen, 2008; Greene, Nystrom, Engell, Darley, & Cohen, 2004; Greene et al.,
2001) have developed an alternative dual-process model of moral judgment

that is in many ways consistent with the SIM. Greene's model posits two natural, ubiquitous, and qualitatively different modes of moral thinking that depend on dissociable, and in some cases competing, systems in the brain (Figure 2). According to Greene, deontological moral judgments, judgments that are naturally regarded as reflecting concerns for rights and duties, are driven primarily by intuitive emotional responses. At the same time, Greene et al., argue that utilitarian/consequentialist judgments, judgments aimed at promoting the greater good, are supported by controlled cognitive processes that look more like moral reasoning. For example, when people are confronted with the possibility of saving five people by pushing one person in front of a runaway trolley, it appears that the inclination to respect the "rights" of the would-be victim is driven by emotional responses that depend on the ventromedial prefrontal cortex (Ciaramelli, Muccioli, Ladavas, & di Pellegrino, 2007; Greene et al., 2001, 2004; Koenigs et al., 2007; Mendez, Anderson, & Shapira, 2005), while the countervailing utilitarian judgment is driven by controlled cognitive processes that depend on the dorsolateral prefrontal cortex (Greene et al., 2001, 2004, 2008).

For present purposes, there are two critical differences between Haidt's SIM and Greene's dual-process model. First, while the SIM posits that reasoned judgment within an individual is, "rare, occurring primarily in cases in which the intuition is weak and processing capacity is high," Greene's dual-process model allows that moral reasoning—especially utilitarian/consequentialist reasoning—may be a ubiquitous feature of moral common sense. Second, according to the SIM, social influence on moral judgment only occurs when one person succeeds in modifying another's intuition. In other words, the SIM includes no social counterpart to the "reasoned judgment" link, which would allow one person's moral reasoning to influence another's moral judgment directly, without first modifying the target's intuition. This last difference, while perhaps seeming trivial, is actually of great social significance, with important implications for the practice of democracy and the pursuit of social progress. If the SIM is correct, then attempting to engage others through their ability to reason, aiming messages at the "head" rather than the "heart," is an exercise in futility. Indeed, depending on what one means by "reasoning," one might say that the SIM does not really allow for "reasoned persuasion" at all. According to the SIM, we can say things in hopes of modifying one another's moral intuitions, but it is impossible to convince someone to put her moral intuitions aside and, instead, reach an alternative, counter-intuitive conclusion based on reasoning. According to the SIM, it is impossible for Adam to turn Greg into a vegetarian (or a supporter of healthcare reform, or gay marriage, or anything else) without first changing the way Greg *feels*. In contrast, the dual-process model suggests that Adam may be able to change Greg's mind, and even his "heart," by starting with his "head," by targeting the system for controlled cognition that is based in the dorsolateral prefrontal cortex. Note that the disagreement here is not over the importance—even dominance—of emotion and intuition in moral psychology and moral discourse. The disagreement is over the reality, or even the mere possibility, of what we regard as genuinely reasoned moral discussion, that is, discussion in which one person's capacity for moral reasoning is directly engaged with another's.

Against this theoretical backdrop, this paper has two goals. First, with respect to the existence and prevalence of individual "reasoned judgment" our aim is simply to present and consider the available evidence. Here, the SIM and dual-process theories differ only in degree, and the decision to favor one model over the other may ultimately come down to one's preferred accounting system. With respect to "reasoned persuasion," the disagreement is more substantial, but the available evidence is more scant. Here, our aim is to review the available evidence, however limited it may be, and to lay a conceptual foundation for research that could provide more conclusive evidence.

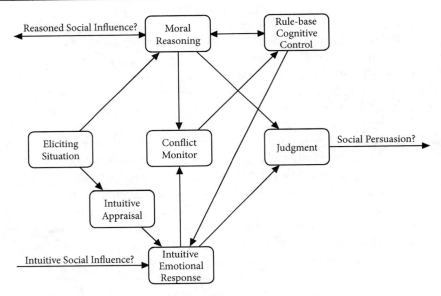

Figure 2. According to Greene et al.'s (2001, 2004, 2008) dual-process model, moral judgments are driven by both intuitive emotional responses and controlled cognitive responses. This model differs from the SIM in two critical ways. First, it emphasizes the role of rule-based, controlled cognitive processes, especially the conscious application of utilitarian moral principles. Second, it allows that social influence may occur when people directly engage one another's capacities for moral reasoning, that is, the conscious evaluation of moral judgments/behaviors for their consistency with moral principles and other moral commitments.

3. What Is Moral Reasoning?

Haidt defines moral reasoning as "conscious mental activity that consists of transforming given information about people in order to reach a moral judgment" (Haidt, 2001). While this definition provides a useful starting point, we believe that it may be too broad, as it would allow any conscious thought process (about people) that affects moral judgment to count as "moral reasoning."

For example, we might engage in conscious reasoning to determine whether Oswald shot JFK, and such reasoning may affect our ultimate judgment concerning Oswald's moral guilt or innocence (Bucciarelli, Khemlani, & Johnson-Laird, 2008). There's little doubt that we often need to make factual inferences in order to reach a moral judgment, that these inferences are instances of reasoning, and that they have an important influence on moral judgment. But this is not moral reasoning in the sense that has been, and remains, controversial in moral psychology.

A related problem concerns the classification of mental activity that is specifically moral, but that may not seem sufficiently reasoned to qualify as "reasoning." If, for example, one consciously thinks to oneself, or says to another in an attempt at persuasion, "Anti-war protesters are communist, fascist, pigs who should go back to Russia!" that may qualify as "conscious mental activity that consists of transforming given information about people in order to reach a moral judgment," but many of us would not want to count this as "moral reasoning." And the same goes for more congenial moral communications, such as many of those delivered in Martin Luther King Jr.'s famous "I Have a Dream" speech, in which persuasion is effected primarily (though not exclusively) through metaphor and imagery. Haidt (2001) regards such communication as "reasoned persuasion." We think this classification is questionable, but our task here is not to quibble over definitions. The more substantive point is that there is, or may be, a kind of moral persuasion that is more reasoned than this—more "head" and less "heart."

Take for example, Adam's argument with Greg. Adam might have said, "Greg, I have a dream . . . that one day cows and humans will stroll together through the pastures of peace . . ." But Adam takes a different approach. Adam points out that animals raised for meat suffer, but he goes further. He claims that the suffering animals experience is not outweighed by the enjoyment that humans gain by eating meat rather than vegetable products, explicitly invoking a utilitarian/consequentialist principle. Greg does not dispute Adam's utilitarian calculus, but attempts to render it irrelevant by claiming that eating meat is natural, implicitly appealing to the principle that what is natural is right or good. And Adam replies by observing that things that Greg himself regards as bad, such as wars of aggression, may be natural, thus invalidating the principle to which Greg has implicitly appealed. And so on.

What, then, is the difference between "I have a dream . . ." and this kind of argumentative persuasion? One might suggest that, ultimately, there is no difference, that Adam's arguments are nothing more than attempts to push intuitively compelling metaphors and images into Greg's head. That may be the case, but, alternatively, it may be that Adam is changing Greg's mind by appealing to his capacity to reason, and not (primarily) by modifying Greg's intuitions. If that's the case, what exactly does it mean for one person to engage another's reasoning?

We propose that moral reasoning, in this more restricted sense, involves an attempt to compel another individual (or oneself) to accept a moral conclusion *on pain of inconsistency*. For the sake of clarity, we will refer to this more restricted kind of moral reasoning as "Moral Reasoning," defined as follows:

> Moral Reasoning: Conscious mental activity through which one evaluates a moral judgment for its (in)consistency with other moral commitments, where these commitments are to one or more moral principles and (in some cases) particular moral judgments.[1]

This definition explains why "I have a dream . . ." need not count as Moral Reasoning. One can be moved to pursue King's dream of racial harmony without any conscious recognition that to do otherwise would be inconsistent with one's other moral commitments. In contrast, Adam's persuasive strategy is to point out that eating meat is inconsistent with a utilitarian principle. This is different from saying, "But think of the poor suffering animals!" Adam is saying, "Think of the poor suffering animals, but also think of the happy meat-eating humans. Do the math, and come to the inexorable conclusion that the animal suffering caused by eating meat is greater than the human happiness caused by eating meat. If you accept the moral principle that we should not do things that make the world an overall less happy (and more suffering) place, then you, too, should be opposed to eating meat." Such a strategy can only be effective in response to an interlocutor who is capable of recognizing logical inconsistency and motivated to avoid it. "I have a dream," in contrast, can be successful in response to anyone who is capable of sharing another's dream.

Our hypothesis is that Moral Reasoning not only happens, but that, for all we know, it may be a pervasive and important aspect of our moral psychology, even if it is relatively rare compared to more intuitive moral reasoning (Pizarro & Bloom, 2003). In what follows we consider the evidence, limited though it may be, that supports this hypothesis.

4. Inducing Moral Reasoning

To determine whether people engage in Moral Reasoning, one might begin by examining how people behave when asked to take a more rational approach to moral judgment. Pizarro, Uhlmann, and Bloom (2003) took this approach in a study employing scenarios like this:

> Barbara wants to kill her husband, John. When they are eating at a restaurant, Barbara slips some poison into John's dish while he isn't looking. Unbeknownst to Barbara, the poison isn't strong enough to kill her husband. However, it makes the dish taste so bad that John changes his order. When he receives his new order, it contains a food that John is extremely allergic to, and which kills him within minutes.

Here, Barbara is a cause of John's death. She intends to kill him, and he does indeed die, but John does not die in exactly the way that Barbara intends. Pizarro and colleagues found that, under normal conditions, subjects assigned less blame to the agent in "causally deviant" scenarios like this one, relative to casually normal scenarios in which harm unfolds exactly as the agent intended. However, when subjects were instructed to first make a "rational, objective judgment," they discounted blame less than when they were first instructed to go with their "intuitive, gut feeling."

Even if one regards the effect observed here as an effect of experimenter demand, the question remains, why did the demand to be more "rational" and "objective" lead subjects to alter their judgments as they did? They must think there is something irrational about blaming Barbara less because her murderous plot failed to unfold exactly as intended. In other words, the subjects appear to be applying some kind of normative standard, a principle, for evaluating judgments of blameworthiness. Taking a bit of liberty, they may be thinking something like this: "Barbara seems less blameworthy when she causes John's death in this weird, coincidental way. But does that really make sense? Her intention is just as bad. The result is just as bad. And she is causally responsible for the bad result. The only reason I can see for reducing her blame is that she just seems less blameworthy. But that does not sound like a very good reason. And I was just asked to be rational, so . . ."

In other words, this appears to be a case of Moral Reasoning, a case in which a judgment is not merely altered through conscious mental activity, but altered in a *principled* way, so as to be consistent with one's other moral commitments ("Deviant causation is not on the list of things that matter for blame"). This interpretation does not necessarily pose a problem for the SIM. One might simply regard this phenomenon as evidence—much needed evidence—that private "reasoned judgment" sometimes happens. And it is worth noting that this does not appear to be a case in which reason resolves a dispute between two competing intuitions. Rather, it appears to be a case in which intuition and reason conflict, as suggested by the fact that the instruction to be "rational" reliably pushes subjects in a particular direction.

These results challenge the SIM in a more serious way if the effect is viewed as a product of social interaction. The subject hears the experimenter's instruction to be "rational" and chooses an answer that he believes will stand up better to social scrutiny. If that's the case, then it appears that one person can influence another person's judgment, not by modifying the target's intuition, but by appealing to the target's capacity to reason, to formulate judgments that are consistent with their other moral commitments.

Of course, it does not follow from this that the target has actually changed his judgment. These subjects may simply be telling the experimenter what they think she wants to hear. However, even if this effect is driven in part by demand, these results still show that one can influence another's judgment simply by urging that person to be "rational." This suggests that people may well have a capacity to engage one another with Moral Reasoning: We know what we're supposed to do when told to be "rational" because this is something that we, at least occasionally, do.

5. Application of Deontological Moral Principles

Among the moral principles discussed and applied by professional and amateur philosophers, the most prominent may be deontological principles. Deontological moral principles prohibit or allow certain types of actions based on the features of those actions, as opposed to their consequences. For example, according to the *action principle*, harm caused by an action is less morally acceptable than harm caused by an omission.

A pair of recent studies (Borg, Hynes, Van Horn, Grafton, & Sinnott-Armstrong, 2006; Cushman, Young, & Hauser, 2006) provides evidence that subjects apply deontological moral principles when making moral judgments in response to hypothetical "trolley" scenarios (Foot, 1978; Greene et al., 2001; Mikhail, 2010; Petrinovich, O'Neill, & Jorgensen, 1993; Thomson, 1985). In Cushman et al.'s study, matched pairs of scenarios were constructed in which harm is caused either through action (e.g., hitting a lever that turns a runaway trolley away from five people and onto one person) or through omission (e.g., refraining from hitting a lever that will turn a runway trolley away from one person and onto five people). In the first phase of the experiment, subjects morally evaluated a series of harmful actions and omissions as described above. In the second phase, subjects were asked to justify their responses to matched pairs of previously evaluated action/omission scenarios. The experimenters then coded each justification with respect to whether the subject provided a clear appeal to the action principle.

Subjects' judgments in the first phase of the experiment did indeed conform to the action principle, with harmful actions evaluated less favorably than harmful omissions. Moreover, in the second phase of the experiment, subjects provided clear appeals to the action principle for 81% of the scenario pairs. This indicates that subjects could have consciously applied the action principle in generating their judgments, as they were able, in the end, to consciously articulate the action principle.

In an unpublished reanalysis of these data (F. Cushman, personal communications, January 2009), the authors asked whether subjects who successfully articulated the action principle after the first phase of the experiment were more likely to have consistently conformed to the action principle in the first phase. That is indeed what happened, suggesting that at least some subjects were consciously applying the action principle during the first phase of the experiment. However, it is also possible that subjects whose judgments best conformed to the action principle during the first phase were more likely to articulate the action principle in the second phase, not because they had consciously applied that principle earlier, but simply because their past behavior made the action principle more accessible during the second phase.

An independent functional magnetic resonance imaging (fMRI) study (Borg et al., 2006) provides convergent evidence for the hypothesis that people consciously apply the action principle in making moral judgments. In this study, subjects were scanned while making judgments about moral dilemmas similar to those listed above. For moral dilemmas involving the action principle (as compared to analogous nonmoral scenarios), the dorsolateral prefrontal cortex (DLPFC) was identified as area of maximal activation. While the activation of the DLPFC does not guarantee that the process in question is conscious, the DLPFC is typically implicated in conscious processing (Dehaene, Changeux, Naccache, Sackur, & Sergent, 2006). More specifically, the DLPFC is widely implicated in controlled cognitive tasks, such as the color-naming Stroop (1935) task, in which one must apply a conscious decision-rule (typically one provided explicitly by the experimenter) in the face of a countervailing prepotent response (MacDonald, Cohen, Stenger, & Carter, 2000; Miller & Cohen, 2001).

Thus, these fMRI data provide further support for the interpretation offered by Cushman et al. for their justification results. If the post-hoc interpretation were correct, one would not expect to see neural activity associated with Reasoning and controlled cognition engaged until after the decision had already been made. But, in this case, the timing of the activation corresponds to the point of decision, rather than points after the decision. Thus, the activation in question is more likely to be indicative of a Reasoning process that led to the decision than a rationalizing process that came after the decision.

In light of these convergent findings, there is good reason to think that, at least in some cases, people consciously apply deontological principles such as the action principle. Even if this is true, however, one might still regard such Reasoning as a kind of post-hoc rationalization. This is because the principle in question may itself have been formulated merely as an attempt to rationalize prior moral intuitions.

This kind of concern opens the door to future research on Moral Reasoning examining whether yesterday's post-hoc rationalizations could be the basis for today's moral reasoning (Greene, 2007). For instance, if, after being given the opportunity to explicitly formulate the action principle for themselves, subjects were given a new set of dilemmas involving actions and omissions, would they apply the action principle even more consistently? If so, this would constitute strong evidence that subjects are capable of engaging in principled deontological Reasoning. Likewise, experiments aimed at disrupting the Reasoning process (e.g., using cognitive load or transcranial magnetic stimulation (TMS)) would provide further evidence for this interpretation.

6. Rejecting Unprincipled Intuitions

Cushman et al. (2006), in addition to examining the action principle, examined the "contact principle," according to which using physical contact to cause harm to a victim (e.g., by pushing) is less morally acceptable than causing harm to a victim without using physical contact (e.g., by dropping the victim through a switch-operated trap door). Subjects' judgments were often consistent with this principle, and, when they were, subjects cited the contact principle 60% of the time. (Note that more recent evidence indicates that these effects are due to the presence of "personal force" rather than physical contact per se; Greene, Cushman et al., 2009.) Moreover, 20% of the subjects not only cited the contact principle, but, upon citing it as the basis for their judgments, went on to reject it as a legitimate moral principle, often stating that the mere presence of physical contact did not seem like a good reason to make a moral distinction between the contact and no-contact dilemmas. In other words, subjects revised their judgments when they became conscious of the fact that their initial judgments were *inconsistent* with their beliefs about what kinds of things ought to make a moral difference.

People's willingness to abandon the contact principle is an example of a more general phenomenon in which judgments about pairs of items change depending on whether the items are presented separately or jointly (Bazerman, Loewenstein, & White, 1992). Such effects are typically observed when joint presentation highlights features of the items that are likely to influence judgment, but that strike people, upon reflection, as irrelevant (or weakly relevant) to the judgments being made. For example, when two dictionaries are evaluated separately, subjects are likely to ignore the number of entries in each dictionary, but attend to the fact that one has a slightly torn cover. But when the dictionaries are evaluated jointly, the number of words becomes more important and the fact that one dictionary has a torn cover becomes less important. Joint evaluation makes people think about what they're thinking about and adjust their judgments accordingly.

A recent study (Paharia, Kassam, Greene, & Bazerman, 2009) demonstrates this phenomenon of "joint/separate reversal" in a moral context. Subjects responded to scenarios in which a major pharmaceutical company increased its profits by dramatically increasing the price of a slow-selling, but desperately needed, cancer drug. In one scenario, the firm *directly* increased the price of the drug. In the other, the firm increased the price of the drug indirectly by selling the rights to market the drug to a smaller company, knowing that that the other company would increase the price. When the two cases were presented separately (between-subjects), the action in the indirect selling case was judged to be more morally acceptable than the action in the direct selling case. But when the two cases were presented jointly (within-subjects), this effect went away. This is presumably because subjects rejected their intuitive tendency to see direct harm as worse than indirect harm, based on a principled conception of what does and does not matter morally when it comes to evaluating harmful actions.

A study examining the role of disgust in moral judgment (Wheatley & Haidt, 2005) makes a similar point. Highly hypnotizable subjects were given a hypnotic suggestion to feel a "flash of disgust" upon hearing affectively neutral words that were embedded within vignettes describing moral violations (e.g., shoplifting, bribery, library theft, etc.). Subjects were asked for judgments concerning how disgusting and how morally acceptable/unacceptable they found each action. When the scenario descriptions included the hypnotic disgust word, subjects judged the actions to be both more disgusting and less morally acceptable, as compared to when the scenario descriptions did not include the hypnotic disgust word. However, the magnitude of the effect was larger for the disgust judgments than for the moral judgments, suggesting that the disgust responses were often countered by some kind of competing response. Wheatley and Haidt also presented subjects with a scenario about a student council representative who finds interesting topics for discussion, doing nothing remotely immoral in the process. Amazingly, some subjects condemned this innocent student when they were hypnotically induced to feel a flash of disgust. Less amazingly, but equally important for present purposes, is the fact that most subjects who were hypnotically induced to experience disgust did not condemn the student council representative. This implies that they overrode their disgust responses, presumably by thinking to themselves something like this: "I get an icky feeling from this person, but I cannot see how he is doing anything wrong, so I guess his behavior is fine." Alternatively, one might propose that this sober response is just as intuitive as the icky feeling. However, even if that is true, this does not explain why subjects so reliably sided with the sober intuition over the icky feeling. This asymmetry in judgment suggests a conscious, principled resolution of the conflict ("But that just makes no sense"). Nevertheless, we cannot rule out the possibility that the sober intuition simply overpowered the icky feeling, without the help of a conscious, principled decision process. As above, studies using fMRI, TMS, or cognitive load could provide support for the hypothesis that such sober judgments in the face of irrational disgust responses are genuinely counter-intuitive and not just differently intuitive.

In short, these studies indicate that people spontaneously reject certain intuitive judgments as unprincipled, so long as they are in a position to appreciate the nature of their intuitions. Moreover, these judgments, at least in some cases, do not appear to be based on countervailing moral intuitions, but rather on more abstract, principled conceptions of what factors ought or ought not carry moral weight.

7. Application of Utilitarian Moral Principles

Consider the following scenario, known as the crying baby dilemma (Greene et al., 2001, 2004):

> It's wartime. You and your fellow villagers are hiding from nearby enemy soldiers in a basement. Your baby starts to cry, and you cover your baby's mouth to block the sound. If you remove your hand, your baby will cry loudly, and the soldiers will hear. They will find you, your baby, and the others, and they will kill all of you. If you do not remove your hand, your baby will smother to death. Is it morally acceptable to smother your baby to death in order to save yourself and the other villagers?

Most people find dilemmas such as this difficult, as indicated by relatively long reaction times (RTs) and divergent judgments between subjects. This difficulty appears to be due to a conflict between two competing responses, an automatic emotional response that opposes "personally" harmful actions (Greene, Cushman et al., 2009; Greene et al., 2001) and a more controlled cognitive response that, in utilitarian fashion, favors minimizing harm. Evidence for the presence of competing responses comes from an fMRI experiment (Greene et al., 2004) demonstrating that dilemmas such as this one preferentially engage the anterior cingulate cortex (ACC), a brain region known for its role in the detection of response conflict (Botvinick, Braver, Barch, Carter, & Cohen, 2001). Likewise, these difficult dilemmas preferentially engage regions within the dorsolateral prefrontal cortex (DLPFC), which is, once again, known for its role in cognitive control processes that resolve response conflicts (MacDonald et al., 2000; Miller & Cohen, 2001). Critically, these regions of DLPFC also exhibit increased activity when people make utilitarian judgments in response to such dilemmas (as compared to RT-matched nonutilitarian judgments), thus supporting a link between utilitarian judgment and controlled cognitive processing. Likewise, a more recent fMRI study demonstrates that utilitarian judgments approving of breaking a promise in order to save additional lives are also associated with increased DLPFC activity (Greene, Lowenberg, et al., unpublished data).

These results suggest that people sometimes Reason their way to moral judgments by applying utilitarian moral principles. To provide further support for this hypothesis, Greene, Morelli, Lowenberg, Nystrom, and Cohen conducted a study in which subjects responded to dilemmas like the one above while simultaneously engaged in a cognitive load task designed to interfere with controlled cognitive processing. Putting subjects under cognitive load was found to have a selective effect on RT, slowing down utilitarian moral judgments while having no effect on nonutilitarian judgments. In other words, a disruption in one's executive processing makes it harder to render utilitarian judgments, but does not interfere at all with one's ability to render nonutilitarian judgments, a result that holds both for subjects with generally utilitarian inclinations and for subjects with generally nonutilitarian inclinations. This result is consistent with the hypothesis that utilitarian judgments are preferentially supported by "top-down" Moral Reasoning processes, and not simply by competing moral intuitions.

However, it should be noted that the load manipulation affected subjects' reaction times, but not their judgments. The reason for this lack of a judgment effect could be traced to a general awareness on the part of the subjects that the load manipulation was causing interference, leading subjects to increase their efforts to overcome the interference. Such a process would be cognitively analogous to the resolution of a speed-accuracy trade-off in favor of accuracy. That is, subjects may avoid making fewer utilitarian judgments by taking longer to make the utilitarian judgments that they make. Like drivers presented with obstacles on the roadway, these subjects may be delayed in, but not prevented from, reaching their destinations.

Three recent behavioral studies provide further evidence for a link between utilitarian judgment and controlled cognition. Hardman (unpublished data) used the Cognitive Reflection Test (CRT), developed by Frederick (2005), to study the relationship between the tendency to override intuitive responses and the tendency to make utilitarian judgments. The CRT asks questions such as the following: "A bat and a ball cost $1.10. The bat costs one dollar more than the ball. How much does the ball cost?" Intuitively, the answer seems to most people to be $0.10. However, a bit of reflection reveals that the correct answer is actually $0.05. Subjects who correctly answered questions like this one were twice as likely to give utilitarian responses to the crying baby dilemma and the footbridge dilemma. Likewise, Bartels (2008) found that individuals with more "rational" intellectual styles tended to make more utilitarian judgments, while individuals with more "intuitive" intellectual styles tended to make fewer utilitarian judgments. Finally, Moore, Clark, and Kane (2008) found that, for a restricted class of dilemmas, individuals with greater working memory capacity tended to make more utilitarian judgments.

Taken together, these studies suggest that utilitarian judgments are preferentially supported by Moral Reasoning. This is because cognitive control generally requires the "top down" application of a guiding rule or principle. As noted above, cognitive control mechanisms play a critical role in conforming behavior to the explicit task demands, particularly when the demands of the task are at odds with a prepotent response, as in the Stroop (1935) task (Botvinick et al., 2001; MacDonald et al., 2000). To apply a rule that overrides an intuitive response, one must first determine that the intuitive response is incompatible with the rule, that is, engage in Moral Reasoning. Moreover, it appears that such determinations are conscious. In our research experience, subjects who make utilitarian judgments in response to moral dilemmas invariably justify their answers by appeal to utilitarian principles. These contrasts starkly with the trouble subjects often have in articulating deontological principles to which their judgments conform (Cushman et al., 2006).

8. Overriding Implicit Negative Attitudes

It is well-known that people's implicit attitudes may differ from the explicit attitudes they profess to hold (Greenwald & Banaji, 1995). For example, most White people profess to have either neutral or positive attitudes toward Blacks, and yet a majority of Whites exhibit an implicit anti-Black/pro-White bias (Nosek et al., 2007). This dark cloud, however, may have a silver lining. Since Martin Luther King Jr. uttered the words "I have a dream . . ." in 1963, we have made great strides toward racial equality—not great enough, but very great. Notably, this has occurred *without* eliminating people's implicit racial biases, or even coming close to doing so. A similar phenomenon exists with respect to attitudes toward gays. For example, Inbar and colleagues (Inbar, Pizarro, Knobe, & Bloom, 2009) have shown that college students at a relatively liberal university, whose explicit attitudes toward gays are overwhelmingly nonnegative, exhibit negative attitudes toward gays on implicit measures. Here, too, the glass may be seen as half full: College campuses are tremendously more gay-friendly than they were a generation ago, despite the continued widespread prevalence of negative implicit attitudes toward gays.

How did this happen? One possibility is that, to the extent that we have made social progress within these domains, implicit negative attitudes toward Blacks and other minorities have been outcompeted by other implicit attitudes, such as positive attitudes toward Blacks and gays, positive attitudes toward equality more generally, or negative attitudes toward discrimination. We have no doubt that this is part of the story. But is it the whole story? Could it be that the voices of the civil rights movement, in addition to reshaping people's moral intuitions, succeeded in causing people to *transcend* their intuitions?

Some evidence suggests that social progress is not simply a matter of replacing one dominant intuition with another. For example, Cunningham and colleagues (Cunningham et al., 2004) have shown that when White people view Black faces they exhibit a strong amygdala response when the faces are presented subliminally, but a weaker amygdala response when the faces are presented superliminally. What's more, the superliminal presentations are associated with increased activity in brain regions associated with cognitive control, including the DLPFC. Likewise, interracial interaction is cognitively depleting (as indicated by reduced Stroop (1935) task performance) for Whites who exhibit strong implicit negative associations with Blacks (Richeson & Shelton, 2003). In other words, people do cognitive work to overcome their biases. If this willingness to actively override bias is a product of social influence—and it is hard to imagine that it is not—this suggests that social influence on moral judgment is not simply a matter of changing intuitions.

Suppose, contrary to this interpretation, that the effect of social influence has been nothing more than to implant in people more congenial implicit attitudes, which compete with the nasty old ones. Under this supposition, one might characterize the cognitive control activity observed in these studies as the engagement of a mechanism that mediates between these competing automatic processes. While it is undoubtedly true that these mechanisms play such a mediating role, both here and elsewhere, the critical question is whether these mechanisms serve as a *neutral party* in such mediations. The supposition that these control mechanisms are neutral is hard to reconcile with the fact that explicit measures show no bias: If biased automatic processes are sufficiently powerful to dominate on implicit measures, then why do they have such little effect on explicit measures? The answer, we propose, is that the control mechanisms are not neutral. Rather, their operations reflects a conscious commitment to *principle*, choosing one of two competing automatic responses based on its conformance with that principle, where the favored response is typically the *weaker* of the two automatic responses (as indexed by implicit measures). As noted above, this is exactly parallel to what happens in the color-naming Stroop task: The automatic tendency to read the word (e.g., "red" written in blue) is stronger than the competing tendency to name the color of the word, but cognitive control mechanisms nevertheless manage to produce the color-naming behavior most of the time. And this is not because some prior process has made color-naming tendency more potent, but because the cognitive control system is actively conforming the subject's behavior to a "principle," that is, the task instructions to follow the color-naming rule.

Thus, it appears that, when it comes to regulating morally unacceptable bias, cognitive control mechanisms are not merely mediating among competing automatic processes. Rather, it appears that they actively select responses that conform to a rule, a principle such as "don't discriminate based on race," such that the response selected may be less intuitive, less automatic, than its competitors. Moreover, we emphasize that the regulation of bias is not merely a case of private "reasoned judgment," although it may be that as well. This is because the tendency to control one's biased intuitions is (we presume) a tendency that has become widespread due to social influence. Our claim then, is that, in addition to shaping one another's moral intuitions through our words and deeds, we transmit to one another moral principles that allow us to transcend our dominant automatic responses, and thus effect important social change.

9. Conclusion

There are good reasons to believe that people engage in Moral Reasoning and that moralists can influence each other, not simply by modifying each others' intuitions, but by transmitting moral principles that may be used to override moral intuitions, including intuitions that would otherwise dominate behavior. People reject judgments based on their own intuitions when those judgments appear to be unprincipled, particularly if they are given a little prodding ("be rational") or put in a situation in which they can identify the factors to which their "unprincipled" intuitions are sensitive. People appear to spontaneously apply utilitarian moral principles, and perhaps deontological moral principles as well. While much of the evidence for Moral Reasoning comes from laboratory experiments with limited ecological validity, there is some evidence to suggest that Moral Reasoning is a potent social force. When it comes to making moral progress, the "head" may be no less indispensible than the "heart."[2]

Notes

1. This definition is inspired in part by John Rawls (1971) notion of "wide-scope reflective equilibrium." For a similar account of the psychology of moral reasoning, see Harman, Mason, and Sinnott-Armstrong (in press).

2. For their very helpful comments and insightful suggestions on earlier drafts of this paper, we thank Jonathan Haidt, Bryce Huebner, Joshua Knobe, Molly Pinter, and Wendell Wallach.

References

Bartels, D. M. (2008). Principled moral sentiment and the flexibility of moral judgment and decision making. *Cognition*, 108(2), 381–417.

Bazerman, M. H., Loewenstein, G. F., & White, S. B. (1992). Reversals of preference in allocation decisions: Judging an alternative versus choosing among alternatives. *Administrative Science Quarterly*, 37(2), 220–240.

Borg, J., Hynes, C., Van Horn, J., Grafton, S., & Sinnott-Armstrong, W. (2006). Consequences, action, and intention as factors in moral judgments: An fMRI investigation. *Journal of Cognitive Neuroscience*, 18(5), 803–817.

Botvinick, M., Braver, T., Barch, D., Carter, C., & Cohen, J. (2001). Conflict monitoring and cognitive control. *Psychological Review*, 108(3), 624–652.

Bucciarelli, M., Khemlani, S., & Johnson-Laird, P. N. (2008). The psychology of moral reasoning. *Judgment and Decision Making*, 3(2), 121–139.

Ciaramelli, E., Muccioli, M., Ladavas, E., & di Pellegrino, G. (2007). Selective deficit in personal moral judgment following damage to ventromedial prefrontal cortex. *Social Cognitive and Affective Neuroscience*, 2(2), 84.

Cunningham, W. A., Johnson, M. K., Raye, C. L., Gatenby, J. C., Gore, J. C., & Banaji, M. R. (2004). Separable neural components in the processing of black and white faces. *Psychological Science*, 15(12), 806–813.

Cushman, F., Young, L., & Hauser, M. (2006). The role of conscious reasoning and intuition in moral judgment: Testing three principles of harm. *Psychological Science*, 17(12), 1082–1089.

Dehaene, S., Changeux, J. P., Naccache, L., Sackur, J., & Sergent, C. (2006). Conscious, preconscious, and subliminal processing: a testable taxonomy. *Trends in Cognitive Sciences*, 10(5), 204–211.

Foot, P. (1978). *The problem of abortion and the doctrine of double effect*. Oxford, England: Blackwell.

Frederick, S. (2005). Cognitive reflection and decision making. *The Journal of Economic Perspectives*, 19(4), 25–42.

Greene, J. D. (2007). The secret joke of Kant's soul. In W. Sinnott-Armstrong (Ed.), *Moral psychology*, Vol. 3 (pp. 35–79). Cambridge, MA: MIT Press.

Greene, J. D., Cushman, F. A., Stewart, L. E., Lowenberg, K., Nystrom, L. E., & Cohen, J. D. (2009). Pushing moral buttons: The interaction between personal force and intention in moral judgment. *Cognition*, 111(3), 364–371.

Greene, J. D., Morelli, S. A., Lowenberg, K., Nystrom, L. E., & Cohen, J. D. (2008). Cognitive load selectively interferes with utilitarian moral judgment. *Cognition*, 107(3), 1144–1154.

Greene, J. D., Nystrom, L. E., Engell, A. D., Darley, J. M., & Cohen, J. D. (2004). The neural bases of cognitive conflict and control in moral judgment. *Neuron*, 44(2), 389–400.

Greene, J. D., Sommerville, R. B., Nystrom, L. E., Darley, J. M., & Cohen, J. D. (2001). An fMRI investigation of emotional engagement in moral judgment. *Science*, 293(5537), 2105–2108.

Greenwald, A. G., & Banaji, M. R. (1995). Implicit social cognition: Attitudes, self-esteem, and stereotypes. *Psychological Review*, 102(1), 4–27.

Haidt, J. (2001). The emotional dog and its rational tail: A social intuitionist approach to moral judgment. *Psychological Review*, 108(4), 814–834.

Haidt, J., Koller, S. H., & Dias, M. G. (1993). Affect, culture, and morality, or is it wrong to eat your dog? *Journal of Personality and Social Psychology*, 65(4), 613–628.

Harman, G., Mason, K., & Sinnott-Armstrong, W. (in press). Moral reasoning. In J. M. Doris & the Moral Psychology Research Group (Eds.), *The handbook of moral psychology*. Oxford, England: Oxford University Press.

Inbar, Y., Pizarro, D., Knobe, J., & Bloom, P. (2009). Disgust sensitivity predicts intuitive disapproval of gays. *Emotion*, 9(3), 435–439.

Koenigs, M., Young, L., Adolphs, R., Tranel, D., Cushman, F., Hauser, M., & Damasio, A. (2007). Damage to the prefrontal cortex increases utilitarian moral judgements. *Nature*, 446(7138), 908–911.

Kohlberg, L. (1969). Stage and sequence: The cognitive-developmental approach to socialization. In D. Goslin (Ed.), *Handbook of socialization theory and research* (pp. 151–235). New York: Academic Press.

MacDonald, A. W., Cohen, J. D., Stenger, V. A., & Carter, C. S. (2000). Dissociating the role of dorsolateral prefrontal cortex and anterior cingulate cortex in cognitive control. *Science*, 288(5472), 1835–1837.

Mendez, M., Anderson, E., & Shapira, J. (2005). An investigation of moral judgement in frontotemporal dementia. *Cognitive and Behavioral Neurology*, 18(4), 193–197.

Mikhail, J. (2010). *Elements of moral cognition: Rawls' linguistic analogy and the cognitive science of moral and legal judgment*. New York: Cambridge University Press.

Miller, E. K., & Cohen, J. D. (2001). An integrative theory of prefrontal cortex function. *Annual Review of Neuroscience*, 24, 167–202.

Moore, A., Clark, B., & Kane, M. (2008). Who shalt not kill? Individual differences in working memory capacity, executive control, and moral judgment. *Psychological Science*, 19(6), 549–557.

Nosek, B. A., Smyth, F. L., Hansen, J. J., Devos, T., Lindner, N. M., Ranganath, K. A., Smith, C. T., Olson, K. R., Chugh, D., Greenwald, A. G., & Banaji, M. R. (2007). Pervasiveness and correlates of implicit attitudes and stereotypes. *European Review of Social Psychology*, 18(1), 36–88.

Paharia, N., Kassam, K. S., Greene, J. D., & Bazerman, M. H. (2009). Dirty work, clean hands: The moral psychology of indirect agency. *Organizational Behavior and Human Decision Processes*, 109(2), 134–141.

Petrinovich, L., O'Neill, P., & Jorgensen, M. (1993). An empirical study of moral intuitions: Toward and evolutionary ethics. *Journal of Personality and Social Psychology*, 64(3), 467–478.

Pizarro, D. A., & Bloom, P. (2003). The intelligence of moral intuitions: Comment on Haidt (2001). *Psychological Review*, 110(1), 197–198.

Pizarro, D. A., Uhlmann, E., & Bloom, P. (2003). Causal deviance and the attribution of moral responsibility. *Journal of Experimental Social Psychology*, 39(6), 653–660.

Rawls, J. (1971). *A theory of justice*. Cambridge, MA: Belknap Press.

Richeson, J. A., & Shelton, J. N. (2003). When prejudice does not pay: Effects of interracial contact on executive function. *Psychological Science*, 14(3), 287–290.

Smetana, J., & Killen, M. (2006). *Handbook of moral development*. Mahwah, NJ: Lawrence Erlbaum Associates.

Stroop, J. R. (1935). Studies of interference in serial verbal reactions. *Journal of Experimental Psychology*, 18, 643–662.

Thomson, J. (1985). The trolley problem. *Yale Law Journal*, 94, 1395–1415.

Turiel, E. (1983). *The development of social knowledge: Morality and convention*. New York: Cambridge University Press.

Wheatley, T., & Haidt, J. (2005). Hypnotic disgust makes moral judgments more severe. *Psychological Science*, 16(10), 780–784.

Chapter 7

Ethics in Everyday Life

In Search of an Ethics
of Personal Relationships

John Hardwig

John Hardwig *earned a PhD from the University of Texas and is currently a philosophy professor and department head at the University of Tennessee at Knoxville. He has written extensively on ethics and social relationships as well as bioethics. In this essay, Hardwig explores the implications of de-personalizing our personal relationships. By drawing a distinction between personal and impersonal relationships and by recognizing differing ethical obligations for each, Hardwig proposes an ethical framework to guide our most cherished human connections.*

Although it's been ten years, I can still see the student, hands on her hips, as she brought my beautiful lecture on Kant's ethics to a grinding halt: "Is Kant saying," she demanded, "that if I sleep with my boyfriend, I should sleep with him out of a sense of duty?" My response: "And when you're through, you should tell him that you would have done the same for anyone in his situation." What could I say?

We do not search for what we already have. Thus my title commits me to the thesis that we do not have an ethics of personal relationships. And that is in fact my view, a view grown out of incidents like this one.

More specifically, I believe that for at least the past 300 years or so, philosophers thinking about ethics have tacitly presupposed a very impersonal context. They have unconsciously assumed a context in which we mean little or nothing to each other and have then asked themselves what principles could be invoked to keep us from trampling each other in the pursuit of our separate and often conflicting interests. Consequently, I contend, what we now study and teach under the rubric of ethics is almost entirely the ethics of impersonal relationships.

Various explanations might be offered as to why philosophers have thought in terms of impersonal relationships. Philosophers have historically been almost exclusively males, and males have generally believed that the public realm where impersonal relationships predominate is much more important and worthy of study than the private and personal dimensions of life. Or perhaps the assumption that we are talking about impersonal relationships reflects the growing impersonality of modern society or an awareness of the increasing ability given us by our technology to affect the lives of people quite remote from us.

However, even if philosophers were not thinking about personal relationships when developing their ethics, it might seem that an ethics adequate to impersonal relationships should work at least as well in personal contexts. For in personal relationships there would be less temptation to callously ignore or to ride rough-shod over each other's interests, owing to the greater meaning each has for the other. Thus it seems reasonable to assume that the principles constituting the ethics of impersonal relationships will work satisfactorily in personal contexts as well.

But this assumption is false. An ethics of personal relationships must, I try to show, be quite different from the ethics of impersonal relationships. Traditional ethics is, at best, significantly incomplete, only a small part of the story of the ethics of personal relationships. Often it is much worse: basically misguided or wrong-headed and thus inapplicable in the context of personal relationships. In fact, much of traditional ethics urges us to act in ways that would be inappropriate in personal contexts; and thus traditional ethics would often be dangerous and destructive in those contexts.

We do not search for what we already have. I do not have an ethics of personal relationships, though I offer some suggestions about what such an ethics would and would *not* look like. Since my views about the ethics of personal relationships depend, naturally enough, on what I take a personal relationship to be, I begin with a brief discussion of the nature and structure of personal relationships.

But I'm going to cheat some: Throughout, I speak of personal relationships as if they were static. Although this is obviously a gross oversimplification, limitations of space and understanding preclude a discussion of the beginnings and endings and dynamics of personal relationships.

So what's a personal relationship? Personal relationships, as opposed to impersonal relationships, are of course relationships such as love, being lovers, friends, spouses, parents, and so on. But these sorts of relationships aren't always very *personal*, since there are all sorts of marriages of convenience, Aristotle's "friendships of utility," Hobbesian power alliances, and many varieties of quite impersonal sexual relationships. Consequently, we need to distinguish what are commonly *called* personal relationships (love, friendship, marriage) from personal relationships in a deeper sense. Even when they are not *personal* in the deeper sense, relationships like love, friendship, and marriage are not exactly impersonal relationships either. So I use the phrase "quasi-personal relationships" to cover such cases, reserving the term "personal relationships" for those relationships which are personal in the deeper sense I hope to explicate. I thus work with a threefold distinction between personal, quasi-personal, and impersonal relationships.

Let us begin with the distinction between personal and impersonal relationships. I want to say two things by way of characterizing personal relationships: (1) If I have a personal relationship with you, I want you. You (and your well-being) are then one of my *ends*. This would seem to be part of what it means to care for or care about another person. (2) If my relationship to you is to be personal, this end must be *you*—precisely you and not any other person. The persons in personal relationships are not substitutable. . . .

First, then, the idea of having you as one of my ends is to be contrasted with both sides of the Kantian dichotomy between respecting you as an end in yourself and treating you as a means to my ends. Kant would have me respect you as a person, just as I would respect any person, simply because you (all) are persons. To respect you as an end in yourself is to recognize that you have value apart from whatever use I might be able to make of you. It is, moreover, to recognize that your goals and purposes have validity independent of whatever goals and purposes I may have and to acknowledge in my action that your goals and purposes have an equal claim to realization. Although respect for you and your goals is a part of a personal relationship, it is not what makes a personal relationship *personal*, valuable, or even a relationship. Instead, having you as one of my ends is valuing you in *relation* to me; it is seeing you and the realization of your goals as part of me and the realization of my goals. This is not, of course, to reduce you to a means to my ends. On the contrary, I want you. You are one of my *ends.*

The second characteristic of a personal relationship—that I want precisely *you*—serves to highlight the difference between this kind of relationship and impersonal relationships, and also to further elucidate the difference between seeing you as one of my ends and seeing you either as an end in yourself or as a means to my ends. The characteristic intentions in personal relationships are different from those in impersonal relationships. It is the difference between:

> wanting *to get* something T and wanting to get *T from you.*
> wanting *to give* T and wanting to give *T to you.*
> wanting *to do* T and wanting to do *T with you.*

The first set of intentions or desires structures impersonal relationships; the second, personal relationships. There is a big difference between wanting to be loved, for example, and wanting to be loved *by you*; a crucial difference between wanting to go to bed (with someone) and wanting to go to bed *with you*. This difference seems to retain its significance whether "T" ranges over relatively insignificant things like taking a walk, having your breakfast made, sharing a ride to a party, and going to a movie, or over crucially important things like baring your soul, receiving love and emotional support, sharing your living space, and having children.

If I want *something* (as opposed to wanting something *from you*), I depersonalize you, reducing you (in my eyes) to an X who is a possessor or producer of certain goods. For it's these good things I want, not you; anyone who could and would deliver these goods would do as well. The language captures the depersonalization nicely: I want "someone who. . . ." It is when I want *something* and you become for me a "someone who" is the possessor or producer of this good that I reduce you to a means to my ends. This kind of desire and the intentions it gives rise to structure an impersonal relationship, though many of what are usually called "personal relationships" are structured by precisely this sort of impersonal desire. . . .

Let us now turn to quasi-personal relationships. These are the relationships that are commonly *called* personal, but that are not personal relationships in the deeper sense I have discussed. Quasi-personal relationships can be analyzed along similar lines. Suppose that it's important to me to have *the kind of friend* or *the kind of wife* who will help me with my work. In such cases, my desire or our relationship is not simply impersonal, for it won't do for me just to get help with my work—I want help from a friend or from a wife. In this intermediate case, the kind of relationship you have to me (wife, lover, loved one, friend, child) is essential to the structure of my desire; a certain kind of relationship is one of my ends.

But our relationship is still abstract or impersonal in a sense. I want something from you *because you are my wife* (lover, friend, child). I'd want the same from *any* wife (lover, friend, kid). Thus *you* are not important to the structure of my desire, *you* are not one of my ends. In such cases, the relationship I want must be defined (by me) in terms of roles and rules for those roles. I call these relationships quasi-personal. They are important for an ethics of personal relationships, for we often get hurt in precisely these sorts of relationships, especially when we believe we are involved in a personal relationship.

Two additional points about personal relationships are important for the ethics of personal relationships. First, although I talk mainly about positive, healthy personal relationships, it is important to recognize that *hatred,* as well as love, can be a personal relationship. As can resentment, anger, contempt. Hatred is personal if I hate *you,* not just some of the things you are or do or stand for, not just "anyone who. . . ." In cases of personal hatred, I may well desire your overall ill-being. Hatred that is personal rather than impersonal is much more thoroughgoing and often more vicious. Good sense suggests that we should get out of or depersonalize relationships dominated by intractable hatred, anger, or resentment. Interestingly, however, haters often don't get out of personal relationships with those they hate. And this calls for explanation. Such explanation must acknowledge that if I continue to hate *you* and to have your ill-being as one of my ends, there must be some sort of bond between you and me. *You are* important to me or I wouldn't devote my life to making *you* miserable. The opposite of love is not hatred; the opposite of love is indifference.

A second point important for the ethics of personal relationships is the possibility of one-sided personal relationships. Suppose I want *you* and you simply want to be loved and protected or to have a certain kind of marriage. Do I then have a personal relationship with you while you have an impersonal or quasi-personal relationship with me? Perhaps. But this surely is not the kind of relationship I will normally want. Such relationships are ripe for exploitation and tragedy. They are, in any case, almost always deeply disappointing, for we usually want *mutually* personal relationships. This means that not only do I want *you* and not just some producer of certain goods and services, but I want you to want *me*, not "someone who. . . ."

Although the logical structure of personal, quasi-personal, and impersonal relationships seems quite distinct, there can be tremendous . . . difficulties facing those of us who would know what kinds of relationships we have. Do I want *you* or do I want *something* (from you)? Do I want a relationship *with you* or do I want a *kind* of relationship with "someone who . . ."? Even if I think I want you, is it because I'm picking up on something that is *you*, or is it because you happen to resemble my childhood sweetheart, perhaps, or because you are so successful? If I cannot fathom my desires and intentions enough to make these discriminations accurately, it would be possible for me not to know whether I have a personal relationship with you, much less whether you have a personal relationship with me. These . . . difficulties notwithstanding, it may be *critically* important—both ethically and psychologically—to know what kinds of relationships we actually do have. Relationships are often made or broken by the issue of whether I want you or "someone who. . . ."

. . . Obviously, these characterizations of personal and quasi-personal relationships are based on my own intuitions, with which others may not agree. Fortunately, my argument does not require that my characterizations be accepted as necessary conditions, much less as necessary and sufficient conditions, for a personal relationship. It is enough for my purposes if it is admitted that many very healthy and beautiful personal relationships have the structure I have ascribed to them and that the reasons we often have for wanting personal relationships are expressed in my formulations.

Now for the ethics of personal relationships. My main contention and basic principle is that ethics must not depersonalize personal relationships, for doing so does violence to what these relationships are; to what is characteristically and normatively going on in them; and to the intentions, desires, and hopes we have in becoming involved in them. Particular persons figure essentially in personal relationships. But most ways of thinking about ethics invite or require us to treat ourselves or our loved ones as a "someone who. . . ." And this leads to many difficulties, both on the level of metaethical theory and on the practical level of ethical or moral prescription. . . .

"I don't want you to take me out," my wife exploded. "I just want you to want to go out with me. If you don't want to go out, let's just forget it." Motives, intentions, and reasons for acting play a *much* larger role in the ethics of personal relationships than they do in the ethics of impersonal relationships. In fact, the motivation of those who are close to us is often more important than the things which result from it. And even when actions are important in personal relationships, it is often because they are seen as symbols or symptoms of underlying feelings, desires, or commitments. Thus actions often seem worthless or even perverse if the motivation behind them is inappropriate.

In impersonal situations and relationships, on the other hand, we are much more content to allow people to do the right thing for the wrong reason and we are often even willing to provide incentives (for example, legal and financial) to increase the chances that they will do the right thing and also that they will do it for the wrong reason. I wouldn't, for example, be very much concerned about the motives of my congressman if I could be sure that he would always vote right. I believe that he should be well paid to increase the chances that he will vote right. But I would be deeply upset to learn that my wife is staying with me primarily for financial reasons. And I might be even more upset if her actions all along had been scrupulously wifelike. An ethics of personal relationships must, then, place more emphasis on motives and intentions, less on actions and consequences than most ethical theories have.

However, the motives that ethicists have found praiseworthy in impersonal contexts are usually inappropriate and unacceptable in personal contexts. Actions motivated by duty, a sense of obligation, or even a sense of responsibility are often unacceptable in personal relationships. A healthy personal relationship cannot be based on this sort of motivation; indeed, it cannot even come into play very often. . . . [It would be] devastating . . . to learn that your spouse of thirty-seven years had stayed in your marriage purely or even primarily out of a sense of obligation stemming from the marriage contract.

For similar reasons, motives of benevolence, pity, or compassion are also not acceptable as the characteristic or dominant motives in personal relationships. Acts of charity, altruism, and mercy are also, in general, out. As are sacrifices of important interests or a sense of self-sacrifice. Paternalism and maternalism are also generally unacceptable among adults in personal relationships. While it might be nice to feel yourself to be charitable, benevolent, or compassionate, who could endure being emotionally involved with someone who saw you essentially or even very often as an appropriate object of benevolence, charity, or pity? Of course, there always will be some occasions when you *are* an appropriate object of these attitudes, and it's desirable that they then be forthcoming . . . so long as they are viewed as exceptions. And yet, even in cases of great misfortune—if I contracted a debilitating disease, for example—I don't think I'd want my wife or friends to stay with me if they were motivated predominantly by pity or benevolence.

If even this much is correct, I think we can draw several lessons that point toward a deeper understanding of ethics in personal relationships. First, personal relationships between adults (and perhaps also between adults and children) are to be entered into and continued out of a sense of strength, fullness, and vitality, both in yourself and in the other, not out of a sense of weakness, need, emptiness, or incapacity.

Anything other than a shared sense of vitality and strength would lead to the unacceptable motives already discussed. Moreover, if I see myself primarily as a being in need, I will be too focused on myself and my needs. I will then tend to depersonalize you into someone who can meet my needs. And I will also be generally unable to freely and joyously give: Since I see myself as not having enough as it is, my giving will seem to me a giving up. (Does this mean that those who most need a first-rate personal relationship will be unable to have one? I'm afraid that this might be true.)

The fact that giving characteristically must be free and joyous points to a second lesson about the ethics of personal relationships: Characteristically and normatively, the appropriate motive for action in personal relationships is simply that we want to do these things. Persons pursue whatever *ends* they have simply because they want to (that's what it means to say that something is an *end*, of course). And in a personal relationship, I and my well-being are ends of yours. From this vantage point it is easy to see why motives should play such a central role in personal relationships and also why *wanting* to do the things we do together is often the only acceptable motivation: That motivation is the touchstone of whether or not we have a personal relationship.

Of course, this is not to imply that personal relationships must rest simply on untutored feelings, taken as brute givens in the personalities of the participants. Indeed, it makes sense to talk about doing things, even for the wrong reasons, in order that doing those things will in time change you, your feelings, and your reasons. But it may be even more important to point out that continual attempts to create the right feelings in oneself are also not acceptable or satisfactory. If you must continually try to get yourself to want to do things with me, or for me, or for our relationship, we must at some point admit that I and my well-being are not among your ends and that we do not, therefore, have a personal relationship.

Nor am I claiming that actions motivated by a sense of duty or obligation, by altruism or self-sacrifice, by benevolence, pity, charity, sympathy, and so on *never* have a place in personal relationships. They may be appropriate in unusual circumstances. But such motives and actions are a fall-back mechanism which I compare to the safety net beneath a high wire act. We may be safer with a net, but the act is no good if the net actually comes into play very often. Similarly, the fall-back mechanisms may, in times of crisis, protect us and *some* of what we want, but they do not and cannot safeguard what is central to personal relationships. Thus when we find ourselves thinking characteristically or even very often in terms of the motives and concepts I have claimed are generally inappropriate in personal relationships, this is a symptom that our relationships are unsound, unhealthy, jeopardized, decayed, or that they never did become the personal relationships we wanted and hoped for. (Compare Hardwig, 1984.)

A third lesson about the ethics of personal relationships can be drawn from these reflections: The distinction between egoism and altruism is not characteristically applicable to personal relationships. Neither party magnanimously or ignominiously sacrifices personal interests, but the two interests are not independent, not really even two. For your ends are my ends too. The distinction between giving and receiving thus collapses. In impersonal contexts, if I respect your (independent) interests, that may be all you want of me. But in a personal context, you will want me to be interested in your interests. For if I am not interested in your interests, your well-being is not one of my ends.

This does not, of course, mean that all interests will be shared, but it means I am interested even in those of your interests I do not share. (I may have no appreciation of operas, but knowing how much they mean to you, it is important to me that your life include them. Operas for you are important to me in a way that operas for others who may love them just as much simply are not.) Nor, of course, am I claiming that there are *never* conflicts of interest in personal relationships. But such conflicts are set within the context of the meaning each has for the other and are therefore seen and handled differently. In personal relationships, conflicts of interest are conflicts within myself, a very different thing from a conflict of interest with someone separate from me.

A fourth lesson about ethics and personal relationships is this: Because personal relationships are ends—indeed, ultimate and incommensurable ends—they cannot and need not be justified by an appeal to some higher value such as love, pleasure, utility, or social utility. Any ethics that attempts to justify personal relationships in terms of more ultimate goods depersonalizes personal relationships. It construes us as wanting these higher goods, not each other.

Nor can the relative merits of personal relationships be adequately assessed in terms of abstract values. Each personal relationship is a good *sui generis*. Irreducibly involving the specific persons that they do, personal relationships cannot be reduced to common denominators that would permit comparison without depersonalizing them. Although persons caught in situations requiring choices between different personal relationships sometimes talk (and probably think) about comparing them in terms of abstract common denominators, evaluating relationships in this way Platonistically reduces our loved ones to mere instantiations of forms, thus depersonalizing them and our relationships to them.

A fifth and final lesson serves to summarize and conclude these reflections. The ethics of personal relationships must see persons in nonatomic terms; it must be based on a doctrine of internal relations. People see themselves in nonatomic terms if they see at least some other individuals not just as means to their well-being, but as part of their well-being. As I suggested earlier, there is no way to explain why I value a relationship with *you* (over and above the goods I desire from you and from this kind of relationship) except by saying that I feel a bond between us. I have come to see myself as a self that can only be fulfilled by a life that includes a relationship with you. Thus I see myself, in part, as part of a larger whole that is *us*. This does not mean that I see you as either a necessary or a sufficient condition for my well-being. If our relationship ends, my world will not fall apart and I may know that it won't. But if our relationship does end, I will have to alter my conception of myself and my well-being. . . .

Granted, we must remember that relationships can be viciously personal as well as gloriously personal. And it does seem plausible to maintain that we don't need an ethics for times when relationships are healthy and going smoothly. But again, I believe that the plausibility of this view reflects the limitations of the ways in which we have thought about ethics. I would contend, instead, that we *do* need an ethics for good times and for healthy, beautiful relationships—an ethics *of aspiration* that would serve to clarify what we aim for in personal relationships and to remind us of how they are best done.

Moreover, even when personal relationships become troubled, strained, or even vicious, it is not always possible or desirable to depersonalize the relationship. And an ethics must not tacitly urge or require us to depersonalize our relationships whenever serious conflicts arise. Within a personal relationship, the depersonalizing stance will often distort the issue beyond recognition. If we leave out my love for you, my turmoil over how often you drink yourself into oblivion vanishes, and with it, the issue that arises between us. For I can acknowledge with equanimity the drinking of others who are not personally related to me. My concern is simply not an impersonal concern that ranges indifferently over many possible objects of concern.

Depersonalizing (or ending) a relationship *may* be the appropriate final step in the face of intractable difficulties. But I would deny that depersonalizing is always the best course even here. For I think we should aspire to learn how to end relationships without depersonalizing them. If we can learn to continue to care and to care personally for our past loves, friends, and partners, we can be left happier, less bitter, wiser about the causes of the difficulties, and better able to go on to other relationships than if we end our relationships in hostility, anger, rejection, or even the kind of indifference characteristic of an impersonal stance.

What, then, is to be done? If we accept my position that we need an ethics of personal relationships and that such an ethics will have to be different from an ethics of impersonal relationships, the field of ethics opens up and ethical theory turns out to be a much less thoroughly explored domain than we might have thought. For my view implies that there are vast, largely uncharted regions beyond what we have come to know as ethics. I have tried to point to this region, but I have hardly begun to explore it.

1.   We need to consider whether personal relationships are always better. If that view is correct, impersonal relationships would be only the result of the limitations of our sense of relatedness, and there would be a constant ethical imperative to personalize social contexts whenever possible and to expand our sense of connectedness. I suspect, however, that some relationships are better left impersonal and also that, because enmity, resentment, disgust, and many forms of conflict are much more bitter and intractable when they are personal, there are situations where depersonalizing is a good strategy. We must also understand more clearly exactly what depersonalizing a relationship involves.

2.   We need an ethics for quasi-personal relationships (love, marriage, friendship) when these relationships are not also *personal* (in the sense I have been trying to explicate). For it is perhaps in such contexts that people are most devastatingly used, abused, and mistreated. Still, quasi-personal relationships have important roles to play, both when they do and when they do not involve a personal relationship: Marriage is also a financial institution; our concept of a parent seeks to insure that children will be protected and raised, even if not loved; even living together is in part an arrangement for sharing the chores of daily life.

3.   We need some way to deal with the conflicts and tensions arising in situations involving both personal and impersonal relationships. Is it moral, for example, for me to buy computer games and gold chains for my son while other children are starving, simply because he is *my son* and I have a personal relationship with him? The issues about the extent to which one can legitimately favor those to whom one is personally related are, for me, deeply troubling and almost impenetrable to my ethical insight. . . .

4.   Then, when we have all this in view, we should perhaps reexamine our "stranger ethics" to see if we need to revise our ethics of impersonal relationships in light of the ethics of personal and quasi-personal relationships.

5.   Finally, we undoubtedly need a more precise understanding of what makes relationships personal, a better grasp on the values of such relationships, and a much more rigorous and developed account of the ethics of personal relationships. For even if the present paper succeeds beyond my wildest dreams, it has only scratched the surface.

Until we have done all these things, it will be premature to make pronouncements about what constitutes "the moral point of view."

Acknowledgment

This paper was begun in 1978 at a National Endowment for the Humanities Summer Seminar directed by Amelie Rorty. It has, in various versions, benefited from many helpful criticisms and suggestions from the members of that NEH seminar, from the Philosophy Departments at East Tennessee State University and Virginia Commonwealth University, from the members of Kathy Emmett's seminar on personal relationships, from the editors of the present volume, and especially from Amelie Rorty and Mary Read English. My many benefactors have left me with a whole sheaf of powerful and important ideas for revising, amending, and qualifying what I've said, but unfortunately too often without the wit and wisdom needed to incorporate their suggestions into this paper.

Eliminating the Provider Role

Pepper Schwartz

Pepper Schwartz *(1945–) is an American sociologist and sexologist teaching at the University of Washington in Seattle. Schwartz is a prolific writer and authority on the subject of sexuality and relationships. She wrote the column "Sex and Health" for* Glamour *magazine for seven years. She has appeared on such television programs as the* Oprah Winfrey Show, Dateline, *and* Dr. Phil. *She was the 2005 president of the Pacific Sociological Association and is a sexuality adviser for WebMD.com*

The linchpin of marital inequality is the provider role—or, to be precise, the provider complex, a combination of roles that give the man the responsibility for financially supporting the family's life-style and the woman all the auxiliary duties that allow the man to devote himself to his work. This division of duties is elemental to traditional marriage; indeed, traditional marriage is defined by it. Even if a man is called on to do some child care and a woman must work outside the home to help the family live better, the real responsibilities of traditional couples are clearly differentiated according to male earning capacity and female caretaking.

The ideology of traditional marriage holds that each sphere has its own honor and power, with homemaking and child raising theoretically as elevated and as important as money making. Money making serves merely as support for the real and consequential outcomes of success: a good home, well-reared children, and a fulfilling life-style. Male and female combine forces to achieve this end, and each gets a vote about family life.

In reality, however, the person who makes the buck makes the rules, or at least the key contested rules. If we could measure each partner's ability to get his or her own way, the provider would win. Research corroborates this belief. In *American Couples,* for example, Philip Blumstein and I found that decision making correlates with income: the person who makes more income has more decision-making power, and the more distance there is between incomes, the greater the control the high earner has.[1] Other studies have come to essentially the same conclusion.[2]

Defenders of traditional marriage offer a corporate metaphor, with husband and wife as equal stock-holders, but the reality is quite different. Sometimes there is rather shocking evidence that the low- or nonearning spouse has few rights concerning even what might be considered essential and elementary family resources. For example, the author of a study of working-class families found that working class women systematically had less access to family cash and in fact lived less well than their husband. Women were less likely to have a car, less likely to eat the same amount as or as well as their husband, and less likely to have similar discretionary spending money or decision-making capacity.[3]

Female earnings, thriftiness, or contribution in kind (producing needed family items such as homemade clothes) are often desired or expected, but they are not seen as replacing or competing with the male right and responsibility to be the provider. Even if the wife has more money because of a job, or windfall, or inheritance, both her husband and she may feel it does not entitle her to power in the relationship. Unless both male and female believe that women are entitled to equal power in the relationship, her earning power will be circumvented or at least modified.[4] One traditional woman I interviewed who had inherited a vast sum of money did not control it independently, nor did she feel she had any particular right to control it more than her husband did. Quite the contrary. She felt that because the man was the provider and the economic head of the household, it was his responsibility to handle all serious economic matters. As soon as the wife received the money, she put it in a joint investment account that her husband controlled. One heiress said, "He's the financial person here. I think it would show a lack of confidence in him if I kept money separate. I think he would wonder if I was not totally committed to our marriage—which I am. I really hand over everything but petty cash, and I didn't think of this as any kind of different category than our other money."

Even women who consider themselves the family accountant do not necessarily view themselves as responsible for the financial well being of the family. Many traditional women keep the family books, oversee investments, and control cash outlay. This work does give them some measure of power in economic decision making, but most of them serve as the family agent rather than as its CEO. They do not think of themselves as the provider or even coprovider; they think of themselves as a supportive team member.

Most women are not taught, formally or informally, to expect to be a provider. If they find themselves divorced or widowed and in charge of their own and their children's survival, they often feel a shocked sense of betrayal because this wasn't the way it was supposed to be. Even if they have been working, they are not prepared for the full weight of what the provider role really entails. They did not pick a job or make choices thinking that their salary or a salary they could earn would determine their life-style.

Despite high divorce rates and larger numbers of single mothers, modern married women are just starting to consider themselves as necessary contributors to the family economy—and yet they still do not consider themselves to be the person who is going to be blamed if the family doesn't do as well as expected. An increasing number of women are starting to earn the same as or more than their spouse, but for most of them, this is a happenstance that is good for life-style, not necessarily a role that is comfortable or welcomed. Women often resent being the more constant or higher earner. One lawyer I interviewed was upset because she had been made a partner in her firm before her husband was, and now he was considering leaving the job and taking a state job that paid a good deal less. She said, "I'm not ambivalent about my success; I'm thrilled. But I am highly ambivalent about Ray's thinking about dropping out—well, not actually dropping out but doing less than he's capable of doing. The idea of being the big earner is something I never really considered. I just assumed that it would be him or that maybe we would be both near equal. Now I can see where he doesn't have quite the drive that I do, and I find that unsettling. It's not a matter of money; it's a matter of me being the more responsible, the more necessary earner, and, honestly, I'm not completely comfortable with that."

Most men also feel uncomfortable with sharing or relinquishing the provider role. They have been socialized to provide for the family and have trouble reconceptualizing this responsibility. A man who loses his job or stagnates in a job that does not meet his financial expectations is troubled enough. When he cannot provide for his family and his wife *can*, a different sort of challenge to his self-concept arises. If this situation happens in a traditional marriage, with neither husband nor wife expecting an economic role reversal, it creates a crisis. The man will almost surely insist on remaining the main decision maker; however, the longer he fails to provide, the more defensive he may become about his right to be head of the family. Typically his wife will support his leadership for quite a while, perhaps indefinitely, but quite possibly his authority will erode once it becomes clear that he cannot fulfill the provider role. His wife may act less differentially, even if she is avoiding the full mantle of provider. He may become aware of the change, and his anger over his loss of status may make a volatile combination with her resentment and worry about being the high earner.

The ideology of the provider role traps traditional couples into an unequal set of standards of successful family functioning. But ideology is not the only way this role orients the relationship. The larger economic system makes the provider role hard to ignore or escape. The fact is that there are still more high-paying "male" jobs than female jobs. Near peers, couples who may start out trying to have a fairly egalitarian relationship, often find themselves sideswiped by the economic facts of the work force; if they want to get ahead, the best way to do so requires following the man's career possibilities, which might necessitate sacrificing the woman's potential success and earnings. The highest number of the highest-paying jobs still go to men. Even in professions that offer men and women very large salaries, such as medicine, the subspecialties that pay the most (e.g., brain surgeon, anesthesiologist) are still heavily male. In prestige professions, women are more likely to be lower on the status and pay ladder. In "pink-collar" jobs, women are usually in the nonunionized, more unstable, and less independent jobs. Many of them are jobs well worth leaving. In the pure service of economic self-interest, many couples who planned to work and stay "balanced" find themselves having to curtail one career to promote another. In the not-too-distant future, this tendency may strike men and women at random, but now the great majority of these decisions end up, sometimes quite unconsciously or reluctantly, putting the man in the provider role.

More often than not, the couple's plans for parenthood help make that decision. Women's attachment to the parenting role plays a part here, as does most couples' mutual intent for the woman to be the main parent. She is expected to stay home with the child anywhere from several months to many years, and she is the designated person for most child-related needs after she returns to work. If both the man and the woman agree that children are best served by being with their mother and that this philosophy requires an episodic relationship with the work world, then the man's role as the main wage earner becomes even more central. Both partners, in an effort to protect the family's central income, conspire not to interrupt or disadvantage the man's work; if a child is suddenly sick, the mother (or a mother surrogate) has to be available to take care of the child.

This arrangement can endure for years. A typical American has two children, and if the couple is financially able, the wife will stay home at least several years during each child's infancy and childhood. The majority of women return to work before their children are in kindergarten, but each woman's designation as primary caretaker modifies the possibility of her being the provider long after the children have left the home.

Given these attitudes and economic facts, it is hardly surprising that the provider role stays allocated to the man and that the provider complex results. Couples agree that it's the best arrangement and that they will deal with the consequences later.

Consequences of the Provider Role

Obedience

The provider role is not easy. It is in many ways a noble role. The man takes on the burden of family survival, and if he is lucky, or talented, or both, he can work hard to create a lifestyle for which his family is grateful and of which he is justifiably proud. The role is endless, though, because the husband can always provide better; he is never off the hook. Especially in countries like the United States that offer increasingly extraordinary consumer goods, elaborate houses and second homes, and electronic toys of fabulous capacities, no amount of money ever seems to be enough. Extremely high earners generally practice conspicuous consumption as proof of what they have achieved. Families with old money may merely need to use their name to get deference and respect, but more anonymous achievers tell the world who they are through their cars, clothes, and houses. Perhaps having a wife who does not need to work shows the world how great the provider truly is. The desire to have massive evidence of success drives workers ad infinitum to further achievements.

Doing one's best requires long days and evenings of work, times of worry and fear, and the danger of mental and physical exhaustion. Providers suffer and sacrifice to provide, and often they want something in return for this effort. At first what they want is appreciation; later they seek obedience.

Most traditional men and women would hardly put it in these terms. They might call it "support" or "holding up the other end of the household." But to be head of the household implies that all other household members hold a lower rank. And while a good and kind ruler should not incur resentment, occasionally the ruler will have to make unpopular decisions or unpopular requests. He might reason that his ability to keep the family going is dependent on the strength of his support services, so he does not think it unfair to get mad when those services seem inadequate. When the dry cleaning is not picked up, or a child or wife's schedule endangers a business commitment, the entire family (not just the provider) is at risk.

The price of the provider role isn't cheap. The more the provider provides or the harder he works to do so, the more he feels entitled to emotional returns and provision of services. One woman in a near-peer relationship complained, "Things have really changed since Max's promotion. When we were both struggling to get ahead, I'd say we both took care of the household pretty equally, and we were even more even on Elaine's [their daughter's] weekly stuff. But between what it took to get to VP and what it takes to maintain it, he palms off just about everything on me now. And what ticks me off most about that, is that unlike before, he doesn't feel at all guilty about it. He just expects me to do things he would feel apologetic about before." Another near-peer wife said, "I swore that I wouldn't be like my mother who was the only one in the household, including my father, who knew where my dad's clothes and underwear and things were. I mean he had no idea where his things were because he expected her to get them for him—and she did for maybe fifty years. She was the housewife, and she was supposed to do everything. He was entitled, you know. And somehow, creeping slowly up from nowhere, though it seems like it started almost against our wills, Pete has started to be more like your old-style husband, expecting everything to be done for him because he's so busy and important."

Economic Control, Psychological Backlash

Traditional marital wisdom has it that all money earned is family income. But interviews of traditional and near-peer marriages show that neither husband nor wife generally feels that way. Women who do not work or who earn much less income than their husbands feel constrained about acting independently with family money. Their fastidiousness is not shared by their husbands; many more men than women make big-ticket purchases without consulting their wife. They feel that the money is their's and they can spend it however they want. Even when there is precious little to begin with, sociologist Jan Pahl finds that, any discretionary income goes disproportionately to the male.[5]

A few traditional and near-peer wives try to retain a bit of control by keeping some separate money, but this is rarely a considerable sum unless the couple is quite well off. The ideology of marriage includes commitment to pooling money; keeping separate money implies incomplete commitment. About 80 percent of all married couples pool their money and resources.[6] At first glance, this might seem to be a far better deal for the wife than for the husband—she gets more than otherwise, and he loses some control over his earnings. Yet if we assume that the male contribution to the pool is greater, his money renders hers virtually unnoticeable. He ends up directing the use of both sources of money.

Women who have husbands who make extraordinary sums of money may live well and have so much discretionary income that their ability to spend freely is never questioned. Yet they too can be severely constrained if they exceed their husband's opinion about how much money should be available. Sometimes these controls are never noticed amid lush circumstances, unless the marriage runs into trouble and dissolves. Many wives at all income levels, but especially those who were very well off, are shocked to find out what their husband feels they are entitled to (or not entitled to) when the marriage ends. The checking account is closed, the charge cards withdrawn and the amount of money available is predicated on very different premises than existed throughout the marriage. The traditional wife or lower-earning near-peer spends pretty much at the pleasure of her husband, as a matter of his generosity and delight in enacting the provider role.

Many wives are aware that if their husband no longer wished to share the bounty with them, they would be in economic peril. This compromises more than an occasional unhappy wife's ability to leave her relationship. And it is an unspoken fear in even well-functioning marriages. Women who are economically controlled and deeply dependent cannot help being a bit afraid of a life without their provider. This cannot help but severely compromise how they act in their relationship.

Even so, the provider complex is a bargain that many women are happy to make. They either do not wish to be a provider or do not believe they could be one if they tried. They may voice serious resentment when their husband is stingy, untrusting, too controlling, or merely less generous than they think is appropriate yet do not generally clamor for an end to the provider role. They would like the provider's privileges to erode, and they would like more shared control and respect, but women who have neither been prepared for the provider role nor taught to want to provide approach it with caution and, often, fear and distaste.

With this lack of enthusiasm for change, it may seem not only impertinent but foolhardy to champion the cause of the minority fraction of couples who do away with this role to be peers. And it would be foolhardy and even cruel to encourage everyone to eliminate the provider role if marital contracts were enforced for life. As bad as the resentment gets and as controlling as the husband might be, many women are content to have less status, power, and respect as long as they and their children are economically supported.

But as the notion of equality spreads, resentments of the provider complex are hard to avoid; they build and build and start to undermine the harmony of the household. They bring emotional conflict and feelings of unfairness that buckle the foundation of the marriage. Tensions over cooperation and respect that are displaced by the provider complex can lead to the end of a marriage, with the wife at risk of being absolutely destitute and certainly much poorer. Divorce will cause an economically dependent woman to drop class status like an elevator cut from its cable.

The traditional wife in a provider complex may do everything she can to maintain the relationship, to the applause of conservatives, who believe that economic dependency will slow the divorce rate. This stance ignores two problems. First, even traditional women will take only so much, especially now that equality is so widely embraced. To the extent that the provider role works against modern women's requirements for love and fairness, marriages will be troubled. When a woman's lack of independence causes her to be a supplicant in her own marriage, honesty will be undermined, along with the emotional directness that helps marriages mature and become more intimate.

Second, for marriages that are abusive, the conservative scenario is a cruel one. If the wife is unable to provide for herself and is in a dysfunctional relationship, she may stay married well beyond what is in her own or the children's best interests. Dependency may force her to stay in a marriage in which her own and the children's lives are endangered.

Economic dependency can cause dishonesty between spouses. Countless housewives, or lower-earning nonpeer wives, resent the fact that their contribution is not appreciated, and they feel they deserve more than they get. They are part of a partnership and should share equally in the profits and the decision making. But they do not feel strong enough or secure enough to insist on a new economic deal. So what do they do? They open up a secret bank account or save up money for the spending their husband might not approve of. This "mad money" is testament to the fact that they think they cannot be an equal partner in deciding the way family money should be spent, saved, or gifted.

Quite a few traditional women I have interviewed have a private discretionary fund that their husband knew nothing about. Even more common—perhaps
almost universal—is that they told him that items cost more than they did—and
they kept the difference. Husbands often hear fictitious price tags because women
are not full partners and do not have the right to buy at the level they feel is appropriate. The more traditional the relationship is, the less likely it is that the husband
shops and has occasion to know what prices really are, and the less likely he is to
question her quotations.

Sometimes her hoarding of cash is not for herself. One traditional woman told
me, "I keep money back so that I can do for the children. He has this idea that they
have to have the same childhood he had. I can't make him see how old-fashioned
that is. So I keep some back, and I give them the allowance that their friends get."
These wives give little gifts of money to the children that the husband would not
approve of, and they collude with their children to keep the information secret so
that the system can continue. As long as the money never enters a joint fund, the
husband doesn't realize that a shadow economy operates in his own household.

Affluent wives use another way of getting around economic dependency:
They fight their insecurity or reward themselves for various insults or services
with a frenzy of consumer energy. They go shopping not as a utilitarian exercise
but as a way to feel good, as a way of punishing their husband, or as a way, sometimes unconsciously computed, of feeling that they are getting as good a deal as
they are giving.

These strategies have other than economic costs to the relationship. They
encourage deceit and dishonesty, erode the capacity for deep friendship, and insti-
tutionalize resentment. If the husband finds out, there may be anger, or patronizing
acceptance, or perhaps pain and confusion about why his wife would not be honest with him. Two traditional husbands have told me they know about their wive's
"little extravagances and caches." These upper-middle-class men felt bemused,
superior, and paternalistic. They *expected* their wives to "skim a little off the top"
and were rather proud that it could be done without economic injury to the household. But it hardly promoted mutual respect between the partners. This example
leads to the next consequence of the provider complex: its effect on husbands'
respect for their wives.

Male Lack of Respect and Ingratitude

Because the provider role polarizes men and women, it inevitably, albeit indirectly,
causes a loss of respect for women in their husbands' eyes. Men appreciate traditional female skills but don't respect those services as much as they say they do.
Even significant economic contribution doesn't get a woman as much credit as
she thinks she is getting. Studies have shown that women who work may think
they are making a great contribution to the welfare of the family and may believe

that their husband feels the same way. Men, however, rate the wife's work as less important than their own and as less of a contribution than the wife does.[7]

Both men and women consider the provider role difficult and demanding. Feelings and fears about responsibility are accepted as a major burden for the provider. It is this ultimate responsibility, beneath all surface issues, that husbands and wives admire and credit. All other labor, while appreciated, is seen as less onerous. No accumulation of effort ever seems to outmatch the provider's contribution. Husbands and wives typically agree that child care is hard and important work, but the fact is that it is considered just a part of a woman's duties, whereas the provider role is deemed to be all-consuming for the man. The message is consistent: Only the provider role releases a person from auxiliary labor.

The traditional and near-peer men in this study consistently underestimated the effort that goes into household work. Certainly someone who has never shopped for children's clothes or spent the day running around doing small errands may have difficulty believing how busy and time-consuming a day is when "nothing important gets done." Most of the middle- and upper-middle-class traditional and near-peer men interviewed believe at some level that wives have an enviable life, with more freedom and less anxiety than they have. Quite a few said that they wish they could have that life—but seemed to say so more for the interviewer's benefit than to express a true desire. When asked, "Why not try it?" the answer was that they could not afford it. Peer husbands, by contrast, did not think about household chores in economic terms. Many actually enjoy these tasks. Like many wives, they like to cook, take pride in their homes—or at least some part of the cleaning or home-making experience—and can think of only a few duties that they wish they could hire someone else to do. A comparison between peer husbands and other husbands on the subject of household tasks shows how little respect and how much avoidance traditional husbands display toward these duties.

Credit is more likely to be given in an area in which the husband has somewhat more participation in, such as child rearing. But even here credit is modified by how difficult he believes child raising to be, and how much he enjoys the subtleties of raising children. The proof of his regard is how much time he gives to his children and how much else he expects his wife to do. Only a few of the traditional husbands interviewed felt guilty about their , working wife's double schedule. They did not see the "second shift" as inequitable because they did not think it-was as difficult as she made it out to be. The provider believes that nothing is quite as hard as being the provider, so even when he thinks his wife is burdened by a second shift of work, he does not see her as being any more burdened than he is.

Wives are upset about this situation. Although some studies have shown that women who believe in the provider role feel that the load of household and child-related duties they carry is equitable, others have found that the weight of underappreciation and overload of responsibilities is hard on women.[8] Most wives who are part of the provider complex feel that they rather selflessly perform their myriad duties. Like the provider's job, their own work is never done, can always be done better, and carries with it high expectations. There is some compensation, of course, since women have been raised to take care of others; many love to cook and clean, and others take satisfaction in knowing that they are talented home-makers and caretakers. They can do without fair credit for their contribution—up to a point. They can bear being taken for granted when they receive some respect. When they do not, they become angry and unhappy even if they don't believe their bargain can, or should, be changed.

Traditional women want appreciation and help. What they get ranges any-where from temporary aid to a husband who is furious that his wife doesn't just do her job and shut up. In some homes, this rage can be an excuse for violence. A recent study showed that the most common argument preceding wife battering was about housework.[9] The homemaking role is a surrogate for the wife's display of obedience to and support of the husband, and any crack the violent husband sees in that picture can drive an angry and insecure man to a physical attack, an attack that puts the not-quite-low-enough wife reassuringly further down.

Most wives receive a far less destructive reaction to their performance of homemaking tasks, but that does not mean they like their treatment. Most wives have bitter complaints—sometimes cloaked in humor, sometimes just hurt and mad. A traditional wife who has been married twenty-five years says that her hus-band's expectations and complaints still make her angry: "When he complains that the towels aren't folded just so, it just drives me wild. He doesn't understand any disorder in the household. He thinks that making sure that two teenagers fold towels is a test of competent motherhood or something, and I simply can't stand when he does that sort of thing." A wife in a near-peer relationship is furious; she and her husband return home from work at about the same time, and he is upset when dinner is not well thought out, ready relatively quickly, or, most important, "hot": "We have continual dialogue about the importance of a hot meal with all the basic food groups. No, I'm not kidding. It's not enough I get something on the table; it has to be well balanced and eye-pleasing. Meanwhile, I am also sup-posed to pick up the cleaning on the way home and things like that which he will help with if he can, but if he can't, I'm supposed to. It's like he will help, he will cook, he will pick up, and he will menu plan if he can—but he doesn't understand what it is as a responsibility, day in and day out. He does his thing and thinks he's about equal. But he's nothing of the sort. And it is almost worse than nothing at all because then he thinks it gives him the right to complain all the time about his three food groups!"

Hundreds of behavioral science studies show that men do significantly less work in the household than women do—and not because of income, opportu-nity, or even employment.[10] One study showed that the *more* women made relative to their husbands, the *more* housework the wife did! The author concluded that women who suddenly earned more than their husbands were deviating so badly from their traditional role that they were madly compensating by doing reassuringly feminine work. Their husbands, embarrassingly cut off from their usual validation, shied away from the housework that a more secure, high-earning husband could afford to do without further damage to his masculinity.[11]

Whether women are earning more, less, or the same, the ideology of the provider sets up women to do "women's work" and men to "help." Men have specific boundaries. Their province usually includes heavy lifting, car maintenance, and lawn-related duties—work that can be done sporadically, perhaps over the weekend. This separate sphere operates even when it is quite clear that doing the job together would be a bonding experience that would help create the family attachment they both say they want. For example, one traditional couple both looked at me in amazement when I suggested that the exhausted new mother should ask her husband to share the nighttime shift with the baby. "Oh, no," she protested. "He couldn't do that. He needs his sleep for work. I can afford to be exhausted. He can't."

Distortion of Men as Partners and Persons

The provider role is an elemental part of how both the male and female rate the man's competence as a partner. Only couples with a drastically different approach to marriage are able to separate a man's worth from his paycheck. Peer men and women try to do it. The black couples I interviewed were most likely to make this distinction, particularly because both husband and wife saw black men as systematically excluded from opportunity through no fault of their own. But these are the exceptions to the rule. Most men and women see a man, his worth, and his work as intertwined.

This is a fragile base for a marriage since the role can be disrupted by outside forces. The economy can go sour, or physical disability can occur, or jobs dry up in a specific sector of the work force—or a man turns out not to be as talented or as successful in his chosen line of work as he, or his wife, thought he would be. If the provider role is a huge part of the husband's status and worth in the relationship, the marriage cannot avoid being devastated by the long-term inability of the husband to perform that role according to expectations.

Even if the man is doing well, expectations may rise higher than his earnings. Just as men are often unreasonable about giving credit for women's roles because they know little about them, women can be extremely demanding about what kind of income generation is possible because they do not understand the vagaries of the economic market the husband struggles to succeed in. Even if the woman does know that "it's a jungle out there," her view of the possible and the necessary is shaded because she is not demanding the same thing from herself that she asks from her husband. She, may be content to work, for example, for a medium salary in a job without higher earning potential. But she expects much more from her husband, and she is prepared to be a much harder judge of him than of herself because she and he have a different mandate. Over time, especially as he is drawn away from the family by the demands of his job, her focus on his adequacy increasingly narrows to the provider role.

The provider role both remains prioritized and is taken for granted. People tend to concentrate on what they don't have rather than on what they have. While both husband and wife have agreed that the husband should be mostly unconstrained in his pursuit of income, once that is not in jeopardy, women tend to take the maintenance of family life seriously. Almost all modem women want their spouse to be their friend, to be knowledgeable and active in the children's lives, to be romantic and communicative in the marriage, and to have shared leisure time with the family. Sooner or later, these expectations and desires are compromised by the pursuit of the provider role because the more dedicated the man is to being a good provider, the more it is likely that he will falter in his family and marital duties. Neither the husband nor the wife may know how much work activities could be cut back without endangering the family's income, and this ambiguity of risk makes it hard for men to make rational decisions about how much of himself can be given back to the family at any given time. It is also true that the better a provider he is, the more likely he enjoys his role and the world he lives in while doing that role. He may not want to be with the family as much as the family, or his wife, wants to be with him. If his wife does not have a job that competes for her emotions and time in the same way his job does, she will channel more of her self into family situations. Women are mostly unsympathetic about the auxiliary effects of men's attachment to the provider role—their desire to be among co-workers, in "optional" work or work-related activities, especially if those activities consume precious time that the family has to preserve carefully if family members are going to have time together.

The outcome is that traditional and near-peer women are in a catch-22. The provider role is duly emphasized, so much so that the man's adequacy as a partner rests on his fulfillment of his wife's expectations. But at the same time, it is seen as a drain and competitor for the family and marriage's needs and time. The difficulty of successfully orchestrating both the provider role and the family and marital role is rarely rationally analyzed. And the thought of deemphasizing the role as an answer to the conflict is all too rare.

Peer Marriage as a Remedy to the Provider Complex

People seek an egalitarian relationship because they want fair treatment, respect, and the right to have equal voice in creating and maintaining a fulfilling marriage. In addition, since the organizing principle of peer marriage is that partners should be best friends, they need to know each other's life and needs well and be able to cooperate without psychological or any other kind of hierarchy. In practical terms, these requirements rule out the provider complex. But more than pragmatics is at issue; this question goes to the definition of marriage. Peer couples are evaluating marriage according to the quality and type of time spent together; they are reinterpreting marriage.

Peer men and women came to reject the provider idea from a variety of experiences. Some come from marriages that failed due to provider-complex pressures on their marital esteem. Some realize that they cannot "have it all" if "all" means maximum income with devoted motherhood and parenthood. But however it happens, the elimination of the provider role represents a fundamental rethinking of marriage, success, and partnership.

How do they do it? What are the costs? From my interviews, I believe that there are some common principles that have to be established in order to subvert the provider complex. Sooner or later, these steps have to be taken. The first step is an ideological one.

Reconceptualizing the Goods to Be Provided

One of the easy ways near peers derail their hopes of an egalitarian relationship is their entrancement with goals that lead to the provider role. If the man is financially successful, the wife gives up all previous demands for his time and cooperation and releases him to as much success as he can provide for them. Peer marriage is different. In order for peers to share economic responsibility and shun the provider role, they must put the marriage *above* their economic success. Couples emphasize the joys of making a good home, as well as the rewards of treating the family economy as a true partnership. It can happen with both persons working—with each doing their fair share and with no expectations that one person is more responsible for family financial success than the other—or with one person working, if each spouse has equal claim to money, its deployment, and overall economic decision making.

Even in my relatively small sample, the scarcity of couples with a nonworking spouse tells us something about how hard it is to get rid of the provider role when only one partner is providing. On the other hand, the fact that there *were* a few—and that some of the others had experienced a period when only one partner worked—means that dual careers or two workers are not essential to peer marriage. More important is the desire to reconceptualize the goods that a marriage provides, achieving wealth and security not as primary goals but rather as by-products of a joint home and work life. If deep friendship and cooperation are the goals, achieved through a system of shared governance, shared responsibilities, and collective ownership, then careers and homes will be designed to sustain, not subvert, peer marriage. Marriage is elevated to its most lofty, most ambitious possibility: a partnership for love and understanding, not a support system for childbearing or male careers.

In the reformed marital model, no one gets all the credit or all the blame for financial success or failure. No one is exempt from child raising or household tasks. Although the division of labor, like income, may not be precisely equal, it is not greatly unbalanced No partner takes a disinterested or uninvolved relationship to the other's territory. There does not need to be a purely androgenous household in which sex role characteristics disappear, but the collaborative nature of the relationship ensures that each person will be strongly represented in the important elements of the couple's everyday life. Perhaps the best way to illustrate some of these modifications of the provider role is to describe a few couples who have done it.

Polly and Greg

Polly and Greg hold a strong commitment to equality, but for very different reasons. Polly, age forty-seven, was an active feminist in the 1970s, traveling this path because she abhorred her parents' quite traditional marriage and vowed that she would rather be single than be dependent. Her father, a well-to-do businessman, had run the family, and her mother almost always obeyed him without question. If there was a conflict, Polly remembered her mother backing down, always supporting her husband when there was a public disagreement over child-related issues. When Polly was older, she chided her mother for her continual acquiescence, and when her mother defended the hierarchical organization of their household, Polly was both sad and furious. She resolved to have a career and never to be subservient to a husband.

Greg, on the other hand, had never given much thought to feminist issues even though he was the same age as Polly and had watched the feminist movement grow on his college campus. The angry debates had never moved him much; he had grown up in an egalitarian household, and so the urgency of the feminists' cause was lost on him. His father and mother were artists, each represented by different galleries and both achieving regional success. Greg would never have called himself a feminist, but it would never have occurred to him to want a traditional wife or expect traditional wifely services. He assumed his wife would work and be his equal; he assumed that everyone would pitch in on household work and pick up after himself or herself. When he met Polly, her desires for maintaining separate control over money, for respecting each other's work and work demands, and for taking a mutual approach to solving everyday issues seemed a natural way to go about a marriage. He found some of Polly's anger about these issues justified, and they looked at some of the traditional relationships of their friends as unfortunate.

When they started out their marriage, Greg was finishing architecture school and Polly was in law school. They were both ambitious, and everything looked good for their future career success. In fact, both became successful. Greg became a principal in a firm that designed airports all over the world, and Polly was made a partner in her law firm. Both worked long hours and were rarely home, a situation that suited them until they decided to have children. They had two children in two years—and even a well-organized combination of pre-school and help from the local college couldn't compensate for the loss of the time they had for each other and the chaotic nature of almost every single day. They could afford the expenses that came with living a good life based on their considerable joint income, but they began to realize how little they were together, how much of their life was handed over to hired caretakers, and how more and more responsibility was subtly accruing to Polly as Greg's business travel grew, and it became impossible for him to share equally in family maintenance. Worse, Polly and Greg were getting on each other's nerves.

Finally, in a series of intense debates, they put everything on the table: her job and how much she liked it and how much income it brought in; his job, and its costs and benefits. They considered how well they wanted to live and the cost of that life-style; then they examined how much they could modify their existing standard of living and still be content with it. The result was a carefully considered compromise. They realized that since Polly was a partner in her firm, she had more flexibility than Greg's work would probably ever allow, so they mutually agreed that Greg would be the person to modify his career. He left his firm and opened a small, mostly one man architecture operation with hired consultants for specific projects. The first few years, he lost money; during this time, they relied on Polly's relatively high income. Over the next decade, however, Greg's practice grew to a respectable amount of work. Neither he nor Polly had any illusions that it would pay as much as his other job had—high-paying jobs in architecture are few and far between—but the change saved their peer marriage.

They have never regretted their choice. In fact, Polly has been thinking of following suit and joining a smaller firm, with even more leeway in her workday. The impact of lowering the intensity of their work has been, in both their opinions, "an amazing salvation of our lives." Greg says, "I was not only making lots of trips, but I would be gone for weeks at a time. That was fine before I was a father, but when Polly and I started raising a family, I knew there was no way I could stay in that firm. She" and I worried about trashing my career. The money was great, I was on a fast track, and it was the kind of work I loved. But Polly and I weren't going to have one of these marriages where nobody sees each other and Polly would have to be making up for all the things I didn't have time to do."

Neither Greg nor Polly feels that Greg has lost status in the relationship. Occasionally Polly will make the "provider mistake" of presuming Greg can do things for the household that she cannot and too many requests and expectations start stacking up, but then Greg will say something and work will get reassigned. Greg also feels that being around the house more has made him enjoy certain kinds of household tasks. He feels more connected to his home and realizes that the flexible time and his more limited ambitions give him the time to be a more complete person: "Now my work gives me flexible hours. Even though I still work maybe fifty hours a week, these are *my* fifty hours. Except for a few meetings a week, I can do my work where I want to. When I worked at my old firm, I could never get away when I wanted to, even if it was important. For example, when Heather fell and hurt herself at day care, they called Polly to come take her for X rays. Polly couldn't be reached, so they called me, and, of course, I said I'd be right down. I went to one of the guys in the office and told him why I had to cancel our meeting, and he acted like I was from Mars. These guys have wives who take orders, and they don't respect me when I tell them my wife has a career too and she doesn't do all the stuff. It's not that I felt I was going to be fired for taking care of my kids. I just didn't like feeling guilty or pressured because I was trying to carry my share of the load in our family."

Polly and Greg knew that when he backed away from the provider role and they decided to share the economic and household responsibilities of their family, they weren't going to get unanimous support for it. Greg's family was horrified. They were proud of his achievements, and they couldn't believe he was "throwing it all away." Polly's mother and father felt she was being selfish and that Greg would always regret his choice and resent her for her part in it. Polly's mother also thought that Polly should have been the one to take less time with her work and allow her husband to shine. Friends were a bit more supportive, but Polly could tell that few of them felt at ease about their lowering their economic ability and changing the direction of Greg's career.

Greg and Polly never have regretted their decision, or ideological tectonic shift. They came to realize that economic success and old fashioned providing were not as important as maintaining their family and their relationship. Even Polly, who once was driven by a feminist's need to prove herself as a provider, now is most interested in making sure that she and Greg safeguard their marriage: "I try never to lose sight of what this life is all about. You can get caught up and so excited about your own success that it is easy to get a warped view of what's important. But you need to step away from it, and you realize that the only thing enduring is the people you love. I've caught myself cursing that I have to go to a school meeting, not because I don't like them but because I wanted to finish some work. Then if I'm thinking clearly, I get my priorities straight and say, 'Screw the office.' I want to be there for Heather."

The fact that Greg had to curtail his career raises a disturbing general point. There may be some jobs that simply *do not allow* for peer marriages. Can an associate in a high-powered law firm, for example, be a peer spouse, while she or he must bill enough hours to be made a partner? In other professions as well, employees are expected to put in years of working long hours to prove their value to the company. Some corporations ask their managers to move almost every year and take several different overseas assignments in quick succession. The schedules of many medical specialties allow almost no personal time. Eventually the whole family may gain prestige, security, and money, and future prospects may be glamorous and exciting. But the price is dear. The job holder is unable to have the kind of flexibility and time that allows for parenting or daily shared experiences. The career runs the relationship. Occasionally, the job holder becomes so successful and powerful that he or she can change the job to fit family and personal goals, but by that time, the family may be grown up. Or, just as likely, by the time a person *can* change the system, he or she *doesn't want* to. By this time, the person has created a way of life and may no longer desire additional time with his or her partner or children. By choosing a job that is hostile or indifferent to personal relationships, a person unconsciously shapes his or her future possibilities for intimacy.

Greg and Polly consciously evolved a joint stance on how jobs and family intertwine. They are aware that the way they live in their marriage makes quite a few friends and colleagues uncomfortable. In fact, during interviews with traditional and near peers, I found that most couples believe that what Polly and Greg are doing can't be done. Both the men and the women worry that they won't be able to live with the psychological or economic ramifications of treating both partners as responsible in all parts of the couple's life. They also sometimes complain that they don't want a two-career life-style but that single-career couples are unequal by definition. Angie and Garrett are an example to the contrary.

Angie and Garrett

Angie has never had a paying job since she graduated from college. She came from a poor and chaotic family in which no one was ever available to help her or her sisters when they needed someone, and she swore that when she married, she would stay home and give her children what they needed. On the other hand, she is strong, intelligent, and independent, and she didn't want to be in a marriage that defined staying home as being a stereotypically junior partner in a relationship.

Fortunately she met Garrett, who wanted a total partnership, who was happy to have a wife who stayed home, but who did not feel that having a homemaker wife gave him any special exemptions from the duties of family life. He had grown up in a family with a non-working mother who was a strong and admired presence in the household. Garrett modeled himself on his intellectually acute and emotionally intense mother and hated his father's oppressive treatment of her. When he looked for a wife, he sought out someone with his mother's strength and vowed not to be a husband in his father's image.

From the beginning, he and Angie shared everyday duties. He went to graduate school while she stayed home with the first of their four children, yet he helped every day with their care. When he joined a research institute, he gave her control of what he absolutely believed to be their mutually held money. When he inherited some family money, that arrangement continued. There has never been a moment in the marriage that they did not counsel together about decisions. And there has never been a time when he believed the money he made to be more his than hers.

In the beginning of the marriage, Angie had a bit more trouble feeling that the money really was hers as much as his. But because they talked a lot and she had everyday control over it, it soon became a mutual responsibility. When Garrett lost his job because of the merger of his institute with another institution, there was no change in how they operated together. They decided to live in reduced circumstances rather than leave their city and take another opportunity, because they both felt that they had established a community and friends worth keeping. They were thrifty and could live decently with Garrett doing occasional consulting. Their emphasis was on their needs as a couple and a family, not on his career or their money.

If anything, money had a bit of a dirty feel to Garrett. His father was constantly giving himself a great deal of credit for being a breadwinner, and he harped on its importance, to the point that Garrett became rebellious. Because he identified with his mother more than his father, he found no dishonor in homemaking, and he copied her fastidiousness as a house cleaner and home organizer. He never developed a knack for cooking but became a superior cleaner and took great pride in his home. Even when he was working full time, he was a full partner in raising the children. He attended every school play, counseled their oldest son when he needed help, and participated in all the family conversations, an involvement that helped him feel that he knew his children as people and not just as their caretaker. He loved Angie, respected her opinions, and was highly sensitive to any dismissal of her from professional men or women. To Garrett, the only marriage worth having is one to a peer; he wanted to be neither oppressed nor oppressor, and he felt lucky to have found a way to have a family that didn't follow in the footsteps of a model that he had never liked and that he knew would never fit him.

Selma and Marco

Angie's and Garrett's willingness to live in reduced circumstances showed the seriousness of their commitment to the marriage and their evaluation of the provider complex. For Selma and Marco, the devaluing of the provider role proceeded and supplanted any desire to make a lot of money. Marco is a young man who wants to be a poet. He is married to Selma, who at age twenty-seven is two years older than he is. Selma is a massage therapist, and they live on an island within commuting distance of a city where she gets occasional work. They are caretakers for a doctor's weekend/summer place, which covers their rent, utilities, plus a small salary for Marco's gardening and handyman job.

Both have college educations; Marco has a teaching credential. But each feels strongly about having a life that revolves around internal satisfaction rather than jobs. Selma says they "are both spiritual people. We both spend time being in nature, meditating, keeping physically strong and in touch with ourselves. We've tried to do this in the city, but it defeats us, so it limits our options. We like being unattached to ownership, to things. We think that things keep you attached to things, and people keep you attached to people."

Right now it is Marco's job as a handyman that keeps a roof over their heads, but they both feel that at any time, the other person could be the one who is more responsible or successful at providing. Providing is not a valued role to them; economics is just a way to protect their combined freedom.

Neither of them enjoys home maintenance very much. They keep their house as minimal as possible and save their money to go on major hikes and outdoor trips. They don't expect much household labor from each other.

They have not had children yet, and they are a little afraid to do so. Both like children, but they are attached to their freedom from creating the kind of income they think might be necessary if they have a child. They go back and forth on the issue; their compromise now is to wait two years and see if they are ready then. They have no doubt, however, that when they do have children, they will take equal control of parenting, just as they have shared everything else in their marriage.

Marlene and Dennis

Marlene and Dennis are outstanding specimens of the yuppie genus. They are in their early thirties and live in a fancy downtown condo. They can afford it because Dennis has been a successful real estate broker, and Marlene does management seminars all over the country. Both have high salaries, although Dennis usually earns more. Dennis met Marlene after a brief, disastrous first marriage.

Dennis was already successful when he met his first wife. He was only in his late twenties but had already bought and sold several expensive properties, and he and his wife started their life together renting an expensive apartment and living what he thought was the life of the beautiful people. His first wife was a hairdresser, and they were constantly invited to fancy parties where people dressed to the hilt—and where drugs were common. He found out that his wife was addicted to cocaine when some very unpleasant characters presented him with a massive unpaid bill. He paid and then tried to get his wife some help with her addiction. It didn't work, and after what he refers to as the "most ghastly years of my life," the marriage ended.

By the time Dennis met and married Marlene, he was financially cautious. He was afraid that too much money floating around was going to cause some horrible excess to take over their life. He didn't have to worry, for Marlene was as thrifty as he was; but she resented the controls he put on the money, the accounting procedures he invoked almost daily, and her sense that she was not trusted to be a full, vested, and responsible partner. She knew the details of his first marriage and was sympathetic, but she wanted full equity in the relationship or no relationship at all.

Dennis came to realize that if he wanted his marriage to last, he had to relinquish his control and instead trust Marlene and the relationship. Eventually they became coproviders, a relationship that required a lot of independence. They kept joint and separate books—sometimes they found out what the other person had made only at tax time—but they kept track of the general economics of their life almost weekly.

Working out an economic bargain helped them with other emotional negotiations. When they decided to have a child, Marlene wanted to make sure that she could slow down without losing her status as a full partner in the marriage; she also wanted him to slow down a bit too. The change was almost impossible. As Marlene said, "We were both A types—tough, on the go, just want to get in as much as we can. So we knew we weren't going to turn into Ma and Pa over this. But I did want to make sure that Dennis wasn't going to disappear and change this relationship into something that wouldn't make me as happy as we've been up to this point."

Dennis loved his work and wasn't ready to modify it much, but more than anything else, he did not want a divorce. Neither of them cut back as much as less compulsively active people might, but they made concessions. They spent more time alone rather than with clients. They made time to do some of the things at home they never had done before. They made a decision to invest wholly in the condo rather than continuing to rent. They made sure that the baby went to both offices, not just one, and that both absorbed the costs for running the household and child care. Marlene spent more time with their child than Dennis did, and her income went down when she stopped traveling as much. But they took care not to hand over the provider role to Dennis, and both of them feel that while their relationship is not the same as before, the most important part, their partnership, is intact.

From Ideology to Practice: Controlling Money Together

As these examples show, attitude is far more important than any specific strategy. Nonetheless, some practical suggestions are possible, the most important of which is to control money as a team. This sounds like a traditional approach except that traditional couples do not act truly corporately as peers must. Some of Garrett and Angie's friends subtly (and not so subtly) told Garrett that he was a fool for not acting like a breadwinner. Garrett said, "When we have dinner parties and Angie speaks up very aggressively about how we're going to plan the future or what car we're going to buy, I get the distinct feeling—and I know she does too—that in some way, she's not supposed to be so unreverential to me. I think most people think it is the man's money, or maybe just that it's the person's money who made it, and they don't like the kind of power and interdependence Angie and I share. You know, I even see this with couples in which both partners work—maybe especially from them. I think some of those women don't think Angie deserves to talk aggressively about, say, how much money we will or won't give Adam at school, because she doesn't make that money. Well, we don't see it that way—never have. Its *our* money. Even our kids had to learn that."

One path to co-management of finances was through experience. Several individuals had suffered financial fiascos in their past that changed forever the way they approached family money. Nina was one of them. She trusted her first husband to take care of everything: insurance, savings, and investments. When he died at a young age from a heart attack, she found out that he was underinsured, that he had made poor investments for which she was personally liable, and that their savings were minimal. It took her years to dig out of the mess she found herself in. When she and Burke became serious about each other, she insisted on being a full economic partner in their marriage. Burke did not agree. He was a stockbroker and felt that he understood much more about money than she did and it was ridiculous for her not to trust him to make good decisions. They almost broke up, but eventually he came to understand that nothing less than full partnership would make her feel comfortable and respected in the marriage. In this case, only the women's intransigence could break down the provider tradition. If Burke had not been able to change, Nina would have broken up with him, and it was only that level of seriousness and commitment to her feelings about money that caused Burke to change. He said, "If I could have made her see the wisdom of my point of view, I would have. I mean I thought she was a real idiot about this, and we really fought about it. But I saw that this was going to be it if I didn't try it her way. And I guess the bottom line was I didn't want to lose her. So I didn't—and I guess it taught me a few things. For one thing, I think she was right. This is a much better way to go about things."

Keeping Private Money

Joint management of joint money is essential. But autonomy for each member is also important. Most people want some privacy and some independence of action. When finances are tight, independence becomes hard, or even impossible, and conflict occurs often because decisions with no good solution available have to be made all the time. The ability to do some private spending is symbolically and practically important, especially for women. Having separate money is one way partners feel that they still have a separate identity, that they have not so merged that they cannot find themselves. Some peer women designed their marriages precisely in order to make sure they did not lose their identity, to make sure they did not "dwindle into wives." These women have a recurring nightmare that one day they will yield just a little too much—do a little too much housework or day care—and find themselves a junior partner in a subordinate position. By maintaining some financial autonomy, they assuage those fears.

Some peer couples, in an effort to give each other leeway and a vote of confidence, keep at least some of their money separate. Sometime they deposit all of it separately. Seven of the couples I interviewed kept their money completely separate, with varying strategies for common expenses. Most had a house account they both put money into. Others casually tried to cover their share: Whoever went shopping paid, or one person covered the utilities and another the mortgage, for example.

Judy and Kenny kept everything separate because Judy was afraid of being trapped again in a relationship like her first marriage. She described her first husband as "a control freak" who doled out money in such small sums that she was constantly having to ask him for more. She found this situation debasing. And because her father was similarly controlling of her mother, for some time she felt that she would never be able to find a man who was not "a petty dictator." But Kenny, a high school teacher, had no intention of being either petty or a dictator. He met Judy at the school where they both taught, and from the beginning, their relationship was easy and friendly. When they moved in together, he respected her desire for independence although sometimes he felt upset that she thought he would dominate her if they pooled their money. But since they both made about the same amount of money, it was easy to keep their finances separate and collaborative. Over the years, they accumulated enough money to buy a house together, but even then, Judy insisted on drawing up the purchase as a business arrangement. Finally, some fifteen years into the relationship, Judy felt comfortable enough that she lost track of who owned what. Still, she liked keeping separate accounts, explaining, "I think that one of the secrets to our relationship is the fact that we don't have to check in with one another about most money issues. We can disagree, we can spend money differently, and we don't get into it. I am just so glad not to be one of those wives that has to say.

'Oh, I'll have to ask Harold about that.' I just could not have borne that in my marriage."

Kenny agrees that keeping private money has helped their relationship: "There are quite a few arguments 1 think we've missed because we didn't know we had them!" In a more serious vein he said, "I don't think any one person should control money. I never really wanted to. I would have done it because that's the way I learned it. My dad was a bookkeeper, and I just naturally thought the man kept track of all the money. But, honestly, it was a relief to be able to share everything."

Sharing Worlds

Eliminating the provider role requires more than just using money equitably; it requires sharing each other's tasks such that mutual respect is naturally encouraged. Sharing such mundane activities as doing the marketing, or taking the children for shoes is the way to understand the importance of these acts, both for the family and as acts of solidarity with each other. Polly always gets home late, so there is no time during the week for her to do any housework or shopping. But Greg doesn't want to end up doing it all just because he is home, and Polly does not want to end put him into the role of househusband, so they wait until the weekend or the occasional late shopping nights. And they do it together, which both see as companionable, well-spent time. There is some backsliding: Greg likes to do outdoor work more than almost any other household work, and he will try to trade it for less welcome tasks. He hated to iron so much that Polly finally took it over and reduced their ironing needs by about 75 percent by buying clothes that do not need pressing. But Polly's biggest gripe—and a common one among peer wives—is that Greg still likes to turn her into the guardian of who does what. She says, "I don't like to be the one who's always making sure we share the 'woman's work.' After all these years together, Greg still doesn't have a household executive's mind for noticing what has to be done—or at least not to my standards." Still, all in all, Polly is grateful and happy about Greg's household participation, which is one of the reasons Greg is happy to do it: "I get a lot of credit for everything I do—a lot from Polly's woman friends, a lot from her, of course. I'm sort of the local house hero. I actually find housework kind of soothing. I like having a clean counter; I positively glow when all the laundry is folded! [He laughs.] Seriously, it can be very satisfying. And I wouldn't feel good if I wasn't doing these things as part of handling our life."

Another peer husband put it this way: "A grim job isn't so grim if you do it together. We're both lazy—but why should only I get away with it? And you know, if you do, you know it. And if you keep getting away with it, you stop being guilty, and you start to feel you're owed that. And soon it's like something you would never do. I think that's an easy way to lose respect for the person you've put it over on."

A Final Admonition: No Larger-Than-Life Players

When you sack the quarterback, you demoralize the team because you have hit at the heart of its ability to play the game. When you sack the provider complex, you strike at the heart of marital hierarchy and also strike down the single most elemental aspect of traditional marriage. This sort of change requires revising not only the relations but also the values of the spouses. One newly elevated value is respect. Peer marriage makes it almost impossible to operate as unfairly as before. There is no one who can command the head-of-household role and hold it individually and absolutely. Polly's father always wanted the family to acknowledge their indebtedness to his largesse: "He found it necessary to remind us maybe daily about how much he was doing for us. He was very generous with material things, and he thought that covered all his responsibilities to us. I never felt that way. Not only did I get tired of his telling us what he had done for us lately, slaving at the office, but I would have gladly taken more time with him instead of us having a new car every year."

Getting rid of the provider role removes the main earner's need—and authority—to demand hosannas for his labor and puts both spouses in the same game. Couples devalue the provider role's mandate for continuing success; in return, they get back family time. Couples who share the provider ambition and go full steam ahead may at least do it together and are not living parallel lives; but there are pitfalls for those who choose to solve the provider dilemma by encouraging full-tilt accomplishment by both partners. Two real problems can emerge: No one is left for household tasks, and the provider role may encourage competition between the partners. Neither is an unsolvable problem, but both are important enough to discuss here.

The Challenge of Competition

Being the provider encourages a "master of the universe" mentality; conversely, being provided for may infantilize the consuming partner. What the provider role does not do is encourage competition between partners. One of the strengths of dividing labor into distinct gender categories is that both spouses can be excellent in their area of accomplishment, and they will be absolutely uncomparable to each other. It is possible that one reason more *pairs* of doctors or lawyers or corporate executives did not show up in this sample of peer marriages is that spouses in these professions were more likely to run their relationship according to more traditional rules—or that the senior earner made so much money, and needed so much work time, that equality and collaboration were unlikely. It is also possible that two ambitious people in similar and competitive fields make conflict more likely—and break-ups more common.

While several peer couples had a business together, worked in the same field, or even shared a firm or practice and were convinced this strengthened their relationship, interviews with other couples showed tensions caused by competition. For example, Lynn and Roger met in medical school on the East Coast. They were both extremely talented and successful; she went into academic medicine and began to get all kinds of honors and job offers, while he ran a more conventional medical practice. His income was much higher than hers; her reputation was far greater. It became increasingly clear to her that he was jealous of the attention she received. When she was offered a prestigious speaking tour to Africa and then shortly after to Latin America, he became increasingly sarcastic and distant. At the time of the interview, the marriage was obviously in trouble. She was going to counseling, but he would not go after the first session, and she felt that the marriage was probably not going to last. She was very committed to her work, very disappointed in Roger, and very worried that no matter what men said, they could not handle a successful and busy woman who did not cater to their ego.

Another couple, also doctors who volunteered for the study, were similarly defeated by competition but in a different way. Wesley and Margaret also met in medical school. They were the stars of the school and graduated number one and two in the class. She was number one. Both had intended to be surgeons, but he felt that they would never see each other if she pursued that specialty, so she went into internal medicine because she felt she could control her hours better. Over the years, he made a lot of money, and they were able to afford a luxurious life-style. He wanted her to be able to travel more and kept urging her to work part time, and finally she did, both because of his urging and her own sense that shorter hours would be good for her and their child. She said she needed the "opportunity to get out from the extreme pressure I was feeling, and take some time for myself. I'm not going to look back at these years and regret that I missed important events in my kid's life."

She did not feel that her husband was competitive with her personally, but she did feel he had become competitive for her time and resented her work because she was not free when he was. He had started devaluing what she could contribute at the clinic versus what she owed to her home and family. Still, she thought she had made a good choice in terms of her family and her marriage. Nevertheless, as she talked about her marriage and this new bargain in it, it seemed clear that she no longer approached the relationship on equal terms. When she talked about an extravagant purchase, she said, "Last time we went to Dallas, Wesley said I could spend $500 on a pair of boots, which we both knew was outrageous." She meant to be talking about some of the fun they were having together but a phrase like "Wesley said I could . . ." indicates a loss of peer status. When a spouse talks about the other's giving permission for anything, something very important has been lost. Margaret may have saved her marriage by changing her career, but it is not clear whether she got the life—or relationship—she wanted. Whether the competition between a husband and wife is a direct clash of egos or merely competition over how much of each other they will have, it has to be solved in a way that keeps equality intact.

The Challenge of Emotional Contribution

In traditional relationships, the division of labor is clear. Part of the woman's assignment is the emotional health of the family and the marriage. She is trained for it. From early on, little girls learn how to be "nice," to be acutely aware of the feelings of others, and to be a caretaker. They are more likely than boys to have babysitting experience, to learn how to cook and to clean—in short, to learn the homemaking and interpersonal skills that make them attractive as partners.

When the provider role is shared, considerably less time is available for caretaking, and the conditions of the work world often distract women from their instincts to nurture and caretake. The experiences of employment may also mute previous characteristics; being a manager or an employee requires an additional layer of skin. Not everyone is nice or fair or friendly. Workers learn that many, perhaps most, of the people they work with do not care about them and that kindnesses may not be reciprocated or appreciated. They may even be seen as a sign of weakness. People who work outside the home get a little tougher because they have to.

The combination of learning survival skills and not having the time or presence of mind to caretake can reduce the general level of emotional sharing in a marriage. Although women have now experienced several decades of work force culture and success in an often impersonal though not necessarily impartial workplace, men have had considerable less practice at taking up their share of the emotional work at home. Even the most well-meaning man may find that his wife feels he is not coming up with his share of the emotional labor that she and the children require and that she is providing to him.

If the couple has time together and if the man spends a lot of time with his children, some of these skills will develop naturally. But if the couple is in a fast-track world, both being intense coproviders, the chance that the male will be an adequate contributor to the emotional well-being of the household is small. Like any other group of skills, intuition, thinking of someone's else's needs, sensing their state of mind, remembering important dates and anniversaries, attending to the children's psychological comfort—all take time to learn and practice to perfect. Coproviders run severe risks if they think that these skills are any less essential to the success of their relationship than economic contribution, or if they think that emotional work somehow will get done in the tiny bits of time they allot for interpersonal interaction. In a traditional relationship, almost all of this emotional work rests on the woman's capabilities. The relationship rises or falls with her skill at keeping everyone communicating, interacting, and feeling good about themselves and others. Theoretically, a peer couple will have two people who can do this for the marriage and for the family. Theoretically, everyone in a peer marriage household benefits from the additional expressive contributions of the husband.

In relaxed households, the peer husband who has taken time to be with the family and the wife who is not running as fast as she can provide emotional comfort and acuity. But the pitfall for the fast trackers is present and real.

Rosemary and Buck have a peer marriage but nearly lost what they set out to construct because they put the relationship on automatic pilot. Both were social workers in the mental health field, with demanding schedules. Both directed large programs and also worked with clients. They worked extraordinarily long days and felt that life and their relationship were good until their twelve-year-old son, David, started hanging out with teenagers who were always in trouble. These episodes scared Rosemary and Buck, and they realized that they had not been spending enough time with David or, it turned out, with each other to give the relationship the emotional balance and ballast that it needed. They had been putting all their emotional talent into their work and hardly any of it into the family. They decided to cut away the nonessentials of their jobs, designed after-school activities to do with David, including counseling, and started getting home in time for dinner. Buck said, "We had a real scare, a real come-to-Jesus moment. It was the time to figure out what we were about, where our priorities were. And there was no question. What we didn't realize is how we'd let our work overwhelm our family needs. It was awful, embarrassing, scary. Now I'm spending a lot more time just talking with David, with Rosemary, with everybody."

A Final Word

The provider role shapes a marriage. Traditional wives who do not work or who act as minor financial contributors and do not have equal economic control in the marriage may think they are full partners in the relationship, yet in conversation, their husbands dismiss them more or do not even refer to them. These wives are more likely to be permission seeking, more likely not to try to extend a strong voice beyond the agreed-upon parameters of their territory in the relationship. They may be given complete control over the children, or household expenses, or even culture and social life, but the man retains veto power. This is not to say there are not good and satisfying provider role relationships. Many couples who are in such relationships do not experience them as lacking anything; if they do sense deficiencies, they would not put the blame on the fact that the man is the provider. Nevertheless, any comparison of these marriages with those that avoid the provider complex, with husband and wife sharing economic and family responsibility, puts the differences between traditional and peer couples in dramatic perspective. The peers are partners. They talk more together. They talk about more subjects together. At their most successful, the men can talk "women's language": the language of people, children, daily duties, and emotional issues. The women can talk "men's talk"; they are full partners in financial planning, spending, keeping the family afloat, and making whatever economic compromises need to be made to bring priorities and finance together. Men in these relationships do not feel totally responsible for economic success. Men and women are more broadly evaluated. By eliminating the provider role and removing what has historically been our highest external definition of success, the couple reaches for idealism. Their real ambition is to be intimate, to create and be a best friend. Economic success cannot be used to justify the family or the marriage. These couples construct a fairer world and perhaps a harder test of love and character.

Peer spouses think of their economic and household collaboration as a major advance, something that makes them irreplaceable to each other. They are members of a team who need each other. And in today's world, the combination of need, valued contribution, and emotional connection is a solid foundation for a strong marriage.

Notes

1. Blumstein and Schwartz, *American Couples*.
2. Marsha Millman, *Warm Hearts and Cold Cash* (New York: The Free Press, 1991); Jan Pahl *Money and Marriage* (New York: St. Martin's Press. 1989).

3. Jan Pahl, *Money and Marriage*.

4. Philip Blumstein and Pepper Schwartz, "Money and Ideology: Their Impact on Power and the Division of Household Labor," in Rae Lesser Blumberg, Ed., *Gender, Family and Economy* (Newbury Park, Calif.: Sage, 1991).

5. Jan Pahl, *Money and Marriage*.

6. Blumstein and Schwartz, *American Couples*; also Judith Treas, "Transaction Costs and the Economic Organization of Marriage," *American Sociological Review*, Vol. 58, No. 5 (Oct. 1993), pp. 723–734.

7. Sue Sprecher and Pepper Schwartz, "Equity and Balance in the Exchange of Contributions in Close Relationships," in Melvin Lerner and Gerald Mikula. *Entitlement and the Affectional Bond* (New York: Plenum, 1993).

8. P. England, and G. Farkas, *Households, Employment, and Gender: A Social, Economic and Demographic View* (New York: Aldine de Gruyter. 1986). Also: Janice Steel and Karen Weltman, "Marital Inequality: The Importance of Resources, Personal Attributes, and Social Norms on Career Valuing and the Allocation of Domestic Responsibilities." *Sex Roles Journal*, Vol. 24, No. 314 (1991). Also Philip Blumstein and Pepper Schwartz, "Money and Ideology: Their Impact on Power and the Division of Household Labor." in Rae Lesser Blumberg. Ed., *Gender, Family and Economy* (Newbury Park, Calif: Sage, 1991).

9. "Sexual Static," in *Health Care Forum* (Health Care Forum, May–June 1987), pp. 25–30.

10. Blumstein and Schwartz, *American Couples*.

11. Julie Brines, "Gender, Economic Dependence and the Division of Labor at Home." *American Journal of Sociology*, forthcoming, 1994; also "The Exchange Value of Housework," *Rationality and Society*, Vol. 5 (1993), pp. 302–340; also Julie Brines and Karen Joyner "The Ties That Bind: Principles of Stability in the Modern Union," manuscript under review, 1994.

Parental Authority and the Rules of the Family

William Damon

William Damon *is a renowned researcher on moral development. He is Professor of Education and the Director of the Center on Adolescence at Stanford University. He has previously taught at Clark University and Brown University. Damon is the editor-in-chief of* New Directions for Child and Adolescent Development *and the editor of the* Handbook of Child Psychology *(1998 and 2005 editions). He is also a Senior Fellow at the Hoover Institution on War, Revolution, and Peace and a member of the national Academy of Education. Among his many publications are* Good Work: When Excellence and Ethic Meet *(2001),* Greater Expectations *(1996), and* The Moral Child: Nurturing Children's Natural Moral Growth *(1988), from which this chapter is taken.*

A family is a small social system; and, like any social system, families have rules of conduct. In many cases, family rules are similar to those of society at large, except that family rules are not written into any formal legal code. Families, like societies at large, have prohibitions against disorder, dishonesty, theft, violence, and incest. Acts of cruelty and hostility breach familial as well as societal regulations. In both family and society, such offenses are discouraged through sanctions like disapproval and punishment.

For children in a family, parents act as the chief enforcers of social regulation. Parents obviously have a great deal of power over children, particularly when the children are young: not only do parents possess the advantages of strength, size, and competence over children, but they also are needed by their children for protection and nurturance. Consequently, parents are in a good position to uphold family rules and to administer sanctions for violations of these rules.

Because family rules often overlap with society's rules, parental enforcements present a double message to children: this is prohibited here and this is wrong in general. In this way, the child's first encounter with societal regulations is likely to occur in the home. A parent's command to stop hitting little sister communicates a sanction against violence, a sanction that the child soon realizes applies well beyond the scope of the family.

For this reason, the parent (or the parent substitute) has a critical and irreplaceable role in the child's moral development. It is the parent who first introduces the child to the laws and logic of the social order. In addition to informing children about sanctions within and beyond the family, this means enforcing these sanctions and communicating to the child their social purpose.

But introducing children to the social order means more than just getting them to obey certain rules. It also means inculcating in children an abiding respect for social order itself. All social systems have principles of hierarchy and regulation that are essential for the systems' functioning as well as their cohesion. If a social system is to work well, these principles must be known, respected, and consistently implemented. Roles and responsibilities must be distributed and members of the social system must cooperate to accept their own allotted positions. This means that authority must be assumed by some and deferred to by others. These roles may be renegotiated over time. Nevertheless, barring a revolution, there must be some shared willingness to follow, at least for a time, the rules and regulations prescribed by the present social order.

Parents' authority and the shared rules of conduct maintained by their authority are essential both for the family's social functioning and for the child's growing moral awareness. The child's respect for this authority is the single most important moral legacy that comes out of the child's relations with the parent. (Other legacies—such as a belief in justice and other moral values—are also crucial, but they are not as much confined to the domain of parental influence). The child's respect for parental authority sets the direction for civilized participation in the social order when the child later begins assuming the rights and responsibilities of full citizenship.

Although parents have at their disposal the power to punish, force is by no means a parent's only means of getting children to respect authority or to comply with social rules. The closely affectionate relationship that most parents enjoy with their children normally induces an inclination to cooperate. Studies by Mary Ainsworth and her colleagues show that young children securely attached to their parents are the ones most likely to comply with family rules.[1] These children actively seek and accept the adult's guidance. In this sense, secure children obey voluntarily from "within" the relationship, rather than out of coercion or fear.

Aside from punishment and love, parents induce good behavior in their children through such strategies as appeals to reason, cajoling, and outright bribery. As an example with dietary rather than moral significance, many parents customarily will hold their children's dessert in ransom until the children have downed at least a token portion of leafy green vegetable. Incentives for moral behavior within the family are structured in much the same way—as are those in the world outside.

The family, then, is the first context for learning society's rules and the obligation to obey. Consequently, it is the primary agent of "socialization" during the
child's early years. But not all families socialize children in the same way. There
is great variation from one family to the next in how children are treated, raised,
and communicated with, as well as in how they are induced to follow social rules.
Such variation accounts for important differences between children in their later
propensities towards moral and not-so-moral behavior.

Through conversations, confrontations, and other exchanges with parents and
siblings, children at an early age discover the social rules implicit in family life.
Judy Dunn and her colleagues have observed toddlers in some of their first intro-
ductions to family rules.[2] Two of Dunn's examples are as follows:

1. Child (16 months) throws biscuit on the floor.

    MOTHER: "What's that? Biscuit on the floor? Where biscuits aren't supposed to be.
        Isn't it?"

    Child looks at mother and nods.

    MOTHER: "Yes. Now what's all this?" (points to toothbrush and toothpaste on
        kitchen table). "Who brought that downstairs?"

    Child looks at mother and smiles.

    MOTHER: "Yes, you did. Where does this live?"

    CHILD: "Bath."

2. Sibling of child (24 months) draws on a piece of jigsaw puzzle. Sibling shows
    mother.

    SIBLING (to mother): Look.

    MOTHER (to sibling): "You're not supposed to draw on them. You should know
        better. You only draw on pieces of paper. You don't draw
        on puzzles."

    CHILD (to mother): "Why?"

    MOTHER (to child): "Because they aren't pieces of paper."

    CHILD: "Naughty."

    MOTHER: "Yes that is a naughty thing to do."[3]

Both of these examples show parents instructing children on common family
rules. The two rules in question are "Put things where they belong," and "Don't
write on things that aren't pieces of paper." In the first example, the child under
observation is the transgressor, whereas in the second example the observed child
only witnesses and comments upon on a sibling's transgression. What the two cases
have in common is that in both a child is familiarized with an unwritten principle

of household regulation. Dunn's observations show an enormous amount of such learning during the second year of life.

How do parents go about making their children aware of unwritten rules? The first example reveals a technique that Dunn found to be among the most common and effective among the families that she observed. "Rather than simply stating the rule, the comments (pointing out the rule) were usually in question form, as if the mothers expected and made 'space' for an answer."[4] Through this kind of Socratic "conversation," the child is led first to giving an example of the rule and then to formulating it in a general way.

From the age of sixteen months onwards, parents engage their children in such conversations with increasing frequency. Where appropriate, the parent may also justify the rule in terms of a sibling's feelings. For example, a parent may refer to a rule against taking another person's things and explain it by saying that the child's sibling would be upset if the child used the sibling's toy without asking first. Dunn believes that this too is a highly effective strategy for helping children understand and accept social rules. Clearly it supports the child's own natural empathic leanings. In a follow-up study, Dunn and Penny Munn found that children who acted most socially mature (with more conciliatory behavior, less teasing with peers, and less prohibited behavior) were children whose parents were most likely to communicate with about rules and the feelings of siblings.[5]

The parent is not the only socializing agent in the family. Siblings often take part in reprimanding one another for breaking rules. Sometimes this is done out of genuine dismay at a forbidden act; other times it is simply part of the child's ongoing efforts to tease a sibling. In the second example above, it seems that as soon as the child has learned the rule under discussion, he joins the mother's efforts to enforce it. The entire family is a network in which any member can place pressure on any other member to comply with accepted family regulations.

Not all family communications lead in fact to compliance. Especially when they are young, children tend to ignore messages that they do not want to hear, such as a demand to stop performing a pleasurable but prohibited act. They are, however, well tuned in to verbal and facial emotional expressions, and respond quickly to anger on the part of a parent. By the second year of life children actively monitor their parents' faces and voices for emotional signals.[6] Communications highly charged with affect are likely to draw their attention.

Dunn reports that the children she observed became most acutely aware of a rule when it was conveyed by the parent with intense negative affect. Similarly, observational studies by Robert Emde have shown that before age two, children generally ignore their parents' commands unless the commands are vigorously pressed with a strong emotional overtone.[7] It is not until well after this time, when children themselves have internalized family rules, that there is a reliable tendency to comply voluntarily. And even then, as every parent knows, such compliance is hardly perfect.

Parental emotions like anger and disgust play a role in communicating to children the urgency of following important rules. But this does not mean that greater displays of parental affect lead to ever greater rule following. Continual, strident expressions of anger are likely to bring about just the opposite. As they become commonplace, such expressions lose their ability to arouse attention; and they create an unruly atmosphere that leads to more rather than less disorder in the family. Further, children are likely to imitate parental outbursts in their own behavior, again to the detriment of household harmony and order. Far more effective for capturing the child's attention in a productive manner are "modulated" emotional expressions that follow directly from genuine provocations on the part of the child. Such modulated expressions not only convey a precise message about wrongdoing and its consequences, but they are also within an affective range that the child can tolerate without tuning out.

Even within middle-class Western family life, parents vary widely in how they communicate about rules of conduct and express emotional reactions to breaches. When variations of economic background, ethnicity, and culture are considered, still sharper differences emerge in these and other child-rearing practices. Some of these differences greatly affect the quality and substance of children's morality. They also provide us with clues about which kinds of social environments may be most conductive to children's moral growth.

Some parents are highly punitive, emphasizing the sanctions that follow prohibited behavior. Others lean more towards persuasion of one kind or another. Some parents regularly "set limits" in order to restrict their children's behavioral choices; others permit their children to express their own values and desires freely. Such differences can be extreme or slight. They can combine with one another, and with other child-rearing patterns, to create a particular style of moral discourse in each family. In some families there is an overall consistency in the child-rearing practice; in others, styles are irregular and inconsistent: families also vary in the extent to which they conduct themselves in a stable as opposed to a fluctuating and inconsistent manner.

There is also much variation in the way that parents act from situation to situation. A father who has just lost his job may be more punitive than during times when he feels fewer career pressures. A child who is sick may find her misdeeds greeted more tolerantly than when she was well. Further, the same parents may treat a first-born differently than a second-born child; or a male child differently than a female child; or a shy child differently than an aggressive one.

It is clear from all this that no two children encounter the same pattern of family experience. Since moral rules and values are communicated to young children primarily in the family context, this means that there must be great variation in how children are introduced to these values. There is also great variation in the specific composition of the values that are introduced. Studies with young children and their families have shown that all of these variations can seriously affect the quality and course of children's moral development. But the moral influence of family child-rearing style is not always the same as popular preconceptions might lead us to believe. A good example of this concerns the much-discussed dimension of parental permissiveness.

In the popular culture, much is made of how permissive or restrictive parents are in enforcing behavioral standards. Depending upon which editorial page columnist one reads, all of our society's current shortcomings can be blamed either on the leniency or strictness with which we have raised our children. In fact, each end of the permissiveness/restrictiveness polarity has gone in and out of vogue several times during the past century. In the course of such shifts in fashion, the media—sometimes inaccurately—have taken child care experts such as John D. Watson and Benjamin Spock to represent one or the other pole. These controversies generally assume that the tone of a child's moral character will be set by the relative permissiveness or restrictiveness of a parent.

Scientific research challenges this assumption. Permissiveness and restrictiveness may play a part within a larger context of parental styles, but in themselves they do not have a direct or predictable influence on children's morality. For example, one of the early studies on this topic, conducted by Robert Sears and his colleagues at Stanford, showed that the relative permissiveness of a parent did not have a noticeable effect on a child's tendency to be aggressive.[8] Only when combined with the parent's degree of punitiveness did permissiveness make a difference. Parents who were *both* permissive and punitive tended to have markedly more aggressive children than either parents who were one and not the other or those who were neither. This combination signifies a parental style that is generally lenient, paying little attention to children's breaches except when they directly affect the parent. But when the breach does annoy the parent, the parent reacts with severe punitive measures. It is this inconsistent and self-indulgent form of parenting that Sears and his colleagues, and other researchers,[9] have found linked with children's aggressiveness. In fact, most studies have found that it is always selective *combinations* of parental practices, rather than single dimensions, that influence children's moral values and behavior.[10] The question that we must answer is, Which combinations are beneficial and which ones are deleterious?

Back in the 1940s, Alfred Baldwin conducted a classic study of family life and its consequences for children's development.[11] Baldwin compared families who conducted their affairs "democratically" (frequently communicating about family rules and policy decisions) with families who were more closed, secretive, and arbitrary about decisions. He also looked at the extent to which these parents effectively controlled their children's conduct. He found that children from families with democracy *without* control were often cruel and disobedient, while children in families with control *without* democracy often lacked initiative and an inner sense of responsibility. The combination of democracy *and* control in the family led to an optimal pattern of assertive kindliness on the part of the child.

More recently, Diana Baumrind has reported similar findings, using somewhat different language to describe them.[12] Baumrind's main categorical distinction is between *authoritarian* and *authoritative* patterns of child rearing. Authoritarian child rearing is a combination of high control and low clarity of communication between parent and child. The authoritarian parent also shuns warmth and nurturance while expecting socially mature behavior. Authoritative child rearing, on the other hand is a combination of high control and clear communication. It also favors warmth and nurturance, while still holding firm and consistent maturity expectations. Both patterns contrast, each in its own way, with permissiveness, which combines *low* control with infrequent maturity demands, but also includes clear communication as well as warmth and nurturance.

Like Baldwin, Baumrind found that parents who clearly communicated with their children while at the same time exerting control and demanding maturity (the "authoritative" ones) frequently had children with an active sense of social responsibility. These children were "friendly rather than hostile to peers, facilitative rather than disruptive of others' work, and cooperative rather than resistive of adult-led activity."[13]

Authoritative parents produce socially responsible children for a number of reasons.[14] First, these parents support the child's natural empathic responses by explicitly confronting children about actions that may be harmful to others. Second, they consistently enforce their commands, thus demonstrating their decisive commitment to these commands. Third, they are direct and honest about their commands rather than indirect or manipulative. Fourth, these parents communicate to their children a general norm requiring obedience to authority, along with the sense that good behavior (and the child's identity as a "good" child) requires compliance with legitimate authority. Fifth, their consistent use of parental authority makes them attractive role models for their children.

Further, authoritative parents impose demands that are challenging but not unrealistic.[15] They push their children to improve their behavior, and this may result in some pressure and some clash of will; but because authoritative parents are also communicative and responsive, they continually tailor their demands to the child's capabilities. This makes their demands moderately, but not overly, tension-producing for the child, an ideal spur for development.[16]

In contrast, both authoritarian and permissive parents shield their children from challenging stress. The former do so by limiting their children's opportunities for exploration, the latter by not confronting their children with the adverse effects of their own acts. As a consequence, children from these two very different family backgrounds have similar difficulties in developing self-reliance, assertiveness, an autonomous sense of social responsibility, and a tolerance for life's ups

and downs. Baumrind found a similar pattern of low self-control and lack of initiative among children from both authoritarian and permissive families. This pattern
of similarity is somewhat surprising, since these two parenting styles seem so
radically opposed to one another. But in fact both sets of parents make essentially
the same two mistakes: First, they fail to confront children regularly and consistently about moral transgressions, and second, they overintrude into the child's
own experience.

Authoritarian and permissive parents make these mistakes quite differently.
Authoritarian parents fail to confront children in a regular and consistent manner
because authoritarian directives stem from the parents' own moods and temper.
The coercive harshness of these parents reflects their own egocentric needs rather
than objective assessments of the child's behavior. Such harshness leads to arbitrary intrusions into the child's life.

Permissive parents, in contrast, are philosophically or temperamentally dis-
inclined towards discipline. As a result, they avoid any confrontations over the
child's transgressions. Yet they, too, intrude in their own way. The intrusion of
permissive parents takes the form of a sentimental overprotectiveness rather than
coercion and punishment. The child is sheltered from experiencing unpleasantness of any type, even when this unpleasantness is simply a realistic consequence
of the child's bad behavior. In many cases, permissive parents also find ways of
preventing teachers and other authority figures from forcing the child to face such
consequences. These parents intrude into their children's school and peer relationships whenever they fear that their children may need protection from a possibly
harsh experience. Although this looks like a gentler and more caring form of intru-
siveness than the authoritarian mode, the adverse effects on children's self-control
and initiative are the same.

Baumrind's work shows how the "authoritative" pattern of firm parental
control mixed with responsiveness, clear communication, and maturity demands
can foster social responsibility (as well as competence) in children. Authoritative
parenting may not be the only means of achieving this end.[17] In fact, Baumrind's
own data reveal a small subset of families in which the same ends were achieved
through an entirely "harmonious" set of relations between parent and child.[18] In
these families, the parent rarely needs to assert control, because the children anticipate the parent's directives and obey without command or discipline. Like children
of authoritative parents, these children from "harmonious" families turned out
competent and socially responsible.

Such family patterns may be far more common in Eastern cultures such as
Japan than in our own society; indeed, a sizable proportion of the few "harmonious" families in Baumrind's own data base were Japanese-Americans. This
suggests that parenting is itself very much influenced by cultural values and practices—a point that we shall return to shortly. It also suggests that there is more

than one viable way to support children's moral growth. Baumrind's own conclusion is that authoritative child rearing is *sufficient but not necessary* for encouraging optimal development.[19] It works, but so do family patterns in which children from the start actively assume responsibility for anticipating parental directives and maintaining family order.

As in any communication, the medium is a large part of the message when it comes to influencing children's values. A parent's manner of expressing and enforcing standards of behavior tells the child a great deal about the parent's own values. A parent's communication style also sets an example for the child's expressive behavior in other social relationships. Accompanying all of the family and child-rearing patterns outlined above, there are several distinct means by which parents attempt to communicate moral values to their young. Some procedures have proven more effective than others for the establishment of long-lasting behavioral standards in children.

Martin Hoffman has identified *power assertion, love withdrawal,* and *induction* as three basic techniques parents can use to transmit values to their children.[20] Power assertion means employing force or punishment as the main means of ensuring the child's compliance with parental standards. In power assertion, the parent's command is justified through the parent's power to enforce rather than through any intrinsic value that the command might have: it is a familial form of might makes right. Love withdrawal means expressing disapproval or disappointment when a child deviates from the standards. This can be accomplished through direct statements—"I don't like you when you act like that"—or through a cold glance or grimace. Induction means ensuring the child's compliance through some form of control, but at the same time drawing the child's attention to the reasons behind the standard. For young children, this often entails giving information about how bad behavior adversely affects others. For example, one common induction used by many parents is to stop a child from pushing his sibling while telling him, "If you keep pushing her like that, she may fall down and cry."

Research has shown that power assertion is a good way of stopping children from doing something dangerous to themselves or others *in the short term.* It may be necessary if a child is about to run into the street or hit her brother on the head with a hammer, but is ineffective for creating permanent change in a child's conduct and values. Once the asserter of power is no longer present, the child tends to revert to the old standards. Without the continued presence of constraint, there is little continued compliance.

In fact, power assertion that is too strenuous may actually *decrease* the child's tendency to follow parental standards. In one clever experiment, one group of children was forbidden to play with a toy in a mild way, while a second group was forbidden the toy under threat of severe punishment.[21] On a later occasion, the children returned to the laboratory and were observed as they approached the forbidden toy. Children from the severe-threat group frequently played with the toy when they thought no one was looking, whereas children from the mild constraint group often said that the toy was boring and not worth playing with. If anything, therefore, severe threats are counterproductive to lasting social influence.

Love withdrawal produces behavioral changes that are some-what longer lasting. Experimental findings have shown that it can be used successfully in teaching children to inhibit their hostile urges towards others.[22] Children whose parents consistently rely on love withdrawal as a disciplinary technique often are self-controlled and respectful of the rights and property of others. But even though it can have an enduring positive effect on children's behavior, love withdrawal does not lead children to develop fully autonomous moral beliefs that they consider their own. Instead, it creates a need for children to conform to parental standards for the sake of their parent's approval. Such a need indeed may continue to assert itself even in the parent's absence, thus motivating the child to maintain her good behavior over time. But this still does not have the staying power of the child's own deep-seated belief in the behavioral standard itself.

Only induction has been found to foster such internalized beliefs. Children exposed to frequent inductions during disciplinary encounters tend to adopt their parents standards as their own. The standards become "functionally autonomous." That is, the standards operate on their own far into the future, despite the parent's absence—and even despite a parent's subsequent disavowal of the standard. For example, a child in whom a parent had successfully induced the standard of honesty could become quite offended later in life if the same parent claimed that cheating on taxes was fine. The standard now exists on its own, wholeheartedly adopted by the child, independent of further parental input.

In general, the optimal conditions for the successful induction of moral beliefs are (1) control of the child's behavior through the minimal external force necessary for achieving such control, combined with (2) provision of information to the child about the rationale for the standard through persuasion, argument, and reasoning.

Control is needed because mere instruction without ensuring behavioral compliance does not "stick." Children quickly forget the message unless they are made to act accordingly. With control, the theory goes, the child performs the proper behavior out of necessity and then gradually begins to believe in the standard represented by this behavior. It is the parent's firm control combined with input about the rationale behind the standard that produces this "internalized" belief. But the parent's control cannot be too forceful: if so, it will remain salient in the child's mind, and force will be all the child remembers from the disciplinary encounter. The goal is to have the child act properly and then to come away from the event remembering why it was important to do so. This is only possible if the informational message is more memorable for the child than the sanctions used to enforce it. The key here is presenting a moral rationale along with a mild form of coercion, so that the child mainly retains the rationale.

The "forbidden toy" experiment provides us with a compelling demonstration of this principle. Mark Lepper and his colleagues have shown that this principle works in the case of positive as well as negative incentives.[23] In other words, inducing children towards behavioral standards through rewards is best done with minimal reward, just as inducing them through enforced control is best done with minimal force. Lepper asked three groups of children to play with Magic Markers, an activity that they normally enjoy on their own. The first two groups were given attractive rewards (a "Good Player" certificate) after they had finished. The third group was given nothing. Weeks later all the children were brought back to the laboratory and given a chance to play with the Magic Markers again if they wanted to. Only the third group leaped at this opportunity. Lepper concluded that he had diminished the autonomous, intrinsic motivation of children in the first two groups by offering them "an unnecessarily salient extrinsic incentive."[24]

These experimental findings may help us better understand the effects of the different child-rearing patterns described by Diana Baumrind. Authoritarian parents rely on coercive disciplinary techniques that are too strenuous and therefore too salient. These parents may get their children to comply in the short run, but over the long haul there is nothing to sustain the desired standard. Permissive parents, on the other hand, fail to provide their children with even the minimum coercions or rewards necessary to change the child's behavior in the first place. Thus, in the end, both sets of parents often see their children engaging in unruly behavior. Authoritative parents combine mild enforcement techniques with clear reasoning and argument. This establishes ideal conditions for children to internalize socially appropriate standards. Hence Baumrind's claim that children whose parents raise them in an authoritative manner are likely to perform socially responsible acts on their own initiative throughout life.

It is important, however, for parents not to allow mild enforcement to become deceitful manipulation by covering up its source or existence—for example, by telling a child that he stopped hitting his sister because he loves her when the real reason was that his father grabbed him and sent him to his room. In other words, parents must represent honestly the extent to which the child is indeed being coerced even if this is an aspect of the encounter that the parent would just as soon have the child forget. Deceiving children into behaving correctly by misrepresenting the situation is objectionable for several reasons, both practical and moral. First, deception as an influence strategy is impractical in the long run, because sooner or later children realize that they are being manipulated. Children, in fact, are keenly aware of "tricks" from an early age.[25] If parents or other adults consistently relied on getting children to misperceive events as part of their moral instruction, children would quickly develop a mistrust for the entire enterprise (as well as for the adults involved). Fortunately, real-life parenting in this case does not often emulate experimenters' manipulative designs.

Further, social influence is generally not accomplished through calculated strategies foisted upon unsuspecting recipients. Rather, it normally comes about through a series of negotiations, cooperative or otherwise, between persons who may or may not be aware that they are influencing one another—and who, as a rule, give little thought to how influence is strategically accomplished.

As a rule, too, moral ends do not derive from immoral means. I do not write this to sermonize, but rather to indicate that what we have here is yet another example of this powerful axiom. Deception cannot work as a means of moral influence because children are not dumb creatures who remain permanently unaware of deceptive practices. Even if a deceptive practice is successful at gaining a child's behavioral compliance, it spins off unwanted messages and other dangerous byproducts. One such message is that dishonesty is condoned by the adults whom one most respects. Diana Baumrind sums up the danger here:

> Manipulative parents are likely to produce manipulative children. Parents' subtle manipulation of children's motivation provides a model for dishonest behavior, which is likely to be detected by children in the home setting.[26]

Because children act as intelligent participants in their social relationships, attempts to influence them must respect their awareness and their many capabilities. This does not mean that children must be given free rein. We have seen that firm parental control can provide important guidance for the child's moral development. But such control is effective only when it is communicated to children openly and directly. It is most effective when coupled with parental reasoning that supports rather than disregards the child's own moral inclinations.

Children not only participate actively in their social relationships; they also develop their own beliefs about these relationships. Such beliefs derive very much from children's own cognitive perspectives: they are not simply a blind reflection of what others would have children believe. This is as much true for children's beliefs about adult-child relations as for their beliefs about any other social relations.

There is a natural developmental progression in the way that children think about adult authority. Children at all ages believe that obeying authority is important. But as they grow older, children change their reasons for obeying, as well as their choices about whom to obey, and under what conditions. These attitudinal changes engender increasingly open and mature (though also increasingly confrontational) adult-child exchanges as children move into adolescence.

Much as in studies of children's early sharing conceptions, children's ideas about authority have been explored by using hypothetical stories and extended questions.[27] One story used for children between the ages of four and twelve is the following:

> This is Peter (Michelle for girl subjects) and here is his mother, Mrs. Johnson (pictures of story characters are shown). Mrs. Johnson wants Peter to clean up

his own room every day, and she tells him that he can't go out and play until he cleans his room up and straightens out his toys. But one day Peter's friend Michael comes over and tells Peter that all the kids are leaving right away for a picnic. Peter wants to go, but his room is a big mess. He tells his mother that he doesn't have time to straighten his room right now, but he'll do it later. She says no, he'll have to stay and miss the picnic.[28]

This story, and others like it, are followed by questions that probe children's ideas about the *legitimacy* of authority (the bases for the authority figure's right to command) and about the *rationale for obedience* (why it is important to do as the authority figure says). Typical questions along these lines are: "What is it about parents that gives them the right to tell kids what to do?" "Why would it be wrong for Peter to ignore his mother and go out anyway?" As the following quotes illustrate, children's answers to such questions change dramatically in the years between infancy and adolescence.

Until age five or so, children believe that they obey because they want to. There is only a shaky understanding that some commands conflict with one's desires and still must be followed. The two children quoted directly below are both four-year-olds:

> Is it all right for Peter's mother to say that? *No.* Why not? *Because he can't go out to play.* But he didn't clean his room like she asked him to. Does that make it all right for her to say that? *No.* Why not? *She wouldn't say something like that.* She wouldn't? Why not? *Her mother only tells him to do good things.*
>
> What do you think Peter should do? *Go to the picnic.* Why should he do that? *Because he wants to and all his friends are going.* But what if his mother says, "No, Peter, you can't go until you clean up your room first?" *He would do what his mom says.* What if Peter really wants to go on the picnic and he doesn't want to clean up his room at all because if he does he'll miss the picnic? *His mommy will let him go out with his friends.* But what if she won't let him? *He will stay home and play with his sister and clean up all his toys in his toy box.* Why will he do that? *Because he wants to.*[29]

By the end of the preschool years, children come more to terms with the realities of parent-child conflict and impending punishment. Parental authority is legitimized by size, strength, and other indications of power. The unpleasant consequences of disobedience provide a forceful rationale for obeying. A fairly typical quote from a five-year-old is the following:

> What should Peter do? *Clean up his room.* Why should he do that? *Because his mother told him to.* Why does he have to do what his mother tells him to? *Because she's the mother.* What difference does that make? *'Cause she's the boss of the house like his father.* What makes them the boss of the house? *Mothers and fathers are bigger and they can spank.*[30]

Children soon learn that parents have more to recommend them than brute strength and power. By middle childhood there is an awareness of other parental virtues that legitimize their authority. Most prominent among these are their superior intelligence and know-how. Obedience is considered a sign of respect for the parent's abilities. It also has a certain reciprocal value: one obeys not only as a necessary gesture of respect, but also as a kind of payback for the parents' protection and nurturance. Because the parent knows a lot, the parent is in a good position to help you, and that fact alone dictates obedience. The following quotes are from three children ages seven and eight:

> Why is it important to do what your mother says? *Because if it's something that you can't do she might help you.* Is that why you do what she tells you to? *Yes, she's the one that can help you the most.* Why is she the one that can help you like that? *Well, she's older and can do a lot of things you can't do.*
>
> What should Peter do? *He should miss the picnic.* How come? *Because if his mother told him to do something he should do it.* Why? *Because if you were sick and asked her for a glass of water she would do it for you.*
>
> What if Peter sneaks out of the house and goes on the picnic anyway? *He shouldn't do that.* Why not? *'Cause his mother told him to stay in and clean his room.* Well, why should he do what his mother says? *Because she's the one taking care of him.* What difference does that make? *Well, after all she's done for him it just doesn't seem fair that he wouldn't do what she says.*[31]

Towards the end of childhood, there is a growing sense that obeying parental authority is in one's best interests because parents care about their children and have more experience than they do. But at the same time there is also a growing sense of equality in the relationship. When the parent is wrong, the child has a right to disagree. At the threshold of adolescence, many children express the belief that obedience is a matter of choice, a voluntary deferral to someone with leadership qualities who cares about one's welfare. There is a situational quality to this choice: should a child know more than the parent about a certain matter, the parent should listen to the child on this topic. The following remarks are from a nine-year-old, but are more typical of children some years older:

> Why does Peter have to listen to his mother? *Because she knows what's best for him.* Is that why she's telling him to clean his room? *Well, she knows it's best for him to learn to do stuff like that.* How does she know that? *'Cause she's a mother and she's learned all about how to raise kids.* What if it were something she didn't know about? Like, suppose the whole family went on a camping trip and nobody knew about camping, nobody had gone camping before except Peter. *Then they should all listen to Peter and he should tell them what to do.* They should all listen to what Peter says? *If he knows the most about camping.* Why should they? *He knows what to do, he should lead the way, and his mother and father better listen.*[32]

Towards the end of childhood, therefore, authority begins to be seen as a consensual relation that serves the interests of all who participate in it. This is a far more constructive way of viewing authority than the respect-for-power perspective of younger children. For one thing, it encourages a voluntary spirit of obedience. For another thing, it further opens the channels of communication between parent and child. When children engage in genuine two way dialogues with parents about choices and values, the parents' opinions are usually heard and taken seriously. When parents' opinions are unilaterally dictated and couched in a context of coercion, they are often lost in the surrounding noise.

Perhaps most importantly, the developing child's new views on authority relations pave the way for a social perspective that will be necessary for adaptation to civilized living. All societies need to delegate authority and need to have such delegations followed and respected. The older child begins to see the social rationale for systems of leadership and followership. Further, the older child understands that authority is legitimate only when it serves the interests of subordinate as well as leader; and that this means that authority figures must have claims to special qualities like experience or talent that enable them to lead effectively. By this logic, children can imagine themselves in leadership positions someday, a sure sign of impending preparation for full citizenship in society.

The important changes that I have described in children's views on authority are natural and widespread, but particular family settings can foster them to a greater or lesser extent. As research has shown, families with clear communication between parent and child-as in Baumrind's "authoritative" pattern of child rearing—are far more conducive to the development of mature beliefs about authority than are families in which parents act in a harshly coercive or laxly permissive manner. In this sense, there is a two-way interplay between children's beliefs and the family atmosphere. In highly communicative families, children readily develop mature ideas about authority; and as children develop more mature authority beliefs, the family atmosphere becomes more democratic and communicative.[33]

In family life around the world, there are wide variations in how parents communicate moral values to their children, as well as in the nature of the values that they choose to express. The most striking contrast is that our own culture promotes the values of independence, liberty, and assertiveness, whereas many others promote the values of interdependence, community, and tradition. Whereas many urban Western societies tend to be similar to our own in this regard, many agrarian sections of Africa, India, and Asia tend to be among the latter (see, for example, the Chapter 6 discussion of children's morality in parts of India).

Beatrice and John Whiting and their colleagues have compared family life in cultural settings as diverse as Okinawa, Mexico, the Philippines, India, Kenya, and New England.[34] They report that children in the United States are weaned earlier and isolated more from the community at large than in any other culture they have studied. Throughout development, they are encouraged to excel over others rather than to blend in with the needs and traditions of the community. All of this has the effect of encouraging autonomy and self-assertiveness in Western children, at the expense of a shared sense of solidarity with others.

The Whitings also found that children in the rural societies they studied—the Philippine, Kenyan, and Mexican children—behave more altruistically than do children from urban societies—the U.S., Okinawan, and Indian children in the Whitings' sample. In rural families, mothers often work in the fields during the day. The children therefore must take on serious household chores and other family responsibilities. They baby-sit with younger siblings and help with the wash and cooking. They even assist with care of the sick and elderly. Such frequent helping activity can accustom children to prosocial behavior as a habitual mode of conduct.

Urban children, particularly in technological societies like the United States, assume relatively little responsibility in the family. One effect of this may be the urban child's propensity towards competitiveness rather than cooperation as a social standard. The anthropologist Millard Madsen conducted several studies contrasting urban and rural children around the world on this dimension, consistently finding the urban children to be more competitive and conflictual and the rural children to be more cooperative and generous in their social interactions.[35]

An important early difference between Western and non-Western children is that the former are far more prone to attention-seeking ("Look at me, Mommy!") than the latter. Studies in Africa by Robert LeVine suggest ways in which parental styles may combine with cultural values to produce such contrasts.[36] LeVine reports that African parents rarely praise their children for good behavior. Rather, they communicate the message that such behavior is to be expected. This means that behavior that conforms to parental standards is largely ignored, whereas deviations from the standards are punished: "Children in those societies observe and imitate, getting corrective feedback when necessary and no feedback when they perform correctly." This, of course, stands in sharp contrast to middle-class American parental communication, which rewards children's good behavior with compliments. LeVine believes that such parental praise only increases the child's tendency to demonstrate the behavior in front of the parent and decreases the child's compliance with parental requests and commands. In addition, parental praise encourages attention-seeking as a generalized mode of activity.

Attention-seeking is an early form of the assertiveness that many parents in our culture intentionally inculcate in their young. Most people in our achievement-oriented society consider assertiveness to be a virtue. It is related to self-confidence, and contributes to personal competence and success. But assertiveness sometimes works against virtues like humility, deference, and self-sacrifice that are more highly valued in cultures that stress the interdependence of persons. Parents in such cultures do not seek to nurture early manifestations of assertiveness such as attention-seeking.

In child-rearing practices, we can see cultures maintaining themselves by transmitting their values to new generations. The transmission of values is not done directly, through lectures or lessons about right and wrong. Rather, it is accomplished through the subtle encouragement or discouragement of behaviors such as attention-seeking. Parents around the world must have an intuitive ability to recognize implications for the culture's heritage in such childhood behaviors.

No society, of course, is a homogeneous whole when it comes to values. Individuals within any society disagree about what is right and wrong, just as they disagree about the best way to raise moral children. Any picture of cultural contrasts is painted with a broad brush, covering over many within-culture inconsistencies. Further, societies change, sometimes acquiring radically new values in the space of one or two generations. This century has witnessed many traditional societies taking on Western values. In some cases, reactions within these societies have led to a rejection of the changes and a reassertion of the old values. In other cases, the tension between the two continues and acts as a socially divisive force.

A recent study by psychologists in mainland China offers us a vivid account of how a society in transition struggles to foster moral values in its children.[37] Professors Jiao, Ji, and Jing were interested in the developmental effects of China's one-child family policy. This policy, implemented by a centralized State Family Planning Commission, has succeeded in dramatically reducing the size of many Chinese families. According to recent surveys, almost three-fourths of married couples in China's major cities and provinces now have only one child. Political leaders in China believe that this shift will have salutary economic consequences. Professors Jiao, Ji, and Jing were curious about the consequences for Chinese children.

The researchers studied almost a thousand kindergarten and elementary school children from rural and urban backgrounds. Children with siblings were compared with only children on a range of social and cognitive dimensions. The researchers went into the children's schools and asked the children's peers to rate how cooperative, friendly, or selfish the children were. In both rural and urban settings, only children were found to be more self-centered than children with siblings. They acted more according to their own interests and tended to share and cooperate less with others. Children with siblings were better liked by their peers and more able to cope with constraints and frustrations.

The researchers conclude that, at least in China, a family environment with siblings is an important part of a child's moral upbringing. "Communal home life," they write, "requires cooperation and collective participation."[38] Children are forced to share their parents' attention with their brothers or sisters and must learn to respond productively to peer pressure. Only children are at a disadvantage here. The researchers cite one observation of "an only child in a kindergarten who did not know how to put his clothes on after the noon nap; he just sat on the bed waiting for the nurse to dress him. If no one came to attend to him, he would just sit there, watching the others get dressed."[39]

Such problems exist in many places around the world. The Whitings have found that only children are less inclined to share and help than are children with younger siblings.

But this seems to be the case mainly in the rural and traditional cultures where children in general tend to be more cooperative and altruistic. It does not seem that only children in contemporary America or other urban Western cultures are markedly more egocentric than their peers from large families. It may be that parents in rural societies do not try as hard as their urban counterparts to compensate for the only child's lack of peer influences.

This problem may be particularly aggravated in a society like China, where the shift to small families has been sudden and mandated. It may be that there has not been enough time for the culture to develop ways of orienting children to prosocial values in the absence of the large family experience.

One can imagine why this research report has created concern among Chinese policy makers. The nation's socialist ethic could not long endure an entire generation of self-centered individualists. If Chinese children are indeed being unintentionally trained to eshew communal values, they will inevitably clash with their culture's primary values at some point in their development. Indeed, there are already reports that contemporary Chinese youth, to the distress of many of their elders, are increasingly attracted to materialism, individualistic achievement, and other Western values. Changing family structure, and the altered early experience that it brings, could be one reason behind this new attraction.

Every society undergoes some generational flux in values: this is how cultures change over time. Parents, it seems, only partially succeed in replicating their own values in the young. This is because even the most effective parents are not perfect inducers of values; and there are many parental practices and family conditions that are ineffective—or even counterproductive. Carolyn Pope Edwards, for example, has described a Kenyan tribe where parents strenuously discourage aggression in their children by beating offenders.[40] Not surprisingly, children from this tribe frequently resort to hitting when confronted with a problem, despite the behavioral standard advocated by their parents.

There is also generational flux because parents are not the only influences on children's moral development. Children often sort out matters of right and wrong among themselves in the context of the social realities within which they find themselves. In so doing, they often come to their own conclusions, regardless of what their parents might say. There is much in the way of moral experience that children encounter outside the home.

Notes

1. Ainsworth, M. D., Blehar, M. C, Waters, E., and Wall, S. (1978) *Patterns of Attachment.* Hillsdale, N.J.: L. Erlbaum Associates.

2. Dunn, J., and Munn, P. (1985) Becoming a family member: Family conflict and the development of social understanding in the second year. *Child Development,* 56, 480–492; see also Dunn, J. (1987) The beginnings of moral understanding. In J. Kagan and S. Lamb (Eds.), *The Emergence of Morality in Young Children.* Chicago: University of Chicago Press, and Dunn, J., and Munn, P., (1986) Sibling quarrels and maternal intervention: Individual differences in understanding and aggression. *Journal of Child Psychology and Psychiatry,* 27, 583–595.

3. Dunn, The beginnings of moral understanding.

4. Ibid.

5. Dunn, J., and Munn, P. (1986) Siblings and the development of prosocial behavior. *International Journal of Behavioral Development,* 9, 265–294.

6. Ekman, P. (1984) Expression and nature of emotion. In K. R. Scherer and P. Ekman (Eds.), *Approaches to Emotion.* Hillsdale, N.J.: L. Erlbaum Associates.

7. Emde, R. Levels of meaning of infant emotions: A biosocial view. In W. A. Collins (Ed.), *Development of Cognition, Affect, and Social Relations* (Minnesota Symposium on Child Psychology, Vol. 13). Hillsdale, N.J.: L. Erlbaum Associates.

8. Sears, R. R., Maccoby, E. E., and Levin, H. (1957) *Patterns of Child Rearing.* Evanston, Ill.: Row Peterson.

9. Maccoby, E. E., and Martin, J. A. (1983) Socialization in the context of the family: Parent-child interaction. In P. H. Mussen (Ed.), *Handbook of Child Psychology* (Vol. 4). New York: Wiley.

10. Ibid.

11. Baldwin, A. (1948) Socialization and the parent-child relationship. *Child Development,* 19, 127–136.

12. Baumrind, D. (1973) The development of instrumental competence through socialization. In A. D. Pick (Ed.), *Minnesota Symposium on Child Psychology* (Vol. 7). Minneapolis: University of Minnesota Press.

13. Ibid.

14. Ibid.

15. Ibid.

16. Ibid.

17. Ibid.

18. Baumrind, D. (1973) Note: Harmonious parents and their pre-school children. *Developmental Psychology,* 4, 99–102.

19. Baumrind, D. (1989) Rearing competent children. In W. Damon (Ed.), *Child Development Today and Tomorrow.* San Francisco: Jossey-Bass.

20. Hoffman, M. L. (1967) Moral internalization, parental power, and the nature of parent-child interaction. *Developmental Psychology*, 5, 45–57.

21. Lepper, M. R., and Green, D. (1975) Turning play into work: Effects of surveillance and extrinsic reward on children's intrinsic motivation. *Journal of Personality and Social Psychology*, 31, 479–486.

22. Hoffman, M. L. (1977) Moral internalization. In L. Berkowitz (Ed.), *Advances in Experimental Social Psychology* (Vol. 10). New York: Academic Press.

23. Lepper, M. R. (1983) Social control processes, attributions of motivation, and the internalization of social values. In E. T. Higgins, D. N. Ruble, and W. W. Hartup (Eds.), *Social Cognition and Social Behavior: Developmental Perspectives*. New York: Cambridge University Press.

24. Lepper, Social control processes.

25. Flavell, J. (1982) *Cognitive Development*. Englewood Cliffs, N.J.: Prentice-Hall.

26. Baumrind, Rearing competent children.

27. Damon, W. (1977) *The Social World of the Child*. San Francisco: Jossey-Bass.

28. Ibid., pp. 174–175.

29. Ibid., p. 182.

30. Ibid., pp. 188–189.

31. Ibid., p. 192.

32. Ibid., p. 199.

33. Youniss, J. (1980) *Parents and Peers in Child Development*. Chicago: University of Chicago Press.

34. Whiting, B. B., and Whiting, J. W. M. (1975) *Children of Six Cultures: A Psychocultural Analysis*. Cambridge, Mass.: Harvard University Press.

35. Madsen, M. C. (1971) Developmental and cross-cultural differences in the cooperative and competitive behavior of young children. *Journal of Cross-Cultural Psychology*, 2, 365–371.

36. LeVine, R. A. (1980) Anthropology and child development. *New Directions for Child Development*, 8, 71–86.

37. Jiao, S., Ji, G., and Jing, Q. (1986) Comparative study of behavioral qualities of only children and sibling children. *Child Development*, 57, 357–361.

38. Ibid.

39. Ibid.

40. Edwards, C. P. (1987) Socialization in Kenya. In J. Kagan and S. Lamb (Eds.), *The Emergence of Morality in Young Children*. Chicago: University of Chicago Press.

The Varieties of Friendship

Aristotle

Aristotle *(383–322 BCE) was a student of Plato and became one of the most influential thinkers in history. He taught in Plato's Academy and subsequently established his own center of learning, the 'Lyceum.' Like Plato, Aristotle wrote on virtually every subject, including logic, physics, biology, psychology, rhetoric, poetry, politics, and ethics. In this selection from his* Nicomachean Ethics, *which is one of the greatest works in moral philosophy, Aristotle examines the nature of friendship, which he considered to be essential to human life.*

The Problems

Common Beliefs about Friendship

After that the next topic to discuss is friendship; for it is a virtue, or involves virtue, and besides is most necessary for our life.

It is necessary in all external conditions . . .

For no one would choose to live without friends even if he had all the other goods. For in fact rich people and holders of powerful positions, even more than other people, seem to need friends. For how would one benefit from such prosperity if one had no opportunity for beneficence, which is most often displayed, and most highly praised, in relation to friends? And how would one guard and protect prosperity without friends, when it is all the more precarious the greater it is? In poverty also, and in the other misfortunes, people think friends are the only refuge.

In all times of life . . .

Moreover, the young need it to keep them from error. The old need it to care for them and support the actions that fail because of weakness. And those in their prime need it, to do fine actions; for 'when two go together . . .', they are more capable of understanding and acting.

And throughout nature . . .

Further, a parent would seem to have a natural friendship for a child, and a child for a parent, not only among human beings but also among birds and most kinds of animals. Members of the same race, and human beings most of all, have a natural friendship for each other; that is why we praise friends of humanity. And in our travels we can see how every human being is akin and beloved to a human being.

For communities as well as for individuals

Moreover, friendship would seem to hold cities together, and legislators would seem to be more concerned about it than about justice. For concord would seem to be similar to friendship and they aim at concord above all, while they try above all to expel civil conflict, which is enmity.

Further, if people are friends, they have no need of justice, but if they are just they need friendship in addition; and the justice that is most just seems to belong to friendship.

It is both necessary and fine

However, friendship is not only necessary, but also fine. For we praise lovers of friends, and having many friends seems to be a fine thing. Moreover, people think that the same people are good and also friends.

Puzzles about Friendship

Still, there are quite a few disputed points about friendship. For some hold it is a sort of similarity and that similar people are friends. Hence the saying 'Similar to similar', and 'Birds of a feather', and so on. On the other hand it is said that similar people are all like the proverbial potters, quarrelling with each other.

On these questions some people inquire at a higher level, more proper to natural science. Euripides says that when earth gets dry it longs passionately for rain, and the holy heaven when filled with rain longs passionately to fall into the earth; and Heracleitus says that the opponent cooperates, the finest harmony arises from discordant elements, and all things come to be in struggle. Others, e.g. Empedocles, oppose this view, and say that similar aims for similar.

Let us, then, leave aside the puzzles proper to natural science, since they are not proper to the present examination; and let us examine the puzzles that concern human [nature], and bear on characters and feelings.

For instance, does friendship arise among all sorts of people, or can people not be friends if they are vicious?

Is there one species of friendship, or are there more? Some people think there is only one species because friendship allows more and less. But here their confidence rests on an inadequate sign; for things of different species also allow more and less.

The Three Types of Friendship

Complete and Incomplete Species of Friendship Correspond to the Different Objects

Now since these causes differ in species, so do the types of loving and types of friendship. Hence friendship has three species, corresponding to the three objects of love. For each object of love has a corresponding type of mutual loving, combined with awareness of it, and those who love each other wish goods to each other in so far as they love each other.

Friendships for Utility and Pleasure are Incomplete

Those who love each other for utility love the other not in himself, but in so far as they gain some good for themselves from him. The same is true of those who love for pleasure; for they like a witty person not because of his character, but because he is pleasant to themselves.

And so those who love for utility or pleasure are fond of a friend because of what is good or pleasant for themselves, not in so far as the beloved is who he is, but in so far as he is useful or pleasant.

Hence these friendships as well [as the friends] are coincidental, since the beloved is loved not in so far as he is who he is, but in so far as he provides some good or pleasure.

And so these sorts of friendships are easily dissolved, when the friends do not remain similar [to what they were]; for if someone is no longer pleasant or useful, the other stops loving him.

Friendship for Utility

What is useful does not remain the same, but is different at different times. Hence, when the cause of their being friends is removed, the friendship is dissolved too, on the assumption that the friendship aims at these [useful results]. This sort of friendship seems to arise especially among older people, since at that age they pursue what is advantageous, not what is pleasant, and also among those in their prime or youth who pursue what is expedient.

Nor do such people live together very much. For sometimes they do not even find each other pleasant. Hence they have no further need to meet in this way if they are not advantageous [to each other]; for each finds the other pleasant [only] to the extent that he expects some good from him. The friendship of hosts and guests is taken to be of this type too.

Friendships for Pleasure

The cause of friendship between young people seems to be pleasure. For their lives are guided by their feelings, and they pursue above all what is pleasant for themselves and what is near at hand. But as they grow up [what they find] pleasant changes too. Hence they are quick to become friends, and quick to stop; for their friendship shifts with [what they find] pleasant, and the change in such pleasure is quick. Young people are prone to erotic passion, since this mostly follows feelings, and is caused by pleasure; that is why they love and quickly stop, often changing in a single day.

These people wish to spend their days together and to live together; for this is how they gain [the good things] corresponding to their friendship.

Complete Friendship Is the Friendship of Good People

But complete friendship is the friendship of good people similar in virtue; for they wish goods in the same way to each other in so far as they are good, and they are good in themselves. [Hence they wish goods to each other for each other's own sake.] Now those who wish goods to their friend for the friend's own sake are friends most of all; for they have this attitude because of the friend himself, not coincidentally. Hence these people's friendship lasts as long as they are good; and virtue is enduring.

Each of them is both good unconditionally and good for his friend, since good people are both unconditionally good and advantageous for each other. They are pleasant in the same ways too, since good people are pleasant both unconditionally and for each other. [They are pleasant for each other] because each person finds his own actions of that kind pleasant, and the actions of good people are the same or similar.

It is reasonable that this sort of friendship is enduring, since it embraces in itself all the features that friends must have. For the cause of every friendship is good or pleasure, either unconditional or for the lover; and every friendship reflects some similarity. And all the features we have mentioned are found in this friendship because of [the nature of] the friends themselves. For they are similar in this way [i.e., in being good]. Moreover, their friendship also has the other things—what is unconditionally good and what is unconditionally pleasant; and these are lovable most of all. Hence loving and friendship are found most of all and at their best in these friends.

These kinds of friendships are likely to be rare, since such people are few. Moreover, they need time to grow accustomed to each other; for, as the proverb says, they cannot know each other before they have shared the traditional [peck of] salt, and they cannot accept each other or be friends until each appears lovable to the other and gains the other's confidence. Those who are quick to treat each other in friendly ways wish to be friends, but are not friends, unless they are also lovable, and know this. For though the wish for friendship comes quickly, friendship does not.

Self-Love Is a Component of Friendship

The Common View Identifies Self-Love with Selfishness

There is also a puzzle about whether one ought to love oneself or someone else most of all; for those who like themselves most are criticized and denounced as self-lovers, as though this were something shameful.

Indeed, the base person does seem to go to every length for his own sake, and all the more the more vicious he is; hence he is accused, e.g., of doing nothing of his own accord. The decent person, on the contrary, acts for what is fine, all the more the better he is, and for his friend's sake, disregarding his own good.

But Facts about Friendship Justify Self-Love

The facts, however, conflict with these claims, and that is not unreasonable.

For it is said that we must love most the friend who is most a friend; and one person is most a friend to another if he wishes goods to the other for the other's sake, even if no one will know about it. But these are features most of all of one's relation to oneself; and so too are all the other defining features of a friend, since we have said that all the features of friendship extend from oneself to others.

All the proverbs agree with this too, e.g., speaking of 'one soul', 'what friends have is common', 'equality is friendship' and 'the knee is closer than the shin'. For all these are true most of all in someone's relations with himself, since one is a friend to himself most of all. Hence he should also love himself most of all.

Hence We Must Distinguish Good and Bad Forms of Self-Love

It is not surprising that there is a puzzle about which view we ought to follow, since both inspire some confidence; hence we must presumably divide these sorts of arguments, and distinguish how far and in what ways those on each side are true.

Perhaps, then, it will become clear, if we grasp how those on each side understand self-love.

The Bad Form of Self-Love is Selfish, Resting on an Incorrect View of the Self

Those who make self-love a matter for reproach ascribe it to those who award the biggest share in money, honours and bodily pleasures to themselves. For these are the goods desired and eagerly pursued by the many on the assumption that they are best; and hence they are also contested.

Those who are greedy for these goods gratify their appetites and in general their feelings and the non-rational part of the soul; and since this is the character of the many, the application of the term ['self-love'] is derived from the most frequent [kind of self-love], which is base. This type of self-lover, then, is justifiably reproached.

And plainly it is the person who awards himself these goods whom the many habitually call a self-lover. For if someone is always eager to excel everyone in doing just or temperate actions or any others expressing the virtues, and in general always gains for himself what is fine, no one will call him a self-lover or blame him for it.

But the Good Form of Self-Love Rests on a Correct View of the Self

However, it is this more than the other sort of person who seems to be a self-lover. At any rate he awards himself what is finest and best of all, and gratifies the most controlling part of himself, obeying it in everything. And just as a city and every other composite system seems to be above all its most controlling part, the same is true of a human being; hence someone loves himself most if he likes and gratifies this part.

Similarly, someone is called continent or incontinent because his understanding is or is not the master, on the assumption that this is what each person is. Moreover, his own voluntary actions seem above all to be those involving reason. Clearly, then, this, or this above all, is what each person is, and the decent person likes this most of all.

Hence he most of all is a self-lover, but a different kind from the self-lover who is reproached, differing from him as much as the life guided by reason differs from the life guided by feelings, and as much as the desire for what is fine differs from the desire for what seems advantageous.

The Justification of Friendship

Friends Do Not Seem to be Needed for Happiness

There is also a dispute about whether the happy person will need friends or not.

For it is said that blessedly happy and self-sufficient people have no need of friends. For they already have [all] the goods, and hence, being self-sufficient, need nothing added. But your friend, since he is another yourself, supplies what your own efforts cannot supply. Hence it is said, 'When the god gives well, what need is there of friends?'

But Friends are the Greatest External Good

However, in awarding the happy person all the goods it would seem absurd not to give him friends; for having friends seems to be the greatest external good.

We Need Friends for us to Benefit

And it is more proper to a friend to confer benefits than to receive them, and proper to the good person and to virtue to do good; and it is finer to benefit friends than to benefit strangers. Hence the excellent person will need people for him to benefit. Indeed, that is why there is a question about whether friends are needed more in good fortune than in ill-fortune; for it is assumed that in ill-fortune we need people to benefit us, and in good fortune we need others for us to benefit.

Solitude Makes Happiness Impossible

Surely it is also absurd to make the blessed person solitary. For no one would choose to have all [other] goods and yet be alone, since a human being is political, tending by nature to live together with others. This will also be true, then, of the happy person; for he has the natural goods, and clearly it is better to spend his days with decent friends than with strangers of just any character. Hence the happy person will need friends.

Friendship Includes Shared Life, and Hence Shared Conversation and Thought

We agreed that someone's own being is choiceworthy because he perceives that he is good, and this sort of perception is pleasant in itself. He must, then, perceive his friend's being together [with his own], and he will do this when they live together and share conversation and thought. For in the case of human beings what seems to count as living together is this sharing of conversation and thought, not sharing the same pasture, as in the case of grazing animals.

Conclusion: Friendship Is Needed for Self-Sufficiency

If, then, for the blessedly happy person, being is choiceworthy, since it is naturally good and pleasant; and if the being of his friend is closely similar to his own; then his friend will also be choiceworthy. Whatever is choiceworthy for him he must possess, since otherwise he will to this extent lack something, [and hence will not be self-sufficient]. Anyone who is to be happy, then, must have excellent friends.

The Proper Number of Friends for a Happy Life

Then should we have as many friends as possible? Or is it the same as with the friendship of host and guest, where it seems to be good advice to 'have neither many nor none'? Is this also good advice in friendship, to have neither no friends nor many?

Friends for Utility and Pleasure Should be Limited

With friends for utility the advice seems very apt, since it is hard work to return many people's services, and life is too short for it. Indeed, more [such] friends than are adequate for one's own life are superfluous, and a hindrance to living finely; hence we have no need of them. A few friends for pleasure are enough also, just as a little seasoning on food is enough.

Friends for Virtue Must be Limited by the Requirements of Living Together

Of excellent people, however, should we have as many as possible as friends, or is there some proper measure of their number, as of the number in a city? For a city could not be formed from ten human beings, but it would be a city no longer if it had ten myriads; presumably, though, the right quantity is not just one number, but anything between certain defined limits. Hence there is also some limit defining the number of friends.

Presumably, this is the largest number with whom you could live together, since we found that living together seems to be most characteristic of friendship. And clearly you cannot live with many people and distribute yourself among them.

Besides, these many people must also be friends to each other, if they are all to spend their days together; and this is hard work for many people to manage. It also becomes difficult for many to share each other's enjoyments and distresses as their own, since you are quite likely to find yourself sharing one friend's pleasure and another friend's grief at the same time.

An Excessive Number of Friends Changes the Character of the Friendship

Presumably, then, it is good not to seek as many friends as possible, and good to have no more than enough for living together; indeed it even seems impossible to be an extremely close friend to many people. For the same reason it also seems impossible to be passionately in love with many people, since passionate erotic love tends to be an excess of friendship, and one has this for one person; hence also one has extremely close friendship for a few people.

This would seem to be borne out in what people actually do. For the friendship of companions is not found in groups of many people, and the friendships celebrated in song are always between two people. By contrast, those who have many friends and treat everyone as close to them seem to be friends to no one, except in a fellow-citizen's way. These people are regarded as ingratiating.

Certainly it is possible to be a friend of many in a fellow-citizen's way, and still to be a truly decent person, not ingratiating; but it is impossible to be many people's friend for their virtue and for themselves. We have reason to be satisfied if we can find even a few such friends.

The Role of Friends in Living Together, in Good Fortune and in Ill Fortune

Have we more need of friends in good fortune or in ill fortune? For in fact we seek them in both, since in ill fortune we need assistance, while in good fortune we need friends to live with and to benefit, since then we wish to do good.

Certainly it is more necessary to have friends in ill fortune, and hence useful friends are needed here. But it is finer to have them in good fortune, and hence we also seek decent friends; for it is more choiceworthy to do good to them and spend our time with them.

The Good Person Will Avoid Causing Pain to His Friends

The very presence of friends is also pleasant, in ill fortune as well as good fortune; for we have our pain lightened when our friends share our distress. Hence indeed one might be puzzled about whether they take a part of it from us, as though helping us to lift a weight, or, alternatively, their presence is pleasant and our awareness that they share our distress makes the pain smaller. Well, we need not discuss whether it is this or something else that lightens our pain; at any rate, what we have mentioned does appear to occur.

However, the presence of friends would seem to be a mixture [of pleasure and pain]. For certainly the sight of our friends in itself is pleasant, especially when we are in ill fortune, and it gives us some assistance in removing our pain. For a friend consoles us by the sight of him and by conversation, if he is dexterous, since he knows our character and what gives us pleasure and pain. Nonetheless, awareness of his pain at our ill fortune is painful to us, since everyone tries to avoid causing pain to his friends.

That is why someone with a manly nature tries to prevent his friend from sharing his pain. Unless he is unusually immune to pain, he cannot endure pain coming to his friends; and he does not allow others to share his mourning at all, since he is not prone to mourn himself either. Females, however, and effeminate men enjoy having people to wail with them; they love them as friends who share their distress. But in everything we clearly must imitate the better person.

He Will Readily Share His Good Fortune with His Friends

In good fortune, by contrast, the presence of friends makes it pleasant to pass our time and to notice that they take pleasure in our own goods.

Hence it seems that we must eagerly call our friends to share our good fortune, since it is fine to do good. But we must hesitate to call them to share our ill fortune, since we must share bad things with them as little as possible; hence the saying 'My misfortune is enough'. We should invite them most of all whenever they will benefit us greatly, with little trouble to themselves.

He Will Show Them Proper Consideration in Their Good and Ill Fortune

Conversely, it is presumably appropriate to go eagerly, without having to be called, to friends in misfortune. For it is proper to a friend to benefit, especially to benefit a friend in need who has not demanded it, since this is finer and pleasanter for both friends. In good fortune he should come eagerly to help him, since friends are needed for this also; but he should be slow to come to receive benefits, since eagerness to be benefitted is not fine. Presumably, though, one should avoid getting a reputation for being a killjoy, as sometimes happens, by refusing benefits.

Hence the presence of friends is apparently choiceworthy in all conditions.

Is There a Duty to Die?

John Hardwig

When Richard Lamm made the statement that old people have a duty to die, it was generally shouted down or ridiculed. The whole idea is just too preposterous to entertain. Or too threatening. In fact, a fairly common argument against legalizing physician-assisted suicide is that if it were legal, some people might somehow get the idea that they have a duty to die. These people could only be the victims of twisted moral reasoning or vicious social pressure. It goes without saying that there is no duty to die.

But for me the question is real and very important. I feel strongly that I may very well some day have a duty to die. I do not believe that I am idiosyncratic, morbid, mentally ill, or morally perverse in thinking this. I think many of us will eventually face precisely this duty. But I am first of all concerned with my own duty. I write partly to clarify my own convictions and to prepare myself. Ending my life might be a very difficult thing for me to do.

This notion of a duty to die raises all sorts of interesting theoretical and metaethical questions. I intend to try to avoid most of them because I hope my argument will be persuasive to those holding a wide variety of ethical views. Also, although the claim that there is a duty to die would ultimately require theoretical underpinning, the discussion needs to begin on the normative level.

I will use "duty," "obligation," and "responsibility" interchangeably, in a pre-theoretical or preanalytic sense, as is appropriate to my attempt to steer clear of theoretical commitments.[1]

Circumstances and a Duty to Die

Do many of us really believe that no one ever has a duty to die? I suspect not. I think most of us probably believe that there is such a duty, but it is very uncommon. Consider Captain Oates, a member of Admiral Scott's expedition to the South Pole. Oates became too ill to continue. If the rest of the team stayed with him, they would all perish. After this had become clear, Oates left his tent one night, walked out into a raging blizzard,and was never seen again.[2] That may have been a heroic thing.

This is a very unusual circumstance—a "lifeboat case"—and lifeboat cases make for bad ethics. But I expect that most of us would also agree that there have been cultures in which what we would call a duty to die has been fairly common. These are relatively poor, technologically simple, and especially nomadic cultures. In such societies, everyone knows that if you manage to live long enough, you will eventually become old and debilitated. Then you will need to take steps to end your life. The old people in these societies regularly did precisely that. Their cultures prepared and supported them in doing so.

Those cultures could be dismissed as irrelevant to contemporary bioethics; their circumstances are so different from ours. But if that is our response, it is instructive. It suggests that we assume a duty to die is irrelevant to us because of our wealth and technological sophistication have purchased exemption for us . . . except under very unusual circumstances like Captain Oates'.

But have wealth and technology really exempted us? Or are they, on the contrary, about to make a duty to die common again? We like to think of modern medicine as all triumph with no dark side at all. Our medicine saves many lives and enables most of us to live longer. That is wonderful, indeed. We are all glad to have access to this medicine. But our medicine also delivers most of us over to chronic illnesses and it enables many of us to survive longer than we can take care of ourselves, longer than we know what to do with ourselves, longer than we even are ourselves.

The costs—and these are not merely monetary—of prolonging our lives when we are no longer able to care for ourselves are often staggering. If further medical advances wipe out many of today's "killer diseases"—cancers, heart attacks, strokes, ALS, AIDS, and the rest—then one day most of us will survive long enough to become demented or debilitated. These developments could generate a fairly widespread duty to die. A fairly common duty to die might turn out to be only the dark side of our life-prolonging medicine and the uses we choose to make of it.

Let me be clear. I certainly believe that there is a duty to refuse life-prolonging medical treatment and also a duty to complete advance directives refusing life-prolonging treatment. But a duty to die can go well beyond that. There can be a duty to die before one's illnesses would cause death, even if treated only with palliative measures. In fact, there may be a fairly common responsibility to end one's life in the absence of any terminal illness at all. Finally, there can be a duty to die when one would prefer to live. Granted, many of the conditions that can generate a duty to die also seriously undermine the quality of life. Some prefer not to live under such conditions. But even those who want to live can face a duty to die. These will clearly be the most controversial and troubling cases; I will, accordingly, focus my reflections on them.

The Individualistic Fantasy

Because a duty to die seems such a real possibility to me, I wonder why contemporary bioethics has dismissed it without serious consideration. I believe that most bioethics still shares in one of our deeply embedded American dreams: the individualistic fantasy. This fantasy leads us to imagine that lives are separate and unconnected, or that they could be so if we chose. If lives were unconnected, things that happened in my life would not or need not affect others. And if others were not (much) affected by my life, I would have no duty to consider the impact of my decisions on others. I would then be morally free to live my life however I please, choosing whatever life and death I prefer for myself. The way I live would be nobody's business but my own. I certainly would have no duty to die if I preferred to live.

Within a health care context, the individualistic fantasy leads us to assume that the patient is the only one affected by decisions about her medical treatment. If only the patient were affected, the relevant questions when making treatment decisions would be precisely those we ask: What will benefit the patient? Who can best decide that? The pivotal issue would always be simply whether the patient herself wants to live like this and whether she herself would be better off dead.[3] "Whose life is it, anyway?" we ask rhetorically.

But this is morally obtuse. We are not a race of hermits. Illness and death do not come only to those who are all alone. Nor is it much better to think in terms of the bald dichotomy between "the interests of the patient" and "the interests of society" (or a third-party payer), as if we were isolated individuals connected only to "society" in the abstract or to the other, faceless members of our health maintenance organization.

Most of us are affiliated with particular others and most deeply, with family and loved ones. Families and loved ones are bound together by ties of care and affection, by legal relations and obligations, by inhabiting shared spaces and living units, by interlocking finances and economic prospects, by common projects and also commitments to support the different life projects of other family members, by shared histories, by ties of loyalty. This life together of family and loved ones is what defines and sustains us; it is what gives meaning to most of our lives. We would not have it any other way. We would not want to be all alone, especially when we are seriously ill, as we age, and when we are dying.

A Burden to My Loved Ones

But many older people report that their one remaining goal in life is not to be a burden to their loved ones. Young people feel this, too: when I ask my undergraduate students to think about whether their death could come too late, one of their very first responses always is, "Yes, when I become a burden to my family or loved ones." Tragically, there are situations in which my loved ones would be much better off—all things considered, the loss of a loved one notwithstanding—if I were dead.

The lives of our loved ones can be seriously compromised by caring for us. The burdens of providing care or even just supervision twenty-four hours a day, seven days a week are often-overwhelming.[4] When this kind of caregiving goes on for years, it leaves the caregiver exhausted, with no time for herself or life of her own. Ultimately, even her health is often destroyed. But it can also be emotionally devastating simply to live with a spouse who is increasingly distant, uncommunicative, unresponsive, foreign, and unreachable. Other family members' needs often go unmet as the caring capacity of the family is exceeded. Social life and friendships evaporate, as there is no opportunity to go out to see friends and the home is no longer a place suitable for having friends in.

We must also acknowledge that the lives of our loved ones can be devastated just by having to pay for health care for us. One part of the recent SUPPORT study documented the financial aspects of caring for a dying member of a family. Only those who had illnesses severe enough to give them less than a 50% chance to live six more months were included in this study. When these patients survived their initial hospitalization and were discharged, about 1/3 required considerable caregiving from their families, in 20% of cases a family member had to quit work or make some other major lifestyle change, almost 1/3 of these families lost all of their savings, and just under 30% lost a major source of income.[5]

If talking about money sounds venal or trivial, remember that much more than money is normally at stake here. When someone has to quit work, she may well lose her career. Savings decimated late in life cannot be recouped in the few remaining years of employability, so the loss compromises the quality of the rest of the caregiver's life. For a young person, the chance to go to college may be lost to the attempt to pay debts due to an illness in the family, and this decisively shapes an entire life.

A serious illness in a family is a misfortune. It is usually nobody's fault; no one is responsible for it. But we face choices about how we will respond to this misfortune. That's where the responsibility comes in and fault can arise. Those of us with families and loved ones always have a duty not to make selfish or self-centered decisions about our lives. We have a responsibility to try to protect the lives of loved ones from serious threats or greatly impoverished quality, certainly an obligation not to make choices that will jeopardize or seriously compromise their futures. Often, it would be wrong to do just what we want or just what is best for ourselves; we should choose in light of what is best for all concerned. That is our duty in sickness as well as in health. It is out of these responsibilities that a duty to die can develop.

I am not advocating a crass, quasi-economic conception of burdens and benefits, nor a shallow, hedonistic view of life. Given a suitably rich understanding of benefits, family members sometimes do benefit from suffering through the long illness of a loved one. Caring for the sick or aged can foster growth, even as it makes daily life immeasurably harder and the prospects for the future much bleaker. Chronic illness or a drawn-out death can also pull a family together, making the care for each other stronger and more evident. If my loved ones are truly benefitting from coping with my illness or debility, I have no duty to die based on burdens to them.

But it would be irresponsible to blithely assume that this always happens, that it will happen in family, or that it will be the fault of my family if they can not manage to turn my illness into a positive experience. Perhaps the opposite is more common: a hospital chaplain once told me that he could not think of a single case in which a family was strengthened or brought together by what happened at the hospital.

Our families and loved ones also have obligations, of course—they have the responsibility to stand by us and to support us through debilitating illness and death. They must be prepared to make significant sacrifices to respond to an illness in the family. I am far from denying that. Most of us are aware of this responsibility and most families meet it rather well. In fact, families deliver more than 80% of the long-term care in this country, almost always at great personal cost. Most of us who are a part of a family can expect to be sustained in our time of need by family members and those who love us.

But most discussions of an illness in the family talk as if responsibility were a one-way street. It is not, of course. When we become seriously ill or debilitated, we too may have to make sacrifices. To think that my loved ones must bear whatever burdens my illness, debility, or dying process might impose upon them is to reduce them to means to my well-being. And that would be immoral. Family solidarity, altruism, bearing the burden of a loved one's misfortune, and loyalty are all important virtues of families, as well. But they are all also two-way streets.

Objections to a Duty to Die

To my mind, the most serious objections to the idea of a duty to die lie in the effects on my loved ones of ending my life. But to most others, the important objections have little or nothing to do with family and loved ones. Perhaps the most common objections are: 1) There is a higher duty which always takes precedence over a duty to die. 2) A duty to end one's own life would be incompatible with a recognition of human dignity or the intrinsic value of a person. 3) Seriously ill, debilitated, or dying people are already bearing the harshest burdens and so it would be wrong to ask them to bear the additional burden of ending their own lives.

These are all important objections; all deserve a thorough discussion. Here I will only be able to suggest some moral counterweights—ideas that might provide the basis for an argument that these objections do not always preclude a duty to die.

An example of the first line of argument would be the claim that a duty to God, the giver of life, forbids that anyone take her own life. It could be argued that this duty always supersedes whatever obligations we might have to our families. But what convinces us that we always have such a religious duty in the first place? And what guarantees that it always supersedes our obligations to try to protect our loved ones?

Certainly, the view that death is the ultimate evil cannot be squared with Christian theology. It does not reflect the actions of Jesus or those of his early followers. Nor is it clear that the belief that life is sacred requires that we never take it. There are other theological possibilities.[6] In any case, most of us—bioethicists, physicians, and patients alike—do not subscribe to the view that we have an obligation to preserve human life as long as possible. But if not, surely we ought to agree that I may legitimately end my life for other regarding reasons, not just for self-regarding reasons.

Secondly, religious considerations aside, the claim could be made that an obligation to end one's own life would be incompatible with human dignity or would embody a failure to recognize the intrinsic value of a person. But I do not see that in thinking I had a duty to die I would necessarily be failing to respect myself or to appreciate my dignity or worth. Nor would I necessarily be failing to respect you in thinking that you had a similar duty. There is surly also a sense in which we fail to respect ourselves if in the face of illness or death, we stoop to choosing just what is best for ourselves. Indeed, Kant held that the very core of human dignity is the ability to act on a self-imposed moral law, regardless of whether it is in our interest to do so.[7] We shall return to the notion of human dignity.

A third objection appeals to the relative weight of burdens and thus, ultimately, to considerations of fairness or justice. The burdens that an illness creates for the family could not possibly be great enough to justify an obligation to end one's life—the sacrifice of life itself would be a far greater burden than any involved in caring for a chronically ill family member.

But is this true? Consider the following case: An 87-year old woman was dying of congestive heart-failure. Her APACHE score predicted that she had less-than a 50% chance to live for another six months. She was lucid, assertive and terrified of death. She very much wanted to live and kept opting for rehospitalization and the most aggressive life-prolonging treatment possible. That treatment successfully prolonged her life (though with increasing debility) for nearly two years. Her 55-year-old daughter was her only remaining family, her caregiver, and the main source of her financial support. The daughter duly cared for her mother. But before her mother died, her illness had cost the daughter all of her savings, her home, her job and her career.

This is by no means an uncommon sort of case. Thousands of similar cases occur each year. Now, ask yourself which is the greater burden:

(a) To lose a 50% chance of six more months of life at age 87?

(b) To lose all your savings, your home, and your career at age 55?

Which burden would you prefer to bear? Do we really believe the former is the greater burden? Would even the dying mother say that (a) is the greater burden? Or has she been encouraged to believe that the burdens of (b) are somehow morally irrelevant to her choices?

I think most of us would quickly agree that (b) is a greater burden. That is the evil we would more hope to avoid in our lives. If we are tempted to say that the mother's disease and impending death are the greater evil, I believe it is because we are taking a "slice of time" perspective rather than a "lifetime perspective."[8] But surely the lifetime perspective is the appropriate perspective when weighing burdens. If (b) is the greater burden, then we must admit that we have been promulgating an ethic that advocates imposing greater burdens on some people in order to provide smaller benefits for others just because they are ill and thus gain our professional attention and advocacy.

A whole range of cases like this one could easily be generated. In some, the answer about which burden is greater will not be clear. But in many it is. Death—or ending your own life—is simply not the greatest evil or the greatest burden.

This point does not depend on a utilitarian calculus. Even if death were the greatest burden (thus disposing of any simple utilitarian argument), serious questions would remain about the moral justifiability of choosing to impose crushing burdens on loved ones in order to avoid having to bear this burden oneself. The fact that I suffer greater burdens than others in my family does not license me to simply choose what I want for myself, nor does it necessarily release me from a responsibility to try to protect the quality of their lives.

I can readily imagine that, through cowardice, rationalization, or failure of resolve, I will fail in this obligation to protect my loved ones. If so, I think I would need to be excused or forgiven for what I did. But I cannot imagine it would be morally permissible for me to ruin the rest of my partner's life to sustain mine or to cut off my sons' careers, impoverish them, or compromise the quality of their children's lives simply because I wish to live a little longer. This is what leads me to believe in a duty to die.

Who Has a Duty to Die?

Suppose, then, that there can be a duty to die which grows out of the burdens that will fall upon our loved ones if we live on. WHO has a duty to die? And WHEN? To my mind, these are the right questions, the questions we should be asking. Many of us may one day badly need answers to just these questions.

But I cannot supply answers here, for two reasons. In the first place, answers will have to be very particular and contextual. Our concrete duties are often situated, defined in part by the myriad details of our circumstances, histories, and relationships. Though there may be principles that apply to a wide range of cases and some cases that yield pretty straightforward answers, there will also be many situations in which it is very difficult to discern whether one has a duty to die. If nothing else, it will often be very difficult to predict how one's family will bear up under the weight of the burdens that a protracted illness would impose on them.

Secondly and perhaps even more importantly, I believe that those of us with family and loved ones should not define our duties unilaterally, especially not a decision about a duty to die. It would be isolating and distance-creating for me to decide without consulting them what is too much of a burden for my loved ones to bear. That way of deciding about my moral duties is not only atomistic, it also treats my family and loved ones paternalistically. They must be allowed to speak for themselves about the burdens my life imposes on them and how they feel about bearing those burdens.

Some may object that it would be wrong to put a loved one in a position of having to say, in effect, "You should end your life because caring for you is too hard on me and the rest of the family." Not only will it be almost impossible to say something like that to one you love, it will carry with it a heavy load of guilt. On this view, you should decide by yourself whether you have a duty to die and approach your loved ones only after you have made up your mind, to say good-bye to them. Your family could then try to change your mind, but the tremendous weight of moral decision would be lifted from their shoulders.

Perhaps so. But I believe in family decisions. Important decisions for those whose lives are interwoven should be made TOGETHER, in a family discussion. Granted, a conversation about whether I have a duty to die would be a tremendously difficult conversation. The temptations to be dishonest could be enormous. Nevertheless, if I am contemplating a duty to die, I and my family should, if possible, have just such an agonizing discussion. It will act as a check on the information, perceptions, and reasoning of all of us. But even more importantly, it affirms our connectedness at a critical juncture in our lives and our life together. Honest talk about difficult matters almost always strengthens relationships.

However, many families seem unable to talk about death at all, much less a duty to die. Certainly most families could not have this discussion all at once, in one sitting. It might well take a number of discussions to be able to approach this topic. But even if talking about death is impossible, there are always behavioral clues—about your caregiver's tiredness, physical condition, health, prevailing mood, anxiety, financial concerns, outlook, overall well-being and so on. And families unable to talk about death can often talk about how the caregiver is feeling, about finances, about tensions within the family resulting from the illness, about concerns for the future. Deciding whether you have a duty to die based on these behavioral clues and conversation about them honors your relationships better than deciding on your own about how burdensome you and your care must be.

I cannot say when someone has a duty to die. Still, I can suggest a few features of one's illness, history, and circumstances that make it more likely that one has a duty to die. I present them here without much elaboration or explanation.

1) A duty to die is more likely when continuing to live will impose significant burdens—emotional burdens, extensive caregiving, destruction of life plans, and, yes, financial hardship—on your family and loved ones. This is the fundamental insight underlying a duty to die.

2) A duty to die becomes greater as you grow older. As we age, we will be giving up less by giving up our lives, if only because we will sacrifice fewer remaining years of life and a smaller portion of our life plans. After all, it's not as if we would be immortal and live forever if we could just manage to avoid a duty to die. To have reached the age of, say, seventy-five or eighty years without being ready to die is itself a moral failing, the sign of a life out of touch with life's basic realities.[9]

3) A duty to die is more likely when you have already lived a full and rich life. You have already had a full share of the good things life offers.

4) There is greater duty to die if your loved ones' lives have already been difficult or impoverished, if they have had only a small share of the good things that life has to offer (especially if through no fault of their own).

5) A duty to die is more likely when your loved ones have already made great contributions—perhaps even sacrifices—to make your life a good one. Especially if you have not made similar sacrifices for their well-being or for the well-being of other members of your family.

6) To the extent that you can make a good adjustment to your illness or handicapping condition, there is less likely to be a duty to die. A good adjustment means that smaller sacrifices will be required of loved ones and there is more compensating interaction for them. Still, we must also recognize that some diseases—Alzheimer's or Huntington's chorea—will eventually take their toll on your loved ones no matter how courageously,resolutely, even cheerfully you manage to face that illness.

7) There is less likely to be a duty to die if you can still make significant contributions to the lives of others, especially your family. The burdens to family members are not only or even primarily financial, neither are the contributions to them. However, the old and those who have terminal illnesses must also bear in mind that the loss their family members will feel when they die cannot be avoided, only postponed.

8) A duty to die is more likely when the part of you that is loved will soon be gone or seriously compromised. Or when you soon will no longer be capable of giving love. Part of the horror of dementing disease is that it destroys the capacity

to nurture and sustain relationships, taking away a person's agency and the emotions that bind her to others.

9) There is a greater duty to die to the extent that you have lived a relatively lavish lifestyle instead of saving for illness or old age. Like most upper middle-class Americans, I could easily have saved more. It is a greater wrong to come to your family for assistance if your need is the result of having chosen leisure or a spendthrift lifestyle. I may eventually have to face the moral consequences of decisions I am now making.

These, then, are some of the considerations that give shape and definition to the duty to die. If we can agree that these considerations are all relevant, we can see that the correct course of action will often be difficult to discern. A decision about WHEN I should end my life will sometimes prove to be every bit as difficult as the decision about whether I want treatment for myself.

Can the Incompetent Have a Duty to Die?

Several mental deterioration springs readily to mind as one of the situations in which I believe I could have a duty to die. But can incompetent people have duties at all? We can have moral duties we do not recognize or acknowledge, including duties that we NEVER recognized. But can we have duties we are UNABLE to recognize? Duties when we are unable to understand the concept of morality at all? If so, do others have a moral obligation to help us carry out this duty? These are extremely difficult theoretical questions. Our notions of moral agency are severely strained by mental incompetence.

I am tempted to simply bypass the entire question by saying that I am talking only about competent persons. But the idea of a duty to die clearly raises the specter of one person claiming that another—who cannot speak for herself—has such a duty. So I need to say that I can make no sense of the claim that someone has a duty to die if the person has never been able to understand moral obligation at all. To my mind, only those who were formerly capable of making moral decisions could have such a duty.

But the case of formerly competent persons is almost as troubling. Perhaps we should simply stipulate that no incompetent person can have a duty to die, not even if she affirmed belief in such a duty in an advance directive. If we take the view that formerly competent people may have such a duty, we should surely exercise extreme caution when claiming a formerly competent person would have acknowledged a duty to die or that any formerly competent person has an unacknowledged duty to die. Moral dangers loom regardless of which way we decide to resolve such issues.

But for me personally, very urgent practical matters turn on their resolution. If a formerly competent person can no longer have a duty to die (or if other people are not likely to help her carry out this duty), I believe that my obligation may be to die while I am still competent --BEFORE I become unable to make and carry out that decision for myself. Surely it would be irresponsible to evade my moral duties by temporizing until I escape into incompetence. And so I must die sooner than I otherwise would have to. On the other hand, if I could count on others to end my life after I become incompetent, I might be able to fulfill my responsibilities while also living out all my competent or semi-competent days. Given our society's reluctance to permit physicians, let alone family members, to perform aid-in-dying, I believe I may well have a duty to end my life when I can see mental incapacity on the horizon.

There is also the very real problem of sudden incompetence due to a serious incompetence—due to a serious stroke or automobile accident, for example. For me, that is the real nightmare. I suddenly become incompetent, I will fall into the hands of a medical/legal system that will conscientiously disregard my moral beliefs and do what is best for me, regardless of the consequences for my loved ones. And that is not at all what I would have wanted!

Social Policies and a Duty to Die

The claim that there is a duty to die will seem to some a misplaced response to social negligence. If our society were providing for the debilitated, the chronically ill, and the elderly as it should be, there would be only very rare cases of a duty to die. On this view, I am asking the sick and debilitated to step in and accept responsibility because society is derelict in its responsibility to provide for the incapacitated.

This much is surely true: there are a number of social policies we could pursue that would dramatically reduce the incidence of a duty to die. Most obviously, we could decide to pay for facilities that provided excellent long-term care (not just health care!) for all chronically ill, debilitated, mentally ill or demented people in this country. We probably could still afford to do this. If we did, sick, debilitated, and dying people might still be morally required to make sacrifices for their families. I might, for example, have a duty to forgo personal care by a family member who knows me and really does care for me. But these sacrifices would only rarely include the sacrifice of life itself. The duty to die would then be virtually eliminated.

I must not, then, live my life and make my plans on the assumption that social institutions will protect my family from my infirmity and debility. To do so would be irresponsible. More likely, it will be up to me to protect my loved ones.

A Duty to Die and the Meaning of Life

A duty to die seems very harsh, and often it would be. It is one of the tragedies of our lives that someone who wants very much to live can nevertheless have a duty to die. It is both tragic and ironic that it is precisely the very real good of family and loved ones that gives rise to this duty. Indeed, the genuine love, closeness and supportiveness of family members is a major source of this duty: we could not be such a burden if they did not care for us. Finally, there is deep irony in the fact that the very successes of our life-prolonging medicine help to create a widespread duty to die. We do not live in such a happy world that we can avoid such tragedies and ironies. We ought not to close our eyes to this reality or pretend that it just doesn't exist. We ought not to minimize the tragedy in any way.

And yet, a duty to die will not always be as harsh as we might assume. If I love my family, I will want to protect them and their lives. I will want not to make choices that compromise their futures. Indeed, I can easily imagine that I might want to avoid compromising their lives more than I would want anything else. I must also admit that I am not necessarily giving up so much in giving up my life: the conditions that give rise to a duty to die would usually already have compromised the quality of the life I am required to end. In any case, I personally must confess that at age fifty-six, I have already lived a very good life, albeit not yet nearly as long a life as I would like to have.

We fear death too much. Our fear of death has lead to a massive assault on it. We still crave after virtually any life-prolonging technology that we might conceivably be able to produce. We still too often feel morally impelled to prolong life—virtually any form of life—as long as possible. As if the best death is the one that can be put off longest.

We do not even ask about meaning in death, so busy are we with trying to postpone it. But we will not conquer death by one day developing a technology so magnificent that no one will have to die. Nor can we conquer death by postponing it ever longer. We can conquer death only by finding meaning in it.

Although the existence of a duty to die does not hinge on this, recognizing such a duty would go some way toward recovering meaning in death. 1) Paradoxically, it would restore dignity to those who are seriously ill or dying. 2) It would affirm the connections required to give life (and death) meaning. I close now with a few words each of these points.

First, recognizing a duty to die affirms my agency and also my moral agency. I can still do things that make an important difference in the lives of my loved ones. Moreover, the fact that I still have responsibilities keeps me within the community of moral agents. My illness or debility has not reduced me to a mere moral patient (to use the language of the philosophers). Though it may not be the whole story, surely Kant was onto something important when he claimed that human dignity rests on the capacity for moral agency within a community of those who respect the demands of morality.

By contrast, surely there is something deeply insulting in a medicine and a bioethics that would ask only what I want (or would have wanted) when I become ill. To treat me as if I had no moral responsibilities when I am ill or debilitated implies that my condition has rendered me morally incompetent. Only small children, the demented or insane, and those totally lacking in the capacity to act are free from moral duties. There is dignity, then, and a kind of meaning in moral agency, even as it forces extremely difficult decisions upon us.

Secondly, recovering meaning in death requires an affirmation of connections. If I end my life to spare the futures of my loved ones, I testify in my death that I am connected to them. It is because I love and care for precisely these people (and I know they care for me) that I wish not to be such a burden to them. By contrast, a life in which I am free to choose whatever I want for myself is a life unconnected to others. A bioethics that would treat me as if I had no serious moral responsibilities does what it can to marginalize, weaken, or even destroy my connections with others.

But life without connection is meaningless. The individualistic fantasy, though occasionally liberating, is deeply destructive. When life is good and vitality seems unending, life itself and life lived for yourself may seem quite sufficient. But if not life, certainly death without connection is meaningless. If you are only for yourself, all you have to care about as your life draws to a close is yourself and your life. Everything you care about will then perish in your death. And that—the end of everything you care about—is precisely the total collapse of meaning. We can, then, find meaning in death only through a sense of connection with something that will survive our death.

This need not be connections with other people. Some people are deeply tied to land (e.g., the family farm), to nature, or to a transcendent reality. But for most of us, the connections that sustain us are to other people. In the full bloom of life, we are connected to others in many ways—through work, profession, neighborhood, country, shared faith and worship, common leisure pursuits, friendships. Even the guru meditating in isolation on his mountain top is connected to a long tradition of people united by the same religious quest.

But as we age or when we become chronically ill, connections with other people usually become more restricted. Often only ties with family and close friends remain and remain important to us. Moreover, for many of us, other connections just don't go deep enough. As Paul Tsongas has reminded us, "when it comes time to die, no one says, 'I wish I had spent more time at the office.'"

If I am correct, death is so difficult for us partly because our sense of community is so weak. Death seems to wipe out everything when we can't fit it into the lives of those who live on. A death motivated by the desire to spare the futures of my loved ones might well be a better death for me than the one I would get as a result of opting to continue my life as long as there is any pleasure in it for me. Pleasure is nice, but it is meaning that matters.

I don't know about others, but these reflections have helped me. I am now more at peace about facing a duty to die. Ending my life if my duty required might still be difficult. But for me, a far greater horror would be dying all alone or stealing the futures of my loved ones in order to buy a little more time for myself. I hope that if the time comes when I have a duty to die, I will recognize it, encourage my loved ones to recognize it too, and carry it out bravely.

Acknowledgements

I wish to thank Mary English, Hilde Nelson, Jim Bennett, Tom Townsend, the members of the Philosophy Department at ETSU and anonymous reviewers of the REPORT for many helpful comments on earlier versions of this paper. In this paper, I draw on material in Hardwig J. "Dying at the Right Time; Reflections on (Un)Assisted Suicide" in LaFollette, H. *Practical Ethics* (London: Blackwell), 1996, with permission.

Notes

1. Given the importance of relationships in my thinking,"responsibility"—rooted as it is in "respond"—would perhaps be the most appropriate word. Nevertheless, I often use "duty" despite its legalistic overtones, because Lamm's famous statement has given the expression "duty to die" a certain familiarity. But I intend no implication that there is a law which grounds this duty, nor that someone has a right corresponding to it.

2. For a discussion of the Oates case, see Tom L. Beauchamp, "What Is Suicide?" in Tom L. Beauchamp & Seymour Perlin, eds., *Ethical Issues in Death and Dying*, (Englewood Cliffs, NJ: Prentice-Hall, 1978).

3. Most bioethicists advocate a "patient-centered ethics"—an ethics which claims only the patient's interests should be considered in making medical treatment decisions. Most health care professionals have been trained to accept this ethic and to see themselves as patient advocates. For arguments that a patient-centered ethics should be replaced by a family-centered ethics see John Hardwig, "What About the Family?" *Hastings Center Report 20*, no. 2 (1990): 5–10; Hilde L. Nelson & James L. Nelson, *The Patient in the Family*, (New York: Routledge, 1995).

4. A good account of the burdens of caregiving can be found in Elaine Brody, *Women in the Middle: Their Parent-Care Years* (New York: Springer Publishing Co., 1990). Perhaps the best article-length account of these burdens is Daniel Callahan, "Families as Caregivers; the Limits of Morality" in Nancy Jecker, ed., *Aging and Ethics: Philosophical Problems in Gerontology*, (Totowa NJ: Humana Press, 1991).

5. Kenneth E. Covinsky, Less Goldman et al., "The Impact of Serious Illness on Patients' Families" 272 (1994): 1839–1844.

6. Larry Churchill, for example, believes that Christian ethics takes us far beyond my present position: "Christian doctrines of stewardship prohibit the extension of one's own life at a great cost to the neighbor . . . And such a gesture should not appear to us a sacrifice, but as the ordinary virtue entailed by a just social conscience." Larry Churchill, *Rationing Health Care in America* (South Bend, IN: Notre Dame University Press, 1988), p. 112.

7. Kant, as is well known, was opposed to suicide. But he was arguing against taking your life out of self-interested motives. It is not clear that Kant would or we should consider taking your life out of a sense of duty to be wrong. See Hilde Nelson, "Death with Kantian Dignity," *Journal of Clinical Ethics*, 7 (1996): 215–21.

8. Obviously, I owe this distinction to Norman Daniels. Normal Daniels, *Am I My Parents' Keeper? An Essay on Justice Between the Young and the Old* (New York: Oxford University Press, 1988). Just as obviously, Daniels is not committed to my use of it here.

9. Daniel Callahan, *The Troubled Dream of Life* (New York: Simon & Schuster, 1993).

California Penal Code
Section 261–269

The Penal Code of California is the foundation for applying criminal law in the state of California. It was originally enacted in 1872 and has been substantially amended and revised since then. Sections 261–269 define the crimes of rape, unlawful sexual intercourse, prostitution, and stipulate the penalties for the crimes described. Section 261.7 defines the meaning of consent under California criminal law.

261. (a) Rape is an act of sexual intercourse accomplished with a person not the spouse of the perpetrator, under any of the following circumstances:

(1) Where a person is incapable, because of a mental disorder or developmental or physical disability, of giving legal consent, and this is known or reasonably should be known to the person committing the act. Notwithstanding the existence of a conservatorship pursuant to the provisions of the Lanterman-Petris-Short Act (Part 1 (commencing with Section 5000) of Division 5 of the Welfare and Institutions Code), the prosecuting attorney shall prove, as an element of the crime, that a mental disorder or developmental or physical disability rendered the alleged victim incapable of giving consent.

(2) Where it is accomplished against a person's will by means of force, violence, duress, menace, or fear of immediate and unlawful bodily injury on the person or another.

(3) Where a person is prevented from resisting by any intoxicating or anesthetic substance, or any controlled substance, and this condition was known, or reasonably should have been known by the accused.

(4) Where a person is at the time unconscious of the nature of the act, and this is known to the accused. As used in this paragraph, "unconscious of the nature of the act" means incapable of resisting because the victim meets any one of the following conditions:

(A) Was unconscious or asleep.

(B) Was not aware, knowing, perceiving, or cognizant that the act occurred.

(C) Was not aware, knowing, perceiving, or cognizant of the essential characteristics of the act due to the perpetrator's fraud in fact.

(D) Was not aware, knowing, perceiving, or cognizant of the essential characteristics of the act due to the perpetrator's fraudulent representation that the sexual penetration served a professional purpose when it served no professional purpose.

(5) Where a person submits under the belief that the person committing the act is someone known to the victim other than the accused, and this belief is induced by any artifice, pretense, or concealment practiced by the accused, with intent to induce the belief.

(6) Where the act is accomplished against the victim's will by threatening to retaliate in the future against the victim or any other person, and there is a reasonable possibility that the perpetrator will execute the threat. As used in this paragraph, "threatening to retaliate" means a threat to kidnap or falsely imprison, or to inflict extreme pain, serious bodily injury, or death.

(7) Where the act is accomplished against the victim's will by threatening to use the authority of a public official to incarcerate, arrest, or deport the victim or another, and the victim has a reasonable belief that the perpetrator is a public official. As used in this paragraph, "public official" means a person employed by a governmental agency who has the authority, as part of that position, to incarcerate, arrest, or deport another. The perpetrator does not actually have to be a public official.

(b) As used in this section, "duress" means a direct or implied threat of force, violence, danger, or retribution sufficient to coerce a reasonable person of ordinary susceptibilities to perform an act which otherwise would not have been performed, or acquiesce in an act to which one otherwise would not have submitted. The total circumstances, including the age of the victim, and his or her relationship to the defendant, are factors to consider in appraising the existence of duress.

(c) As used in this section, "menace" means any threat, declaration, or act which shows an intention to inflict an injury upon another.

261.5. (a) Unlawful sexual intercourse is an act of sexual intercourse accomplished with a person who is not the spouse of the perpetrator, if the person is a minor. For the purposes of this section, a "minor" is a person under the age of 18 years and an "adult" is a person who is at least 18 years of age.

(b) Any person who engages in an act of unlawful sexual intercourse with a minor who is not more than three years older or three years younger than the perpetrator, is guilty of a misdemeanor.

(c) Any person who engages in an act of unlawful sexual intercourse with a minor who is more than three years younger than the perpetrator is guilty of either a misdemeanor or a felony, and shall be punished by imprisonment in a county jail not exceeding one year, or by imprisonment pursuant to subdivision (h) of Section 1170.

(d) Any person 21 years of age or older who engages in an act of unlawful sexual intercourse with a minor who is under 16 years of age is guilty of either a misdemeanor or a felony, and shall be punished by imprisonment in a county jail not exceeding one year, or by imprisonment pursuant to subdivision (h) of Section 1170 for two, three, or four years.

(e) (1) Notwithstanding any other provision of this section, an adult who engages in an act of sexual intercourse with a minor in violation of this section may be liable for civil penalties in the following amounts:

(A) An adult who engages in an act of unlawful sexual intercourse with a minor less than two years younger than the adult is liable for a civil penalty not to exceed two thousand dollars ($2,000).

(B) An adult who engages in an act of unlawful sexual intercourse with a minor at least two years younger than the adult is liable for a civil penalty not to exceed five thousand dollars ($5,000).

(C) An adult who engages in an act of unlawful sexual intercourse with a minor at least three years younger than the adult is liable for a civil penalty not to exceed ten thousand dollars ($10,000).

(D) An adult over the age of 21 years who engages in an act of unlawful sexual intercourse with a minor under 16 years of age is liable for a civil penalty not to exceed twenty-five thousand dollars ($25,000).

(2) The district attorney may bring actions to recover civil penalties pursuant to this subdivision. From the amounts collected for each case, an amount equal to the costs of pursuing the action shall be deposited with the treasurer of the county in which the judgment was entered, and the remainder shall be deposited in the Underage Pregnancy Prevention Fund, which is hereby created in the State Treasury. Amounts deposited in the Underage Pregnancy Prevention Fund may be used only for the purpose of preventing underage pregnancy upon appropriation by the Legislature.

(3) In addition to any punishment imposed under this section, the judge may assess a fine not to exceed seventy dollars ($70) against any person who violates this section with the proceeds of this fine to be used in accordance with Section 1463.23. The court shall, however, take into consideration the defendant's ability to pay, and no defendant shall be denied probation because of his or her inability to pay the fine permitted under this subdivision.

261.6. In prosecutions under Section 261, 262, 286, 288a, or 289, in which consent is at issue, "consent" shall be defined to mean positive cooperation in act or attitude pursuant to an exercise of free will. The person must act freely and voluntarily and have knowledge of the nature of the act or transaction involved.

A current or previous dating or marital relationship shall not be sufficient to constitute consent where consent is at issue in a prosecution under Section 261, 262, 286, 288a, or 289.

Nothing in this section shall affect the admissibility of evidence or the burden of proof on the issue of consent.

261.7. In prosecutions under Section 261, 262, 286, 288a, or 289, in which consent is at issue, evidence that the victim suggested, requested, or otherwise communicated to the defendant that the defendant use a condom or other birth control device, without additional evidence of consent, is not sufficient to constitute consent.

261.9. (a) Any person convicted of seeking to procure or procuring the sexual services of a prostitute in violation of subdivision (b) of Section 647, if the prostitute is under 18 years of age, shall be ordered by the court, in addition to any other penalty or fine imposed, to pay an additional fine in an amount not to exceed twenty-five thousand dollars ($25,000).

(b) Every fine imposed and collected pursuant to this section shall, upon appropriation by the Legislature, be available to fund programs and services for commercially sexually exploited minors in the counties where the underlying offenses are committed.

262. (a) Rape of a person who is the spouse of the perpetrator is an act of sexual intercourse accomplished under any of the following circumstances:

(1) Where it is accomplished against a person's will by means of force, violence, duress, menace, or fear of immediate and unlawful bodily injury on the person or another.

(2) Where a person is prevented from resisting by any intoxicating or anesthetic substance, or any controlled substance, and this condition was known, or reasonably should have been known, by the accused.

(3) Where a person is at the time unconscious of the nature of the act, and this is known to the accused. As used in this paragraph, "unconscious of the nature of the act" means incapable of resisting because the victim meets one of the following conditions:

(A) Was unconscious or asleep.

(B) Was not aware, knowing, perceiving, or cognizant that the act occurred.

(C) Was not aware, knowing, perceiving, or cognizant of the essential characteristics of the act due to the perpetrator's fraud in fact.

(4) Where the act is accomplished against the victim's will by threatening to retaliate in the future against the victim or any other person, and there is a reasonable possibility that the perpetrator will execute the threat. As used in this paragraph, "threatening to retaliate" means a threat to kidnap or falsely imprison, or to inflict extreme pain, serious bodily injury, or death.

(5) Where the act is accomplished against the victim's will by threatening to use the authority of a public official to incarcerate, arrest, or deport the victim or another, and the victim has a reasonable belief that the perpetrator is a public official. As used in this paragraph, "public official" means a person employed by a governmental agency who has the authority, as part of that position, to incarcerate, arrest, or deport another. The perpetrator does not actually have to be a public official.

(b) As used in this section, "duress" means a direct or implied threat of force, violence, danger, or retribution sufficient to coerce a reasonable person of ordinary susceptibilities to perform an act which otherwise would not have been performed, or acquiesce in an act to which one otherwise would not have submitted. The total circumstances, including the age of the victim, and his or her relationship to the defendant, are factors to consider in apprising the existence of duress.

(c) As used in this section, "menace" means any threat, declaration, or act that shows an intention to inflict an injury upon another.

(d) If probation is granted upon conviction of a violation of this section, the conditions of probation may include, in lieu of a fine, one or both of the following requirements:

(1) That the defendant make payments to a battered women's shelter, up to a maximum of one thousand dollars ($1,000).

(2) That the defendant reimburse the victim for reasonable costs of counseling and other reasonable expenses that the court finds are the direct result of the defendant's offense.

For any order to pay a fine, make payments to a battered women's shelter, or pay restitution as a condition of probation under this subdivision, the court shall make a determination of the defendant's ability to pay. In no event shall any order to make payments to a battered women's shelter be made if it would impair the ability of the defendant to pay direct restitution to the victim or court-ordered child support. Where the injury to a married person is caused in whole or in part by the criminal acts of his or her spouse in violation of this section, the community property may not be used to discharge the liability of the offending spouse for restitution to the injured spouse, required by Section 1203.04, as operative on or before August 2, 1995, or Section 1202.4, or to a shelter for costs with regard to the injured spouse and dependents, required by this section, until all separate property of the offending spouse is exhausted.

263. The essential guilt of rape consists in the outrage to the person and feelings of the victim of the rape. Any sexual penetration, however slight, is sufficient to complete the crime.

264. (a) Except as provided in subdivision (c), rape, as defined in Section 261 or 262, is punishable by imprisonment in the state prison for three, six, or eight years.

(b) In addition to any punishment imposed under this section the judge may assess a fine not to exceed seventy dollars ($70) against any person who violates Section 261 or 262 with the proceeds of this fine to be used in accordance with Section 1463.23. The court shall, however, take into consideration the defendant's ability to pay, and no defendant shall be denied probation because of his or her inability to pay the fine permitted under this subdivision.

(c) (1) Any person who commits rape in violation of paragraph (2) of subdivision (a) of Section 261 upon a child who is under 14 years of age shall be punished by imprisonment in the state prison for 9, 11, or 13 years.

(2) Any person who commits rape in violation of paragraph (2) of subdivision (a) of Section 261 upon a minor who is 14 years of age or older shall be punished by imprisonment in the state prison for 7, 9, or 11 years.

(3) This subdivision does not preclude prosecution under Section 269, Section 288.7, or any other provision of law.

264.1. (a) The provisions of Section 264 notwithstanding, in any case in which the defendant, voluntarily acting in concert with another person, by force or violence and against the will of the victim, committed an act described in Section 261, 262, or 289, either personally or by aiding and abetting the other person, that fact shall be charged in the indictment or information and if found to be true by the jury, upon a jury trial, or if found to be true by the court, upon a court trial, or if admitted by the defendant, the defendant shall suffer confinement in the state prison for five, seven, or nine years.

(b) (1) If the victim of an offense described in subdivision (a) is a child who is under 14 years of age, the defendant shall be punished by imprisonment in the state prison for 10, 12, or 14 years.

(2) If the victim of an offense described in subdivision (a) is a minor who is 14 years of age or older, the defendant shall be punished by imprisonment in the state prison for 7, 9, or 11 years.

(3) This subdivision does not preclude prosecution under Section 269, Section 288.7, or any other provision of law.

264.2. (a) Whenever there is an alleged violation or violations of subdivision (e) of Section 243, or Section 261, 261.5, 262, 273.5, 286, 288a, or 289, the law enforcement officer assigned to the case shall immediately provide the victim of the crime with the "Victims of Domestic Violence" card, as specified in subparagraph (G) of paragraph (9) of subdivision (c) of Section 13701.

(b) (1) The law enforcement officer, or his or her agency, shall immediately notify the local rape victim counseling center, whenever a victim of an alleged violation of Section 261, 261.5, 262, 286, 288a, or 289 is transported to a hospital for any medical evidentiary or physical examination. The victim shall have the right to have a sexual assault counselor, as defined in Section 1035.2 of the Evidence Code, and a support person of the victim's choosing present at any medical evidentiary or physical examination.

(2) Prior to the commencement of any initial medical evidentiary or physical examination arising out of a sexual assault, a victim shall be notified orally or in writing by the medical provider that the victim has the right to have present a sexual assault counselor and at least one other support person of the victim's choosing.

(3) The hospital may verify with the law enforcement officer, or his or her agency, whether the local rape victim counseling center has been notified, upon the approval of the victim.

(4) A support person may be excluded from a medical evidentiary or physical examination if the law enforcement officer or medical provider determines that the presence of that individual would be detrimental to the purpose of the examination.

265. Every person who takes any woman unlawfully, against her will, and by force, menace or duress, compels her to marry him, or to marry any other person, or to be defiled, is punishable by imprisonment pursuant to subdivision (h) of Section 1170.

266. Every person who inveigles or entices any unmarried female, of previous chaste character, under the age of 18 years, into any house of ill fame, or of assignation, or elsewhere, for the purpose of prostitution, or to have illicit carnal connection with any man; and every person who aids or assists in such inveiglement or enticement; and every person who, by any false pretenses, false representation, or other fraudulent means, procures any female to have illicit carnal connection with any man, is punishable by imprisonment in the state prison, or by imprisonment in a county jail not exceeding one year, or by a fine not exceeding two thousand dollars ($2,000), or by both such fine and imprisonment.

266a. Every person who, within this state, takes any person against his or her will and without his or her consent, or with his or her consent procured by fraudulent inducement or misrepresentation, for the purpose of prostitution, as defined in subdivision (b) of Section 647, is punishable by imprisonment in the state prison, and a fine not exceeding two thousand dollars ($2,000).

266b. Every person who takes any other person unlawfully, and against his or her will, and by force, menace, or duress, compels him or her to live with such person in an illicit relation, against his or her consent, or to so live with any other person, is punishable by imprisonment pursuant to subdivision (h) of Section 1170.

266c. Every person who induces any other person to engage in sexual intercourse, sexual penetration, oral copulation, or sodomy when his or her consent is procured by false or fraudulent representation or pretense that is made with the intent to create fear, and which does induce fear, and that would cause a reasonable person in like circumstances to act contrary to the person's free will, and does cause the victim to so act, is punishable by imprisonment in a county jail for not more than one year or in the state prison for two, three, or four years.

As used in this section, "fear" means the fear of physical injury or death to the person or to any relative of the person or member of the person's family.

266d. Any person who receives any money or other valuable thing for or on account of placing in custody any other person for the purpose of causing the other person to cohabit with any person to whom the other person is not married, is guilty of a felony.

266e. Every person who purchases, or pays any money or other valuable thing for, any person for the purpose of prostitution as defined in subdivision (b) of Section 647, or for the purpose of placing such person, for immoral purposes, in any house or place against his or her will, is guilty of a felony punishable by imprisonment in the state prison for 16 months, or two or three years.

266f. Every person who sells any person or receives any money or other valuable thing for or on account of his or her placing in custody, for immoral purposes, any person, whether with or without his or her consent, is guilty of a felony punishable by imprisonment in the state prison for 16 months, or two or three years.

266g. Every man who, by force, intimidation, threats, persuasion, promises, or any other means, places or leaves, or procures any other person or persons to place or leave, his wife in a house of prostitution, or connives at or consents to, or permits, the placing or leaving of his wife in a house of prostitution, or allows or permits her to remain therein, is guilty of a felony and punishable by imprisonment pursuant to subdivision (h) of Section 1170 for two, three or four years; and in all prosecutions under this section a wife is a competent witness against her husband.

266h. (a) Except as provided in subdivision (b), any person who, knowing another person is a prostitute, lives or derives support or maintenance in whole or in part from the earnings or proceeds of the person's prostitution, or from money loaned or advanced to or charged against that person by any keeper or manager or inmate of a house or other place where prostitution is practiced or allowed, or who solicits or receives compensation for soliciting for the person, is guilty of pimping, a felony, and shall be punishable by imprisonment in the state prison for three, four, or six years.

(b) Any person who, knowing another person is a prostitute, lives or derives support or maintenance in whole or in part from the earnings or proceeds of the person's prostitution, or from money loaned or advanced to or charged against that person by any keeper or manager or inmate of a house or other place where prostitution is practiced or allowed, or who solicits or receives compensation for soliciting for the person, when the prostitute is a minor, is guilty of pimping a minor, a felony, and shall be punishable as follows:

(1) If the person engaged in prostitution is a minor 16 years of age or older, the offense is punishable by imprisonment in the state prison for three, four, or six years.

(2) If the person engaged in prostitution is under 16 years of age, the offense is punishable by imprisonment in the state prison for three, six, or eight years.

266i. (a) Except as provided in subdivision (b), any person who does any of the following is guilty of pandering, a felony, and shall be punishable by imprisonment in the state prison for three, four, or six years:

(1) Procures another person for the purpose of prostitution.

(2) By promises, threats, violence, or by any device or scheme, causes, induces, persuades, or encourages another person to become a prostitute.

(3) Procures for another person a place as an inmate in a house of prostitution or as an inmate of any place in which prostitution is encouraged or allowed within this state.

(4) By promises, threats, violence, or by any device or scheme, causes, induces, persuades, or encourages an inmate of a house of prostitution, or any other place in which prostitution is encouraged or allowed, to remain therein as an inmate.

(5) By fraud or artifice, or by duress of person or goods, or by abuse of any position of confidence or authority, procures another person for the purpose of prostitution, or to enter any place in which prostitution is encouraged or allowed within this state, or to come into this state or leave this state for the purpose of prostitution.

(6) Receives or gives, or agrees to receive or give, any money or thing of value for procuring, or attempting to procure, another person for the purpose of prostitution, or to come into this state or leave this state for the purpose of prostitution.

(b) Any person who does any of the acts described in subdivision (a) with another person who is a minor is guilty of pandering, a felony, and shall be punishable as follows:

(1) If the other person is a minor 16 years of age or older, the offense is punishable by imprisonment in the state prison for three, four, or six years.

(2) If the other person is under 16 years of age, the offense is punishable by imprisonment in the state prison for three, six, or eight years.

266j. Any person who intentionally gives, transports, provides, or makes available, or who offers to give, transport, provide, or make available to another person, a child under the age of 16 for the purpose of any lewd or lascivious act as defined in Section 288, or who causes, induces, or persuades a child under the age of 16 to engage in such an act with another person, is guilty of a felony and shall be imprisoned in the state prison for a term of three, six, or eight years, and by a fine not to exceed fifteen thousand dollars ($15,000).

266k. (a) Upon the conviction of any person for a violation of Section 266h or 266i, the court may, in addition to any other penalty or fine imposed, order the defendant to pay an additional fine not to exceed five thousand dollars ($5,000). In setting the amount of the fine, the court shall consider any relevant factors including, but not limited to, the seriousness and gravity of the offense and the circumstances of its commission, whether the defendant derived any economic gain as the result of the crime, and the extent to which the victim suffered losses as a result of the crime. Every fine imposed and collected under this section shall be deposited in the Victim-Witness Assistance Fund to be available for appropriation to fund child sexual exploitation and child sexual abuse victim counseling centers and prevention programs under Section 13837.

(b) Upon the conviction of any person for a violation of Section 266j or 267, the court may, in addition to any other penalty or fine imposed, order the defendant to pay an additional fine not to exceed twenty thousand dollars ($20,000).

(c) Fifty percent of the fines collected pursuant to subdivision (b) and deposited in the Victim-Witness Assistance Fund pursuant to subdivision (a) shall be granted to community-based organizations that serve minor victims of human trafficking.

(d) If the court orders a fine to be imposed pursuant to this section, the actual administrative cost of collecting that fine, not to exceed 2 percent of the total amount paid, may be paid into the general fund of the county treasury for the use and benefit of the county.

267. Every person who takes away any other person under the age of 18 years from the father, mother, guardian, or other person having the legal charge of the other person, without their consent, for the purpose of prostitution, is punishable by imprisonment in the state prison, and a fine not exceeding two thousand dollars ($2,000).

269. (a) Any person who commits any of the following acts upon a child who is under 14 years of age and seven or more years younger than the person is guilty of aggravated sexual assault of a child:

(1) Rape, in violation of paragraph (2) or (6) of subdivision (a) of Section 261.

(2) Rape or sexual penetration, in concert, in violation of Section 264.1.

(3) Sodomy, in violation of paragraph (2) or (3) of subdivision (c), or subdivision (d), of Section 286.

(4) Oral copulation, in violation of paragraph (2) or (3) of subdivision (c), or subdivision (d), of Section 288a.

(5) Sexual penetration, in violation of subdivision (a) of Section 289.

(b) Any person who violates this section is guilty of a felony and shall be punished by imprisonment in the state prison for 15 years to life.

(c) The court shall impose a consecutive sentence for each offense that results in a conviction under this section if the crimes involve separate victims or involve the same victim on separate occasions as defined in subdivision (d) of Section 667.6.

Can Professionalism Still Be a Viable Ethic?

William M. Sullivan

William M. Sullivan *works on the Preparation for the Professions Program. He also directs the Cross Professions Seminar, comparing education across professions, drawing out common themes and identifying distinct practices in professional education. Sullivan is the author of* Work and Integrity: The Crisis and Promise of Professionalism in America *(2004) and a co-author of* Educating Lawyers: Preparation for the Profession of Law *(2007), and* Habits of the Heart: Individualism and Commitment in American Life *(2007). Prior to his work at Carnegie, Sullivan was professor of philosophy at La Salle University. He earned a PhD in philosophy at Fordham University.*

The Unlikely Persistence of Professionalism

We are living in a time when the professions seem an odd fit, if not a bad one, with the world of work. Today's ascendant images of work have made shibboleths of individual "competitiveness" and strategic "flexibility" in career. While the professions are central to the knowledge economy, their structures of corporate membership and loyalty rarely figure in descriptions of work's future. That future is often depicted as a globalizing march toward a "frictionless capitalism" based upon information and communications technology, a global market from which individuals may profit but to which they must unquestioningly submit. Professionals, by contrast, have preferred to work in regulated markets and advance their claims to authority on the basis of a pledge of fiduciary responsibility, quality of service, and accountability. In both the United States and Britain the professions, including law, medicine, the clergy, the academy and others, continue to stand out in the occupational sphere by the unique way they organize their work, recruit and train their members, and deliver their services.

The professions demand long apprenticeships, carried out in formal educational institutions, which are centered on mastery of complex skills and bodies of knowledge. Professionals work in peculiar labor markets. These are often regulated by the state yet governed largely by standards which the professions themselves have set. Perhaps most significantly, professions such as medicine, law, and the academy are still reluctant to embrace the ubiquitous imagery of business and industry, clinging instead to values of institutional mission, and public service. Despite the fact that each of these fields has become more like business (including widening differences in income and opportunity between the upper and lower reaches of each profession), it is as though the professions harbor their own, quite different notions of good work and a good society which are somehow at odds with market-and-technology utopianism that is so much a part of this era.

In fact, I will argue that professionalism in both the United States and Britain points toward an alternative conception of work and society. It is an ideal of social partnership between the public and functional groups which organize to advance social values in the interest of those they serve. The professions are responsible for key public values such as health, civil regulation and social justice, technological safety, the reliability of public information, and education. It is this responsibility and orientation toward public goods that distinguishes professionals from other "knowledge workers." While professionals are often engaged in generating or applying new ideas and advanced processes, they are directly pledged to ideals of public service.

This kind of social partnership demands both accountability and responsibility on the part of the professions. It also calls for active participation and public concern on the part of citizens whom the professions serve. This reciprocity is what I have called civic professionalism.[1] The immediate question concerns the prospects for professionalism as a civic ethic at a time when public interest and participation in civic affairs continues to decline, while the conditions of professional work link skills less with public purposes than with market advantage.[2]

Despite the fact that each of these fields has become more like business (including widening differences in income and opportunity between the upper and lower reaches of each profession), it is as though the professions harbor their own, quite different notions of good work and a good society which are somehow at odds with market-and-technology utopianism that is so much a part of this era.

The Significance of the Professions

The ideals bound up with professionalism have been only imperfectly realized in any professional field. But the persistence of these aspirations is itself noteworthy. "Professions are defined," notes historian Sheldon Rothblatt, "by an ethic of service. All agree that education, whether apprenticeship or science, has been the central feature of professional identity."[3] Equally true, the professions are highly skilled occupations with a distinctive corporate form of organization. But they are more than this. In their corporate organization they represent a project for bringing into the capitalist marketplace the spirit of public service. In professions, the claims of public safety and welfare have established a beachhead squarely within the realm of self-interested market transactions.

The structure of professions embodies the proposition that capital, specifically human or intellectual capital, ought to be treated as a public trust rather than simply an individual possession to be traded upon without regard for the consequences to others. Consequently, the professions are organized so that individuals must submit to the corporate organization in order to acquire their specialized skills and, equally important, can only benefit personally from the employment of this "human capital" by applying it according to standards that are established and, in aspiration at least, monitored for the public benefit. Of all job categories, professionals have traditionally shown the greatest degree of involvement in their work, along with the greatest attachment to its intrinsic rewards as opposed to income and status.[4] In many ways, the professions have indeed provided models of "good work."[5]

Professions operate within an explicit contract with society as a whole. In exchange for privileges such as monopoly on the ability to practice in specific fields, professions agree to provide certain important social services. In exchange for the privilege of setting standards for admission and authorizing practice, professions are legally obliged to discipline their own ranks for the public welfare. The basis of these contracts is a set of common goals shared by the public and for which different professions undertake responsibility. So, medicine, nursing, and public health are chartered for the maintenance and improvement of society's health, just as education exists to promote the goal of an educated citizenry, law to secure social justice, or engineers to ensure safety.

These are public values. In economic parlance, they are public goods, meaning that they are values from which all benefit and which depend on everyone's cooperation, but to which no individual market actor has a strong incentive to contribute. The professions are publicly chartered to make it their primary concern to sustain such public goods. They are, therefore, in an important sense public occupations even when they work outside government or publicly-supported institutions. In theory, though ambiguously in American practice, the professions' natural ally is government, in its vital function as the guardian of citizen's common values.

The major economic and social changes of the past three decades have powerfully affected professional life during the past three decades. Analysts such as Derek Bok have pointed to the great shift in compensation, and also prestige, within professional ranks since the 1970s. The trend has been away from public-sector employment such as government and education toward the service of business and private-sector activities. One major result has been the growth in income disparity within professional ranks, directing the paths toward both wealth and prestige into the profit-making arena and away from public service.[6] Steven Brint has summarized these developments as a movement away from an earlier conception of professionalism as "social trusteeship" toward the embrace of a notion of the professional as the purveyor of "expert" services in an increasingly stratified and competitive marketplace.[7] The move toward merging legal and accounting firms to provide a portfolio of business services that occurred just before the late 1990s stock market bubble burst, can stand as an example of the trend.

At the same time, some professions, most notably law, have grown vastly in size. Public policy has simultaneously relaxed controls on intra-professional competition. The result has been a more desperate scramble for livelihood, with the consequence of vast discrepancy between the incomes of elite firms and that of the solo practitioner. In many areas the professional world, like American business, has become "leaner and meaner."[8] Other fields, such as teaching, have never recovered from the post-1970 fall of public confidence in the schools, the largest drop in status of any professional field.[9] Medicine, perhaps most notoriously, is in the midst of major changes, largely in reaction to drastic changes in its regulatory and organizational context, a context which the profession is less and less able to control.

The professions are publicly chartered to make it their primary concern to sustain such public goods. They are, therefore, in an important sense public occupations even when they work outside government or publicly-supported institutions.

Institutionalizing Vocation

These unmistakable trends have reduced the cohesion of professional organizations. The larger social climate has put professions on the defensive. It has led many to question both the value and viability of the professional organization of work. It is important to remember that the modern professions are the products of the creative period of institution-building that occurred around the turn of the twentieth century. They grew up and prospered in the industrial society of the past century. However, in the wake of the idealism of the 1960s, it seemed to more than a few observers that they were witnessing a different sort of transformation of the professions. Movements and groups espousing "professions for the people" and professionals for "social responsibility" seemed harbingers of a more egalitarian future. As called for by radical intellectuals at the time, professionals would renounce their aloof, authoritative status and redirect their expertise by joining the "people" in spontaneous, egalitarian associations. Professional schools were to be redesigned into self-managing collectives with strong lay participation in both teaching and management.

The source of this ferment was a moral complaint. The charges against professionals were arrogance and unjustified "paternalism." These charges grew from a new emphasis upon the "autonomy" of patients, clients, students, and the public. However, the context for this incipient revolt of the "people" against their often well-intentioned tutors was a society with stronger public institutions than America has now, as well as general elite support of public goals such as health coverage for all, workplace safety, and environmental protection. In keeping with the major social movements of the time, such as Civil Rights and the Women's Movement, were both democratization of access to public goods and democratization in the way in which professional services were provided and professionals recruited and educated.

The late-60s movements for professional reform have found an antiphonal echo in today's ubiquitous incantations of the "free market." Today's anti-professionalism comes from the anti-state, individualistic populism of those Conservatives who oppose professions as conspiracies for the restraint of trade. In the United States, from the late 1960s onward, public opinion polls measured a dramatic loss of public confidence in major public institutions, including many of the traditional professions associated with them. This loss of trust has never been reversed.[10] However, since the political triumph of Conservatism in the 1980s, with the Thatcher government in Britain and the Reagan presidency in the United States, public policy has not attempted to make the professions better serve public goals. Rather, it has been generally hostile to the idea that government, or delegated corporate bodies such as professions, can or should carry out projects of public purpose— except in a few limited cases such as national defense, though even there various kinds of "privatization" have been attempted. On the contrary, it is alleged that all problems can be better addressed through "market solutions." In historical fact, the decline of industrial unions with their largely male membership has found its analogue in the fate of less-prestigious professional fields such as teaching, nursing, and social work, which have been overwhelmingly staffed by women.

To defend professional prerogatives requires granting society an existence independent of individuals competing in the market. It is to give collective action in the form of politics a certain priority over individual action aiming to fulfill private desires. But it is also to take seriously the professions' own obligation to see that standards of practice are maintained by their own members for the protection of the public.

The concept which the free market ideologues have found suspicious and finally indigestible is the notion of vocation. Professionals have traditionally been ascribed vocations as well as careers or jobs. A century ago, the idea of calling was the basis of the argument for professional control of markets and training. Such "market shelters" would provide a structural foundation for professional identity and long-term commitment. The wave of new professions such as social work and journalism were one result of this movement, along with an expansion and restructuring of the traditional learned fields.[11] While the value of a calling still resonates, it is often understood as only applicable in a few highly prestigious spheres. So, apart from the directly religious sense of calling, it is widely understood that both in the arts and in science, contributions of value require nothing less than the whole of a person's life and devotion. However, the idea of institutionalizing vocation, of making it a regular, established feature of daily work, is the essence of the professional project. It continues to inspire emulation from outside the organized professions. For many, it defines the very meaning of good work as "work of expert quality that benefits the broader society."[12] But it also provokes assault.

The core of the problem emerges in discussions of academic tenure. In the U.S., most arguments in favor of giving tenure to professors, or school teachers, have been based upon notions of preserving freedom—of research or thought. That tenure might be justified because it provides the conditions for a life committed to pursuits deemed of lasting public value is rarely heard. On the contrary, the idea of job tenure is likely to arouse suspicions of abused privilege and featherbedding. Americans are likely to respond with shock or scorn to the news that civil servants in Germany, including most of what we would call professionals, hold tenure as a matter of course. Certainly the Thatcher government must have thought that way when it moved to abolish academic tenure in the U.K.[13]

The idea of tenure, like the notions of vocation and profession, stems from another image of the good society and the good life than that espoused by free market ideologues. Tenure and vocation, after all, are not essentially *economic* concepts which can be defined and justified in terms of the supposed efficiency of markets. On the contrary, they are *social* and *political* notions related to ideas of the well-being of society and the formation of citizens: goals and language quite foreign to the market regime in its extreme formulations currently popular. From this simplistic point of view, professional tenure can only appear as a restrictive practice that introduces undesirable "friction" into the continuous flow of price information in the labor market. To defend professional prerogatives requires granting society an existence independent of individuals competing in the market. It is to give collective action in the form of politics a certain priority over individual action aiming to fulfill private desires. But it is also to take seriously the professions' own obligation to see that standards of practice are maintained by their own members for the protection of the public.

The Challenge of Professional Reform: Renewing the Civic Partnership

To become a professional is not only to take up an occupation. It is to assume a civic as well as an economic identity. The core of professionalism is the idea that by functioning as lawyer, engineer, doctor, accountant, architect, teacher or nurse, an individual carries on a public undertaking and affirms public values. With this identity comes a certain public status and authority, as is granted both by custom and the profession's social contract, but professionalism also means duties to the public. Professionals must be seen to contribute to the public value for which the profession stands.

The larger public seems instinctively to understand this. There is widespread expectation that professionals should be accountable beyond the measure of profit and loss, because the professional ethic rests upon a fiduciary basis. Amid the general outcry over the revelations of fraud and malfeasance as the U.S. financial bubble exploded in 2002, the sharpest outrage was directed at the law and accounting firms. Quite correctly, both officials and the public at large saw the leading lawyers and accountants of those organizations as guilty of an insolent repudiation of public trust. They therefore judged these professionals corrupt and so more odious, if not more reprehensible, than mere business leaders of companies like Enron and WorldCom. Like hypocrisy, moral outrage is premised upon accepted standards of value.

It is not that assertions of good faith on the part of the organized bar or medicine have been lacking in recent years. Rather, the public has seen these professions (in the other sense) as gestures which must be redeemed by concerted action.

What has been missing, then, is not understanding or even appreciation of the value of professionalism so much as trust that professional groups are serious about their purposes. It is not that assertions of good faith on the part of the organized bar or medicine have been lacking in recent years. Rather, the public has seen these professions (in the other sense) as gestures which must be redeemed by concerted action. What has been missing is action in which the professions take public leadership in solving perceived public problems, including the problems of abuse of privilege and refusal of public accountability.

The emphasis upon the efficiency of markets, which in practice often means stimulating competition, threatens essential features of the professional-client relationship. This is true in many areas, such as health care, legal services, and education. As powerful third-party organizations pressure physicians toward emphasizing economic efficiency at the expense of clinical judgment, the result has been to recast physician's practices as "profit-centers" rather than groups of healers. Strong cultural trends, abetted by new information technology, inculcate a ceaseless search for the best "deal" in every area of life, recasting patients as consumers, and narrowing professional roles to fit short-term encounters. These developments have helped to "empower" lay people in ways that can help undercut abuses of professional authority. In that way they are to be welcomed. Yet, these trends toward increased commercialization seriously risk reshaping relationships between professionals and clients for the worse, substituting a calculus of cost and benefit for ethical relations of care and trust. So, in law the role of counselor becomes less possible in a context of truncated relationships, pushing lawyers even further into the role of adversarial agent. In this climate, professionals will find themselves unable to act as guardians of the values they profess unless they can re-engage the public over the nature and value of what they do for the society at large.

So, it is important to ask about all the professions: What connects knowledge and craft with the public good? Ethical codes and legal regulation play an indispensable part, to be sure. They are critical for upholding the institutional framework that supports all our lives. But as the professional failures exposed by the collapse of Enron and its ilk have made vividly clear, codes and laws are not, in themselves, enough. They cannot wholly take the place of that spirit or ethos, the sense *of l'esprit de corps* that is essential to the identity of a profession. To be effective in the world, moral conviction needs a context in which the right way is taken to be the typical practice as well. In illustration, one could point to Deborah Rhode's recent analysis of the legal profession's fall in public legitimacy. Rhode argues cogently that this is the result of a pervasive demoralization of a profession that has literally begun to lose its defining public purpose. As a result, its individual members, while objectively very significant to American life, feel alienated and powerless.[14]

Rhode directly links the profession's current ills to a failure to understand and practice professionalism in a full, activist, civic sense. "The central challenge for the legal profession," Rhode writes, "is how to strengthen a sense of ethical obligation and to inspire a richer sense of what it demands in practice."[15] However, Rhode argues that this will not be easy to do, even with plenty of good will. Like medicine, the legal profession has evolved into what is in many ways a series of fragments rather than a unified professional field. This makes acting together as a profession a rare and difficult achievement. Rhode sums up the situation by saying that: "Commercialism and incivility are increasing; collegiality and collective responsibility are in decline. The priority of profits and the resulting sweatshop schedules have squeezed out time for public service and family commitments . . ."[16] The public is deliberately kept at arm's length, and denied input into professional decision-making and self-disciplining. The consequence, she emphasizes, is the paradox of a prominent and influential profession whose members feel powerless in the face of the profession's most crippling ills.

The upshot of this analysis is that the loss of morale among legal practitioners leaves the profession currently unable to address and solve its own most pressing problems. The reason for this sense of powerlessness lies not in weakness of character on the part of individual lawyers. It stems from weak professional solidarity, manifest in the failure of the organized bar to take leadership in reform. Individual practitioners cannot long or effectively confront the reforming pressures that analysts such as Rhode have catalogued without strong support from an organized profession that is trying to meet its public obligations. There is an important reminder here of the indispensable value of the professions' contract with society. In the absence of the exercise of professional responsibility at the level of collective organization, individual practitioners are simply not able to function effectively.

The Potential of Civic Leadership

What is needed, then, is collective empowerment of practitioners. Such movements in different professions must be in real dialogue with their publics and open to public accountability. Professional organizations can help this process by promoting and disseminating models of high performance practice and self-reflective problem solving in ways that enlist the initiative of individual practitioners. But reform also requires public leadership on the part of professional groups to inspire loyalty to public aims and genuine commitment to public accountability. Professionalism can only flourish when key leaders within a profession take leadership in enforcing high standards of practice, while inviting public response and involvement in the profession's efforts to clarify its mission and responsibilities.

Within medicine there have been stirrings of such a renewed professional movement. Several foundations associated with internal medicine, the American Board of Internal Medicine Foundation and the ACP-ASIM Foundation, joined by the European Federation of Internal Medicine, has issued a "Charter on Medical Professionalism."[17] The Preamble to the Charter sets out the notion that medicine's contract with society is based upon three thinks: first, placing the interests of patients as first priority; second, "setting and maintaining standards of [physician] competence and integrity; third, "providing expert advice to society on matters of health." The Charter emphasizes not only patient welfare, but patient autonomy as well, suggesting more participatory relationships between doctors and patients. Finally, the Charter's Preamble notes that the contract depends upon "public trust in physicians," which in turn rests upon "the integrity of *both individual physicians* and the *whole profession* (my emphasis)."

At the same time, a strong movement for a "new professionalism" has emerged in the United Kingdom, spurred by serious scandals in the mid-1990s. The British understanding of the "new professionalism," as described by Sir Donald Irvine, has three features. These themes represent a pledge by the medical bodies and individual physicians to do three things: to maintain the knowledge and skills needed for good patient care; second, to foster respect, communication, and patient-guided care, including the promotion of access to quality health care for all; and third, to be accountable, both on the part of individual physicians and collectively through professional self-monitoring in cooperation with public regulation.[18] Like the Professionalism Charter, the British version of the "new professionalism" emphasizes both individual physician responsibility and the collective accountability of the profession. "In future as doctors," concludes Donald Irvine, "we must take our professionalism—and with it professional regulation—as our basic professional asset . . . as a living thing, the contemporary embodiment of medical culture."[19] Distinguishing such living culture from a merely inert concept, Irvine would have physicians embody their common love for their profession and its mission in effective organization of a kind that reaches out to the public by opening up professional practice and, especially, self-organization, to scrutiny and evaluation.

What is needed, then, is collective empowerment of practitioners. Such movements in different professions must be in real dialogue with their publics and open to public accountability.

These are significant proposals. To support and spur these and similar movements of civic professionalism, the schools which educate professionals are an essential site. The movement of professional education into the university a century ago was a crucial part of that larger effort to establish the modern professions on a rational and public basis. That effort to raise standards and improve the technical competence of basic practice has been largely successful. Today, however, the big need is to rediscover *the formative* dimension of these large and impressive educational operations. Every field confronts the challenge of providing an apprenticeship that includes both theoretical knowledge and practical know-how. But each profession must also, if it wishes to survive and prosper, lay a foundation for a lifetime's identity and solidarity as a member of the profession. The new professionalism requires a fuller preparation for commitment to the mission of the profession, a preparation that integrates cognitive abilities and practical skills with judgment and patterns of practice that can advance as well as sustain the profession's "essential asset" of genuine professionalism.

Here, the academy can make a significant contribution. One of the strongest values of the academic profession has been the fostering of habits of scholarship and research. The renewal of civic professionalism needs ways to better educate future professionals in those academic virtues of reflective criticism and systematic investigation. These academic skills are not specific to professional schools. Rather, they are of the essence of what makes the academy a distinctive institution. They are as much a part of the liberal arts as they are of professional training. Here the historical accident of the professional schools' cohabitation of the academic realm with the arts and sciences needs to be turned to better effect. The qualities of good research and scholarship, openness and mutual criticism, peer review, and the free dissemination of findings need to be applied more fully to the professional schools' understanding of their own pedagogical purposes. At the same time, the heritage of the liberal arts, especially the formative concerns of the traditional humanities, can give depth and staying power to the quest to shape future professionals for a new professionalism.

Notes

1. William M. Sullivan, *Work and Integrity: The Crisis and Promise of Professionalism in America* Second Edition, (San Francisco: Jossey-Bass, forthcoming).

2. See: Robert C. Putnam, *Bowling Alone: The Collapse and Revival of American Community* (New York: Simon and Schuster, 2000). On the relation of the professions' civic claims to these trends, see: Steve Brint and Charles S. Levy, "Professions and Civic Engagement: Trends in Rhetoric and Practice, 1875–1995," in Theda Skocpol and Morris P. Fiorina, Civic *Engagement in American Democracy* (Washington D.C.: Brookings Institution, 1999), pp. 163–210.

3. Sheldon Rothblatt, "How 'Professional' Are the Professions? A Review Article," *A Comparative Study in Society and History* Vol. 37, No. l, January 1995, pp. 194–204, 195.

4. Derek Bok, *The Cost of Talent: How Executives and Professionals are Paid and How It Affects America* (New York: Free Press, 1993) p. 12.

5. See, for instance, the study of description of professional work in the fields of journalism and genetic research in Howard Gardener, Mihaly Csikszenmihalyi, and William Damon, *Good Work: Where Excellence and Ethics Meet* (New York: Basic Books, 2001).

6. Derek Bok,

7. Steven Brint, *In An Age of Experts: The Changing Role of Professionals in Politics and Public Life* (Princeton NJ: Princeton University Press, 1994), pp. 202–209.

8. For attempts to understand what has happened to law, see: Anthony Kronman, *The Lost Lawyer: Failing Ideals of the Legal Profession* (Cambridge MA: Harvard University Press, 1993); Deborah L. Rhode, *In The Interests of Justice: Reforming the Legal Profession* (New York: Oxford University Press, 2000).

9. Bok, *Cost of Talent*, pp. 57–58.

10. Robert C. Putnam, *Bowling Alone: The Collapse and Revival of American Community* (New York: Simon and Schuster, 2000).

11. For the American context, see Robert M. Crunden, *Ministers of Reform: The Progressives' Achievement in American Civilization* (New York: Basic Books, 1982).

12. Howard Gardner, Mihaly Gikszentmtfialyi, and William Damon, *Good Work* p. xi.

13. See the illuminating discussion by Nicholas Boyle, *Who Are We Now? Christian Humanism and the Global Market from Hegel to Heaney* (Notre Dame, IN: Notre Dame University Press, 1998), pp. 13–34.

14. Deborah L. Rhode, *In the Interests of Justice.*

15. Ibid. p. 213.

16. Ibid. p. 208.

17. "Medical Professionalism in the New Millennium: A Physician Charter, *Annals of Internal Medicine,* 5 February 2002, Vol. 136, No. 3. pp. 243–246.

18. Sir Donald Irvine, "The New Professionalism," *The Lancet,* 1999, Vol. 353, pp. 1174–1177. See also his *The Doctor's Tale: Professionalism and Public Trust* (Abingdon UK: Radcliffe Medical Press, 2003).

19. Donald Irvine, *Doctor's Tale*, p. 205.

Combating Ethical Cynicism and Voicing Values in the Workplace

Mary C. Gentile

Mary C. Gentile *is a Senior Research Scholar at Babson College and the Director of the Giving Voice to Values curriculum. She is also a senior advisor at the Aspen Institute Business & Society Program. She was previously a faculty member and manager of case research at Harvard Business School. The Giving Voice to Values curriculum focuses on the question of ethical action. Arguing that the key problem in applied ethics is often not distinguishing between right and wrong, but in being able to act on one's values despite opposing pressures, Gentile offers practical advice to facilitate ethical action.*

A leader cannot create a values-driven culture with rules and mission statements alone. Using techniques such as pre-scripting, rehearsal and peer coaching, leaders can learn to listen and employees can learn to speak. The result is a circle of practice that removes values from the realm of aspiration and positions them squarely within the realm of everyday business. Readers will learn how to create such a circle in this article.

Recent events have contributed to an ever-growing cynicism and even a sense of futility about the values and ethics of global business institutions. We have seen, for example, the creation and marketing of investment vehicles allegedly designed to fail, so that those in the know could short them; the knowing disregard of credit-worthiness requirements by banks and mortgage brokers; the practice of "cooking the books" over long time periods until seemingly solid and successful businesses collapse under the weight of their own false information, and the prioritizing the importance of time and financial pressures over safety requirements in the mining and extractive industries.

The costs of such transgressions have had a troubling multiplier effect, causing financial, human and environmental devastation. Beyond that, they contributed to a crisis of faith in the marketplace that paradoxically, makes it even more difficult to fix what ails us. The more business leaders and employees believe that the system is corrupt, the less likely they are to feel empowered or motivated to behave differently. Research and experience suggest that among the most prevalent reasons for the failure of individuals to address problems in the workplace are a fear of retaliation, a sense that they are alone with their concerns and the belief that their efforts will be ignored anyway.[1]

Whose Job Is It, Anyway?

So what's a business leader to do, particularly when it comes to values and ethics? How can he or she address and counter this sense of futility? This can be a daunting challenge particularly because the received wisdom is that everything "starts at the top."

This was driven home to me recently when I was delivering a public lecture about how to voice one's values in the workplace. I noticed a smartly dressed gentleman in the front row who was fidgeting in his seat and growing increasingly agitated. As I completed my remarks and invited comments, his hand shot up so fast I thought his chair might tip over. Wondering what was on his mind, I invited him to speak:

> "I am the owner and CEO of my own very successful retail company and I care a great deal about values, but let me tell you that it is just not possible for employees to act ethically if the CEO does not create the culture and make it possible. This is not about individual action; it's about leadership."

And as he spoke, a number of heads in the audience were bobbing up and down in agreement. Of course in one sense there is no question that a primary responsibility of organizational leaders is to set the tone and communicate what is important in an organization, what is allowed and where the boundaries of action lie. But taken to its extreme, this perspective runs the risk of exaggerating the CEO's power, on the one hand, and the helplessness of the employees, on the other, fueling that very sense of futility discussed above.

The B.P. oil spill in the Gulf in the summer of 2010 is a case in point. Every morning for months, stunned citizens opened the newspapers or turned on their computers, only to hear of more unheeded warning signals and more apparently known safety risks that had contributed to the environmental and financial devastation. One had to wonder why anyone didn't speak up? But then as the story unfolded, there were indeed accounts of engineers at B.P. who had raised questions, and of managers at Transocean who had expressed concerns, and of federal regulators with the Minerals Management Service who had complained—all to no avail!

From one vantage point, this dismal story can be seen as proof that the CEO quoted above is right when he argues that individual employees have no power to make change, and that it's up to organizational leaders to counter the cynicism that can silence an otherwise well-intended employee. But from another perspective, this story suggests a dual-sided leadership and management agenda. In reality, there is a complicated dance that takes place between organizational leaders and their employees. Employees need to learn to voice and enact their values more effectively and persuasively; it's not enough to just speak up. Just as with any managerial decision, they need to learn to frame and explain their position in an actionable form. And leaders need to create a culture where those messages are welcomed, encouraged and in which they can be heard. This means, first of all, learning to hear dissenting voices.

Choreographing the Dance

The recognition that management is not a solo performance and that values-driven leadership behaviors are not only possible but required from any and every seat in the house suggests the need for a much more pragmatic, action-oriented approach to business ethics than the one that is usually undertaken. The typical best practices involve setting and communicating a mission statement and corporate values; external and internal statements from the CEO and senior leaders of the organization; employee training on the relevant laws, regulations and corporate policies, often illustrated by case examples; and a set of consequences - positive incentives as well as the threat of punishment—established to support the rules. It is, indeed, a very top-down approach but it doesn't necessarily address the underlying concern expressed by that CEO quoted above. In other words, setting and communicating rules and guidelines from the top is not necessarily the same as creating a culture that encourages, enables and welcomes the voicing of values.

In fact, the typical approaches to ethics and compliance, although necessary, are not sufficient to counter the sense of futility discussed above. This is because they are too often viewed as paying mere lip service as well as the fact that those employees who would want to take these values and policies seriously are too often ill prepared to do so effectively. A new, very practical, action-oriented approach is required to help them develop the necessary skills, the toolkit and the confidence required for "Giving Voice To Values" (GVV).

There are five distinctive features of this approach:

1. **Asking a different question:** Rather than using rules and policies to address the question, "What is the right thing to do?" in a particular situation, the GVV approach asks and answers the question, "When I know what the right thing to do is, how do I get it done?" That is, this approach to thinking and training about ethical conflicts in the workplace starts from the assumption that managers very often already know what is right. GVV then focuses on figuring out, pre-scripting and practicing what they need to say and do in order to be heard. This approach is not

about preaching or arguing or even merely inspiring; it's about building the "muscle memory" for voicing values by means of actual rehearsal, individually, in organizational training sessions, or by means of internal coaching.

For, example, one can imagine that some of the employees at B.P. or Transocean raised concerns about the materials and processes being used in a group meeting, but were quickly shut down or even ignored. Or maybe they approached their boss one-on-one, who expressed sympathy but explained that his or her hands were tied by financial and time constraints. Or maybe these employees were forceful, even angry, in expressing their concerns but once silenced, they went off to stew and build resentment, fueling the kind of counter-productive cynicism described earlier. And perhaps they each screwed up the courage to take individual stands, when it could have been easier, safer and more effective to coordinate their voices.

If however, they had planned their arguments in much the same way that a manager would plan and orchestrate the campaign for a new product launch or a new customer focus or even a new internal audit system, they may have been more successful. If they had "normalized" the challenge they were facing—after all, the tension between time and money on the one hand, and care and safety on the other, is nothing new—they may have been more able to speak calmly; to gather necessary supporting data and arguments; to find others who shared their view and build a more powerful and coordinated coalition; to strategize about who needed to be approached; in what sequence and with what arguments tailored to their interests and points of view. Instead of isolated individuals sporadically and randomly popping up with complaints only to be shut down, like a tragic game of "whack-a-mole," they might have orchestrated a steady drumbeat of credible voices and positions.

Although the GVV approach is about empowering every employee to speak effectively, it also means that the CEO and other executives need to share—when they speak to employees—how they found ways to craft effective scripts and action plans in the service of their values. Rather than simply exhorting their ranks to "do the right thing," they can model just exactly how that might happen. This is one of the most powerful mechanisms they can use to send the signal that they would, indeed, listen if employees came forward, thereby countering the sense of futility that too often silences them.

2. **Spotlighting positive examples:** Research and experience support the power of storytelling for building and sharing organizational culture.[2] Too often, however, when organizations, and their leaders and employees turn to the topic of values, the emphasis is on the negative stories. There

can be a sort of "scared straight" approach that is often more disempowering than anything else.

On the contrary, sharing the stories of times when individuals have, indeed, found ways to respond to the all-too-common values challenges in an organization can have a profound impact. This can be particularly so if the stories are not shared as examples of heroism, but rather as roadmaps and toolkits to be mined for effective strategies. The point is not to celebrate the individual hero, but rather to counter the fear that no one actually does this and to provide concrete examples of how it might be done well. The stories can be disguised but the more real and closer the situation feels to the kinds of challenges employees face themselves and the more details about just what was said and done are included, the greater the impact they can make.

3. **Playing to individual strengths:** Again, the "Giving Voice To Values" approach to a common management development tool—self-assessment—turns conventional strategies on their heads. Although the focus here is on ethics and values, the GVV emphasis is not on "values clarification"—assessing what one's core values are—but rather on identifying and using one's communication and style preferences to become more effective at voicing values. In other words, rather than preach to assertive risk-embracing managers that they should be more cautious and restrain themselves, this approach would say "Embrace that risk-taking personality and use it take risks in the service of your best values." Or, on the other hand, rather than exhort the more conservative and reticent employees to be bolder, the GVV approach would say. "Find a way to frame your values conflict so that acting on your values appears safer than not doing so."

    This perhaps counter-intuitive approach grew out of interviews with managers who had, in fact, successfully voiced and acted on their ethical values in the workplace. It was found that the individual who saw him or herself as aggressive viewed enacting values as a more assertive position, while the individual who saw him or herself as fearful viewed voicing values as a less risky stance. They worked with their self-concept instead of against it. Instead of thinking they had to become a different sort of person altogether in order to behave ethically, they found that they could simply be more of who they believed they were already.

    Some of the self-assessment questions to consider include:
    -   How do I define my personal, organizational and professional sense of purpose? The broader and more explicit the definitions are, the more they can enable values-driven behaviors.
    -   What is my personal risk profile?

Both risk-embracing and risk-averse individuals can find ways to voice their values. They simply need to re-frame the challenge to fit their predisposition.

- What is my preferred communication style?

Values can be expressed in many ways: as arguments, well-timed questions, invitations, or expressions of concern. Too often, employees feel that they need to be whistle-blowers or give self-righteous little speeches. This is often not the most effective strategy. The more comfortable one is with the style, the more likely one is to use it.

4. **Pre-Scripting:** One of the most powerful and effective strategies that organizations and their leaders can use to empower voice and combat a sense of futility in the workplace around voicing values is to provide opportunities to literally pre-script their responses to values conflicts. That is, use informal conversations, team meetings as well as formal training sessions to provide the opportunity to identify the most frequently heard "reasons and rationalizations" for NOT acting on one's values. Employees can then work together to craft persuasive responses to those arguments and practice delivering them.

Interestingly, when this is done, it quickly becomes evident that the rationalizations for not acting ethically are finite and fairly predictable. And perhaps most importantly, they are vulnerable to refutation.[3]

The most common categories of argument tend to be:
- It's standard operating procedure: that is, everyone does this and it's expected.
- It's not material: that is, it's only a little wrong.
- It's not my responsibility: that is, someone else has the power, the legitimacy or the requirement to address this.
- Appeals to loyalty: I don't want to hurt my colleague, my team, my friend, my boss, etc.

The pattern of these arguments has been familiar to most of us since childhood, and similarly, so have the responses. But they need to be framed in the language of the organization, the industry or the particular project. And they need to be normalized through rehearsal with one's peers.

For example, if a certain behavior is really expected, why are there rules and regulations against it? And what were the negative consequences that made those rules necessary? And what are the costs of ignoring them? Regarding "materiality," some behaviors involve binary choices; that is they are either off or on. Fraud is not triggered by degree, for example. If they appeal to "responsibility," they are already admitting that they agree that there is a problem. The question then becomes more about tactics, persuasion and strategies. And "loyalty" is a reciprocal concept, so it is always possible to re-frame the concern to ask: Where is my colleague's loyalty to me if they are asking me to put my own career, reputation and values at risk out of loyalty to them? And so on.

The responses, of course, need to be refined and often the strategies used are less about arguing than they are about finding win/win's or framing new questions or quantifying the costs of not enacting one's values just as clearly as one has quantified the feared consequences of doing so. Anticipating these arguments in advance, thinking through their vulnerabilities beforehand, and defusing their impact are powerful tools.

5. **Peer coaching:** Building formal and informal opportunities to practice the scripting described above, and to work with one's colleagues to refine and familiarize oneself with them is perhaps the most effective remedy for organizational cynicism and the feeling of futility described at the top of this essay. Practicing the "scripts" and working with colleagues to make them more persuasive creates the sense of a community of values-driven actors who are countering the feeling of isolation and making it more likely that employees can and will act.

Countering the Cynicism

Each of these five behaviors is both a key component of a more action-oriented training program around values-driven leadership and behavior in an organization, as well as a mechanism that any individual—from the top of an organization to the bottom and back again—can practice and apply on their own. Together, these behaviors are a powerful antidote to a sense of futility and cynicism that is fueled by, and then ironically, reinforces, the tragic erosion of trust in businesses today.

A business leader cannot create a values-driven culture with rules and mission statements alone. And employees will not be effective if they merely speak out for their values, without thinking about how to help those expressions be heard and without offering to help find ways to address them. Organizational leaders and their reports must act their way into an organization that can appreciate and positively respond to expressions of values and attempts to enact them. Through pre-scripting, rehearsal and peer coaching, leaders learn to listen and employees learn to speak, creating a circle of practice that removes values from the realm of aspiration and positions them squarely within the realm of everyday business practice.

Notes

1. "Debunking Four Myths About Employee Silence," James R. Detert, Ethan R. Burris and David A. Harrison, *Harvard Business Review*, June 2010.

2. This phenomenon has been studied and explored by numerous scholars and practitioners, from Gareth Morgan to Joanne Martin to David Cooperrider to Stephen Denning.

3. See more on responding to "reasons and rationalizations" in Gentile, Mary C., "Keeping Your Colleagues Honest," *Harvard Business Review*, March 2010.

Voicing Values, Finding Answers

Mary C. Gentile

Why do business schools find it so difficult to integrate ethics into the curriculum? Although standalone business ethics courses are unquestionably important, the topic becomes marginalized if ethics issues are not also integrated into core courses. Perhaps the subject of ethics doesn't always make it into core courses because both faculty and students are unsure whether it is really possible for people to act on their values in the workplace.

For example, when accounting faculty want to integrate questions of ethics into their courses, they often address the topic of "cooking the books." They discuss the pressures employees face to engage in unethical practices, such as altering earnings reports. They emphasize the consequences of such actions and the regulatory safeguards that exist to prevent them. All the while, they might consider the whole exercise to be futile if they don't know how to teach students to handle such situations when they arise—or if they believe it would be fruitless for young managers even to bring up those issues with their employers.

This is not to say that faculty need to have all the answers about how young executives should behave if confronted with these situations. But they should

---

A new program—a collaboration between the Aspen Institute and the Yale School—helps students learn to speak up when confronted by ethically complex situations.

---

believe there's a way to find the answers and that it's important to try. The distinction between not knowing the answers and not believing they exist is one that faculty, students, *and* managers all struggle to understand.

To help educators prepare students to speak up on ethical issues, The Aspen Institute Business & Society Program in New York City and the Yale School of Management in New Haven, Connecticut, have collaborated on a research and curriculum development initiative called Giving Voice to Values (GVV). Students hear from business practitioners who have acted on their values; they learn strate-gies to communicate values-based arguments in the workplace; and they develop "scripts" to help them articulate their values not only in front of their peers, but also in the real world.

A Practical Approach

Traditional ethics classes are best at illuminating students' options in situations where the ethical boundaries are unclear. The goal with GVV, on the other hand, is to help students determine a course of action when they believe they know what they *should* do but feel disempowered, unsure, or unable to find a way to act on that knowledge.

"So many students struggle with the question: How can I act on what I know is right?" says Jerry Goodstein, a professor in the department of management and operations at Washington State University-Vancouver. Goodstein notes that when students are given opportunities to explore ethical situations, drawing on their own experiences and the experiences of others, they better understand what might help or hinder their ability to voice their values. GVV helps move them "from ethi-cal intent to ethical action," he says.

In the GVV curriculum, students and practitioners are explicitly asked, "If you were going to act on your values, what *would* you say or do?" To help stimu-late this discussion, faculty present students with GVV case studies, then discuss sample scripts and action plans that can be used in similar situations. When GVV cases don't resolve positively, the teaching plans offer discussion questions and readings from which students can draw recommendations to alter the outcome.

For instance, the "Reporting" module shows how three managers—one senior executive, one middle manager, and one new manager fresh from his bachelor's degree—handle values conflicts linked to falsified records. In the module, the man-agers hear many of the common arguments in favor of such practices; students learn what they might be able to say if they're faced with similar ethical dilemmas.

Giving Voice to Values doesn't downplay the obstacles inherent in values conflicts with peers and bosses, and it doesn't deny that people tend to make rationalizations to justify their actions. Rather, the GVV program lets students know that, despite the risks and complexities of ethically challenging situations, people *can* speak up about their values and take effective action.

"GVV shifts the focus away from debates about what the 'right' answer to an ethical challenge might be and places the focus on how to act on one's val-ues in a particular situation," says Michael C. Jensen, Jesse Isidor Straus Professor of Business Administration Emeritus at Harvard Business School in Cambridge, Massachusetts. "This approach provides people the opportunity to practice han-dling the discomfort, threats, isolation, and embarrassment people face in such situations."

There is much to be learned from looking at how and why some people voice their values in the workplace—even when they understand the risks and acknowledge the obstacles. These individuals make a great effort to know themselves and better understand others, so they can try to avoid self-justifying rationalizations about their failure to act. They think strategically about how to implement their values, thereby diminishing the risks they face; and when the risks are unavoidable, they prepare themselves for repercussions. They also learn to communicate openly and clearly about their values, making sure they gather the information they need to make considered decisions.

The Complete Program

Seven pillars support the GVV curriculum:

One: Acknowledging shared values. Although there are quibbles about the details, research reveals that there is a short list of values that individuals generally share, regardless of their cultures, religions, or eras. While disagreements about some values are real, they need not prevent people from working together on common goals.

Two: Choosing to act. The GVV program includes a classroom exercise that helps students recognize that all individuals are capable of acting on their values, even if they have not always chosen to do so. One goal with this exercise is to debunk the idea that people are either good or bad. Another goal is to encourage students to think about factors that encourage them to act on their values—factors that are "enablers"—as well as those that discourage them, or serve as "disablers." Students learn strategies for strengthening their individual enablers and counteracting their disablers.

Students also learn that individuals are likely to grow more sure of themselves each time they speak up. One series of cases, called "Lisa Baxter—Developing a Voice," follows a woman from her earliest days as a junior strategy consultant to her current role as senior vice president of a major consumer products firm. Every time she takes a stand during her career, her actions are feasible for someone at her particular level. In the final case, she draws on all the skills and confidence she has developed as she stands up to the chairman of the board over her decision to fire a favored executive. In the debrief of the case, students examine the ten "enablers" that made it possible for her to develop a powerful voice— "enablers" that students can pursue for themselves.

The GVV program lets students know that, despite the risks and complexities of ethically challenging situations, people can speak up about their values and take effective action.

Three: Normalizing values conflicts. If students expect to face values conflicts in their careers, they'll understand that these situations are a normal part of business, and they won't be disabled by surprise when conflicts arise. Instead, they'll retain their sense of competency; they'll speak up without freezing or trying to evade the problem altogether.

Four: Defining professional purpose. If students accept an explicitly broad definition of their purpose in doing business, they will have more leverage when they confront values conflicts. They will know that their goals aren't merely to make the next deal or please their bosses, and they can call on a wide set of arguments to make their cases.

Five: Understanding the self. Because GVV is built on the idea of appealing to students' strengths—as opposed to preaching about the need to conquer their weaknesses—the program emphasizes self-knowledge and positive alignment with personal values. The curriculum includes sample assessment tools, including one exercise called "Framing a Life Story," which helps students understand what matters to them and how they define success.

Six: Using one's voice. If they're going to speak up about values conflict in the workplace, students must first understand that there are different ways to voice their values. For instance, they can make assertions, ask questions, provide new research, try persuasion, negotiate, set examples, or identify allies. They also need to understand that various techniques work better in some circumstances than in others and that they may be more comfortable with one method over another. In addition, they need to learn that the organizational setting and the personal style of the leader could affect what approach they might take to express their values—and even the likelihood that they will speak up at all.

Most important, the GVV approach allows students to develop actual scripts and practice voicing their values in front of their peers, using the style of expression that suits them best, and then to receive coaching from their classmates. The premise is that, once they have scripted and spoken their values in the safe classroom setting, they will be more likely to speak up when necessary in the workplace.

Seven: Preparing responses. Students learn to anticipate and respond to the typical "reasons and rationalizations" that peers and bosses will give for ethically questionable behavior. One module in the GVV curriculum, "Scripts and Skills," includes a set of short cases, annotated readings about decision-making biases and framing, and teaching plans that help students script responses to frequently heard rationalizations.

For instance, in the case called "Naivete or Boldness?" the COO of a hospital faces a conflict with her CEO over the potential sale of the institution. She believes that the decision is based on inaccurate financial data and that the sale will negatively affect the quality of health services in the region. Her CEO, new to the organization himself and facing an inherited financial crisis, has just appointed her to this senior post, and she does not want him to question her loyalty. She suspects that if she does not get on board, she may have to leave the hospital.

The teaching plan for the case delineates many well-demonstrated decision-making biases—such as social proof, false consensus, sunk costs, overoptimism, and self-serving bias—and suggests ways for the COO to turn these to her advantage as she makes her case to the CEO. Students learn that if they understand these biases, they might be able to frame their own positions more persuasively.

All of the cases presented in the GVV curriculum are quite brief, usually three pages or less. They do not conclude by asking students what the subjects should do, as most business school cases do. Merely asking that question raises the issue of whether the subjects *should* act on their values. Instead, the cases present protagonists who want to act on their values and want to know how to do so. What should they say? To whom? At what time?

Although the cases are inspired by actual experiences, they are disguised. This allows students to explore not only what *did* happen, but what *could* happen, depending on their choices.

Values in the Classroom

The Giving Voice to Values curriculum and approach have been or soon will be piloted in 20 sites, and many other schools and businesses are reviewing it. One popular exercise, called "A Tale of Two Stories," has students detail two ethically challenging situations, one in which they did speak up and one in which they did not. This module has been integrated into orientation sessions at some schools, turned into a standalone workshop, integrated into core courses, and used as an elective within some MBA programs.

The unique nature of the GVV curriculum makes it easy for faculty to adapt it to a wide variety of needs. For example:

■ Maureen Scully, assistant professor in management at the University of Massachusetts-Boston, teaches "issue selling in organizations" in the core MBA course called Organizational Analysis and Skills. Last year, she used the "Tale of Two Stories" exercise to get students thinking about strategic and political actions they could use in the workplace when they're trying to "sell" a values-driven position to management.

Scully says that after one student described a situation in which she did not report a coach who was sexually harassing students, the class discussed what factors had combined to keep her silent and what she could have done differently. Another student described a time he challenged company management when homophobia was affecting employees in the workplace. He actually lost his job shortly after speaking up, but he remained glad he had voiced his values.

An international student, who had been very quiet in class until this point, told a story about the time she objected when her boss fired a middle-aged man who had just been diagnosed with cancer. Scully notes that sharing her experience during this class period seemed to be a turning point for this student, who became much more outspoken during the rest of the course.

Because the "Tale of Two Stories" exercise unfolded during the ninth week of class, says Scully, the students had already built up a level of trust with each other and wanted to tell the stories in plenary sessions rather than in small groups. She feels the impact was extraordinary. "We realized we had given students analytical tools at a structural level and managerial skills at a team level, but we hadn't given them enough tangible leadership skills at the individual level," she says. "Because

---

The Giving Voice to Values curriculum recognizes the fact that all managers encounter value conflicts in the workplace—instances when their own values conflict with what they are asked to do.

GVV grounds the discussion in the students' own experiences, the session is memorable and practical." The school has since decided to incorporate the same material across all ten sections of the course.

■ Last May, Minette Drumwright, associate professor at the University of Texas-Austin, also used "A Tale of Two Stories" as part of the ethics component of the EMBA program. In addition, she gave students an exercise from the "Scripts and Skills" module.

Drumwright had students consider how the new manager of a highly productive sales group could deal with unethical sales practices. Several sales managers in the class shared both the firm policies and the individual approaches that could work in such a situation. Had this topic been posed as a typical ethical dilemma, these same experienced students might have adopted a cynical "seen it all" stance. Instead, these students joined a class discussion that debated informed and sophisticated ways to handle the challenge.

Drumwright's class was so successful that she is now proposing an elective course in which EMBA students would research and write caselets about situations where people did speak up about their values. They would develop the teaching notes—and then teach the cases to the next incoming cohort of EMBA students.

■ At the Yale School of Management, Ira Millstein and Anne Simpson invited the GVV initiative to develop customized cases for their corporate governance course. The cases— "The Backdating Scandal" and "The Independent Director's Challenge"—place particular emphasis on voicing dissent in the corporate boardroom, often an environment rife with strong personal loyalties and complex group dynamics.

Millstein and Simpson assigned three teams to prepare scripts and action plans for each case and present them in class. As the presentations went on, students became increasingly sophisticated and more forward-thinking. Instead of simply scripting the most persuasive arguments for the values-driven position, they began to anticipate the second and third round of counter-arguments from the people they wanted to persuade, and they developed the next layers of argument and strategy. Some students even envisioned that they might not be able to prevail; at that point, they presented their conclusion that the position was still important to take because they needed to differentiate themselves from the actions of the board.

Adapting for the Future

Currently there are more than 175 pages of material available in the Giving Voice to Values curriculum. The Aspen Institute and the Yale School of Management are developing more materials, sometimes in partnership with faculty who have expertise in or a desire to teach about particular topics. Aspen and Yale also are disseminating the basic pedagogy of the approach so that faculty can use it independently in their classes. In addition, Aspen and Yale are in discussion with several faculty about designing research to examine what kind of impact this curricular approach has on students once they return to work.

At the same time, Aspen and Yale are finding opportunities to develop materials across cultures. For example, faculty from the Goa Institute of Management and the Indian School of Business are developing GVV cases and teaching plans based on India-specific situations. Aspen also recently conducted a Student Attitude Survey in China and is considering ways to use that data to develop similar methods there. Although the GVV interviews suggest many similarities across cultures, the concept of "voice" may be culturally determined, and country-specific realities may influence which approach will work best for an individual who wishes to speak up.

The Giving Voice to Values curriculum recognizes the fact that all managers encounter value conflicts in the workplace—instances when their own values conflict with what they are asked to do. It can be extremely difficult for individuals to take a stand if they feel they are in the minority, if they don't have the time to come up with a workable alternative, or if they don't want to risk presenting an incomplete response to a senior member of the organization.

The GVV approach equips individuals with tested responses to the most common ethical challenges they will face in their careers. It helps students develop the self-confidence and clarity of thought to voice their values in the workplace—and perhaps change the way business is done.

The Life You Can Save: How to Do Your Part to End World Poverty

Peter Singer

Peter Singer *(1946–) is one of the most widely read and influential contemporary moral philosophers. He is currently the Ira W. DeCamp Professor of Bioethics at Princeton University. Working within a preference utilitarian approach, Singer has pursued the application of his approach, which he refers to as personism to sometimes controversial areas like animal liberation, abortion, euthanasia, and infanticide. In recent years, Singer has concentrated on the question of global poverty and argued that people who are economically well-off have an undeniable moral imperative to make a greater effort to reduce poverty, especially by donating to charitable causes that help the poor.*

1. Saving a Child

On your way to work, you pass a small pond. On hot days, children sometimes play in the pond, which is only about knee-deep. The weather's cool today, though, and the hour is early, so you are surprised to see a child splashing about in the pond. As you get closer, you see that it is a very young child, just a toddler, who is flailing about, unable to stay upright or walk out of the pond. You look for the parents or babysitter, but there is no one else around. The child is unable to keep his head above the water for more than a few seconds at a time. If you don't wade in and pull him out, he seems likely to drown. Wading in is easy and safe, but you will ruin the new shoes you bought only a few days ago, and get your suit wet and muddy. By the time you hand the child over to someone responsible for him, and change your clothes, you'll be late for work. What should you do?

I teach a course called Practical Ethics. When we start talking about global poverty, I ask my students what they think you should do in this situation. Predictably, they respond that you should save the child. "What about your shoes? And being late for work?" I ask them. They brush that aside. How could anyone consider a pair or shoes, or missing an hour or two at work, a good reason for not saving a child's life?

In 2007, something resembling this hypothetical situation actually occurred near Manchester, England. Jordon Lyon, a ten-year-old boy, leaped into a pond after his stepsister Bethany slipped in. He struggled to support her but went under himself. Anglers managed to pull Bethany out but by then Jordon could no longer be seen. They raised the alarm, and two police community support officers soon arrived; they refused to enter the pond to find Jordan. He was later pulled out, but attempts at resuscitation failed. At the inquest on Jordon's death, the officers' inaction was defended on the grounds that they had not been trained to deal with such situations. The mother responded: "If you're walking down the street and you see a child drowning you automatically go in that water . . . You don't have to be trained to jump in after a drowning child."[1]

I think it's safe to assume that most people would agree with the mother's statement. But consider that, according to UNICEF, nearly 10 million children under five years old die each year from causes related to poverty. Here is just one case, described by a man in Ghana to a researcher from the World Bank:

> Take the death of this small boy this morning, for example. The boy died of measles. We all know he could have been cured at the hospital. But the parents had no money and so the boy died a slow and painful death, not of measles but out of poverty.[2]

Think about something like that happening 27,000 times every day. Some children die because they don't have enough to eat. More die, like that small boy in Ghana, from measles, malaria, and diarrhea, conditions that either don't exist in developed nations, or, if they do, are almost never fatal. The children are vulnerable to these diseases because they have no safe drinking water, or no sanitation, and because when they do fall ill, their parents can't afford any medical treatment. UNICEF, Oxfam, and many other organizations are working to reduce poverty and provide clean water and basic health care, and these efforts are reducing the toll. If the relief organizations had more money, they could do more, and more lives would be saved.

Now think about your own situation. By donating a relatively small amount of money, you could save a child's life. Maybe it takes more than the amount needed to buy a pair of shoes—but we all spend money on things we don't really need, whether on drinks, meals out, clothing, movies, concerts, vacations, new cars, or house renovation. Is it possible that by choosing to spend your money on such things rather than contributing to an aid agency, you are leaving a child to die, a child you could have saved?

Poverty Today

A few years ago, the World Bank asked researchers to listen to what the poor are saying. They were able to document the experiences of 60,000 women and men in seventy-three countries. Over and over, in different languages and on different continents, poor people said that poverty meant these things:

- You are short of food for all or part of the year, often eating only one meal per day, sometimes having to choose between stilling your child's hunger or your own, and sometimes being able to do neither.
- You can't save money. If a family member falls ill and you need money to see a doctor, or if the crop fails and you have nothing to eat, you have to borrow from a local moneylender and he will charge you so much interest as the debt continues to mount and you may never be free of it.
- You can't afford to send your children to school, or if they do start school, you have to take them out again if the harvest is poor.
- You live in an unstable house, made with mud or thatch that you need to rebuild every two or three years, or after severe weather.
- You have no nearby source of safe drinking water. You have to carry your water a long way, and even then, it can make you ill unless you boil it.

But extreme poverty is not only a condition of unsatisfied material needs. It is often accompanied by a degrading state of powerlessness. Even in countries that are democracies and are relatively well governed, respondents to the World Bank survey described a range of situations in which they had to accept humiliation without protest. If someone takes what little you have, and you complain to the police, they may not listen to you. Nor will the law necessarily protect you from rape or sexual harassment. You have a pervading sense of shame and failure because you cannot provide for your children. Your poverty traps you, and you lose hope of ever escaping from a life of hard work for which, at the end, you will have nothing to show beyond bare survival.[3]

The World Bank defines extreme poverty as not having enough income to meet the most basic human needs for adequate food, water, shelter, clothing, sanitation, health care, and education. Many people are familiar with the statistic that 1 billion people are living on less than one dollar per day. That was the World Bank's poverty line until 2008, when better data on international price comparisons enabled it to make a more accurate calculation of the amount people need to meet their basic needs. On the basis of this calculation, the World Bank set the poverty line at $1.25 per day. The number of people whose income puts them under this line is not 1 billion but 1.4 billion. That there are more people living in extreme poverty than we thought is, of course, bad news, but the news is not all bad. On the same basis, in 1981 there were 1.9 billion people living in extreme poverty. That was about four in every ten people on the planet, whereas now fewer than one in four are extremely poor.

South Asia is still the region with the largest number of people living in extreme poverty, a total of 600 million, including 455 million in India. Economic growth has, however, reduced the proportion of South Asians living in extreme poverty from 60 percent in 1981 to 42 percent in 2005. There are another 380 million extremely poor people in sub-Saharan Africa, where half the population is extremely poor—and that is the same percentage as in 1981. The most dramatic reduction in poverty has been in East Asia, although there are still more than 200 million extremely poor Chinese, and smaller numbers elsewhere in the region. The remaining extremely poor people are distributed around the world, in Latin America and the Caribbean, the Pacific, the Middle East, North Africa, Eastern Europe, and Central Asia.[4]

In response to the "$1.25 a day" figure, the thought may cross your mind that in many developing countries, it is possible to live much more cheaply than in the industrialized nations. Perhaps you have even done it yourself, backpacking around the world, living on less than you would have believed possible. So you may imagine that this level of poverty is less extreme than it would be if you had to live on that amount of money in the United States, or any industrialized nation. If such thoughts did occur to you, you should banish them now, because the World Bank has already made the adjustment in purchasing power: Its figures refer to the number of people existing on a daily total consumption of goods and services—whether earned or home-grown—comparable to the amount of goods and services that can be bought in the United States for $1.25.

In wealthy societies, most poverty is relative. People feel poor because many of the good things they see advertised on television are beyond their budget—but they do have a television. In the United States, 97 percent of those classified by the Census Bureau as poor own a color TV. Three quarters of them own a car. Three quarters of them have air conditioning. Three quarters of them have a VCR or DVD player. All have access to health care.[5] I am not quoting these figures in order to deny that the poor in the United States face genuine difficulties. Nevertheless, for most, these difficulties are of a different order than those of the world's poorest people. The 1.4 billion people living in extreme poverty are poor by an absolute standard tied to the most basic human needs. They are likely to be hungry for at least part of each year. Even if they can get enough food to fill their stomachs, they will probably be malnourished because their diet lacks essential nutrients. In children, malnutrition stunts growth, and can cause permanent brain damage. The poor may not be able to afford to send their children to school. Even minimal health care services are usually beyond their means.

This kind of poverty kills. Life expectancy in rich nations averages seventy-eight years; in the poorest nations, those officially classified as "least developed," it is below fifty.[6] In rich countries, fewer than one in a hundred children die before the age of five; in the poorest countries, one in five does. And to the UNICEF figure of nearly 10 million young children dying every year from avoidable, poverty-related causes, we must add at least another 8 million older children and adults.[7]

Affluence Today

Roughly matching the 1.4 billion people living in extreme poverty, there are about a billion living at a level of affluence never previously known except in the courts of kings and nobles. As king of France, Louis XIV, the '"Sun King," could afford to build the most magnificent palace Europe had ever seen, but he could not keep it cool in summer as effectively as most middle-class people in industrialized nations can keep their homes cool today. His gardeners, for all their skill, were unable to produce the variety of fresh fruits and vegetables that we can buy all year-round. If he developed a toothache or fell ill, the best his dentists and doctors could do for him would make us shudder.

But we're not just better off than a French king who lived centuries ago. We are also much better off than our own great-grandparents. For a start, we can expect to live about thirty years longer. A century ago, one child in ten died in infancy. Now, in most rich nations, that figure is less than one in two hundred.[8] Another telling indicator of how wealthy we are today is the modest number of hours we must work in order to meet our basic dietary needs. Today Americans spend, on average, only 6 percent of their income on buying food. If they work a forty-hour week, it takes them barely two hours to earn enough to feed themselves for the week. That leaves far more to spend on consumer goods, entertainment, and vacations.

And then we have the superrich, people who spend their money on palatial homes, ridiculously large and luxurious boats, and private planes. Before the 2008 stock market crash trimmed the numbers, there were more than 1,100 billionaires in the world, with a combined net worth of $4.4 trillion.[9] To cater to such people, Lufthansa Technik unveiled its plans for a private configuration of Boeing's new 787 Dreamliner. In commercial service, this plane will seat up to 330 passengers. The private version will carry 35, at a price of $150 million. Cost aside, there's nothing like owning a really big airplane carrying a small number of people to maximize your personal contribution to global warming. Apparently, there are already several billionaires who fly around in private commercial-sized airliners, from 747s down. Larry Page and Sergey Brin, the Google cofounders, reportedly bought a Boeing 767 and spent millions fitting it out for their private use.[10] But for conspicuous waste of money and resources it is hard to beat Anousheh Ansari, an Iranian-American telecommunications entrepreneur who paid a reported $20 million for eleven days in space. Comedian Lewis Black said on Jon Stewart's *The Daily Show* that Ansari did it because it was "the only way she could achieve her life's goal of flying over every single starving person on earth and yelling 'Hey, look what I'm spending my money on!'"

While I was working on this book, a special advertising supplement fell out of my Sunday edition of *The New York Times:* a sixty-eight-page glossy magazine filled with advertising for watches by Rolex, Patek Philippe, Breitling, and other luxury brands. The ads didn't carry price tags, but a puff piece about the revival of the mechanical watch gave guidance about the lower end of the range. After admitting that inexpensive quartz watches are extremely accurate and functional, the article opined that there is "something engaging about a mechanical movement." Right, but how much will it cost you to have this engaging something on your wrist? "You might think that getting into mechanical watches is an expensive proposition, but there are plenty of choices in the $500–$5000 range." Admittedly, "these opening-price-point models are pretty simple: basic movement, basic time display, simple decoration and so on." From which we can gather that most of the watches advertised are priced upward of $5,000, or more than one hundred times what anyone needs to pay for a reliable, accurate quartz watch. That there is a market for such products—and one worth advertising at such expense to the wide readership of *The New York Times*—is another indication of the affluence of our society.[11]

If you're shaking your head at the excesses of the superrich, though, don't shake too hard. Think again about some of the ways Americans with average incomes spend their money. In most places in the United States, you can get your recommended eight glasses of water a day out of the tap for less than a penny, while a bottle of water will set you back $1.50 or more.[12] And in spite of the environmental concerns raised by the waste of energy that goes into producing and transporting it, Americans are still buying bottled water, to the tune of more than 31 billion liters in 2006.[13] Think, too, of the way many of us get our caffeine fix: You can make coffee at home for pennies rather than spending three dollars or more on a latte. Or have you ever casually said yes to a waiter's prompt to order a second soda or glass of wine that you didn't even finish? When Dr. Timothy Jones, an archaeologist, led a U.S. goverment-funded study of food waste, he found that 14 percent of household garbage is perfectly good food that was in its original packaging and not out of date. More than half of this food was dry-packaged or canned goods that keep for a long time. According to Jones, $100 billion of food is wasted in the United States every year.[14] Fashion designer Deborah Lindquist claims that the average woman owns more than $600 worth of clothing that she has not worn in the last year.[15] Whatever the actual figure may be, it is fair to say that almost all of us, men and women alike, buy things we don't need, some of which we never even use.

Most of us are absolutely certain that we wouldn't hesitate to save a drowning child, and that we would do it at considerable cost to ourselves. Yet while thousands of children die each day, we spend money on things we take for granted and would hardly notice if they were not there. Is that wrong? If so, now far does our obligation to the poor go?

2. Is It Wrong Not to Help?

Bob is close to retirement. He has invested most of his savings in a very rare and valuable old car, a Bugatti, which he has not been able to insure. The Bugatti is his pride and joy. Not only does Bob get pleasure from driving and caring for his car, he also knows that its rising market value means that he will be able to sell it and live comfortably after retirement. One day when Bob is out for a drive, he parks the Bugatti near the end of a railway siding and goes for a walk up the track. As he does so, he sees that a runaway train, with no one aboard, is rolling down the railway track. Looking farther down the track, he sees the small figure of a child who appears to be absorbed in playing on the tracks. Oblivious to the runaway train, the child is in great danger. Bob can't stop the train, and the child is too far away to hear his warning shout, but Bob can throw a switch that will divert the train down the siding where his Bugatti is parked. If he does so, nobody will be killed, but the train will crash through the decaying barrier at the end of the siding and destroy his Bugatti. Thinking of his joy in owning the car and the financial security it represents, Bob decides not to throw the switch.

The Car or the Child?

Philosopher Peter Linger developed this variation on the story of the drowning child to challenge us to think further about how much we believe we should sacrifice in order to save the life of a child. Lingers story adds a factor often crucial to our thinking about real-world poverty: uncertainty about the outcome of our sacrifice. Bob cannot be certain that the child will die if he does nothing and saves his car. Perhaps at the last moment the child will hear the train and leap to safety. In the same way, most of us can summon doubts about whether the money we give to a charity is really helping the people it's intended to help.

In my experience, people almost always respond that Bob acted badly when he did not throw the switch and destroy his most cherished and valuable possession, thereby sacrificing his hope of a financially secure retirement We can't take a serious risk with a child's life, they say, merely to save a car, no matter how rare and valuable the car may be. By implication, we should also believe that with the simple act of saving money for retirement, we are acting as badly as Bob. For in saving money for retirement, we are effectively refusing to use that money to help save lives. This is a difficult implication to confront. How can it be wrong to save for a comfortable retirement? There is, at the very least, something puzzling here.

Another example devised by Unger tests the level of sacrifice we think people should make to alleviate suffering in cases when a life is not at stake:

> You are driving your vintage sedan down a country lane when you are stopped by a hiker who has seriously injured his leg. He asks you to take him to the nearest hospital. If you refuse, there is a good chance that he will lose his leg. On the other hand, if you agree to take him to hospital, he is likely to bleed onto the seats, which you have recently, and expensively, restored in soft white leather.

Again, most people respond that you should drive the hiker to the hospital. This suggests that when prompted to think in concrete terms, about real individuals, most of us consider it obligatory to lessen the serious suffering of innocent others, even at some cost (even a high cost) to ourselves.[16]

The Basic Argument

The above examples reveal our intuitive belief that we ought to help others in need, at least when we can see them and when we are the only person in a position to save them. But our moral intuitions are not always reliable, as we can see from variations in what people in different times and places find intuitively acceptable or objectionable. The case for helping those in extreme poverty will be stronger if it does not rest solely on our intuitions. Here is a logical argument from plausible premises to the same conclusion.

First premise: Suffering and death from lack of food, shelter, and medical care are bad.

Second premise: If it is in your power to prevent something bad from happening, without sacrificing anything nearly as important, it is wrong not to do so.

Third premise: By donating to aid agencies, you can prevent suffering and death from lack of food, shelter, and medical care, without sacrificing anything nearly as important.

Conclusion: Therefore, if you do not donate to aid agencies, you are doing something wrong.

The drowning-child story is an application of this argument for aid, since ruining your shoes and being late for work aren't nearly as important as the life of a child. Similarly, reupholstering a car is not nearly as big a deal as losing a leg. Even in the case of Bob and the Bugatti, it would be a big stretch to suggest that the loss of the Bugatti would come close to rivaling the significance of the death of an innocent person.

Ask yourself if you can deny the premises of the argument. How could suffering and death from lack of food, shelter, and medical care not be really, really bad? Think of that small boy in Ghana who died of measles. How you would feel if you were his mother or father, watching helplessly as your son suffers and grows weaker? You know that children often die from this condition. You also know that it would be curable, if only you could afford to take your child to a hospital. In those circumstances you would give up almost anything for some way of ensuring your child's survival.

Putting yourself in the place of others, like the parents of that boy, or the child himself, is what thinking ethically is all about. It is encapsulated in the Golden Rule, "Do unto others as you would have them do unto you." Though the Golden Rule is best known to most westerners from the words of Jesus as reported by Matthew and Luke, it is remarkably universal, being found in Buddhism, Confucianism, Hinduism, Islam, and Jainism, and in Judaism, where it is found in Leviticus, and later emphasized by the sage Hillel.[17] The Golden Rule requires us to accept that the desires of others ought to count as if they were our own. If the desires of the parents of the dying child were our own, we would have no doubt that their suffering and the death of their child are about as bad as anything can be. So if we think ethically, then those desires must count as if they were our own, and we cannot deny that the suffering and death are bad.

The second premise is also very difficult to reject, because it leaves us some wiggle room when it comes to situations in which, to prevent something bad, we would have to risk something *nearly* as important as the bad thing we are preventing. Consider, for example, a situation in which you can only prevent the deaths of other children by neglecting your own children. This standard does not require you to prevent the deaths of the other children.

"Nearly as important" is a vague term. That's deliberate, because I'm confident that you can do without plenty of things that are clearly and inarguably not as valuable as saving a child's life. I don't know what *you* might think is as important, or nearly as important, as saving a life. By leaving it up to you to decide what those things are, I can avoid the need to find out. I'll trust you to be honest with yourself about it.

Analogies and stories can be pushed too far. Rescuing a child drowning in front of you, and throwing a switch on a railroad track to save the life of a child you can see in the distance, where you are the only one who can save the child, are both different from giving aid to people who are far away. The argument I have just presented complements the drowning-child case, because instead of pulling at your heartstrings by focusing on a single child in need, it appeals to your reason and seeks your assent to an abstract but compelling moral principle. That means that to reject it, you need to find a flaw in the reasoning.

You might now be thinking to yourself that the basic argument—that we should donate to aid agencies when by doing so we can prevent suffering and death without giving up anything nearly as important—isn't all that controversial. Yet if we were to take it seriously, our lives would be changed dramatically, for while the cost of saving one child's life by a donation to an aid organization may not be great, after you have donated that sum, there remain more children in need of saving, each one of whom can be saved at a relatively small additional cost. Suppose you have just sent $200 to an agency that can, for that amount, save the life of a child in a developing country who would otherwise have died. You've done something really good, and all it has cost you is the price or some new clothes you didn't really need anyway. Congratulations! But don't celebrate your good deed by opening a bottle of champagne, or even going to a movie. The cost of that bottle or movie, added to what you could save by cutting down on a few other extravagances, would save the life of another child. After you forgo those items, and give another $200, though, is everything else you are spending on as important, or nearly as important, as the life of a child? Not likely! So you must keep cutting back on unnecessary spending, and donating what you save, until you have reduced yourself to the point where if you give any more, you will be sacrificing something nearly as important as a child's life—like giving so much that you can no longer afford to give your children an adequate education.

We tend to assume that if people do not harm others, keep their promises, do not lie or cheat, support their children and their elderly parents, and perhaps contribute a little to needier members of their local community, they've done well. If we have money left over after meeting our needs and those of our dependents, we may spend it as we please. Giving to strangers, especially those beyond ones community, may be good, but we don't think of it as something we *have* to do. But if the basic argument presented above is right, then what many of us consider acceptable behavior must be viewed in a new more ominous light. When we spend our surplus on concerts or fashionable shoes, on fine dining and good wines, or on holidays in faraway lands, we are doing something wrong.

Suddenly the three premises laid out above are much harder to swallow. You may now be questioning whether a moral argument that has such radically demanding implications can possibly be sound. And so it's worth stepping back a moment to look at how this argument fits into some of our most respected ethical traditions.

Traditional Views on Helping the Poor

In the Christian tradition, helping the poor is a requirement for salvation. Jesus told the rich man: "If you want to be perfect, go, sell your possessions and give to the poor." To make sure his message wasn't missed, he went on to say that it is easier for a camel to go through the eye of a needle than for a rich man to enter the kingdom of God.[18] He praised the Good Samaritan who went out of his way to help a stranger.'[19] He urged those who give feasts to invite the poor, the maimed, the lame, and the blind.[20] When he spoke of the last judgment, he said that God will save those who have fed the hungry, given drink to the thirsty, and clothed the naked. It is how we act toward "the least of these brothers of mine" that will determine, Jesus says, whether we inherit the kingdom of God or go into the eternal fire.[21] He places far more emphasis on charity for the poor than on anything else.

Not surprisingly, early and medieval Christians took these teachings very seriously. Paul, in his second letter to the Corinthians, proposed that those with a surplus should share with the needy: "Your surplus at the present time should supply their needs, so that their surplus may also supply your needs, that there may be equality."[22] The members of the early Christian community in Jerusalem, according to the account given in the Acts of the Apostles, sold all their possessions and divided them according to need.[23] The Franciscans, the order of monks founded by Francis of Assisi, took a vow of poverty and renounced all private property. Thomas Aquinas, the great medieval scholar whose ideas became the semi-official philosophy of the Roman Catholic church, wrote that whatever we have in "superabundance"—that is, above and beyond what will reasonably satisfy our own needs and those of our family, for the present and the foreseeable future—"is owed, of natural right, to the poor for their sustenance." In support of this view, he quoted Ambrose, one of the four original "Great Doctors" or teachers of the Church. He also cited the Decretum Graciani, a twelfth-century compilation of canon law that contains the powerful statement, "The bread which you withhold belongs to the hungry: the clothing you shut away, to the naked: and the money you bury in the earth is the redemption and freedom of the penniless."

Note that "owed" and "belongs." For these Christians, sharing our surplus wealth with the poor is not a matter of charity, but of our duty and their rights. Aquinas even went so far as to say: "It is not theft, properly speaking, to take secretly and use another's property in a case of extreme need: because that which he takes for the support of his life becomes his own property by reason of that need."[24] This isn't just a Roman Catholic view. John Locke, the favorite philosopher of America's founding fathers, wrote that "charity gives every man a title to so much our of another's plenty, as will keep him from extreme want, where he has no means to subsist otherwise."[25]

Today, some Christians are seeking a renewed focus on the message of the gospels. Jim Walks, founder and editor of the Christian magazine *Sojourners,* likes to point out that the Bible contains more than three thousand references to alleviating poverty—enough reason, he thinks, for making this a central moral issue for Christians.[26] Rick Warren, author of *The Purpose Driven Life* and pastor of the Saddleback Church, visited South Africa in 2003 and came across a tiny church operating from a dilapidated tent and sheltering twenty-five children orphaned by AIDS. This was, Warren says, "like a knife in the heart: I realized they were doing more for the poor than my entire megachurch." Since then, with his encouragement, more than 7,500 Saddleback Church members have paid their own way to developing countries to do volunteer work fighting poverty and disease. Once they have seen the situation for themselves, many warn to keep helping. Warren himself now says, "I couldn't care less about politics, the culture wars. My only interest is to get people to care about Darfurs and Rwandas."[27]

Helping the poor is also strongly emphasized in Judaism, the source of many of those three thousand biblical references to helping the poor. The Hebrew word for "charity," *tzedakah,* simply means "justice" and, as this suggests, for Jews, giving to the poor is no optional extra but an essential part of living a just life. In the Talmud (a record of discussions of Jewish law and ethics by ancient rabbis) it is said that charity is equal in importance to all the other commandments combined, and that Jews should give at least 10 percent of their income as *tzedakah.*[28]

Islam, too, requires its adherents to help those in need. Each year, Muslims above a minimum level of wealth must give *zakat* in proportion to their assets (not income). For gold and silver—which today are understood to include cash and other liquid assets—the requirement is to give 2.5 percent every year. In addition, one may give *sadaqa,* which may include both money and labor—for example, digging a well so that travelers will have water, or helping build a mosque. *Unlike zakat, sadaqa* is optional.

Judaism, Christianity, and Islam are related traditions with their roots in the same part of the world. The Chinese tradition is quite distinct and, it is sometimes said, more focused on how one acts to those with whom one is in some relationship, especially familial; yet here, too, it is possible to find a very strong statement of our obligations to the poor. Mencius, who lived about three hundred years before the Christian era, is regarded as the most authoritative interpreter of the Confucian tradition, and in terms of his influence on Chinese thought is second only to Confucius himself. One of the works that describes his teachings recounts a visit he paid to the court of King Hui of Liang. On arriving, he met the king and said to him:

> There are people dying from famine on the roads, and you do not issue the stores of your granaries for them. When people die, you say, "It is not owing to me; it is owing to the year." In what does this differ from stabbing a man and lulling him, and then saying "it was not I, it was the weapon?"[29]

There is nothing new about the idea that we have a strong moral obligation to help those in need. In one-on-one situations where rescue is easy, our intuitions tell us that it would be wrong not to do it. We all see or read appeals to help those living in extreme poverty in the world's poorest countries. And yet most of us reject the call to "do unto others." I'll turn now to some of the reasons we give for our failure to act.

3. Common Objections to Giving

You may think of yourself as a charitable person. Most Americans do, and the $306 billion they donated to charities in 2007, three quarters of which came directly from individuals, lends support to that belief. In the United States, charitable giving is around 2.2 percent of gross national income. That's significantly more than in any other country, and about double the level of charitable giving in most other rich nations. About seven in every ten households in the United States made some form of gift to charity in 2007.[30] Americans also give time: Nearly 30 percent do some kind of volunteer work, most with religious, educational, or community organizations, with the average amount given being about 50 hours a year. In contrast to financial donations, however, when it comes to volunteering, the United States lags behind several European nations, especially the Dutch, who give more than twice as much of their time. When financial donations and volunteering are combined, the United States ranks as the world's third most generous nation, behind the Netherlands and Sweden.[31]

But beneath these encouraging numbers is a slightly less encouraging picture, at least as concerns those who live in extreme poverty. According to "Giving USA 2008," the most authoritative report on U.S. charity, the largest portion of the money Americans give, fully a third of it, goes to religious institutions, where it pays for the salaries of the clergy and for building and maintaining churches, synagogues, and mosques. Some of that—but by the most optimistic estimate, less than 10 percent—is passed on as aid for developing countries. The next biggest sector is education, including universities, colleges, and libraries. Again, a small percentage of that goes toward scholarships to students from developing countries, or to fund research that can help reduce poverty and disease. "Giving USA 2008" lumps donations to international aid organizations together with gifts to other organizations that do not give aid to the poor but, for example, run international exchange programs or work for international peace and security. This entire category received only 4.3 percent of all American charitable giving. According to statistics from the Organisation for Economic Co-operation and Development (OECD), U.S. private philanthropy for foreign aid amounts to only 0.07 percent of the nation's gross national income (that's just 7 cents for every $100 of income).[32]

As someone who has chosen to read this book, you are probably among those who give to charity or who volunteer in their community; despite that, you may be less inclined to give a substantial portion of your income to save the lives of those living in extreme poverty in faraway places. Charity begins at home, the saying goes, and I've found that friends, colleagues, students, and lecture audiences express that resistance in various ways. I've seen it in columns, letters, and blogs too. Particularly interesting, because they reflect a line of thought prevalent in affluent America, were comments made by students taking an elective called Literature and Justice at Glennview High (that's not its real name), a school in a wealthy Boston suburb. As part of the reading for the course, teachers gave students an article that I wrote for *The New York Times* in 1999, laying out a version of the argument you have just read, and asked them to write papers in response.[33] Scott Seider, then a graduate student at Harvard University researching how adolescents think about obligations to others, interviewed thirty-eight students in two sections of the course and read their papers.[34]

Let's look at some of the objections raised by these varied sources. Perhaps the most fundamental objection comes from Kathryn, a Glennview student who believes we shouldn't judge people who refuse to give:

> There is no black and white universal code for everyone. It is better to accept that everyone has a different view on the issue, and all people are entitled to follow their own beliefs.

Kathryn leaves it to the individual to determine his or her moral obligation to the poor. But while circumstances do make a difference, and we should avoid being too black-and-white in our judgments, this doesn't mean we should accept that everyone is entitled to follow his or her own beliefs. That is moral relativism, a position that many find attractive only until they are faced with someone who is doing something really, really wrong. If we see a person holding a cat's paw on an electric grill that is gradually heating up, and when we vigorously object he says, "But it's fun, see how the cat squeals," we don't just say, "Oh, well, you are entitled to follow your own beliefs," and leave him alone. We can and do try to stop people who are cruel to animals, just as we stop rapists, racists, and terrorists. I'm not saying that failing to give is like committing these acts of violence, but if we reject moral relativism in some situations, then we should reject it everywhere.

After reading my essay, Douglas, another Glennview student, objected that I "should not have the right to tell people what to do." In one sense, he's correct about that. I've no right to tell you or anyone else what to do with your money, in the sense that that would imply that you *have* to do as I say. I've no authority over Douglas or over you. On the other hand, I do have the right of free speech, which I'm exercising right now by offering you some arguments you might consider before you decide what to do with your money. I hope that you will want to listen to a variety of views before making up your mind about such an important issue. If I'm wrong about that, though, you are free to shut the book now, and there's nothing I can do about it.

It's possible, of course, to think that morality is not relative, and that we should talk about it, but that the right view is that we aren't under any obligation to give anything at all. Lucy, another Glennview High student, wrote as follows:

If someone wants to buy a new car, they should. If someone wants to redeco-
rate their house, they should, and if they need a suit, get it. They work for their
money and they have the right to spend it on themselves.

You've probably already had this thought: You've worked hard to get where
you are now, so haven't you earned a right to enjoy it? This seems both fair and
reflective of our basic economic values. Yet, when thinking about fairness, you
might also consider that if you are a middle-class person in a developed country,
you were fortunate to be born into social and economic circumstances that make it
possible for you to live comfortably if you work hard and have the right abilities.
In other places, you might have ended up poor, no matter how hard you worked.
Warren Buffett, one of the world's richest people, acknowledged as much when
he said: "If you stick me down in the middle of Bangladesh or Peru, you'll find
out how much this talent is going to produce in the wrong kind of soil." Nobel
Prize-winning economist and social scientist Herbert Simon estimated that "social
capital" is responsible for at least 90 percent of what people earn in wealthy societies. Simon was talking about living in a society with good institutions, such as an
efficient banking system, a police force that will protect you from criminals, and
courts to which you can turn with reasonable hope of a just decision if someone
breaches a contract with you. Infrastructure in the form of roads, communications,
and a reliable power supply is also part of our social capital, "without these, you
will struggle to escape poverty, no matter how hard you work. And most of the
poor do work at least as hard as you. They have little choice even though most
people in rich nations would never tolerate the working conditions in poor countries. Work in poor countries is more likely to involve hard physical labor, because
there are fewer machines to do the job; office workers in poor countries in the trop-
ics rarely have the luxury of air-conditioning. If poor people are not working it is
likely because unemployment is higher in poor nations than in rich ones, and that
is not the fault of the poor.

Lucy said that people have a right to spend the money they earn on themselves. Even if we agree with that, having a *right* to do something doesn't settle
the question of what you *should* do. If you have a right to do something, I can't
justifiably force you not to do it, but I can still tell you that you would be a fool to
do it or that it would be a horrible thing to do, or that you would be wrong to do
it. You may have a right to spend your weekend surfing, but it can still be true that
you ought to visit your sick mother. Similarly, we might say that the rich have a
right to spend their money on lavish parties, Patek Philippe watches, private jets,
luxury yachts, and space travel, or, for that matter, to flush wads of it down the toi-
let. Or that those of us with more modest means shouldn't be forced to forgo any
of the less-expensive pleasures that offer us some relief from all the time we spend
working. But we could still think that to choose to do these things rather than use

the money to save human lives is wrong, shows a deplorable lack of empathy, and means that you are not a good person.

If we have the right to do as we wish with our money, that right would supply an objection to any attempt to force the rich to give their money away, or to attempts to take it from them, for example by taxation. I don't agree that we have such a right, but I am not arguing here for higher taxation or any other coercive means of increasing aid. I am talking about what we should *choose* to do with our money if we are to live ethically. At the same time, I'm not arguing against a governmental role in reducing global poverty. Whether governments should play such a role is simply a separate question from the argument I am making. My aim is to convince you, the individual reader, that you can and should be doing a lot more to help the poor.

Libertarians resist the idea that we have a duty to help others. Canadian philosopher Jan Narveson articulates that point of view:

> We are certainly responsible for evils we inflict on others, no matter where, and we owe those people compensation . . . Nevertheless, I have seen no plausible argument that we owe something, as a matter of general duty, to those to whom we have done nothing wrong.[35]

There is, at first glance, something attractive about the political philosophy that says: "You leave me alone, and I'll leave you alone, and we'll get along just fine." It appeals to the frontier mentality, to an ideal of life in the wide-open spaces where each of us can carve out our own territory and live undisturbed by the neighbors. At first glance, it seems perfectly reasonable. Yet there is a callous side to a philosophy that denies that we have any responsibilities to those who, through no fault of their own, are in need. Taking libertarianism seriously would require us to abolish all state-supported welfare schemes for those who can't get a job or are ill or disabled, and all state-funded health care for the aged and for those who are too poor to pay for their own health insurance. Few people really support such extreme views. Most think that we do have obligations to those we can help with relatively little sacrifice—certainly to those living in our own country, and I would argue that we can't justifiably draw the boundary there. But if I have not persuaded you of that, there is another line of argument to consider: If we have, in fact, been at least in part a cause of the poverty of the world's poorest people—if we are harming the poor—then even libertarians like Narveson will have to agree that we ought to compensate them.

Some people imagine that the wealth of the world is a static quantify, like a pie that must be divided among a lot of people. In that model, the bigger the slice the rich get, the less there is for the poor. If that really were how the world works, then a relatively small elite would be inflicting a terrible injustice on everyone else, for just 2 percent of the world's people own half the world's wealth, and the richest

10 percent own 85 percent of the wealth. In contrast, half the world's people have barely 1 percent of the world's assets to split among them.[36] But the world's wealth is not fixed in size. The world is vastly richer now than it was, say, a thousand years ago. By finding better ways to create what people want, entrepreneurs make themselves rich, but they don't necessarily make others poorer. This book is about absolute poverty, not about being poor relative to how wealthy your neighbors are; in absolute terms, entrepreneurs increase the world's wealth. So the unequal distribution of the world's wealth—startling though it is—is not sufficient to show that the rich have harmed the poor.

There are many ways in which it is clear, however, that the rich *have* harmed the poor. Ale Nodye knows about one of them. He grew up in a village by the sea, in Senegal, in West Africa. His father and grandfather were fishermen, and he tried to be one too. But after six years in which he barely caught enough fish to pay for the fuel for his boat, he set out by canoe for the Canary Islands, from where he hoped to become another of Europe's many illegal immigrants. Instead, he was arrested and deported. But he says he will try again, even though the voyage is dangerous and one of his cousins died on a similar trip. He has no choice, he says, because "there are no fish in the sea here anymore." A European Commission report shows that Nodye is right: The fish stocks from which Nodye's father and grandfather took their catch and fed their families have been destroyed by industrial fishing fleets that come from Europe, China, and Russia and sell their fish to well-fed Europeans who can afford to pay high prices. The industrial fleets drag vast nets across the seabed, damaging the coral reefs where fish breed. As a result, a major protein source for poor people has vanished, the boats are idle, and people who used to make a living fishing or building boats are unemployed. The story is repeated in many other coastal areas around the world.[37]

Or consider how we citizens of rich countries obtain our oil and minerals. Teodoro Obiang, the dictator of tiny Equatorial Guinea, sells most of his country's oil to American corporations, among them Exxon Mobil, Marathon, and Hess. Although his official salary is a modest $60,000, this ruler of a country of 550,000 people is richer than Queen Elizabeth II. He owns six private jets and a $35 million house in Malibu, as well as other houses in Maryland and Cape Town and a fleet of Lamborghinis, Ferraris, and Bentleys. Most of the people over whom he rules live in extreme poverty, with a life expectancy of forty-nine and an infant mortality of eighty-seven per one thousand (this means that more than one child in twelve dies before its first birthday).[38] Equatorial Guinea is an extreme case, but other examples are almost as bad. In 2005, the Democratic Republic of the Congo exported minerals worth $200 million. From this, its total tax revenues were $86,000. Someone was surely making money from these dealings, but not the people of the Congo.[39] In 2006, Angola made more than $30 billion in oil revenue, about $2,500 for each of its 12 million citizens. Yet the majority of Angolans have no access to basic health care; life-expectancy is forty-one years; and one child in four dies before reaching the age of five. On Transparency International's corruption perception index, Angola is currently ranked 147th among 180 countries.

In their dealings with corrupt dictators in developing countries, international corporations are akin to people who knowingly buy stolen goods, with the difference that the international legal and political order recognizes the corporations not as criminals in possession of stolen goods but as the legal owners of the goods they have bought. This situation is, of course, profitable for corporations that do deals with dictators, and for us, since we use the oil, minerals, and other raw materials we need to maintain our prosperity. But for resource-rich developing countries, it is a disaster. The problem is not only the loss of immense wealth that, used wisely, could build the prosperity of the nation. Paradoxically, developing nations with rich deposits of oil or minerals are often worse off than otherwise comparable nations without those resources. One reason is that the revenue from the sale of the resources provides a huge financial incentive for anyone tempted to overthrow the government and seize power. Successful rebels know that if they succeed, they will be rewarded with immense personal wealth, they can also reward those who backed their coup, and they can buy enough arms to keep themselves in power no matter how badly they rule. Unless, of course, some of those to whom they give the arms are themselves tempted by the prospect of controlling all that wealth . . . Thus the resources that should benefit developing nations instead become a curse that brings corruption, coups, and civil wars.[40] If we use goods made from raw materials obtained by these unethical dealings from resource-rich but money-poor nations, we are harming those who live in these countries.

One other way in which we in the rich nations are harming the poor has become increasingly clear over the past decade or two. President Yoweri Museveni of Uganda put it plainly, addressing the developed world at a 2007 meeting of the African Union: "You are causing aggression to us by causing global warming. . . . Alaska will probably become good for agriculture, Siberia will probably become good for agriculture, but where does that leave Africa?"[41]

Strong language, but the accusation is difficult to deny. Two-thirds of the greenhouse gases now in the atmosphere have come from the United States and Europe. Without those gases, there would be no human-induced global warming problem. Africa's contribution is, by comparison, extremely modest: less than 3 percent of the global emissions from burning fuel since 1900, somewhat more if land clearing and methane emissions from livestock production are included, but still a small fraction of what has been contributed by the industrialized nations. And while every nation will have some problems in adjusting to climate change, the hardship will, as Museveni suggests, fall disproportionately on the poor in the regions of the world closer to the equator. Some scientists believe that precipitation will decrease nearer the equator and increase nearer the poles. In any case, the rainfall upon which hundreds of millions rely to grow their food will become less reliable. Moreover, the poor nations depend on agriculture to a far greater degree than the rich. In the United States, agriculture represents only 4 percent of the economy; in Malawi it is 40 percent, and 90 percent of the population are subsistence farmers, virtually all of whom are dependent on rainfall. Nor will drought be the only problem climate change brings to the poor. Rising sea levels will inundate fertile, densely settled delta regions that are home to tens of millions of people in Egypt, Bangladesh, India, and Vietnam. Small Pacific Island nations that consist of low-lying coral atolls, like Kiribati and Tuvalu, are in similar danger, and it seems inevitable that in a few decades they will be submerged.[42]

The evidence is overwhelming that the greenhouse gas emissions of the industrialized nations have harmed, and are continuing to harm, many of the world's poorest people—along with many richer ones, too. If we accept that those who harm others must compensate them, we cannot deny that the industrialized nations owe compensation to many of the world's poorest people. Giving them adequate aid to mitigate the consequences of climate change would be one way of paying that compensation.

In a world that has no more capacity to absorb greenhouse gases without the consequence of damaging climate change, the philosophy of "You leave me alone, and I'll leave you alone" has become almost impossible to live by, for it requires ceasing to put any more greenhouse gases into the atmosphere. Otherwise, we simply are not leaving others alone.

> America is a generous nation. As Americans, we are already giving more than our share of foreign aid through our taxes. Isn't that sufficient?

Asked whether the United States gives more, less, or about the same amount of aid, as a percentage of its income, as other wealthy countries, only one in twenty Americans gave the correct answer. When my students suggest that America is generous in this regard, I show them figures from the website of the OECD, on the amounts given by all the organization's donor members. They are astonished to find that the United States has, for many years, been at or near the bottom of the list of industrialized countries in terms of the proportion of national income given as foreign aid. In 2006, the United States fell behind Portugal and Italy, leaving Greece as the only industrialized country to give a smaller percentage of its national income in foreign aid. The average nation's effort in that year came to 46 cents of every $100 of gross national income, while the United States gave only 18 cents of every $100 it earned.

In four different surveys that asked Americans what portion of government spending (not national income) goes to foreign aid, the median answers ranged from 15 percent to 20 percent. The correct answer is less than 1 percent.

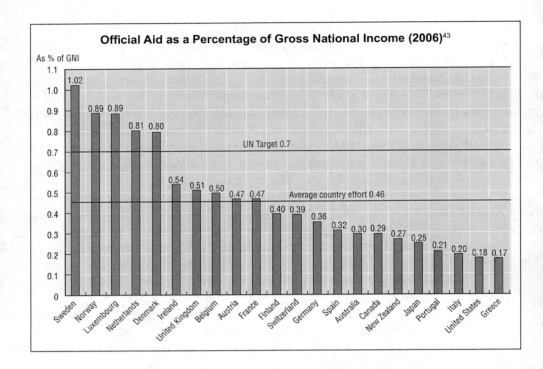

Official Aid as a Percentage of Gross National Income (2006)[43]

Asked what share of Americas national income the United States gives in foreign aid, 42 percent of respondents believed that the nation gives more than four times as much as it actually gave, while 8 percent of Americans thought that the United States gives more than 100 times the actual amount![44]

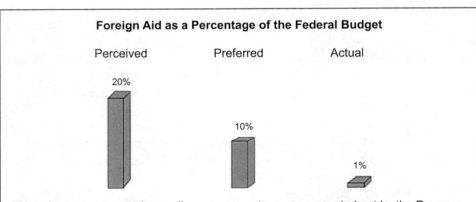

Foreign Aid as a Percentage of the Federal Budget

Perceived   Preferred   Actual

20%

10%

1%

The columns represent the median responses to a survey carried out by the Program in International Policy Attitudes (PIPA) in 2000. Other surveys carried out by PIPA and by *The Washington Post* yielded similar results.

A majority of people in these surveys also said that America gives too much aid—but when they were asked how much America should give, the median answers ranged from 5 percent to 10 percent of government spending. In other words, people wanted foreign aid "cut" to an amount five to ten times greater than the United States actually gives!

Some contend that these figures for official aid are misleading because America gives much more than other countries in private aid. But although the United States gives more private aid than most rich nations, even its private giving trails that of Australia, Canada, Ireland, and Switzerland as a percentage of national income, and is on a par with giving by people in Belgium and New Zealand. Adding U.S. nongovernmental aid, of 7 cents per $100 earned, to U.S. government aid leaves America's total aid contribution at no more than 25 cents of every $100 earned, still near the bottom of the international aid league.[45]

Philanthropic responses undermine real political change.

If those on the right fear that I am encouraging the state to seize their money and give it to the world's poor, some on the left worry that encouraging the rich to donate to aid organizations enables them to salve their consciences while they continue to benefit from a global economic system that makes them rich and keeps billions poor.[46] Philanthropy, philosopher Paul Gomberg believes, promotes "political quietism," deflecting attention from the institutional causes of poverty—essentially, in his view, capitalism—and from the need to find radical alternatives to these institutions.[47]

Although I believe we ought to give a larger portion of our income to organizations combating poverty, I am open-minded about the best way to combat poverty.[48] Some aid agencies, Oxfam for example, are engaged in emergency relief, development aid, *and* advocacy work for a fairer global economic order. If, after investigating the causes of global poverty and considering what approach is most likely to reduce it, yon really believe that a more revolutionary change is needed, then it would make sense to put your time, energy, and money into organizations promoting that revolution in the global economic system. But this is a practical question, and if there is little chance of achieving the kind of revolution you are seeking, then you need to look around for a strategy with better prospects of actually helping some poor people.

Giving people money or food breeds dependency.

I agree that we should not be giving money or food directly to the poor, except in emergencies like a drought, earthquake, or flood, where food may need to be brought in to stop people from starving in the short term. In less dire situations, providing food can make people dependent. If the food is shipped in from a developed nation, for example the United States, it can destroy local markets and reduce incentives for local farmers to produce a surplus to sell. We need to make it possible for people to earn their own money, or to produce their own food and meet their other needs in a sustainable manner and by their own work Giving them money or food won't achieve that. Finding a form of aid that will really help people is crucial, and not a simple task, but as we'll see, it can be done.

Cash is the seed corn of capitalism. Giving it away will reduce future growth.

Gaetano Cipriano contacted me after reading one of my articles because he thought that as an entrepreneurial capitalist, he could offer a helpful perspective. The grandson of immigrants to America, he owns and runs EI Associates, an engineering and construction firm based in Cedar Knolls, New Jersey, that has assets of around $80 million. "Cash is the seed corn of capitalism" is his phrase. Gaetano told me that he deploys his capital to the best of his ability to promote profits and enduring growth, and that giving more of it away would be "cutting my own throat." But he does not spend extravagantly. "I do not live in a splendid house," he told me. "I have no second home. I drive a 2001 Ford Explorer with 73,000 miles. I belong to a nice squash club, and have four suits and two pairs of black shoes. When I take vacations they are short and local. I do not own a boat or a plane." While he does give to charity, he does it "at a level which is prudent and balanced with sustainable growth." If he were to give much more money away, it would have to come out of sums that he now reinvests in his business. That, in turn, would reduce his future earnings and perhaps the number of people he is able to employ, or how well he can pay them. It would also leave him with less to give if, later in life, he decides that he wants to give more.

For similar reasons, we can agree that it's a good thing Warren Buffett did not give away the first million dollars he earned. Had he done so, he would not have had the investment capital he needed to develop his business, and would never have been able to give away the $31 billion that he has now pledged to give. If you are as skilled as Buffett in investing your money, I urge you to keep it until late in life, too, and then give away most of it, as he has done. But people with less-spectacular investment abilities might do better to give it away sooner.

Claude Rosenberg, who died in 2008, was founder and chairman of RCM Capital Management, an institutional money management firm, so he knew something about investing, but he also knew a lot about philanthropy. He founded a group called New Tithing and wrote *Wealthy and Wise: How You and America Can Get the Most Out of Your Giving.* He argued that giving now is often a better value than investing your money and giving later, because the longer social problems are left unchecked, the worse they get. In other words, just as capital grows when invested, so the costs of fixing social problems are likely to grow. And, in Rosenberg's view, the rate at which the cost of fixing social problems grows is "exponentially greater" than the rate of return on capital.[49] In support of this belief

Rosenberg pointed to the cascading impact of poverty and other social problems, not just on one person but on future venerations and society at large. The claim is a broad one, difficult to prove or disprove; but, if it is true for poverty in the United States, then it is even more likely to hold for poverty in developing countries, in part because it is easier to get a high percentage return when starting from a low base. Of course, that assumes that there are things we can do in developing countries that will be effective in reducing poverty.

> What if you took every penny you ever had and gave it to the poor of Africa . . . ? What we would have is no economy, no ability to generate new wealth or help anybody.

This objection comes from Colin McGinn, a professor of philosophy at the University of Miami.[50] It isn't clear whether McGinn's "you" is you, the individual reader, or the group an American Southerner might refer to as "y'all." If you [insert your name], took every penny you ever had and gave it to the poor of Africa, our national economy would not notice. Even if every reader of this book did that, the economy would barely hiccup (unless the book's sales exceed my wildest dreams). If *everyone* in America did it, the national economy would be ruined. But, at the moment, there is no cause for worry about the last possibility: there is no sign of it happening, and I am not advocating it.

Because so few people give significant amounts, the need for more to be given is great, and the more each one of us gives, the more lives we can save. If everyone gave significantly more than they now give, however, we would be in a totally different situation. The huge gulf between rich and poor means that if everyone were giving, there would be no need for them to take every penny they ever had and give it all to Africa. As you'll see before the end of this book, quite a modest contribution from everyone who has enough to live comfortably, eat out occasionally, and buy bottled water, would suffice to achieve the goal of lifting most of the world's extremely poor people above the poverty line of $1.25 per day. If that modest contribution were given, we would no longer be in a situation in which 10 million children were dying from poverty every year. So whether a small number of people give a lot, or a large number of people give a little, ending large-scale extreme poverty wouldn't cripple out national economy. It leaves plenty of scope for entrepreneurial activity and individual wealth. In the long run, the global economy would be enhanced, rather than diminished, by bringing into it the 1.4 billion people now outside it, creating new markets and new opportunities for trade and investment.

> People do have special relationships with their families, their communities, and their countries. This is the standard equipment of humanity, and most people, in all of human history, have seen nothing wrong with it.[51]
>
> —Alan Ryan, philosopher and warden of New College, Oxford

It is true that most of us care more about our family and friends than we do about strangers. That's natural, and there is nothing wrong with it. But how far should preference for family and friends go? Brendan, a Glennview High student, thought that instead of going to aid for the poor, money "can be better spent helping your family and friends who need the money as well." If family and friends really *need* the money, in anything remotely like the way those living in extreme poverty need it, it would be going too much against the grain of human nature to object to giving to them before giving to strangers. Fortunately, most middle-class people in rich nations don't have to make this choice. They can take care of their families in an entirely sufficient way on much less than they are now spending, and thus have money left over that can be used to help those in extreme poverty. Admittedly, saying just where the balance should be struck is difficult. I'll return to that question later in the book.

Kiernan, another Glennvicw High School student, made a point similar to Alan Ryan's:

> [Giving what we don't need to the poor] would make the world a better, more equal place. But it is like a little kid buying a pack of candy, keeping one piece, and giving the rest away. It just doesn't happen.

The issue raised by all these remarks is the link between what we humans are (mostly) like, and what we *ought* to do. When Brendan O'Grady, a philosophy student at Queen's University in Ontario, posted a blog about this issue, he got the following response from another Canadian philosophy student Thomas Simmons:

> Of course I do not want people to die, but I just feel generally unattached to them. I have no doubt that it I were to take a trip to places where people are starving then I might think differently, but as it stands now they are just too far removed. In not making these donations, I am implicitly valuing the affluence of my own life over the basic sustenance of many others. And, well, I guess I do. Am I immoral for doing so? Maybe.[52]

When O'Grady queried this, Simmons clarified his position: "I don't intend to make a moral defense, but rather just reveal my personal feelings—that is, just to explain how I feel." The distinction between describing how things are and saying how they ought to be is also relevant to what Kiernan and Alan Ryan are saying. The fact that we tend to favor our families, communities, and countries may explain our failure to save the lives of the poor beyond close boundaries, but it does not justify that failure from an ethical perspective, no matter how many generations of our ancestors have seen nothing wrong with it. Still, a good explanation of why we behave as we do is an important first step toward understanding to what extent change is possible.

Notes

I. Saving a Child-

1. BBC News, September 21, 2007, http://news.bbc.co.uk/2/hi/uk_news/engiand/manchester/7006412.stm.

2. Deepa Narayan with Raj Patei, Kai Schafft, Anne Rademacher, and Sarah Koch-Schulte. *Voices of the Poor: Can Anyone Hear Us?* Published for the World Bank by Oxford University Press (New York, 2000), p. 36.

3. This is a compilation of things said by the poor, cited in ibid., p. 28.

4. World Bank Press Release, "New Data Show 1.4 Billion Live on Less Than US$1.25 a Day, But Progress Against Poverty Remains Strong," August 26, 2008, http://go.worldbanlt.org/T0TEVOV4E0. The estimate is based on price data from 2005, and does not reflect increases in food prices in 2008, which are likely to have increased the number below the poverty line. For the research on which the press release is based, see Shaohua Chen and Martin Ravallion, "The Developing World Is Poorer Than We Thought, But No Less Successful in the Fight Against Poverty," Policy Research Working Paper 4073, World Bank Development Research Group, August 2008, www-wds.worldbank.org/external/default/WDSContentServer/IW3P/IB/2008/08/26/000158349.20080826113239/Rendered/PDF/WPS4703.pdf.

   For further discussion of World Bank statistics, see Sanjay Reddy and Thomas Pogge, "How *Not* to Count the Poor," www.columbia.edu/-"Sr793/count.pdf, and Martin Ravallion, "How *Not* to Count the Poor: A Reply to Reddy and Pogge," www.columbia.edu/-sr793/wbreply.pdf.

5. Robert Rector and Kirk Anderson, "Understanding Poverty in America," Heritage Foundation Backgrounder #1713 (2004), www.heritage.org/Research/Welfare/bgl713.cfm. Rector and Anderson draw on data available from the 2003 U.S. Census Bureau report on poverty and on various other government reports.

6. United Nations, Office of the High Representative for the Least Developed Countries, Landlocked Developing Countries and the Small Island Developing States, and World Bank, World Bank Development Data Group, "Measuring Progress in Least Developed Countries: A Statistical Profile" (2006), tables 2 and 3, pp. 14–15. Available at www.un.org/ohrils/.

7. United Nations Development Program, *Human Development Report 2000* (Oxford University Press, New York, 2000) p. 30; *Human Development Report 2001* (Oxford University Press, New York, 2001) pp. 9–12, p. 22; and World Bank, *World Development Report 2000/2001*, overview, p. 3, www.woridbank.org/poverty/ wdrpoverty/report/overview.pdf, for the other figures. The *Human Development Reports* are available at http://hdr.undp.org.

8. James Riley, *Rising Life Expectancy: A Global History* (New York: Cambridge University Press, 2001); Jeremy Laurance, "Thirty Years: Difference in Life Expectancy Between, the Worlds Rich and Poor Peoples," *The Independent* (UK), September 7, 2007.

9. "Billionaires 2008," *Forbes*, March 24, 2008, www.forbes .com/forbes/2008/0324/0S0.html.

10. Joe Sharkey, "For the Super-Rich, It's Time to Upgrade the Old Jumbo," *The New York Times,* October 17, 2006.

11. "Watch Your Time," Special Advertising Supplement to *The New York Times,* October 14, 2007. The passage quoted is on p. 40.

12. Bill Marsh, "A Battle Between the Bottle and the Faucet," *The New York Times,* July 15, 2007.

13. Pacific Institute, "Bottled Water and Energy: A Fact Sheet," www.pacmst.org/topics/water_and_sustainability/bottled_water/bottled_water_and_energy.html.

14. Lance Gay, "Food Waste Costing Economy $100 Billion, Study Finds," Scripps Howard News Service, August 10, 2005, www.knoxstudio.com/shns/story.cfm?plc=GARBAGE-08-10-05.

15. Deborah Lindquist, "How to Look Good Naked," Lifetime Network, Season 2, Episode 2, July 29, 2009. As relayed by Courtney Moran.

16. Peter Unger, *Living High and Letting Die* (New York: Oxford University Press, 1996).

17. For further discussion see Peter Singer, *The Expanding Circle,* (Oxford: Clarendon Press, 1981), pp. 136,183. For futher examples, see www.unification.net/ws/theme015.htm.

18. Luke 18:22–25; Matthew 19:16–24.

19. Luke 10:33.

20. Luke 14:13.

21. Matthew 25:31–46.

22. Second Letter to the Corinthians, 8:14,

23. Acts 2:43–47; see also 4:32–37.

24. Thomas Aquinas, *Summa Theologica,* II-II, Question 66, Article 7.

25. John Locke, *Two Treatises of Government,* Book I, Paragraph 42.

26. Erin Curry, "Jim Wallis, Dems Favorite Evangelical?" *Baptist Press,* January 19, 2005, www.bpnews.net/bpnews.asp?ID=19941.

27. Nicholas Kristof, "Evangelicals a Liberal Can Love," *The New York Times,* February 3, 2008.

28. Babylonian Talmud, Bava Bathra 9a; Maimonides, Mishneh Torah, "Laws Concerning Gifts for the Poor," 7:5.

29. Mengzi [Mencius] Liang Hui Wang I, http://chinese.dsturgeon.net/text.pl?node=16028&ifk=en.

30. Center on Philanthropy at Indiana University, *Giving USA 2008: The Annual Report on Philanthropy for the Year 2007,* Glenview, IL: Giving USA Foundation, 2008, pp. 9, 48. The comparative figure covers the period 1995–2002, and is from the Comparative Nonprofit Sector Project at the Center for Civil Society Studies at the Johns Hopkins Institute of Policy Studies, Table 5, www.jhu.edu/~cnp/PDF/compatable5_dec05.pdf.

31. Eli Portillo and Sadie Latifi, "American Volunteer Rate a Steady 28.8%," *San Diego Union-Tribune,* June 13, 2006. The comparative data are again from the Comparative Nonprofit Sector Project.

32. *Giving USA 2008*, pp. 9–14, 40; Organisation for Economic Cooperation and Development (OECD), Statistical Annex of the 2007 Development Co-operation Report, www.oecd.org/dataoecd/52/9/1893143.xls, Table 7e. The "most optimistic" estimate for the percentage of religious giving that goes to foreign aid comes from the Hudson Institutes Index of Global Philanthropy, 2008. This suggests that religious institutions contribute $8.8 billion to foreign aid. It also gives a total figure for U.S. private philanthropy almost four times as high as the OECD figure. Some of the discrepancy can be explained by the broader scope of the Index of Global Philanthropy figures—which include, for example, time worked by volunteers, costed at average U.S. wage levels—but it nevertheless remains unclear how this figure can be reconciled with the OECD or the Giving USA data. See Center for Global Prosperity, Index of Global Philanthropy, Hudson Institute, 2008, available at http://gpr .hudson.org/.

33. Peter Singer, "The Singer Solution to World Poverty," *The New York Times Sunday Magazine*, September 5, 1999.

34. Glennview High School is Seider's fictional name for the school, and the names of the students are also pseudonyms. Material about Glennview High School students is drawn from Scott Seider, "Resisting Obligation: How Privileged Adolescents Conceive of Their Responsibilities to Others," *Journal of Research in Character Education*, 6:1 (2008), pp. 3–19, and Scott Seider, *Literature, Justice and Resistance: Engaging Adolescents from Privileged Groups in Social Action*, unpublished doctoral dissertation, Graduate School of Education, Harvard University.

35. Jan Narveson, "(We Don't Owe Them a Thing!' A Tough- minded but Soft-hearted View of Aid to the Faraway Needy," *The Monist*, 86:3 (2003), p. 419.

36. James B, Davies, Susanna Sandstrom, Anthony Shorrocks, and Edward N. Wolff, "The World Distribution of Household Wealth," Worldwide Institute for Development Economics Research of the.United Nations University, Helsinki (December 2006), www.wider.unu.edu/research/2006-2007/2006-2007-1/wider-wdhw-launch-5-12-2006/wider-wdhw-report-5-12-2006.pdf.

37. Sharon Lafraniere, "Europe Takes Africa's Fish, and Boatloads of Migrants Follow," *The New York Times*, January 14, 2008, and Elizabeth Rosenthal, "Europe's Appetite for Seafood Propels Illegal Trade," *The New York Times*, January 15, 2008.

38. See Leif Wenar, "Property Rights and the Resource Curse," *Philosophy & Public Affairs* 36:1 (2008), pp. 2–32. A more detailed version is available on Wenar's website: www.wenar.staff.shef.ac.uk/PRRCwebpage.html.

39. Paul Collier, *The Bottom Billion* (New York: Oxford University Press, 2007).

40. See Leonard Wantchekon, "Why Do Resource Dependent Countries Have Authoritarian Governments?" *Journal of African Finance and Economic Development* 5:2 (2002), pp. 57–77; an earlier version is available at www.yale.edu/lekner/pdf/1999-l1.pdf. See also Nathan Jensen and Leonard Wantchekon, "Resource Wealth and Political Regimes in Africa," *Comparative Political Studies*, 37 (2004), pp. 816–841.

41. President Museveni was speaking at the African Union summit, Addis Ababa, Ethiopia, February 2007, and the speech was reported in Andrew Revkin, "Poor Nations to Bear Brunt as World Warms," *The New York Times*, April 1, 2007.

42. Andrew Revkin, op. cit., and "Reports from Four Fronts In the War on Warming," *The New York Times*, April 3, 2007; Kathy Marks, "Rising Tide of Global Warming Threatens Pacific Island States," *The Independent* (UK), October 25, 2006.

43. Organisation for Economic Co-operation and Development *(OECD), OECD Journal on Development: Development Cooperation Report 2007,* p. 134, www.oecd.org/dac/dcr. The table is reproduced by kind permission of OECD, See also *Statistical Annex of the 2007 Development Co-operation Report,* www.oecd.org/dataoecd/52/9/1893 143.xls, Fig. 1e.

44. Program on International Policy Attitudes, www.worldpublicopinion.org/pipa/articles/home_page/383.php?nid=&id=&pnt=383&lb=hmpg1. The table is reproduced by kind permission of the Program on International Policy Attitudes, and is taken from "Americans on Foreign Aid and World Hunger: A Survey of U.S. Public Attitudes" (February 2, 2001), http://65.109.167.118/pipa/pdf.feb01/ForeignAid "Feb01_rpt.pdf.

45. Organisation for Economic Co-operation and Development (OECD), Statistical Annex of the 2007 Development Co-operation Report, www.oecd.org/dataoecd/52/9/1893143. xls, Table 7e. If we accept the much higher estimate of U.S. private philanthropy in the Hudson Institute's Index of Global Philanthropy, America's total aid contribution rises to 0.42 percent, which is more respectable, although still slightly below the average country effort for official aid. The Index of Global Philanthropy figures are not suitable for international comparisons, however, as we lack figures calculated on a similar basis for most other countries.

46. See, for example, Anthony Langlois, "Charity and Justice in the Singer Solution," in Raymond Younis (ed) *On the Ethical Life* (Newcastle upon Tyne: Cambridge Scholars, forthcoming); Paul Gomberg, "The Fallacy of Philanthropy," *Canadian Journal of Philosophy* 32:1 (2002), pp. 29–66.

47. Gomberg, *op, cit,* pp. 30, 63–64.

48. See Andy Lamey's response to Anthony Langlois's paper in the volume referred to in n. 17, above.

49. Claude Rosenberg and Tim Stone, "A New Take on Tithing," *Stanford Social Innovation Review,* Fall 2006, pp. 22–29.

50. Colin McGinn, as quoted by Michael Specter in "The Dangerous Philosopher," *The New Yorker,* September 6, 1999.

51. Alan Ryan, as quoted by Michael Specter in "The Dangerous Philosopher," *The New Yorker,* September 6, 1999.

52. http://www.muzakandpotatoes.com/2008/02/peter-singer-on-affluence.html.